Introduction to
FORENSIC PSYCHOLOGY

Dedicated to
Gina, Ian, Soraya, and Jim
for your love and support

Introduction to
FORENSIC PSYCHOLOGY

Curt R. Bartol
Castleton State College

Anne M. Bartol
Castleton State College

SAGE Publications
International Educational and Professional Publisher
Thousand Oaks ■ London ■ New Delhi

For information:

Sage Publications, Inc.
2455 Teller Road
Thousand Oaks, California 91320
E-mail: order@sagepub.com

Sage Publications Ltd.
1 Oliver's Yard
55 City Road
London EC1Y 1SP
United Kingdom

Sage Publications India Pvt. Ltd.
B-42, Panchsheel Enclave
Post Box 4109
New Delhi 110 017 India

Printed in the United States of America

Library of Congress Cataloging-in-Publication Data

Bartol, Curt R., 1940-
Introduction to forensic psychology / by Curt R. Bartol and Anne M. Bartol.
    p. cm.
Includes bibliographical references and index.
ISBN 0-7619-2606-2 (cloth: alk. paper)
    1. Forensic psychology.   I. Bartol, Anne M.   II. Title.
RA1148.B37 2004
614'.15—dc222   2003021875

04   05   06   07   10   9   8   7   6   5   4   3   2   1

Acquisitions Editor:	Jerry Westby
Editorial Assistant:	Vonessa Vondera
Production Editor:	Kristen Gibson
Copy Editor:	Gillian Dickens
Typesetter:	C&M Digitals (P) Ltd.
Proofreader:	Kris Bergstad
Cover Designer:	Glenn M. Vogel

Contents

V. PSYCHOLOGY AND THE COURTS   245

List of Boxes, Tables, and Figures

Preface

This text is designed to be a core text in undergraduate courses in forensic psychology. It is also addressed to general readers and mental health professionals who are looking for a basic overview of the field.

Although many people associate forensic psychology with criminal profiling, crime scene investigations, and serial murder, the field is much broader in scope than commonly believed. In fact, forensic psychology is an engaging yet difficult field to survey because of its topical diversity, wide range of application, and very rapid growth. For our purposes, forensic psychology will refer *broadly* to the production and application of psychological knowledge and research findings to the civil and criminal justice systems. The book is organized around five major subareas of the field: (1) police psychology, (2) the psychology of crime and delinquency, (3) victimology and victim services, (4) psychology and law or legal psychology, and (5) correctional psychology (including institutional and community corrections for both adults and juveniles). Victimology and victim services represent the newest areas in which forensic psychologists are beginning to participate in increasing numbers.

The text will concentrate on the *application* side of the field, focusing on research-based forensic practice. Throughout the book, we emphasize the professional application of psychological knowledge, concepts, and principles to both the civil and criminal justice systems. The topics included in the text are largely dictated by what forensic psychologists and psychologists practicing in forensic settings do on a day-to-day basis. Consequently, we will cover such subjects as threat assessment for schools, child custody evaluations, competency evaluations of criminal defendants and of the elderly, counseling services to victims of crime, death notification procedures, screening and selection of law enforcement applicants, the assessment of posttraumatic stress disorder, and the delivery and evaluation of intervention and treatment programs for juvenile and adult offenders. The practice of forensic psychology involves investigations, research studies, assessments, consultation, the design and implementation of treatment programs, and expert courtroom testimony.

One of the major goals of the text is to expose readers to the many careers related to forensic psychology. From our years of teaching, it has become apparent that an overriding concern of many students is to discover what kinds of employment opportunities are available in their chosen major or favorite subject area once they graduate. In an effort to answer some of these questions, most chapters contain insert boxes that provide examples of the various careers in forensic psychology or boxes including samples of current (but disguised) employment ads that describe the educational and other requirements for the various positions. The first chapter is especially focused on the career base of forensic psychology. Because students often latch onto the word *forensic* without realizing the many branches of practice contained within the label, the chapter first covers the forensic sciences *in general*. It then moves on to the various levels of graduate training, internships, and fellowships relevant to forensic *psychologists*. It will become very clear to the aspiring forensic psychologist at the outset that he or she will have to pursue several years of graduate education (perhaps even postdoctoral training) and, in many cases, certification and licensure to practice. However, we also wish to emphasize that forensic psychology can be an enormously rewarding career filled with the personal satisfaction of knowing that one can make a difference in the lives of others.

Another major goal of the text is to emphasize the multicultural perspective that is an integral part of the day-to-day work of forensic psychologists. Well-trained forensic psychologists recognize that ethnic and racial sensitivity is critical to successful practice, and they know they must be constantly vigilant to the injustices that can result from a monocultural perspective. Therefore, throughout the book, we have tried to pay careful attention to the issue of cultural diversity, as well as to relevant issues involving mental and physical disabilities, sexual orientation, and gender discrimination.

Numerous topics in this book deserve far more attention than we have been able to give them here. We have not reviewed the empirical research or covered the legal and clinical ground that would be expected in a more advanced text. Nevertheless, we hope that this introductory material will prompt readers to explore topics of interest in more depth. The text should serve as an overview of the field of forensic psychology and an invitation to learn more about this very attractive and exciting career option.

Some features of the text should make it relatively accessible, even to readers without extensive background in psychology. Key terms appear in boldface in the text narrative, and lists of key concepts and review questions appear at the end of the book. The text includes extensive references that will aid readers to find more material on the subject areas covered. Material in boxes not only provides more information about career options—as mentioned above—but also should prompt discussion on contemporary issues relevant to the practice of forensic psychology. For example, there are boxes relating to physician-assisted suicide, the mentally ill and homeless, school shootings, expert testimony, and cognitive-behavioral treatment.

Acknowledgments

I t is common for authors to acknowledge at least one individual without whom a book would not have been produced—or at least would have taken much longer to arrive. In this case, we are extremely grateful to two "sage" editors. Former Senior Editor Terry Hendrix persuaded us—over dinner at one of Vermont's finest country inns—to submit a book proposal to Sage. Senior Acquisitions Editor Jerry Westby diplomatically found the right balance between patience and gentle prodding that resulted in the final product. Jerry is truly a skillful master at orchestrating the whims of authors while keeping the project moving forward. We are especially grateful for his enthusiastic guidance and good humor throughout the course of writing this book. Reviewers of chapters provided excellent suggestions and thoughtful recommendations, which have been incorporated whenever possible. The reviewers were Dr. Mike Aamodt, Radford University, Radford, Virginia; Dr. Andrea Barnes, Alliant International University, Alhambra, California; Dr. John Edens, Sam Houston State University, Huntsville, Texas; Dr. Jane Tyler Ward, Cedercrest College, Allentown, Pennsylvania; Dr. Norman Simonson, University of Massachusetts, Amherst; Dr. Kelly Goodness, University of Texas, Dallas; and Dr. Art Lurigio, Loyola University, Chicago.

Other individuals from the editorial staff at Sage who made this book possible are Associate Editor Ben Penner, who provided a thoughtful summary of early reviews and was instrumental in leading us to developing the final chapter structure for the book; Ben was always there to accommodate our whims and concerns. To begin the editorial process, the manuscript was turned over to our very capable copyeditor, Gillian Dickens. We are grateful for her patience, efficiency, and careful attention to the many details required to produce the final text. Our Production Editor, Kristen Gibson, capably supervised the many behind-the-scenes tasks about which we remain blissfully ignorant.

In addition to our daughter and son and their spouses—to whom this book is dedicated—many other family members, friends, and students have been an important part of our lives throughout the writing of this book. A few deserve special mention. Forensic graduate students Michele Macumber, Melissa Burbank, and Erica O'Toole patiently and cheerfully provided research assistance. Two special, long-time friends and colleagues in psychology, Professors Kevin Fleming and Virginia Philo, are part of our extended family. They have never wavered in their support, have never been acknowledged, but always make us laugh. We hope they know that they are treasured.

PART I

Introduction

CHAPTER 1

Forensic Psychology

Introduction and Overview

When the space shuttle *Columbia* disintegrated upon reentry into the Earth's atmosphere on February 1, 2003, "forensic investigators" from various federal agencies were immediately sent to the crash sites in an effort to identify the causes of the accident. They were forensic scientists trained to uncover evidence that may or may not eventually end up in a court of law. The term *forensic* thus refers to anything pertaining or potentially pertaining to law, both civil and criminal. Forensic investigations were undertaken after *Columbia's* disintegration in the event that human factors—for example, terrorism, sabotage, or negligence—might have caused the tragedy. Investigations of this sort almost invariably occur whenever there are unexpected and unexplained events that are not obvious natural disasters.

Forensic science has become an all-encompassing professional activity and a popular career choice among students. Nearly every conceivable profession, including psychology, has a forensic specialization. Many people are confused about the various "forensic" areas and

assume that professionals within these fields do largely the same thing. It will become clear, however, that they do not. Although **forensic psychology** is the exclusive subject of this text, it is helpful to begin with illustrations of other forensic sciences for comparison purposes. In other words, it is important for readers to know at the outset what forensic psychology is *not*.

Examples of the forensic professions, in addition to forensic psychology, include forensic engineering, forensic linguistics, forensic medicine, forensic computer investigation, forensic pathology, forensic anthropology, forensic archaeology, **forensic psychiatry,** forensic social work, and forensic accounting. The focus of each discipline is evident from the terms. Forensic linguistics, for example, is concerned with the in-depth evaluation of language-related characteristics of text, such as grammar, syntax, spelling, vocabulary, and phraseology, either to profile an offender or to determine whether specific writing samples are from the same author (Black, 1990). Forensic anthropology refers to the identification of skeletal, badly decomposed, or otherwise unidentified human remains using the science of physical anthropology. Forensic pathology is that branch of medicine concerned with diseases and disorders of the body that relate to questions that might come before the court. The forensic pathologist—popularized in television shows such as *CSI* and in the novels of Patricia Cornwell—examines the bodies of crime victims for clues about the victim's demise. Forensic anthropologists and forensic pathologists often work in conjunction with homicide investigators to identify a decedent, discover evidence of foul play, and help establish the age, sex, height, ancestry, and other unique features of a decedent from skeletal remains.

Forensic laboratories are usually maintained or sponsored by governmental agencies specifically to examine physical evidence in criminal and civil matters. The scientists working in these laboratories are expected to prepare reports and provide courtroom testimony on the physical evidence if needed (see Box 1.1). Alternately, private

---

BOX 1.1 Examples of Employment Ads for Forensic Scientists

Forensic Scientist—Level 1

Qualifications

Master's degree in chemistry, biology, physics, or forensic science from a regionally accredited college or university, including or supplemented by 20 credits in chemistry and 3 years of satisfactory experience performing forensic laboratory analyses in the specialty area *or* baccalaureate degree with a major in chemistry, biology, physics, or forensic science from a regionally accredited college or university, including or supplemented by 20 credits in chemistry and 4 years of satisfactory experience performing forensic laboratory analyses.

Responsibilities

Include the analysis of evidence in one of the following forensic science specialties: forensic chemistry, criminalistics, questioned document examination, or firearms or toolmark examination; the preparation of written reports; and testifying in court. Perform other duties as related.

Forensic Scientist—Level 2

Minimum Qualifications

Shall have a minimum of a bachelor's degree in the natural or physical sciences. Have a minimum of 18 months' experience performing the duties of a Forensic Scientist 1–Questioned Documents or its equivalent in another laboratory. If applicable, have gained experience in testimony as an expert witness and have established his or her credentials as an expert in various courts of record.

Responsibilities

Will be proficient in all of the duties of a Forensic Scientist 1–Questioned Documents. Will be expected to perform appropriate analysis on case work that is technically of limited complexity using standard established procedures. Will plan and execute analyses, including proper quality control procedures, using instrumentation and techniques as necessary. Results will be interpreted and findings reported for court purposes. Will be expected to maintain and enhance his or her expertise and maintain technical proficiency in the field of forensic questioned documents.

laboratories provide services to government agencies on a contract basis. Scientists from both public and private laboratories may be asked to examine and testify about latent fingerprints, hair fibers, firearms and ballistics, explosives and fire debris, toxic material, and other pertinent evidence found at or near a crime scene or tragic accident. Some forensic labs are better at investigating certain types of evidence than others. For example, the U.S. Fish and Wildlife Services Forensic Laboratory is often summoned to help law enforcement officers investigate possible law violations when evidence includes animal parts or carcasses. The Food and Drug Administration (FDA) Forensic Center in Cincinnati is better equipped for, and experienced in, ultratrace elemental analysis (Stehlin, 1995). The lab's chemists can find contaminants in microscopic amounts, such as parts per trillion.

The FDA lab was instrumental in investigating a major product-tampering case that occurred in the United States in 1982. Seven persons in the Chicago area collapsed and died soon after taking Tylenol capsules. The capsules had been purchased in six different stores, and victims included a 12-year-old girl, a woman who had just returned from the hospital after giving birth, and three members of one family. Chemical investigation revealed that the capsules had been laced with cyanide. FDA chemists developed fingerprinting-like techniques that allowed authorities to trace the cyanide back to the specific manufacturer and distributor (Stehlin, 1995). The cyanide compound was identified as potassium cyanide with a purity of 90%. The compound is usually used in industries involved in metal electroplating, metal extraction, and both photographic and cinematographic film processing. Unfortunately, despite the fact that the poison was identified and the source was traced, the perpetrator was never found.

A wave of similar product tamperings took place soon after the Tylenol incident, involving Lipton's Cup-A-Soup (1986), Excedrin (1986), Tylenol (again in 1986), Sudafed (1991), and Goody's Headache Powder (1992). Cyanide was also discovered in grapes from Chile in 1989. The FDA lab continues to apply the "fingerprinting" techniques to identify the cyanide origins, and since 1980, FDA chemists have developed techniques to screen for more than 250 of the most toxic poisons commonly available to the public (Stehlin, 1995).

Since the increased threat of terrorism in recent years and events such as the anthrax scare that followed the September 11, 2001 terrorist attacks in New York and Washington, D.C., quick forensic chemical detection methods such as those described above have become especially critical. Also critical, though, are forensic techniques that can address more common crimes, such as drug trafficking, computer crimes, and a wide variety of white-collar offenses that involve fraudulent documents. We highlight a few of these techniques below.

Example of Forensic Science: Forensic Entomology

Forensic laboratories often employ scientists who specialize in **forensic entomology,** which is the study of insects as it relates to legal issues. This specialty is becoming increasingly important in criminal and civil investigations. For example, entomological investigations of termite infestation may be used to support civil litigation dealing with real estate, pest control, or landlord-tenant disputes. In another context, forensic entomology may be useful in investigations of food contamination. Scientists try to determine where an infestation occurred (e.g., which plant or store), when it occurred, and whether it was accidental or the possible result of human tampering. (Whether there actually was negligence or evil intent, though, is left to the courts to decide.)

In criminal investigations, forensic entomology is used to determine the time since death (postmortem interval), the location of the death, placement or movement of the body, and manner of death. For instance, because insects will feed first on soft-tissue areas of the head, such as the eyes and nasal passages, and any open wounds, they often will neglect undamaged flesh that will be left intact to harden. Consequently, the feeding patterns of insects often provide invaluable clues about the nature of death.

Forensic entomology can also be applied to investigations of drug trafficking. Insects are sometimes found in drugs, and the identity of these insects can help in pinpointing where the drugs were produced or packed.

Another Example: Questioned Documents

Still another science represented in forensic laboratories is forensic document examination. This science analyzes handwriting, print fonts, the authenticity of signatures, alterations in documents, charred or water-damaged paper, the significance of inks and papers, photocopying processes, writing instruments, sequence of writing, and other elements of a document to establish authorship and authenticity. The process is often called **questioned document examination or analysis.** The questioned document may be a check, a threatening letter, a hold-up note, a credit application or receipt, a will, an investment record, a tax form, or a medical record (Morris, 2000). Questioned document analysis can be applied to many types of investigations, including fraud, homicide, suicide, sexual offenses, blackmail, bombings, and arson. Questioned handwriting analysis, for example, may include the forensic examination of a signature, handwritten letter, entries on a form, or even graffiti on a wall (Morris, 2000). A forensic document examiner (FDE) may be asked to examine and render opinions on the authorship of writing on building walls, recover engraved or obliterated writing on different types of surfaces, or determine the brand or model of typewriters, printers, embossers, inks, and printing processes (Morris, 2000).

An intriguing example of forensic document examination can be found in the search for Jack the Ripper, the serial killer who brutally murdered five prostitutes in separate incidents in London's East End in 1888. The case was never solved, although many professional and amateur investigators have tried to identify the killer for years. Recently, crime writer Patricia Cornwell (2002) carried on an extensive investigation of the murders and wrote a book on her findings, *Portrait of a Killer: Jack the Ripper—Case Closed.* Cornwell believes that Jack the Ripper was Walter Sickert (1860–1942), a renowned impressionist painter who walked the East London streets during the same time period as Jack the Ripper.

Apparently, letters confirmed as having been written by the Ripper are kept in the Public Record Office in London. The British government gave Cornwell permission to view these letters and about 500 others letters claiming to be from the notorious serial killer. During her investigation, Cornwell was also able to obtain two pieces of Sickert's own stationary. Although extensive handwriting analysis has not proved successful—the Ripper probably disguised his handwriting—a watermark and other characteristics of the paper were far more revealing. According to Cornwell, the stationery was on Gurney Ivory Laid and was produced exclusively by a small manufacturer for personal use. Typically during production, the sheets were guillotined to size and then folded into quires of 24 sheets. The sheets were then given a final "bim," a distinguishing mark because each bim is slightly different from the other. The match between the short-edge cuts on the 4 identified sheets (2 from the Ripper and 2 from Sickert's stationery) indicates they came from the same quire of paper. According to Cornwell, this evidence is the strongest so far to implicate Sickert as the infamous Ripper.

Closely related to forensic document analysis is forensic ink analysis, a little-known crime-fighting tool that is sometimes used to show that certain documents have been backdated or altered. Most of the ink analysis today is done by the U.S. Secret Service's Forensic Services Division, "which maintains the world's largest library of ink samples with more than 7,000 entries" (Maremont, 2003, p. A4). There is also a small group of private forensic experts who do ink analysis, primarily for medical malpractice suits, patent battles, or cases involving disputed wills. The ink analysis is especially effective in examining the ink of ballpoint pens which contain a variety of different dyes and drying properties. Ink analysis played a role in the 1973 conviction of mass murder Juan Corona, who hacked to death 25 migrant workers near Yuba City, California (Maremont, 2003). Usually, however, ink analysis is used in investigations of business fraud or, in rare cases, by the Internal Revenue Service for income tax cases.

Computer Evidence Recovery

Computer evidence recovery, also called forensic data recovery, involves e-mail and Internet analysis, along with sophisticated hard drive and diskette recovery techniques of orphaned, fragmented, and erased data. A computer evidence recovery specialist has the training to search, seize, and analyze magnetic media originating from a variety of operating systems pursuant to the execution of a search warrant or subpoena. The major goal of the specialist or investigator is to recover the data without modifying the original media or the image of the media. Without specialized training, a law enforcement officer armed with a search warrant would not be advised to open computer files from the office of a person suspected of Internet fraud or one suspected of distributing child pornography.

Katy Clark (2002) points out that "forensic data recovery is a field that is swiftly becoming an important, as well as lucrative, industry" (p. 36). Quoting Kevin Ripa, president of a forensic data recovery company in Canada, Clark writes, "Data recovery is a necessary and vital investigative tool. It is the wave of the future for lawyers" (p. 26). In divorce cases, for example, lawyers may subpoena spouses' personal computers to obtain evidence of an extramarital affair or other

malfeasance. Computer evidence recovery is used in a wide variety of investigations, such as financial fraud, embezzlement, sexual harassment, child pornography, program vandalism, identity theft, document forgery, software piracy, narcotics trafficking, and money laundering. The data evidence recovery process involves an analysis of the computer make and capacity, the computer's time and date settings, hard drive partitions, data and operating system integrity, computer virus evaluation, files, and software. The analysis will also usually involve careful evaluation of shadow data, which is the information that remains on a disk even after the data are ostensibly erased, damaged, or lost. Many people engaging in various forms of illegal activity think they are safe by making deletions or using software designed to cover their tracks, not realizing that a well-trained computer data recovery expert can access almost any information sent or received.

Forensic data recovery also may be a powerful tool to clear a person of wrongdoing. For example, Clark describes a case of a successful businessman living in an upscale neighborhood, happily married with two children, who was accused of accessing and distributing child pornography. One evening, police appeared at his door to execute a search warrant. They seized his computer, took him into custody, and charged him with distribution of child pornography, though he strongly denied the allegations. His attorney contacted a computer evidence recovery service, which was able to demonstrate that the pornography was stored in his computer on dates the man wasn't even in town. Apparently, he had unknowingly downloaded a "Trojan Horse," enabling the computer cracker to have access to his computer. (A computer cracker is someone who maliciously breaks into computers for the purpose of damaging data or sending out viruses, whereas a hacker tries to get through holes in computer codes to prove a point or play a joke.) The computer specialist was able to prove that someone else had been storing the pornography on the individual's computer without his knowledge.

Thus far, we have discussed forensic sciences while barely mentioning forensic psychology. Today, television, movies, and popular novels provide numerous graphic examples of forensic examinations of evidence such as human hair, DNA, semen traces, carpet fibers, gunshot wounds, ballistics, and explosives. The scientists depicted typically have access to state-of-the-art equipment, and they are often glamorous and/or have complex emotional lives. Many students express a keen interest in the forensic sciences and seriously consider pursuing a career in the field without fully understanding what it is or what is required to reach their goal. As is apparent from the above illustrations, forensic investigations usually require expertise in chemistry, biology, physics, and/or other sciences, including the science of computer technology. The field of forensic psychology requires a very different type of preparation and is significantly different in content, as we will now demonstrate.

Forensic Psychology: An Overview

Forensic psychology—like many specialties in psychology—is difficult to define precisely. As John Brigham (1999) writes, if you ask a group of psychologists who interact with the legal system in some capacity, "Are you a forensic psychologist?" many will say yes, some will say no, and a majority will probably admit they really do not know. Referring to his own testimony in court, Brigham notes that, when asked the question, his most accurate current response would be, "Well, it depends." As Brigham points out, the professional literature on the subject adopts one of two prominent definitions. Some of the literature defines forensic psychology *broadly* as the *research* and *application* of psychological knowledge to the legal system, whereas some of it prefers a more narrow definition, limiting forensic psychology to the *application* and *practice* of psychology as it pertains to the legal system.

We (Bartol & Bartol, 1987) offered the following definition: "We view forensic psychology broadly, as both (1) the research endeavor that examines aspects of human behavior directly related to the legal process . . . and (2) the professional practice of psychology within, or in consultation with, a legal system that embraces both civil and criminal law" (p. 3). Ronald Roesch (cited in Brigham, 1999, p. 279) suggests a narrow definition: "Most psychologists define the area more narrowly to refer to clinical psychologists who are engaged in clinical practice within the legal system." This definition may be too restrictive because it seems to imply a specialty called "forensic *clinical* psychology." The broad definition, on the other hand, includes not only clinicians (also called practitioners) but also social, developmental, counseling, cognitive, experimental, industrial-organizational, and school psychologists—some but not all of whom are clinicians. The common link is their contribution to the legal system.

In this text, we will continue to adopt a broad definition of forensic psychology but will focus primarily on forensic practice and what psychologists working in the field actually do. That is, we emphasize the professional *application* of psychological knowledge, concepts, and principles to civil and ·criminal justice systems. It should be understood, however, that this application must be based on solid research; thus, the research prong of our original definition (Bartol & Bartol, 1987) has not disappeared. The practice of forensic psychology, as it will be treated here, includes investigations, studies, evaluations, advice to attorneys, advisory opinions, and depositions and/or testimony to assist in the resolution of disputes relating to life or property in cases before the courts or other lawful tribunals. It can—and does—encompass situations before they reach the court as well as those situations following the court decision. It includes activities as varied as the following: courtroom testimony, child custody evaluations, screening and selection of law enforcement candidates, and clinical services to offenders and staff in correctional facilities. It also includes research and theory building in criminology; the design and implementation of intervention, prevention, and treatment for youth offenders; and counseling of victims of crime.

Over the past 25 years, forensic psychology has grown rapidly. As noted by Tucillo, DeFilippis, Denny, and Dsurney (2002),

A growing number of clinicians provide expert witness testimony addressing a variety of issues, such as competency to stand trial, criminal responsibility, child custody, personal injury or handicap, and suitability to work in law enforcement. In addition to this major trend in clinical psychology and neuropsychology, developmental and experimental psychologists have come into demand for their expert opinions on such matters as the reliability of eyewitness testimony and lie detection. (p. 377)

This growth is also reflected in the development of professional organizations devoted to research and practice in the field, significant increases in the number of books and periodicals focusing on the topic, and the establishment of standards for practitioners working in the discipline (Otto & Heilbrun, 2002). (See Box 1.2 for important historical benchmarks in forensic psychology.)

BOX 1.2   Historical Benchmarks in Forensic Psychology

1893—First psychological experiment on the psychology of testimony, conducted by J. McKeen Cattell of Columbia University.

1903—Louis William Stern of Germany established a periodical dealing with the psychology of testimony (*Betrage zur Psychollogie der Aussage*).

1908—Publication of Hugo Münsterberg's *On the Witness Stand,* arguably one of the first professional books on forensic psychology. The book launched Münsterberg's career in forensic psychology, and some scholars consider Münsterberg, a Harvard professor of psychology, the father of forensic psychology.

1911—J. Varendonck was one of the earliest psychologists to testify in a criminal trial held in Belgium.

1913—First time that psychological services were offered within a U.S. correctional facility (a women's reformatory in the state of New York).

1917—William Marston developed the first modern polygraph.

1917—Louis Terman was the first American psychologist to use psychological tests in the screening of law enforcement personnel.

1918—First inmate classification system developed by psychologists was established by the New Jersey Department of Corrections. New Jersey also became the first state to hire full-time correctional psychologists on a regular basis.

1921—First time an American psychologist testified in a courtroom as an expert witness (*State v. Driver,* 1921).

(Continued)

BOX 1.2 (Continued)

1922—Karl Marbe, a psychology professor at the University of Wurzburg, Germany, became the first psychologist to testify at a civil trial.

1922—Psychologist-lawyer William Marston became the first to receive a faculty appointment in forensic psychology, an appointment as "professor of legal psychology" at American University. Marston also conducted the first empirical research on the jury system.

1931—Howard Burtt's *Legal Psychology* was published—the first *textbook* in the forensic area written by a psychologist.

1961—Hans Toch edited one of the first texts on the psychology of crime, *Legal and Criminal Psychology.*

1964—Hans J. Eysenck formulated the first comprehensive and testable theory on criminal behavior advanced by a psychologist and published it in the book *Crime and Personality.*

1968—Martin Reiser became the first full-time police psychologist in the United States. He was hired by the Los Angeles Police Department and became instrumental in establishing police psychology as a profession.

1972—Under the guidance and leadership of the American Association for Correctional Psychology (AACP), Stanley Brodsky, Robert Lewinson, and Asher Pacht, correctional psychology became recognized as a professional career.

1974—The first successful interdisciplinary psychology and law program was developed at the University of Nebraska–Lincoln.

1978—The American Board of Forensic Psychology began professional certification of diplomates in forensic psychology.

1991—American Academy of Forensic Psychology and American Psychology Law Society published *The Specialty Guidelines for Forensic Psychologists.*

2001—American Psychological Association recognized forensic psychology as a specialty.

For our purposes, forensic psychology will be divided into five subspecialties: (1) police psychology, (2) psychology of crime and delinquency, (3) victimology and victim services, (4) legal psychology, and (5) correctional psychology. Police psychology and correctional psychology tend to be the more *applied* branches of forensic psychology, whereas the psychology of crime and delinquency and legal psychology tend to be more *research* focused. Nevertheless, legal psychology in particular can also be very applied. Victimology and victim services also represent a mixture of both, with victimology being the research and victim services the application component. However, we must be careful not to apply an exclusive focus to any one of the five subspecialty areas, because each one has both research and applied aspects. Furthermore, psychologists conducting research in one area of forensic psychology may consult with or train practitioners in other areas. Likewise, the clinical experience of applied psychologists helps to inform theory development and suggest hypotheses to research psychologists. Finally, many practitioners do engage in research, although a very common complaint among them is the lack of time and resources for doing that.

Specific examples of some of the things that forensic psychologists (depending on their specialty) may be asked to do include the following:

Police Psychology

- assist police departments in determining optimal shift schedules for their employees,
- assist police in developing psychological profiles of serial offenders,
- establish reliable and valid screening procedures for law enforcement officer positions at various police and sheriff departments,
- train police officers on how to deal with mentally ill citizens,
- provide counseling services to officers after a shooting incident.

Psychology of Crime and Delinquency

- evaluate the effectiveness of preschool intervention strategies designed to prevent violent behavior during adolescence,
- conduct research on the development of psychopathy,
- consult with legislators and governmental agencies as a research policy adviser on the prevention of stalking,
- consult with school personnel on identifying troubled youth who are potentially dangerous,
- develop a psychological test for assessing risk among the mentally ill.

Victimology and Victim Services

- evaluate and treat persons who are the victims of crime or witnesses of crime;
- conduct psychological assessments for personal injury matters having to do with such things as auto accidents, product

liability, sexual harassment and discrimination, and medical negligence or workers' compensation;
- educate and train victim service providers on psychological reactions to criminal victimization, such as posttraumatic stress disorder;
- assess, support, and counsel those who provide death notification services;
- educate service providers on the impact of multiculturalism when victims seek mental health and support services.

Legal Psychology

- conduct child custody evaluations, visitation risk assessments, and child abuse evaluations;
- assist attorneys in jury selection through community surveys and other research methods;
- perform evaluations of a defendant's competency to stand trial;
- consult with attorneys and the courts concerning custody decisions, conflict resolution, and the validity of assessment procedures used in the evaluation of various psychological conditions;
- conduct competency evaluations for the civil court.

Correctional Psychology

- establish reliable and valid screening procedures for correctional officer positions at correctional facilities;
- evaluate the effectiveness of a variety of existing programs (a process called program evaluation) for juvenile and adult offenders, such as victim-offender reconciliation programs, teen courts, or health education programs;
- develop a stress management program for correctional personnel;
- assess the development of a system for classifying prison inmates for placement within a correctional facility.

It should be noted that the above list would be shortened considerably if we were to adopt a more narrow definition of forensic psychology. The work settings in which forensic psychologists are found include, but are not limited to, the following:

- Private practice
- Family courts, drug courts, and mental health courts
- Child protection agencies
- Victim services
- Domestic violence courts and programs
- Forensic mental health units (governmental or private)
- Sex offender treatment programs
- Correctional institutions (including research programs)
- Law enforcement agencies (federal, state, or local)
- Research organizations (governmental or private)
- Colleges and universities (teaching and/or research)
- Juvenile delinquency treatment programs
- Legal advocacy centers (e.g., for the mentally ill and developmentally disabled)

Forensic Psychology Compared to Forensic Psychiatry

Psychologists, especially clinical, counseling, and forensic psychologists, are often confused with psychiatrists by the public and the media. Today, the lines of separation between the two professions are becoming increasingly blurred. Clinical, counseling, and some forensic psychologists, along with psychiatrists, are trained to provide direct treatment services to persons with emotional, cognitive, or behavioral problems. Psychiatrists are medical doctors (MDs) (or, in some cases, doctors of osteopathy [DOs]) who specialize in the prevention, diagnosis, and treatment of mental, addictive, and emotional disorders. Psychologists do not hold a medical degree.

Another major distinction between the two has been the license to prescribe drugs, including psychoactive drugs. Traditionally, psychologists have not been permitted by law to prescribe any medication. Now, even that distinction is beginning to disappear. On March 6, 2002, New Mexico became the first state in the United States to allow properly trained psychologists to prescribe psychoactive drugs, or drugs intended to treat mental disorders. At this writing, four other states have pending legislation on prescription privileges for psychologists: Georgia, Illinois, Hawaii, and Tennessee. Psychologists in Guam gained prescription privileges in 1999.

Many psychiatrists, like psychologists, work in a variety of forensic settings, including the court, correctional facilities, and law enforcement. Psychiatrists who are closely associated with the law are often referred to as forensic psychiatrists. In some areas, such as issues relating to insanity determination by the courts, psychiatrists are more visible—and sometimes more preferred—than psychologists. As we will discuss in a later chapter, this reflects a greater comfort on the part of some judges with the medical model approach to mental disorder (Melton, Petrila, Poythress, & Slobogin, 1997). Law-related research, however, tends to be the bailiwick of psychologists, although some psychiatrists are engaged in conducting and publishing such research also.

Careers in Psychology

Since the 1970s, there has been an enormous expansion of the profession of psychology in general (Reed, Levant, Stout, Murphy, & Phelps, 2001). Psychology encompasses a wide spectrum of topics ranging from engineering designs (human factors) to animal behavior and has a place in every imaginable setting. Psychologists can be found in "personnel selection and training, developing user-friendly computer software, the delivery of psychological services to victims of natural and man-made disasters, the profiling of serial killers, the creation of effective commercials that increase the sale of a product, and so on" (Ballie, 2001, p. 25). Currently, there are 155,000 members of the **American Psychological Association (APA)** alone. The APA, based in Washington, D.C., is the largest association of psychologists worldwide. Another 12,000 psychologists from the United States and abroad and whose specialties span the entire spectrum of scientific, applied, and teaching specializations are members of the **American Psychological Society (APS)**, the second largest psychological organization in the United States. It is estimated that there are at least 300,000 practicing psychologists worldwide who provide a wide range of services (Donn, Routh, & Lunt, 2000; Lunt & Poortinga, 1996). In addition to the APA and APS, psychologists belong to many other professional organizations at the national, state, and local levels.

Education and Training

About 75,000 undergraduate psychology majors graduate each year from the nation's colleges and universities (American Psychological Association, 2003d; B. Murray, 2002b). Starting salaries range from $18,000 to $45,000, depending on the job type and location, with an average of approximately $29,000. Psychology majors most often find employment in the areas of management, teaching, counseling, social work, and sales. As most psychology majors become quickly aware, the bachelor's degree does provide a basic foundation in the field of psychology, but it does not adequately prepare a person to be a professional psychologist. The minimum educational requirement for psychologists is the graduate degree. In addition, specialization in psychology usually begins at the graduate level, although many undergraduate programs offer concentrations in certain areas, such as social psychology, education psychology, or human development. Graduate programs in psychology most often offer graduate degrees in experimental, biopsychology, developmental, cognitive, clinical, counseling, school, and industrial/organizational

psychology. The last four represent the more applied or practitioner's side of psychology. Most recently, as we will see shortly, forensic psychology has become a fifth applied branch in the field, although the other four applied sectors have historically made significant contributions to various forensic topics and settings.

Graduate Training: Master's Level

At the master's level, clinical, counseling, and school psychology attract the most students (B. Murray, 2002b). In some states, graduates of master's degree programs in psychology—with the appropriate clinical training—may be eligible for licensure as psychological associates (LPAs) or psychologist—master's level (MacKain, Tedeschi, Durham, & Goldman, 2002). In other states, graduates with master's degrees in psychology are not allowed to practice *psychology* (at least not use the label) and are instead licensed with *nonpsychology* titles, such as licensed mental health counselor, marriage and family therapist, or psychotherapist (MacKain et al., 2002).

In a survey conducted in North Carolina, Sally Joy MacKain and her associates (2002) asked state and private employers if they employed LPAs. Through this method, they were able to identify 345 master's-level psychologists working within the state. The researchers discovered that 158 were employed at mental health centers, 108 were with the state department of corrections, 54 were working at residential centers that serve the mentally retarded and developmentally disabled, and 25 were employed at state psychiatric hospitals. Employers indicated that LPAs were as marketable as other master's-trained clinicians, such as social workers and counselors. Eighteen percent of the employers stated they were more likely to hire psychologists than other master's-trained clinicians, and 49% said they were "just as likely to hire them." In fact, some employers reported difficulty in finding enough LPAs for their positions. Salaries for LPAs ranged from $27,000 to $45,000 with a median of $30,500, a range similar to that of other master's-level clinicians.

In addition to employers, MacKain et al. (2002) also surveyed 60 LPAs. More than half the graduates interviewed (54%) stated they were definitely planning or were considering entering a doctoral program within the next 5 years, suggesting that the opportunities presented by the LPA alone may be limited. Of the LPAs, 36% were employed in community mental health centers, 24% were working in state corrections or the courts, 16% were involved in private inpatient or outpatient facilities, 10% were in university or college settings, and 8% were in nonprivate agencies.

Currently, there is no accreditation of master's programs in psychology through the APA. However, since 1995, applied master's programs have been able to seek accreditation from the Master's Accreditation Council (MPAC) (Hays-Thomas, 2000). Approximately 14,500 master's degrees in psychology are awarded each year (American Psychological Association, 2003d).

Graduate Training: Doctoral Level

At the doctoral level, clinical psychology attracts the largest number of students of all the applied specialties and is considered the entry-level credential for the independent practice of psychology (American Psychological Association, 1978; Hayes-Thomas, 2000). Every year, approximately 1,200 students earn PhDs and another 700 students earn PsyDs in clinical psychology (B. Murray, 2002a). The PhD degree (Doctor of Philosophy) requires a dissertation and is well accepted in the academic world as appropriate preparation for scientists and scholars in many fields across the globe (Donn et al., 2000). It is regarded primarily a researched-based degree. A dissertation refers to a substantial paper based on the PhD candidate's original research, which should make a significant contribution to the research literature. The PsyD (Doctorate in Psychology) is a graduate degree designed primarily for students who wish to become practitioners rather than researchers. The first PsyD program was established in 1968 by Donald R. Peterson at the University of Illinois (Peterson, 1968). Although many PhD psychologists have questioned the soundness of the PsyD since its early beginnings, especially in view of its limited research focus, the degree has received increasing professional recognition in recent years and has attracted the interest of many students. More than 50 institutions have awarded 9,000 PsyDs during the past 30 years. Overall, approximately 4,300 doctoral degrees in psychology are awarded each year (American Psychological Association, 2003d).

Licensure

By 1977, every state in the United States required a license to practice psychology, and all Canadian provinces regulated the practice in 1990 (Tucillo et al., 2002). In 1987, in an effort to encourage standardized licensing requirements, the APA developed the Model Act for State Licensure of Psychologists (see American Psychological Association, 1987) to serve as a prototype for drafting state legislation (Tucillo et al., 2002). One of the chief criteria to qualify for licensing is possession of the doctoral degree. Professional psychologists are also ethically obligated to comply with the standards pertaining to their practice, as outlined by the **Ethical Principles of Psychologists and Code of Conduct—2002** (American Psychological Association, 2003a). Guidelines are also offered in a number of areas associated with research and clinical practice. A good example is the **"Specialty Guidelines for Forensic Psychologists"** (Committee on Ethical Guidelines for Forensic Psychologists, 1991). Among other things, the "Specialty Guidelines" assert that "forensic psychologists are responsible for a fundamental and reasonable level of knowledge and understanding of the legal and professional standards that govern their participation as experts in legal proceedings" (p. 658). An important distinction between standards and guidelines should be noted. Psychologists are expected to comply with standards, and there is an enforcement mechanism in place in case they do not. For example, a violation in the *code of ethics* could result in a complaint to the APA's Professional Conduct Board and, ultimately, loss of one's license to practice psychology (although such drastic consequences are rare). By contrast, the *guidelines* are aspirational; psychologists are strongly encouraged—but not required—to abide by them.

Employment

The most recent survey on where psychologists with new doctorates find employment indicated that about three fourths are employed in higher education or human service settings (such as schools or hospitals) (D. Smith, 2002c). The rest were working in business, government, or private practice. About 25% of new doctorates find employment in academic positions at 4-year colleges and universities. Most of the graduates have a strong foundation in research methodology and analysis that allows them to work in a variety of occupations. "Rather than being stereotyped as a professor or therapist, more and more psychologists are being seen as applied scientists" (Ballie, 2001, p. 25).

The Applied Specialties

Although the subspecialties of applied psychology may have distinct features, journals, associations, and interests, they also have many things in common. The similarities between counseling psychology and clinical psychology, in particular, are far greater than the differences. The clinical psychologist typically experiences 9 or 12 months of supervised internship in a clinical setting, where the theories and methods acquired in graduate training can be applied to human behavior problems. The counseling psychologist has received much the same training as the clinical psychologist, including the internship. In the past, the major distinction between the two was their focus. The counseling psychologist was trained to evaluate and treat (counsel) persons with adjustment problems, such as those

relating to education, job, and personal and marital relationships. The clinical psychologist was trained to evaluate and treat persons suffering more serious behavior and mental problems found in mental hospitals or psychiatric clinics. This distinction is rapidly becoming blurred, however.

Both counseling and clinical psychologists are employed in a wide assortment of settings, including college and university counseling centers, university research and teaching positions, independent practice, health care settings, hospitals, and the legal-forensic system. About 40% of the doctoral-level practitioners are in private or independent practice (Reed et al., 2001). Both counseling and clinical psychologists (at the doctorate level) are licensed in all 50 states, usually under the same designation of "licensed practicing psychologist."

In clinical and counseling practice throughout the United States, psychologists are finding that their clients are often from cultural backgrounds different from their own. "The majority of service providers are European Americans with middle-class values and orientation; a sizeable portion of the diverse client populations are African-Americans and underserved with mixed values and orientations" (E. F. Morris, 2001, p. 563). In addition, psychologists are encountering in their practices more persons of Latino, Asian, Native American, and Arabic heritage. It is extremely crucial for practicing psychologists to be sensitive to the cultural values and norms held by persons to whom they are providing service. This may be especially important for forensic psychologists, who are often called on to assist in making decisions that may drastically affect the life of someone they are evaluating or treating. Clinical and counseling psychologists who are service providers to diverse populations should at a minimum be aware of their own assumptions and biases regarding cultures that are different from their own, understand their clients' worldviews, and use only culturally appropriate interventions and techniques (Erickson & Al-Timini, 2001; Sue, Arredondo, & McDavis, 1992). It is interesting to note that only half of the doctoral-level clinicians in one survey felt competent to provide services to African Americans despite their training exposure and diverse clientele (Allison, Crawford, Echemendia, Robinson, & Kemp, 1994; E. F. Morris, 2001).

The APA has begun to take notice of this important issue by publishing its "Guidelines for Providers of Psychological Services to Ethnic, Linguistic, and Culturally Diverse Populations" (American Psychological Association, 1993). The guidelines emphasize, for example, that psychologists "consider the validity of a given instrument or procedure and interpret resulting data, keeping in mind the cultural and linguistic characteristics of the person being assessed" (p. 46). In addition, the guidelines further recommend that "psychologists who do not possess knowledge or training about an ethnic group seek consultation with, and/or make referrals to, appropriate experts as necessary" (p. 46). It should also be recognized by forensic psychologists that the legal system they are working with might be unprepared to deal with many complex issues not only of culture, ethnicity, and race but also of sexual orientation. Same-sex marriages or unions, adoptions by gay and lesbian couples, custody evaluations when one party seeking custody is gay or lesbian, and same-sex domestic violence are examples.

School psychology is a specialty involved in the evaluation, diagnosis, and reduction of social, emotional, and cognitive problems of school-age children. In many ways, the tasks of school psychologists are very similar to those of child clinical psychologists, but school psychologists tend to be more focused on the school environment and its influences on the child. They work not only with children with problems but also with parents, teachers, and school administrators. Many school psychologists do not have the PhD or other doctorate degree, but many states provide certification and licensing for school psychologists who have the requisite master's degree and an internship within a school setting. Currently, there is a major shortage of qualified school psychologists nationwide (Dittmann, 2002). Compounding this shortage is the fact that approximately 45% of the students in public schools are from racial or ethnic minorities, often with very different linguistic experiences (Sue, Bingham, Porché-Burke, & Vasquez, 1999). As we will see shortly, school psychologists are increasingly becoming involved in forensic settings.

Industrial/organizational (I/O) psychologists help develop strategies that build better organizations and improve the well-being of employees. They work in a variety of areas within the organization, including selection and placement, training and development, organizational development and change, performance measurement and evaluation, quality of work life, consumer psychology, and human factors. The I/O psychologist may assist in fashioning accommodations for the disabled, offer employee workshops on sexual harassment, or counsel employees who have experienced workplace victimization. The training for this specialty usually involves a heavy emphasis on research design, statistics, knowledge of the research literature as it relates to organizations, and a 1-year internship within a relevant organization.

Forensic Psychology as a New Specialty

In August 2001, the Council of Representatives of the American Psychological Association voted to recognize forensic psychology as another specialty. Although this is an important step forward, recall that other specialties also provide services in forensic settings. It is too early to tell whether these psychologists will change their affiliations or will identify with more than one specialty. It should be noted that the council adopted a narrow rather than broad definition of forensic psychology. "It was ultimately decided that the petition for specialization should define forensic psychology narrowly, to include the primarily clinical aspects of forensic assessment, treatment, and consultation" (Otto & Heilbrun, 2002, p. 8). At this point, it is not clear whether the new specialty embraces the wide variety of settings discussed in this text. Although we follow the direction of the petition by focusing primarily on the clinical aspect of forensic psychology, we also interpret *clinical* broadly. It includes services provided across the five areas outlined earlier in the chapter: police psychology, psychology of crime and delinquency, victimology and victim services, legal psychology, and correctional psychology.

Educational and Training Requirements in Forensic Psychology

The growth in the field is demonstrated by the recent development of several graduate programs in forensic psychology (at both the master's and doctoral levels) throughout the world, particularly in Canada, the United States, the United Kingdom, and Australia. There has also been considerable growth in *training* opportunities in forensic psychology at the predoctoral, internship, and postdoctoral levels (Otto & Heilbrun, 2002) (see Boxes 1.3 and 1.4). In recent years, a discernible expansion has also occurred

---

BOX 1.3   Postdoctoral Fellowship in Forensic Psychology

The University of _____ is accepting applicants for postdoctoral fellowships beginning September 1. The fellowship is a full-time, 1-year training program in forensic psychology that develops skills in the application of clinical psychology to various legal issues. The program includes specially designed seminars in criminal, civil, juvenile, family, personal injury, worker's compensation, landmark mental health cases, legal regulation of psychology and law, correctional psychology, and special issues in forensic psychology. Interdisciplinary faculty. Intensive supervision of clinical evaluations and experiences. Patients from wide variety of legal agencies. PhD in clinical psychology from an APA-accredited school required.

BOX 1.4   Description of Psychology Internship at a Metropolitan Detention Center

The training offered by the Metropolitan Detention Center (MDC) Psychology Internship Program is designed to provide well-rounded training experience leading to the development of a clinical generalist. The primary goal of the program is to provide training as preparation for professional practice, consolidating the knowledge, skills, and abilities acquired through graduate training. To accomplish this goal, the program stresses development of competence in psychological assessment, intervention, and consultation. Interns are selected based on their preparation for more intensive work in these areas, their ability to provide psychological services, and their capacity for professional growth.

The MDC internship is considered a full-time position and offers a stipend of approximately $30,000 for the year. It assumes 40 hours a week of direct clinical services, assessment, research,

(Continued)

BOX 1.4 (Continued)

consultation, and supervision activities. Release time for attending dissertation defense, meetings of the intern's research committee, and professional conferences can be arranged with the director of training and the chief psychologist.

The services provided by the Psychology Department at the MDC are primarily brief in nature. They include psychological screenings of newly admitted inmates, brief treatment of adjustment symptoms, crisis intervention, and suicide risk assessment and prevention. The center also conducts forensic evaluations for the federal courts, psychological assessment for other referral questions, drug abuse treatment, and consultation with staff for inmate management concerns and personal issues. Some opportunities exist to provide brief and long-term treatment in individual and group formats.

---

in the number of doctoral programs in clinical and counseling psychology that offer at least one or more courses, practica, or internships in forensic psychology. Many colleges and universities offer courses in forensic psychology, legal psychology, or psychology and law at the undergraduate level.

Most of the graduate programs in the United States concentrate on either clinical or counseling psychology as it relates to corrections or on social psychology as it relates to legal psychology or psychology and law. Some universities offer a combined JD (law degree) and PhD as part of the academic package, although, partly due to the academic rigor and time involved, the "package" has become less popular to students in recent years. Formal programs offering specific degrees in police psychology are virtually nonexistent in the United States and Canada, although there are several programs called "investigative psychology" in the United Kingdom. Canada leads the world in research in correctional psychology, and the curricula in Canadian forensic programs reflect this strong research or empirical attention. Students graduating from any of the worldwide graduate programs are expected to be able to analyze, organize, apply, and transmit existing knowledge in the field of forensic psychology, broadly defined. We will return to the specific educational and training requirements for each of the five major areas in forensic psychology when we discuss the areas in more detail shortly.

Although there are few formal doctoral programs in the discipline, the American Board of Professional Psychology has awarded diplomate status in forensic psychology since the mid-1980s. A **diplomate** is a professional designation signifying that a person has been certified as having advanced knowledge, skills, and competence in a particular specialty. Diplomate certification in forensic psychology attests to the fact that an established organization of peers has examined and accepted the psychologist as being at the highest level of excellence in his or her field of forensic practice. The psychologist must be licensed to qualify for diplomate status.

Many other national and state certification boards have emerged during the past 10 years, including the American Board of Psychological Specialties (ABPS), which is affiliated with the American College and Board of Forensic Examiners. Criteria used by the various boards and organizations to grant credentials or titles vary widely (Otto & Heilbrun, 2002). Note that certification usually requires knowledge and competence in both the applied and research components of the discipline, but it is largely for those psychologists who provide services to the courts and possess doctorates in psychology.

The American Academy of Forensic Psychology and the American Psychology Law Society published, in 1991, the *Specialty Guidelines for*

Forensic Psychologists (*SGFP*) referred to earlier (Committee on Ethical Guidelines for Forensic Psychologists, 1991). "The primary goal of the SGFP is to improve the quality of forensic psychological services by providing guidance to psychologists delivering services to courts, members of the bar, litigants, and persons housed in forensic, delinquency, or correctional facilities" (Otto & Heilbrun, 2002, p. 7). We now turn to a discussion of the five major areas in the practice of forensic psychology to be covered throughout the text. (See Box 1.5 for examples of employment opportunities for forensic psychologists.)

BOX 1.5   Examples of Forensic Psychology Employment Ads

Forensic Psychologist sought by Forensic Associates to join the multidisciplinary treatment team of the Forensic Unit, a 35-bed acute inpatient forensic psychiatric treatment facility. Experience conducting personality, cognitive, and forensic assessments, as well as group and individual psychotherapy required. PhD in psychology and eligibility for state licensure required.

Forensic Neuropsychologist (Licensed or Licensed Eligible): Forensic Division at Medical Center has two positions available. Clinical duties include forensic evaluations of competency to stand trial, criminal responsibility, and dangerousness. Expert witness testimony in district courts throughout the state is also expected. Experience in neuropsychological evaluation without forensic experience will be considered.

Forensic Psychologists (**2 positions**): Opportunity to join a growing forensic program with a new facility currently under construction. The forensic psychologist will provide assessment and psychotherapy services to long-term adult clientele on medium-secure forensic and female units. Seeking skilled clinicians with solid psychological testing skills. Experience with competency/sanity evaluations, expert witness testimony, and forensic clientele preferred. Offering an excellent salary and benefits package commensurate with experience.

Forensic Psychologist: The University Law School is inviting applicants for a forensic psychologist at either the assistant or associate professor level, depending on experience and expertise. The successful candidate will be involved in conducting forensic evaluations of both adults and juveniles, conducting comprehensive training of forensic evaluators on contract from the Department of Mental Health, supervising clinical practicum and postdoctoral students, serving as the clinical adjunct in classes offered at the Law School, and conducting research on topics of interest. To apply for this position, the applicant must have 3 to 5 years' experience conducting forensic evaluations, be eligible for licensure, and be interested in developing research interests in addition to carrying out clinical and teaching responsibilities.

Forensic Psychologist: The university is seeking applicants for assistant professor with forensic expertise. The duties of this tenure track position include teaching graduate and undergraduate courses in forensic psychology, clinical and research supervision of graduate students, maintaining an active program of research on forensic topics, and participation in the clinical and law-psychology programs. The successful applicant should be prepared to teach courses in legal psychology, forensic assessment, and forensic research methodology. Qualifications include aPhD in clinical or counseling psychology, clinical and research experience with forensic issues, a record of achievement in scholarship, and teaching and license eligibility. Experience with quantitative methods preferred.

Police Psychology: An Overview

Police psychology is the research and application of psychological principles and clinical skills to law enforcement and public safety (Bartol, 1996). The term *police psychology* is somewhat imprecise because it appears to exclude other law enforcement agents, such as deputy sheriffs, fish and wildlife agents, airport security, marshals, constables, and many types of other state and federal agents. The term *law enforcement* is more encompassing. However, critics of that term note that enforcement of the law is only one of many tasks performed by police and that law is often enforced selectively. The real work of police is maintaining order, providing service, keeping the peace, or being coproducers—with citizens—of public safety. Rather than adopt one or the other viewpoint—each has its merits—we will use *police* and *law enforcement officers* interchangeably and broadly to include the wide variety of agents listed above.

The relationship between psychology and law enforcement has waxed and waned over the years, with considerable forensic psychology involvement followed by a period of overall quiet. Overall, though, as law enforcement agencies have become more professional, law enforcement supervisors and directors better educated, and the public more critical and concerned, there has been a substantial increase in the need for services provided by forensic psychologists. They perform preemployment psychological assessments, fitness-for-duty evaluations (FFDEs), special unit evaluations, hostage team negotiations, and deadly force incident evaluations. Special unit evaluations include the selection and training of special weapons and tactics teams (SWATs), tactical response teams (TRTs), and hostage negotiation teams (HNTs). Forensic psychologists are also increasingly asked to do investigative-type activities, such as criminal profiling, psychological autopsies, handwriting analysis, and eyewitness (or earwitness) hypnosis. Larger police departments usually hire full-time, in-house police psychologists, whereas the smaller departments usually use psychological consultants.

In a survey of 152 police psychologists (Bartol, 1996), 89% of the respondents said they had PhD degrees, followed by EdD degrees (4.5%), master's degrees (3.6%), and PsyD degrees (2.7%). Most of the PhDs had obtained their degrees in clinical psychology (60.7%), counseling (17%), or industrial/organizational psychology (8%). Twenty-five percent of the respondents were women. Participants in the nationwide survey were also asked to indicate the type of services they provided to police during a typical month, as well as the amount of time they usually spent at each activity. Respondents said that preemployment screening and assessment consumed the largest percentage (34.3%) of their time. A significant amount of time was also spent in providing services to officers and their families (28.7%), followed by fitness-for-duty evaluations (6.8%), training of personnel (6.9%), and administrative work (3.9%).

Currently, there are no formal graduate programs in the United States specifically focused on police psychology. It is best for students entering the field to earn a doctorate in psychology (especially clinical, counseling, or industrial/organizational) and, while in the graduate program, work with a faculty member who is involved in those areas. It is also advisable to complete a doctoral or postdoctoral internship in an agency or organization that deals directly with police organizations. A few police departments do offer pre- or posttraining in police psychology, such as the Los Angeles Police Department (LAPD), the Los Angeles Sheriff's Department (LASD), the Metro-Dade Police Department in Florida, and the New York Police Department (NYPD). There may be others at the larger police departments across the nation. An internship usually involves a formal schedule of supervision and training, as well as an opportunity for some degree of police training, ranging from ride-alongs to attendance at a police academy. Regardless of the career path taken, it is critical that a person interested in police psychology become highly familiar with the nature of police work, the policies and procedures, and an understanding of the police culture. Some practitioners estimate that for police psychologists to be highly effective, the "police culture socialization process" may take up to 3 years beyond the usually academic and clinical training (Finn & Tomz, 1997). An aspiring police psychologist should also plan on being available 24 hours a day for the agency and be willing to work in different locations (e.g., on the street, at the academy, or in an officer's home). It is not, however, necessary to become a police officer before accomplishing these goals; in fact, it may be a disadvantage. Many police officers would prefer to talk to someone outside of the agency, especially when it comes to confidentiality (Finn & Tomz, 1997).

Psychology of Crime and Delinquency

The psychology of crime and delinquency is the *science* of the behavioral and mental processes of the adult and juvenile offender (Bartol, 2002). It is primarily concerned with how criminal behavior is acquired, evoked, maintained, and modified. Recent research has focused on the offender's cognitive versions of the world, especially his or her thoughts, beliefs, and values and how they can be changed. It assumes that various criminal behaviors are acquired by daily living experiences, in accordance with the principles of learning, and are perceived, coded, processed, and stored in memory in a unique fashion for each individual. Criminal psychology examines and evaluates prevention, intervention, and treatment strategies directed at reducing criminal behavior.

Research in crime and delinquency has discovered, for example, that chronic violence usually develops when children do poorly in school, do not get along with peers, have abusive parents, and attend schools that cannot control disruptive and violent behavior (Crawford, 2002). Research has also found that social rejection by peers and others can lead to serious, violent offending.

"A great deal of psychological functioning is predicated on belonging to the group and enjoying the benefits, both direct and indirect, of that belongingness" (Benson, 2002, p. 25). When this sense of belongingness is removed or restricted, a feeling of isolation and social exclusion occurs that tends to produce significant changes in behavior, such as an increase in aggression, violence, and other maladaptive behaviors. Under these conditions, human behavior may become impulsive, chaotic, selfish, disorganized, and even destructive. School shooters, for example, frequently express a sense of social isolation and rejection.

Researchers have also found, however, that well-designed and carefully executed prevention programs can prevent violence and a lifelong career path of crime. For example, the Fast Track Prevention Program, developed by researchers at Duke University, Pennsylvania State University, Vanderbilt University, and the University of Washington, has shown highly promising results in reducing juvenile crime. We will discuss more such programs in the chapters on crime and delinquency. Of late, applied psychologists working in school settings have found an increased need for their services, as we noted above. This has led to a keen interest in a new subdivision of school psychology.

Forensic School Psychology

Educational programs are required in correctional and psychiatric facilities for young people throughout the country, and some states have established special school districts within these facilities (Crespi, 1990). The challenges for forensic school psychologists within these contexts are considerable. Although the primary focus of public and private schools is obviously education, education in most correctional or psychiatric settings is secondary to the reasons for confinement. Rehabilitation of the juveniles—which includes but is not limited to education—is crucial. Consequently, assessment and counseling services are critical roles for the school psychologist within these settings. Although many forensic school psychologists primarily work with mentally disordered offenders and youth in correctional facilities, they also work with public and private schools on issues that potentially relate to the legal system.

> Forensic school psychologists routinely interact with a multitude of legal issues: Local school concerns about discharge; possible placement into residential school programs and its concomitant implications for the youngster's home school district; the limitations of client privilege; tactics during contested special education cases; and expectations of judges, attorneys, and facility staff pertaining to mental status and the client's legal commitment. (Crespi, 1990, p. 84)

The need for additional consultation with school psychologists within the public and private schools systems across the country took on chilling urgency in the late 1990s when a rash of school shootings made headlines. Communities across the nation that had previously had a low profile—West Paducah, Kentucky; Jonesboro, Arkansas; Pearl, Mississippi; Springfield, Oregon— suddenly became well known. The most striking case was the mass murder of 12 students and one teacher at Columbine High School in Littleton, Colorado, in April 1999. Twenty other students were injured, some seriously, during that incident. The two teenage boys who were responsible for the shootings apparently committed suicide in the school library during the tragedy. To the public and news media, the shooters appeared to be two ordinary boys from normal middle-class families living in a suburb of Denver. Although there had been a number of school shootings prior to Columbine (there had been at least 10 school shootings between 1996 and 1999), the Columbine shootings prompted a great deal of alarm and concern from parents across the United States. In addition, the media and some experts were quick to generalize about the "sky-rocketing school violence problem" and demanded some kind of threat or risk assessment

to identify those youth who might have similar intentions. Such an assessment would occur, for example, when a student makes a spoken or written threat to harm classmates or teachers. Once a youth has been assessed, he or she may then be counseled in the school setting or in the community or may even be expelled from school. That assessment task often falls to the school psychologist.

Despite the media attention directed to Columbine and the other school tragedies, it is important to keep school violence in perspective. The school shootings described occurred during a time when juvenile violent crime was decreasing nationwide. Whenever the news media highlight certain events and dramatize their significance, the events seem to be more widespread and frequent to people than they really are. This phenomenon is called the **availability heuristic.** Therefore, although the shootings were terrible and tragic, they were not representative of the juvenile crime picture as a whole. Furthermore, although the media understandably report incidents of children having guns on school premises, there is no documentation that this is a widespread problem. Although it is important to be alert for possible dangers facing school-age children and the adults who work with them in the schools, the reality is that the risk of victimization in the school environment is smaller than in private homes or the community at large (O'Tool, 2000).

Unfortunately, at present, there are very few formal training programs specializing in **forensic school psychology.** However, with the continual increase of youth confined in correctional facilities across the country in need of education and the push to make our schools a safer place, this discipline would seem to have a very promising future.

Victimology and Victim Services

Victimology refers to the study of persons who have experienced either actual or threatened physical, psychological, social, and/or financial harm as the result of the commission or attempted commission of crime against them. The harm may be direct or primary (against those who experience it and its consequences firsthand) or indirect or secondary (against family members, relatives, survivors, or friends who experience the harm because of their closeness to the victim) (Karmen, 2001).

Violent victimization of children, such as terrifying abductions, school shootings, and sexual attacks, can disrupt the course of child development in very fundamental ways and can be associated with emotional and cognitive problems over the course of the life span (Boney-McCoy & Finkelhor, 1995). In adults, there is strong evidence that the effects of criminal victimization—such as assault, robbery, and burglary—are both pervasive and persistent (Norris & Kaniasty, 1994). Until recently, psychological services were received by a very small fraction of crime victims (2%-7%) (Norris, Kaniasty, & Scheer, 1990). In fact, it has only been within the past 30 years that criminal victimology has become recognized as a scientific and professional field of study (Karmen, 2001). Increasingly, forensic psychologists are beginning to play major roles in the research, evaluation, and treatment of crime victims from diverse cultural contexts and age groups. These activities will be covered in greater depth in Chapters 7, 8, and 9.

Students wishing to pursue a research career in victimology probably should obtain a research doctorate in psychology, criminal justice, social work, or sociology. Those desiring careers as practitioners in the field would be advised to obtain a PhD in clinical or counseling psychology or an MSW in social work. There are other training opportunities and career paths, however. Over the past 25 years, for example, the field of victim services has become a rapidly growing profession. Today, there is greater understanding of victims' issues due to legislation enacted to support victims' rights, increased funding for victim services, the efforts of victim advocates, and active research in victimology. Victim services concentrating on victims of sexual assault, domestic violence, and partner, child, and elder abuse have especially grown in recent years. More

recent legislation will certainly broaden the scope of understanding and services for victims across a wide spectrum. Examples of this recent legislation are the Victims of Trafficking and Violence Prevention Act of 2000 and the USA Patriot Act of 2001, which—among its least controversial provisions—addresses the needs and concerns of victims of terrorist acts.

A small number of community colleges and universities are beginning to offer specific training designed for victim service providers. Beginning in 1989, the California State University–Fresno (CSUF) offered the first Victim Services Institute with Victims' Services Certification to graduates of the institute. The program became so popular that the university, in 1991, developed the first victimology major (BA) and, by 1992, the first graduate concentration in victimology (Walker & Kilpatrick, 2002). The University of New Haven offers degree concentrations and certificate programs at both graduate (MS) and undergraduate (BS) levels. Other colleges or universities offering certification or degrees in crime victim or survivor services include Washburn University, Kansas City Community College, Red Rocks Community College, and Sam Houston State University. In the very near future, many other colleges and universities will be offering academic credit and degrees in this emerging area.

The National Victim Assistance Academy (NVAA), funded and sponsored by the U.S. Department of Justice's Office of Victims of Crime (OVC), has led the way in developing curriculum standards to be used at the national and state levels. The NVAA currently offers two distinct levels of training and education: (1) the Foundation Level Academy and (2) the Advanced Topic Series. The Foundation Level Academy, which began in 1995, is a comprehensive, 40-hour, academic-based course of study in victimology, victims' rights, and victim services for victim services professionals and allied professionals. The Advanced Topic Series are workshops consisting of 20 to 24 hours of academic-based training in selected concentrations, such as program management, specific training/education skills, and techniques.

Legal Psychology

Legal psychology is an umbrella term for the scientific study of a wide assortment of topics reflecting the close relationship between psychology and the courts. These topics include competencies and criminal responsibility (insanity defense), civil commitment, the psychology of the jury, the psychology of evidence, child custody determinations, family law issues, eyewitness identification, and the effects of pretrial publicity on jury decision making. As treated here, legal psychology includes both research and application of behavioral and social science to criminal and civil courts.

A caveat is in order, however. It is not unusual to see the terms *legal psychology, psychology and law,* and *forensic psychology* used interchangeably in academic and professional literature. Although we use *legal psychology* here as a subarea of forensic psychology, we recognize that this is not a universal approach. We also recognize the considerable overlap between legal psychology and the other subareas we have carved out. The psychology of evidence, for example, is of intense interest to police psychologists, who might be advising the law enforcement community on facial composites or the reliability of eyewitness testimony. The legal psychologist is far more likely than the police psychologist to be conducting research in these areas, however. Likewise, legal psychology and victimology intersect when psychologists perform risk assessments and some custody evaluations. The point here is to emphasize that the various subareas of forensic psychology are not mutually exclusive. (See Box 1.6 for an example of a specialization that may be valuable in several subareas of forensic psychology.)

BOX 1.6 Forensic Neuropsychology

The term *forensic neuropsychology* refers to the application of knowledge from the neuropsychological profession to legal matters. Neuropsychology is the study of the psychological effects of brain and neurological damage and dysfunction on human behavior. Clinical neuropsychology is the applied branch of the field that focuses on the assessment and diagnosis of the neurological damage. Forensic neuropsychologists provide information in legal cases on such things as dementia, brain damage, and intellectual functioning. The neuropsychologist may be asked to testify on the extent of a person's impairment and be expected to answer questions pertaining to employment fitness, the need for a guardian or health care provider, chances of full recovery, and/or the extent of rehabilitation. Over the past two decades, the predominant application of forensic neuropsychology has been directed at civil cases involving disability determination, worker's compensation, personal injury cases, and the mental ability of a person to make financial, health, and general living decisions. Neuropsychology is also increasingly used in criminal cases, such as in the evaluation of a defendant's competency to stand trial or for determining whether an insanity defense could be supported.

Neuropsychological assessment procedures and tests include measures that evaluate general intelligence, language, memory, attention, thought processes, perceptual-motor functioning, and emotional status.

Forensic neuropsychology is a profession that is developing very rapidly and has a very bright and promising future. The best career route for a student interested in this field is to pursue a PhD in clinical psychology with a heavy emphasis on biopsychology and an internship focusing on clinical neuropsychology. Many neuropsychologists are certified by the American Board of Clinical Neuropsychology.

One of the numerous topics holding considerable interest for legal psychologists is the psychology of false confessions. Most people are aware that suspects—for a wide variety of reasons—sometimes confess to crimes they did not commit. A suspect may be afraid, may want the notoriety attached to confessing, may desire to protect the real perpetrator, or simply may believe that no one will believe in his or her innocence. What surprises many people, however, is the fact that some suspects who are truly innocent come to believe they are truly guilty. Current research strongly suggests that skillful manipulation by law enforcement officers can lead to such false confessions (Kassin, 1997; Kassin, Goldstein, & Savitsky, 2003; Kassin & Kiechel, 1996). Legal psychologists have been at the forefront of studying this bizarre phenomenon.

Another topic of interest to legal psychologists is the creation of facial composites from the memory of eyewitness. Composites are considered indispensable aids to criminal investigation by most police agencies. Composites are reconstructions of faces through memory, and they are built either with the help of an artist's sketching skills or by using the various commercial kits available to law enforcement. In recent years, kits have been replaced by computer-based systems where features are stored on disks and the face is put together on a video display unit. Research by forensic psychologists, however, has revealed that computer systems are no more accurate in developing accurate facial composites than kits or artists (Koehn & Fisher, 1997; Kovera, Penrod, Pappas, & Thill, 1997). So far, this research has consistently found that facial composites developed from the memory of eyewitnesses are poor models of the "real" face of the offender.

Family Forensic Psychology

Forensic psychologists are becoming increasingly involved in family law, and family forensic psychologists are leading the way in dealing with the many new and emerging issues in this area. For example, the 2000 census indicates that there has been a baby boom in gay and lesbian families as well as a dramatic increase of cohabitating, single-parent, and grandparent-led families (Grossman & Okun, 2003).

> These changes impact family formation, maintenance, and dissolution and challenge traditional concepts of what a family is and how families function. Family courts are struggling with unprecedented issues over visitation and custody with lesbian, gay, and cohabitating parents who split up; whether surrogate mothers or donors of eggs or sperm have any parental rights; and the implications of children who are doing well living with a grandparent when a parent is released from jail and wants to reclaim these children. (Grossman & Okun, 2003, p. 163)

In addition, family forensic psychologists are concerned with

> abuse; adoption; alternative families; child support; divorce, including custody, relocation, and conflict resolution; elder law, including estate planning; family business; guardianship; juvenile justice; paternity; reproductive and genetic technologies; and other areas such as termination of parental rights. Family forensic psychology is involved in civil and criminal cases when the understanding of family dynamics and family systems is essential, for example, in cases involving visitation to prisons, release programs, and impact of sentencing on family members. (Grossman & Okun, 2003, p. 166)

The best-known areas of **family forensic psychology** involve child custody, family violence, and the assessment and treatment of juveniles, all topics that will be covered in some detail later in the book. We will describe the other newer topics as we encounter them throughout various sections of the text.

Correctional Psychology:
An Overview

Correctional psychology is arguably the fastest growing branch of forensic psychology. The number of persons incarcerated in the United States is now over 2 million and growing daily. Although only a portion (7%–10%) of these individuals qualify as "chronic offenders," it is estimated that each chronic offender costs society about $1.3 million over the course of the offender's lifetime (Crawford, 2002). In addition, more than 4 million persons are under correctional supervision in the community, such as on probation or parole. Clearly, there is a great need for the services of correctional psychologists.

Correctional psychologists are sometimes distinguished from psychologists working in correctional facilities or with correctional populations in the community. The correctional psychologist typically has "specific academic and/or program training in correctional philosophy, systems, offender management, forensic report writing, treatment aimed at reducing recidivism, and outcome research" (Althouse, 2000, p. 436). Many—if not most—psychologists working in corrections do not have this specific background. Nevertheless, they offer valuable services to corrections. For our purposes, we will use the terms interchangeably.

In 1974, psychologist Ned Megargee remarked, "By and large, psychology as a scientific discipline has not made a substantial contribution to the applied area of corrections" (p. 44). Correctional psychology has changed dramatically since the 1970s, however. In recent years, correctional and research psychologists have made substantial contributions to corrections, particularly pertaining to inmate classification systems, psychological assessments, program/treatment evaluation, crisis intervention strategies, and substance abuse treatment approaches. As the number of opportunities in corrections has proliferated for psychologists, psychologists have increasingly discovered that correctional psychology is an exciting, rewarding, and challenging field (Richardson, 2003).

The correctional psychologist's major goal is to help in inmate rehabilitation, treatment, and reintegration into the community. Direct inmate services may include crisis intervention, long-term and short-term therapy, group therapy, and substance abuse treatment. Psychologists in these settings administer a wide variety of psychological assessment techniques (intellectual, personality, aptitude, vocational, and educational), interpret results, and prepare comprehensive reports. Their recommendations are considered in decisions to release prisoners, change their security levels, and/or assign them to a variety of programs. The above services also are offered to offenders who are serving their sentences, or the end of their sentences, in the community—specifically, those on probation or parole.

Correctional psychologists also offer consultative services relating to corrections staff, which may include screening and selection, employee assistance counseling, and mental health consultation with hostage negotiation or crisis support teams. Research opportunities are often available, particularly—although not exclusively—in the larger prison systems.

The Federal Bureau of Prisons (BOP), an agency of the U.S. Department of Justice, employs doctoral-level clinical or counseling psychologists, licensed or license-eligible general staff psychologists, and substance abuse specialists. The BOP currently supports a team of more than 350 psychologists and 650 mental health/substance abuse treatment specialists in more than 100 federal correctional institutions nationwide. The BOP is organized nationally into six regions and has its headquarters in Washington, D.C. It is one of the largest employers of psychologists in the United States. Entry-level salaries range from $41,000 to $80,000, commensurate with experience. More experienced psychologists generally receive salaries ranging from $70,457 to $91,589 (GS-14). Salaries at state correctional facilities vary according to region but, in most instances, probably pay slightly less than the BOP.

Research psychologists often study the psychological effects of correctional systems on prisoner behavior. Topics include the general effect of imprisonment on special populations of offenders, such as the mentally disordered or the elderly; the effects of crowding; the effects of isolation; and the outcome of various rehabilitative programs. Interestingly, psychologists in this setting are sometimes criticized for aligning themselves with prison administrators or failing to acknowledge the detrimental effects of incarceration. Nevertheless, many correctional psychologists find great personal and professional satisfaction working in these settings. In addition, as we will note in Chapter 12, there is ample evidence to support the positive impact of psychology on the correctional system (see, generally, APA's *Monitor on Psychology,* 2003).

Boothby and Clements (2000) conducted an extensive survey of 830 psychologists working in state and federal prisons (but not jails) across the United States; 59% held a doctorate. All psychologists in federal prisons held doctorates, whereas state prisons employed master's- and doctoral-level psychologists about equally. According to the survey, correctional psychologists spend most of their time on administrative tasks (30%), followed by direct treatment of inmates (26%) and psychological testing and assessment (18%). Very little time was devoted to research (6%). In the same survey, the psychologists expressed a wish that they had more time to offer direct treatment. An additional report based on material obtained in this survey (Boothby & Clements, 2002) will be covered in Chapter 12.

Psychologists working in correctional facilities are guided by a series of recently updated standards developed by the **American Association for Correctional Psychology** (AACP) (Standards Committee, 2000). (See Box 1.7 for a description of the AACP.) These standards provide the minimum acceptable levels for psychological services offered to offenders, whether they are adults or juveniles, held in local, state, or federal facilities, as well as in the community. They cover a wide range of principles as well as services, including

---

BOX 1.7 American Association for Correctional Psychology

The American Association for Correctional Psychology (AACP) is an organization of behavioral scientists and practitioners who are concerned with the delivery of high-quality mental health services to criminal offenders and with promoting and disseminating research on the etiology, assessment, and treatment of criminal behavior. Students interested in correctional psychology are encouraged to become members of the organization. The goals of AACP are:

- To promote the development of psychological practice in criminal justice and law enforcement settings
- To contribute toward appropriate teaching of the psychology of crime, delinquency, and criminal justice
- To support the development and application of effective treatment approaches for individuals in the care of the criminal justice system
- To stimulate research into the nature of criminal behavior, to exchange such scientific information, and to publish the reports of scholarly studies of criminal behavior
- To concern ourselves with relevant public, professional, and institutional issues that affect or are affected by the practice of psychology in the criminal justice system

licensure, staffing requirements, confidentiality issues, duty to warn, professional development, informed consent, segregation, and a host of other topics relating to this work.

Defining Forensic Psychology—A Recap

The foregoing sections indicate that the field of forensic psychology, as we define it broadly, provides ample opportunities for psychologists interested in interacting with some aspect of the law. We have devoted separate sections of this book to each of the five subareas defined above. It should be noted that those who favor a narrow definition of forensic psychology are referring primarily to the *clinical practice* that falls under our subareas of *legal psychology* and *correctional psychology*.

Otto and Heilbrun (2002) posit that if forensic psychology (particularly legal psychology) is to continue to grow and develop as a viable discipline, it has to become more mainstream. Currently, they note, a relatively small group of forensic specialists devote themselves full-time to this field, whereas a much larger group of psychologists provide occasional forensic services or provide such services only within a circumscribed area, such as child custody evaluations. They argue that forensic psychology, as a field, must acknowledge the fact that forensic practice is occurring at a variety of levels and for different reasons. The field must develop a plan to ensure that forensic practice overall is well informed and competent. This plan is especially needed in the area of forensic testing and assessment.

Otto and Heilbrun (2002) and Bersoff and his colleagues (1997) suggest that forensic psychology should recognize three levels of psychologists or clinicians who provide services in the field. First, there would be the "legally informed clinician," who has a basic education in law relevant to professional practice, "including information about confidentiality, privileged communication, and response to subpoenas for clinical records or personal notes" (Otto & Heilbrun, 2002, p. 15). Second, there would be the "proficient clinician," who has a midlevel expertise gained from academic coursework, professional training, and a supervised experience in forensic psychology. His or her knowledge should consist of relevant law, procedures, and ethics applicable to the kinds of forensic practice in which the individual engages. The third group would be the "specialist clinician," who would demonstrate the highest level of expertise obtained through formal training in forensic psychology at the graduate and postgraduate levels. His or her training should include intensive and in-depth understanding of the relevant law and legal procedures as well as knowledge about a range of relevant psychological procedures and issues. Whether these three levels of expertise eventually become recognized remains to be seen.

Summary and Conclusions

As recently as 25 years ago, the term *forensic psychology* had barely been introduced into psychological or legal literature. Today, as we have seen, it is a commonly encountered term, but it still defies definition. Although the consensus might seem to favor a narrow definition limiting it to clinical practice, the contributions of research psychologists may be undermined by such an approach. In addition, it is important to consider the context in which forensic psychology is practiced. Limiting forensic psychology to work with civil and criminal courts and correctional systems—which seems to be the consequence of a narrow definition—does not recognize well enough the law-related functions performed by psychologists working with law enforcement or victims. Finally, the many contributions of psychologists who study the psychology of crime and delinquency deserve to be included in this field. The legal system surely can benefit, for example, from research on the developmental paths to delinquency or research on the prevention and control of sex offending.

We have persisted, then, in advocating for a broad definition of forensic psychology, one that could divide it into the five subareas covered in this chapter. In fact, in structuring this book, we came very close to adding a sixth area, the forensic school specialization discussed under crime and delinquency. Given the rapid development and increasing need for services within the educational system, it may be only a matter of time before such a subarea of forensic psychology is warranted.

Likewise, family forensic psychology, discussed under legal psychology but having obvious relevance to other subspecialties, may be deserving of the same special attention. In each of the areas discussed, numerous career opportunities exist. Both undergraduate and graduate programs have rapidly seen the need for preparation for careers in forensic psychology, and professionals themselves are regularly offered opportunities for licensing, certification, and continuing education.

PART II

Police and Investigative Psychology

CHAPTER 2

Police Psychology

History and Practice

Today, approximately 18,000 agencies qualify as law enforcement agencies in the United States. They exist at four levels of government: federal, state, county, and local or municipal. As law enforcement departments have become more professional and the public has demanded more accountability, the role of psychological services to law enforcement has become more critical and prevalent. In addition, a wide range of private and public safety agencies also exists. Some are private security agencies, and others are supported by public funding, such as campus police departments on public university and college campuses.

Psychologists involved in providing psychological services to law enforcement participate in a wide variety of tasks, including helping in the screening and selection of employees, conducting **fitness-for-duty evaluations,** assessing deadly force incidents, and doing special unit evaluations. Special unit evaluations include the selection and training of special weapons and tactical teams (SWATs), tactical response teams (TRTs), and hostage negotiation teams (HNTs). Psychologists also provide counseling or psychotherapy services, such as may be required after a shooting incident when an officer uses deadly force or witnesses a police colleague killed in the line of duty. In addition, it is estimated that about 7% of police contacts involve people who are mentally disordered (Borum, Deane, Steadman, & Morrissey, 1998). Research has shown that most people with severe mental problems—either mental illness or mental retardation—will experience at least one arrest, and many will be arrested more than once (McFarland, Faulkner, Bloom, Hallaux, & Bray, 1989). Consequently, psychologists may be asked to assess the situation, such as making a referral or talking to the individual, or train police officers on effective strategies for dealing with these specialized populations. Psychologists also participate in the development of training, research, and implementation of effective mental health programs for public safety personnel, including critical incident stress debriefings (commonly abbreviated CISDs), crisis intervention techniques, stress management, and referral to other providers. Critical incidents refer to tragedies, death, serious injuries, hostage situations, and other threatening situations that the police frequently encounter. CISDs are commonly implemented in public safety departments (including emergency service personnel) across the United States, Canada, the United Kingdom, and other parts of the world (Miller, 1995).

Many psychologists providing some or all these services prefer to call themselves "police psychologists." As defined in Chapter 1, *police psychology* is the research and application of psychological principles and clinical skills to law enforcement and public safety. As also mentioned in Chapter 1, a police psychologist does not have to be a present or former police officer to be an effective service provider to law enforcement agencies. However, the police psychologist must be highly familiar with and knowledgeable about what policing involves. (See Box 2.1)

Entry into the field of police psychology for most psychologists usually begins by providing consulting services to police agencies, such as screening and selection, or psychotherapy or counseling of police officers and their families. Claiming to be an expert, without earning the acceptance and respect of a police agency, however, will likely lead to limited success. On the other hand, if the psychologist proves effective, trustworthy, and credible, the department may begin to request a variety of other services such as help with management problems, shift work assignments, fitness-for-duty evaluations, or evaluating officers who have applied for promotion. Ride-along programs, in which the psychologist accompanies police officers in patrol cars, are usually helpful in educating the psychologists about the realities of the police experience (Hatcher, Mohandie, Turner, & Gelles, 1998). As experience accumulates, the psychologist may be asked to do many other things, such as evaluating an alleged use of excessive force incident, or become a member of the hostage/crisis negotiation team. "The invitation to the psychologist to participate in the hostage/crisis negotiation team

---

BOX 2.1   Examples of Employment Ads for a Police Psychologist

The Smithsville Police Department (SPD) Behavioral Science Services is seeking to fill a number of police psychologist positions: A police psychologist provides a range of psychological services to sworn and civilian members of the SPD. Duties include but are not limited to individual and couples counseling, teaching, supervisory/managerial consultation, health education, research, and program development. The police psychologists will periodically serve after-hours on-call, during which time they may receive emergency calls regarding psychological emergencies or respond as part of the crisis negotiations team. All candidates must be fully licensed or licensable in the state. Successful candidates must clear a thorough background check prior to being offered employment.

The City of Green Springs Police Department seeks a licensed psychologist to conduct clinical fitness-for-duty assessments as well as psychological evaluations of all applicants. Will be expected to implement programs, training, and organizational consultations; act as expert and resource on personnel matters; provide counseling and therapy for officers and others in support of critical or emergency situations; and recommend improvement to existing programs and procedures. *Qualifications include the following:* PhD in psychology and current license or ability to obtain same. Experience with psychological evaluations, forensic psychology, crisis intervention, stress management, and marital/family/children/teen counseling is highly recommended.

appears to depend upon three factors: (1) mutual acceptance, (2) professional credibility (timely provision of critical information and behavioral analysis), and (3) an ability to function in the field setting" (Hatcher et al., 1998, p. 462). We will discuss the roles of the police psychologist as an integral member of the hostage/crisis negotiation team later in the chapter.

In this chapter, we will also briefly touch on some key issues involved in police behavior, such as discretion and the use of force. The competent police psychologist also must be well informed about current psychological research relating to police strategies, such as research on lineups, eyewitnesses, and the identification of suspects.

We begin this chapter with a review of the history of police psychology, including its origin in the tasks of police screening and selection. Because very little has been written on police psychology in general, it is helpful to travel this historical route to gain a basic understanding of the foundations and activities of the police psychologist.

Trends in Police Psychology

Beginnings of the Profession

Precisely when police psychology began is unclear. Viteles (1929) discovered that police departments in Germany were using psychologists in a variety of ways at least as early as 1919. Chandler (1990) noted that in 1966, the Munich (Germany) police were employing a full-time in-house psychologist to train officers to deal with patrol problems, such as crowd control. An in-house psychologist is one who is retained as a regular employee of the agency, in contrast to a psychological consultant, who is independent of the agency but contracted to provide special services. Today, the great majority of police psychologists are consultants (Bartol, 1996).

In the United States, police psychology probably began as a viable profession in 1968 when Martin Reiser, EdD, was hired as a full-time in-house psychologist by the Los Angeles Police Department

(LAPD). A year later, in 1969, Reiser presented a paper at the Western Psychological Association Convention in Vancouver titled "The Police Department Psychologist." The presentation was later published in 1972. Chandler (1990) suggests that the presentation of the paper probably marks the official beginning of American police psychology.

There is little doubt that Reiser was the most prolific writer on police psychology in this country throughout the 1970s. He also established the first graduate student internship in police psychology at the LAPD, in conjunction with the California School of Professional Psychology. However, it remains debatable whether Reiser was the first full-time psychologist employed by a police department in the United States. It is likely that some psychologists were employed by American police agencies prior to 1969, but their work may have become lost in history. Reiser (1982) himself, in a collection of published papers, asserted that he was not at all sure he was the first full-time police psychologist in the United States. For now, though, we will refer to the year 1968—the year he was officially hired—as the "beginning" of police psychology until we learn otherwise.

Four discernible but overlapping historical trends in police psychology can be delineated: (1) mental and aptitude screening of law enforcement, (2) personality assessment and the search for the "police personality," (3) stress management and other clinical services, and (4) fairness in testing. In the first trend, psychologists tried to identify the intellectual skills and aptitude required to be an effective police officer. The second focused on the development of personality measures that could distinguish effective officers from less effective ones. It was also concerned with the search to discover the elusive "police personality." The third trend, stress management, refers to the development of psychological techniques for identifying and controlling stressful conditions often encountered in law enforcement. To carry out their duties effectively, law enforcement officers must be able to cope with a wide variety

---

BOX 2.2   Dr. Martin Reiser's Advice to Psychologists Consulting With Police

---

One major difficulty described by Police Psychologist Martin Reiser when consulting with police is the amount of suspicion and distrust directed at the psychologist by law enforcement officers. Changing these negative percepts requires openness and sensitivity on the part of the psychologist. All too often, Reiser observes, consultants approach the police like professors talking down to first-year college students. An attitude of humility and the willingness to listen are useful behaviors at the beginning of the police relationship.

Reiser recommends that the aspiring police psychologist have training in clinical, organizational, educational, and research psychology. In addition, experience in teaching, program evaluation and development, organizational consultation, counseling and therapy, and research design would be helpful.

Reiser also believes that the police consultant needs to be patient and open-minded because of the slowness of change so characteristic of bureaucratic organizations. In some cases, the consultant will need to be tolerant of the many frustrations inherent in the quasi-military structure of many police organizations.

Confidentiality is especially important when providing therapy, assessment, and research to law enforcement. And if possible, the police consultant should maintain offices outside of the police facility for assessment and therapy work. This would increase the utilization of services by officers who might otherwise fear being seen by supervisors or peers while visiting the "shrink's" office.

For "in-house" police psychologists (those who work for the department as employees rather than consultants), the perennial problem of limited resources for psychological purposes can be ameliorated by developing an internship with colleges and universities on a quid quo pro basis—supervision and licensing credit in exchange for services to the police department.

Source: Reiser and Klyver (1987).

---

of stress that results from the job. Fairness in testing, the fourth trend, refers to the requirements that all people should have an equal chance of being selected on the basis of individual merit and qualifications. Each trend will be examined more closely in the following pages.

The First Trend: Mental and Aptitude Testing

Even before police psychology officially began, psychologist Louis Terman (1917), using the Stanford-Binet Intelligence Scale (one of the earliest "IQ" tests), tested the intelligence of applicants for several firefighter and police officer positions for the city of San Jose, California, in 1916. Their ages ranged from 21 to 38, with a median age of 30. Much to his surprise, Terman discovered that a large majority of the candidates were functioning near what he considered "dull normal" range of intelligence. More specifically, only three candidates obtained an IQ score over 100, the score considered average for the general population. College freshmen averaged 116 on the Stanford-Binet at that time. The education level of these applicants for the public safety positions was limited, with only four of the applicants having attended high school and none going beyond the sophomore year.

On the basis of his experience with the intellectual capabilities of school-age children,

Terman concluded that police and firefighting positions apparently attracted individuals of below average intelligence. He recommended that all candidates who scored below 80 on the Stanford-Binet be eliminated automatically from further job consideration for public safety positions. He also urged police administrators to keep the cognitive ability scores and compare them with later job performance, but apparently this was never done. As a result of Terman's project, an IQ score of 80 was established as an arbitrary score to indicate ability to perform public safety responsibilities during that time.

A contemporary of Terman, psychologist Louis Thurstone, was also interested in the value of mental testing in the screening and selection of police officers. Thurstone (1922) administered the Army Intelligence Examination (the Army Alpha) to 358 various ranking male employees of the Detroit Police Department. The Army Alpha was an intelligence measure designed by the U.S. military during World War I as a *quick* classification device for placing recruits into various training programs. Thurstone found that the police officers at all ranks scored below average on the scale. In fact, the more experienced the police officer was, the lower was his intelligence. The average score for the 307 patrol officers was 71.44, the 34 sergeants averaged 54.71, and the 17 lieutenants 57.80 (the average score for 1½ million recruits on the Alpha was 100). Similar findings were reported in a later study conducted in California 2 years later (Fernald & Sullivan, 1924). Like Terman, Thurstone concluded that law enforcement simply did not attract intelligent individuals. He further surmised that the more intelligent individuals who entered police service quickly left for other occupations, where their ability and intelligence were presumably better recognized. The less intelligent remained on the force and were promoted through the ranks. However, it should be mentioned that the early versions of the Army Alpha had many flaws and significant problems in accurately measuring intelligence. At the very least, the Army Alpha demonstrated marginal validity in its ability to classify people on the basis of intellectual functioning. Therefore, these scores may not have accurately reflected the "intelligence" of the officers who took the exam—or of the army recruits, for that matter.

Law enforcement officers were vindicated, however, when Stanford Professor Maude Merrill (1927) administered a newer version of the Army Alpha to 113 applicants for positions to the police force of Palo Alto, California (population of 11,500 at the time), between 1924 and 1926. Although the overall average score was 104—slightly above average on the scale—the median Alpha score of the men selected for the police force was 136, a score substantially above average. Even more impressive was the finding that those officers who remained on the force for at least 2 years had achieved significantly higher scores on the Alpha (143.5) and were better educated. Essentially, the hired officers had even higher average Alpha scores than the college students at Stanford University (located in Palo Alto). As an explanation for these highly intellectual officers at the Palo Alto PD, Merrill believed the police chief (Chief Zink) was partly responsible. Merrill (1927) wrote,

The Chief is not only in thorough sympathy with the use of scientific methods in police work but has been well trained and has himself contributed to the development of such methods in that field. Perhaps the organization itself under capable leadership offers an incentive to capable, intelligent men in police work. (p. 515)

Improvement in professionalism and in rewards of law enforcement work over the years began to attract significantly more intellectually capable law enforcement officers. In later studies, law enforcement officers obtained at least average intelligence scores across a wide spectrum of law enforcement agencies (C. C. Gordon, 1969; Matarazzo, Allen, Saslow, & Wiens, 1964). In a review of the literature, Poland (1978) notes that "if police agencies can attract applicants with some college education, they have an applicant pool of above average intelligence" (p. 376).

As encouraging as it may be to know that law enforcement personnel are not substandard intellectually, this tells us little about the relationship between intelligence level and actual job performance. Is high intelligence—as measured by traditional IQ tests—a predictor of superb or even satisfactory functioning as a law enforcement officer? Or does some other form of intelligence, such as street sense or social intelligence—represent a better indicator of effective performance? It should be noted that despite Poland's (1978) comment about the value of a college education, college-educated officers have not been found to be better on the job overall. However, they have been shown to have better communication skills and have earned promotions at a higher rate than non-college-educated officers (Cole & Smith, 2001).

In general, intelligence and ability tests have been useful predictors of police academy performance but less valuable for predicting how well an officer actually performs in the field (Henderson, 1979; Spielberger, Ward, & Spaulding, 1979). Screening of applicants for law enforcement positions, then, should go beyond simply using standardized intelligence tests. A multiassessment procedure involving standardized tests plus other measures and screening procedures should be used.

The Second Trend: Personality Assessment

This trend was initially prompted by six different Presidential Commissions on Law Enforcement and Crime during the 1960s, all of which emphasized the value of properly selected law enforcement officers. Implicit in these far-reaching recommendations was the pressing need for reliable and valid testing that would evaluate the intellectual capacity, emotional stability, and personality characteristics of law enforcement personnel.

During this era, police officers across the country came under intense scrutiny as they dealt—sometimes brutally—with peaceful civil rights protesters and antiwar demonstrations. In 1967, the Task Force on the Police (President's Commission on Law Enforcement and the Administration of Justice, 1967) concluded that police were too often out of touch with the communities they served and underscored the lack of adequate screening in most law enforcement agencies. The commission asserted,

> Screening out candidates whose emotional stability makes them clearly unfit for police work—through psychological tests and psychiatric interviews—should also improve the capacity of police forces to improve community relations. . . . While there is not one psychological test which can reliably identify all candidates who are emotionally unfit for police service, a combination of tests and oral psychiatric interviews can pinpoint many serious character defects. (pp. 164–165)

In keeping with the recommendations of this and other commissions, the U.S. Congress provided funds from the Law Enforcement Assistance Administration (LEAA) for law enforcement agencies to retain the services of mental health professionals, including properly trained police psychologists. Because the funding was intended to identify the emotions, personality, and prejudices of police officers, psychologists—especially police psychologists—were expected to become more test conscious and sophisticated about the power and capabilities of personality inventories and psychological tests.

Five years later, the National Advisory Commission on Criminal Justice Standards and Goals also recommended that every law enforcement agency "employ a formal process for the selection of qualified police applicants. This process should include a written test of mental ability or aptitude, an oral interview, a physical examination, a psychological examination, and an in-depth background investigation" (Spielberger, 1979, p. xi).

Extent of Psychological Testing in Law Enforcement Agencies

Following the federal recommendations and guidelines, did law enforcement agencies respond to the push for having diversified psychological testing as a prominent component in the selection process? To answer this, it helps to compare the results of studies conducted before and after the federal government stepped in. In a survey conducted during the early 1960s on the use of psychological tests in metropolitan police departments, Narrol and Levitt (1963) found that 85% of the departments reported using some type of psychological testing, broadly defined. Almost all the reporting departments indicated they primarily used mental or aptitude instruments and found little need to measure emotional stability, judgment, or personality in general. Moreover, the testing programs were described only vaguely. The departments appeared to be using them as a symbolic gesture to appease the community rather than as empirically conceived instruments of valid selection. Most of the tests were little more than unstandardized intelligence or aptitude tests of questionable design or validity. Concurrent or predictive validity—the measures of how the tests actually related to performance—were unknown or not even examined by most departments. Only 22% of the departments reported using "personality measures" in their selection process, and only one department reported doing any original research to determine the validity of the tests it used.

Nearly 10 years later, Murphy (1972) conducted a comprehensive survey of 49 state police agencies and 258 local and municipal police departments employing at least 100 officers. Although the data revealed no discernible shift in the percentage of departments using psychological exams, he did find a substantial shift away from questionable aptitude, intelligence, or projective tests and toward better developed and empirically based objective personality inventories. Departments were adopting more standardized and somewhat more valid psychological measures of personality and emotional status. Surprisingly, the survey indicated that, compared to the local and municipal departments, state police agencies were slower at adopting psychological measures in the screening process. More specifically, although 44% of the local or municipal police departments used "psychological examinations" to screen police candidates, only 13% of the state law enforcement agencies used them.

Most of the tests reported in the Murphy (1972) survey were objective, paper-and-pencil personality inventories. The Minnesota Multiphasic Personality Inventory (MMPI) was by far the most common personality measure used, with 48.75% of the agencies using it alone or in combination with other psychological instruments. Murphy further learned that 41.25% of the agencies also used a "psychiatric interview" as part of their screening procedure.

Fifteen years after the Murphy study, in a nationwide survey designed to measure the extent to which law enforcement agencies used psychological services, Delprino and Bahn (1988) reported that 52% of the municipal and state police departments responding indicated they used psychological screening on police applicants. In a more recent survey of 155 agencies, Cochrane, Tett, and VandeCreek (2003) found that 91% of the municipal police departments use personality measures in their selection procedures, a dramatic increase from the Delprino and Bahn survey conducted more than a decade earlier. Although the departments used a wide variety of screening instruments, Cochrane et al. discovered that the most frequently used personality measures were the Minnesota Multiphasic Personality Inventory—Revised (71.6%), the California Psychological Inventory (24.5%), the Sixteen Personality Factor—Fifth Edition (18.7%), and the Inwald Personality Inventory (11.6%). In addition, more than 90% of the departments used a background investigation along with a medical exam, interview, and application. More than half of the agencies also said they use drug testing, measures of physical fitness, and the polygraph in the screening process.

Research on Personality Assessment

The **personality assessment** trend has two research offshoots, the first being a search for the police personality (Lefkowitz, 1975). Law enforcement agencies were asking (and hoping), "Does policing draw a certain kind of personality, and can we identify the 'successful' personality as opposed to the 'unsuccessful' personality?" The second research offshoot involved an effort to identify or develop personality measures that could select out and possibly select in. **Screening-out procedures** try to eliminate those applicants who demonstrate significant signs of psychopathology or emotional instability or who lack the *basic* ability or mental acuity to perform the job in a safe and responsible manner. Screening-out procedures are the procedures most commonly applied by police psychologists when screening police candidates. **Screening-in procedures,** on the other hand, are intended to identify those attributes (almost invariably personality) that distinguish one candidate over another as being potentially a more effective officer. Implicit in this approach is the ability to rank order applicants, allowing agencies to select the top candidates from a pool that passed the initial screening procedures. This approach assumes that there are traits, habits, reactions, and attitudes that distinguish an outstanding cop from a satisfactory one. To date, there is virtually no evidence that psychologists have reached this laudable goal in any satisfactory, valid manner, however. Carefully conducted research and sophisticated analysis, though, may well achieve this goal in the future.

The search for the "police personality" has been much less promising, and few police psychologists today actually pursue it. It is clear that law enforcement draws a wide spectrum of personalities, most of which do a commendable job of policing across a wide range of tasks and responsibilities. Consequently, further attempts to discover a particular type of personality "best suited" for law enforcement are unlikely to be productive.

On the other hand, screening out ineffective or undesirable police officers remains a challenging but reasonable goal. One of the very first steps in achieving this goal is to recognize and understand the nature of the daily tasks expected of law enforcement officers. This requires the identification and analysis of the skills, abilities, knowledge, and psychological characteristics that are needed to do the job, a process called **job analysis.** In the past, many law enforcement screening procedures have been based on intuition and "gut feeling" rather than a comprehensive analysis of job requirements. However, without a job analysis to justify the choice of psychological measures, it is extremely difficult for the screener to know what he or she is looking for—let alone measure it. Job analyses have revealed that successful police officers need to have good judgment and common sense, appropriate decision-making skills, interpersonal skills, a solid memory, good observation talents, and communication skills (both oral and written) (Spielberger, 1979). Integrity and trustworthiness are certainly other important traits. Although the emphasis that each agency places on the above characteristics may differ slightly, they tend to be universal psychological requirements for law enforcement. Thus, police psychologists often recommend a screening out of applicants who demonstrate a lack of these attributes. Mental disorders and serious behavioral problems, of course, are clear reasons for refusal to hire or for termination.

There is a lack of consensus concerning which personality inventory or measure is most useful in the screening process. As the surveys described above indicated, the following six personality measures are currently the most commonly used in the screening of law enforcement officers:

- The Minnesota Multiphasic Personality Inventory—Revised (MMPI-2)
- The Inwald Personality Inventory (IPI)
- The California Psychological Inventory (CPI)
- The Personality Assessment Inventory (PAI)
- The NEO Personality Inventory—Revised (NEO PI-R)
- The Sixteen Personality Factor—Fifth Edition (16-PF)

The MMPI-2 has drawn the greatest amount of research of all personality inventories and is, by far, the most commonly used in the screening of law enforcement applicants. For instance, Cochrane et al. (2003) report that in their national survey of municipal police departments, 72% said they regularly use the MMPI-2 in their officer screening process. The original MMPI was developed during the late 1930s and early 1940s as a diagnostic tool for psychiatric screening. The items and scales were developed empirically based on the abnormal behaviors and symptoms that differentiated psychiatric patients from nonpsychiatric patients (nurses and visitors to the Minnesota State Mental Hospital), who we can only assume were "normal."

The second version of the MMPI (MMPI-2), published in 1989, has a standardization sample that, compared to the original MMPI, is far more representative of the country as a whole, and the distribution of African Americans, Latinos, Asians, Native Americans, and other minorities is considerably more in balance with their distribution across the nation. Consequently, the MMPI-2 is more appropriate for testing a broad range of ethnically diverse people. Based on the available research, MMPI-2 scores are less likely to discriminate on the basis of race or ethnic origin. The available data suggest that all groups, on average, score basically the same on the scales (Pope, Butcher, & Seelen, 2000). On the original MMPI, there was some evidence that some racial or minority groups did score somewhat differently on certain MMPI subscales. Thus, the inventory

had the potential of placing certain groups at a disadvantage during the screening process. The MMPI-2 has made some meaningful strides in correcting this problem. Second, the MMPI-2 eliminated a number of outdated and objectionable items found on the original MMPI. There were invasion-of-privacy issues inherent in the test that very much needed to be corrected. The MMPI-2 is relatively free of intimate, privacy intrusions.

The research on the power of the MMPI-2 to predict police officer performance has shown mixed results (Bartol, 1996). Some studies show promise, but others have concluded that some preemployment screening instruments are superior to the MMPI-2. Most of the research on the MMPI as it relates to law enforcement has been of the concurrent validation variety, whereby the personality characteristics of already employed police officers are assessed and used to establish predictors of good performance. **Concurrent validity** is the degree to which a test identifies a person's *current* performance on the dimensions and tasks the test is supposed to measure. Typically, the inventory is administered to officers representing varying degrees of success in law enforcement work, with "success" determined by supervisory ratings. For example, if a high percentage of officers evaluated by supervisors as "successful" respond differently to questions on a scale of the MMPI-2 than a group of "unsuccessful" officers, the scale is considered a good evaluator of *current* on-the-job performance.

Research that examines the current performance of individuals already on the force has a critical limitation, however, because it ignores the important personality characteristics of those officers who were hired but dropped out because of various problems during the course of their career path. Thus, significant segments of the population are missed. One of the primary reasons for using any screening instrument is to discover the potential dropouts or failures as soon as possible in their careers, which could save both time and money.

Predictive validation is a more useful and rigorous research procedure than concurrent-related validation, but it is rarely implemented because it requires a longitudinal design in which officers must be followed over an extended period of time, usually several years. **Predictive validity** is the degree to which a test *predicts* a person's subsequent performance on the dimensions and tasks the test is designed to measure. If a test or inventory claims to be able to predict which candidates develop into good or outstanding police officers, its predictive validity should be high, discriminating those who eventually perform well from those who do not. If there is empirical evidence that the instrument does have predictive validity, a test is a powerful device for the screening and selection of candidates prior to entry into law enforcement. Officers are tested during a preemployment stage and then followed over their careers to see how the initial testing results could have predicted eventual problems. Some research focusing on predictive validity of the MMPI and MMPI-2 has been conducted and shown some promise, provided the intent is to identify psychopathology or behavioral problems (Bartol, 1991). Far too much of the research on the MMPI-2 has incorrectly assumed that the inventory has the capacity to appraise both emotional status and *normal* personality traits, however. The MMPI and MMPI-2 were both originally designed to identify possible psychopathology and behavioral deviations and *not* normal personality traits. To force the instrument into doing something it is not equipped to do is unlikely to produce encouraging results. In summary, then, the MMPI-2 has better use as a screening-out measure to identify candidates least suited for law enforcement work, rather than as a screening-in measure to confirm the existence of positive attributes.

The IPI is a 310-item, true-false questionnaire that has 26 scales. The IPI was specifically designed to measure the suitability of law enforcement and public safety candidates based on a variety of personality traits and behavioral patterns (Inwald, 1992). It was developed to measure both normal personality traits and deviant behavioral patterns, such as job difficulties, substance abuse, driving violations, absence abuse (missing excessive days of work), and antisocial attitudes. The IPI also contains a 19-item validity scale called "Guardedness," which is intended to identify those individuals resistant to revealing negative information about themselves (the MMPI-2 has a similar "Lie" scale). As Inwald (1992) states, "When a candidate denies such items, a strong need to appear unusually virtuous is indicated" (p. 4). If this score is low, the other scale scores may be affected due to socially desirable responses from the respondent.

Robin Inwald (the author of the IPI) and her associates continue to do research in an effort to improve the reliability and validity of the IPI. So far, the research suggests that the IPI, in *some* situations, does slightly better than the MMPI-2 in predicting the performance of public safety personnel and probably is a useful instrument when used in combination with other screening instruments. One strength of the IPI is that it has good face validity. **Face validity** refers not to what the test actually measures but to what it superficially *appears* to measure (Anastasi, 1988). If a test "looks valid" or if it appears to measure what should be measured, it has face validity. In reality, there may be no empirical support for these assumptions. Face validity does have some value because examinees believe the exam is at least pertinent to the job for which they are applying. In addition, Otto et al. (1998) emphasize the importance of face validity for application in the legal context because any measuring instrument should look pertinent and relevant to the legal questions at hand. However, unless other types of validity are also ensured, a test with high face validity has little overall worth with regard to measuring what it is supposed to measure.

Currently, the IPI is used in the preemployment screening process by about 12% of all municipal police departments across the country (Cochrane et al., 2003). The IPI has remained at roughly that percentage of use in preemployment screening over the past decade.

The CPI (Gough, 1987) contains 462 true or false questions designed to measure various features of the normal personality. An earlier version, called Version I, has 480 questions. The inventory is to be used with both adolescents and adults to predict how individuals will behave and react in a variety of interpersonal situations (Murphy & Davidshofer, 1998). The items are grouped into 20 scales developed to measure attributes of personality involved in interpersonal behavior and social interaction (Murphy & Davidshofer, 1998). Norms of law enforcement applicants are available from the publisher (Consulting Psychologists Press, Inc.). The nationwide survey conducted by Cochrane et al. (2003) revealed that approximately 25% of the departments responding indicated that they used the CPI in their screening procedure.

Some success has been reported for the ability of the CPI to predict performance, both during training and in the field. Topp and Kardash (1986) compared the CPI scores of police recruits who passed academy training with the scores of those who failed or resigned from the academy prior to graduation. Based on CPI score patterns, the researchers described those who graduated as more outgoing, stable, venturesome, confident, controlled, and relaxed. In a recent comprehensive meta-analysis assessing the overall validity of personality measures as predictors of the job performance of law enforcement officers, Varela, Boccaccini, Scogin, Stump, and Caputo (in press) discovered that prediction was strongest for the CPI compared to the MMPI or IPI. Varela and his coauthors reasoned that one possible explanation for the superior performance of the CPI is that the CPI is designed to measure *normal* personality traits, in contrast to the MMPI-2, which—as we mentioned previously—is designed to measure psychopathology. They write,

Personality measures that are designed to assess normal personality traits, such as the CPI, may be more useful in this context because they provide information that is not obtained during the initial screening process. For instance, the CPI was designed to provide information about consistent style of interpersonal behavior. Because being a successful police officer requires effective interpersonal skills, the CPI may be a useful measure for predicting this important aspect of officer performance.

The PAI (Morey, 1991) is a self-administered, objective inventory of adult personality that provides information on "critical clinical variables." The PAI contains 344 statements. Respondents are asked to rate the degree each statement is true of themselves on a 4-point scale (1 = *very true*, 2 = *mainly true*, 3 = *slightly true*, 4 = *false*). Responses to statements determine scores on 4 validity scales, 11 clinical scales, 5 treatment scales, and 2 interpersonal scales. Research suggests that the PAI may be a decent predictor of violence, suicide, aggression, and substance abuse and may be a reasonable instrument to use in the selection of police officers. However, considerably more research needs to be done before any firm conclusions can be made about its suitability in this context.

The NEO PI-R (Costa & McCrae, 1992) is specifically designed to measure the five major domains of personality, called the "Big Five." They are (1) extraversion, (2) agreeableness, (3) conscientiousness, (4) emotional stability (neuroticism), and (5) openness to experience. The NEO PI-R contains six trait or facet measures that define each of the five personality domains. Taken together, the 5 domain scales and 30 facet scales of the NEO PI-R facilitate a comprehensive and detailed assessment of normal adult personality. At first, the five-factor model of personality as measured by the NEO was thought to be the answer to the ongoing search for a comprehensive and valid measure of personality and was met with enthusiasm by those involved in personnel selection. So far, though, the NEO has had mixed success. In a meta-analytic study, Barrick and Mount (1991) found that, except for openness to experience, the other four Big Five domains correlated significantly but only moderately with police performance. J. Black (2000) investigated the predictive validity of the NEO PI-R in police officers in New Zealand. He administered the NEO PI-R to recruits at the beginning of training and then analyzed how well the NEO PI-R scales predicted outcomes at the end of training. He found significant relationships between the conscientiousness, extraversion, and neuroticism domains and several performance measures conducted during the training. Similarly, Detrick, Chibnall, and Luebbert (in press) examined the predictive validity of the NEO PI-R in relation to police academy performance in a large metropolitan area of the midwestern United States. They found that high scores on three facets of the neuroticism domain, and lower scores on one facet scale of the conscientiousness domain, were related to performance during academy training. Disciplinary and absenteeism factors were predicted by multiple facets. The Vulnerability facet scale also emerged as a significant predictor of nongraduation. Overall, the authors concluded that the study provided support for the validity of the NEO PI-R as predictor of police academy performance. However, to what extent the NEO PI-R measures performance *in the field* is unknown.

The 16-PF is another instrument designed to measure normal adult personality traits. The inventory contains 185 items that require a person to answer along a 3-point Likert-type scale. The items are grouped into 16 primary factor scales representing the dimensions of personality initially identified by Raymond Catell (Murphy & Davidshofer, 1998). The inventory was based on a series of factor-analytic studies of items that contained personality dimensions that differentiate normal individuals. The 16-PF has been heavily researched and consistently demonstrates solid reliability and validity. The Cochrane et al. (2003) survey reported that the 16-PF was used by about 19% of the police departments in their preemployment screening procedures. Only a very limited amount of research has been done on its ability as a valid predictor of law enforcement performance, however.

Situational Testing

Because psychological tests administered to law enforcement candidates have not demonstrated high predictive validity, some police psychologists have constructed test situations that resemble as closely as possible the working conditions actually encountered in police work. In a situational test, the applicant is placed in simulated police situations where he or she is observed and rated on how well he or she responds. Proponents of such situational tests argue that paper-and-pencil tests, such as intelligence tests and personality inventories, do not require candidates to do anything that approximates actual police work. Situational tests were used extensively by the American, British, and German military during World War II to select officers and special services personnel. Although there were few data to support the value of these tests in predicting success, they have a strong intuitive appeal and remain popular today.

Chenoweth (1961) was among the first to suggest that situational tests be used for the selection of police officers. Later, Diliman (1963), R. B. Mills and his colleagues (1969, 1976), and Tagatz and Hess (1972) began to explore the use of such tests through research.

Diliman (1963) reported the first application of situational tests to police screening in a study involving a police force in Albuquerque, New Mexico. He devised two situations typical of police work in that city, with one requiring an officer to interview an uncooperative hit-and-run suspect and the other requiring the officer to deal with a man stopped for speeding in the process of driving his pregnant wife to the hospital. Police academy recruits were used as subjects. In each situation, the recruit's responses were taped and rated by a group of judges, who scored the responses for both frequency and dominance. Frequency referred to the actual number of responses made by the recruit, and dominance referred to the overriding or "repetitive theme" of the recruit's response pattern. As a criterion measure, the recruits were ranked by the commandant of the academy according to their potential as police officers. The relationships between frequency and dominance of responses and the commandant's ratings were highly significant for the first situation but considerably less so for the second.

In light of the inconsistent relationship between academy performance and field performance frequently reported in other studies (e.g., Spielberger, 1979), the usefulness of this situational study to the selection of police officers is questionable. It is not even known whether frequency and dominance of responses contribute to successful police work. Also, it is unwise to rely on one person's assessment (the commandant's, for example) of who will and will not become a successful officer.

The only other published attempt to apply situational tests to police selection was reported by Robert Mills and his colleagues in Cincinnati (Mills, McDevitt, & Tonkin, 1966). The Mills group constructed scenarios of a variety of situations commonly encountered in some aspect of police work. The overall results were discouraging and did not support the value of situational tests for the selection of police officers.

It should be mentioned that, although psychologists are not highly involved in **situational testing,** this is a common way for law enforcement supervisors to select applicants. Most departments employ some variant of the "oral board," which requires a candidate to submit to questions fired by three to five supervising officers. Candidates are asked, for example, what they would do if they stopped a car for speeding and discovered the driver was the captain's son. Police departments also routinely use the polygraph in the screening process.

Situational tests can be time-consuming and expensive, particularly when they involve role-playing as opposed to asking candidates what they would do in a given situation. They require special equipment as well as technical and professional assistance. More important, there is little guarantee that the tests, though apparently job related, have any value in predicting who will

succeed in law enforcement and who will not. Moreover, candidates cannot be expected to know how to handle situations until they receive the proper training. The notion that test content that appears job related increases the validity of the test is misguided. On the contrary, there is evidence that carefully selected paper-and-pencil exams are more accurate in assessing and predicting good police officers than other procedures that are currently used. Unfortunately, the preference for job-related content over seemingly irrelevant but predictive tests is not uncommon in personnel selection.

Personality Measures of Police Corruption

The term *police corruption* covers a wide range of illegal behaviors that represent a violation of the public trust. Accepting bribes, confiscating drugs or drug money, planting evidence, and soliciting sexual activity in exchange for giving a suspect a "break" are all illustrations. Can police psychologists assist departments in selecting out candidates who are likely to be engaged in corrupt activities?

The Defense Personnel Security Research Center (PERSEREC) conducted one of the most extensive studies on the ability of personality measures to identify eventual police corruption and misconduct. The PERSEREC began the Police Integrity Study in 1992, using the four commonly used personality inventories in law enforcement: the MMPI-2, IPI, 16-PF, and CPI. Sixty-nine departments met all the prerequisites for participation and supplied personality test data on 878 officers, of whom 439 demonstrated misconduct and 439 did not. The preemployment personality inventories most frequently administered to those officers when they originally applied to their respective departments was the MMPI-2 (92.7%), followed by the CPI (41.0%), 16-PF (11.2%), and IPI (11.0%).

Overall, the study concluded that only modest improvements in combating corruption could be made by using the personality data collected. The few personality inventories that had any success tended to indicate that those officers who engaged in misconduct or corruption during their careers had more of the following characteristics:

- difficulty getting along with others,
- delinquent histories,
- indications of maladjustment, immaturity, irresponsibility, and/or unreliability.

Basically, the study found that the single best predictor of corruption was not a personality measure.

> None of the pre-employment psychological tests currently being used by law enforcement departments appears to offer a general scale or dimension that can reliably and validly differentiate officers at the beginning of their career likely to violate the public trust later in their career. (Boes, Chandler, & Timm, 2001, p. 35)

Rather, the strongest predictor was posthire misconduct. Officers who got into trouble for misconduct early in their careers were most likely to be punished for later acts of corruption. Furthermore, the study found that the decision of whether or not to engage in acts of corruption is largely shaped by environmental factors, such as opportunity combined with the values particular police subcultures allowed or condoned by certain departments. However, as will be discussed in the section on criminal profiling in Chapter 3, the tendency toward misconduct, including misconduct and corruption by police officers, is more likely to be some combination of personality interacting with the situation, rather than personality or situation alone.

Conclusions on Personality Testing for Law Enforcement Personnel

Although many different assessment techniques and personality inventories are currently used in the screening, selection, and promotion of law enforcement officers, it is usually not known whether many of these testing procedures are valid predictors of effective on-the-job law enforcement performance (criterion-related validity). This is a sobering fact because any selection procedure should ultimately be validated. Before a test can be meaningful and useful, it must have validity, which tells us whether the instrument measures what it is supposed to measure. For example, if a psychological test is designed to predict how well applicants will perform in law enforcement, we must have solid, empirical evidence that it in fact does predict performance on the job. If not, the test is essentially useless as a predictor of future performance. Empirical investigations evaluating relationships between initial selection standards (predictors) and the actual job performance of law enforcement officers should be undertaken.

There are many different kinds of validity, but one of the more important types is predictive validity. To repeat what was said earlier in this section, **predictive validity** is the degree to which a test predicts a person's subsequent performance on the dimensions and tasks the test is supposed to measure. If a test claims to be able to predict which candidates develop into good or outstanding police officers, its predictive validity should be high, discriminating those who eventually perform well from those who do not. If there is empirical evidence that the instrument does have predictive validity, a test is a powerful device for the screening and selection of candidates prior to entry into law enforcement. Obviously, a device that could do this would save both the candidate and the agency valuable time as well as potential difficulty and embarrassment.

Suppose we have a very high incidence of citizen complaints within a particular department. The complaints not only affect public confidence in the department but also result in a high turnover rate. In an effort to identify both the individuals most prone to citizen complaints and the situations engendering them, the police psychologist administers a battery of psychological tests or inventories before the officers are hired and follows them over a number of years, collecting supervisory reports, police affidavits, and any documents pertaining to the complaints. The psychologist then correlates the preemployment measures with these documents, paying particular attention to those officers who leave or against whom complaints are filed. If all goes well, the psychologist should be able to identify those tests or inventories that predict poor police-citizen relationships and use those specific measures in future screening of police officers for those departments.

We should be careful to add a note of caution with respect to the above illustration, however. The best way to deal with citizen complaints may not be to screen out ahead of time those who are most susceptible to them. Rather, the best way may be to improve training, communication with the public, and working conditions, thus minimizing the opportunity for stress to appear. An important thing to remember about predictive validity, therefore, is that it predicts adaptability to the status quo or to the situation as it exists. When the situation changes, the predictive validity of an instrument also changes.

As suggested by the above example, single psychological tests as predictors of effective law enforcement performance take considerable and carefully designed research. This is partly due to the diversity and complexity of behaviors required of law enforcement officers, but it is also due to varying work situations across departments. Police duties range from preventing and detecting crime to investigating accidents, intervening in disputes, handling domestic disturbances, and responding to a wide range of requests from the public. The smaller the department, the more varied the responsibilities of individual officers. It is not unusual to find a local, small-town law enforcement officer offering first-aid tips to an elementary school class and, on the same day, dealing with a violent domestic altercation. Because specialization is a luxury very small departments cannot afford, it is very difficult to establish objective performance criteria on which to base predictions. Some officers may perform very competently on some tasks while failing at others. The officer who relates exceptionally well to fun-loving teenagers may perform poorly in crisis situations involving depressed adults.

To tap the heterogeneity of law enforcement activities, screening devices should contain a number of predictors based on a multitude of behaviors, and few psychological measures are able to do this. In addition, because law enforcement work differs substantially from one jurisdiction to another, a test may be adequate for a given department but may not suffice elsewhere. Rural or small-town law enforcement may require different behaviors and talents than metropolitan or urban law enforcement work. Also, many states have sheriffs departments that often offer very different services from those of municipal or state law enforcement agencies.

Another obstacle to validating psychological tests or inventories is determining what, precisely, constitutes successful performance. Interjudge agreement about performance ratings is often difficult to obtain, even within one department. What one supervisor considers superior performance in the field may be only average performance to another supervisor. Predictors of success, therefore, are elusive.

The broad scope of law enforcement, together with the urgent need for more vigorous and sophisticated methods of study, warn us that we should expect few solid conclusions in the research literature as to what are adequate predictors of success or failure in law enforcement work. As expected, the literature is littered with inconclusive or mixed results. This does not mean that reliable and valid psychological assessment is beyond reach. It may mean, though, that a successful testing program may have to be tailor-made to the needs of a particular agency. In addition, it is certainly acceptable to "screen out" those candidates who exhibit gross indicators of problems, such as mental disorder, highly aggressive or antisocial behaviors, or poor judgment.

The Third Trend: Stress Management

The third trend is best represented by the term *stress*, which became the overriding theme from the mid-1970s to the early 1980s. More than ever before, police psychologists were called on to identify and dissipate stress, which, if left unmanaged or untreated, could result in an array of psychological and physical health problems for the officer and potentially put the public at risk for faulty judgment and decision making. *Stressors, burnout, posttraumatic stress disorder (PTSD),* and *critical incident trauma* became standard terms in the police psychologist's vocabulary. Whether police officers actually experienced more stress than persons in other high-risk occupations (e.g., air traffic control) remained highly questionable, however. Nevertheless, there was little doubt that stress played a major role in the lives of law enforcement officers at all levels of the organization. The focus on stress was significant because it moved police psychologists away from their traditional testing functions and into a much larger realm of opportunity and services. Consequently, psychologists began to offer not only stress management but also crisis intervention training, hostage negotiation training, domestic violence workshops, and substance abuse and alcohol treatment.

Some reports indicate that there is more stress in police work today than there was 10 or 20 years ago (Finn, Talucci, & Wood, 2000). One survey of Baltimore police officers found that approximately 10% of officers experience high levels of stress. In addition, these officers are much more likely than others to report poor physical and psychological health, family problems, alcohol abuse, and depression. Today, police officers see new sources of stress in the high level of violent crime and in what they perceive as greater public scrutiny and adverse publicity. They also indicate that police camaraderie has declined significantly in recent years. Community policing, an approach whereby police and citizens work more closely together in

positive endeavors, has added new pressures. Although the benefits of community policing are apparent, some officers find it difficult to adapt to its accompanying changes in strategies and policies.

Occupational Stressors in Law Enforcement

During the 1970s, considerable research interest was directed at the effects of stress that are unique to, or more pronounced among, law enforcement officers. Many researchers, as well as the officers and their families, consider law enforcement to be one of the most stressful of all occupations, with correspondingly reported high rates of divorce, alcoholism, suicide, and other emotional and health problems (Finn & Tomz, 1997). "Police officers regularly deal with the most violent, impulsive, and predatory members of society, put their lives on the line, and confront miseries and horrors that the rest of us view from the sanitized distance of our newspapers and TV screens" (L. Miller, 1995, p. 592). However, persons in many occupations may argue that they face more physical danger than law enforcement officers. Construction workers, miners, stunt pilots, firefighters, and demolition workers are all exposed to potential death and physical injury. Paramedics and other medical personnel, though less likely to be exposed to physical harm, contend that theirs is as stressful as any occupation. However, perhaps few occupations encounter the wide variety of stressors, ranging from organizational demands (e.g., shift work) to the nature of police work itself (e.g., exposure to violence, suffering, and tragedy at all levels), as consistently as law enforcement.

Despite limited resources in recent years, many law enforcement agencies have implemented stress programs not only to benefit officers and their families but also to improve efficiency, morale, and image and to help ensure that officers are in the best condition to protect and serve the public. Psychologists interesting in working with law enforcement play an integral part in these programs.

Types of Police Stress

Law enforcement officers face a number of sources of stress particular to their field. During the past 10 years, some officers have reported new or increasing sources of stress, including those that result from the implementation of community policing, negative publicity, and reduced resources (Finn & Tomz, 1997). A common strategy employed in the police stress literature is to divide the occupational stressors identified by police officers into four major categories: (1) organizational, (2) external, (3) task related, and (4) personal. **Organizational stress** refers to the emotional and stressful effects that the policies and practices of the police department have on the individual officer. They include poor pay, excessive paperwork, insufficient training, inadequate equipment, weekend duty, shift work, inconsistent discipline and enforcement of rules, limited promotional opportunities, poor supervision and administrative support, and poor relationships with supervisors or colleagues. Organizational stressors in major departments may also include antagonistic subcultures within the department, such as intense competition between specialized units, precincts, or even shifts.

One recent study reveals that excessive shift work contributes to more errors in judgment and greater increases in stress than perhaps any other factor in the police environment (Vila & Kenney, 2002). Some officers work more than 14 hours a day on a regular basis, and some "moonlight" for extra income. Excessive hours on the job not only interfere with sleep and eating habits but also raise havoc with family life and responsibilities. Furthermore, irregular hours often interfere with social get-togethers and family activities, isolating the officer even more from social support systems. Also, the organizational structure of large police departments often promotes office politics, lack

of effective consultation, nonparticipation in decision making, and restrictions on behavior. Currently, organizational stressors are considered as the most prevalent and frustrating source of stress for most law enforcement personnel (Finn & Tomz, 1997).

Task-related stress is generated by the nature of police work itself, such as inactivity and boredom, situations requiring the use of force, responsibility of protecting others, the use of discretion, the fear that accompanies danger to oneself and colleagues, dealing with violent or aggressive individuals, making critical decisions, frequent exposure to death, continual exposure to people in pain or distress, and the constant need to keep one's emotions under close control. Police officers also fear air- or blood-borne diseases, either intentional (e.g., terrorists) or accidental. Task-related stress also deals with role conflict, such as being at once an enforcer of the law, a social worker, a counselor, and a public servant (Finn & Tomz, 1997). Stressful assignments, such as undercover duty or drug raids, also play a role in the stress equation. More recently, budget cutbacks and fiscal uncertainty due to the economy have resulted in concerns about job security and opportunity advancement. Many departments in recent years have undergone downsizing or hiring and promotional freezes because of across-the-board budget cuts (Finn & Tomz, 1997).

External stress refers to an officer's ongoing frustration with the courts, the prosecutor's office, the criminal justice process, the correctional system, the media, and public attitudes. Available data suggest that for every 100 felony arrests, 43 are typically dismissed or not prosecuted (Finn & Tomz, 1997). Although this is not necessarily a bad thing, police often find it troubling. Moreover, many law enforcement officers feel court appearances are excessively time-consuming, and they are often frustrated over what they perceive as inefficiency and "unjust" court decisions.

Personal stressors involve marital relationships, health problems, addictions, peer group pressures, feelings of helplessness and depression, discrimination, sexual harassment, and lack of accomplishment. Some officers worry about their competency to do the job well or worry about doing something against regulations. Many police officers feel that the nature of their work has an adverse effect on their home life and social life.

Although much of the above research was conducted in the 1970s, the problems continue to exist. In 1994, the U.S. Congress authorized the Law Enforcement Family Support (LEFS) Program to assist in reducing the harmful effects of stress experienced by law enforcement officers in their families. The Department of Justice Office of General Counsel clarified the term *law enforcement personnel* to include correctional, probation, and parole officers. Consequently, the program was renamed the Corrections and Law Enforcement Family Support (CLEFS) Program. The program consists of demonstration and research grants to provide programs for local police departments as well as periodically to state and local agencies or organizations representing law enforcement and correctional personnel.

Although criminal justice literature frequently mentions exceedingly high divorce rates and general marital unhappiness among law enforcement officers, documentation is very difficult to obtain. Borum and Philpot (1993), in their study, found that divorce rates among police families were no higher than those found in the general population. Yet, there is little doubt that the whole family suffers the stressors inherent in law enforcement. In one study of 479 spouses of police officers, 77% reported experiencing unusually high amounts of stress from the officers' job (Finn & Tomz, 1997). The most common sources of spousal stress include the following (Finn & Tomz, 1997):

- shift work and overtime;
- an officer's cynicism, need to feel in control at home, or inability or unwillingness to express feelings;

- the fear that the officer will be hurt or killed;
- the officer's and other people's excessively high expectations of their children;
- avoidance, teasing, or harassment of children because of their parent's job;
- the presence of a gun in the home.

Summary

In light of the above data, it is not surprising that police departments are increasingly hiring full-time police psychologists or psychological, counseling, or mental health consultants who are available not only to consult on cases but also to offer their services to individual officers and their families. Delprino and Bahn (1988) reported that 53% of police agencies studied used counseling services for job-related stress. About one third of these agencies also hired psychologists to provide relevant workshops and seminars. In addition, many family support groups are appearing throughout the country, frequently at the instigation of police spouses who band together to discuss and solve common problems.

Peer counseling programs are available in many departments, but many police officers prefer to work with mental health professionals who are knowledgeable about police work but who are *not* police officers themselves (Finn & Tomz, 1997). Officers are often resistant to discuss with other police officers problems that are generally unacceptable within the police culture, such as sexual dysfunction, fear of getting hurt, or inability to use force when necessary in the line of duty. On the other hand, psychologists must be careful *not* to try to act and talk like police officers as a means of gaining acceptance, or they may be labeled as "cop wannabes." Richard Smith, a police psychologist with the Michigan State Police Behavioral Science Unit, warns that the more you try to be like a cop, the higher the danger of looking like a clown (cited in Finn & Tomz, 1997).

The Fourth Trend: Fairness in Testing

The legal consequences of using psychological measures for employee screening and selection has become a prominent issue in recent years. Legislation has prompted all law enforcement agencies to examine their employment practices and to demonstrate that groups of applicants are not being unfairly discriminated against in screening, selection, and promotion procedures. The emergence of "community policing" has also meant a new role for police officers and a pressing need for more women and ethnic minorities to be added to the force. In the community policing model, departments are encouraged to seek candidates who can demonstrate intercultural sensitivity and interpersonal skills for dealing with a wide spectrum of minority groups. Community policing is a collaborative effort between law enforcement and the community that identifies problems of crime and disorder and ideally involves all elements of the community in the search for solutions to these problems. It is based on the close, mutually beneficial ties between law enforcement and community members. To achieve a better representation of the local communities in police departments, some police agencies have undertaken initiatives to recruit larger numbers of women and police officers representing various ethnic and racial groups. In addition, they strive to establish screening and selection procedures that facilitate the hiring of such individuals.

This positive reaching out to previously underrepresented groups—which is the essence of affirmative action programs—does *not* mean that departments adopt quotas in which they deliberately hire to achieve a given percentage of women or a specific racial or ethnic group. Nor does it mean that they hire unqualified candidates. Failure to recognize this, however, has led to court challenges to these recruitment strategies. To date, departments seeking to bring qualified women and minorities on board have overcome these challenges.

As noted by Cole and Smith (2001), before the 1970s, many police departments did not hire non-Whites. However, the makeup of departments changed beginning in the late 1970s. A survey of the nation's 50 largest cities discovered that, between 1983 and 1992, 29% of the departments reported an increase of 50% of more in the number of Black officers, and 20% reported a similar increase in the number of Latino officers (Cole & Smith, 2001). In 1993, police officers representing racial and ethnic minorities made up approximately 20% of all local police departments across the country (Bureau of Justice Statistics, 1993).

Gender Issues in Policing

During the past two decades, increasing concern that selection procedures may be screening out women as well as racial and ethnic minority groups has been raised (National Center for Women & Policing, 2000). Women remain a small minority in law enforcement nationwide, comprising less than 14.3% of the sworn police officers, with an annual increase of only 0.5% over the past several years (Bureau of Justice Assistance, 2001; National Center for Women & Policing, 2000). The rate of increase has slowed significantly over the past five years. The larger the department, the higher the proportion of women police officers (Cole & Smith, 2001). For example, approximately 20% of the sworn officers on the Detroit police force are women (Cole & Smith, 2001). The major impediment for women gaining a greater proportion of representation in some of the law enforcement agencies across the country is the common perception that policing is a male-oriented profession, requiring physical strength and a display of physical prowess for many of the tasks. Consequently, many women are reluctant to apply, especially when a department has the reputation of being hostile toward women or has a high female officer turnover rate.

Researchers also have found that women are making some slow progress in acquiring promotions and administrative positions, although they still encounter continuing resistance from police managers, supervisors, and administrators (Martin, 1989, 1992). Less than 4% of supervisory positions are held by female officers, though the percentages are higher in larger departments (Meloy, 2000).

Worden (1993) found very few differences between male and females officers in their *attitudes* toward policing. She writes, "Overall, female as well as male police officers were predictably ambivalent about restrictions on their autonomy and the definition of their role, only mildly positive about their public clientele, complimentary of their colleagues, and unenthusiastic about working conditions and supervisors" (p. 229). She attributes (cautiously) much of this gender similarity in policing to "occupational socialization," a process that seems to wash out many of the major differences in gender roles. Occupational socialization refers to the learning of attitudes, values, and beliefs of a particular occupational group (Van Maanen, 1975). In general, women have the ability to become socialized into the police culture as successfully as men.

Morris (1996) reports that among New York Police Department (NYPD) officers, women (and minorities) received substantial social and psychological support from their police colleagues, and the women officers described mostly positive professional and social interactions while on the job. The one major gender difference identified by Morris was that women officers, compared to their male colleagues, were less likely to socialize off the job with other police officers. Their closest personal friends also tended to be outside the police community. This observation is not surprising if we consider that women police officers are likely to have families, including dependent children, to whom they prefer to give their off-duty attention.

Accumulating research, both in this country and internationally, indicates that the style of law enforcement used by women as a group may be more effective than the policing styles employed by men as a group (Bureau of Justice Assistance, 2001). For example, many law enforcement administrators and many members of the public are convinced that female officers are more skillful at defusing potentially dangerous or violent situations (Balkin, 1988; Bell, 1982; Weisheit & Mahan, 1988). Johnson (1991) reports evidence that women officers seem to have a "gentling effect" when dealing with the public. Moreover, Worden (1993) found that women police officers seem to be guided more by altruistic and social motives than men, who tended to be more motivated toward the financial rewards of the occupation. The research to date demonstrates that, overall, women officers are better at defusing and de-escalating potentially violent confrontations with citizens and less likely to become involved in incidents of excessive force (Bureau of Justice Assistance, 2001). Moreover, women officers as a group generally possess better communication and social skills than their male colleagues and are better able to facilitate the cooperation and trust required to implement a community policing model (Bureau of Justice Assistance, 2001). It is also likely that women officers respond more effectively in dealing with situations involving violence against women (such as domestic abuse or sexual assault), although more research is needed in the area. Consequently, hiring more women is likely to be an effective way of addressing the problems of excessive force and citizen complaints and also of improving community policing in general. It should also reduce the problem of sex discrimination and sexual harassment by changing the climate of the agency.

The Americans With Disabilities Act of 1990

In 1990, Congress passed what has become known as the **Americans With Disabilities Act (ADA)**, which became fully effective 2 years later, on July 26, 1992. The federal law guarantees equal opportunity for individuals with disabilities in state and local government services, public accommodations, employment, transportation, and telecommunications.

The ADA continues to be the most far-reaching public law in the United States since the Civil Rights Act of 1964, affecting some 43 million Americans defined by the law as physically or mentally disabled. The police psychologist who designs employment screening, selection, and promotional procedures for police agencies would be wise to be very familiar with all the nuances of the act. The ADA prohibits employers (with 15 or more employees) from discriminating against any qualified person with a disability who can perform the essential (as opposed to marginal or incidental) functions of the job he or she holds or seeks. A qualified individual with a disability is an employee or job applicant who meets the legitimate skill, experience, education, or other requirements of a job. The ADA does not spell out clearly who qualifies as disabled, although it specifically excludes from that category persons with sexual disorders, compulsive gamblers, kleptomaniacs (persons with a compulsive need to steal), pyromaniacs (those with a compulsive need to set fires), homosexuals, and persons with disorders resulting from current illegal use of drugs. The exclusion of homosexuals reflects the current recognition that homosexuality is not a mental disorder and is not covered under the term *disability*. In the years since the passage of the ADA, the courts—including the U.S. Supreme Court—have addressed some of its unanswered questions. Most recently, the Court has issued a number of rulings limiting the reach of the law. In a recent case, for example, the Court ruled that the disability covered by the law had to be one that restricted activities that are of central importance to most people's lives. In the Court's opinion, carpal tunnel syndrome was not considered such a disability (*Toyota v. Williams,* 2002). In addition, a company may refuse to hire a person with a disability for a job that could ultimately exacerbate the problem (*Chevron v. Echazabal,* 2002). The latter ruling seems to be especially pertinent to law enforcement.

The ADA prohibits questions or questionnaires pertaining to past medical history or that otherwise elicit information about disabilities before the employer has made a job offer. The job offer can be conditioned on successfully passing a medical examination. Tests that measure simply an applicant's ability to perform a task are not considered to be medical examinations. This raises a problem with respect to many psychological inventories. Some items on the MMPI-2, for example, ask about medical history or center on medical or health problems. Does this mean that the MMPI-2 cannot be used, or does it mean only that those items that delve into medical history must be deleted? The ADA further prohibits using qualification standards, employment tests, or other selection criteria that screen out individuals or a class of individuals with disabilities unless the standard, test, or other selection criterion is shown to be directly job related and is consistent with business or occupational necessity. It could be argued, for example, that the ability to run is critical to work as a patrol officer and that a person confined to a wheelchair could be screened out of such a position on that basis. The person should not be screened out of working as a dispatcher, in a clerical or administrative position, or on special assignments that do not require street patrol. On the other hand, the cases become more difficult when we are dealing with mental or psychological impairments compared to physical impairments (Goodman-Delahunty, 2000). An alcoholic, for example, is a person with a disability and is protected by the ADA if he or she is qualified to perform the essential functions of the job. Unless the agency can firmly establish that the individual will be intoxicated while on the job, the agency may be required to assume that the applicant can perform the essential aspects of the job until proven otherwise. The alcoholic, however, must adhere to the same standards of conduct as other nondisabled employees even when poor performance or behavior is caused by or is related to drug use or alcoholism (Goodman-Delahunty, 2000). It should be noted that drug testing is not prohibited by the ADA.

Most ADA litigation to date has centered on whether a condition constitutes a disability within the meaning of the act (Goodman-Delahunty, 2000). A case-by-case approach has been the general rule. Police agencies typically have not been required to make extensive accommodations when the issues pertain to serious emotional problems or mental impairments (Rostow, Davis, Levy, & Brecknock, 2001).

According to the ADA, test procedures and materials must be administered in such a manner that the test results accurately reflect the applicant's or employee's skills, aptitude, or other relevant abilities that are necessary for the job (Bartol & Bartol, 2004). This suggests that hiring agencies will be expected to adapt testing procedures if they impede the performance of persons with a disability. For example, we might begin to see more Braille versions of self-administered paper-and-pencil tests or other testing accommodations that allow a wide range of people with disabilities to take the exam.

The ramifications of the ADA for psychological testing and assessment are substantial and will continue to draw considerable legal attention in the years to come (Bartol & Bartol, 2004). It is also the kind of legislation that can promote serious conflicts between mental health professionals and lawyers. For example, a key question at this point is whether the diagnostic labels placed on many mental disorders qualify as disabilities. If they do, we can expect to see increasing challenges to the validity of these labels and the instruments and methods used to produce them.

In balancing an individual's rights under the ADA and an organization's right to know of an applicant's physical and mental fitness, the Equal Employment Opportunity Commission (EEOC) has divided disability inquiries into two stages: (1) preoffer of employment and (2) postoffer/prehire. At the preoffer stage, a police agency, for example, must not ask applicants any health or fitness questions that elicit information about disabilities, again leaving out many items on the MMPI-2 as well as questions that were often asked in interviews. The agency *may* ask general

"job performance" questions. At the postoffer/prehire stage, a police department may make direct inquiries about disabilities and may require applicants to undergo medical and psychological examinations. Such postoffer inquiries are allowed because the employer, by making a conditional offer of employment, can rescind that offer only if it can be shown that the person is unable to perform the essential functions of the job even with reasonable accommodation.

The ADA affects law enforcement agencies beyond accommodating and providing for equal opportunity for employment within the agency. The ADA affects nearly everything that police officers do, from receiving citizen complaints; interviewing witnesses; arresting, booking, and holding suspects; operating telephone ("911") emergency centers; providing emergency medical services; and enforcing the laws. In all these activities, the agency must try to make reasonable accommodations in their services to people who are disabled.

Special Circumstances in Policing

The following sections describe some of the areas in which police psychologists or other psychologists working with law enforcement agencies are most likely to be involved. Dealing with excessive force issues; helping police officers deal with the mentally disordered; evaluating critical (shooting) incidents, police suicides, or attempts at suicide; giving fitness-for-duty evaluations and special unit evaluations; and participating in crisis/hostage-taking incidents are all situations in which competent services are expected from police psychologists.

Excessive Force

The repeated showings of the videotape documenting the L.A. police beating of Rodney Glen King on the early morning hours of March 3,

1991, created nationwide concern about excessive force by law enforcement. Primarily as a result of the King incident, the Department of Justice called for research that would identify the nature, extent, and strategies for controlling the use of force by the nation's law enforcement personnel (Scrivner, 1994).

When the level of force exceeds the level considered justifiable under the circumstances, it is called **excessive force.** Excessive force is unacceptable behavior demonstrated by an individual officer, or it might be a pattern and practice of an entire law enforcement agency. In many instances, excessive force probably reflects some combination of both.

Prior to the 1970s, the police had wide discretion in the use of force, including deadly force (Blumberg, 1997). Police agencies often had poorly defined or nonexistent policies regarding the use of force generally. Mark Blumberg (1997) writes that, prior to 1970,

> Investigations into police shootings were sometimes conducted in a half-hearted manner, and police agencies often did not keep records of all firearm discharges by officers. In addition, social science research on this topic was practically nonexistent and no meaningful attempt to measure the incidence of police killings on a national basis had been undertaken. (p. 507)

How common is the use of force by police officers today? And under what circumstances or in what contexts does it occur? After all, police officers are in one of the very few occupations that is permitted and sometimes encouraged to use force (Brooks, 1997). The National Institute of Justice (NIJ) (Adams et al., 1999) released a report summarizing what is known about police use of force. The report found that

- police use force infrequently;
- police use of force typically occurs at the lower end of the force spectrum, involving grabbing, pushing, or shoving;

- use of force typically occurs when police are trying to make an arrest and the suspect is resisting.

Another source of information about police use of force comes from surveys conducted on the general population concerning their contacts with law enforcement. In 1996, the U.S. Census Bureau interviewed a national randomly selected sample of 6,421 persons age 12 or older (Greenfeld, Langan, & Smith, 1997). Interviewers determined that 1,308 persons out of the total had face-to-face contact with the police during that year. Of those 1,308 persons, only 14 (less than 1%) said they were hit, pushed, choked, threatened with a flashlight, restrained by a police dog, threatened with or actually sprayed with chemical or pepper spray, threatened with a gun, or experienced some other form of force. Unfortunately, the small number of persons who were the subject of police force prevents a reliable comparison of police use of force experienced by Black, Latino, or other minority or ethnic respondents. These data suggest, however, that the use of police force is a relatively rare phenomenon. Additional data from citizen complaints, use-of-force reports, and observational methods consistently indicate that only a small percentage of police-public interactions involve the use of force (Adams et al., 1999). As mentioned above, available data also indicate that most uses of force are at the lower end of the force spectrum, mostly grabbing or holding. This finding is not a surprise, considering that police officers are trained to use force progressively along a continuum, and the usual departmental policy requires that officers use the least amount of force necessary to accomplish their goals.

Police psychologist Ellen Scrivner (1994), in a report sponsored by the NIJ, investigates some of the psychological attributes characteristic of officers who engage in excessive force. Police psychologists assigned to conduct fitness-for-duty evaluations should be knowledgeable about the behaviors outlined in the report. Scrivner identifies five different officer profiles that are prone to excessive force complaints or charges:

1. officers with personality patterns that reflect a lack of empathy for others and antisocial, narcissistic, and abusive tendencies;

2. officers with previous job-related experiences, such as involvement in justifiable police shootings;

3. officers who experienced early career stage problems having to do with their impressionability, impulsiveness, low tolerance for frustration, and general need for strong supervision;

4. officers who had a dominant, heavy-handed patrol style that is particularly sensitive to challenge and provocation;

5. officers who had personal problems such as separation, divorce, or perceived loss of status that caused extreme anxiety and destabilized job functioning.

Unfortunately, the Scrivner (1994) study focused primarily on the psychological profiles of individual police officers. Little attention was given to the properties of entire police organizations that may implicitly (or explicitly) promote or condone excessive force within their ranks. For example, an agency may have an aggressive policing policy that encourages confrontational tactics that increase the probability of violence on the part of officers as well as members of the public. As Adams et al. (1999) state, "A major gap in our knowledge about excessive force by police concerns characteristics of police agencies that facilitate or impede this conduct" (p. 11). Adams and his colleagues further assert that

> many formal aspects of the organization—such as hiring criteria, recruit training, in-service programs, supervision of field officers, disciplinary mechanisms, operations of internal affairs, specialized units dealing with ethics and integrity, labor unions, and civilian oversight mechanisms—plausibly are related to the levels of officer misconduct. (p. 11)

As suggested above, knowledgeable police psychologists should also realize that, in some cases, the law enforcement agency itself might be a major factor in implicitly (or explicitly) encouraging the use of excessive force by its officers. Possibly, agencies may be placed on a continuum signifying the degree of aggressive policing they advocate in the community, especially in areas that have high crime rates. At one pole, the agency advocates that minimum force be applied when dealing with suspects, but at the other pole, the agency encourages force—and, if necessary, excessive force—in dealing with the suspects.

In summary, research data consistently show that only a small minority of police officers engage in excessive force in dealing with the public. Fortunately, an "early warning system," used by an increasing number of departments, can help identify problem officers early and intervene through counseling or training to correct problem behaviors (Walker, Alpert, & Kenney, 2001). **Early warning systems** are data-based management tools, usually consisting of three basic phases: (1) selection, (2) intervention, and (3) postintervention monitoring (Bartol & Bartol, 2004). The criteria by which officers are selected vary from agency to agency but usually include some threshold combination of citizen complaints, civil litigation, firearms discharge or use-of-force reports, high-speed pursuits, and resisting-arrest incidents (Walker et al., 2001). Some early research on the effectiveness of early warning systems suggests that they are effective, especially if used in combination with department-wide attempts to raise standards of performance and improve the quality of police services.

Dealing With the Mentally Disordered

Law enforcement officers are routinely the first line of response for situations dealing with mentally disordered citizens in crisis (Borum et al., 1998). Moreover, police encounters with mentally disordered citizens are frequent and are perceived by police agencies to present a significant operation problem (Borum et al., 1998). According to one of the leading experts in the area, psychologist Linda Teplin (2000), officers who encounter a mentally disordered person creating a disturbance generally have three basic choices: (1) transport the person to a psychiatric facility, (2) arrest the person, or (3) resolve the matter on the spot. In practice, these choices have some positives and some negatives. Transporting an irrational person is fraught with bureaucratic obstacles and the legal challenges of obtaining involuntary civil commitment or treatment. In addition, not all psychiatric facilities will accept mentally disordered persons considered dangerous to others or those who have substance abuse problems. An arrest is often the only option available to the officer when individuals do not appear to be disturbed enough to be accepted by a psychiatric facility but the deviance is sufficient enough not to be ignored. This option is especially preferred when the person is unknown by the police, in contrast to the "neighborhood characters" whose strange but harmless behaviors are well known by the police who patrol the area.

BOX 2.3   Help for the Homeless With Mental Illness

Police psychologists and police officers across the country are teaming up to find effective responses to problems of homeless people who suffer from mental illness. These individuals often come into conflict with the law through minor, public order, or property offenses such as disturbing the peace, public intoxication, vandalism, trespassing, and shoplifting. Almost everyone agrees that jails are no place for the mentally ill. Although some communities are establishing mental health courts (see Chapter 9), others have taken a different approach that bases services within police departments rather than the courts.

The following is the description of a program in Marin County, California, as described in a recent issue of *Monitor on Psychology*.

The program was the brainchild of Joel Fay, who holds a PsyD and has been a police officer for more than 25 years. According to Fay, both police and mental health agencies were frustrated with the cycle of individuals being arrested, going to jail, being released, getting brief treatment, dropping out, and being arrested once again. Now, police and members of the community develop and carry out an outreach plan for each individual. "We have a no-quit and never-give-up-policy. Once a person is referred to us, we never stop trying to get that person into treatment."

Every police department in the county has a designated mental health liaison. Fay himself is the liaison officer for the San Rafael Police Department. Liaison officers act as a resource for other officers and represent their department at countywide meetings of a forensic multidisciplinary team. At these meetings, various agency representatives share information and pool resources to help the mentally ill. Police, the district attorney's office, mental health agencies, probation officers, and housing programs are all represented on the team.

The *Monitor* article ends with a quote from Fay that summarizes the essence of police psychology. "There can be a tremendous connection between the mental health field and law enforcement. . . . If you find a way of talking to each other, you'll find that we're working toward the same goal and a lot could be accomplished."

Source: Smith (2002a).

The arrest approach is criticized by many mental health professions who contend that arresting the mentally disordered is essentially criminalizing mentally disordered behavior. Teplin (2000) believes there is *some* validity to this contention. However, she points out that many mental health hospitals or psychiatric facilities do not accept many of the mentally disordered persons brought in by the police (usually because of drastic budget reductions), and the police are left in many cases with only the arrest option. "Consequently, jails and prisons may have become the long-term repository for people with mental disorders" (Teplin, 2000, p. 12). An estimated 16% of inmates in U.S. prisons and jails are considered to have mental disorders (Ditton, 1999). The research on this issue finds that police try to resolve the problem on the spot 72% of the time, make an arrest 16% of the time, and initiate emergency hospitalization 12% of the time (Teplin, 1986, 2000).

One of the recommendations made by Teplin is that police officers must receive adequate training in recognizing and handling individuals with mental disorders. In addition, police officers must have a clear set of procedures on how to handle such persons. This responsibility often rests with the police psychologists or consulting psychologists to provide training workshops specifically designed to help officers develop strategies for dealing with those who are mentally disordered. Psychologists can also help by developing referral sources for mentally disordered individuals who may need to be protected from themselves.

In recent years, a number of communities have established specialized courts (mental health courts) to deal with these difficult issues. Although there are wide differences in how they operate and in the resources available to them, the goal of these courts is to divert individuals from the criminal process and offer closely monitored treatment, preferably in the community. We will discuss these courts in more detail in Chapter 9. In addition, some of the large law enforcement agencies have developed police-based specialized units for dealing with special populations, including the mentally ill. (See Box 2.3)

Postshooting Traumatic Reactions

A **postshooting traumatic reaction** (PSTR) represents a collection of emotions and psychological response patterns that may occur after a law enforcement officer shoots a person in the line of duty. The reaction is especially likely when the victim dies. Fortunately, most law enforcement officers complete their career without ever firing a weapon in the line of duty. About 600 individuals are shot and killed each year, and another 200 are wounded by law enforcement officers (More, 1992). L. Miller (1995) estimates that in the United States, two thirds of the officers involved in shootings demonstrate moderate to severe psychological problems after the shooting, and about 70% leave the force within 7 years after the incident. Unfortunately, PSTR has not been subjected to well-executed empirical research, and most of the information on the topic comes from anecdotal or self-report surveys. As Zeling (1986) writes, "The study of post shooting trauma is illustrative of a concept in police psychology that is widely accepted yet has little empirical support" (p. 410).

Solomon and Horn (1986) surveyed 86 law enforcement officers who had been involved in a critical incident involving a shooting. The researchers found that one of the most prominent psychological effects that occurred during the incident were perceptual distortions involving time, sight, and sound. Eighty-three percent of the officers reported that they experienced a distortion of time during the shooting. Most of them said that time seemed to slow down to a point where everything appeared to be happening in slow motion. One officer remembered thinking, "How come I'm moving so slowly?" On the other hand, some officers thought everything speeded up during the event. Other officers reported visual distortions (56%), and many experienced auditory (sound) distortions (63%). The most frequent visual distortion was "tunnel vision," in which the officer became so focused on one object that everything else at the scene went unnoticed. This phenomenon is frequently experienced by victims of a terrifying event as well. Some officers reported seeing everything more vividly and in greater detail than normal. Auditory distortions centered on not hearing sounds (such as the shots fired, shouts, commands given) or hearing them less or more intensely.

Following the incident, officers experienced a number of psychological reactions. The five most common were a heightened sense of danger, anger, sleep difficulties, isolation/withdrawal, and flashbacks. Specifically, officers involved in shooting incidents often lost their sense of invincibility and began to perceive their job as more dangerous than they originally thought. They were often angry at the victim of the shooting, at the department, at colleagues, or at society in general for putting them in the position of having to shoot someone. They had difficulty both falling asleep and staying asleep because of thoughts of the episode. Many needed to withdraw for a while, including taking leaves of absence, to get their thoughts together and to work through what happened. Finally, reoccurring thoughts of the scene intruded into their daily lives.

Solomon and Horn (1986) found that these common reactions varied widely in intensity. About 37% of the officers described their reactions as mild, 35% as moderate, and 28% as severe. The intensity of these reactions is similar to that reported by Stratton, Parker, and Snabbe (1984). The researchers (Solomon & Horn, 1986; Stratton et al., 1984) also agree that the intensity of the reaction depends partly on the perceived "fairness" of the shooting incident.

> Being outnumbered, having a limited field of fire due to bystanders, going against a shotgun when armed with a revolver, and having to shoot someone who points an unloaded weapon (unknown to the officers), are examples of factors affecting the "fairness" of the situation. (Solomon & Horn, 1986, p. 390)

The standard operating procedure in large agencies after a critical incident—such as a shooting—is to immediately contact the on-duty postshooting peer support team members and the police psychologist. The psychologist will consult with supervisors to determine whether he or she should arrange to meet with the involved officers at that time or see the officer at a later time. Police psychologists generally realize that police officers have a reputation for shunning mental health services under a wide range of circumstances (L. Miller, 1995). L. Miller (1995) notes that some officers have

> a notion of the psychotherapy experience as akin to brain-washing, a humiliating, infantilizing experience in which they lie on a couch and sob about their toilet training. More commonly, the idea of needing "mental help" implies weakness, cowardice, and lack of ability to do the job. (p. 596)

Despite these apprehensions, many agencies require that the involved officer or officers receive immediate attention from both the peer support group and the police psychologist, regardless of the circumstances. It is also standard procedure at most agencies for the involved officer to immediately be placed on administrative leave for 3 days or longer. During that administrative leave, it is usually common practice to recommend that the officer see the police psychologist for critical incident stress debriefings (CISDs). Usually, the CISD takes place within 24 to 72 hours after the critical incident and normally consists of a single group meeting that lasts approximately 2 to 3 hours (L. Miller, 1995). Thereafter, affected personnel may be seen individually or in groups.

Fitness-for-Duty Evaluations

The **fitness-for-duty evaluation (FFDE)** is conducted to determine the psychological ability of individuals to perform their essential job functions. The FFDE usually requires a much more extensive assessment than the preemployment psychological screening evaluation.

The order or request for the FFDE comes from the department supervisor or head and is normally conducted by a police psychologist or qualified licensed psychologist who is highly familiar with police psychology issues and research. It is ordered or requested when an officer displays behavior that raises serious questions as to whether he or she is fit to carry out public safety duties. Behavior that may prompt concerns include such things as one or more complaints of unnecessary or excessive force or any conduct indicating the officer has difficulty controlling his or her behavior. Other behaviors may include irrational verbal statements, evidence of hallucinations or delusions, suicidal statements or behaviors, inappropriate or excessive use of alcohol, use of illegal drugs, or behavioral signs of mental instability, serious depression, or emotional overreactions. Stone (1995) estimates that excessive force questions accounted for 19% of FFDE referrals. If the officer's behavior immediately or directly threatens safety, a supervisor or chief may immediately relieve the officer of duty or reassign him or her until a FFDE is completed. However, any long-term decision to reduce an officer's rank and/or duties or terminate that individual may be subject to a legal challenge.

Police officers, emergency personnel, and firefighters who witness an especially disturbing event—such as the deaths of young children; the terrorist attacks on the World Trade Center on September 11, 2001; plane crashes; or catastrophes involving fellow colleagues—may exhibit intense emotional or psychological reactions. In some cases, evaluations are needed to determine whether the officer (or firefighter) has the mental and psychological stability to continue as an effective officer (or firefighter) on the street, at least for the foreseeable future. Some agencies require evaluations as standard procedure after a critical incident (such as a fatal shooting).

Psychologists conducting the FFDE are advised to employ a variety of methods in their assessments, including psychological tests and a standard clinical interview that assesses mental status. They should obtain background information from files, the officers themselves, and other

significant parties if possible. The evaluations must be done with the informed consent of the officer, but the examiner is under no obligation to explain the results to the officer. The "owner" of the FFDE is essentially the agency requesting the evaluation. On the other hand,

the agency is not entitled to any more psychological information regarding an employee than is necessary to document the presence or absence of job-related personality traits, characteristics, disorders, propensities, or conditions that would interfere with the performance of essential job functions. (International Association of Chiefs of Police [IACP], 2002, p. 6)

The FFDE report usually includes the psychological measures used, a conclusion regarding the determination of fitness for duty, and a description of the functional limitations of the officer. In most instances, the FFDE report is provided to the department as a confidential personnel record. Periodic evaluations of the officer may also be necessary. The IACP (2002) recommends that the psychologist conducting the FFDE include performance evaluations, commendations, testimonials, internal affairs investigation, preemployment psychological screening, formal citizen/public complaints, use-of-force incidents, officer-involved shootings, civil claims, disciplinary actions, incident reports of any triggering events, medical/psychological treatment records, or other supporting or relevant documentation related to the officer's psychological fitness for duty. The IACP further recommends that personality, psychopathology, cognitive, and specialized tests that have been validated be used in the assessment process.

The FFDE is not limited to law enforcement but can be used by any occupational group. In addition, in law enforcement agencies, unsworn employees, such as dispatchers, administrative assistants, and community service officers, may be referred if there is reason to believe that the employee cannot perform his or her job in a safe or effective manner due to a mental health problem (Fischler, 2001).

Police Suicide

Data on the prevalence or frequency of police suicide are extremely difficult to obtain. The common assumption is that suicide among police officers is one of the highest of any occupational group in the nation (Violanti, 1996). It is estimated that twice as many officers (about 300 annually) die by their own hand as are killed in the line of duty (Miller, 1995). Moreover, most victims are young patrol officers with no record of misconduct, and most shoot themselves while off-duty (Miller, 1995). A recent study of police suicide conducted by Aamodt and Stalnaker (2001), however, suggests that the suicide rate among police officers may be significantly lower than commonly believed. Aamodt and Stalnaker point out that the incident reports usually compare the rates of police suicide to the rates found in the general population. According to Aamodt and Stalnaker, if researchers would compare the police suicide rate to the rates found in that sector of the population that is comparable to police officer age, gender, ethnic/minority, and racial group, they would discover that the police suicide incidence is significantly lower than often reported. Similar results have also been reported by Stack and Kelley (1999).

Police suicide may result from a number of factors, including psychological reactions to critical incidents, relationship difficulties, internal investigations, financial difficulties, frustration and discouragement, and easy access to weapons (Herndon, 2001). The overwhelming reason for police suicide, however, appears to be difficulties in marital or intimate partner relationships, followed by legal problems and internal investigations (Aamodt & Stalnaker, 2001).

If suicide rates for law enforcement personnel are lower than those found in the general population, this might be explained by several factors. These include the sophisticated screening procedures and rigorous evaluations at the time of hiring, increased use of stress awareness training, better police training, increased counseling opportunities, and the many services provided by police psychologists and other psychologists working closely with police agencies.

BOX 2.4   Always on Call

Psychologist Ellen Kirschman lives a varied professional life as a consultant to law enforcement departments across the United States. She provides crisis intervention after stressful incidents, works with families of law enforcement officers, assists field training officers, and provides critical incident training—among many other contributions. Kirschman—with police psychologist Lorraine Greene—also cofounded a Web site for families of law enforcement officers, which provides access to online support services (www.policefamilies.com).

Kirschman's consulting work, described in a recent edition of *Monitor on Psychology,* is representative of service provided by police psychologists who work independently of any one police department. Although she keeps regular weekly office hours with one or more departments, she also travels across the country offering workshops, speaking at police academies, and helping train officers to provide peer support. (Many police and correctional psychologists have discovered that officers often respond better to support from colleagues than from outside mental health professionals.)

In the *Monitor* article, Kirschman comments that, because police work 24 hours a day and 7 days a week, police psychologists must be available "24–7." The work is obviously demanding. Yet Kirschman suggests it is extremely satisfying. "My view is that I am working with healthy people who have difficult jobs and a lot of job stress—as opposed to working with a sick population."

Source: Smith (2002b).

Special Unit Evaluations

Psychological assessments are also done as standard procedure for members of special teams, such as SWATs and TRTs, undercover agents, and narcotics, internal affairs, and crisis/hostage negotiation teams, to determine if they are psychologically fit to undergo the pressures and judgment requirements of high-stress positions. Normally, team members are evaluated on a yearly basis to identify problems before they develop into more serious behavioral patterns that would interfere with effective job performance. Successful members of SWAT teams, for example, tend to be "self-disciplined, conscientious, adherent to rules, comfortable accepting rules, conforming, and helpful" (Super, 1999, p. 422). However, very little research has focused on the validity of assessment procedures used to identify special team selection. As concluded by Super (1999), "There is a serious need for rigorous research regarding psychological assessment and special unit appointments" (p. 422).

Hostage-Taking Incidents

An area where police psychologists often serve as consultants involves hostage-taking incidents. A hostage situation is characterized by a person (or persons) holding victims against their will and who are used to obtain material gain, deliver a sociopolitical message, or achieve personal advantage. Typically, the hostage taker threatens to take the lives of victims if certain demands are not met within a specified time period. A barricade situation is one in which an individual has fortified or barricaded himself or herself in a residence or public building or structure and threatens violence either to himself or herself or to others. Included in the broad hostage-taking category are abductions and kidnappings, vehicle abductions (including aircraft or other forms of public transportation), and some acts of terrorism.

Most police experts classify hostage takers into four very broad categories: (1) political activists or terrorists, (2) prisoners, (3) individuals who have committed a crime, and (4) individuals with mental disorders (Fuselier, 1988; Fuselier & Noesner, 1990). Political terrorists, who take hostages primarily to gain publicity for their cause, are considered the most difficult to deal with. Their demands often go beyond the authority of the local police departments and usually require the involvement of federal officials (Fuselier, 1988). According to Fuselier (1988), political terrorists take hostages for four basic reasons:

(a) to show the public that the government cannot protect is own citizens; (b) to virtually guarantee immediate coverage and publicity for their cause; (c) to support their hope that after repeated incidents the government will overreact and place excessive restrictions on its citizens; and (d) often to demand the release of members of their group who have been incarcerated. (p. 176)

The hostage taker who committed a crime is usually trapped while committing the crime, such as robbery or domestic violence, and is trying to negotiate some form of escape. Prisoners, on the other hand, usually take hostages (usually correctional personnel) to protest conditions within the correctional facility. Persons with mental disorders take hostages for a variety of reasons but primarily to establish their sense of control over their life situations. Research *suggests* that more than 50% of all hostage-taking incidents are perpetrated by individuals with mental disorders (Borum & Strentz, 1993).

In the early 1970s, the FBI and police departments began to set up specialized hostage negotiation teams that included a designated negotiator, tactical assault team (TAC), command structure, and support personnel (Butler, Leitenberg, & Fuselier, 1993; Fuselier, 1981).

Psychologists are usually part of the support team. Today, the "third generation" of crisis/hostage teams usually has five designated primary members: (1) the primary negotiator (the primary talker), (2) the secondary negotiator (monitors negotiations and offers suggestions), (3) the intelligence officer (seeks and organizes incoming information), (4) the psychologist (whose functions will be described shortly), and (5) the tactical liaison (maintains communications with SWAT and command) (Hatcher et al., 1998). Psychologists rarely are the primary negotiators (less than 7%), usually because of their limited training and experience in hostage negotiations. Even if the psychologist has advanced training and experience in such matters, it is recommended that he or she be used as a negotiation consultant to maintain a more objective role in assessing the situation (Fuselier, 1988).

Individuals aspiring to be on the crisis/negotiation teams as psychologists, however, should realize that multiyear training—as expected of all crisis/negotiation team members—is necessary to become an effective member of the team. Some of that training may require some "street experience" such as ride-alongs with experienced officers and as informed observers in hostage/barricade situations. "The chaos of the field or street situation, the military-like police command structure, and presence of real personal risk can come as quite a shock, no matter how professionally well trained one is" (Hatcher et al., 1998, p. 463).

An estimated 30% to 58% of law enforcement agencies with a crisis/hostage negotiation team use a mental health professional in some capacity, of which 88% are psychologists as opposed to psychiatrists, social workers, and other professionals (Butler et al., 1993; Hatcher et al., 1998). However, the use of psychologists on crisis/hostage negotiation teams appears to be on the increase (Hatcher et al., 1998). In hostage and barricade situations, four types of roles for non–law enforcement personnel have developed: (1) the consultant/adviser, (2) the integrated team member, (3) the primary negotiator, and (4) the primary controller (Hatcher et al., 1998). The psychologist is most likely to be in the consultant/adviser role with a variety of tasks. "Pre-incident, psychologists provide selection, training, police input, and conceptual development services to law enforcement" (Hatcher et al., 1998, p. 464). During the selection process, the psychologist would assist in identifying personnel who are likely to be effective and skillful negotiation team members. To date, however, studies have not been done to determine what selection procedures and psychological tests are best at determining the effectiveness of negotiation team members.

Approximately 40% of agencies use psychologists for advice at the scene of hostage-taking or barricade incidents (Hatcher et al., 1998). The on-scene psychologists might be expected to profile and assess the suspect, possibly trying to determine his or her motivation, vulnerabilities, and dangerousness. In addition, the psychologists might be expected to suggest some dialogue strategies or psychological tactics that are likely to defuse the situation. The on-scene psychologists also might be asked to assess the hostages with the goal to determine which hostages may engage in behaviors that may enhance or diminish their chances of survival. In some situations, the hostage taker may expect the hostages to do the talking during the incident. According to Hatcher et al. (1998), "The successful resolution of most hostage incidents requires that the crisis/hostage negotiation team devote almost equal interest to managing the hostages as to managing the hostage taker" (p. 465).

The psychologist, as an adviser/consultant, may assist in witness interviews and the review of other collateral information on the incident (Hatcher et al., 1998). Family members, friends, neighbors, coworkers, employers, and even hostages who escaped during the situation may provide important pieces of information that will lead to an understanding of the hostage taker and help in the eventual resolution of the incident. Those psychologists well trained and experienced in hostage negotiations can also offer useful analysis in the decision-making strategy to the team.

Research by Butler et al. (1993) discovered that police agencies that used a psychologist to assess suspects reported significantly fewer incidents in which the hostage taker killed or seriously injured a hostage. More specifically, police agencies that used a psychologist reported more hostage incidents ending by negotiated surrender and fewer incidents resulting in the serious injury or death of a hostage. The data confirmed the observation that psychologists can make valuable contributions in resolving hostage incidents with a lessened chance of injury or death.

One final but very important topic in which psychologists could provide enormous assistance relates to police interrogations and the many dangers of psychologically coercing a suspect to confess to something he or she did not do. The police psychologist could be especially helpful in providing balanced training to interrogators and educating them about the extant research in the area.

Police Interrogation and False Confessions

The primary aim of police interrogation is to obtain a confession from a suspect or to gain information that may lead to a conviction. Skillful interrogation involves the application of psychological principles and concepts. Experienced police interrogators use a wide variety of methods and techniques that are tailored to their personality and style. The U.S. Supreme Court has granted law enforcement wide latitude in trying to obtain confessions from suspects (see generally, Leo, 1996). Police are allowed to lie or trick suspects, pretending they have eyewitness testimony or evidence that does not exist. For example, April Witt (2001, p. A01), writing for the *Washington Post*, describes the interrogation experience of a 17-year-old high school student (Dennis Green) suspected of a homicide. He was

being interrogated by homicide detectives of Prince George's County, Maryland.

"I had been asking to get a lawyer when it appeared they thought I did it for real, and they weren't going to give up until they got what they wanted," Green said. "They said, you are not getting a phone call until I hear what I want to hear."

The teenager was relieved when a man wearing a jacket emblazoned "forensics" entered the interrogation room, swabbed the teenager's hand, and said he was performing a scientific test to determine if Green had fired a gun recently. Finally, they'd believe that he didn't shoot anyone, Green recalled thinking.

"When they come back and the test is negative, I'll forgive you and then I can just go home," Green remembered telling a detective.

The "test" apparently was a bit of interrogation room theatrics designed to persuade Green to confess. Green said a detective told him that the test showed he had not only fired a gun but he had used a .22—a degree of specificity that an authentic gunshot residue test does not provide. (Witt, 2001)

Although police interrogators can use a wide variety of psychological tactics, they are not permitted to use *coercion* to extract confessions. The confession must be freely and voluntarily given if it to be used as evidence in court. At this point, no one can accurately estimate the rate of police-induced **false confessions** across the country or the number of wrongful convictions caused by false confessions (Leo & Ofshe, 1998). It should be understood at the outset, though, that most convictions are the result of the evidence acquired at the crime scene or through witness reports rather than through interrogations and a confession from the suspect.

In this section, we will focus only on the nature of false confessions rather than discuss all the psychological strategies that may used be during interrogation procedures. We believe that false or coerced confessions present far more challenge to the police psychologist than the development of more effective interrogative strategies or the training in such strategies. As stated by Leo and Ofshe (1998), a confession is universally treated as damning and compelling evidence of guilt, which is likely to dominate all other case evidence and lead a trier of fact to convict the defendant. When suspects confess to crimes they did not commit, it is the responsibility of all those involved to establish the validity of those confessions and to stress to police interrogators the many dangers of psychological pressure and coercion. Leo and Ofshe point out that American police are poorly trained about the dangers of interrogation and false confession. "Rarely are police officers instructed in how to avoid eliciting confessions, how to understand what causes false confessions, or how to recognize the forms false confessions take or their distinguishing characteristics" (p. 437). This is one important training service that police psychologists should be able to provide.

People confess to crimes they did not commit primarily to become a celebrity, to expedite things if they feel they will not be believed, to protect others, or for a variety of other reasons. And some people confess to a crime they did not commit because they come to believe (usually through persuasion) that they actually did do it.

One of the leading psychological experts on false confessions is Saul Kassin (1997). In a summary of the research literature, Kassin and Wrightsman (1985) were able to identify three types of false confessions: (1) voluntary, (2) coerced-compliant, and (3) coerced-internalized. The first type refers to a self-incriminating statement made without any external pressure from law enforcement. A well-known example of this type of voluntary confession, Kassin (1997) notes, is when more than 200 people came forward and confessed to kidnapping the Charles Lindbergh baby, the most famous kidnapping case in U.S. history. Charles Lindbergh was an American hero who was the first man to fly the Atlantic Ocean alone. On March 1, 1932, the first-born child of Lindbergh and his wife Anne was kidnapped for ransom and later found dead. The child was 20 months old. Although Bruno Richard Hauptmann was convicted and executed for the crime, doubts about his guilt have persisted around the case for years. Apparently, a large number of other individuals have confessed to the crime, ostensibly in an effort to receive recognition or fame.

The coerced-compliant and the coerced-internalized false confessions, as their name implies, involve pressure from police officers. Research has indicated that skillful manipulation, deception, or suggestive tactics under stressful conditions may lead to false confessions (Gudjonsson, 1992; Kassin, 1997). Under these circumstances, even an innocent person may come to believe that he or she is guilty of the crime. Kassin (1997) attributes much of the coerced false confession phenomenon to such psychological concepts as compliance and internalization, processes first identified by Kelman (1958). Compliance is a form of conformity in which we change our public behavior—but not our private beliefs or attitudes—to appease or reduce social pressure or threats from others. Internalization, on the other hand, refers to changes in our private thoughts or beliefs because we sincerely believe in the issue or perspective.

Coerced-compliant false confessions, Kassin (1997) concludes, are most likely to occur after prolonged and intense interrogation experiences, especially in situations when sleep deprivation is a feature. The suspect, in desperation to avoid further discomfort, admits to the crime even though this person knows he or she is innocent. This is an example of compliance without internalization.

In June 2001, the *Washington Post* examined the tactics of Prince George's homicide detectives, who were able to coerce four men to confess to crimes they did not commit (Witt, 2001). The detectives used a variety of highly coercive methods and threats, including extremely long hours of interrogation combined with sleep deprivation, and ignored or refused the suspect's request for a lawyer. In one case, the suspect was slammed against the wall, threatened with execution, and deprived of sleep until he confessed. All four suspects were later exonerated by DNA and other evidence. In addition to these cases, the *Post* found in its review of hundreds of police and court documents that the detectives had habitually used coercive methods and violated the rights of suspects during interrogation over a period of years. Some of the interrogations lasted more than 32, 35, 51, and even 80 hours.

Coerced-internalized false confessions, on the other hand, occur when innocent persons— who are tired, confused, and highly psychologically vulnerable—come to believe that they actually committed the crime (Kassin, 1997; Kassin & Kiechel, 1996). This is an example of compliance eventually developing into an internalization of the belief. In addition, the pressures to confess may not necessarily originate from police offices but may come from family members, friends, religious figures, and colleagues who communicate to the suspect that he or she will feel better by doing the right thing and admit to the offense (or atone for his or her sins) (McCann, 1998).

Perhaps the most famous case of what *may* be a coerced-internalized confession is that of Paul Ingram, a deputy sheriff from Olympia, Washington. In 1988, his two daughters accused him and a number of others (actually 30 members of the sheriff's department were accused) of satanic ritual abuse and sexual abuse. The charges grew out of events sponsored by Ingram's church, the Church of Living Water. As a suspect, Graham was subjected to 23 interrogations by detectives over a 5-month period, hypnotized, provided with graphic details of the crime, pressured by his church minister, who believed he was "80% evil," to confess, went through exorcism by this same minister to purge the demons from him, and was told by a court-appointed therapist that sex offenders often repress memories of their crimes (Fizel, 1997; Kassin, 1997). Ingram, saying he did not want his daughters to suffer through a trial, confessed, pleaded guilty, and was convicted of six counts of third-degree child rape. He received a 20-year sentence. It should be noted that Ingram was the first person who actually pleaded guilty to satanic ritual abuse. Ingram was released on April 8, 2003, after serving 14 years of his 20-year sentence. Upon release, he was required to register as a sex offender in the state of Washington and was rated as a Level 3 sex offender, the highest risk to reoffend. Many people believe that Ingram was rightly convicted, even if the details surrounding his crimes were exaggerated. However, there has never been any forensic or physical evidence to establish that any of the ritual abuse or sexual abuse ever took place.

Summary and Conclusions

Individual psychologists have likely consulted with various law enforcement agencies in the United States throughout the 20th century, but police psychology as a subfield of applied psychology was not officially recognized until the late 1960s. Since then, it has expanded rapidly. Police psychologists today participate in the screening and selection of law enforcement candidates, conduct promotional exams and fitness-for-duty evaluations, provide counseling services to officers as well as their families, offer workshops in stress management, and assist in hostage negotiations training (see Box 2.4). In addition, there is a rich store of psychological research on topics relating to law enforcement work. Examples of such research include police handling of those with mental disorders, excessive force, adaptations to stress, gender differences in policing, police response to crisis situations, and reliability and validity of various instruments for use in screening. All of these topics were covered in this chapter.

A review of the history of police psychology identifies four overlapping trends in the services offered: (1) mental and aptitude screening, (2) personality assessment, (3) stress management and other clinical services, and (4) fairness in testing. Although it is difficult to discern precisely how much of a police psychologist's practice relates to each of these, we might provide the educated guess that by far the greatest percentage of time is spent doing a combination of personality assessments for screening purposes and clinical services. As used here, clinical services includes a wide variety of training and workshops provided to law enforcement departments, in addition to individual and group counseling of officers.

As noted in the chapter, the search for a "police personality" has proved futile. Police work attracts a wide variety of people and for many different reasons, and most of them do a commendable job. Although some researchers have identified a police personality that they believe includes negative elements such as authoritarianism and cynicism, such features are more likely to be developed on the job, sometimes in frustration over department policies or a perceived lack of public understanding. The screening of candidates for officer positions, then, is more likely to be fruitful when it screens out undesirable officers. We discussed the use of the MMPI-2 in this context. The inventory, though, should be carefully validated according to the needs of a particular agency and should also offer departments probability statements that an individual will or will not succeed at various law enforcement tasks. In recent years, the Personality Assessment Inventory (PAI) has also received favorable research results, in the sense that it has identified positive traits that are often associated with success in law enforcement. Again we must emphasize, though, that a universal, ideal "police personality" likely does not exist.

Psychologists have a good deal to offer law enforcement in the way of stress management and other clinical services. Police work ranks high among stressful occupations. We discussed a number of occupational stressors that officers encounter, including those that are organizational, external, task related, and personal. Women officers continue to be a minority (about 15%–20%) of the law enforcement population. Although men and women are equally competent at police work, research suggests that there are differences in their styles, which sometimes produce differences in stress. Women seem to be guided more by altruistic and social motives and

are often reported as being better able to "defuse" potentially violent situations. Men are more likely than women to report external burnout. However, we must be cautious in making these generalizations. We emphasize that the weight of the research has demonstrated that, overall, both men and women are good at police work.

Police psychologists in recent years have been giving more attention to legal issues relating to procedures used in hiring and promotional exams. The trend in many departments to adopt community policing has led to an even greater need for representation of women and racial and ethnic minority groups on police forces. Screening and selection procedures must be scrutinized carefully to ensure that these groups are not unfairly dropped from the applicant and promotional pools. In addition, the Americans With Disabilities Act prohibits employers from discriminating against disabled persons who can perform essential functions of the job. The ADA has already led to changed testing procedures in many departments; numerous departments give the MMPI only after a conditional offer of employment, for example, but others have deleted items that inquire about health-related issues.

In recent years, considerable attention has been given to police discretion and strategies for handling those with mental disorders, who—because of their visibility in the homeless population of many cities—often come into contact with police. Specialized training in dealing with those with mental disorders and individuals with disabilities is now offered by many departments, and mental health courts have been established. These specialized courts will be discussed in Chapter 9.

The chapter ended with coverage of special topics in police psychology, including fitness-for-duty evaluations, hostage negotiations, and the psychology of false confessions. FFDEs are often conducted following a critical incident experienced by an officer or group of officers—such as a shooting or a tragic accident involving the death of a child. Officers who have recently experienced an inordinate amount of stress in their personal

CHAPTER 3

Investigative Psychology

Investigative psychology, the application of psychological research and principles to the investigation of criminal behavior, is a term coined by David Canter, the director of the Centre for Investigative Psychology at the University of Liverpool in England. Investigative psychology probably began in 1985, when Canter was called to Scotland Yard to explore the possibilities of integrating existing investigation procedures and techniques with psychological principles (Canter, 1995). Eventually, he developed a graduate program in investigative psychology at the University of Surrey in England and, 10 years later, moved to the University of Liverpool to direct a graduate program in investigative psychology there.

From a psychological perspective, three fundamental questions characterize all criminal investigations (Canter & Alison, 2000, p. 3):

1. What are the important behavioral features of the crime that may help identify and successfully prosecute the perpetrator?

2. What inferences can be made about the characteristics of the offender that may help identify him or her?

3. Are there any other crimes that are likely to have been committed by the same person?

These questions are central to the entire process of investigative psychology. In this chapter, we broaden the field of investigative psychology slightly to include topics of psychological autopsies, suicide-by-cop, the polygraph, forensic hypnosis, and facial composites based on information provided by eyewitnesses. We will begin by exploring an activity that has prompted considerable media attention, psychological profiling.

Profiling: The Psychological Sketch

Profiling—one of the tasks often associated with investigative psychology—requires sketching the significant psychological and demographic features of a person or persons. In some instances, the profile summarizes the psychological features of persons who *may* commit a crime, such as identifying potential terrorists who plan to hijack or blow up a plane. In the United States, for example, the nation's major airlines have used a profiling system known as the Computer Assisted Passenger Prescreening System (CAPPS) (Armstrong & Pereira, 2001). CAPPS, a more limited version of the passenger prescreening systems used in Europe and Israel, was created after the midair explosion of TWA flight 800 over Long Island Sound in 1996, which resulted in the deaths of 230 people. At first, it was thought that the explosion was the result of a terrorist attack, but further investigation several months later revealed the cause to be frayed electrical wiring in or near the fuel tanks located in the mid-section of the aircraft.

CAPPS uses basic data disclosed by passengers when they reserve and buy tickets—such as their names, addresses, and how they paid for tickets—to look for patterns that identify potential terrorists. For example, passengers who purchase one-way tickets, pay in cash, travel alone, buy tickets for passengers with different last names on the same credit card, and buy tickets with the same credit card shortly after another transaction are targeted for further investigation or closer surveillance (Armstrong & Pereira, 2001). The federal government uses similar profiles in its search for drug couriers and potential terrorists. The Drug Enforcement Administration (DEA) and the Department of Homeland Security, for example, have developed lists of likely characteristics of offenders.

Do these profiling techniques actually work? CAPPS did flag two of the four hijackers abroad American Airlines Flight 77 (which crashed into the Pentagon) as suspicious when they checked in at Dulles Airport on the morning of September 11, 2001. Unfortunately, neither man was questioned or searched at the airport, although their bags were carefully scanned before being loaded onto the plane. After the attacks on September 11, passengers as well as baggage were searched, a practice that continues today, as all air travelers are well aware. In reference to the drug courier profiles, critics have argued that although they discover evidence of drug trafficking, they are also so broad in their description that they can apply to a great number of passengers and result in the temporary detention and questioning of numerous innocent individuals.

After the terrorist attacks of September 11 and with the heightened threat of more terrorism, psychologists and behavioral scientists were asked to further develop profiles that would help security personnel identify potential terrorists from passenger lists. These profiles usually take into consideration the clothes the passenger is wearing, the person's nationality, travel history, behavioral patterns while at the airport, and even the book that he or she may have just purchased at the airport bookshop. That is, to improve their ability to identify potential terrorists, profile researchers would examine the buying habits, dress patterns, and cultural and social backgrounds of previous airline terrorists.

Profiling of potential hijackers is not new. To digress briefly, the word *hijack* originated in the Midwest around 1912 to 1920 and is a shortened form of a command meaning, "Hold your hands up high, Jack" (Dailey & Pickrel, 1975b). Apparently, it was first used by bands of individuals who habitually robbed farmers and eventually came to mean the use of force or trickery to compel individuals to do things they do not want to do. In 1961, *Time* magazine coined the term *skyjacking* to refer to the seizure of aircraft.

After the first official hijacking of an American aircraft occurred in 1961 (see Box 3.1), a trickle of skyjackings continued until the epidemic years between 1968 and 1978. In 1968, there were 36 skyjackings, 20 of them involving American aircraft, with most diverted to Cuba (Arey, 1972). This "contagion effect" became even more apparent in 1969 with 71 skyjackings, 58 of which were diverted to Cuba from the United States and other parts of the world. Some skyjackers were homesick Cubans, some claimed to be political activists, but most apparently wanted to become significant and newsworthy.

BOX 3.1   Early History of Skyjackings

The first official hijacking of an American aircraft occurred in 1961, but the first recorded skyjacking of aircraft had taken place 30 years earlier when a group of political activists in Peru seized a plane and used it to shower sections of Peru with propaganda pamphlets (Arey, 1972). Following the Peruvian hijacking and up to 1961, there were a total of 32 "skyjackings" throughout the world, although none of them involved American aircraft. John Dailey and Evan Pickrel (1975b) relate a story of an Alaska airline that used to frisk passengers shortly after World War II and take away all guns, knives, and alcoholic beverages. It was common practice for the pilots of this airline to carry guns as part of their regular flight equipment and lock themselves in the cockpit.

On May 5, 1961, shortly after the infamous Bay of Pigs invasion of Cuba by American-supported guerillas, the first "official" hijacking of an American aircraft occurred when Antilio Ortez, armed with knife and revolver, demanded that the pilot of a National Airlines Convair 440 fly him to Cuba. His expressed intention was to warn Castro of an assassination attempt—information he apparently thought would gain him special recognition in the Cuban leader's eyes. The plane landed successfully in Cuba. Ortez left the plane under the custody of the Cuban authorities and was never heard from again. Shortly thereafter, the airliner was allowed to return to Florida. On July 24 of that same year, homesick Cuban Wilfredo Oquendo took over an Eastern Airlines Electra with 38 aboard and diverted it from its Tampa destination to Havana. The incident ended in the same way as the earlier skyjacking, with the skyjacker captured and never heard from again.

Sixty-nine skyjackings occurred in 1970, and similar instances continued until the United States began to clamp down on airport security. One of the incidences that attracted extensive media attention was the case of D. B. Cooper.

D. B. Cooper: The Mysterious Hijacker

On a dark and rainy day in November 24, 1971, a day before Thanksgiving, a man boarded a Northwest Airlines Boeing 727 in Portland, Oregon, under the name of Dan Cooper. Moments after takeoff, the smartly dressed and middle-aged Cooper handed a flight attendant a note that warned the flight crew he had a bomb. He told the crew he wanted $200,000 in cash and four parachutes. On his demand, the plane landed at the Seattle-Tacoma International Airport, where it was refueled and the 36 passengers and two crewmembers were released. Authorities at that location also met his demands for the money and parachutes. On takeoff, Cooper ordered the plane to fly toward Mexico via Reno at no more than 10,000 feet at low air speed (170 miles per hour) with landing gear down and flaps at 15 degrees. This drag made the plane less aerodynamic and increased fuel consumption to a point where the plane was forced to land in Reno for refueling. After once again taking off, Cooper asked the remaining flight attendant to show him how to lower the rear stairs in the back of the 727. Then he ordered the flight attendant into the cockpit, closed the door, and at some point over southwest Washington, he bailed out with the cash tied to him. The weather outside was 7 degrees below zero, and the wind chill approached 70 below zero. Cooper was wearing only a suit, an overcoat, and casual shoes. He was never found.

However, the Cooper story became well known with much speculation about whether he lived or died from his jump. Books, posters, T-shirts, rock songs, and a movie—*The Pursuit of D. B. Cooper*—starring Robert Duvall and Treat Williams document the considerable ongoing interest in the heist. Even a restaurant in Salt Lake City was named after him. His daring feat also illustrates a good example of the **contagion** or **copycat effect**. Cooper himself may have been reacting to the early rash of skyjackings mentioned above. However, his demand for money and a parachute prompted others to do the same. Of the 19 foiled hijacking attempts in 1972, 15 demanded both money and parachutes. During the same year, three hijackers demonstrated that it was possible to survive a jump from a 727 by parachuting out the back (all were later captured or shot). The Federal Aviation Administration (FAA) soon required all 727s to be fitted with a device that automatically locks the rear door while in flight. The idea of demanding a ransom and parachutes may not have originated with Cooper, however. A hijacker, with a gun, tried to take over an Air Canada plane just 12 days prior to the Cooper hijacking. The hijacker demanded money and parachutes but was subdued by the flight crew when he tried to put on the parachute. Cooper, though, decided to use a bomb in a briefcase instead of a gun, a plot that he may have copied from the 1970 movie *Airport*.

Not long after the Cooper skyjacking, in August 1972, the FAA issued a directive that all U.S. carriers had to either search or deny boarding to those who fit a certain profile (Daily & Pickrel, 1975a). The profile had been developed by FAA psychologists in response to the rash of skyjackings in the late 1960s and early 1970s. They had concluded that, in general, skyjackers were different from the usual air traveler of that time in such aspects as socioeconomic class and mannerisms in the airport terminal (Daily & Pickrel, 1975a). The "typical" skyjacker was

generally an "unsuccessful" member of society, was inadequate socially and occupationally, was lacking in resourcefulness, appeared to have substantial feelings of helplessness or hopelessness, and perhaps was suicidal. Apparently, the skyjacking was a way of improving his or her situation and gaining some control and significance in the world. However, although the skyjacker profile was helpful at first, it eventually proved inadequate and incomplete because cultural, social, political, and security forces are always in a state of flux. Consequently, the most useful profiles must be continually evaluated and updated with new information.

The preboarding procedure mandated by the FAA seemed to work. During the years 1973 and 1974, only four American aircraft were involved in skyjackings, none of which turned out to be successful in terms of getting the skyjacker flown to the desired destination (Civil Aeronautics Board, 1975).

Other psychologists and psychiatrists also were involved in developing profiles. The skyjacking profile offered by a well-known psychiatrist at the time, David Hubbard, was both dogmatic and offensive, to put it mildly. Hubbard concluded from his investigation of hijackers that "they are not strong, masculine supermen but weak, longtime losers, men who have failed at life and love. They tend to be passive, effeminate, latently homosexual, and afraid of their eldest sisters and mothers" (*Time*, November 13, 1972, p. 51). The validity of the Hubbard skyjacker profile has never been established by systematic, empirical research, nor is it accepted by a vast majority of professional profilers.

Over the years, interest in profiling has waxed and waned, and it is often fueled by sensational media events. After a series of school shootings in the 1990s, considerable attention was directed at developing profiles of the type of high school student who would be likely to open fire on classmates or school officials. When the Washington D.C. area was terrorized by sniper shootings in the fall of 2002, sniper profiles were the rage. However, despite its enormous media interest—including depictions of profilers in the entertainment media—profiling is not a frequent investigative activity of police officials or psychologists. Many police psychologists question the technique. In a nationwide survey of police psychologists, for example, 70% said they did not feel comfortable profiling and seriously questioned its validity and usefulness (Bartol, 1996). Still, the topic is an important one, and in the sections to follow, we will cover it in three forms: criminal profiling, psychological autopsies, and geographical profiling.

Criminal Profiling

Criminal profiling is the process of identifying personality traits, behavioral tendencies, geographical location, and demographic or biographical descriptors of an offender (or offenders) based on characteristics of the crime (Bartol & Bartol, 2004). The primary goal of criminal profiling is to narrow the field of possible suspects to a more reasonable number from the hundreds or thousands of possible suspects within a specific population. Profiling is also a form of prediction. Based on crime scene information and the behavioral patterns or habits of the offender, the profiler tries to "predict" who the offender or offenders might be and where and how the next crime may occur. To a very large extent, the profiling process is dictated by the quality of the data collected on previous offenders who have committed similar offenses. It should be emphasized, at the outset, that profiling—even in its most sophisticated form—rarely can point directly to *the* person who committed the crime. Instead, the process helps develop a manageable set of hypotheses for identifying who *may* have been responsible for the crime. If done competently, a profile will provide some statistical probabilities of the demographic, geographic, and psychological features of the offender. More important, it should eliminate large segments of the population from further investigation.

The term *profiling* is used in several ways to identify different kinds of information. The

---

BOX 3.2   The FBI Academy Behavioral Science Unit

The FBI Behavioral Science Unit is one of the instructional components of the FBI's Training Division at Quantico, Virginia. Its mission is to develop and provide programs of training, research, and consultation in the behavioral and social sciences for the FBI and law enforcement community that will improve or enhance their administration, operational effectiveness, and understanding of crime. This work includes conducting high-impact research and presenting a variety of cutting-edge courses on topics such as applied criminal psychology, clinical forensic psychology, crime analysis, death investigation, interpersonal violence, research methodology, stress management in law enforcement, and violence in America.

The Behavioral Science Unit conducts specialized and applied training in the above disciplines as they pertain to law enforcement for new agents, FBI services and symposia, the FBI National Academy Program, international police officers, field police schools, and criminal justice-related organizations and conferences.

The Behavioral Science Unit also coordinates with and supports other FBI units, such as the National Center for the Analysis of Violent Crime (NCAVC) and the Critical Incident Response Group (CIRG), which provides operational assistance to the FBI field offices and law enforcement agencies. The Behavioral Science Unit does not presently recruit from outside the FBI.

Source: Behavioral Science Unit, FBI Academy. Available: www.fbi.gov

term we use here—**criminal profiling**—refers to identifying and describing essential information about a suspect. Psychological profiling refers to a behavioral sketch of an individual who may or may not be a suspected offender. **Crime scene analysis,** or the more technical terms *criminal investigative analysis* and *crime scene investigation,* pertains to developing a rough behavioral or psychological sketch of an offender based on clues identified at the crime scene. Sometimes the terms are used interchangeably, causing confusion for the public, researchers, and students alike. *Racial profiling,* on the other hand, is defined as

> police-initiated action that relies on the race, ethnicity, or national origin rather than the behavior of an individual or information that leads the police to a particular individual who has been identified as being, or having been, engaged in criminal activity. (Ramirez, McDevitt, & Farrell, 2000, p. 53)

Racial profiling has become so well known to ethnic/minorities or people of color during traffic stops that they began to label the phenomenon "driving while Black" or "driving while Brown" (abbreviated as DWB) as a play on the legally accepted term DWI (driving while intoxicated). Racial profiling is based on the assumption by some law enforcement officials that ethnic or racial minorities are most often used as couriers of illegal drugs or other contraband. This unwarranted assumption has led to a disproportionate number of "pretext" stops of members of minority groups. A pretext stop is one in which a driver is pulled over for a mild traffic infraction, such as crossing the center line or driving a vehicle with a defective taillight. The stop allows the officer to conduct a visual search of the vehicle and, under some conditions, order drivers and even passengers out of the car.

Psychological profiling was used by the U.S. Office of Strategic Services (OSS) during World War II in an effort to identify the tendencies and thought processes of Adolf Hitler (Ault & Reese, 1980). It is very likely, though, that the technique predated the OSS by several hundred years in earlier efforts to understand the thinking of kings and military leaders. David Canter—whom we credited with coining the term *investigative psychology*—and his colleague Laurence Alison point out that psychological profiling is basically an offshoot of psychological testing (Canter & Alison, 2000).

An excellent example of crime scene or criminal investigative analysis can be found in an article by Raymond Knight and his colleagues (Knight, Warren, Reboussin, & Soley, 1998). "This technique attempts to derive hypotheses about the personality of the offender from analysis of a crime scene, victim information, and current knowledge of offenders from previous research" (Knight et al., 1998, p. 47).

Criminal profiling has gained popularity in law enforcement circles since first used by the Federal Bureau of Investigation in 1971 (Pinizzotto & Finkel, 1990). In more recent years, criminal profiling has intrigued the public through such films as *Silence of the Lambs* and TV series such as *CSI: Crime Scene Investigation, CSI: Miami, Crossing Jordan,* or *Autopsy* in the United States and *Cracker* in the United Kingdom. Despite the media attention and popular TV and movie depictions of highly successful and probing profilers employing sophisticated techniques to identify the offender, reality is far from that picture. If the number of actual success stories in profiling is compared to the total number of misses or failures, the ratio of hits to misses might be close to chance. Furthermore, it should be emphasized early in this section that there are very few full-time employment opportunities for professional criminal profilers, even highly experienced ones. Although a fascinating area, students aspiring to become forensic psychologists should keep their career options open to the many other forensic areas that are growing and emerging each year and not narrow their career interests to such limited topics as criminal profiling.

However, it is also very important to understand the many aspects of profiling as it is such a pervasive and ultimately important topic in the field of forensic psychology. One of the first questions that the public asks the forensic psychologist is about criminal profiling. Moreover, in contrast to the *applied* aspects of criminal profiling, the one area that drastically needs attention from forensic psychologists is profiling *research*. In other words, it is critical that we learn how reliable or valid the various profiling procedures and methods currently used are and how (or if) they can be improved to allow meaningful application to law enforcement and other forensic realms. Consequently, in this section, we will spend some time going over the key concepts in the field, the current state of the "art," and the available research.

Contrary to popular belief, criminal profiling is not and should not be restricted to serial murder or serial sexual assaults. It has considerable *potential* value when applied successfully to crimes such as arson, burglary, shoplifting, and robbery and to white-collar crimes such as bank fraud or embezzlement. However, because of the limited research base available, its effectiveness in these areas has yet to be demonstrated.

More recently, computer-based models of offender profiles based on extensive statistical data collected on similar offenses have been introduced. With the necessary empirical research, they may hold considerable promise in advancing the accuracy of criminal profiles. But, so far, there are very little research data on the utility, reliability, and validity of computer-based profiling. This point leads us to the general topic of predictions of human behavior.

Dynamic and Static Risk Factors in Prediction

An important issue in the prediction and profiling of human behavior is the distinction between **dynamic risk factors** and **static risk factors** (Andrews & Bonta, 1998; Andrews, Bonta, & Hoge, 1990). Dynamic risk factors are those that change over time and situation. For example, our

attitudes, values, and beliefs have considerable potential for change, in contrast to static risk factors, such as our gender, birth order, ethnic background, and biological parents. In short, dynamic factors can change, whereas static factors cannot.

Dynamic factors can be subdivided into stable and acute dynamic factors (Hanson & Harris, 2000). **Stable dynamic factors,** although they are changeable, usually change slowly and may take months or even years to change. **Acute dynamic factors,** on the other hand, change rapidly (days, hours, or even minutes) and include such things as mood swings, emotional arousal, and alcohol or other drug-induced effects. Hanson and Harris (2000) found that acute dynamic factors, such as anger and subjective distress, were better predictors of the tendency of sex offenders to reoffend than were the more stable dynamic factors, such as the sex offender's attitudes about women.

This is important to profiling because serial offenders, whether serial rapists, burglars, arsonists, serial killers, or pedophiles, often change their **modus operandi (MO)** as they become more proficient at their crime—or, as noted by Turvey (2002), it may change due to an offender's deteriorating mental state or the increased use of drugs or alcohol.

The MO—the actions and procedures an offender uses to commit a crime successfully—can be considered a stable dynamic factor. It is a behavioral pattern that the offender learns as he or she gains experience in committing the offense. Burglars are continually changing their procedures and techniques to better accomplish their goals, and serial killers often become more daring and risky in their selection of victims. Because the offender generally changes the MO until he or she learns which method is most effective, investigators may make a serious error if they place too much significance on the MO when linking crimes. Turvey (2002) also points out that some offenders improve their MO through educational and technical materials. "Professional journals, college courses, textbooks, and other educationally oriented media available at a public library, or now via the Internet, can provide offenders with knowledge that is useful toward refining their particular MO" (Turvey, 2002, p. 232). Turvey further illustrates his point by asserting that "arsonists may read *Kirk's Fire Investigation* (DeHaan, 1997); rapists may read *Practical Aspects of Rape Investigation* (Burgess & Hazelwood, 1995); murderers may read *Practical Homicide Investigation* (Geberth, 1996); and bank robbers may subscribe to security magazines" (p. 232). In addition, many offenders read newspaper, magazine, and television accounts of their crimes, which sometimes provide clues that the police have identified concerning the MO. Such accounts may prompt the offender to alter his or her methods of operations. In some instances, the offender may perfect the MO by engaging in a career or profession that enhances the methods used, such as joining a volunteer fire department or even becoming a fire investigator.

A similar but distinct feature is the signature. The **signature** is thought to be related to the unique cognitive processes of the offender and, because it is relatively consistent in its characteristics, may be more useful in the profiling process. In other words, the signature probably has greater stability than the MO, although both are stable, dynamic factors.

The signature is a symbolic communication by the offender that goes beyond what is necessary to commit the crime. For example, some burglars tailor their styles (or their signature) to convey messages to victims and investigators, hoping to induce some strong emotional reactions from the victims, such as fear or anger. The burglar may leave a frightening or threatening note or "violate" some personal item, such as intimate clothing, a photograph, or a diary. Consequently, the emotional reactions of burglarized victims often run the gamut from anger and depression to fear and anxiety (Brown & Harris, 1989).

Related to the signature is the issue of psychopathology. Experienced profilers have argued for many years that profiling serial violent offenders is most successful when the offender exhibits some form of psychopathology at the scene of the crime, such as sadistic torture, evisceration, postmortem slashings and cuttings, and other mutilations (Pinizzotto, 1984). The reasoning behind this assertion is that when a person is mentally disordered, he or she demonstrates greater consistency in behavior from situation to situation. However, whether persons with mental disorders are more consistent in their behavioral patterns than stable individuals remains very much open to debate, and systematic empirical research on the topic is lacking.

Additional Crime Scene Concepts

During the 1980s, the FBI's **Behavioral Science Unit (BSU)** (see Box 3.2) interviewed incarcerated sexual murderers in an effort to identify some common behavioral characteristics and motives of serial killers (Ressler, Burgess, & Douglas, 1988; Ressler, Burgess, Hartman, Douglas, & McCormick, 1986). In the late 1980s, further study focused on the behavioral and motivational features of serial rapists (Hazelwood & Burgess, 1987, 1995). One of the outcomes of these studies was the development of a typology that classifies crime scenes as organized, disorganized, or mixed. An **organized crime scene** suggests planning and premeditation on the part of the offender. The crime reveals signs that the offender maintained control of himself or herself and the victim(s) and took considerable cautions to elude apprehension. In addition, it is also apparent that the victim or victims were selected rather than being randomly attacked. A **disorganized crime scene,** on the other hand, shows that the offender committed the crime without premeditation or planning. Essentially, the crime scene looks chaotic, indicating the offender acted on impulse, rage, or some other intense emotional state. High emotions tend to "disorganize" a person's thought processes and behavior. Think of what happens when a person becomes uncontrollably angry. Often, the disorganized offender obtains his or her victim or victims by chance. The victim is simply at the wrong place at the wrong time. The **mixed crime scene** has both organized and disorganized aspects. For example, a crime may have begun as a carefully planned one but quickly deteriorated into a disorganized crime when things failed to go as originally planned and unanticipated strong emotions set in.

This manner of looking at a crime scene is rarely as neat as portrayed here, however, and some recent research (Kocsis, Cooksey, & Irwin, 2002) suggests that the organized-disorganized classification scheme may have very limited usefulness. It is probably more realistic to assume that crime scenes exist somewhere along a continuum, with the organized label at one pole of the continuum and the disorganized label at the other. Otherwise, we would be trying to fit crime scene analysis into an unrealistic classification system or **typology.** In contemporary psychology, the term *typology* refers to a particular system for classifying personality or other behavioral patterns. Usually, the typology is used to classify a wide assortment of behaviors into a more manageable set of brief descriptions. However, placing individuals into behavioral categories is based on the fundamental assumption that behavior is consistent across time and place. Crime scene typologies are constructed on the premise that human behavior (e.g., of the offender) is largely the same from situation to situation. The concept of typologies will be discussed again in Chapters 5 and 6 when sexual assaults and criminal violence are covered.

Another concept sometimes encountered in crime scene analysis is **undoing.** Undoing is a behavioral pattern found at the scene in which the offender tried to psychologically "undo" the crime. For example, a distraught or emotionally upset offender, who kills the victim, may try to undo his or her actions by placing the body in bed, gently placing the head on a pillow, and neatly covering the body with blankets. Or he or she may place the victim upright in a chair, trying desperately to return the victim to a natural-looking state.

Trophy taking is another behavioral pattern sometimes encountered in crime scene analysis. Although it is more common in violent crime, it may also occur in burglary as well. A crime scene **trophy** is a meaningful souvenir taken by the offender to remember the incident, to psychologically control the victim, or both. It could be anything, from a piece of clothing, a photograph, a piece of jewelry, or—in the case of a murdered victim—a body part. Trophy taking may be also part of a signature of the offender. One of the more infamous trophy takers in recent years was the serial killer Jeffrey Dahmer, who collected body parts in glass jars filled with formaldehyde as well as photographs depicting victims at various stages of their deaths.

Staging is another behavioral pattern sometimes found at a suspected suicide, accidental death, or crime scene. Staging is the intentional alteration of a suicide or crime scene prior to the arrival of the police. It is usually done for one of two reasons: either to redirect the investigation away from the most logical suspect or to protect the victim or the victim's family (Douglas & Munn, 1992). Staging is frequently done by someone who has a close association or relationship with the victim. For example, the victim may have become an accidental death victim by practicing autoerotic asphyxia. **Autoerotic asphyxia** refers to obtaining sexual excitement from hypoxia (lack of oxygen), usually through near strangulation, such as a near hanging. Holmes and Holmes (2002) estimate that as many as 1,000 accidental deaths each year may be attributed to autoerotic asphyxia. Douglas and Munn (1992) report that in nearly one third of all autoerotic fatalities, the victim is nude, and in about another third, the victim has cross-dressed (e.g., male in female clothing). Most victims are young, White, middle-class, unmarried males (Holmes & Holmes, 2002). Distressed family members who discover the victim in a "compromised" condition may feel compelled to alter the situation (dressing the victim and hiding paraphernalia), perhaps to make it appear as either a homicide or a suicide. This topic leads us into the next form of profiling, the psychological autopsy.

The Psychological Autopsy

Recently, the attempt to reconstruct the personality profile and cognitive features (especially intentions) of *deceased* individuals has gained some popularity. This postmortem psychological analysis is called **reconstructive psychological evaluation** (RPE), **equivocal death analysis** (EDA) (Poythress, Otto, Darnes, & Starr, 1993), or, more commonly, **psychological autopsy** (Brent, 1989; Ebert, 1987; Selkin, 1987), the term used here. EDA, or the equivocal death psychological autopsy (EDPA), is usually reserved for those investigations conducted by law enforcement officials, especially the FBI, who primarily examine the crime scene material and other information directly available to the police (Canter, 1999; Poythress et al., 1993). Psychological autopsies differ from criminal profiling in two important ways: (1) the profile is constructed on a dead person, and (2) the identity of the person is already known.

The psychological autopsy was originally devised to assist certifying officials to clarify deaths that were initially ambiguous, uncertain, or equivocal as to the *manner* of death (Shneidman, 1994). The method was first used in 1958, when the Los Angeles medical examiner/coroner consulted the L.A. Suicide Prevention Center for assistance in determining the cause of an unusually high number of equivocal deaths (La Fon, 2002). The term *manner* has special significance in any death investigation. Basically, "the manner of death refers to specific circumstances by which a death results" (La Fon, 2002, p. 158). There are five generally accepted manners of death: natural, accident, suicide, homicide, and undetermined (La Fon, 2002).

Today, the psychological autopsy is primarily undertaken in an effort to make a reasonable determination of what may have been in the mind of the deceased person leading up to and at the time of death—particularly if the death appears to be a suicide. La Fon (2002) identifies two basic types of psychological autopsy: suicide psychological autopsy (SPA) and EDPA. The goal of the SPA is to identify and understand the psychosocial factors that contributed to the suicide. The goal of the EDPA, on the other hand, is to determine the reasons for the death. In most instances, the psychological autopsy (or the SPA) is done for insurance purposes. Although some insurance policies do compensate the family if the cause of death is determined to be suicide, many policies do not. Consequently, if the manner of death is equivocal, it is in the best financial interest of the insurance company to hire a forensic psychologist to do a complete psychological autopsy to determine whether the death was more likely the result of suicide or some other cause. The forensic psychologist would do this

> by looking at lifestyle, behavioral history, as well as the characterogical elements that contribute to that history: the degree of ambivalence, the clarity of cognitive functioning, the amount of organization or obsession, the state of turmoil or agitation, and the amount of psychic pain. (Shneidman, 1994, p. 76)

The following brief description of an incident illustrates the conditions that might call for a psychological autopsy:

> The man believed to have drowned in the Greenwood Lake has been identified as a 55-year-old Smithfield resident. The man was last seen floating at Johnson's Cove, where the Attleboro Sailing Club anchors its boats, at about 4 p.m. Tuesday. The Smithfield police said the man had called for a dinghy; after retrieving oars, a man on shore looked away for a moment, and when he looked back, the man was gone. There was no indication that drugs or alcohol were a factor in the disappearance, and it is

unknown what caused the man to go under. Was this a suicide, foul play, or an accident?

A vast majority of the psychological assessments to uncover a person's thoughts and feelings prior to their death have been done in the United States, usually in civil or criminal litigation (Canter, 1999). The procedure consists largely of conducting interviews with family members and people who knew the decedent, the examination of personal documents (suicide notes, diaries, and letters), and other materials, such as the autopsy by the medical examiner, other medical reports, and police reports. Mental health professionals who develop psychological autopsies do their own interviews, conduct background investigations, and examine other pertinent information that they believe will contribute to a meaningful report.

According to La Fon (2002), the U.S. military is one of the major consumers of psychological autopsies. "Each branch of the Armed Forces including the Navy, Army, and Air Force, have the task of conducting an EDPA for every equivocal death that occurs either on base property or to military personnel" (La Fon, 2002, p. 160). Both civilian and military forensic psychologists conduct these autopsies. In most cases, the beneficiaries of the deceased military personnel receive remuneration regardless of the cause of death.

In the legal contexts, the psychological autopsy is frequently conducted to reconstruct the possible reasons for a suicide and ultimately to establish legal culpability on the part of other persons or organizations. For example, if a police officer shoots himself on the steps of the state capital building, the message he was trying to send to all those concerned may be unclear. Family members of the deceased, convinced the department had poor stress management techniques and/or nonexistent early detection procedures for identifying emotional problems in their officers, may sue the department for emotional and financial damages. Under these conditions, a mental health professional may be retained to do a reconstruction of the victim's mental state during and before the incident. Psychological autopsies have also been part of civil proceedings in the private sector, where it was necessary to ascertain whether certain events on the job affected the persons—such as various kinds of harassment by fellow workers or supervisors—or whether certain job-related accidents prompted the eventual suicide. Failure of the company or organization to have adequate policies and procedures in place for handling problems of this sort may be sufficient reason to find the company liable.

Unfortunately, the reliability and validity of the psychological autopsy has yet to be demonstrated and awaits further research. Poythress et al. (1993) warn that

> persons who conduct reconstructive psychological evaluations should not assert categorical conclusions about the precise mental state or actions suspected of the actor at the time of his or her demise. The conclusions and inferences drawn in psychological reconstructions are, at best, informed speculations or theoretical formulations and should be labeled as such. (p. 12)

Ault, Hazelwood, and Reboussin (1994) posit that a psychological autopsy is an investigative technique that is ultimately "a professional opinion based on years of law enforcement experience with indirect assessment and violent death" (p. 73). Selkin (1994) argues that clear, definitive procedures for carrying out psychological autopsies have yet to be developed, and investigators have a long way to go before standardized methods for conducting the psychological autopsy are established.

Poythress et al. (1993) make three recommendations for forensic psychologists to follow when doing psychological autopsies or equivocal death analyses. First, the use of these procedures and techniques should not be extended to nondeath situations (such as burglary or kidnapping), at least until the reliability and validity of the methods are clearly established. Second, in legal and quasi-legal contexts, psychologists who conduct reconstructive psychological evaluations should not make conclusions about the *precise* mental state or actions suspected of the actor at the time of his or her demise. Third, psychologists, mental health professionals, and social scientists should be careful not to mislead consumers about the accuracy of conclusions drawn from these psychological reconstructions, unless the research data support such conclusions. Currently, the research data are inconclusive about the accuracy of such methods, and clearly more well-executed research needs to be undertaken before firm conclusions about the validity of psychological autopsies can be made.

Geographical Profiling and Mental Mapping

One of the more interesting features of offending patterns is that they often occur or cluster within certain geographical areas, such as a specific area of a city. There are two major ways these crime patterns may be analyzed: geographical profiling and geographical mapping. **Geographical profiling** refers to the analysis of geographical locations associated with the spatial movements of a *single* serial offender, whereas **geographical mapping** is concerned with analyzing the spatial patterns of crimes committed by numerous offenders over a period of time. In a sense, geographical mapping focuses on identifying the "hot spots" of certain types of crime. The procedure has been used in Europe since the first half of the 19th century and began to be used in the United States during the early 1900s. Geographical profiling, on the other hand, is a recent development.

In 1995, D. Kim Rossmo wrote a doctoral dissertation at Simon Frasier University's School of Criminology (Vancouver, British Columbia) on a method of geographical profiling that has become a promising tool for serial offender identification (Bartol & Bartol, 2004). Rossmo, who became the detective inspector in charge of the Vancouver Police Department's Geographic

Profiling Section, developed a computer program called Criminal Geographic Targeting (CGT). It is designed to analyze the geographical or spatial characteristics of an offender's crimes. Basically, the program creates a topographical map that assigns different statistical probabilities to various areas that seem to fall into the offender's "territory." The primary goal of the technique is to pinpoint the location of the offender's residence and/or base of operations. The CGT takes into account known movement patterns, possible comfort zones, and hypothesized "hunting patterns" for victims of a specific offender.

Rossmo (1997) classifies the "hunting patterns" of the offenders into four groups: (1) hunter, (2) poacher, (3) troller, and (4) trapper. Some serial offenders tend to commit their crimes within a certain region (are geographically stable), but some are more transient (move from place to place). "Hunters are those criminals who specifically set out from their residence to look for victims, searching through the areas in their awareness spaces that they believe contain suitable targets" (Rossmo, 1997, p. 167). The crimes of the hunter tend to be geographically stable and often occur near the offender's place of residence or neighborhood. Poachers tend to be more transient, usually traveling some distance from their residence or neighborhood in search of their victims. The third group, the trollers, are not specifically searching for victims but rather randomly encounter them during the course of some other activity. The fourth group, the trappers, create situations to draw victims to themselves. "Trapping" may be accomplished either through entertaining suitors, placing want ads, taking in boarders, or assuming positions or occupations where potential victims come to them. Rossmo recommends that geographical profiling be combined with criminal profiling for maximum effectiveness in developing probabilities for offender identification. In addition, he admonishes that geographical profiling is essentially an investigative tool that does not necessarily solve crimes but should help in the surveillance or monitoring of specific locations.

Having reviewed various forms of profiling, it is important that we turn our attention briefly to psychological concepts relative to the prediction of human behavior. The ultimate goals of profiling are both identification and prediction. Psychologists have long been involved in the enterprise of behavioral prediction, with the assumption that if we can predict with reasonable accuracy, we can prevent and treat those behaviors that are most dangerous to society and to the individual. If we can predict that an individual will be violent, for example, we can take steps to prevent the violence, including offering treatment addressing the violent tendencies.

Unfortunately, as we saw in the earlier discussions of static and dynamic factors, predicting behavior is not easy or simple. In fact, with respect to violent behavior, psychologists today prefer the term *risk assessment,* whereby they provide probabilities that a person will display violent behavior at some point in the future. Psychological profiles, autopsies, and geographical profiling assume to a large extent that psychologists can predict (or postdict [after the fact]) human behavior.

Why Is Profiling So Inaccurate?

Contemporary researchers on profiling (Alison, Bennell, Ormerod, & Mokros, 2002; Alison & Canter, 1999) identify two main flaws with the current state of criminal profiling. One is the assumption that human behavior is consistent across a variety of situations; the other is the assumption that offense style or crime scene evidence is related to specific psychological characteristics. The second point refers to the tendency of profilers to believe that specific clues gathered at the crime scene (such as signatures) reveal certain generalizable psychological characteristics and thought patterns of certain types of offenders. Alison et al. (2002, p. 116) further assert that

(a) most current profiling methods rely on a naïve and outdated understanding of

personality and the trait approach; (b) global traits, or broad personality types, are unlikely to be useful in predicting criminal behavior; (c) it is unlikely that the classification of offenders into broad personality types would enable the profiler to relate clusters of sociodemographic characteristics to different types; (d) a theoretical framework that emphasizes the importance of Person × Situation interactions in generating behavior may lead to a more productive research endeavor; (e) profiling should be used with extreme caution in criminal investigations, and not at all as evidence in court, until research demonstrates its predictive validity. (p. 116)

The above points underscore the observation that many professional profilers tend to rely on unsubstantiated assumptions about personality theory, the power of that personality or disposition to virtually override the influence of all situations, and the validity and accuracy of the profiling process itself. They rely too heavily on "gut feelings," believing they have special knowledge to put the pieces of the puzzle together, and too little on science.

A common error is the failure to consider the power of the situation to influence behavior. And remember, part of the situation is the victim and all the characteristics brought to the incident by that individual or individuals. As noted by Jenkins (1993), "The failure to consider victim-oriented factors often leads researchers to misunderstand the nature of such activity" (p. 462). The lack of a victimology perspective generates confusion and often leads to further flaws in the development of offender profiles. Jenkins strongly asserts that an overlooked tool available to profilers is examining characteristics of the victim because "offenders and victim comprise a common and interdependent ecology" (p. 463). Cromwell, Olson, and Avary (1991) also discuss the importance of the victim perspective in their study of burglary. Cromwell and his colleagues contend that the activities of the victim play a critical role in how burglars pick a home to burglarize, how they enter, and how long they remain. Cromwell et al. believe that "most burglaries in the jurisdictions studied appeared to result from a propitious juxtaposition of target, offender, and situations" (p. 47).

Profiling is ultimately based on the assumption that human behavior is consistent across time (transtemporal consistency) and place (transsituational consistency). The profile process, by its very nature, presupposes that crime scene clues provide the skillful investigator with clues of the perpetrator's personality traits, habits, and even thought processes. Furthermore, there is an assumption that key factors of the personality identified at the crime scene should generalize to other situations, including future crimes.

The ability to predict the behavior and tendencies of individuals across different situations (transsituational consistency) is very much open to debate. For example, some researchers (e.g., Mischel, 1968; Mischel & Peake, 1982) argue that human behavior across different situations is inconsistent and that notions of stable behavioral dispositions or personality traits are largely unsupported. Research by Merry and Harsent (2000) cogently illustrates that most criminal behavior, such as burglary, changes as the dynamics of the situation changes. Consequently, crime scene activity is likely to be different from crime to crime. Although transsituational consistency remains highly questionable, consistency across time or temporal consistency is acknowledged. As long as situations are similar, people will likely respond the same way over their life spans. But when situations change, behavior is apt to change. Therefore, criminal behavior that has been reinforced in a particular context is more apt to recur in a similar context than across a wide variety of different settings. A person who had engaged in a lifetime of burglary, for instance, is more likely to burglarize again if surrounded by similar psychosocial situations that have a perceived reward value. Therefore, there is transtemporal consistency in behavior if the perceived situation is the same. On the other hand, if his or her environment has changed substantially (e.g., long-time partner in crime has died, or the person has aged to the point where physical agility has substantially deteriorated), the burglarizing is less likely to continue.

Mischel and Peake (1982) conclude, on the basis of their research findings, that behavior is highly dependent on the nature of the situation and that humans discriminate between situations and respond accordingly. Can we expect a shy child to be socially withdrawn on *all* occasions—even with family? He or she may be shy when meeting strangers (transtemporal consistency) but not shy in familiar, family situations. Consider the typical skyjacker profile, identified by Dailey and Pickrel (1975a) and discussed earlier. Lacking resourcefulness and having feelings of helplessness are examples of mood states and behavioral patterns that may well *not* have transsituational consistency. In fact, Hanson and Harris (2000) would call these acute dynamic risk facts, which are highly changeable. Although research by Bem and Allen (1974) and Kenrick and Springfield (1980) does suggest that *some* behaviors are consistent across both time and place, it is clear that *most* are not.

Transsituational consistency is a critical issue in the formulation of any classification system or profile system, but we have seen that it is risky to assume it exists. Yet belief in "personality profiles" persists, not only with respect to criminal behavior but also in areas involving employment screening. Thus, a company may want to know what type of person makes the best salesperson, or a law enforcement agency may want to know who from a pool of applicants will make the best officer.

The intricate interaction of personality and situation creates problems for profilers. Personality research and theory building, 20 or 30 years ago, emphasized the person to the exclusion of the situation. It was assumed that personality structures and traits were the center and driving force of all human behavior. Once these attributes were delineated, accurate prediction was almost guaranteed. In this sense, to say an individual had an aggressive personality was to infer a corresponding list of behaviors, most of them negative. As we have noted, however, the situation and the meaning of that situation for the person are crucial variables. Rather than relying on a global conclusion that an officer has an "aggressive personality," an agency would do well to try to determine how the officer handles himself or herself in various situations.

The above discussion emphasizes that accurate assessment and prediction require not only an evaluation of the person but also an evaluation of the psychosocial environment within which the behaviors we are trying to predict occur. Failure to consider the context of the behavior is destined to produce disappointing results.

Profiling is a nomothetic enterprise in that it tries to make *general* predictions about offenders based on clusters of data gathered from previous offenders. **Nomothetic** refers to the search for general principles, relationships, and patterns by examining and combining data from many individuals. Research psychology is largely nomothetic as opposed to idiographic in scope. The **idiographic** approach emphasizes the intensive study of one individual. A case study of the coping behaviors of an individual or the biography of a famous person is an example of the idiographic approach. Profiling that relies exclusively on the idiographic approach is in far more danger of missing the mark than profiling based on the nomothetic approach, especially if the nomothetic approach emphasizes the situational variables as much as validly possible. Yet many profilers and clinicians prefer exclusive use of the idiographic approach, even though research has continually revealed that predictions based on statistical probability, calculated from research on clusters of offenders under various conditions, are far more accurate.

There are other problems with profiling as well. Some recent studies indicate that a large proportion of the conclusions and predictions contained within profiles are both ambiguous and unverifiable (Alison, Smith, Eastman, & Rainbow, 2003; Alison, Smith, & Morgan, 2003).

Some of the statements are so vague that they are open to a wide range of multiple interpretations. Moreover, there seems to be a tendency for police investigators to "creatively interpret" the ambiguous information contained within profiles to fit their own biases about the case or the suspect. They select those aspects of the profile that they perceive as fitting the suspect while ignoring the many conclusions and predictions that do not seem to fit.

If a suspect does arise during the investigation officers may wish to actively ignore the information that does not fit the suspect, perhaps, unwittingly, exaggerate the merits of the information that might fit and not appreciate the extent to which the information could fit a wide range of individuals. (Alison, Smith, & Morgan, 2003, p. 193)

The strong preference to have one's views confirmed is known as **confirmation bias.** "When it operates, it places us in a kind of closed cognitive system in which only evidence that confirms our existing views and beliefs gets inside; other information is sometimes noticed but is quickly rejected as false" (Baron & Byrne, 2000, p. 8). In short, confirmation bias is the tendency to notice and remember information that lends support to our views on something, such as a suspect. It is a tendency that might be prevalent not only in the subjective interpretations of a profile but also in its creation.

Although there are many flaws in current profiling methods, if conducted appropriately, profiling could have a promising and extremely useful future. If profilers took into account the interaction between the person and the situations (and the influence of the victim), the science of profiling could lead to more accurate and helpful sketches of the offender. In addition, profilers should abandon the traditional and naive understanding of trait theory and rely more on contemporary psychological theory and research on human behavior. They should look for the conditional probability of certain behaviors occurring under certain situations instead of assuming that behavior remains consistent across all situations. All of this will require greater reliance and involvement in well-executed scientific research.

The Polygraph

The polygraph—commonly called the "lie detector"—does not really detect lies or deception but only the psychophysiological responses that accompany emotional reactions to guilt, shame, and anxiety. The instrument usually records heart rate, blood pressure, breathing rate, and skin conductance. Skin conductance refers to how well the skin conducts a small, imperceptible electrical current that is affected by slight changes in perspiration. Presumably, when one tries to deceive, there are telltale bodily or physiological reactions that can be measured with sophisticated equipment and detected by a trained examiner called a polygrapher. In addition to observing the physiological measures, the skillful polygrapher makes behavioral observations and notations to infer truth or deception in the subject being examined. There is little doubt that the polygraph can accurately measure and record the physiological responses. Whether it can detect actual lying and deception is another matter.

A Brief History of the Polygraph

The modern polygraph has been used in some form for nearly a century, and much cruder versions of its components existed as far back as 300 B.C. (Trovillo, 1939). The Bedouins of Arabia, for example, required the authors of conflicting statements to lick a hot iron. The one whose tongue was not burned was considered truthful (Smith, 1967). The ancient Chinese required suspects to put rice powder in their mouths and then spit it out (Smith, 1967). If the powder was dry, the individual was lying. The common

principle underlying these and other similar methods used throughout history is that the tense, nervous person (the one who is lying) has less saliva (dry mouth and tongue) and thus is more likely to have their tongue burned, spit drier rice powder, or even be less able to swallow the "trial slice" of bread, as practiced centuries ago in England.

The idea of lie detection caught on rapidly in the United States during the 1920s and 1930s after John Larson was asked by the chief of police in Berkeley, California, to develop a "lie detector" to solve a case under investigation (Barland & Raskin, 1973). This instrument, according to Barland (1988), became "the first true polygraph used for lie-detection purposes" (p. 75). A number of well-publicized successes by Larson and one of his students, Leonarde Keeler, catapulted the polygraph into the limelight. Eventually, Keeler began to teach a 2-week course for police and military examiners, which soon developed into a 6-week course (Barland, 1988; Keeler, 1984). The increasing demand for polygraph examiners resulted in the formation of at least 30 polygraph schools across the United States (Barland, 1988).

Current Usage of the Polygraph

During its early beginnings in the United States, the polygraph was used almost exclusively in criminal investigations. However, as criminal suspects became less interested in incriminating themselves, and as civil libertarians challenged the instrument's validity, the use of the polygraph has become less common. Furthermore, the U.S. Congress severely limited the extent to which *private* employers can use the polygraph with the passage of the **Employee Polygraph Protection Act,** enacted in 1988. This law has, in effect, ended preemployment polygraphic screening by *private* employers as well as the periodic testing of employees to verify their good behavior (Iacono & Patrick, 1999). We still see examples of suspects volunteering to take a polygraph to clear their names or the polygraph used in counterintelligence investigations. For the most part, however, its major uses are in personnel selection or screening by *government* agencies.

Today, U.S. governmental counterintelligence polygraph tests far outnumber the tests given at other organizations or all other agencies (Krapohl, 2002). Furthermore, polygraph screening of police, law enforcement, or governmental security applicants has either remained the same or increased in recent years. Meesig and Horvath (1995) report that approximately 99% of the large police agencies and 95% of the small police departments in the United States require the polygraph as an integral and indispensable part of their preemployment screening procedures.

Currently, a variety of private and government-sponsored polygraphy schools are in operation, almost all of which are accredited by the American Polygraphy Association. The most prestigious and intensive is the one operated by the Department of Defense. The Department of Defense Polygraphy Institute (DoDPI) trains all polygraphers employed by federal agencies, with the exception of the CIA, as well as polygraphers employed by many local and state agencies. The DoDPI also includes a research arm, staffed primarily by doctoral-level psychologists (Iacono & Patrick, 1999). Other polygraphy schools vary widely in training and rarely include a research component. The typical polygraph examiner in the United States today does not have graduate psychological or research training; not all polygraph examiners are licensed or graduates of accredited schools. In addition, the profession has "almost no input or oversight from psychology" (Iacono & Patrick, 1999, p. 467).

Many polygraph examiners also have shifted to computerization—called computerized polygraph systems (CPS)—to replace the conventional chart or graph method. Physiological data are stored digitally and are plotted with a printer. Software allows the computer to provide a probability statement as to the likelihood that a person was truthful when responding (Iacono & Patrick, 1999).

Traditional Procedures Used by Polygraphers

Polygraphers use several polygraph techniques or approaches to determine deception or truthfulness during the examination. The most commonly used procedure for lie detection in criminal investigations is the **control question technique (CQT)**, developed by John Reid (Bashore & Rapp, 1993; Reid & Inbau, 1977). The most commonly used procedure for detection in preemployment screening is the **relevant/irrelevant question technique,** developed by Lykken (1981). Critics of these traditional polygraph procedures have argued that the fundamental assumptions on which they are based are flawed and that there is essentially no sound scientific support for their validity (Bashore & Rapp, 1993). These critics believe that these frequently used procedures have not been subjected to rigorous scientific investigation and that the claims of their validity by their proponents are largely based on subjective evaluations. Today, the polygraph continues to be a highly controversial topic on philosophical, legal, theoretical, scientific, and ethical grounds. In a survey of scientists knowledgeable about the polygraph, Iacono and Lykken (1997) found that a majority of the respondents

> believed that polygraphic lie detection is not theoretically sound, claims of high validity for these procedures cannot be sustained, the lie test can be beaten by easily learned countermeasures, and polygraph test results should not be admitted into evidence in courts of law. (p. 462)

Despite the controversy—and as mentioned above—polygraphs continue to be used in a wide variety of governmental contexts, including criminal investigations, counterintelligence and national security screening, and civil litigation and postconviction assessments. The last category includes situations in which the polygraph is used with sex offenders to detect deception in an effort to control recidivism. For example, in

1998, a survey revealed that 35 states were using polygraph testing for monitoring convicted sex offenders (Consigli, 2002).

Countermeasures

Countermeasures are anything that an examinee might do to "fool" the polygraph and the examiner (Bartol & Bartol, 2004). Many types of countermeasures are possible, but most fall into the categories of physical, mental, hypnosis, biofeedback, or drugs. The most common physical countermeasures are either pain or muscle tension. For example, in an effort to deceive the polygrapher, biting one's lip or tongue or subtly jabbing oneself with a pin may induce enough pain to promote a physiological response that masks the subject's response to questions from the polygrapher.

Available research suggests that mental countermeasures may be as effective in deceiving the polygraph as physical ones (Ben-Shakhar & Dolev, 1996; Honts, Devitt, Winbush, & Kircher, 1996). Mental countermeasures include any deliberate attempt by an examinee to alter his or her thought patterns during the polygraph test to deceive the polygrapher. Examples would include counting backwards from 100, thinking of a sexually arousing scene, imagining walking your dog on a promising spring morning, or thinking of a very peaceful scene (such as canoeing on moonlit lake on summer evening). Any thought that either minimizes the emotional impact of relevant questions or increases physiological arousal across all questions qualifies as a mental countermeasure. Although physical countermeasures are often detectable by experienced polygraphers, mental countermeasures are far more difficult to detect (Ben-Shakhar, 2002).

It should be emphasized, however, that research indicates that spontaneous countermeasures in which the examinee tries to influence the outcome of the polygraph without forethought, planning, or training are largely ineffective (Honts & Amato, 2002). Untrained respondents who use physical, behavioral, and cognitive measures to deceive the polygrapher are rarely successful. In addition, there is very little evidence that drugs—sometimes referred to as "general state countermeasures" because they influence the entire neurophysiological systems—can be used as an effective countermeasure to polygraph testing (Honts, 1987; Honts & Amato, 2002). And this includes alcohol (Honts & Perry, 1992). Hypnosis has also been tried as a countermeasure. The primary strategy in the use of hypnosis as a countermeasure is to induce a form of amnesia for the behavior in question. However, there is no evidence to date that hypnosis is an effective countermeasure in untrained respondents either (Gudjonsson, 1988).

An important issue concerning the use of the polygraph in criminal investigations is its accuracy with psychopaths, who are portrayed as skilled liars and manipulators with a limited capacity for anxiety or guilt (Patrick & Iacono, 1989). The possibility that psychopaths might be able to beat the polygraph is a concern because most of the research reveals that psychopaths—who will be discussed in detail in Chapter 4—constitute a sizable proportion of violent and repetitive offenders. Although the evidence on the issue remains unclear, some preliminary data from Patrick and Iacono (1989) suggest that under certain conditions, guilty psychopaths can be detected at about the same rate as guilty nonpsychopaths.

Although individuals are not likely to beat the polygraph on their own, training in physical and mental countermeasures *may* be effective (Ben-Shakhar, 2002; Krapohl, 2002). Charles Honts and his research group (Honts, Hodes, & Raskin, 1985; Honts, Raskin, & Kircher, 1987) report that a significant proportion of highly motivated respondents can be trained to beat polygraph tests. The possibility of effective countermeasures is especially pertinent when the polygraph is used for espionage purposes. Spies and intelligence agents are probably well trained and largely effective in the use of countermeasures for defeating polygraph results.

Honts and Amato (2002) report that scientific studies examining the effects of countermeasure training on the polygraphic results will be very limited in the foreseeable future, however. This is partly due to the fact that research on counter-measures is difficult to conduct unless one has access to considerable resources and governmental financial support. Since the beginning of the 1990s, polygraphic research in the United States has been centered at the DoDPI (Honts & Amato, 2002). Currently, the DoDPI has a policy that all countermeasures research on the polygraph will be classified and not open to the scientific community or the general public. Apparently, the federal government does not want current employees or future applicants to governmental jobs to learn of any effective ways to control the results of the polygraph.

Research on the Polygraph

Many researchers continue to be very wary of the polygraph and its overall accuracy. Historically, professional field polygraphers have claimed extraordinary accuracy rates, ranging from 92% to 100% (Bartol & Bartol, 2004). Most biopsychologists and research psychologists find these statistics highly questionable. In addition to occasional arithmetical errors, none of the published reports gave any details of the methods and procedures used or of the criteria used to decide accuracy rates. Currently, the research conducted under laboratory or controlled conditions indicates that the correct classification of truthful and deceptive examinees ranges between 70% and 80% (Krapohl, 2002). However, the accuracy can be increased slightly through careful and intensive training of the examiner. Furthermore, in lab studies, computerized polygraph systems, in contrast to human evaluations, are slightly more accurate for detecting both innocent and deceptive respondents (Kircher & Raskin, 2002). Polygraphic research conducted under realistic or field conditions is rare, however.

The accuracy of the polygraph in detecting who is telling the truth and who is deceptive is a highly complicated issue.

A number of factors—such as the specific technique used, the nature of the population tested, the issues to be resolved, the context of the examination, whether one is trying to detect truth or deception, the training of the examiner, what cues the examiner considers besides the polygraphic data, or even whether one is examining the victim or the suspect—all must be carefully considered before any tentative conclusions can be advanced. (Bartol & Bartol, 2004, p. 285)

Many professional polygraphers believe that the polygraph may be more accurate with criminal suspects than with victims (Barland, 1988). Many of these polygraphers also believe that people who have committed property crimes (theft, burglary) are more difficult to detect than those who have committed violent crimes, such as physical or sexual assault, robbery, or murder, primarily because the emotional baggage is usually higher for the latter than for the former (Horvath, 1977). The polygraph is also believed to be more accurate when a suspect denies having physically committed a specific, illegal act and less accurate when the suspect admits the act but denies criminal intent (Barland, 1988). In other words, it is more difficult to determine what a person was thinking than what a person actually did.

Forensic Hypnosis

Hypnosis is a procedure during which a mental health, health, or forensic professional suggests to a person that he or she try to experience changes in sensations, perceptions, thoughts, and behavior. It is a procedure that should be used only by highly trained and properly credentialed professionals. Hypnosis is usually established by what is commonly referred to as an induction procedure.

Although there are many different induction procedures, most center on suggestions for relaxation, calmness, and well-being. Induction instructions usually include asking the participant to imagine or think about pleasant experiences or things. During the induction, the participant may be sitting comfortably or lying down while concentrating on a "target" (such as a lit candle) while listening to the hypnotist's voice. The participant is usually encouraged to drift into a sleep-like state while always hearing the hypnotist's voice. Overall, most people find the experience very pleasant and relaxing.

People differ widely in their responses and susceptibility to hypnosis. "Some people respond to almost all suggestions, some respond to a few or none, and most respond to some suggestions but not others" (Braffman & Kirsch, 1999, p. 578). The ability to be hypnotized is believed to be an enduring and stable attribute, which peaks during the life cycle in late childhood and declines gradually thereafter (Spiegel & Spiegel, 1987). Among the factors that are important in inducing hypnosis are (1) the level of trust the participant places on the hypnotist, (2) the participant's motivation and desire to cooperate, (3) preconceived notions the participant has about hypnosis, and (4) the context and reasons for the hypnosis (e.g., entertainment or critical information gathering). Trust, motivation, a strong belief in hypnotism's powers, and a serious context (such as a criminal investigation) inspire most people to become hypnotized, but this does not mean that they will accurately recall events. Apparently, what distinguishes truly being hypnotized from simple behavioral compliance is the person's ability to experience suggested alterations in perception, memory, and mood (Orne, Whitehouse, Dinges, & Orne, 1988).

A person's ability to experience hypnotic suggestions is most often inhibited by fears and concerns arising from some common misconceptions. Contrary to some depictions of hypnosis in books, movies, or television, people who have been hypnotized do not lose control over their behavior. Hypnotized individuals remain aware of who and where they are, and unless some form of temporary forgetfulness is specifically suggested, they usually remember what transpired during the hypnosis. It has long been known that all the experiences and responses that are elicited during hypnosis can also be produced in a normal state without hypnotic induction (Braffman & Kirsch, 1999). Hypnosis does, however, increase suggestibility. As noted by Braffman and Kirsch (1999), "The only thing which characterizes hypnosis as such and which gives any justification for calling it a 'state' is its generalized hypersuggestibility" (p. 578). The hypersuggestibility aspect, however, is the one feature that is most troubling to forensic investigators and researchers concerned with recollections of witnesses or victims of crime incidents. In fact, "The subject's willingness to accept fantasy as reality during the hypnotic experience, together with the often dramatic vividness of recollections in hypnosis, may inspire great confidence that the recalled material is true to fact" (Orne et al., 1988, p. 25). This *induced* confidence, for example, may soundly convince the witness that his or her ambiguous view of the offender was much clearer than it really was.

Hypnosis has long been used in a variety of ways: as a form of entertainment (getting some people in an audience to do humorous things presumably without their awareness), as a method to encourage people to give up smoking or lose weight, as a procedure in several branches of medicine for pain reduction, and as a means of enhancing the memory of eyewitnesses and victims in the criminal justice system. A common belief among some practitioners is that hypnosis can exhume long-forgotten or buried memories, such as repressed memories of sexual abuse. This belief has frequently been bolstered by anecdotal or clinical claims describing cases in which previously inaccessible memories have been brought to light by the mysterious hypnotic trance. Enhancement or revival of memory through hypnosis is known as **hypnotic hypermnesia.** Enhancement or recovery of memory through *nonhypnotic* methods, such as free association, fantasy, recall technique, is called **nonhypnotic hypermnesia.**

Despite its long and varied history, precisely how hypnosis works remains a mystery. Nor do we understand why some persons are readily susceptible to its influence but others are impervious. We do know that hypnosis seems to have little significant biological changes on bodily functioning other than those that occur in normal relaxation. We know also that hypnosis is not the same as sleep or a form of sleepwalking. But we know little more than this.

Currently, two major theoretical perspectives have been proposed for explaining the mechanisms behind its effects. One perspective, known as the **hypnotic trance theory,** assumes that hypnosis represents a *special state of consciousness* that promotes a high level of suggestibility and changes in bodily experiences. Under this special state of consciousness, the theory maintains, the hypnotized person may be able to do things that he or she could not do under a normal state of consciousness. For example, the person might regress to childhood and vividly remember or act out events that have been repressed or put out of consciousness for an extended period of time. While in the trance, participants may be instructed to feel little or no pain or to perform acts that they are unable to do when not hypnotized. The hypnotic trance theory holds that individuals can be instructed or trained to sense, feel, smell, see, or hear things not normally possible under normal consciousness. For some individuals, hypnosis can substantially improve their ability for remembering things. Generally, trance theory contends that the deeper the "hypnotic trance," the more intense, detailed, and vivid a scene becomes to the participant. Historically, the most influential perspective on hypnotic trance theory was from Ernest Hilgard (1986), who died in October 2001. The research evidence supporting this position, however, is very slim and overall not very convincing.

The second major theory is referred to as the **cognitive-behavioral viewpoint,** which contends that respondents are not in a special state of consciousness when they *appear* hypnotized. Rather, hypnosis is a product of certain attitudes, motivations, and expectancies toward the "hypnotic state"—not a "true" alteration of consciousness. According to the cognitive-behavioral viewpoint, people who have a positive attitude toward hypnosis and are highly motivated to be hypnotized actually role-play the "trance" by closely following many of the suggestions provided by the hypnotist. For example, when the hypnotist suggests to them that they feel relaxed, they will try and probably will feel relaxed. Or when the hypnotist suggests their eyes will tear up from staring so long at the target, their eyes will begin to tear.

Theodore X. Barber, one of the chief spokespersons of the cognitive-behavioral perspective (Barber, Spanos, & Chaves, 1974), has hypothesized that the good hypnotic respondent is one who not only has the proper mixture of attitude, motivation, and expectancy but also has the ability to think and imagine with the hypnotist. According to Barber, the good hypnotic respondent is similar to a person watching a captivating video or movie. This person experiences—sometimes intensely—the emotions and actions portrayed by the actors on the screen. In this sense, the "hypnotized" person is mesmerized by the imagery created in his or her mind.

Martin Orne (1927–2000) (1970; Orne, Dinges, & Orne, 1984), once one of the world's foremost authorities on hypnosis, hypothesized a similar viewpoint to the cognitive-behavioral theory, arguing that role-playing accounts for much of the so-called hypnotic phenomenon. That is, participants act the way they *think* a truly hypnotized individual would act. Orne believed that "a prerequisite for hypnosis is the willingness to adopt the role of the 'hypnotic subject,' with its implicit social contract for uncritical acceptance of appropriate suggestions administered by the hypnotist" (Orne et al., 1988, p. 23). The "hypnotic subject" is willing to relinquish his or her sense of reality temporarily, hold any critical thinking in abeyance, and concentrate on what the hypnotist says. He called this state "trance logic" to describe the behavior of hypnotized participants who appeared to display a "peaceful coexistence between illusion and reality" (Kihlstrom, 2001, p. 754). Orne has found in his research that the material described under so-called hypnotic trances is often inaccurate and embellished with many intervening events that occur between the initial incident and the hypnotic session. It appears that some hypnotic participants are highly susceptible to distortions, suggestions, and leading questions posed by the hypnotist. Particularly if the interrogator is a police officer convinced of the powers of hypnosis, he or she is apt to inadvertently suggest events, details, or behaviors that were not present during the crime. The hypnotized witness or victim, eager to please the interrogator, can easily imagine a scene decorated with subjective fantasies and thoughts in line with the suggestions of the questioner. Under these suggestible conditions, the hypnotized participant may begin to be convinced of the accuracy and power of hypnosis to the same degree as the hypnotist. Furthermore, the participant also may become increasingly convinced of the accuracy of his or her revised account of the imagined scene, in contrast to the original (prehypnotic) account.

Orne became well known as a result of his skillful evaluation of Kenneth Bianchi, the accused "Hillside Strangler" who terrified women and young girls in the Greater Los Angeles area in the late 1970s (see Box 3.3). Bianchi maintained under hypnosis that his alter personality, "Steve Walker," had committed the murders. Bianchi argued that because he was suffering from a multiple personality disorder, he should not be held responsible for the serial murders. Ultimately, he was hoping for a successful insanity defense. Orne, however, was able to convince the court that Bianchi was merely playacting the different personalities while pretending to be hypnotized. Bianchi, because of Orne's testimony, dropped the multiple personality act and agreed to testify against his comurderer, Angelo Buono, and to accept a life sentence without the possibility of parole. Orne's critical perspective on forensic hypnosis influenced more than 30 state Supreme Court decisions as well as the U.S. Supreme Court (Kihlstrom, 2001). He also developed guidelines for forensic hypnosis that were adopted by the Federal Bureau of Investigation (Kihlstrom, 2001).

When forensic hypnosis is used as a method to recall events that may be either several hours or several years old, the fundamental assumption is that human memory functions like a videotape. All the events and details are stored completely and accurately and, with the proper procedure, can be recalled or brought to consciousness intact. This assumption, however, is without much research support (Bartol & Bartol, 2004). Human perception and memory are flawed and permeated with inaccuracies and distortions. The frailties of perception and memory, combined with the highly suggestive medium under which hypnosis is conducted, provide a situation in which critical inaccuracies have a high probability of occurring. Memory recall under hypnosis is highly malleable and manipulable, especially in highly suggestible respondents (Haber & Haber, 2000). Therefore, leading or suggestive questions may have a substantial effect on the respondents' recall of events after they are hypnotized (Kebbell & Wagstaff, 1998). The danger is particularly high when the forensic examiner is untrained or uninformed about the power of questioning suggestible respondents. In addition, the tendency to make up things to fill the gaps in memory appears to be greater under hypnosis (Orne et al., 1988).

It is important, therefore, that the forensic psychologist be aware of the research and the many dangers of poorly conducted interrogations or interviews when hypnosis is used. As noted by Scheflin, Spiegel, and Spiegel (1999), "When hypnosis is used for forensic purposes, strict guidelines must be scrupulously followed" (p. 491). Hypnosis can be a useful tool if used properly and with the understanding that it is no shortcut or replacement for standard investigative procedures (Scheflin et al., 1999). It can help, for instance, when trauma has occurred and it is

BOX 3.3   The Case of the Hillside Strangler

At least 12 women and girls, ranging in ages from 12 to 27, were victims of the Hillside Strangler, who terrorized the Los Angeles area between 1977 and 1978. The name "Hillside Strangler" was assigned to this serial killer because the nude bodies of many of the young women were conspicuously displayed on the hillsides in the Los Angeles area.

Kenneth Bianchi, who eventually pled guilty to the Hillside killings, had a very checkered career, holding at least 12 different jobs during a 9-month period following graduation from high school. During that time, he engaged in a wide variety of illegal activities, ranging from the use of stolen credit cards to the pimping of juvenile prostitutes. Although his life's ambition was to become a police officer, Bianchi also claimed to be a psychologist by falsifying his degrees and credentials. At age 26, he began to live with a woman in a common-law relationship who bore him a son. Soon after the birth of the son, Bianchi's common-law wife moved to Bellingham, Washington, where Bianchi soon joined her. However, soon after his arrival, the police in Bellingham had compelling evidence that Bianchi may have murdered two university students in that small city. Bianchi was arrested on January 11, 1979, and charged with their murders. Surprisingly, an investigation also revealed that the killings in Washington followed a pattern very similar to those of the Hillside Strangler in California.

Bianchi had seen a film shortly before his arrest called *Sybil,* in which Sally Field played a schizophrenic suffering from multiple personalities set in motion by childhood abuse. In the film, one of the personalities Sybil displayed was a spiteful, vicious, manipulating alter ego who chronically tormented the normally pleasant and sedate Sybil. Apparently, Bianchi got his inspiration from the film to play a person haunted by a lustful, murderous alter ego out of his control. In his mind, Bianchi thought his uncontrollable "other person" would provide the key ingredient for a successful insanity defense and absolve him of the crimes.

Under hypnosis during a forensic examination, Bianchi revealed his alter ego as Steve Walker, who admitted killing the two Bellingham women. But evildoer Steve Walker didn't stop there; he went on to confess to the Hillside Strangler murders while implicating Bianchi's cousin, Angelo Buono, as playing a major role in the killings. After two other forensic experts examined Bianchi and found his "performance" convincing, the police brought in one of the world's best-known experts on hypnosis, psychiatrist Martin T. Orne. During a forensic interview, Orne, doubtful about the veracity of exhuming multiple personalities through hypnosis, set a trap for the unsuspecting Bianchi. Orne told Bianchi in passing that multiple personality disorders almost always contain at least three different persons. Bianchi took the bait, and during the next hypnotic session, he introduced three more characters, including a prominent one called "Billy."

Orne's testimony, combined with the testimony of another expert, completely undermined the validity of Bianchi's multiple personality claim, and he was offered a plea bargain: to come clean and to testify against his cousin. In return, he would receive a life sentence without the possibility of parole. Bianchi, realizing his act was up, accepted the plea bargain to avoid the death penalty. Because of Bianchi's testimony, his cousin, Buono, was convicted of nine murders but was spared the death penalty by the jury. He died in prison on September 21, 2002, at age 67 after apparently suffering a heart attack in his cell. Bianchi, as part of the plea bargain, pled guilty to five murders and is currently serving a 118-year sentence at the Walla Walla State Penitentiary in the state of Washington.

difficult for the person to mentally or physically revisit the scene without the relaxation and concentration states that can be accomplished through hypnosis.

Facial Composites in Criminal Identification

Facial composites are reconstructions of faces by witnesses. They are constructed either with the help of an artist's sketching skills or by using the various commercial kits available to law enforcement, such as the American Identikit and the British Photofit. The Identikit includes photographic features printed on transparencies. Witnesses superimpose the transparencies through the guidance of trained personnel until they put together a composite of a face. The Photofit, on the other hand, consists of an assortment of photographed or drawn facial features that witnesses can move about like pieces of a jigsaw puzzle to reconstruct a face. The photographic features are printed on cards that can be inserted into a specially designed facial frame to produce a composite. (See Box 3.4 for a description of facial composite kits.)

In recent years, there has been an attempt to replace kits with computer-based systems in which features are stored on disks and the face is put together on a video display unit (Davies et al., 2000). Computer-based systems can substantially expand the number and variety of facial features and also have an extensive capacity for various slight manipulations of those features. One system, called the Mac-a-Mug Pro, has the capacity to generate nearly 100 times the number of faces that a standard noncomputerized kit can

---

BOX 3.4   Facial Composite Kits

Facial composites are invaluable tools in many criminal investigations. Nothing compares to an excellent composite artist who can draw the image by hand. When a composite artist is unavailable, however, mechanical and computer software kits may provide adequate substitutes. Mechanical examples include the American Identikit and the British Photofit. Computer examples include the CD-Fit, E-Fit (Electronic Facial Identification Technique), and the Mac-A-Mug Pro systems. The Identikit and Photofit include an assortment of photographed or already drawn facial features that witnesses can move about like pieces of a jigsaw puzzle to construct a face. The Identikit has photographic features printed on transparencies, whereas the Photofit has photographic features printed on cards. Computer-based systems consist of features stored on CDs, which allow a witness to put together a face on a video screen. The Mac-A-Mug Pro, currently the most popular computer kit, was developed from the line-drawn features of the original Identikit but uses an expanded library of features, particularly accessories, such as hats, glasses, and masks, and has the capacity to make nearly 100 times the number of faces offered by mechanical systems (Davies, van der Willik, & Morrison, 2000). A number of additional adjustments can be made to the composite—for example, it may be "aged" by the addition of appropriate facial lines. E-Fit is made for Windows and was developed in England for Scotland Yard. This forensic technology contains the world's largest database of human facial features, hairstyles, and accessories.

When skeletal remains are found and the victim cannot be identified, facial reconstructions can be made using a technique known as two-dimensional or three-dimensional forensic art. The procedure uses the skull to reproduce the facial characteristics so that the victim can be more easily identified.

produce (Davies et al., 2000). The ultimate test of usefulness, however, depends on which system (computer based, standard kits, or artist sketch) can consistently produce the most accurate facial composite for identification.

Many law enforcement experts believe that facial composites drawn by artists are superior to other composite reproductions. Unfortunately, very little research has been done that identifies a superior method for reconstructing faces from witness memory. Research has demonstrated, however, that accurate memory for faces is extremely difficult to achieve. The reconstruction of faces requires a number of complicated steps. A witness is expected to transform his or her perceptions of the face to memory and then, at a later time, transform the image into an accurate verbal description. At that point, the professional or trained compositor continues the process by trying to transform the descriptions (often very imprecise) into a comprehensive image (usually through trial and error), which eventually approximates the perceived face. Compounding the process even further is the potential contamination that may have occurred during police interviews about what the witness saw or heard. Police often make many errors when interviewing witnesses, including asking too many short-answer or leading questions and interrupting frequently (Koehn & Fisher, 1997).

Another important factor in the perception of faces is the processing of the human brain. Most people process faces in the right hemisphere of the brain, which "perceives" faces as a *whole*. It normally does not "see" faces as separate components, such as hair, nose, chin, eyes, ears, and mouth; rather, it relies on immediate recognition all at once. Thus, it is "unnatural" for a person to be required to describe a face in a piecemeal fashion so that a composite of the exact or highly similar face can be reproduced. Consequently, the likelihood of misrepresentation and inaccuracy throughout this difficult transformation process is very high. Until a system is developed that is grounded on more "natural" total facial recognition instead of relying on estimations of facial parts to construct a composite, the best

approach is to use artist sketching based on open-ended verbal descriptions of a witness.

Identifying the Offender: Other Procedures

Police officers routinely interview witnesses to a criminal incident. Typically, this task requires attempts at some form of identification of the offender and, as described above, especially the facial features. The identification of suspects by witnesses begins as soon after the offense as possible. Police usually obtain verbal descriptions of the perpetrators from witnesses or show photographs to obtain a preliminary identification. In some instances, the police will have witnesses scan photos of individuals with previous records, either to identify the specific offender or to obtain an approximation of the offender's appearance. Some police agencies routinely ask witnesses to examine a group of photographs (photoboards, photospreads, or mug shots) fairly well matched to the physical characteristics described by the witnesses, including the person the police suspect to be the guilty party. This section will examine the many pitfalls of other procedures designed to gather identification clues of the offender.

Identifying the Face

Courts, particularly criminal courts, rely heavily on eyewitness recognition as critical evidence either for or against the defendant. As we learned in the previous section, an accumulation of scientific studies, however, demonstrates that the accurate recognition of a relatively unfamiliar face is an extremely complex and error-ridden task (Bartol & Bartol, 2004). Research also reveals that the accuracy of facial recognition depends greatly on the type of face being recalled. For reasons unknown, some faces are easier to identify than others. Highly unique faces, for example, are better recognized than plain or average faces (Cohen & Carr, 1975; Going & Read, 1974), and distinct faces are easier to recognize than are typical faces (Chiroro & Valentine, 1995; MacLin & Malpass, 2001). Faces high and low in attractiveness also are easier to recognize than faces judged to be of medium attractiveness (Shepherd & Ellis, 1973). Not surprisingly, the longer a person views a face, the better the recognition of the face at a later time (MacLin, MacLin, & Malpass, 2001).

Unconscious Transference

On occasion, witnesses sometimes identify persons they have seen at some other time and place as the perpetrators of a more recent crime. This phenomenon, called **unconscious transference,** occurs when a person seen in one situation is confused with or recalled as a person seen in another situation. It is called "unconscious" because people do not realize they are doing it. A witness may have had limited exposure to a face (e.g., in a grocery store) and, on seeing the face at a later time, concludes that it is the offender's. Loftus (1979) believes that unconscious transference is another feature of the fallible and malleable nature of human memory, where earlier input becomes "tangled up" with later input. As we noted above, research has continually shown that human memory is not like a videotape or DVD that stores things exactly as seen. Rather, memory is continually changing or being revised in line with our cognitive beliefs and versions of the world.

The phenomenon of unconscious transference illustrates that it is highly possible that a fast-food worker, who is witness to a robbery of the restaurant, might incorrectly identify as the perpetrator an occasional customer who may have some of the features of the actual culprit. However, for unconscious transference to occur, the previous encounters with the innocent face must have been relatively brief. *Frequent* encounters with customers by the witness are unlikely to trigger unconscious transference involving those particular customers.

Own-Race Bias (ORB)

There is now considerable evidence that people are much better at discriminating between faces of their own race or ethnic group than faces of other races or ethnic groups (Bartol & Bartol, 2004). Researchers call this phenomenon **own-race bias** (ORB), or it is sometimes referred to as "own-race effect" or "cross-race effect." Scientific research across a wide band of cultures and countries has documented ORB, and it exists across diverse ethnic groups (Meissner & Brigham, 2001; Sporer, 2001). Unfortunately, the majority of errors due to ORB are false alarms. False alarms refer to those situations when a witness identifies the wrong person as the offender. Although the frequency of false alarms seems to be increasing in our society, racial attitudes or prejudice do not seem to account for this phenomenon in a majority of cases (Meissner & Brigham, 2001).

Although there are several possible explanations for ORB, the most popular is called the **differential experience hypothesis.** The hypothesis states that individuals will have greater familiarity or experience with members of their own race and will thus be better able to discern differences among its members. Furthermore, it is the frequency of meaningful and positive contacts with other races that develops the skill to differentiate between racial or ethnic faces (MacLin & Malpass, 2001; Yarmey, 1979). For example, having close friends of other races is more likely to promote better facial recognition than having frequent but casual exposure. This other-race effect is obviously a critical aspect in the identification of suspects by eyewitnesses.

Pretrial Identification Methods

Lineups and Photospreads

Pretrial identification methods are especially vulnerable to biases and error, running from very blatant practices to more subtle innuendo, an aspect that police psychologists should be very aware of. For example, a police investigator suggesting to an undecided witness that she should look more closely at "the second one from the right" represents subtle innuendo.

Because the witness will look for a suspect in the lineup who fits the description he or she gave the police, the physical characteristics of the members in the lineup are a crucial factor. In other words, they should have similar characteristics—such as age, physical stature, race, hairstyle, and facial hair—that were included in the original witness description. It is also well known that, before appearing in lineups, many suspects will try to change their appearance to mislead eyewitnesses, a tactic that is often successful (Cutler, Penrod, & Martens, 1987). If the witness remembered the offender as a 6'6" individual with black, curly hair and a beard, the lineup is obviously biased if only one person in six fits that description. No matter how many foils are standing in the line, the test is effectively limited to the number of participants who resemble the suspect, a condition called **functional size** of the lineup.

Nominal size of the lineup, on the other hand, refers to the actual number of members within the lineup who may or may not resemble the suspect. Therefore, in a lineup of six persons, the functional size will decrease as the physically dissimilar members of a lineup increase. For a lineup to be considered fair, its functional size should approximate the nominal size. If, by employing various measures and statistical tests, it is determined that all the members of a six-member lineup have an equal probability of being selected on the basis of crucial characteristics, the functional size is six. If only three resemble the suspect, the functional size is three and the nominal size is six.

Another area of pretrial identification that must be closely monitored is **commitment bias.** When a witness has initially identified a face, even an incorrect one, he or she will be more likely to choose the face again. Commitment bias is most likely to occur when witnesses are eager to please police investigators and who further assume that the police have good evidence against someone in the pretrial identification process. Because of commitment bias, a witness who initially identifies a suspect, but with some doubt, is more likely to identify the suspect in subsequent exposures with greater conviction. Each subsequent identification promotes greater confidence in the witness because he or she will continue to make public commitment to the police that the suspect is clearly the one.

A controversial identification procedure is called the **show-up.** "A show-up is an identification procedure in which police present a single suspect to the eyewitness(es) to see if the eyewitness(es) will identify that person as the perpetrator" (Wells, 2001, p. 795). Unlike the lineup, there are no distractors or foils in a show-up procedure. A show-up is legal in the United States as long as it occurs soon after the offense (within hours) or under circumstances that would make a lineup impracticable or impossible. Research shows that show-ups are far more likely to lead to mistaken identification than lineups (Wells, 2001). This is because in a lineup, the error of mistakenly identifying a suspect is spread out among the foils and distractors. In the show-up situation, on the other hand, there is only one choice, right or wrong.

Recently, the American Psychology-Law Society (AP-LS), in an effort to make certain that forensic psychologists and other personnel in the criminal justice system were aware of ways to improve lineup procedures, published a comprehensive document known as the *Police Lineups* white paper (Wells, 2001). The document made four recommendations for implementing valid procedures in conducting lineups or photospreads (see Wells et al., 1998). First, the panel recommended that the person *putting together* the lineup or photospread know which member of the lineup or photospread is the suspect; however, the person *administering or conducting* the lineup should *not* know. In addition, the eyewitness should be informed that the person administering the lineup does not know which person is the suspect in the case. This recommendation is designed to prevent the witness from looking for subtle clues or identifying information from the officer administering the lineup. Second, eyewitnesses should be clearly told that the suspect might *not* be in the lineup or photospread. Under these conditions, the witness will not feel compelled to make an identification if he or she does not believe the suspect is in the lineup. Third, the suspect should not stand out in the lineup or photospread as being clearly different from the distractors, based on the eyewitness's (or eyewitnesses') previous description. Fourth, a clear statement should be taken from the eyewitness at the time of identification, prior to any feedback from the police that would inform the witness whether he or she had chosen the "right" suspect. This last recommendation is based on the observation that witnesses are often susceptible to inadvertent or intentional communication about the suspect during or immediately after the lineup occurs. Findings from the white paper were incorporated into a 44-page government guide for law enforcement officers working with eyewitness identification (Reno, 1999). The guide provides very useful, detailed recommendations for specific procedures to be followed by all those involved in eyewitness identifications, and the well-informed police psychologist would be wise to be highly familiar with it.

Summary and Conclusions

Investigative psychology is perhaps the newest area of specialization for forensic psychologists, having begun in 1985 with the work of David Canter in England. It focuses on identifying features of a crime and likely characteristics of its perpetrator. Investigative psychology also includes broader areas, such as psychological autopsies, the polygraph, forensic hypnosis, and facial composites, all covered in this chapter.

Essentially, we have included a variety of areas in which psychologists provide consulting services to law enforcement agencies in their investigations of crimes.

Profiling, though a relatively infrequent enterprise when conducted by forensic psychologists, has gained considerable media attention. We discussed profiling in three different contexts: criminal profiling, psychological autopsies, and geographical profiling. If done correctly, criminal profiling can provide statistical probabilities of features of an offender, but it is far from a foolproof procedure. Dynamic factors, both stable and acute, can wreak havoc with efforts to construct the "profile" of an offender. Perpetrators may change their procedures and techniques as they become more skilled and more daring. Psychological autopsies—more formally called reconstructive psychological evaluation—are performed after a person has died and the cause of the death is uncertain or equivocal. The psychologist conducting the autopsy tries to reconstruct the victim's behavior and thought processes leading up to the death. This procedure is often used in cases of apparent but questionable suicide. Psychological autopsies are also used—though less frequently—in civil cases in an effort to determine whether a third party may have contributed to the death. For example, an employer may have failed to respond appropriately to signals of extreme emotional distress and/or threats of suicide. As yet, there is no established, standard method for conducting a psychological autopsy, and its validity has yet to be demonstrated.

Geographical profiling analyzes spatial characteristics of a crime to yield probabilities of a perpetrator residing in a particular location. We described four "hunting patterns" that are examined. Geographical profiling is used primarily to solve serial crimes, in which a pattern of offending occurs over time. It is more likely to yield positive results when combined with criminal profiling, although we must caution that the scientific status of the latter remains in question.

We discussed some of the reasons profiling is difficult. Chief among these is the fact that much of human behavior is not consistent across different situations. Dynamic factors of an individual, particularly those that are acute—such as mood swings and drug-induced effects—contribute to this lack of consistency. In addition, crime scene evidence does not necessarily relate to specific psychological characteristics of the perpetrator. Although some professional profilers are cautious about the power of their predictions, others are too ready to rely on unsubstantiated assumptions, some of which are based on outdated interpretations of personality theory. In sum, profiling—though fascinating to the public—is an enterprise that must be approached with extreme caution, at least until research demonstrates that it has predictive validity.

The polygraph is not strictly an investigative technique in the narrow sense because it is used in a wide variety of criminal and civil contexts. In law enforcement, it is used primarily in the selection of candidates for law enforcement positions and much less in criminal investigation. Results from polygraph tests are not admitted into courts against criminal defendants, but they have been allowed in some courts to support a defendant's contention that he or she did *not* commit the crime. It appears that the polygraph is also being used more extensively in counterintelligence and by federal agencies than it has been in the past. Like the other techniques discussed in this chapter, the polygraph has not garnered impressive research results with respect to reliability and validity. Nevertheless, some researchers do support its use in limited situations and when administered by highly trained polygraphers.

We ended the chapter with a discussion of forensic hypnosis, the use of facial composites during criminal investigations, and the construction of police lineups. Hypnosis is a controversial topic, particularly when used to elicit repressed memories of traumatic events in victims of crime. It may also be used to enhance recall of nonvictim eyewitnesses to a crime. Although the weight of the scientific evidence is still very much against its use, research over the past decade has begun to challenge early assumptions. By contrast, the research on facial composites—specifically those generated by computer or by commercial composite kits—is quite unequivocal and pessimistic. In recent years, psychologists have made significant research contributions relating to the construction and administration of police lineups. Some of their recommendations have been incorporated into government guidelines used by law enforcement officers nationwide.

PART III

Criminal Psychology

CHAPTER 4

The Development of Habitual Criminal Behavior

Crime can be defined as "an intentional act in violation of the criminal law committed without defense or excuse, and penalized by the state as a felony or misdemeanor" (Tappan, 1947, p. 100). Criminal behavior, therefore, is intentional behavior that violates a criminal code. It is intentional in that it did not occur accidentally or without justification or excuse. To be held criminally responsible, a person must have known what he or she was doing during the criminal act and must have known that it was wrong. To convict someone of a criminal offense, the prosecution (the government) generally must prove that the defendant committed a *voluntary act* (*actus reus*) intentionally, or with a *guilty* state of mind (*mens rea*). The statute defining the offense will specify what actions and what mental states (together called "elements") constitute a particular crime (La Fond, 2002). If a case goes to trial, the judge or jury can convict the defendant only if the prosecutor proves all elements beyond a reasonable doubt (the burdens of proof are illustrated in Box 10.1 in Chapter 10). However, if a defendant pleads guilty, the prosecutor is spared the burden of doing so, and a conviction is still entered on the record.

The spectrum of criminal behavior is extremely wide, ranging from minor traffic violations to murder. In 2002, the public became much more aware of corporate crimes, a category of offenses that has long captured the interests of criminologists who believe that extensive harm is perpetrated by persons in power. Although many people from all socioeconomic groups break laws, only a few become persistent offenders who commit numerous serious crimes, including crimes of a violent nature. Consequently, we restrict our discussion to offenders who demonstrate a habitual, persistent offending history of committing serious crimes. We will especially concentrate on those offenders who often follow a *lifelong* criminal career of engaging in a wide variety of criminal offenses. Good examples of repetitive, chronic offenders will be found in the life course–persistent offender discussed in the following section on juvenile delinquency, as well as the section on the psychopath reviewed later in the chapter.

In the next two chapters, we will narrow our focus to crimes involving sexual assault, intimidation, and violence, such as murder, stalking, hate crime, and arson—crimes that lend themselves particularly well to psychological research and theory. The purpose of the present chapter is to provide an overview of criminal behavior, with a focus on the developmental factors that are involved in the formation of serious or repetitive criminal behavior. Empirical research indicates that persistent antisocial behavior does not normally begin in adulthood but begins quite early in life, with signs sometimes appearing even during the preschool years (Moffitt, 1993a, 1993b). Consequently, the best place to start is by examining the developmental trajectory of the emerging juvenile offender. Before we do, though, it is important to avoid the temptation to seize on one cause or single explanation of crime. The causes of crime and delinquency are multiple, complex, and probably result mostly from some complicated interaction of several influences. Although "the crime problem" as a whole can be attributed to any number of broad societal factors—racism, poverty, glorification of violence, sexism, and the availability of handguns are examples—the cause of a given individual's criminal behavior is unlikely to be unidimensional.

The Juvenile Offender

Definition of Juvenile Delinquency

Juvenile delinquency is an imprecise, social, clinical, and legal label for a wide variety of law- and norm-violating behavior. At first glance, a simple legal definition appears to be adequate: *Delinquency is behavior against the criminal code committed by an individual who has not reached adulthood.* But the term *delinquency* has numerous definitions and meanings beyond this one-sentence definition. In some states, the legal definition also includes status offending, which is not behavior against the "adult" criminal code but is behavior prohibited *only* for juveniles. For

example, running away, violating curfew laws, and truancy all qualify as status offenses.

In addition, social, legal, and psychological definitions of delinquency overlap considerably. Social definitions of delinquency encompass a broad gamut of youthful behaviors considered inappropriate, such as aggressive behavior, truancy, petty theft, vandalism, drug abuse, sexual promiscuity, and even incorrigibility. The behavior may or may not have come to the attention of the police and, in fact, often does not. If the behavior is known to the police, it is not unusual for "social delinquents" to be referred to community social service agencies or to juvenile courts, but these youth do not qualify for the legal definition of delinquent unless they are found at a court hearing to have committed the crime for which they are charged. Therefore, *legally speaking,* a **juvenile delinquent** is one who commits an act against the criminal code and *who is adjudicated delinquent by an appropriate court.* The legal definition is usually restricted to persons younger than age 18, but states vary in their age distinctions. A handful of states give criminal courts, rather than juvenile courts, automatic jurisdiction over juveniles at age 16. Furthermore, all states allow juveniles to be tried as adults in criminal courts under certain conditions and for certain offenses.

Psychological or *psychiatric* definitions of *delinquency* include the symptom-based labels of "conduct disorder" or "antisocial behavior." **Conduct disorder** (often abbreviated CD) is a diagnostic designation used to represent a group of behaviors characterized by *habitual* misbehavior, such as stealing, setting fires, running away from home, skipping school, destroying property, fighting, being cruel to animals and people, and frequently telling lies. Under this definition, the "delinquent" may or may not have been arrested for these behaviors. Some of the behaviors, in fact, are not even against the criminal law. CD is described more fully in the fourth edition of the American Psychiatric Association's (1994) *Diagnostic and Statistical Manual of Mental Disorders,* commonly referred to as the *DSM-IV,* and the more recent, slightly modified version of the manual, referred to as the *DSM-IV-TR* (American Psychiatric Association, 2000). The *TR* stands for "text revision." The *DSM-IV* divides conduct disorders into two categories, depending on the onset of the misbehaviors. If the misconduct began in childhood (before age 10), it is called *conduct disorder: childhood-onset type.* If the misconduct began in adolescence, it is called *conduct disorder: adolescent-onset type.*

The more psychological term *antisocial behavior* is usually reserved for more serious habitual misbehavior, which involves actions that are directly harmful to the well-being of others. It is to be distinguished, however, from **antisocial personality disorder,** a psychiatric diagnostic label reserved primarily for *adults* at least 18 years of age who displayed conduct disorders as children or adolescents and who continue serious offending well into adulthood. Our main focus throughout this chapter will be on the chronic, repetitive offender who moves from adolescence to adulthood in a continuing cycle of offending and reoffending.

Although many psychologists do subscribe to the designations of conduct disorder and anti-social behavior, a growing number of psychologists also approach the issue of crime and delinquency with an emphasis on developmental and cognitive processes in an effort to describe and understand offending behavior. For example, Moffitt's (1993a) developmental theory provides a cogent sketch of explaining crime from a developmental prospective, and Hare's (1996) concept of criminal psychopathy offers an intriguing delineation of the emotional, cognitive, and biopsychological factors involved in repetitive, serious offending over a lifetime. We will review each of these perspectives shortly. First, it is important that we gain some perspective on the nature and extent of juvenile offending in the United States.

The Nature and Extent of Juvenile Offending

The amount of delinquent behavior—both what is reported and unreported to law enforcement agencies—is essentially an unknown area (Krisberg, 1995). We simply do not have complete data on the national incidence of juvenile delinquency, broadly defined. Although incomplete, we do have some statistics collected by law enforcement agencies, the courts, and juvenile correctional facilities.

Unlawful acts committed by juveniles can be divided into five major categories:

1. Unlawful acts against persons

2. Unlawful acts against property

3. Drug offenses

4. Offenses against the public order

5. Status offenses

Most referrals to juvenile court are for crimes against property (45%), followed by offenses against the public order (21%), crimes against persons (23%), and drug offenses (11%) (Sickmund, 2003). The first four categories are comparable in definition to crimes committed by adults. **Status offenses,** on the other hand, are acts that only juveniles can commit and that can be adjudicated only by a juvenile court. As discussed earlier, typical status offenses range from misbehavior, such as violations of curfew, underage drinking, running away from home, and truancy, to offenses that are interpreted very subjectively, such as unruliness and ungovernability (beyond the control of parents or guardians). The most common status offenses referred by law enforcement agencies are underage drinking (92%), running away from home (40%), ungovernability (11%), and truancy (10%) (Sickmund, 2003).

The juvenile justice system historically has supported differential treatment of male and female status offenders. Adolescent girls, for example, have often been detained for incorrigibility or running away from home, when the same behavior in adolescent boys was ignored or tolerated. As we approached the end of the 20th century, about three times as many girls were detained for status offenses as boys (U.S. Department of Justice, 1988). In recent years, as a result of suits brought on behalf of juveniles, many courts have put authorities on notice that this discriminatory approach is unwarranted. For example, the status offense of runaway has now dropped to a 3 to 2 ratio, with three females taken into custody for every two males (Federal Bureau of Investigation [FBI], 2002b; Sickmund, 2003). The largest proportion of status offenses that involve females are runaways (61%), truancy (46%), ungovernability (45%), and underage drinking (29%) (Sickmund, 2003). The practice of confining status offenders in correctional institutions is also diminishing.

It has been argued that, because status offenses lend themselves to so much subjectivity, they should be removed from the purview of all state juvenile courts (American Bar Association, 1979). Some states have clearly moved in this direction. On the other hand, many states do not call status offenders "delinquents" but do allow their detention and/or supervision. They are presumed to be in need of protection either from their own rash behavior or the behavior of others. The statutes allowing this are usually referred to as PINS or CHINS laws (person or child in need of supervision). Under these laws, runaways or incorrigible youngsters are subject to juvenile court jurisdiction, often at the instigation of their parents, even though they may not have committed an act comparable to a crime. These statutes also allow juvenile or family courts to address the needs of neglected and dependent children.

Youth crime data are collected from a mixture of sources: (1) official records of police arrests, such as the FBI's Uniform Crime Reports (UCR); (2) reports from victims, such as the National Crime Victimization Survey (NCVS); (3) self-reports of delinquent involvement, in which national samples of youth are asked to complete questionnaires about their own behavior, such as in the National Youth Survey (Elliott, Ageton, & Huizinga, 1980) and Monitoring the Future (MTF); (4) juvenile court processing, as reported by the National Center for Juvenile Justice (NCJJ); (5) juvenile corrections, as reported in

the monograph *Children in Custody* (*CIC*); and (6) probation and parole statistics, as reported in various governmental publications. The last three sources of information have the major disadvantage of greatly underestimating the number of actual offenses because, even more than in the criminal system, a very high proportion—perhaps a majority—of cases are either undetected or dismissed before reaching the courts. In other words, because of parental involvement, negotiations, and community programs, many offenders are diverted before they go to juvenile court. To add to the problem of obtaining statistics on juvenile offenders, juvenile court dockets do not always reflect serious offending. Referrals by parents, schools, probation officers, and other courts, either for status offenses or for supervision, make up much of a court's delinquency workload. Because of this confusion, perhaps the most complete official nationwide compilation of juvenile offenses today remains the FBI's UCR. Consequently, we will focus on the juvenile offending data as presented in this document.

The Uniform Crime Reports

The FBI's UCR, first compiled in 1930, is the most frequently cited source of U.S. crime statistics. The UCR is an annual document containing accounts of crime *known to law enforcement* agencies across the country, as well as *arrests*. It is important to note that the UCR does not include conviction data. It is strictly law enforcement information. The UCR is available on the FBI Web site at www.fbi.gov.

The document represents the cooperative statistical effort of nearly 17,000 city, county, and state law enforcement agencies voluntarily reporting data on crimes brought to their attention. During 2001, law enforcement agencies that did report represented 92% of the total U.S. population, as established by the Bureau of Census. Even census data are not perfect, however, because numerous individuals, such as the

Table 4.1   Juvenile Arrests for Index Crimes, 2001

Offense Charged	Total Arrests, All Ages	Under Age 18	Under Age 10
Total index crimes	1,554,737	407,106	7,007
Violent crimes	**434,391**	**67,002**	**1,013**
Murder	9,426	957	6
Forcible rape	18,576	3,119	34
Robbery	76,667	18,111	95
Aggravated assault	329,722	44,815	878
Property crimes	**1,120,346**	**340,104**	**5,994**
Burglary	198,883	61,623	1,390
Larceny-theft	806,093	238,605	3,859
Motor vehicle theft	102,607	33,563	68
Arson	12,763	6,313	677

Source: Federal Bureau of Investigation (2002b, p. 244).

homeless, transients, and persons traveling or studying abroad, are not reached by census workers. It should also be noted that federal law enforcement agencies do not report through the traditional UCR program; instead, they are expected to report to a new redesigned UCR program called the **National Incident-Based Reporting System (NIBRS),** to be discussed shortly.

The UCR divides crimes in several ways, including by age, gender, and race of persons arrested, as well as by city and region of the country. Crimes are also categorized according to seriousness. The seriousness category is based on the **hierarchy rule,** which stipulates that in incidents in which a number of offenses have been committed, only the most serious offense should be reported. For example, if an offender robs a bank, assaults a bank teller, steals a car, and murders the bank security officer, only the murder will be reported in the traditional UCR data. The hierarchy rule, therefore, promotes an underestimation of crime because only one crime is identified from a multiple number of offenses committed at one point in time.

According to the UCR format, serious crimes that are indicators of the crime problem are called **index crimes** (or Part I offenses). However, this distinction may be misleading. For instance, larceny-theft is categorized as an index crime, whereas fraud, embezzlement, child sexual abuse, stalking, and drug offenses—all crimes about which the public is concerned—are classified as nonindex crimes. The UCR recognizes eight index crimes: (1) murder and nonnegligent manslaughter, (2) forcible rape, (3) robbery, (4) aggravated assault, (5) burglary, (6) larceny-theft, (7) motor vehicle theft, and (8) arson. Table 4.1 illustrates the distribution of juvenile arrests for these offenses for 2001.

The UCR is no longer the sole method of recording police data on reported crimes and arrests. Since 1989, the FBI has collected data through the NIBRS. The NIBRS collects data on crime incidents (there is no hierarchy rule) and arrests within 22 categories. For each offense known to law enforcement within these categories, incident, victim, property, offender, and arrestee information are gathered when available. The goal of the NIBRS is to modernize crime information and address many of the shortcomings that had been identified in the UCR. To date, 22 state programs have been certified for NIBRS participation (FBI, 2002b). Currently, a

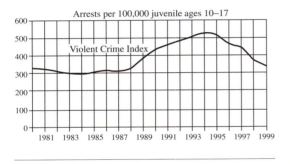

Figure 4.1 Arrests for Juvenile Crimes

Source: Office of Juvenile Justice and Delinquency Prevention (2001).

total of 4,192 law enforcement agencies contribute to the NIBRS data bank, representing 17% of the total U.S. population.

A term commonly used by the Department of Justice and reported in the UCR is **clearance rate,** which refers to the proportion of reported crimes that have been solved. The FBI (2000) considers a crime cleared "when at least one person is arrested, charged with the commission of an offense, and turned over to the court for prosecution" (p. 201). For juveniles (persons younger than age 18), "a clearance by arrest is recorded when an offender under age 18 is cited to appear in juvenile court or before other juvenile authorities" (FBI, 2000, p. 201). Crimes may also be cleared by exceptional means when circumstances outside the control of law enforcement (such as death of the alleged offender) eliminate the possibility of making an arrest.

Arrests for juvenile crime, particularly violent crime, peaked in 1994 and have been decreasing steadily since then (see Figure 4.1). After more than a decade of increases, homicides by juveniles dropped in 2001 by 62%. (For adults, homicides decreased by 29%.) Overall, the juvenile arrest rate for violent crime has dropped 21% during the past decade (1992 to 2001). (For adults, violent crime declined nearly 9%.) Similarly, the juvenile arrest rate for property crimes has dropped by 32% during that same time frame. (For adults, the property crime rate fell by 23%.) These arrest *rates* are for every

100,000 inhabitants within that age bracket. Consequently, these figures take into consideration changes in populations during that time.

Nationally, juveniles made up about 17% of the persons arrested in the United States during 2001. They were arrested for 15% of the violent crime and 31% of the property crime. It should be mentioned that many criminologists prefer these clearance rates to raw arrest data in measuring juveniles' contributions to the crime problem. This is because juveniles often commit crime in groups, and therefore arrest data inflate their involvement. It should also be emphasized that crime and arrest rates move in cycles, often due to the social, economic, and political climates that occur within a society at any given time. Therefore, although rates have decreased in recent years, they may—for a variety of reasons—also suddenly increase in future years.

One point needs to be clear at the outset: A small percentage of offenders are responsible for a large proportion of the total crimes committed (Chaiken, 2000; Coid, 2003). In any given population, the most persistent 5% or 6% of offenders are responsible for at least 50% to 60% of known crimes (Farrington, Ohlin, & Wilson, 1986; Lynam, 1997). It is also important to note that only 3% to 15% of reported serious offenses ever result in a police contact (Bartol, 2002). Self-report surveys suggest that serious, repetitive juvenile offenders escape detection about 86% of the time (Elliott, Dunford, & Huizinga, 1987). These figures clearly indicate that measures of juvenile offending substantially underestimate the overall juvenile crime rate. In addition, frequent offenders usually do not specialize in any one particular kind of offending, such as theft, larceny, or drug trafficking. Instead, they tend to be involved in a wide variety of offenses, ranging from minor property crimes to highly violent ones.

We do not intend to dwell on offending statistics, except to provide some perspective on official offending rates and to emphasize that juvenile and adult offending have significantly decreased in recent years. At this point, however, it is time to turn our attention to identifying some of the known major individual causes of crime, beginning with developmental factors.

Developmental Factors in Juvenile Delinquency

Over the past three decades, the psychological study of crime has shifted away from accepting personality traits as major determinants of criminal and delinquent behavior toward a more interactive cognitive and developmental focus. Eron et al. (2002) note that the contemporary study of crime and delinquency has shifted into two main areas. First, there has been a growing interest in the social and cognitive aspects of violence, including social information-processing skills, specific beliefs, and cognitive scripts. Second, there has been an increasing attempt to understand the influence of multiple contexts (e.g., school, peers, and families) in the learning and continuation of criminal behavior. This includes trying to understand the importance of social relationships and other developmental influences.

There is solid research evidence that serious, persistent delinquency patterns begin in early childhood. It is also clear that learning experiences begin early and build on themselves. Researchers have discovered discernible differences in impulsiveness, social skills, and feelings for others between young children who ultimately became serious delinquents and those who did not. Even around age 5, aggressive, belligerent children are unpopular and are excluded from peer groups (Dodge & Pettit, 2003; Patterson, 1982). In fact, Coie, Underwood, and Lochman (1991) contend that aggressiveness is the single most important reason for a child to be rejected by peers.

As a group, highly aggressive, disruptive children demonstrate social and interpersonal skills that fall below average for their age. Those children who continue offending into adolescence and young adulthood are troublesome in school, beginning as early as the first grade (Dodge & Pettit, 2003; Farrington, 1987), and perform below average in most school achievement tasks (Kelly, 1980; Schafer & Polk, 1967). Low achievement, a limited vocabulary, and poor verbal reasoning demonstrated in early childhood have been found to correlate significantly with later pervasive delinquency (Farrington, 1979).

Many other developmental factors have been identified as contributing to a child's developmental trajectory toward a life of committing serious crime and violence. The experience of physical abuse in early life significantly increases the risk of future antisocial conduct (Dodge & Pettit, 2003; Mayfield & Widom, 1996). On the other hand, warmth and appropriate behavioral management by parents have been found to have very positive outcomes on the developmental trajectories of their children (Dishion & Bullock, 2002; Dodge & Pettit, 2003). The amount of exposure that a child has to aggressive peers in day care or preschool also appears to have significant effects on a child's later aggressive behavior (Sinclair, Pettit, Harrist, & Bates, 1994). In addition, children who spend large amount of time in unsupervised after-school self-care in the early elementary grades are also at high risk of participating in antisocial behavior (Bates et al., 1994).

Peer acceptance is also crucial during early development. Children who are liked and accepted by their peer group in the early school years are far less likely to become antisocial in their later years (Laird, Jordan, Dodge, Pettit, & Bates, 2001; Rubin, Bukowski, & Parker, 1998). "Those children who were rejected for at least 2 or 3 years by second grade had a 50% chance of displaying clinically significant conduct problems later in adolescence, in contrast with just a 9% chance for those children who managed to avoid early peer rejection" (Dodge & Pettit, 2003, p. 353).

Stealing is another early predictor of delinquency. In fact, in a literature review by Loeber and Dishion (1983), *habitual* stealing—as reported by parents and teachers—emerged as one of the strongest predictors of later delinquency. Many children "experiment" with some minor theft, but the key word is *habitual.* Furthermore, youngsters who engaged in habitual stealing, even at the elementary school level, also tended to be simultaneously demonstrating other problem behaviors such as lying, bullying, truancy, and running away. Frequent dishonesty appears to be another behavioral pattern that predicts quite early a tendency toward repetitive offending (Farrington, 1979; Loeber & Dishion, 1983).

Developmental Theory

Research conducted by Terrie Moffitt (1993a, 1993b) and her colleagues indicates that a very helpful way to understand delinquency is to view it as developing along at least two developmental paths. Because the Moffitt theory is one of the dominant theories in the psychology of delinquency today, it is important that we cover the perspective in some detail. We must emphasize at the outset that, although most of Moffitt's research identifies the *two* paths that will be covered below, more recent research by Moffitt and others suggests strongly that a two-path theory is not sufficient.

On one path we see a child developing a lifelong trajectory of delinquency and crime at a very early age, probably around 3 or even younger. Moffitt (1993a) reports that

> across the life course, these individuals exhibit changing manifestations of antisocial behavior: biting and hitting at age four, shoplifting and truancy at age ten, selling drugs and stealing cars at age sixteen, robbery and rape at age twenty-two, and fraud and child abuse at age thirty. (p. 679)

These individuals, whom Moffitt calls **life course–persistent** (**LCP**) offenders, continue their antisocial ways across all kinds of conditions and situations.

Moffitt finds that many of these LCP offenders exhibit neurological problems during their childhoods, such as difficult temperaments as infants, *attention deficit disorders* or *hyperactivity* as children, and learning problems during their later school years (Moffitt, 1993a, 1993b). Some of these neurological problems are present before and/or soon after birth. Judgment and problem-solving deficiencies are often apparent when the children reach adulthood.

LCP offenders generally commit a wide assortment of aggressive and violent crimes over their lifetimes. Moreover, LCPs as children miss opportunities to acquire and practice prosocial and interpersonal skills at each stage of development. This is partly because they are rejected and avoided by their childhood peers and partly because their parents and other caretakers become frustrated and give up on them (Coie, Belding, & Underwood, 1988; Coie, Dodge, & Kupersmith, 1990; Moffitt, 1993a). Furthermore, disadvantaged living conditions, inadequate schools, and violent neighborhoods are factors that are very likely to exacerbate the ongoing and developing antisocial behavioral pattern. Based on available data, the number of LCPs in the male juvenile offender population is estimated to be somewhere between 5% and 10% (Moffitt, Caspi, Dickson, Silva, & Stanton, 1996). "Less than 10% of males should show extreme antisocial behavior that begins during early childhood and is thereafter sustained at a high level across time and across circumstances, throughout childhood and adolescence" (Moffitt, 1993a, p. 694). Less than 2% of females can be classified as early starters in a persistent career of crime (Coid, 2003).

The great majority of "delinquents" are those individuals who *begin* offending during their adolescent years and stop offending somewhere around their 18th birthday. In essence, these adolescent delinquent behaviors arise from peer and social environmental factors, and the offending tends to be temporary. Moffitt labels these individuals **adolescent limited** (**AL**). Moffitt (1993a) estimates that a majority of adolescents are involved in some form of antisocial behavior during their teens, but then the antisocial behavior stops as they approach the responsibilities of young adulthood.

The developmental histories of the ALs do not demonstrate the early and persistent antisocial problems that members of the LCP group manifest. However, the frequency—and, in some cases, the violence level—of the offending *during the teen years* may be as high as that of the LCP youth. In effect, the teenage offending patterns of ALs and LCPs may be highly similar during the teenage years (Moffitt et al., 1996).

> The two types cannot be discriminated on most indicators of antisocial and problem behavior in adolescence; boys on the LCP and AL paths are similar on parent-, self-, and official records of offending, peer delinquency, substance abuse, unsafe sex, and dangerous driving. (Moffitt et al., 1996, p. 400)

That is, a professional could not easily identify the group classification (AL or LCP) simply by examining juvenile arrest records, self-reports, or the information provided by parents *during the teen years.*

The AL delinquent is most likely to be involved in offenses that symbolize adult privilege and demonstrate autonomy from parental control (Bartol, 2002). Examples include vandalism (usually school property), drug and alcohol offenses, theft, and status offenses such as running away or truancy. In addition, AL delinquents may engage in crimes that are profitable or rewarding, but they also have the ability to abandon these actions when more socially approved behavioral patterns become more rewarding and acceptable to significant others. For example, the onset of young adulthood brings on new opportunities, such as leaving high school for college, obtaining a full-time job, and entering a relationship with a prosocial person. AL delinquents are quick to learn that they have something to lose if they continue offending into adulthood. During childhood, in contrast to LCP children, AL youngsters have

learned to get along with others. Research has consistently shown that social rejection by peers in the elementary school grades is a potent risk factor for the development of antisocial behavior problems in adolescence and adulthood (Dodge & Pettit, 2003; Laird et al., 2001). Therefore, by adolescence, AL youth normally have a satisfactory repertoire of academic, social, and interpersonal skills that enable them to "get ahead" and develop normal, lasting relationships. Their developmental histories and personal dispositions allow them the option of exploring new life pathways, an opportunity not usually afforded the LCP youth.

A growing body of research is finding, though, that a simple dual developmental path may not adequately capture all the variations in criminal careers (Donnellan, Ge, & Wenk, 2000). Using data from three studies of crime and delinquency conducted in London, Philadelphia, and Racine, Wisconsin, some researchers (D'Unger, Land, McCall, & Nagin, 1998; Nagin, Farrington, & Moffitt, 1995; Nagin & Land, 1993) have identified four developmental paths that perhaps more comprehensively reflect the reality of offending patterns. The four paths are (1) the adolescent-limited offenders, (2) the life course–persistent offenders (also called "high-level chronic offenders"), (3) the low-level chronic offenders (LLCs), and (4) a nonoffending pattern (NCs). The ALs followed Moffitt's (1993a, 1993b) hypothesized offending pattern, beginning in their early teens, peaking at around age 16, and then showing a steady decline during their late teens and early adulthood (Nagin et al., 1995). The LLCs on the other hand, exhibited a rise in offending through early adolescence, reached a plateau by mid-teens, and remained at the same offending level well past age 18. The LCPs demonstrated their usual pattern of beginning antisocial behavior early and at a high level throughout their lifetimes. Interestingly, research by White, Bates, and Buyske (2001) suggests that it might be meaningful to introduce a fifth category, characterized by youth who engage in relatively little delinquency in early adolescence but for whom delinquency increases from late adolescence into adulthood.

Daniel Waschbusch (2002) reports that "disruptive behavior problems in childhood typically include hyperactivity, impulsivity, inattention, oppositional behaviors, defiance, aggression, and disregarding the rights of others" (p. 118). These disruptive behavior problems affect 5% to 10% of children and adolescents and account for more than 50% of referrals to mental health clinics. When left untreated, disruptive children are likely to experience peer rejection, have problems in school, demonstrate difficulties getting along with others, and exhibit delinquent behaviors. Similarly, four of the most prominent features of LCPs or serious, persistent offenders that are continually reported in the research literature are (1) hyperactive-impulsive-attention problems, (2) conduct problems, (3) below-average intelligence (or IQ), and (4) poor interpersonal or social skills. It is important, therefore, that we cover each in some detail.

Attention Deficit/Hyperactivity Disorder (ADHD) and Delinquency

The term **attention deficit/hyperactivity disorder** (or ADHD) encompasses a wide variety of terms frequently used in mental and educational contexts, such as minimal brain dysfunction (MBD), hyperactivity, attention deficit disorder (ADD), or hyperactive-impulsive attention (ADHD) problems or simply "hyperactivity." We will use the term most commonly used today, *ADHD*. All the terms, however, refer basically to three central behaviors: (1) excessive motor activity (cannot sit still, fidgets, runs about, is talkative and noisy), (2) impulsivity (acts before thinking, shifts quickly from one activity to another, interrupts others, does not consider consequences of behavior), and (3) inattention (does not seem to listen, is easily distracted, loses things necessary for tasks or activities).

Another symptom cluster that should not be confused with ADHD is **oppositional defiant disorder (ODD)**, which has often been linked to crime (Kosson, Cyterski, Steuerwald, Neuman, & Walker-Matthes, 2002). ODD symptoms include arguing with adults, refusing adults' requests, deliberately tying to annoy others, blaming others for mistakes, and being spiteful or vindictive (Kosson et al., 2002).

Although ADHD is the leading psychological diagnosis for children living in the United States (Flory, Milich, Lynam, Leukefeld, & Clayton, 2003; Nigg, John, et al., 2002), estimates of the incidence of ADHD in school-age children range widely from 1% to 20% (American Psychiatric Association, 2000; Developmental Disabilities Branch, 2000). To date, however, no systematic nationwide research has been conducted to identify the extent, seriousness, or nature of ADHD. The research has consistently revealed that boys outnumber girls, but the ratios reported have ranged from 2:1 to 9:1 (Root & Resnick, 2003). Black children appear to receive the diagnosis more often than other racial or ethnic minority children, although the reasons for this finding are debatable (Root & Resnick, 2003). It is important to realize that all children (and adults) have certain levels of inattention, overactivity, and impulsivity in situations, but for the diagnostic label of ADHD to be assigned, the symptoms must be unusually persistent and pronounced (Root & Resnick, 2003). Although most studies have been carried out in the United States and Europe, research has also supported the validity of ADHD in developing countries (Rohde et al., 2001) and across different cultures (Barkley, 1998). Furthermore, a significant percentage of ADHD children show the same persistent symptoms into adulthood (Nigg, Butler, Huang-Pollock, & Henderson, 2002; Mannuzza, Klein, Bessler, Malloy, & LaPadula, 1998). In other words, many people do not "outgrow" ADHD. The observation that ADHD is prevalent among adults is a recent conclusion, however, and remains somewhat controversial (Barkley, 1998; Faraone, Biederman, & Friedman, 2000; Nigg, John, et al., 2002)

Educators note that ADHD children have difficulty staying on task, remaining cognitively organized, sustaining academic achievement in the school setting, and maintaining control over their behavior. ADHD is a puzzling problem, the cause of which is largely unknown. Some scientists contend that ADHD children are born with a biological predisposition toward inattention and excessive movement; others maintain that some children are exposed to environmental factors that damage the nervous system. Loeber (1990) reveals how exposure to toxic substances during the preschool years often interferes with a child's neurological development, often resulting in symptoms of ADHD. For example, children exposed to low levels of lead toxicity (from paint) are more hyperactive and impulsive and are easily distracted and frustrated. They also show notable problems in following simple instructions. Some researchers observe that ADHD children do not possess effective strategies and cognitive organization with which to deal with the daily demands of school. These children often have particular difficulty in understanding and using abstract concepts. ADHD children also seem to lack cognitive organization skills for dealing with new knowledge and information.

More recent research suggests that one of the primary causal factors appears to be inhibitory problems due to neuropsychological deficits (Barkley, 1997, 1998; Nigg, Butler, et al., 2002). The inhibitory problems may be primarily due to motor (behavioral) control (Nigg, 2000). Overall, the extant research underscores the possibility that the causes of ADHD are probably multiple and extremely difficult to tease out of the many ongoing interactions occurring between the nervous system and the environment.

Although many behaviors have been identified as accompanying ADHD, the major theme is that ADHD children are perceived as annoying and aversive to those around them. ADHD children are continually seeking and prolonging interpersonal contacts and eventually manage to irritate and frustrate those people with whom they interact (Henker & Whalen, 1989). Because of these annoying and socially inappropriate behaviors, they are often rejected by peers,

especially if they are perceived as aggressive (Henker & Whalen, 1989). This pattern of peer rejection appears to continue throughout the developmental years (Dodge & Pettit, 2003; Reid, 1993). In many ways, ADHD appears to be more a disorder of interpersonal relationships than simply a disorder of hyperactivity. Some researchers find that ADHD children generally lack friendship and intimacy (Henker & Whalen, 1989). Moffitt (1990) reports that children between the ages of 5 and 7 who demonstrate the characteristics of both ADHD and delinquent behavior not only have special difficulty with social relationships but also have a high probability of demonstrating these problems into adolescence and beyond.

Experts argue that the most common problem associated with ADHD is delinquency and substance abuse (Beauchaine, Katkin, Strassberg, & Snarr, 2001). The data strongly suggest that youth with symptoms of both ADHD and delinquent behavior are at very high risk for developing lengthy and serious criminal careers (Mannuzza et al., 1998; Moffitt, 1990; Pfiffner et al., 1999; Satterfield, Swanson, Schell, & Lee, 1994). David Farrington (1991), in his well-regarded research, also found that violent offenders often have a history of hyperactivity, impulsivity, and attention deficit problems. The relationship between ADHD, delinquency, and adult crime is an area demanding much more research by forensic psychologists interested in studying crime and delinquency during their careers.

The most common method of treatment for ADHD is medication (especially methylphenidate, more commonly known as Ritalin, and its derivatives). However, although it apparently helps many children, many others exhibit numerous side effects, some of them severe. Counseling and psychotherapy are often used, often in conjunction with medication, but with limited success with this puzzling phenomenon, particularly over the long term. As many practitioners realize, ADHD children generally demonstrate multiple problems that can be best treated through treatment strategies that include all the factors impinging on the child at any given time (see Root & Resnick, 2003, for an excellent review). These treatment approaches are called "multisystemic" and will be dealt with more fully in Chapter 13.

Conduct Disorders

ADHD frequently co-occurs with a diagnostic category called "conduct disorders" (Coid, 2003; Offord, Boyle, & Racine, 1991; Reid, 1993). Waschbusch (2002) reports, for instance, that about 50% of disruptive children exhibit the basic symptoms of both ADHD and conduct disorders (CD). If disruptive children have the symptoms of one, about half the time they have the symptoms of the other. Not only does the presence of CD increase the symptoms of ADHD, but the combination of the two is an especially powerful predictor of a lifelong course of violence, persistent criminal behavior, and drug abuse (Flory et al., 2003; Molina, Bukstein, & Lynch, 2002; Pfiffner et al., 1999). As mentioned previously, conduct disorder consists of a cluster of maladaptive behaviors characterized by a variety of antisocial behaviors. Examples of this misbehavior include stealing, fire setting, running away from home, skipping school, destroying property, fighting, telling lies on a frequent basis, and being cruel to animals and people. CD is generally considered to be a serious childhood disorder because it appears to be a precursor to chronic criminal behavior during adulthood (Lahey et al., 1995). According to the *DSM-IV* (American Psychiatric Association, 1994), the central feature of conduct disorder is the *repetitive* and *persistent* pattern of behavior that violates the basic rights of others. The *DSM-IV* recognizes two types of conduct disorder: childhood onset and adolescent onset. Childhood-onset CD occurs when the pattern begins before the age of 10. This pattern often worsens as the child gets older and is more likely to lead into serious and persistent criminal behavior into adulthood (Frick et al., 2003). "In addition, children in the

childhood-onset group are characterized by more aggression, more cognitive and neuropsychological disturbances, greater impulsivity, greater social alienation, and more dysfunctional backgrounds than are children in the adolescent-onset group" (Frick et al., 2003, p. 246).

On the other hand, adolescent-onset CD is characterized by the absence of any maladaptive behavior before the age of 10. After age 10, adolescent-onset CDs tend to exhibit fewer problems in interpersonal and social skills but do reject traditional rules and formal procedures. They often associate with deviant peers in forbidden activities to show their independence and self-perceived maturity (Frick et al., 2003). In many respects, the two types of CDs follow the developmental paths of Moffitt's (1993a, 1993b) LCPs (childhood onset) and ALs (adolescent onset).

Behavioral indicators of childhood-onset CDs can be observed in their interactions with parents or caretakers well before school entry (Reid, 1993). For instance, children who are aggressive, difficult to manage, and noncompliant in the home at age 3 often continue to have similar problems when entering school. Furthermore, as we noted, these behaviors show remarkable continuity through adolescence and into adulthood. CD children frequently have significant problems with school assignments, a behavioral pattern that often results in their being mislabeled with a "learning disability." It is important to note that students with genuine learning disabilities are not necessarily conduct disordered, however. In other words, the two designations may overlap, but each is also a distinct categorization. Similar to ADHD children, aggressive CDs are at high risk for strong rejection by their peers (Reid, 1993). This rejection generally lasts throughout the school years and is very difficult to change (Reid, 1993). As described above, children who are consistently socially rejected by peers miss critical opportunities to develop normal interpersonal and social skills. Lacking effective interpersonal skills, these youth may meet their needs through more aggressive means, including threats and intimidation.

An estimated 6% to 16% of the male population is believed to have behavioral features of CD (American Psychiatric Association, 2000). The prevalence in girls ranges from 4% to 9.2% (Cohen, Cohen, & Brook, 1993; Zoccoulillo, 1993). A study by Anna Bardone and her colleagues (Bardone, Moffitt, & Caspi, 1996) found that CD patterns in girls are a strong predictor of a lifetime of problems, including poor interpersonal relations with partners/spouses and peers, criminal activity, early pregnancy without supportive partners, and frequent job loss and firings. Similar to CD boys, CD girls—without intervention—often lead a life full of interpersonal conflict.

Again, we must remind ourselves that there are multiple factors associated with delinquency, including serious and chronic offending. The previous section has focused on various deficiencies within the individual—hyperactivity, conduct disorder, and impulsivity, to name a few. Children live within a social system, however. The behavior and reactions of adults such as parents, caretakers, and teachers significantly affect the child's behavior. In some cases, the "deficiencies" described here are due to abuse, maltreatment, neglect, or simply ignorance about effective child-rearing techniques. In these, as well as in other cases, intervention by competent and caring adults can avert a lifetime of continual offending.

Cognitive Ability and Crime

The supposed connection between intelligence and delinquency is a controversial topic. Indeed, the concept of intelligence itself is controversial. Ask two dozen experts on intelligence about what "intelligence" really is and you will likely get two dozen different answers. We will leave this point for the time being but will return to it shortly.

Moffitt (1993a) hypothesizes that the more serious, persistent offenders (LCPs) should demonstrate lower intelligence or cognitive ability

than ALs. For example, she writes, "The verbal deficits of antisocial children are pervasive, affecting receptive listening and reading, problem solving, expressive speech and writing, and memory" (p. 680).

Nearly three decades ago, criminologists Travis Hirschi and Michael Hindelang (1977), on the basis of an extensive review of the research literature at that time, made a similar observation. Research, they said, continually found a robust and consistent relationship between IQ and delinquency. As a group, delinquents generally scored significantly lower on intelligence measures than nondelinquents. More recent empirical studies continue to find that, on average, delinquents score eight IQ points lower than nondelinquents on standard intelligence tests (Lynam, Moffitt, & Stouthamer-Loeber, 1993), and some studies even report lower IQ scores for delinquents (Vermeiren, De Clippele, Schwab-Stone, Ruchkin, & Deboutte, 2002).

Lynam et al. (1993) point out that there are at least three possible explanations for the IQ-delinquency connection. One explanation is that the less bright delinquents are the ones most likely to be caught. However, Moffitt and Silva (1988) found no support for this explanation. The researchers examined the IQ scores of two groups of self-reported delinquents: those who had been detected by the police and those who remained undetected. Results showed two important things: (1) the two groups did not differ from one another in their average IQ scores, and (2) both groups scored significantly below a comparison group of nondelinquent juveniles.

A second explanation, according to Lynam et al. (1993), is that the relationship is spurious. That is, a third factor might account for the relationship, such as social or ethnic background rather than intelligence. For example, it may be argued that boys from lower social classes tend to have lower IQ scores than boys from higher social classes, and boys from lower classes are also overrepresented among adjudicated delinquents (Lynam et al., 1993). Consequently, some might argue that social class—not intelligence—is responsible for both relationships. However, research has consistently found the IQ-delinquency relationship even when social class has been controlled or accounted for (Lynam et al., 1993).

A third explanation is that either low IQ leads to delinquency or, conversely, delinquency leads to a lower IQ. Lynman and his colleagues (1993) maintained that low intelligence leads to delinquency, rather than the other way around. In short, limited cognitive ability—as measured by standard intelligence tests—appears to play a critical role in the development of delinquency and crime. One of the interpretations of this relationship entertained by Lynam et al. (1993) was that low IQ usually leads to poor school performance, which in turn may encourage delinquent behavior. However, in the Lynam et al. study, the connection of poor school performance and delinquency was found *only* for Black youth and not for White youth. That is, when the researchers compared Black and White boys who were both performing poorly in school, it was only the Black boys who were at risk for engaging in delinquency. The reasons for this unexpected finding are unclear.

A more recent study by Donnellan et al. (2000) helps clarify some of the above findings, particularly as they related to the association among intelligence, race or ethnicity, and delinquency. Donnellan et al. used a large and diverse sample of juvenile delinquents ($N = 4,065$) whose arrest records were collected over 20 years (beginning in 1964). Cognitive ability of the group was measured by 12 different cognitive or intelligence tests. According to the authors, this longitudinal study was the first investigation to empirically evaluate Moffitt's (1993a) cognitive ability hypothesis while following the developmental paths of a large sample of delinquents into early adulthood.

Of the sample, 888 offenders qualified as ALs, and 774 offenders were classified as LCPs. The remainder (2,403) was classified as "other" and was not included in the final analysis. The researchers found support for the Moffitt

(1993a) hypothesis for Whites and Latinos, but not for African Americans. Specifically, in 9 of the 12 cognitive tests used, White AL offenders had significantly higher scores than White LCPs. In the Latino sample, AL offenders had significantly higher scores in 6 of the 12 cognitive tests. However, there were no significant differences between ALs and LCPs in any of the cognitive tests for African Americans. The researchers suggest that the reasons for the racial differences may reside in the opportunities afforded youth living in various social environments. That is, many African American youth live in unfavorable circumstances that offer greater risks for continued criminal activity, thereby "washing out" any empirical differences between ALs and LCPs. These unfavorable circumstances are characterized by such things as employment and educational discrimination, general poverty, a lack of readily available prosocial role models, and/or a lack of widespread educational and economic opportunities. It should be noted that these social circumstances were even more prevalent during the period of time covered by the study (1964–1984) than they are today.

Three important points were made by the Donnellan et al. (2000) study. First, there is some solid support for the Moffitt (1993a) hypothesis when it pertains to Caucasians and only modest support in the Latino context, at least over that period of time. Second, it highlights the importance of considering the social ecology or context when considering the relationship between crime and cognitive abilities. In short, race and ethnicity may play a larger role in life course–persistent offending than suggested by the Moffitt hypothesis. The third point relates less to the cognitive controversy than to the AL-LCP dichotomy. As we mentioned when we first introduced Moffitt's research, classifying juvenile offenders into two basic categories is insufficient to account for the many youth who fall somewhere between the two extremes. Donnellan et al. found that there were a large number of individuals (59%) who did not fit neatly into either the AL or LCP grouping. It should be mentioned that Moffitt and her associates also had difficulty classifying 58% of the juvenile offenders into an AL or LCP typology in an earlier study (Moffitt et al., 1996). These results clearly suggest that additional developmental paths may have to be introduced to account for delinquent offenders.

Another important point also needs to be emphasized: "Individuals differ from one another in their ability to understand complex ideas, to adapt effectively to the environment, to learn from experience, to engage in various forms of reasoning, to overcome obstacles by thought" (Neisser et al., 1996, p. 77). Furthermore, although these differences can be substantial, they are rarely consistent. A person's intellectual performance will vary on different occasions, in different domains—as judged by different criteria—and across the life span. In the past two decades, there has been a concentrated effort to develop the idea of broader, multiple intelligences, rather than just one single type of intelligence, and to have an appreciation of abilities that previously either were ignored or considered not very important in understanding human behavior. Today, it has become apparent that intelligence exists in multiple forms and relates to a wide assortment of abilities. Howard Gardner (1983), in his book *Frames of Mind,* for example, describes seven independent intelligences or talents. They are (1) linguistic or language based, (2) logical-mathematical, (3) spatial (used in getting from one place to another or in packing a suitcase), (4) musical, (5) bodily kinesthetic (such as what athletes or ballet dancers have), (6) insight into oneself, and (7) ability to understand and relate to others. Standard cognitive tests measure only the first three. Even if we presume that standard tests are valid (and caution is urged here), the delinquents who scored low on the standard tests may well be higher in other types of intelligence. Gardner added that there are probably many other forms of intelligence. For example, how do we account for wisdom, synthesizing ability, intuition, metaphoric capacities, humor, and good judgment (Gardner, 1986, 1993)?

Gardner (1983) considered the last two of the seven—insight into oneself and understanding others—features of emotional intelligence, and a deficiency in this form of intelligence may play a prominent role in human violence. Individuals who chronically engage in violence may lack significant insight into their own behavior and possess little sensitivity toward others. They tend to misread emotional cues from others and become confused and angry in ambiguous social situations. For example, highly aggressive children often have a **hostile attribution bias.** That is, children prone to unusually aggressive actions are more likely to interpret ambiguous actions of others as hostile and threatening than less aggressive children. Research consistently indicates that highly aggressive and violent adolescents "typically define social problems in hostile ways, adopt hostile goals, seek few additional facts, generate few alternative solutions, anticipate few consequences for aggression, and give higher priority to their aggressive solutions" (Eron & Slaby, 1994, p. 10). These hostile cognitive styles, combined with deficient interpersonal skills, are more likely to result in aggression and violence in certain social situations.

Highly aggressive and antisocial children appear to be less equipped cognitively for dealing with ambiguous or conflictual situations. Research strongly supports the idea that highly aggressive individuals possess biases and cognitive deficits for dealing and solving problematic social encounters with others (Pepler, Byrd, & King, 1991). Research also indicates that chronic delinquent offenders are deficient in being able to cognitively put themselves in the place of others or to empathize (Pepler et al., 1991). As a result, these youth are less concerned about the negative consequences of violence, such as the suffering of the victim or the social rejection they receive from their peers.

Ironically, although the early research on IQ and delinquency can be criticized for its lack of attention to social factors, it is likely that intelligence, in a broader sense, *does* play a role. Most particularly, Gardner's (1983) emotional intelligence may be a key factor in the development of habitual offending. More important, however, early school failure seems to play a more critical role in the development of delinquency and crime than measures of intelligence predict (Dodge & Pettit, 2003). In addition, research indicates that retention in kindergarten and in the early grades—being "held back"—has significant detrimental effects on healthy development (Dodge & Pettit, 2003). Closely related to the developmental issues of juvenile crime is psychopathy, a behavioral pattern and symptomatology that reflects many of the same features of conduct disorders, ADHD, and, more broadly, the LCP. Psychopathy has become the central focus of research in forensic psychology focusing on adult criminal behavior and correctional psychology in recent years. Even more recently, juvenile psychopathy has become the subject of considerable debate and research directed at establishing its validity and implications. Because psychopathy is such an important topic in forensic psychology, we return to it again later in the chapter.

School Violence

In the 1990s, a rash of school shootings across the United States made headlines and brought the topic of school violence into sharp focus. Communities that had previously had a low profile—West Paducah, Kentucky; Jonesboro, Arkansas; Pearl, Mississippi; Springfield, Oregon—suddenly became notorious. The most infamous case was the mass murder of 12 students and 1 teacher at Columbine High School in Littleton, Colorado, in April 1999. The two teenage boys who did the shooting apparently committed suicide during the incident. An additional 20 students were injured. To the public and news media, the shooters appeared to be two ordinary boys from normal middle-class families living in an affluent suburb of Denver. Although there had been a number of school shootings prior to Columbine (there had been at least 10 school shootings between 1996 and 1999), the Columbine shooting prompted a great deal of alarm and concern nationwide. In addition, the media and some experts were quick to make gross generalizations about the school violence problem. O'Toole (2000, p. 4) lists the usual wrong or unverified impressions of school shooters often promoted by the news media (see Box 4.1).

Despite the media attention given to Columbine and other schools, it is important to keep school crime, including violence, in perspective. Note that the school shootings described above occurred during a time when juvenile violent crime on the whole was going

---

BOX 4.1   Public Myths About School Shooters

News coverage magnifies a number of widespread incorrect or unverified impressions of school shooters. Among them are the following:

- School violence is an epidemic.
- All school shooters are alike.
- The school shooter is always a loner.
- School shootings are exclusively revenge motivated.
- Easy access to weapons is *the* most significant risk factor.
- Unusual or bizarre behaviors, interests, and hobbies are the hallmarks of the student destined to become violent.

Source: O'Tool (2000, p. 4).

down; thus, although the shootings were terrifying, they were not representative of the juvenile crime picture. Furthermore, although the media understandably report incidents of children having guns on school premises, there is no documentation that this is a widespread problem. Although it is important to be alert to possible dangers facing school-age children and the adults who work with them in the schools, the reality is that the risk of victimization is smaller in that environment than in private homes or the community at large. Still, each school-based attack has had a stressful and lasting effect on the school in which it occurred, the surrounding community, and the nation as a whole. Consequently, although many parents, teachers, and school officials across the nation are pleased that the *nationwide* statistics of school crime and violence are decreasing, they—understandably—want their children and the children in their local district to have a safe school environment. One way to improve the safety of youth at our nation's schools is through threat assessment, a strategy in which many mental health professionals and forensic psychologists are becoming increasingly involved.

Threat Assessment

Threat assessment is a set of investigative and operational activities designed to identify, assess, and manage individuals who may *pose* a threat of violence to *identifiable targets,* such as the school environment (Borum, Fein, Vossekuil, & Berglund, 1999). "A threat is an expression of intent to do harm or act out violently against someone or something. A threat can be spoken, written, or symbolic—for example, motioning with one's hands as though shooting at another person" (O'Tool, 2000, p. 6).

Threat assessment is innovative in two ways: (1) it does *not* rely on descriptive, demographic, or psychological profiles, and (2) it does *not* rely directly on verbal or written threats as a threshold for risk (Borum et al., 1999). More specifically,

threat assessment is different from "profiling" in that it looks at the pathways of ideas, thinking patterns, and behavior that may lead to violent action. Profiling, as we noted in Chapter 3, is designed to reduce the number of possible suspects within any given population by sketching the "type" of person who may have committed a certain category of crime. Threat assessment, on the other hand, concentrates on determining the *seriousness* of a threat that has already been made and—if the assessment suggests it is serious—setting up procedures and strategies to protect the intended target. "Instead of looking at demographic and psychological characteristics, the threat assessment approach focuses on a subject's thinking and behaviors as a means to assess his/her progress on a pathway to violent actions" (Borum et al., 1999, p. 328).

Therefore, the crucial step in threat assessment is to determine whether the threatener is *making* a threat or *posing* a threat. Thousands of threats are made on public officials (and schools) every year, but a vast majority of them are not based on real intentions to carry them out. On the other hand, those who *pose* a threat are regarded as serious and may not even communicate their intentions to the threatened target directly. Interestingly, none of the 43 people who attacked a public figure (such as the U.S. president) over the past 50 years in the United States ever communicated a threat directly to the intended target (Borum et al., 1999; Fein & Vossekuil, 1999). However, in several of the school shooting cases, the shooters had communicated their intentions to other students who either did not take them seriously, did not tell adults, or, in one case, even turned out to watch. It should be emphasized that all threats are taken seriously and evaluated; the threat assessment tries to distinguish who is serious and who is not.

Because of their expertise in working with threat against public figures and other members of the public, several federal agencies, including the FBI and the Secret Service, have put together threat assessment guidelines to help school personnel, students, and parents identify warning signs of potential violence directed at the school environment. In response to the demand for such, the U.S. Secret Service has been especially involved, establishing the Secret Service National Threat Assessment Center (NTAC) (see Box 8.1 in Chapter 8). In June 1999, following the attack at Columbine High School, the U.S. Secret Service and the U.S. Department of Education launched a collaborative effort called the Safe School Initiative (Borum et al., 1999). This included an intensive study of 37 U.S. school shootings involving 41 perpetrators that have occurred over the past 25 years (see Box 4.2). The focus of the project was a thorough examination of the thinking, planning, and behaviors engaged in by students who carried out school attacks. In addition, the perceived rash of school violence has thrust mental health professionals and school psychologists into the role of assisting school districts and the local communities in the development of prevention and treatment programs directed at juvenile violence (Evans & Rey, 2001). It also has initiated considerable applied research by forensic psychologists across the country.

According to the FBI (O'Tool, 2000), threats may be divided into four types: (1) direct, (2) indirect, (3) veiled, and (4) conditional. A *direct* threat specifies a target and is delivered in a straightforward, clear, and explicit manner. For example, a caller might say, "I placed a bomb in the school cafeteria and it will go off at noon today." An *indirect* threat is more vague and ambiguous. The specific motivation, the intention, and the target are unclear and open to speculation.

BOX 4.2 Secret Service Safe School Initiative Report

What we know about school shooters:

- Attackers talk about their plans to others. Prior to most incidents, the attacker told someone about his idea or plan. In more than three fourths of incidents, the attacker told a friend, schoolmate, or sibling about his idea for a possible attack before taking action.
- Attackers make plans. Incidents of targeted violence at school are rarely impulsive. In almost all incidents, the attacker developed the idea to harm the target before the attack.
- There is no stereotype or profile. There is no accurate or useful profile of the "school shooter." The personality and social characteristics of the shooters vary substantially.
- Attackers had easy access to guns. Most attackers had used guns previously and had access to guns. In nearly two thirds of incidents, the attackers obtained guns used in the attack from their own home or that of a relative.
- School staff are often first responders. Most shooting incidents were not resolved by law enforcement intervention. More than half of the attacks ended before law enforcement responded to the scene. In these cases, faculty or fellow students stopped the attacker.
- Attackers are encouraged by others. In many cases, other students were involved in some capacity. In almost half of the cases, friends or fellow students influenced or encouraged the attacker to act.
- Bullying can be a factor. In a number of cases, bullying played a key role in the decision to attack. A number of attackers had experienced bullying and harassment that were long-standing and severe.
- Warning signs are common. Most attackers engaged in some behavior prior to the incident that caused concern or indicated a need for help.

Source: U.S. Secret Service (2000).

"If I wanted to, I could kill many at the school at anytime." This is the type of threat that had most frequently been made, according to the Safe School Initiative (SSI).

A *veiled* threat strongly implies but does not explicitly threaten violence. For example, a student might receive an anonymous note in his locker that reads, "We would be better off without you around anymore." The message clearly hints at a potential violent act but leaves the seriousness and meaning of the note for the threatened victim to interpret. A *conditional* threat is most often seen in extortion cases. It often warns that a violent act will occur unless certain demands or terms are met, such as occurred during the Washington, D.C., sniper killings in the fall of 2002. The message: "If you don't pay us 10 million dollars, none of your children will be safe." Without the condition attached, this would have been a veiled threat.

Researchers from the SSI have concluded that those involved in school shootings did not "just snap"; they planned their attacks (Vossekuil, Fein, Reddy, Borum, & Mozeleski, 2002). In many cases, the incident was planned at least 2 weeks beforehand. Interestingly, the researchers found that when juveniles plan targeted violence, they often tell at least one person about their plans, give out specifics before the event takes place, and obtain the weapons they need— usually from their own home or a relative's home. Unfortunately, the person or persons who were told about the impending incident were peers and friends, and rarely did these informed youth bring the information to an adult's attention. Another observation from the SSI report was that, in many school shootings, friends and fellow students influenced or encouraged the attacker to act. For example, Evan Ramsey, age 16, who killed his principal and a student and wounded two others in Bethel, Alaska, in 1997, explained, "I told everyone what I was going to do." In fact, so many students had heard about his planned attack that 24 students crowded the lobby mezzanine to watch. One student even brought a camera to record the event.

According to the SSI report, for more than half of the school shooters, the motive was revenge. In many cases, longstanding bullying or harassment played a key role in the decision to attack. However, there are many other motives or reasons for school violence. O'Tool (2000) suggests a list:

> Threats are made for a variety of reasons. A threat may be a warning signal, a reaction to fear of punishment or some other anxiety, or a demand for attention. It may be intended to taunt; to intimidate; to assert power or control; to punish; to manipulate or coerce; to frighten; to terrorize; to compel someone to do something; to strike back for an injury, injustice or slight; to disrupt someone's or some institution's life; to test authority, to protect oneself. The emotions that underlie a threat can be love; hate; fear; rage; or desire for attention, revenge, excitement, or recognition. (p. 6)

In summary, it should be emphasized that there is no accurate or useful profile of "the school shooter" or threatener. According to the SSI report, the personality and social characteristics of the shooters vary considerably. They came from a variety of social backgrounds and varied in age from 11 to 21 years of age. Family situations ranged from intact families to foster homes. Academic performance ranged from excellent to failing. Most were not diagnosed with any mental disorder, and a majority had no history of drug or alcohol abuse. However, more than three fourths of school shooters did threaten to kill themselves, made suicidal gestures, or tried to kill themselves before their attacks. Nevertheless, serious, longstanding, major depression did not appear to be a prominent feature in their backgrounds.

Most school shooters did have easy access to guns. In nearly two thirds of the incidents, school shooters obtained guns from their own home or from that of a relative. The SSI report suggests, therefore, that although guns may be easy to obtain for many youth, when the notion of an attack exists, any effort to acquire, prepare, or use a weapon may signal an attacker's progression from a thought to an action.

The Criminal Psychopath

Probably no topic has caught the attention of forensic psychologists interested in the development of habitual criminal behavior more in recent years than the topic of psychopathy. The term **psychopath** is currently used to describe a person who demonstrates a discernible cluster of psychological, interpersonal, and neuropsychological features that distinguish him or her from the general population. In addition, the psychopath, according to this definition, may or may not engage in habitual criminal behavior. Many psychopaths have no history of serious antisocial behavior, and the converse may be true. That is, many persistent, serious offenders are not necessarily psychopaths. For our purposes here, the term *criminal psychopath* will be reserved for those psychopaths who demonstrate a wide range of persistent antisocial behavior. As a group, they tend to be "dominant, manipulative individuals characterized by an impulsive, risk-taking and antisocial life-style, who obtain their greatest thrill from diverse sexual gratification and target diverse victims over time" (Porter et al., 2000, p. 220). As further noted by Stephen Porter and his colleagues (2000), "Given its relation to crime and violence, psychopathy is arguably one of the most important psychological constructs in the criminal justice system" (p. 227).

General Behavioral Characteristics of Psychopaths

Hervey Cleckley (1941) was one of the first to outline the behavioral characteristics of psychopaths. He was a professor of psychiatry and neurology at the Medical College of Georgia during the 1930s and remained there until the 1950s. Cleckley is credited with completing one of the most comprehensive works on the psychopath, titled *The Mask of Sanity.* The book went through five editions, and his clear writing style, in combination with the subject area, captivated public and scholarly interests for many years.

Cleckley (1941) identified what he thought were 10 cardinal behavioral features characteristic of the true psychopath: (1) selfishness (also called egocentricity), (2) an inability to love or give genuine affection to others, (3) frequent deceitfulness or lying, (4) lack of guilt or remorsefulness (no matter how cruel the behavior), (5) callousness or a lack of empathy, (6) low anxiety proneness, (7) poor judgment and failure to learn from experience, (8) superficial charm, (9) failure to follow any life plan, and (10) cycles of unreliability. By no means do all researchers in the field of psychopathy agree with this list, but the behavioral features outlined serve as a starting point for further discussion in this section.

An important distinction underlying much of the behavioral descriptions is what Quay (1965) refers to as the psychopath's profound and pathological stimulation seeking. According to Quay, the actions of the psychopath are motivated by an excessive *neuropsychological* need for thrills and excitement. It is not unusual to see psychopaths drawn to such interests as racecar driving, skydiving, and motorcycle stunts.

Antisocial Personality Disorder and Psychopathy

Psychiatrists, clinical psychologists, and mental health workers often use the term *antisocial personality disorder* to summarize many of the same features found in the criminal psychopath. Antisocial personality disorder refers specifically to an individual who exhibits "a pervasive pattern of disregard for, and violation of, the rights of others that begins in childhood or early adolescence and continues into adulthood" (American Psychiatric Association, 1994, p. 645).

In other words, the antisocial personality disorder appears closely aligned with the persistent offender, such as the LCP offender.

It should be emphasized that, although there are many behavioral similarities, the terms *antisocial personality disorder* and *psychopathy* are not synonymous. Antisocial personality disorder (ASP) refers to broad behavioral patterns based on clinical observations, whereas psychopathy refers not only to specific behavioral patterns but also to measurable cognitive, emotional, and neuropsychological differences. In addition, ASP is so broad in its scope that anywhere between 50% and 80% of male inmates qualify as meeting its criteria (Correctional Services of Canada, 1990; Hare, 1998; Hare, Forth, & Strachan, 1992). Only 11% to 25% of male inmates meet the criteria for psychopathy (Hare, 1996; Simourd & Hoge, 2000). These data suggest that the construct of psychopathy may be a more precise indicator—and a better predictor of violence—than the more global construct of ASP.

Prevalence of Criminal Psychopathy

Overall, Hare (1998) estimates that the prevalence of psychopaths in the general population is about 1%, whereas in the adult prison population, estimates range from 15% to 25%. Some researchers (e.g., Simourd & Hoge, 2000) wonder, however, whether these estimates are not somewhat inflated. Simourd and Hoge (2000) report that only 11% of their inmate population could be identified as criminal psychopaths. The inmates used in the Simourd and Hoge study were not simply inmates in a medium-security correctional facility. All 321 were serving a current sentence for violent offending, more than half of them had been convicted of a previous violent offense, and almost all of them had extensive criminal careers. Therefore, percentage estimates of criminal psychopathy within any given population should be tempered by the type of facility, as well as the cultural, ethnic, and age mix of the targeted population.

Offending Patterns of Criminal Psychopaths

Although some psychopaths have little contact with the criminal justice system, many have continual contact with the system because of persistent, serious offending. For example, Gretton, McBride, Hare, O'Shaughnessy, and Kumka (2001) point out that criminal psychopaths generally "lack a normal sense of ethics and morality, live by their own rules, are prone to use cold-blooded, instrumental intimidation and violence to satisfy their wants and needs, and generally are contemptuous of social norms and the rights of others" (p. 428).

Criminal psychopaths manifest violent and aggressive behaviors—including verbal abuse, threats, and intimidation—at a much higher rate than found in other populations (Hare, Hart, & Harpur, 1991). In some cases, this persistent offending is extremely violent in nature. Criminal psychopaths are "responsible for a markedly disproportionate amount of the serious crime, violence, and social distress in every society" (Hare, 1996, p. 26). Hare (1996) posits, "The ease with which psychopaths engage in . . . dispassionate violence has very real significance for society in general and for law enforcement personnel in particular" (p. 38). Hare refers to a 1992 report by the FBI that found that nearly half of the law enforcement officers who died in the line of duty were killed by individuals who closely matched the personality profile of the psychopath. In addition, the offenses of psychopathic sex offenders are likely to be more violent, brutal, unemotional, and sadistic than those of other sex offenders (Hare, Clark, Grann, & Thornton, 2000). Some serial murders described as unusually sadistic and brutal also tend to have many psychopathic features (Hare et al., 2000; Stone, 1998). It should be emphasized, though, that very few psychopaths are serial killers!

The relationship between psychopathy and sexual offending appears to be a complex one. For example, the prevalence of psychopaths among child molesters is estimated to be from 10% to 15%; among rapists, it is between 40% and 50% (Gretton et al., 2001; Porter et al., 2000). Research also indicates that rapists who have psychopathic characteristics are more likely to have "nonsexual" motivations for their crimes, such as anger, vindictiveness, sadism, and opportunism (Hart & Dempster, 1997).

Many of the murders and serious assaults committed by nonpsychopaths occurred during domestic disputes or extreme emotional arousal. On the other hand, this pattern of violence is rarely observed for criminal psychopaths (Hare et al., 1991; Williamson, Hare, & Wong, 1987). Criminal psychopaths frequently engage in violence as a form of revenge or retribution or during a bout of drinking. Many of the attacks of nonpsychopaths are toward women they know well, whereas many of the attacks of criminal psychopaths are directed toward men who are strangers. Hare et al. (1991) observe that the violence committed by criminal psychopaths was callous and cold-blooded "without the affective coloring that accompanied the violence of nonpsychopaths" (p. 395).

According to Porter et al. (2000), research suggests that psychopaths reoffend faster, violate parole sooner, and perhaps commit more institutional violence than nonpsychopaths. In one study (Serin, Peters, & Barbaree, 1990), the number of failures of male offenders released on unescorted temporary absence program was examined. The failure rate for psychopaths was 37.5%, whereas none of the nonpsychopaths failed. The failure rate during parole was also examined. Although 7% of nonpsychopaths violated parole requirements, 33% of the psychopaths violated their requirements. In another study (Serin & Amos, 1995), 299 male offenders were followed for up to 8 years after their release from a federal prison. Sixty-five percent of the psychopaths were convicted of another crime within 3 years, compared to a reconviction rate of 25% for nonpsychopaths. Quinsey, Rice, and Harris (1995) found that within 6 years of release from prison, more than 80% of the

psychopaths convicted as sex offenders had violently recidivated, compared to a 20% recidivism rate for nonpsychopathic sex offenders.

High recidivism rates are also characteristic of psychopathic adolescent offenders. According to Gretton et al. (2001), these offenders are more likely than other adolescent offenders to escape from custody, violate the conditions of probation, and commit nonviolent and violent offenses over a 5-year follow-up period. The high recidivism rates among adult and juvenile offenders have prompted some researchers to conclude that there was "nothing the behavioral sciences can offer for treating those with psychopathy" (Gacono, Nieberding, Owen, Rubel, & Bodholdt, 1997, p. 119), partly because psychopaths tend to "be unmotivated to accept their problematic behavior and often lack insight into the nature and extent of their psychopathology" (Skeem, Edens, & Colwell, 2003, p. 26). Other researchers take a decidedly different perspective and believe that untreatability statements concerning the psychopath are unwarranted (Salekin, 2002; Skeem, Monahan, & Mulvey, 2002; Skeem, Poythress, Edens, Lilienfeld, & Cale, in press; Wong, 2000). There is *some* evidence that psychopaths who receive larger "doses" of treatment are less likely to demonstrate subsequent violent behavior than those who receive less treatment (Skeem, Edens, & Colwell, 2003).

Psychological Measures of Psychopathy

Currently, the most popular instrument for measuring criminal psychopathy is the 22-item **Psychopathy Checklist (PCL)** (Hare, 1980) and its 20-item revision (**PCL-R**) (Hare, 1991). More recently, the PCL-R has been published in a second edition, which includes new information on its applicability in forensic and research settings; has been expanded for use in offenders in other countries; and includes updated normative and validation data on male and female offenders. A 12-item short-form version has also been developed, called the **Psychopathy Checklist: Screening Version (PCL:SV)** (Hart, Cox, & Hare, 1995; Hart, Hare, & Forth, 1993), as well as the **Psychopathy Checklist: Youth Version (PCL:YV)** and the **P-Scan: Research Version.** The P-Scan is a screening instrument that serves as a *rough* screen for psychopathic features and as a source of working hypotheses to deal with managing suspects, offenders, or clients. It is designed for use in law enforcement, probation, corrections, civil and forensic facilities, and other areas in which it would be useful to have some information about the possible presence of psychopathic features in a particular person. Of course, the P-Scan needs much more research before it can be used as a valid instrument in practice. All five checklists are conceptually and—with the exception of the P-Scan—empirically similar.

The instruments are largely based on Cleckley's (1941) conception of psychopathy but are specifically designed to identify psychopaths in male prison, forensic, or psychiatric populations. Because the PCL-R is currently the most frequently used instrument as both a research and clinical instrument, it will be the center of attention for the remainder of this section. The PCL:YV is beginning to be researched more extensively and will be covered in more detail in the section on the juvenile psychopath.

The PCL-R assesses the affective (emotional), interpersonal, behavioral, and social deviance facets of criminal psychopathy from various sources, including self-reports, behavioral observations, and collateral sources, such as parents, family members, friends, and arrest and court records, which can help to establish the credibility of self-reports (Hare, 1996; Hare et al., 1991). In addition, item ratings from the PCL-R, for instance, require some integration of information across multiple domains, including behavior at work or school; behavior toward family, friends, and sexual partners; and criminal behavior (Kosson et al., 2002). Typically, highly trained examiners use all this information to score each item on a 0- to 2-point scale, depending on the extent to which an individual has the disposition described by each item on the checklist (0 = *consistently absent,* 1 = *inconsistent,* 2 = *consistently present*). Scoring is, however, quite complex and requires substantial time, extensive training, and access to a considerable amount of background information on the individual. A score of 30 or above usually qualifies a person as a primary psychopath (Hare, 1996). In some research and clinical settings, cutoff scores ranging from 25 to 33 are often used (Simourd & Hoge, 2000). Hare (1991) recommends that persons with scores between 21 and 29 be classified as "middle" subjects who show many of the features of psychopathy but do not fit all the criteria. Scores below 21 are considered "nonpsychopaths."

So far, the research has strongly supported the reliability and validity of the PCL-R for distinguishing criminal psychopaths from criminal nonpsychopaths and for helping correctional psychologists in risk assessments of inmates (Hare, 1996; Hare et al., 1992). The topic of risk assessment will be discussed again in Chapters 9 and 10. In addition, the instrument provides researchers and mental health professionals with a universal measurement for the assessment of psychopathy that facilitates international and cross-cultural communication concerning theory, research, and eventual clinical practice (Hare et al., 2000). Currently, the PCL-R is increasingly being used as a clinical instrument for the diagnosis of psychopathy across the globe, although it appears to be most powerful in identifying psychopathy among North American White males (Hare et al., 2000).

Core Factors of Psychopathy

One of the things that has clearly emerged from the research on the PCL-R is that psychopathy is multidimensional in nature. One statistical procedure designed to find different dimensions or factors in test data is called **factor analysis.** When expert ratings of psychopathy on the PCL-R were submitted to a factor analysis, at least two behavioral dimensions or factors emerged (Hare, 1991; Harpur, Hakstian, & Hare,

1988; Hart et al., 1993). Factor 1 reflects the interpersonal and emotional components of the disorder and consists of items measuring remorselessness, callousness, and selfish use and manipulation of others. The typical psychopath feels no compunction about using others strictly to meet his or her own needs. Factor 2 is most closely associated with a socially deviant lifestyle, as characterized by poor planning, impulsiveness, an excessive need for stimulation, proneness to boredom, and a lack of realistic goals. In criminal psychopaths, some researchers have found that Factor 1 appears to be associated with planned predatory violence, whereas Factor 2 appears to be related to spontaneous and dishinhibited violence (Hart & Dempster, 1997). Factor 1 is also linked to resistance and inability to profit from psychotherapy and treatment programs (Seto & Barbaree, 1999). (Treatment of the criminal psychopathy will be discussed in Chapter 11.) Factor 2 appears related to socioeconomic status, educational attainment, and cultural/ethnic background, whereas Factor 1 may be more connected with biopsychological influences (Cooke & Michie, 1997). Research also suggests that Factor 1 may be a more powerful indicator of psychopathy than Factor 2 (Cooke, Michie, Hart, & Hare, 1999).

More recent research with both children and adults, however, reveals that there may be *three* behavioral dimensions at the core of psychopathy rather than just the original two (Cooke & Michie, 2001; Frick, Bodin, & Barry, 2000; Kosson et al., 2002). Cooke and Michie (2001), for example, found from their factor analysis of PCL-R data that psychopathy probably consists of three core factors: (1) arrogant and deceitful interpersonal style, (2) impulsive and irresponsible behavioral style (highly similar to the original Factor 2), and (3) deficient affective experience. Factors 1 and 3 are actually subdivisions of the original Factor 1 reported in earlier studies. The term *deficient affective experience* refers to the lack of sincere positive emotions toward others and the demonstration of callousness and lack of empathy. The terms *arrogant* and *deceitful interpersonal style*, on the other hand, refer to the

glibness, superficial charm, and the grandiose sense of self-worth that are so characteristic of the psychopath.

Recent research has shown that adult psychopaths usually exhibit significant antisocial behavior in their childhoods (Seagrave & Grisso, 2002). It is reasonable, therefore, to expect researchers to begin searching the developmental trajectory of psychopathy to identify tomorrow's psychopaths. The next section examines what we currently know about the childhood of the psychopath.

Juvenile Psychopathy

One of the serious shortcomings of the extensive research conducted on psychopathy is that it has focused almost exclusively on White adult males (Frick et al., 2000). Consequently, research on juvenile (adolescent and child) psychopathy is limited, but it is rapidly growing. However, attempts to apply the label *psychopathy* to juvenile populations "raise several conceptual, methodological, and practical concerns related to clinical/forensic practice and juvenile/criminal justice policy" (Edens, Skeem, Cruise, & Cauffman, 2001, p. 54). Some debate has focused on whether psychopathy can or should be applied to juveniles at all. Can features of adult psychopathy be found in children and adolescents in the first place? Others are concerned that—even if psychopathy can be identified in adolescents—the label may have too many negative connotations. More specifically, the label implies that the prognosis for treatment is poor, a high rate of offending and recidivism can be expected, and the intrinsic and biological basis of the disorder means little can be done outside of biological interventions. A third debate contends that psychopathy assessments of youth must achieve a high level of confidence before they can be employed in the criminal justice system (Seagrave & Grisso, 2002).

Several instruments for measuring preadult psychopathy have been developed in recent years, including the Psychopathy Screening Device (PSD) (Frick, O'Brien, Wootton, & McBurnett, 1994), the Childhood Psychopathy Scale (CPS) (Lynam, 1997), and the PCL:YV (Forth, Kosson, & Hare, 1997). All three instruments are currently being used primarily as research measures rather than as clinical-diagnostic measures and, as Seagrave and Grisso (2002) point out, may eventually have important implications for the prevention of future serious delinquency. Consequently, they may soon become extensively used in forensic clinical practice. According to Seagrave and Grisso,

It is not overstated to imagine that juvenile psychopathy measures will become one of the most frequently used instruments in forensic assessments of delinquency cases of any kind within a few years after they are made generally available to forensic clinical examiners. (p. 220)

The PCL:YV, designed for assessing psychopathy in adolescents age 13 or older, is a modified version of the PCL-R. Basically, the instrument attempts to assess psychopathy across the youth's life span, with an emphasis on school adjustment and peer and family relations. Similar to the adult PCL-R, the PCL:YV requires a lengthy standardized, semistructured clinical interview and a review of documents by a well-trained psychologist. Scores of 0 (*consistently absent*), 1 (*inconsistent*), or 2 (*consistently present*) for each of the 20 behavioral dimensions of psychopathy represent the scoring system. The instrument—like the PCL-R—generates a total score and two factor scores. Factor 1 reflects an interpersonal/affective dimension and includes items that measure glibness/superficial charm, grandiosity, manipulativeness, dishonesty, and callousness. Factor 2 reflects behavioral or lifestyles features such as impulsiveness, irresponsibility, early behavioral problems, and lack of goals.

The PSD is a behavior rating scale in which some of the items on the PCL-R were rewritten for use with children (Frick et al., 2000).

Currently, the PSD comes in three versions: (1) a teacher version, (2) a parent version, and (3) a self-report version. Using the teacher and parent versions of the PSD, Frick et al. (1994) found (through a factor analysis) that juvenile psychopathy may be made be up of two major dimensions. One dimension was labeled callous-unemotional and the other impulsivity-conduct problems. Later, however, Frick et al. (2000) found evidence (again through a factor analysis) to support a *three*-dimensional core for childhood psychopathy. Two of the factors (callous-unemotional and impulsivity) were similar to the core dimensions found for adults in Frick et al.'s earlier study. However, the construct of impulsivity seems to be much more complex in children than in adults, and the researchers discovered that the construct may be subdivided into impulsivity and narcissism (grandiose sense of self-worth).

One of the major problems of identifying juvenile psychopaths is that psychopathy may be very difficult to measure reliably because of the transient and constantly changing developmental patterns across the life span, especially during the early years. For example, psychopathic symptoms in childhood may look very different from those exhibited in adulthood (Hart, Watt, & Vincent, 2002). That is, some of the behavioral patterns of children and adolescents may be similar to psychopaths for a variety of reasons but may not really be signs of psychopathy. Children in an abusive home often demonstrate an abnormally restricted range of emotions that are similar to the emotional characteristics of psychopathy. Actually, they may be the child's way of coping in a very stressful home environment (Seagrave & Grisso, 2002). Furthermore, "Some adolescent behavior may . . . appear psychopathic by way of poor anger control, lack of goals, and poor judgment, but is actually influenced by parallel developmental tasks encountered by most adolescents" (Seagrave & Grisso, 2002, p. 229). Going against the rules is part of many adolescents' attempts to gain autonomy from adult dominance, such as found in adolescent-limited offending. In addition, adult criminal psychopaths often have been psychologically scarred by years of drug and alcohol abuse, physical fighting, lost opportunities, and multiple incarcerations (Lynam, 1997). Consequently, adult psychopaths may present a very different population pool compared to the juvenile psychopath.

Edens, Skeem, et al. (2001) also point out that some of the items on the various psychological measures of psychopathy (especially the PCL-R and the PCL:YV) are inappropriate for use with adolescents. For example, some items focus on such things as the lack of goals and irresponsibility. If these features are not present, then the adolescent might receive scores in the psychopathy direction. However, adolescents generally have not crystallized their life goals and responsibilities to any great extent, and consequently such items "seem less applicable as definitive markers of psychopathy for adolescence than for adults" (Edens, Skeem, et al., 2001, p. 58). We must be careful, then, not to generalize what we know about the adult psychopath to a juvenile who has been given the same label.

Nevertheless, many researchers are persisting in their attempts to identify juvenile psychopaths and measure psychopathic tendencies. In a study examining the prevalence rate of psychopathy among children, Skilling, Quinsey, and Craig (2001) found in a sample of more than 1,000 boys in Grades 4 to 8 that 4.3% of the sample could be classified as psychopathic on every measure employed in the study. These data suggest that the percentages reported in the prison population may not be as inflated as some researchers suppose.

Lynam (1997) designed a research project that compared juvenile and adult psychopaths. Using the CPS, Lynam reported results that suggested that psychopathy begins in childhood and can be measured reliably in children ages 12 and 13. Lynam found that psychopathic children, like their adult counterparts, were the most aggressive, severe, frequent, and impulsive offenders, a characteristic that was stable across time. Moreover, he discovered that the CPS was a better predictor of serious delinquency than

socioeconomic status, previous delinquency, IQ, or impulsivity.

Research so far does indicate that there is some validity in measures of juvenile psychopathy (Edens, Skeem, et al., 2001; Kosson et al., 2002; Murrie & Cornell, 2002), but a vast majority of the researchers also believe that much more research needs to be done before forensic psychologists can make valid recommendations to the courts. Edens, Skeem, et al. (2001, p. 74) report that, although some researchers "have implied or asserted that assessments of psychopathy will aid in deciding whether to transfer juvenile offenders to the adult court system, whether to decertify adolescents already transferred to the adult system, and/or what type of sentence juveniles should receive, the research still has a way to go before forensic psychologists can confidently make such recommendations." In addition to the ethical issues discussed above, Edens, Skeem, et al. admonish that the extant research remains unclear as to whether juvenile psychopathy is related to persistent violence in adulthood or whether juvenile psychopathy is untreatable, as commonly supposed for adult psychopathy. Given the emphasis usually placed on the juvenile justice system on offender rehabilitation, the second point is especially important. Edens, Skeem, et al. conclude that "it is imperative that we learn more about the stability, nature, and manifestations of psychopathy during the adolescent years, and develop and refine age-appropriate risk assessment tools based on this knowledge" (p. 77).

The Female Psychopath

Similar to the research on juvenile psychopathy, very little research has been conducted on the extent to which psychopathy exists in females. There are few statistics on the ratio of male to female psychopaths, but it has been generally assumed that males far outnumber their female counterparts. Based on PCL-R data, Salekin, Rogers, and Sewell (1997) reported that the prevalence rate of psychopathy for female offenders in a jail setting was 15.5%, compared to a 25% to 30% prevalence rate estimated for men. In another study, Salekin, Rogers, Ustad, and Sewell (1998) found, using a PCL-R cutoff score of 29, that 12.9% of their sample of 78 female inmates qualified as psychopaths. In a more recent investigation involving 528 adult women incarcerated in Wisconsin, Vitale, Smith, Brinkley, and Newman (2002) reported that 9% of their participants could be classified as psychopaths, using the recommended cutoff score of 30 on the PCL-R. Because the known psychopathic population is dominated by men, little research has been directed at women, although both Hare and Cleckley included female psychopaths in some of their work. Nevertheless, Hare's PCL and PCL-R (Hare, 1980, 1991) have been developed almost exclusively on male criminal psychopaths. Some preliminary studies using the PCL-R suggest that female criminal psychopaths may demonstrate different behavioral patterns than male criminal psychopaths (Hare, 1991; Vitale et al., 2002).

There is some preliminary evidence that female psychopaths may be less aggressive and violent than male psychopaths (Mulder, Wells, Joyce, & Bushnell, 1994). Female psychopaths may also recidivate less often than male psychopaths (Salekin et al., 1998). In fact, the evidence suggests that psychopathic female inmates may have recidivism rates that are no different from the recidivism rates reported for nonpsychopathic female inmates (Salekin et al., 1998).

Recent research using the PCL-R shows considerable promise in identifying gender differences in psychopathy. Salekin et al. (1997) have found evidence of at least two broad categories of female psychopaths. One category appears to be characterized by a lack of empathy or guilt, interpersonal deception, sensation seeking, and proneness to boredom. The other group appears to be characterized by early behavioral problems, promiscuous sexual behavior, and adult antisocial (not violent) behavior. In recent years, we have seen a renewed interest in studying the female psychopath.

Racial/Ethnic Differences

Kosson, Smith, and Newman (1990) noticed that most measures of psychopathy have been developed using White inmates as subjects. In their research, they found that psychopathy, as measured by Hare's PCL (Hare, 1980), does exist in African American male inmates in a pattern that resembles White male inmates. However, Kosson et al. found one important difference. African American criminal psychopaths tended to be less impulsive than White criminal psychopaths. This finding raises some questions as to whether the PCL is entirely appropriate to use with African American inmates. On the other hand, Vitale et al. (2002) found no significant racial differences in the scores and distributions of female psychopaths. More specifically, Vitale et al. reported that 10% of the 248 incarcerated White women who participated in their study reached the cutoff scores of 30 or higher on the PCL-R compared to 9% of the 280 incarcerated African American women who had similar scores. A meta-analysis by Skeem, Edens, and Colwell (2003) supports the conclusion that the differences between Blacks and Whites are minimal. Questions remain, however, as to the potential differences among other minority or disadvantaged groups.

Some researchers, though, have raised the intriguing and serious issue of whether the stigmatizing diagnosis of psychopathy is likely to be used in a biased manner among minority or disadvantaged groups (Edens, Petrila, & Buffington-Vollum, 2001; Skeem, Edens, & Colwell, 2003; Skeem, Edens, Sanford, & Colwell, 2003). In essence, the consequence of being diagnosed a psychopath is becoming more serious (Skeem, Edens, Sanford, & Colwell, 2003). As pointed out by Skeem, Edens, and Colwell (2003), Canada and the United Kingdom use the diagnosis of psychopathy to support indeterminate detention for certain classes of offenders. Furthermore,

There is evidence that psychopathy increasingly is being used as an aggravating factor in the sentencing phase of US death penalty cases, where it has been argued that the presence of these personality traits renders a defendant a "continuing threat to society." (Skeem, Edens, & Colwell, 2003, p. 17)

And, as we learned in the juvenile psychopathy section, there is concern that a diagnosis of psychopathy may be used to justify decisions to transfer juvenile offenders to the adult criminal justice system, typically based on the assumption that psychopathy is untreatable. Therefore, any differences in psychopathy scores related to race, ethnicity, or age would raise significant criminal justice and public policy issues (Skeem, Edens, & Colwell, 2003). Edens, Petrila, & Buffington-Vollum (2001) suggest that perhaps the PCL-R should be excluded from capital sentencing until more solid research on its ability to predict future dangerousness in minority and disadvantaged individuals is established. It would be wise, therefore, for forensic psychologists to refrain from using diagnostic indicators of psychopathy at the sentencing phase until considerably more research is undertaken.

Summary and Conclusions

Criminal behavior involves an extremely wide range of human conduct and is committed by individuals of all ages and across all social classes. In this chapter, we have been concerned with that subset of criminal behavior that includes persistent, serious offending over time. Consequently, we have examined early origins of that offending by focusing on developmental factors associated with the antisocial acts of chronic juvenile offenders. In addition, we have examined offending patterns over the life span by focusing on the criminal psychopath.

As a group, juvenile offenders grow out of crime—which is to say, they do not grow up to become chronic adult offenders. From the statistics on juvenile arrests, it is impossible to tell how many different juveniles are involved (some are

arrested more than once) as well as which of these particular juveniles will become long-term offenders. We know from the research that a small percentage (5%–6%) of offenders is responsible for a large proportion of juvenile crime. We know also that chronic offenders do not specialize but rather are involved in a wide variety of offenses. Forensic psychologists attempt to identify those juveniles who are at risk of serious, chronic offending. They are also involved in providing treatment for these juveniles, a topic we will return to in Chapter 13.

In their attempts to identify juveniles at risk, many psychologists today have adopted developmental or cognitive approaches. Developmental studies—such as those conducted by Terrie Moffitt and her colleagues—suggest that differences in impulsivity, aggressiveness, social skills, and empathy for others can distinguish persistent from nonpersistent offenders. Moffitt's (1993a) dual-pathway hypothesis (LCP vs. AL offenders) has contributed significantly to theory development in this area. Most recently, though, Moffitt as well as other researchers suggest that more than two developmental pathways are needed.

The most recent developmental studies have identified such factors as early exposure to aggressive peers and rejection by peers as contributing to later antisocial conduct. Developmental theory also suggests that conduct disorders, differences in cognitive abilities, and ADHD all play a significant role in facilitating chronic antisocial behavior in children and adolescents. However, they certainly do not "cause" it. Although each of these correlates with delinquency, a cautionary note is necessary. "Deficiencies" in children may well be due to abuse, neglect, or lack of resources or understanding on the part of the adults in their lives. Focusing on behavioral problems in children without attending to their broader social systems is unwarranted.

The topic of school violence became salient after highly publicized school shootings in the 1990s. Although victimization in school is a problem, it must be kept in perspective. Studies show that serious school crime is declining and that children are safer in school than in many communities and, unfortunately, many homes. Nevertheless, forensic psychologists have been increasingly asked to conduct threat assessments when school officials are concerned that a particular student or students may pose a threat to others in the school.

We discussed in some detail the criminal psychopath, a designation that has been given to a significant minority of adults. Although it is estimated that only 1% of the total adult population would qualify as psychopathic, estimates of imprisoned psychopaths have reached 15% (although some believe these estimates are inflated). Psychopaths are problematic, not only because of their offending patterns but also because of their resistance to change. For this reason, a diagnosis of psychopathy may be the "kiss of death" at capital sentencing. A variety of instruments are offered to measure psychopathy,

the most widely known being Robert Hare's (1991) PCL-R. We noted that gender, race, and ethnicity differences in psychopathy are beginning to merit research attention.

Although there is debate over whether the concept of psychopathy can be applied to juveniles, efforts to develop instruments for measuring this construct are robust and ongoing. At this point, they are used only in research. However, the concept of juvenile psychopathy—*if such a construct exists*—may have important implications for the prevention of serious delinquency. It is not unlikely, therefore, that instruments to measure it will enter forensic practice in the near future. Nevertheless, as in the adult population, psychopathy is likely to be limited to a very small subset of juvenile offenders. Even so, the concerns expressed by many researchers should be very carefully considered. A psychopathic label placed on a juvenile may virtually guarantee his or her transfer to a criminal court.

CHAPTER 5

Psychology of Violence and Intimidation

Violence both terrifies and fascinates us. Although we are concerned about perceived increases in violent crime rates and fearful of becoming victims of violence, we also support images and depictions of violent activity in the entertainment media and often demand such details in the news media. Interestingly, violence is somewhat difficult to define precisely because it has so many meanings and conjures up such a broad spectrum of images (Newman, 1979). Moreover, it occurs in many situations and under a wide variety of conditions, and there are numerous explanations for why it occurs.

Violence is commonly defined as *physical force* exerted for the purpose of inflicting injury, pain, discomfort, or abuse on a person or persons or for the purpose of damaging or destroying property. Such physical force, however, may be condoned by society. We allow police to use reasonable force against an individual resisting arrest, a football player to tackle his opponent, a soldier to kill his enemy, and crime victims to protect themselves from serious bodily harm. It is the violence committed without justification that

we are concerned with in this chapter, specifically criminal violence.

It should be noted that *violence* and *aggression* are not interchangeable terms. Whereas **violence** involves physical force, **aggression** may or may not involve such force. Aggression can be defined as behavior perpetrated or attempted with the intention of harming another individual (or group of individuals) physically or psychologically (Bartol, 2002). A protester who blocks someone's entry into a facility is performing an aggressive act, not a violent act. Refusing to speak to someone who has insulted you in the past is an aggressive act, not a violent act. Thus, all violent behavior is aggressive behavior, but not all aggressive behavior is violent behavior. Although the concept of aggression has been studied extensively by psychologists, we are concerned primarily in this chapter with the subset that is violent behavior. Nevertheless, nonviolent aggression will also have its place, particularly when we discuss crimes of intimidation.

Two increasingly interconnected streams of research on violence have emerged in recent years. One research stream has examined the many characteristics and demographics of the individual violent offender; the other has examined the immediate contexts and environments in which violence most often occurs (Hawkins, 2003). Studies focusing on the former have examined the social, psychological, and biological factors in interpersonal offending. Studies on the latter tradition have examined family, peer, local community, and neighborhood effects on varying levels of violence. In recent years, each area of research has recognized the importance of the other. That is, researchers acknowledge that both individual factors and environmental influences must be taken into account in their efforts to understand violence. Research has shown, for example, that the relationships among racial/ethnic composition; feelings of anger, resentment, and frustration; and homicide rates are contingent—at least in part—on the level of economic deprivation, joblessness, drug use, and number of gangs within a given community (Johnson & Chanhatasilpa, 2003).

Forensic psychologists frequently encounter violence—as well as aggression in general—sometimes even on a daily basis. Their clients may threaten to harm others. They may be asked to assess the risk of violence in a given individual. They may themselves be placed at risk of violence. They may be offering psychological services to victims of violence. In a court setting, they may be asked to testify about the effects of violence on a victim of a crime or a plaintiff in a civil suit. Therefore, an understanding of the prevalence, the causes, and the effects of violence is critical for forensic psychologists. We will begin this chapter with data on violent crime, including information on gender and race/ethnic differences. This will be followed by a discussion of theoretical perspectives on violence offered by research psychologists. We then focus on the specific violent crimes of homicide and workplace violence. The chapter ends with a discussion of crimes of intimidation, which represent a form of aggression that may or may not result in violence but produce fear in their victims. The following chapter is devoted to another very disturbing violent crime, sexual assault.

UCR Data on Violent Crime

In the Uniform Crime Reports (UCR), four index crimes are classified as violent crimes: murder and nonnegligent manslaughter, forcible rape, robbery, and aggravated assault. Together, these crimes comprise the violent crime rate reported annually to the public. In addition, arrest data on the above crimes as well as the nonindex crime of simple assault are also provided. According to the UCR, aggravated assault accounts for the largest share of violent crimes known to police (approximately 63%), and murder accounts for the smallest share (approximately 1%) (see Figure 5.1). Personal weapons, such as hands, fists, and feet, were used in 31% of the violent crimes committed in 2001, firearms in 26%, and knives or cutting instruments in 15% of the incidents. Other dangerous weapons were used in the remaining 28% of violent offenses.

In 2001, the clearance (or solved) rate for murder was 62%. The clearance rates for aggravated assault, forcible rape, and robbery were 56%, 44%, and 25%, respectively. Nationally,

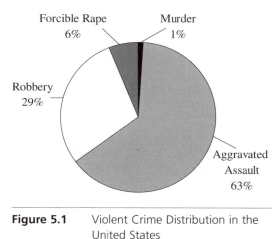

Figure 5.1   Violent Crime Distribution in the United States

Source: Federal Bureau of Investigation (2002a).

44% of total arrests for violent crime in 2001 were of persons younger than age 25, 29% were younger than age 21, and 15% were younger than age 18 (Federal Bureau of Investigation [FBI], 2002b).

The geography of violence is largely distributed across two locations—in the home and on the street. Until recently, much of the emphasis on stopping violent crimes has been directed at the more visible street crimes and less on violence within the homes. Street crimes are far more likely to come to the attention of police and thus more likely to be represented in official statistics. However, women and children are more likely to be harmed by violence in their homes and by people they know than by strangers on the street. Thus, both researchers and law enforcement officials have given increasing attention to studying, preventing, and responding to this category of violent crime. We will address this issue more completely in Chapters 7 and 8, in which we discuss the effects of violent crime on its victims.

Gender, Race, and Ethnic Differences in Criminal Violence

UCR data consistently indicate that males account for 87% to 90% of total arrests for violent crimes in any given year. Males account for about 90% of the annual arrests for murder, females the remaining 10% (FBI, 2002b). This ratio is characteristic of other countries as well (Bartol, 2002). Arrest rates for aggravated assault are slightly different, showing a ratio of 80% male and 20% female. Although women's violent crime rate increased faster than the men's rate for a brief period in the mid-1990s, women continue to be far underrepresented in the violent crime statistics. The two dominant explanations for the gender discrepancies in violent offending are (1) socialization factors (women are less likely

than men to be encouraged to be violent) and (2) biological factors (some researchers have linked the male hormone testosterone to aggression). Women also are said to have less opportunity to commit the violent street crimes that come to the attention of police. Thus, some theorists have suggested that violence perpetrated by women may go undetected and unreported because it is more likely to occur in the privacy of the home. Even if this were so, it would be unlikely to narrow the gender gap in violent offending because much male violence in the home also goes undetected and unreported.

Although gender differences in violent offending have garnered some interest, it is racial and ethnic differences that have produced the most commentary. Race differences in crime and violence remain emotionally and politically charged and divisive topics in the United States and in many other societies around the world (Hawkins, 2003). National surveys conducted in the United States, for example, suggest that a majority of White respondents believe Blacks and Latinos are more prone (innately and culturally) to violence than Whites or Asians (Bobo & Kluegel, 1997). These beliefs demonstrate the continual existence of persisting racial stereotypes as misguided explanations of criminal violence in this country.

Official crime data can be partly blamed for perpetrating these stereotypes. According to these data, African Americans in the United States are involved in criminal homicide and other forms of violence at a rate that far exceeds their numbers in the general population. For example, although African Americans make up about 12% of the U.S. population, they accounted for more than 50% of all arrests for violent crimes in 2001 (FBI, 2002b). These figures probably reflect social inequalities, such as lack of employment and educational opportunities, racial oppression in its many forms, discriminatory treatment at the hands of the criminal justice system, and law enforcement practices in inner-city areas where many African Americans reside. It is extremely important to emphasize that race or ethnic differences in violent crime are not due to genetic or biological factors, such as racial differences in innate aggressive traits. As we shall see shortly, researchers have explored and sometimes uncovered links between biology and aggression, but these links are not racially or ethnically related.

Latinos are now projected to become the largest ethnic minority group in the United States within the next few years. More specifically, the Latino population in the United States more than doubled between 1980 and 2000, from 14.5 million to an estimated 35.3 million. The Latino population currently equals the African American population as the largest ethnic minority group (Martinez, 2002). A large proportion of this Latino population growth is due to a rise in the number of recent immigrants. Empirical research on Latino crime is surprisingly scarce (Martinez, 2003). However, we would expect the crime rates within the Latino communities (barrios) to be high because more than a third of all Latinos are younger than 18 years of age, many if not most are high school dropouts, and this population is generally at high risk for violent crime. Martinez (2002) writes,

All of the ingredients are present for an epidemic of Latino youth violence—their parents are poor, and these youth face a national backlash, are singled out for discrimination, compete for low-paying jobs with other ethnic minorities, and reside in impoverished areas often shaped by drugs and gangs, at least in the popular media's imagination. (p. 5)

Some preliminary data, however, suggest that the Latino violence rate falls significantly *below* the rates found for economically deprived African American and White communities (Martinez, 2002; Reidel, 2003). Martinez (2002) attributes these findings partly to the fact that Latinos generally have high rates of labor

force participation—despite being traditionally characterized as the working poor—and have close and highly supportive ties to the local community and family. Although there are many influences that play a role, this labor-relationship pattern probably reduces violent crime involvement and criminal activity in general. Still, much more research needs to be undertaken before meaningful conclusions about the relationship between violence and Latino ethnicity can be advanced.

Interestingly, research findings from industrialized nations across the globe do not lend themselves to simple explanations for the different rates of violence among groups, cultures, or subcultures. "Group differences in rates of crime and violence observed in those areas of the world do not appear to be easily explained by traditional notions of minority versus majority, white versus nonwhite, and possibly economically disadvantaged versus advantaged" (Hawkins, 2003, p. xxiii). After years of research into the many causes of crime, Farrington, Loeber, and Stouthamer-Loeber (2003) were forced to conclude the following in reference to the overrepresentation of violent Black crime:

We are left with [the] conundrum of why African-American boys are more violent. . . . The challenge for future researchers is twofold: to explain the remainder of the racial difference in behavior, and to explain the even greater disproportionateness in official violence. (p. 237)

We must be careful not to focus exclusively on any one racial or ethnic group, however, to the exclusion of others. Although great attention has been paid to the street crimes of African American males, the research microscope has ignored other groups. There is an indication, for example, that intimate partner and family violence may be far more prevalent among Asian Americans than among other ethnic groups. In the National Violence Against Women Survey conducted in

1999, 25% of Asian women indicated they had been physically or sexually assaulted by family members or intimates (Lee, 2002). Overall, many puzzles remain in any attempts to explain the ethnic and racial distribution of violence and its changes over time (Hawkins, 2003).

Much more research needs to be conducted on ethnic minorities and crime across a variety of settings and environments. Using simple dichotomies such as Black, Latino/Hispanic, Asian, Native American, Muslim, and White does not truly capture the multiethnic mixture characteristics of communities across the nation. Cultures and subcultures are complex and psychologically rich, and meaningful research investigations on ethnic/minority differences in violence require a deep appreciation of this complexity. Practicing forensic psychologists must become highly knowledgeable about the beliefs, attitudes, values, traditions, and expected behaviors of each ethnic/minority group or subculture with which they interact if they are to be effective and helpful to offenders and their victims. *Ethnocentrism,* or viewing others strictly through one's own cultural perspectives, often encourages people—including mental health professionals— to form stereotypes and biases that limit their ability to assess and treat those from diverse backgrounds (Feindler, Rathus, & Silver, 2003). An understanding of violence involves an examination of the demands and expectations that cultures place on people, especially the poor, the oppressed, and the disenfranchised.

Theoretical Perspectives on Violence

Criminal violence can be classified along several continuums. For example, one continuum can represent the amount of planning involved in the act. At one pole, the act is highly calculated and planned (cold-blooded), but at the other pole, the act can be characterized as highly impulsive and emotionally driven behavior with virtually no

planning (e.g., crimes of passion). In psychological literature, violence may represent different forms of aggression, ranging from instrumental aggression to reactive aggression, with equal elements of both occurring at the middle sections of the continuum. **Instrumental violence** "occurs when the injury of an individual is secondary to the acquisition of some other external goal" (Woodworth & Porter, 2002, p. 437). The external goal may be money, status, security, or material goods. **Reactive violence**—also called expressive violence—refers to physical violence precipitated by a hostile and angry reaction to a perceived threat or dangerous situation. Reactive violence, therefore, "is often the impulsive and unthoughtful response to a provocation, real or imagined" (American Psychological Association, 1996, p. 8). An angry person who "flies off the handle" and shoots a friend over a petty argument represents an obvious example. More often than not, the aggressor—once the emotions calm down—cannot believe what he did or understand how he could lose control to that level. In many cases, though, it is difficult to clearly differentiate whether the violence is instrumental or reactive—it appears to include some mixture of both instrumental and reactive factors. Consequently, violent actions often fall in the middle ranges of the instrumental-reactive continuum, similar to what is found in the normal curve (see Figure 5.2).

An interesting question emerges when we examine these two polar opposites on the violence continuum in reference to the criminal

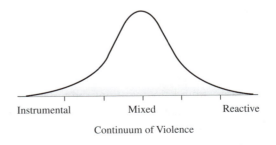

Instrumental   Mixed   Reactive

Continuum of Violence

Figure 5.2   Continuum of Violence

psychopaths discussed in Chapter 4. Are they more likely to commit instrumental or reactive forms of violence? Recall that psychopaths demonstrate a lack of empathy or remorse and shallow emotions in general. However, they are also impulsive and highly reactive to provocative situations. Woodworth and Porter (2002) have initiated some research into this area by studying both psychopathic and nonpsychopathic offenders who committed homicide. According to Woodworth and Porter, psychopaths tend to engage in the more instrumental, goal-driven (e.g., to obtain money or drugs) homicides, whereas nonpsychopathic offenders engage in predominately reactive, spontaneous violence (e.g., in the context of a heated argument). Psychopaths who murdered were primarily motivated to advance their own cause and exhibited little empathy or concern for their victims. Woodworth and Porter were surprised, though, at the overall level of instrumental violence characterizing *all* homicides, whether committed by psychopaths or nonpsychopaths. The majority of the offenders did not simply "snap" and kill their victims in an uncontrollable emotional rage. The researchers suggest that future research should examine whether the results might generalize to other types of criminal violence, offenders, and subcultures.

The Causes of Violence

The causes of violence are multiple. The psychological literature usually divides these causes into four highly overlapping categories: (1) biological, (2) socialization, (3) cognitive, and (4) situational factors.

The *biological factors* refer to the wide array of neurological, physiological, or chemical influences on aggression and violence. Recent advances in the neurosciences have revealed that biological factors, interacting with the social environment, may have some significant influences on child development. The exact nature of these influences remains largely unknown. Child development researchers have found links between aggression and brain damage resulting from a variety of environmental factors. These include (1) toxic materials found in the environment (e.g., lead paint), (2) traumatic head injury (e.g., as the result of child abuse or accident), (3) dietary deficiencies (especially prenatal), (4) alcohol and drug ingestion by the mother during critical fetal developmental stages, and (5) birth trauma. Once the deficits occur, attempts to remove or remedy the biological cause may include active biological treatment in the form of medication. However, and more important, a supportive and competent social environment has also been found to neutralize or reduce the effects that these biological factors exert on any propensity toward violence.

Socialization factors refer to those processes through which a person learns patterns of thinking, behavior, and feeling from his or her early life experiences (American Psychological Association, 1996). More specifically, "Scientists use the term socialization to describe the process by which a child learns the 'scripts' for specific social behavior, along with the rules, attitudes, values, and norms that guide interactions with others" (American Psychological Association, 1996, p. 3). Furthermore, children can learn as much from observing significant or admired others in their environment as from their own experiences. Considerable research indicates that aggressive, antisocial, and violent behaviors are often learned from significant others (including TV, movie, or fictional characters) and are held in reserve for response to specific social situations.

Cognitive factors refer to the ideas, beliefs, and patterns of thinking that emerge as a result of interactions with the world during a person's lifetime. Research has revealed that violent individuals have different ways of processing information and interpreting that information. "They tend to perceive hostility in others when there is no hostility" (American Psychological Association, 1996, p. 5). As the reader may recall from Chapter 4, this notable tendency is referred to as *hostile attribution bias*. Violent people are also less efficient at thinking of nonviolent ways to solve social conflicts and disagreements. They also tend to be more accepting of violence and believe it is acceptable to behave that way. Some young males—especially members of violent groups or gangs—have adopted the belief that it is acceptable to react to every perceived or imagined sign of disrespect with aggression. Aggressive children and adolescents have more antisocial, violent beliefs than their nonaggressive peers (Shahinfar, Kupersmidt, & Matza, 2001).

Situational factors refer to the characteristics of the environment, such as stress or aggression in others, that encourage or engender violent behavior. As pointed out by many researchers, "Often we seek the causes of violence in the person and ignore the contributing effects of the situation" (American Psychological Association, 1996, p. 6). Almost any aversive situation—such as continuous loud noise, unpleasant smells, and crowded, unpleasant living conditions—can provoke aggression and violence in those persons submitted to such conditions. Neighborhoods, schools, family, and peers can all be conducive to the development of violent behavior. The presence of weapons increases the chances that the conflict will occur in the first place and that it will have lethal consequences once it does occur.

It is also clear that children who grow up in deprived environments where poverty, frustration, and hopelessness are prevalent are at much greater risk of later involvement in violence than other children. Childhood aggression can predict adult violence in some individuals. Research has discovered that approximately 10% of highly aggressive children grow up to account for 50% to 60% of the majority of violent crimes (Bartol, 2002). During their childhood, these individuals exhibit aggression, disobedience, and disruptions at home and in the school; are disliked and avoided by peers; are neglected by parents and teachers; and are likely to fail in school, eventually dropping out. Unsupervised and susceptible to

the pernicious influence of other delinquent youth, they grow up to be antisocial, aggressive, and violent young adults. They are likely to become involved in abusive spousal relationships, and they often abuse their own children. But not every child growing up under these conditions follows this destructive path, and the example of such children has provided valuable insights into how to design prevention programs.

Despite the complexity and multitude of causes, human violence is ultimately a learned behavior. And because it is learned, it can be unlearned or altered, or conditions can be changed so that it is not learned in the first place. Furthermore, violence is a behavior that is acquired early in life—in many cases, *very* early in life, as we saw in Chapter 4. Consequently, prevention of violence should likewise begin very early in life.

The Effects of Violent Media

Over the past 40 years, a significant amount of research literature has strongly supported the observation that media violence viewing is one factor contributing to the development of aggression and violence (Huesmann, Moise-Titus, Podolski, & Eron, 2003). The majority of the research has focused on the effects of watching dramatic violence on TV and film. A wide variety of research projects have continually arrived at the same fundamental conclusion: Exposure to dramatic violence on TV and in the movies is related to violent behavior.

In addition to the hundreds of research findings, three major national studies have concluded that *heavy* exposure to televised violence is one of the most significant causes of violence in society (American Psychological Association, 2003c). They are the Surgeon General's Commission Report (1972), the National Institute of Mental Health's Ten-Year Follow-Up (1982), and the American Psychological Association's Task Force on Television in Society (1992). According to the

APA, these reports indicate that viewing a steady diet of violence on the screen has the following negative effects (American Psychological Association, 2003c):

- It increases the viewer's fear of becoming a victim, with a corresponding increase in self-protective behaviors and increased distrust of others.
- It desensitizes the viewer to violence. That is, viewers often become less sensitive to the pain and suffering of others.
- It encourages some individuals to become more involved in violent actions.
- It demonstrates how desired goods and services can be obtained through the use of aggression and violence.
- Sexual violence in X- and R-rated video-tapes has been shown to increase sexual aggression in some males.

It is important to distinguish between short-term and long-term effects of media on aggressive behavior and violence. Long-term effects occur as a result of learning and storing violent and aggressive material into the cognitive system that eventually "crystallizes" and is difficult to change as the child gets older. Young children are especially open to new learning, and these early experiences often have a greater impact during the early developmental years than learning events that occur during adulthood. Moreover, "In recent theorizing, long-term relations have been ascribed mainly to acquisition through observational learning of three social-cognitive structures: schemas about a hostile world, scripts for social problem solving that focus on aggression, and normative beliefs that aggression is acceptable" (Huesmann et al., 2003, p. 201). **Observational learning** refers to the very strong tendency of human beings to imitate any significant or admired person or model they observe. Children are especially prone to do this. Consequently, observation of specific aggressive behaviors around them increases children's likelihood of behaving exactly that way. Over time

and with frequent exposure to aggressive behavior, children develop beliefs (schemas) that the world is basically a hostile place, that aggression is an acceptable social behavior, and that the best way to solve conflicts and to get things is to be aggressive.

Huesmann and his colleagues (2003) found strong long-term effects of media violence observed in early childhood that carried over into adulthood:

> Overall, these results suggest that both males and females from all social strata and all levels of initial aggressiveness are placed at increased risk for the development of adult aggressive and violent behavior when they view a high and steady diet of violent TV shows in early childhood. (p. 218)

Media violence encourages, stimulates, and reinforces aggressive behavior. Furthermore, aggressive children tend to enjoy aggressive media. Huesmann et al. (2003) suggest that "aggressive children feel happier and more justi-fied if they believe they are not alone in their aggression, and view media violence to make them feel happier because it convinces them that they are not alone" (p. 202). Huesmann et al. also posit that media violence appears to have *short-term* effects on adults, but the real *long-term* effects seem to occur only with children. The effects not only are found in already violence-prone children but also affect almost all children.

In addition, the Huesmann et al. (2003) study found that violent films and TV programs that have the most deleterious effects on children are not always the ones that adults and critics per-ceive as most violent. What type of scene is the most deleterious to children? "It is one in which the child identifies with the perpetrator of the violence, the child perceives the scene as telling about life like it is, and the perpetrator is rewarded for the violence" (Huesmann et al., 2003, p. 218). In other words, violent media that portray an admired perpetrator as successful through the use of violence appear to have a greater impact on the child's observational learning of aggression and violence over the long haul. The researchers suggest that the easiest way to reduce the effects of media violence on children is to restrict children's exposure to such violence. The persons in the best position to do this, particularly with young children, are parents or caretakers.

Violent Video Games

The effect of violent video games on violence became a serious topic for study after a series of school shootings that occurred during the late 1990s. The shooters were often students who habitually played violent video games. For example, Eric Harris and Dylan Klebold, the Columbine (Colorado) High School students who murdered 13 persons and wounded 23 before killing themselves, were fascinated with the bloody video game *Doom*, the earliest and most successful of all violent video games. "Harris created a customized version of Doom with two shooters, extra weapons, unlimited ammunition, and victims could not fight back—features that are eerily similar to aspects of the actual shootings" (Anderson & Bushman, 2001, p. 353).

Recent research also suggests that violent video games increase or encourage aggressive behavior not only in children but also in young adults (Anderson & Bushman, 2001). Experimental and nonexperimental studies with males and females support this conclusion. Analyses further reveal that exposure to violent video games increases aggression-related thoughts and feelings and decreases prosocial behavior (Anderson & Bushman, 2001). The long-term effect of heavy exposure to violent video games over the course of a person's life remains unknown at this time. It is, however, probably similar in its effects on children and adolescents as reported for violent TV and films. Still, we must be careful not to make a quick cause-and-effect conclusion on the effects of violent video games until all the evidence is in. It may be that

certain violent-prone individuals are drawn to violent video games and will demonstrate violent actions regardless of the amount of exposure to violent video games they experience.

Criminal Homicide

Homicide is the killing of one person by another. **Criminal homicide** is causing the death of another person without legal justification or excuse. The criminal law recognizes two major levels of criminal homicide, murder and manslaughter. **Murder** is reserved for the "unlawful killing of one human by another with malice aforethought, either expressed or implied" (Black, 1990, p. 1019). **Manslaughter** refers to an *unintended* killing that results from *unjustifiable* conduct that places others at risk (Morawetz, 2002). The individual who aimlessly fires a loaded weapon, even if he or she does not "intend" to kill anyone, is still responsible for that person's death if the victim happens to be in his or her path. Manslaughter also includes an *intended* killing "for which there is mitigation, acts that are provoked by the victim, or that result from temporary and understandable circumstances that compromise the actor's normal responsibility" (Morawetz, 2002, p. 398). For example, a father who comes upon a car accident, discovers that his daughter has been killed, and chokes to death the inebriated driver of the car that hit her would likely be charged with nonnegligent manslaughter, not murder. Most states have additional gradations in their homicide statutes, depending on the level of seriousness. First-degree murder, for instance, is usually considered a capital offense, punishable by death or life in prison. The UCR include both murder and "nonnegligent" manslaughter under the term *criminal homicide* for reporting purposes.

According to the UCR, approximately 15,980 persons were murder victims in 2001 (FBI, 2002b). The murder rate in the nation during that year was 5.6 murders for every 100,000 inhabitants. The murder trend in the United

States has decreased over the past decade. More specifically, the 2001 murder rate represents a 12.2% decrease from the 1997 rate and a 32.7% drop from the 1992 rate. The murder rate as reported in the UCR is based solely on police investigations as opposed to the determination of a court, medical examiner, coroner, jury, or other judicial body. In other words, the UCR provides data on the homicides known to police and—if solved—on the persons arrested. It does not tell us whether the persons arrested were convicted. Not included in the UCR murder statistics are deaths police believe were caused by negligence, suicide, accidents, or justifiable homicide.

During 2001, UCR contributing agencies submitted supplemental information concerning 13,752 homicides. The Supplementary Homicide Report (SHR) collects data on the age, sex, and race of both the victim and the offender; the type of weapon used, the relationship of the victim to the offender; and circumstances surrounding the incident. The circumstances are listed in Table 8.1 in Chapter 8. The relationship of the victim to the offender will also be reported in Chapter 8, which deals with violent victimology.

Criminal homicide, like sexual assault, is a heterogeneous phenomenon, associated with different contexts, motivations, and types of offenders (Woodworth & Porter, 2002). Consequently, any attempt to make broad generalizations about people who commit criminal homicide—particularly murder—is risky. Nevertheless, researchers have drawn tentative conclusions about the types of individuals who commit this ultimate violent act. Most murders are single-incident offenses involving only one victim—and murderers generally do not commit another murder, even after release from prison. The "typical murder" is committed either during the course of committing another offense—most particularly a robbery—or is perpetrated against an intimate or an acquaintance. The "typical murder" also is committed during early adulthood, between the ages of 18 and 25.

An unknown number of murderers kill themselves after they have committed their crimes—typically very shortly thereafter and in the same location. The clinical characteristics of homicide-suicide are similar across the globe. Perpetrators of homicide-suicide are mostly men (95% in the United States), and the homicide victims are usually women (85% in the United States) (Hillbrand, 2001). In a majority of cases, the offender and victim(s) are relatives. Most cases involve one killer and one victim (90%). Despair, hopelessness, and depression are common among perpetrators; in fact, the clinical or psychological characteristics are more typical of suicide than homicide. For example, there is no lifelong pattern of impulsivity or violence.

A distinct form of homicide-suicide involves politically motivated terrorists who commit acts such as suicide bombings. In such incidents, a single terrorist may strap himself or herself with explosives that are later detonated at targeted locations. Otherwise, as in the September 11, 2001, bombing of the World Trade Center and the Pentagon, these may be perpetrated by individuals acting in small groups. Individuals who commit homicide-suicide, whether or not politically motivated, seldom utter threats or give warnings of the impending killings.

It is the atypical murder such as the homicide-suicide that holds the most fascination for the public as well as the greatest amount of psychological attention, although the attention does not rise to the level of hard empirical data. Forensic psychologists are also most likely to consult with reference to the atypical murder. A psychologist may be asked, for example, for a profile of a serial killer or asked to assess the risk that he will strike again within a given locality. Consequently, in the following sections, we devote more coverage to these atypical crimes. It should be noted, though, that the topic of single or typical murders reoccurs in Chapters 7 and 8, when we discuss the effects of violent crime on victims. Persons whose loved ones have been murdered or who themselves have survived an attempt to kill them often seek the help of forensic psychologists and other clinicians in coping with their traumatic experiences.

Multiple Murder

Multiple murder (also called multicide) is usually divided into three somewhat overlapping major offending patterns based on the timing of the act. **Serial murder** usually refers to incidents in which an individual (or individuals) separately kills a number of individuals (usually a minimum of three) over time. The time interval—sometimes referred to as the "cooling-off" period—may be days or weeks but more likely months or years. **Spree murder** normally refers to the killing of three or more individuals *without* a cooling-off period, usually at two or three different locations. A convenience store robber who kills some individuals at the store and kills a number of others during a countywide chase would be an example of a spree murderer. A classic example is illustrated by Charles Starkweather. In 1958, 19-year-old Starkweather went on an 8-day killing spree in Nebraska during which he and his 14-year-old girlfriend, Caril Ann Fugate, murdered 10 persons, including her parents. Starkweather was executed by electric chair on June 25, 1959, and Fugate was sentenced to life in prison. She was paroled in 1977. The Starkweather episode formed the basis for several movies, including Oliver Stone's 1994 film *Natural Born Killers*. Compared with serial and mass murderers, spree murderers have received very little research attention and will not be discussed in detail below.

Mass murder involves the killing of three or more persons at a single location with *no* cooling-off period between the killings. The FBI identifies two types of mass murder: classic and family. An example of a classic mass murder is when an individual barricades himself inside a public building, such as a fast-food restaurant, randomly killing the patrons and any other persons he has contact with. This very scenario occurred in 1991, when George Hennard smashed his pickup truck through a restaurant window in Killeen, Texas, and fired on a lunch-time crowd with two semiautomatic handguns. He killed 22 people and then killed himself. In a family mass murder—by far the more common of the two—at least three family members are killed by another family member or relative. Very often, the perpetrator kills himself (or herself), so family mass murders often also illustrate homicide-suicides.

What the public knows about multiple murder is largely based on misinformation and myth. The more sensational aspects of serial murder, for example, associate it with sexual sadists who prey on strangers to satisfy sexual fantasies.

Violent serial crime is a topic that is, almost by its nature, prone to sensationalism. To say that the violent serial offender holds a certain amount of fascination for the public would be a tremendous understatement, as evidenced by the numerous books, movies, television dramas, and documentaries that are produced each year on the subject. (Petee & Jarvis, 2000, p. 211)

Researchers and scholars do not seem immune to the alluring features of multiple murder either. Fox and Levin (1998) have observed that the scholarly accounts are too often based on media sources or unstructured interviews with convicted offenders: "Indeed, the ratio of scholarly books to research articles is unusually high, reflecting an abundance of speculation and a paucity of hard data" (pp. 409–410). It is with this caveat in mind that we review the following information.

What little empirical research on multiple murder has been conducted has occurred within the past 20 years, largely in response to high-profile multiple homicide incidents, such as the serial offenders David Berkowitz ("Son of Sam"), Ted Bundy, Robert Yates, John Wayne Gacy, Donald Harvey, Jeffrey Dahmer, and Gary Ridgway. Ridgway, known as the "Green River Killer," pleaded guilty in November 2003 to the murders of 48 women, more than any other serial killer in U.S. history to date. In the past, researchers and criminologists have assumed that multiple murderers were basically similar to single-victim offenders and consequently did not require special study. Recent research, however, has revealed that multiple murder does involve different motivations, victims, demographics, and psychological features that differentiate much of it from the more ordinary single-victim homicide.

The considerable variation in the behavioral, emotional, and cognitive features of multiple murderers has prompted some researchers (Holmes & DeBurger, 1988; Holmes & Holmes, 1998; Ressler et al., 1988) to develop typologies or classification systems that allow some appreciation of the complexity of the crime. We will cover one of these typologies later in the chapter.

Although multiple murders receive considerable media attention because of their drama and sensationalism, they are statistically rare occurrences. The frequent onslaught of violence and multiple murder in the entertainment media eventually develops the impression that these incidents are much more frequent than they actually are. When multiple murders actually do occur, news media depict repetitive, graphic, and dramatic accounts of the violence. The normal cognitive reaction of people watching is to store the vivid details and then have these details ready at the "top of their mind" for future references. The result of this process is the public's tendency to conclude that violence and multiple murders are dramatically increasing when they really are not. This phenomenon is called the **availability heuristic** and is based on the observation that humans prefer cognitive simplicity and are often strongly influenced by what they see and hear most often and most recently. Mass and serial murders *seem* to be on the increase in the United States because accounts in the media are readily available. However, a careful review of the data simply does not lend support to this perspective. Even if statistics sometimes indicate that serial murders have increased, this apparent increase may be due to better communication and computer systems between state and federal law enforcement agencies over the past 20 years. For example, the **Violent Criminal Apprehension Program** (ViCAP) (see Box 5.1) is designed to communicate with and help the nation's law enforcement agencies to investigate, identify, track, apprehend, and prosecute violent serial offenders.

BOX 5.1   VICAP: Sharing Data to Solve Violent Crime

ViCAP—the Violent Criminal Apprehension Program—is an FBI-sponsored data information center for crimes of violence, particularly murder. Law enforcement officials across the United States are able to enter information on solved cases into the database, as well as request the FBI's assistance in solving particularly difficult cases. The cases examined by ViCAP include the following:

- solved or unsolved homicides or attempts, especially those that (1) involve an abduction; (2) are apparently random, motiveless, or sexually oriented; or (3) are known or suspected to be part of a series;
- missing persons, in which the circumstances indicate a strong possibility of foul play and the victim is still missing; and
- unidentified dead bodies, in which the manner of death is known or is suspected to be homicide.

As cases are entered into the database, they are compared continually against all other cases to detect signature aspects of homicide—such as a note left at the scene—and similar patterns

(Continued)

BOX 5.1 (Continued)

(e.g., victim's age, season of the year). If ViCAP analysts detect similar patterns, as they would in the case of serial murder, the law enforcement agencies involved are notified. ViCAP can then assist agencies in coordinating an investigation, such as obtaining search warrants and conducting laboratory tests.

The FBI refers to ViCAP as a "timeless tool" because it carries information from many years back. For example, in 1989, Pennsylvania law enforcement officers entered a case that had been solved in 1951 in which a man had murdered a young girl. Shortly after that, Illinois law enforcement officers entered an unsolved murder case from 1957, also involving the death of a young girl. ViCAP analysts noticed similarities in the two cases, allowing Illinois investigators to solve the murder in their state after nearly 40 years.

Source: Federal Bureau of Investigation, 2000. Available: www.fbi.gov/programs/vicap/vicap.htm

---

Serial Killers

Despite the extensive commentary and media interest, there has been surprisingly little empirical research on serial murder. Most of the scientific research is limited to archival research or case studies. "The literature on serial murder is largely the product of broad-based descriptive study of large numbers of cases of serial killers or the result of individual case studies" (Skrapec, 2001, p. 46). Consequently, most of the following information will be descriptive in nature, and the identification of motives will be largely based on the self-reports provided by the killers themselves. Self-reports, although informative, are not the most objective measures available. They provide only information pertaining to what offenders want to reveal. Before we discuss serial killers, though, it is important to keep in mind a very useful statement noted by Candice Skrapec (2001, p. 52) from the work of Kluckhohn and Murray (1953, p. 53). To paraphrase, every human is, in certain respects, (a) like all other humans, (b) like some other humans, and (c) like no other human. That is, there are many characteristics of serial killers that are common to everyone, there are *some* identifiable commonalities between serial killers, and then there are a few significant differences.

What does a serial killer look like? Physically, serial killers can be placed on a continuum, with Theodore Bundy, the handsome, charming, intelligent law student who brutally killed dozens of women, at one pole, to Arthur Shawcross, the dour, rumpled, aging serial killer of prostitutes in the Rochester, New York, area at the other pole. There is no one identifiable serial killer type based on physical appearance, social class, or personality attributes.

Serial killers have many of the same personality traits or behavioral features as the general public. However, the one trait that appears to separate them from the norm is their exceptional interpersonal skill in their presentation of self (Fox & Levin, 1998). Their ability to charm and "fool" others often elevates them beyond suspicion and makes them difficult to apprehend. This may explain why victims allow serial killers into their homes or go willingly with them on dates or other engagements. In reference to this issue, Joseph Fisher (1997) describes a serial killer who held two communities in constant fear for several months. He writes,

Perhaps most unsettling for the community was the behavior of the victims; some of whom were reported to have gone willingly with their killer even though they may have known what lay ahead. This blind trust and the killer's exploitation of that trust seemed to have an eerie, supernatural quality. (pp. xiii-xiv)

It is a mistake to assume that serial murderers are seriously mentally disordered in the clinical sense of that term. Some are, but most are not. Although their thought patterns may be considered to be extremely aberrant when it comes to sensitivity and concern for other human beings, a vast majority of serial killers fail to qualify as psychotic or "crazy" in the traditional diagnostic categories of mental disorders. Serial killers have developed versions of the world characterized by values, beliefs, perceptions, and general cognitive processes that facilitate repetitive murder, often in a brutal, demeaning, and cold-blooded manner. They are drawn to committing murders that draw interest and send spine-chilling fear into the community, and their motives appear incomprehensible to the general public. The motives of many serial killers seem to be based on psychological rewards of control, domination, media attention, and excitement rather than material gain. But the labels "sick," "crazy," or "psychotic" explain little and offer little hope in the quest for understanding the processes in the development of this behavior.

Unlike the typical single-victim murderer who commits the homicide in early adulthood, serial murderers generally begin their careers of repetitive homicide at a relatively late age, usually in their late 20s or early 30s. Jenkins (1988) concludes that most begin their killings between the ages of 24 and 40, and Holmes and Holmes (1998) report that most known serial killers are between the ages of 25 and 35. The National Center for the Analysis of Violent Crime (NCAVC) reports that the average age of serial killers at the time of their first murder is 27.51 years and at their last murder 32.11 years. The age of their victims, on the other hand, varies widely, ranging from infants to the very old. Arthur Shawcross, for example, murdered at least 11 adults, but his first two victims were children.

Although some serial killers have extensive police records, the records mainly reflect a series of petty theft, embezzlement, and forgery rather than a history of violence (Jenkins, 1988). Single-victim homicide often involves family, intimates, or acquaintances, whereas serial murder most often involves strangers, especially if the offender is male. Female serial murderers present a different story, however, because they most often murder those with whom they share a relationship such as husbands, intimates, and acquaintances.

An examination of the victim selection of known male serial murderers will reveal that they prefer victims offering easy access and transience. Often their disappearance is not reported to police. For example, victims are often prostitutes, runaways, young male drifters, and itinerant farm workers whose families and friends may not immediately realize that they are missing. With experience, improving skills, and a need for greater challenge, serial killers often move to more difficult victims, such as university or college students, children, the elderly, or the solitary poor. Very rarely do serial murderers break in and terrorize, torture, and kill middle-class strangers in their homes.

The geographic location preferred by serial killers most often tends to be a specific location. For some unknown reason, serial murderers seldom kill victims in the communities where they (the murderers) were born. They do, however, often select victims near their *current* residence or place of work. Hickey (1997) estimates, for example, that 14% of serial killers use their homes or workplaces as the preferred location, whereas another 52% commit their murder in the same general location or area, such as the same neighborhood or city. This tendency suggests that geographical profiling may be an invaluable aid in the identification of serial murderers. However, this still leaves more than 30% of offenders who apparently commit crime across a much wider geographical area.

Serial killers are primarily males, and they often have a preference for one gender over the other. Jeffrey Dahmer, for instance, murdered at least 17 young males in Wisconsin and Ohio during the early 1990s. Dahmer drugged, strangled, dismembered, and, in some cases, consumed the flesh of his victims. John Wayne Gacy sexually assaulted and killed at least 33 boys in Illinois during the 1970s. He buried most of his victims in the dirt basement of his house. Robert Yates, on the other hand, murdered at least 17 prostitutes and homeless women in the state of Washington during the 1990s. Gary Ridgway targeted women in the Seattle area during the 1980s and 1990s, mainly runaways and prostitutes.

According to Hickey (1997), approximately 20% of serial killers are Black. Research data on Latino and other minority sex killers are virtually nonexistent. The incomplete data on ethnic/racial distribution of serial killers probably rest in part on how serial murder is identified and investigated. For example, law enforcement agencies may be less likely to investigate African American victims as casualties of serial murder if they are found in a rundown apartment complex located in a crime-infested neighborhood. Under these circumstances, law enforcement officials are more likely to conclude that the victim is simply another fatality—perhaps due to drug trafficking—in a high-violence crime area.

A serial murderer may choose his victims because they hold profound meaning for him in the terms of his life experiences (Skrapec, 2001). Interviews and descriptions of serial killers suggest that one of the dominant motives for their behavior is the power and control over another person's life that the crime offers them. "For these killers, murder is a form of expressive, rather than instrumental, violence" (Fox & Levin, 1998, p. 415). In keeping with the control theme, serial killers, unlike typical murderers, usually do not use a firearm to murder their victims. Although they may use a firearm to intimidate and control their victims, serial killers prefer a method of killing that provides the maximum amount of control and dominance over the victims. Choking, stabbing, and other methods of delayed death are ways the killer can control the life-or-death mastery over the helpless victims.

Serial killers also tend to be inspired by detailed and elaborate fantasies rich with themes of dominance (Fox & Levin, 1998; Skrapec, 1996). Prentky et al. (1989), for instance, found that 86% of the 25 serial killers they studied had violent fantasies on a regular basis, compared with only 23% of the 17 single-victim murderers. However, it should be mentioned that a majority (58%) of the serial killers in their sample had above-average intelligence compared to only 29% of the single-victim murderers. Therefore, the two groups were not completely matched in all important factors. In reference to this difference, Prentky et al. state, "While intelligence seems to have little bearing on the quality or content of the fantasy, it does influence how well fantasy is translated into behavior (i.e., how organized the crime is) and how successfully the offender eludes apprehension" (p. 888). The researchers further state that "fantasy, as it is defined in this study, is an elaborated set of cognitions (or thoughts) characterized by preoccupation (or rehearsal), anchored in emotion, and originating in daydreams" (p. 889). Furthermore, the more the fantasy is rehearsed in the mind of the potential killer, the stronger the association between the fantasy content and the actual behavior becomes, eventually lowering the restraints that normally would inhibit acting out the fantasy itself. Eventually, the individual will actually act on the fantasy. At this point, Prentky et al. suggest, the serial killer engages in a series of progressively more accurate "trial runs" in an attempt to enact the fantasy as it is imagined. In other words, the killer will continue to try to improve on his cognitive script through trial and error. Because the trial runs can never quite match the fantasy entirely, the need to restage the fantasy with a new victim is always there. As Fox and Levin (1998) note, "The killer's crime can increase in severity as he constantly updates his fantasy in a never-ending spiral of image and action" (p. 417).

Many serial killers augment their fantasies with hard-core pornography, which often contains themes of violence, dominance, and bondage

(Fox & Levin, 1998). Police investigators often uncover extensive libraries of films and tapes that portray acts of rape and murder. It is not clear, however, whether the violent pornography engenders thoughts of violence or whether violent-prone individuals prefer violent pornography. The answer may lie in some combination of both.

Many serial killers also collect memorabilia or souvenirs of their victims, such as items of clothing, audiotapes or photographs of the murder, and—in rare cases—body parts. Called trophies, these "souvenirs" vividly remind the killer of the incident, enhancing his fantasies even further.

One link noted in case studies of serial killers is that some of them have served time in the military (Castle & Hensley, 2002). Presumably, the military provides a socially approved context through which some serial killers learn the skills and neutralization techniques that make killing easier. However, further research into this observation will need to be conducted before even tentative conclusions can be made.

Serial Killer Typologies

In contemporary psychology, the term *typology* refers to a particular system for classifying personality or behavioral patterns. Usually, the typology is used to classify a wide assortment of behaviors into a more manageable set of brief descriptions. There are many problems with typologies, however, such as considerable overlap between categories. Rarely is one classification independent and separate from the others. In addition, some individuals can qualify for two or more classifications at once. For example, if the typology is based primarily on motive, the offender may demonstrate a combination of motives for the crime. Moreover, placing individuals into various categories is based on the questionable assumption that behavior is consistent across both time and place. Still, typologies are useful in highlighting the complexity of human behavior and the variety of motives and scripts. Several typologies of serial killers have been

proposed in recent years, but we will concentrate only on the Holmes and DeBurger (1985, 1988) and Holmes and Holmes (1998) scheme for illustrative purposes.

Holmes and DeBurger (1985, 1988) classify serial killers into a typology based on motive. The typology outlines four types: (1) visionary, (2) mission oriented, (3) hedonistic, and (4) power/control. The **visionary type** is driven by delusions or hallucinations that compel him (or her) to kill a particular group of individuals. According to Holmes and DeBurger, this serial killer is psychotic—which is atypical because serial killers are not usually mentally disordered—and suffers from a severe break with reality. He or she is probably the most difficult to understand for investigators and the public alike. The crime scene is chaotic and has an abundance of physical evidence, often including fingerprints and even the murder weapon (Holmes & Holmes, 1998). When the visionary type does kill, it will usually be well within his comfort zone (near his residence, place of recreation, or workplace). Therefore, geographical profiling would seem to be a very useful tool in the detection of this offender. Unlike most serial killers, however, the visionary murderer has no ideal victim type (IVT). That is, there are rarely any common physical (hair color, sex, age, or race), occupational, or personality traits that connect the victims. In addition, the murder is usually spontaneous and characterized by very little planning, and the victim is simply in the wrong place at the wrong time.

The **mission-oriented type** believes that there is a particular group of people who are considered undesirable and who must be destroyed or eliminated. The undesirables may be prostitutes, homosexuals, "street people," or members of a particular religious, racial, or minority group. Unlike the visionary type, this serial killer is not psychotic or clinically crazy. The visionary group may be subdivided into subgroups, depending on whom or what is advocating the killing. Two of the most common subgroups are the *demon mandated* and the *God mandated*.

The **hedonistic type** strives for pleasure and thrill seeking, and, in their minds, people are simply objects to use for one's own enjoyment. According to Holmes and Holmes (1998), hedonistic killers may be divided into three subtypes based on the primary motive for the murder: lust, thrill, and comfort. The *lust* serial killer's primary motive is exclusively sex, even if the victim is already dead (an activity called necrophilia). "He kills for sex; it is a propelling element in the motivation to kill and in the enjoyment he receives from his activities" (Holmes & Holmes, 1998, p. 93). Furthermore, "The killer kills in ways that reflect both the fantasy and the manner in which the fantasy is to be satisfied" (Holmes & Holmes, 1998, p. 93). The lust killer, according to Holmes and Holmes, is always seeking the IVT that is sexually appealing to him. Ted Bundy, for example, reported that the way a woman walked and talked was an important factor in his victim selection.

The *thrill* killer is primarily motivated to induce pain or a terrified reaction from the victim. The pain and terror engendered, in combination with the process of the murder itself, are highly stimulating and exciting for the killer. Usually, the killer has no relationship with his victim, although he may have followed her for some time. Similar to the lust killer, the thrill murderer selects victims based on certain physical characteristics that feed into his fantasies.

The motive for the *creature-comfort* killer is to acquire activities (business interests) or objects (money) that provide a comfortable and luxurious lifestyle. The killer's victims presumably stand in the way of achieving this. "The comfort killer's main objective is to enjoy life and to be sufficiently in control of immediate circumstances so that 'the good life' can be attained" (Holmes & Holmes, 1998, p. 119). Moreover, "overt, blatant displays of fatal aggression are not characteristics of this type; most comfort-oriented murderers tend to kill quietly if the situation permits" (Holmes & Holmes, 1998, p. 119). For the comfort killer, the act of murder is incidental to the pursuit of material gain and a comfortable lifestyle. Presumably, comfort killers dispose of their victims when they have identified a potential new "mark." In many ways, comfort killers resemble the behavioral characteristics of a criminal psychopath. Some writers (Holmes, Hickey, & Holmes, 1991) have pointed out that female serial killers often fall into this category.

The **power-control** individual obtains satisfaction from the absolute life-or-death control he has over the victim. Sexual components may or may not be present, but the primary motive is the extreme power and dominance over the helpless victim. These killers also tend to seek specific victims who appear especially vulnerable and easy to victimize.

Mass Murder

Compared to serial murder, relatively little research has been done on mass murderers. Perhaps this is because mass murder, although horrible and troubling, is not as intriguing, mysterious, or frightening as serial murder. Furthermore, mass murder usually happens suddenly and unpredictably—then rarely is there any sequel. A long-term search for the perpetrator is not necessary. It is often clear who the offender is, although the motives are sometimes unclear. Some earlier FBI investigators (Douglas, Ressler, Burgess, & Hartman, 1986) have found it useful to divide mass murder into two major types: *classic* and *family.* Due to the many global examples of mass murder publicized in recent years, a third category—terrorist mass murder—should probably be added. Although the United States encountered these primarily in the 1995 bombing of the Federal Building in Oklahoma City in which 168 people were killed, as well as in the terrorist attacks on September 11, 2001, in which 3,047 people were killed, other countries have encountered terrorist mass murder on a regular basis.

As mentioned earlier, an example of a classic mass murder is the person who barricades himself inside a public building—such as a restaurant or school—and randomly kills persons with whom he has contact. A family mass murder is when at least three family members are killed (usually by another family member). Most often, the incident occurs within the family residence. In one rural town, a woman was dropped off at her home after spending an evening working with friends on crafts for a church fair. She walked into the house and was confronted by her 17-year-old son, who had shot to death his father and younger brother and sister. He killed his mother, wrote a note revealing his actions, and then killed himself. The boy had sexually assaulted his sister, who threatened to reveal her victimization to her parents.

It is commonly assumed that suicide is a primary motive of many mass murderers. In other words, the individual planned to die at the crime scene after killing as many as possible, either at his own hand or by police gunfire. However, Grant Duwe (2000), on the basis of his examination of 495 mass killings over a 21-year time period, concluded that only 21% of mass murderers committed suicide, whereas another 2% attempted suicide, and 3% were fatally shot by the police. It appears that family mass murders are most likely to result in the perpetrator's taking his or her life.

The motives of mass murderers are highly variable. "The motivations for mass murder can range from revenge to hatred, from loyalty to greed; and the victims can be selected individually, as members of a particular category or group, or on a random basis" (Fox & Levin, 1998, p. 430). However, a majority of mass murderers are driven by revenge, and their victims are apparently chosen because of what they have done or what they represent (Fox & Levin, 1998). Mass murderers are frequently described as frustrated, angry people who feel helpless about their lives. They are usually between the ages of 25 and 45 (average age at time of murder is approximately 30), and they are generally convinced

there is little chance that things will get better for them. Their personal lives have been failures by their standards, and they have often suffered some tragic or serious loss, such as losing a job or being abandoned by a spouse or partner. George Hennard, the 35-year-old described earlier who drove his pickup truck into the plate glass window of a restaurant in Texas, killing 22 patrons and wounding 27, had lost his cherished job as a merchant marine. He also apparently had an intense hatred of women and minorities. The 17-year-old described above who killed his family and himself does not fit the above profile, however. His crime appears to be one motivated by guilt for past actions and fear of what would occur if these actions were revealed.

Mass murderers are often socially isolated and withdrawn people who lack a strong social network of friends or supporters. Compared with serial murderers, they are more likely to be mentally disordered in the clinical sense. Their isolation is probably due to some combination of an active dislike of people and their own inadequate social and interpersonal skills. Attacking several or many others at one time provides these lonely, angry people a chance to get even, to dominate others, to take control, and to gain recognition.

Mass murderers often take a very active interest in guns. Unlike serial murder, about two thirds of the mass killings (both traditional and family) involved the use of guns, usually semiautomatic firearms with high magazine capacities (Duwe, 2000). In other words, they prefer weapons that make it easier to kill many people quickly.

The data reported by Duwe (2000) do not bear out reports claiming that most mass murders take place at the workplace. For example, workplace massacres are quite rare, accounting for only 4% of the total incidents, whereas 27% of the incidents involved offenders who killed their victims in a public place. The remainder took place within a residential setting, often involving family members or acquaintances. Consequently, a majority of mass murders can be classified as family mass murders.

Workplace Violence

Workplace violence is a complex phenomenon, encompassing a wide assortment of threatening and injurious behaviors that occur within one's place of employment. Workplace violence is somewhat of a misnomer because it refers not only to the more physically violent incidents but also to the subtle behavior that *threatens* violence, such as coercion, intimidation, outright threats, and harassment. In fact, although the media report the more serious violence, the incidents that actually occur most frequently in the workplace are *threats* of violence (Budd, Arvey, & Lawless, 1996). It is estimated that approximately 7% of those in the workforce are threatened every year, amounting to more than 6 million workers in the United States (Barling, Rogers, & Kelloway, 2000). Persons who report being *physically* assaulted in the workplace average around 2.5% of the U.S. workforce or approximately 2 million workers per year (Gregorie & Wallace, 2002).

Nevertheless, approximately 1,000 employees are murdered in the workplace each year (Gregorie & Wallace, 2002), and an additional 1.5 million workers are victims of nonhomicidal violence, not including threats. Homicide is the third leading cause of death in American workplaces and the second leading cause of fatal occupational injury for women (Iowa Injury Prevention Research Center, 2002). Firearms are used in about 80% of the workplace homicides. Retail sales workers (especially fast-food and convenience store employees) tend to be the most frequent victims, largely because robbery is the primary motive of job-related homicides (Occupational Safety and Health Administration, 2001).

One third of victims of workplace violence between 1993 and 1999 reported that they believed that the perpetrator was under the influence of alcohol or drugs at the time of the crime (Bureau of Justice Statistics, 2001b). In approximately 8 out of 10 workplace homicides, the perpetrators and victims were strangers. Coworkers and former coworkers were responsible for 7% of the workplace homicides, and husbands and boyfriends were responsible for 3% of the workplace homicides (Bureau of Justice Statistics, 2001b). Although retail workers tend to be the most frequent victims of *homicide,* other occupational groups are at greater risk of *violence* in general because of the nature of their job. Police officers are victims of the highest rate of workplace violence, followed by correctional officers, taxi drivers, private security guards, and bartenders. In the 1980s, the term *going postal* became part of the national lexicon after a series of workplace shootings by distressed postal workers. In actuality, postal workers were no more likely to commit workplace violence than other occupational groups, but the convergence of several crimes among this group led to the misconception. Occupational risks for workplace violence per 1,000 workers are listed in Box 5.2.

Physical workplace violence has been classified into four major types on the basis of the assailant's relationship to the workplace (California Occupational Safety and Health Administration, 1995; Gregorie, 2000; LeBlanc & Kelloway, 2002). In the first type, the assailant does not have a legitimate relationship to the workplace or to the victim. He or she usually enters the workplace to commit a criminal action, such as a robbery or theft. Robbery is the principal motive for most workplace homicide, accounting for 85% of the workplace deaths (Gregorie & Wallace, 2000). The second type of assailant is the recipient of some service provided by the workplace or victim and may be either a current or a former client, patient, or customer. Most often, this individual is unhappy with the product or service he or she received from the agency or company. The third type has an employment-related involvement with the workplace, either as a current or former employee, supervisor, or manager. This assailant is often referred to as a "disgruntled employee" who enters the workplace to punish or get back at some individual or the agency or company in general. Disgruntled employees account for

---

BOX 5.2   Occupational Risks for Workplace Violence

Highest rates of workplace violence per 1,000 workers:

Police officers: 306.0

Correctional officers: 217.9

Taxi drivers: 183.8

Private security guards: 117.3

Bartenders: 91.3

Mental health professionals: 79.5

Gas station attendants: 79.1

Convenience and liquor store clerks: 68.4

Mental health custodial workers: 63.3

Junior high/middle school teachers: 57.4

Bus drivers: 45.0

Special education teachers: 40.7

High school teachers: 28.9

Nurses: 24.8

Source: Bureau of Labor Statistics (1999).

---

approximately 10% of workplace homicides (Gregorie & Wallace, 2000). The fourth type has an indirect involvement with the workplace because of a relationship with an employee, such as a current or former spouse or partner. Often, this situation concerns domestic violence or spousal/partner abuse.

Few systematic studies have examined the predictors or causes of workplace violence. Most of the work to date has focused on either (a) describing the assailant or (b) identifying the job characteristics that increase the risk for violence (LeBlanc & Kelloway, 2002). Considerably more research needs to be done on identifying the causes and implementing preventive measures in the workplace. Nevertheless, many places of employment have been sensitized to this issue

and have increased their levels of security in response to fear and uneasiness among employees. This may be due, at least partly, to the dramatic increase in workplace violence litigation in recent years (Kaufer & Mattman, 2002). The legal action and civil lawsuits at this point in time concentrate on four major areas: (1) negligent hiring (failure to screen employees properly), (2) negligent retention (failure to terminate unsuitable and threatening employees), (3) negligent supervision (failure to monitor performance), and (4) inadequate security (Kaufer & Mattman, 2002). Consequently, legal and regulatory obligations for employers to provide safe and secure work environments are bound to increase, and mandatory prevention and training programs are likely to be commonplace across all private and public organizations in the near future. As should be apparent, forensic psychologists increasingly are called on to assess the risk of violence in an individual about whom fellow workers or supervisors are concerned. Perhaps more important, however, psychologists working within workplace settings should be attuned to the culture of the workplace and play a critical role in facilitating a working environment that promotes cooperation and mutual respect among and between employees and supervisory personnel.

Although we have thus far discussed only violence and threats of violence in the workplace, we must emphasize that other workplace issues also merit careful attention. Discrimination—be it on the basis of race, gender, ethnicity, or age—remains of major concern. One particular form of discrimination—sexual harassment—is also noteworthy. Between 1990 and 1997, charges of sexual harassment in the workplace increased nearly threefold, from 6,127 to 15,889 nationwide (Goodman-Delahunty, 1999b). Sexual harassment claims also have comprised an increasing percentage of all of the gender-based discrimination suits filed in courts, reaching 64% in 1997 (Goodman-Delahunty, 1999b). Although not a criminal action, harassing behavior may lead to stalking, which may in turn lead to violence. Likewise, racial and ethnic discrimination in the workplace also may lead to violence. In addition, discrimination in all of its contexts has similarities to bias crimes and to crimes of intimidation, to which we now turn our attention.

Hate or Bias Crimes

Hate crimes—also called **bias crimes**—are criminal offenses motivated by an offender's bias against a group to which the victim either belongs or is believed to belong. Note that neither hatred nor prejudice alone is sufficient to constitute a hate crime. There must be an underlying criminal offense—for example, an assault, vandalism, arson, or murder—that is *motivated* by the hatred or prejudice. When individuals are

charged with bias crimes, prosecutors must be able to establish evidence of this motivation.

The groupings—or protected categories—most commonly identified are race, religion, gender, disability, sexual orientation, and ethnicity. It is important to note that these are inclusive categories; that is, bias crime statutes protect all members of all races (not just Blacks or Whites) and persons of all sexual orientations (not just homosexuals). In addition, statutes in some states also provide penalties for bias crimes against certain age groups (e.g., the elderly) or members of the military. The **Hate Crime Statistics Act** of 1990 requires the FBI to collect data and provide information on the nature and prevalence of violent attacks, intimidation, arson, or property damage directed at persons or groups because of bias against their race, religion, sexual orientation, or ethnicity. In September 1994, the Violent Crime and Control and Law Enforcement Act amended the Hate Crime Statistics Act to include physical and mental disabilities in the data collection. Note that gender—commonly covered in hate crime statutes—is not one of the specified categories. Also in 1994, Congress passed the Hate Crime Sentencing Enhancement Act, which provides for longer sentences for such crimes. In 1996, due to dramatic increases in the burning of places of worship (especially African American churches located in the southeastern sections of the United States), the Church Arson Prevention Act was signed into law. More recently, the Hate Crime Prevention Act of 1999 prohibits persons from interfering with an individual's civil or constitutional rights, such as voting or employment, by violence or threat of violence due to his or her race, color, religion, or national origin.

Based on national statistics, hate crimes appear to account for a relatively small percentage of all criminal violence. The total number of hate crimes identified between 1997 and 1999 was less than 3,000 nationwide (Strom, 2001). We cannot take comfort in these seemingly low numbers, however. Documenting hate or bias crimes is difficult because the intentions of the offender are not always obvious or clear-cut. Consequently, law enforcement agencies record hate crimes only when the investigation reveals facts sufficient to conclude that the offender's actions were bias motivated. Evidence most often used to support the existence of bias includes oral comments, written statements, or gestures made by the offender at the time of the incident or drawings or graffiti left at the crime scene (Strom, 2001). In addition, there is wide state-to-state variation in the degree to which law enforcement officers are trained and encouraged to recognize and record hate crimes.

Available data indicate that a majority of hate crimes are motivated by racial bias (44.9%), followed by ethnic/national origin bias (21.6%), religious bias (14.3%), sexual orientation bias (14.3%), and disability bias (0.3%) (FBI, 2002b). Examples of a disability bias include biases against a person with AIDS, a mental disorder, or mental retardation. Hate crimes on college campuses demonstrate a wide spectrum of criminal conduct, ranging from threats to bombings. They occur at virtually every type of college or university and in every part of the country and are a significant problem on many campuses (Wessler & Moss, 2001). Offenders may include students, former students, or nonstudents.

Approximately 64% of hate crimes are directed at individuals, whereas the remaining targets are businesses, religious institutions, or other institutions and organizations. More than four out of five violent hate crimes reported in the FBI's National Incident-Based Reporting System (NIBRS) involve the victimization of a single individual within a single incidence (Strom, 2001). The majority of persons (three fourths) suspected of committing hate crimes are White males. NIBRS data indicate that more than a third of persons arrested for hate crimes are younger than 18, and more than half are younger than age 25 at the time of arrest. Younger persons (younger than age 18) are more likely to be arrested for property-related offenses, such as vandalism, whereas older persons are more likely to be arrested for violent hate crime. Hate crime

violence appears to have its roots in an individual's learned prejudice against particular social groups. This learned prejudice, combined with fear, can escalate into violence when a member of the prejudicial group believes his or her lifestyle is under attack. Interestingly, two thirds of those arrested for hate crimes reside in the locality in which the crime occurred.

Stalking: The Crime of Intimidation

Stalking is defined as "a course of conduct directed at a specific person that involves repeated physical or visual proximity, nonconsensual communication, or verbal, written, or implied threats sufficient to cause fear in a reasonable person" (Tjaden, 1997, p. 2). The term refers to

> repeated and often escalating unwanted intrusions and communications, including loitering nearby; following or surveying a person's home, making multiple telephone calls or other forms of unwanted direct and indirect communications, spreading gossip, destroying personal property, harassing acquaintances or family members, sending threatening or sexually suggestive "gifts" or letters, and aggressive and violent acts. (Abrams & Robinson, 2002, p. 468)

Stalking is as old as the history of human relationships, and yet it has only been within the past two decades that the behavior has been recognized as unlawful (Beatty, Hickey, & Sigmon, 2002). The release of films such as *Fatal Attraction* (Paramount Pictures, released 1987), *Sleeping With the Enemy* (20th Century-Fox, released 1991), and *Cape Fear* (Universal Studios, released 1991), contributed to increasing salience about this problem in the minds of the public. Increased coverage by the news media of the stalking of celebrities (e.g., David Letterman, Rebecca Schaeffer) also led to stalking becoming a household term. Some commentators refer to stalking as the "crime of the nineties" (Sheridan & Davies, 2001). At the present time, and for some unexplained reason, stalking *appears* to be regarded as a serious social problem *only* in the English-speaking world (Mullen, Pathé, & Purcell, 2001).

Stalking is an extremely frightening, emotionally distressful, and depressing crime of intimidation. Anti-stalking laws exist in all 50 states, the District of Columbia, and Canada. Although most states define stalking in their statutes as the willful, malicious, and repeated following and harassing of another person, some include such activities as lying-in-wait, surveillance, nonconsensual communication, telephone harassment, and vandalism (Tjaden & Thoennes, 1998a). Some states require that at least two stalking incidents occur before the conduct is considered criminal.

One of the most comprehensive studies on stalking was conducted by the Center for Policy Research and published in a monograph titled *Stalking in America: Findings From the National Violence Against Women Survey* (Tjaden & Thoennes, 1998b). The project, cosponsored by the National Institute of Justice and Centers for Disease Control and Prevention, was a nationally representative phone survey of 8,000 women and 8,000 men, 18 years or older. The survey, conducted between November 1995 and May 1996, provides empirical data on the prevalence, characteristics, and consequences of stalking.

The survey found that 8% of women and 2% of men reported that they had been stalked at some point in their lives (Tjaden, 1997). In most instances, the stalking lasted less than 1 year, but some individuals were stalked for more than 5 years. According to the research reported by Mullen et al. (2001), however, repeated unwanted communications and imposed contacts that go on for more than 2 weeks are highly likely to last for months or even years. Researchers believe that the motives of most stalkers are to control, intimidate, or frighten their victims.

The stalker was male 87% of the time, and the victim was female 80% of the time. Eighty percent of the stalkers are believed to be White, at least 50% are between the ages of 18 and 35, and many earn above-average incomes. In most stalking incidents, the victims (particularly women) knew their stalker. Approximately half of the female victims were stalked by current or former marital or cohabiting partners, and a majority of these women (80%) had been physically assaulted by that partner either during the relationship, during the stalking episode, or during both. In about a third of the cases, the stalkers vandalized the victim's property, and about 10% of the time, the stalker killed or threatened to kill the victim's pet. Only 7% of the victims thought their stalkers were mentally disordered, psychotic, crazy, or abusers of alcohol or drugs.

Another comprehensive study of stalking was cosponsored by the National Institute of Justice and the Bureau of Justice Statistics (Fisher, Cullen, & Turner, 2000). The project involved a phone survey of 4,446 female students at 223 colleges and universities, conducted from February to May 1997. The primary screening question used to measure stalking was the following: "Since school began in fall 1996, has anyone—from stranger to an ex-boyfriend—repeatedly followed you, watched you, phoned, written, e-mailed, or communicated with you in other ways that seemed obsessive and made you afraid or concerned for your safety?"

The key findings of the study were the following:

- Thirteen percent of the college women had been stalked since the school year began.
- Of the victims, 80.3% knew or had seen their stalker before.
- Stalking incidents last on average for about 2 months.
- Thirty percent of the women reported being injured emotionally and psychologically from being stalked.
- In 10.3% of incidents, the victim reported that the stalker forced or attempted sexual contact.
- Overall, 83.1% of stalking incidents were not reported to police or campus law enforcement.

It should also be noted that some mental health professionals who deal regularly with persons having mental or emotional difficulties have become the victims of stalking by their clients (Gentile, Asamen, Harmell, & Weathers, 2002). The stalkers of mental health professionals may be either single or divorced at the time of the stalking (Gentile et al., 2002). The majority of these clients (62%) were diagnosed as having a mood disorder. In another survey, about two out of three university counselors had experienced some type of harassing behavior or stalking behavior from a current or former client (Romans, Hays, & White, 1996).

In an effort to better understand stalkers, some researchers have proposed typologies or classification systems. One of the first systematic studies on stalkers was done by Zona, Sharma, and Lane (1993) in their work with the Los Angeles Police Department's Threat Management Unit. These researchers developed a classification system that focused on individuals who stalked entertainment celebrities and divided stalkers into three behavioral clusters: (1) erotomanic, (2) love obsessional, and (3) simple obsessional (these categories will be defined below). A few years later, researchers shifted their focus from "star stalkers" to men who stalked their ex-partners (Emerson, Ferris, & Gardner, 1998; Kurt, 1995). Star stalkers were assumed to be predominately mentally disordered persons who were driven by delusions in their pursuit of their favorite celebrity, whereas ex-partner stalkers were seen as asserting their power over women through violence and intimidation (Mullen et al., 2001). The most common stalking typology, outlined by Beatty et al. (2002), consists of four broad categories: (1) simple obsession stalking, (2) love obsession stalking, (3) erotomania stalking, and (4) vengeance stalking. The term *obsession* refers to recurrent ideas, thoughts, impulses, or images that a person tries to control or satisfy through various actions. It should be emphasized that this typology has not been validated by empirical research but should serve as a springboard for future research and hypothesis development. The following descriptions of the four stalker categories follow Beatty et al.'s (2002) definitions.

Simple obsession stalkers are the most common, accounting for 60% of the stalkers, and represent behavior that is a continuation of a previous pattern of domestic violence and psychological abuse in an intimate relationship. Consequently, the targeted victim is often a former spouse, and the majority of offenders are males. These stalkers appear to be more intelligent and better educated than most stalkers (Meloy & Gothard, 1995). The stalking is hypothesized to be prompted by the offender's feelings of low self-esteem and helplessness. Apparently, the offender increases his own self-esteem by demeaning and demoralizing his former spouse and may take drastic steps if he perceives the victim is trying to remove herself from the controlling situation. Simple obsession is the category of stalking that is most likely to result in murder.

Love obsession stalkers and their victims tend to be casual acquaintances, such as neighbors or coworkers, but may also involve complete strangers, such as a celebrity. The primary motivation of these stalkers is to establish a personal relationship with the targeted victim. Like simple obsession stalkers, these individuals may have very low self-esteem and may be haunted by feelings of helplessness and depression. Presumably, these stalkers believe that by associating with persons who display exceptional qualities and high status, they can correspondingly raise their own levels of self-esteem and worthiness. Often, the love obsession stalker is so desperate to develop a relationship with the victim that he or she is willing to accept a negative or destructive relationship, sometimes resorting to violence in an effort to win the attention of the unwilling victim. A classic example of this type of stalker is John Hinckley, who was convinced he could win the love of actor Jodi Foster by shooting President Ronald Reagan.

Erotomania stalking is considered highly delusional, and the offender is often plagued by serious mental disorders, most often schizophrenia. Erotomania stalkers believe that the relationship with their victim already exists, in contrast to the simple and love obsession stalkers. Erotomania stalkers are usually less dangerous to the victims, but their irrationality is troubling and unpredictable to the victims. Margaret Ray, the woman who stalked talk show host David Letterman for nearly 10 years, illustrates this type of stalker. She apparently believed throughout that time that she was Letterman's wife and the mother of his child. She was discovered on his New Canaan, Connecticut, property on many occasions; was arrested driving his car; and sent him flowers and candy. Eventually, the troubled woman committed suicide by kneeling in front of a speeding train in Colorado.

Vengeance stalkers are quite different from the other three types because they do not seek a personal relationship with their targeted victims. Instead, these stalkers try to elicit a particular response, such as fear, or change of behavior, such as moving to another area, from their victims. Vengeance is their prime motivation. An illustration of this kind of stalker is when an employee who is fired from his job begins to stalk and harass the supervisor whom he believes is responsible for the firing, in hopes of ruining the supervisor's life.

Political stalkers use the weapon of terror to accomplish a political goal and to get a person or group to refrain from some activity. In the abortion context, for example, some persons who are against a woman's right to choose may stalk and threaten physicians with violence if they perform abortions.

When Does Stalking Usually Stop?

What terminates stalking? Some stalkers stop pursuing their current victim when they find a new "love" interest. About 18% of the victims in the Center for Policy Research Survey indicated that the stalking stopped when stalkers entered into a relationship with a new person. Law

enforcement interventions also seem to help. Fifteen percent said the stalking ceased when their stalkers received a warning from the police. Interestingly, more formal interventions such as arrest, conviction, or restraining orders do not appear to be very effective—perhaps serving to antagonize the stalker. When it comes to persistent, frightening stalking that creates risks to personal safety, the survey suggests that the most effective method may be to relocate as far away from the offender as possible, providing no information of one's whereabouts to the stalker or to individuals who might communicate that information.

Predictions of Violence in Stalking Cases

Many stalking victims want to know the likelihood that they will become the victim of a violent act (Rosenfeld & Harmon, 2002). "Determining which stalkers represent a significant risk of violence, and differentiating those individuals from the remaining offenders who may pose less risk of physical harm, has clear and significant implications for victims, clinicians, and the legal system" (Rosenfeld & Harmon, 2002, p. 685).

In an effort to identify features that may differentiate violent stalkers from nonviolent stalkers, Rosenfeld and Harmon (2002) analyzed 204 stalking and harassment cases referred for court-ordered mental health evaluations in New York City. Results supported the findings of previous researchers (e.g., Palerea, Zona, Lane, & Langhinrichsen-Rohling, 1999) who found that former spouses or intimates of stalkers were most at risk.

Specifically, intimate stalkers threatened persons and property (including physical violence toward the victim), were more likely to "make good" on their threats by following them with some form of violent behavior, and used more physical approach behaviors in contacting their victims than non-intimate stalkers. These results illustrate the importance of accounting for the presence of an intimate relationship when assessing for violence risk in stalking cases. (Palerea et al., 1999, p. 278)

Violent *threats* and drug abuse also appear to be significant predictors of stalking violence. Rosenfeld and Harmon (2002) also found that variables such as the stalker's prior criminal history and previous violent *behavior* did *not* emerge as good predictors of violence. This was surprising because Palerea et al. (1999) report that a history of violence was the strongest predictor in their data. However, Rosenfeld and Harmon had access to much more information—official records of arrest and convictions as well as stalker self-report and victim reports—than the Palerea group. Palerea et al. used data obtained form 223 police files maintained by the Los Angeles Police Department. Consequently, the difference between the two studies might be a function of the quality and quantity of the data collected. Research so far has not indicated that psychiatric history is associated with violence against persons or property. Quite possibly, though, if the stalkers were divided into an empirically based typology, more significant results in this regard might be more forthcoming.

Cyberstalking

Cyberstalking is analogous to traditional forms of stalking in that it incorporates persistent behaviors that engender apprehension and fear. However, with the advent of new technologies, traditional stalking has taken on entirely new forms through mediums such as e-mail and the Internet. It is possible that such incidents may be more common than traditional forms of stalking. This is because the basic apparatus of the Internet, including free e-mail and chat rooms, facilitate contact with an immense field of potential victims. Unsolicited e-mail is one of the most common forms of harassment, including hate, obscene, or threatening mail. Other forms of harassment include sending the victim viruses or high volumes of electronic junk mail (spamming). E-mail stalking can result from an attempt to initiate a relationship, repair a relationship, or threaten and traumatize a person. It is often accompanied by traditional stalking such as threatening phone calls, vandalism of property, threatening mail, and physical attacks (Gregorie, 2000).

Chat rooms and e-mail have provided far-reaching and unregulated opportunities for cyberstalkers to harass unsuspecting victims. In addition, there is a considerable amount of personal information available through the Internet, and cyberstalkers can easily and quickly locate private information about a target.

Summary and Conclusions

Violence, the definition of which requires some display of physical force, is essentially atypical human behavior when we compare it with the vast amount of human behavior that is non-violent. Nonetheless, it remains a fascinating area of study as well as a pervasive aspect of popular culture. In fact, as we saw in this chapter, the increasingly violent images in the media have prompted research studies that in turn have led to calls for limiting the exposure of children—particularly young children—to these images. We saw that aggression, a construct frequently studied by psychologists, does not necessarily result in the physical force that we defined as violence. In addition, society actually condones some forms of violence, which further complicates any attempts to prevent it, predict it, or treat those who display violence or who are its victims.

The chapter focused primarily on criminal violence as it is defined in the law and in crime statistics. The four index violent crimes—murder and nonnegligent manslaughter, forcible rape, aggravated assault, and robbery—together comprise about one third of the total crime index. Persons arrested for these crimes are predominantly male (87%–90%), although the violent crime rate for females began to increase faster than the male rate in the 1990s. Women continue to appear in arrest statistics far less often than men, however, a phenomenon for which a variety of explanations has been proposed. The most common explanations relate to either socialization or biological differences.

Race and ethnic differences in violent crime have received greater attention, and these differences are among the most troubling to researchers and policymakers alike. African Americans, particularly African American males, continue to make up a disproportionate part of official statistics on violent crime. The chapter emphasized that numerous social factors can explain these differentials and guarded against attributing any biological factors to the differences. In addition, we warned against focusing on one racial group to the exclusion of others, noting that researchers are beginning to explore differences among ethnic groups.

Psychologists and criminologists as a group often discuss violence as being either instrumental or reactive/expressive or some combination of both. Studies suggest that the great majority of criminal violence—including homicide—is instrumental. Offenders commit the crime to achieve a particular goal, be it material goods, recognition, or political change. Psychologists and criminologists also have explored biological, social, cognitive, and situational factors as explanations for violent behavior. At present, it appears that a combination of all four categories of factors is the best way to approach the study of violence. We emphasize, though, that—although some researchers have found biological links to aggression—any biological predisposition can be attenuated with careful attention to social, cognitive, and situational factors. To use one example, the social environment of a child who is highly aggressive as the result of some brain damage can be modified to make it less likely that that child will display violent behavior.

The chapter gave considerable attention to criminal homicide, the violent crime that is the least frequent but has received considerable research attention. The separate violent crime of sexual assault will be discussed in detail in the following chapter. The typical homicide is the single killing committed either in the course of another felony—most often a robbery—or committed against a relative or acquaintance. Young adult males are the most likely perpetrators of these single murders. Atypical murders—particularly those that qualify as multiple murders (serial, spree, and mass murders) have most fascinated and frightened the public. We discussed in detail both serial and mass murderers because they have been the subject of considerable scholarly commentary and research attention.

Serial murderers—so called because of the time interval between their killings—generally begin their murderous behavior at a later age than single murderers. Most are male, but their victims may be male or female—they generally show a preference for one or the other. Although there is no "serial murderer personality" or profile, serial murderers as a group appear to be persuasive and to delude their victims into thinking that they pose no danger to them. Serial murderers *as a group* are not mentally disordered in the traditional sense; that is, they do not fit traditional diagnostic categories of mental illnesses, although some qualify as criminal psychopaths. In some typologies of serial murderers, however, one type does display psychotic behavior. The best-known typology (Holmes & Holmes, 1998) divides serial murderers into visionary, mission-oriented, hedonistic, and power/control types, with the visionary murderer being the most likely to engender a clinical diagnosis. Mass murderers—who kill three or more individuals during one incident—are generally divided into classic and family types, but a terrorist mass murder type should also be added. Although there are highly publicized illustrations of mass murders in public places, most seem to be family murders. When the perpetrator is a member of the family, he or she is also likely to commit suicide in conjunction with the incident. Compared with serial murderers, mass murders are more likely to be isolated, disenchanted, and ineffective individuals whose crime is precipitated by what they perceive as a tragic loss, such as abandonment by a significant person or loss of employment.

Workplace violence includes homicides, but the vast majority of workplace violence incidents do not end in death. In fact, the vast majority of incidents are not actually violence but rather threats of violence. Study of this phenomenon has increased in recent years, as has litigation on the part of employees who believe their employers did not adequately protect them from threats or from actual violent incidents. Forensic psychologists have critical roles not only in alerting employers to potentially violent individuals in the workplace but also in facilitating a working environment that fosters acceptance and cooperation among all employees. However, a substantial portion of workplace violence is committed by outsiders or by former workers or supervisors.

The chapter ended with a discussion of bias crimes and stalking. Of the two, bias crimes qualify more directly as criminal violence, if the underlying offense is a violent crime—and data indicate that in the majority of cases, it is. Although the federal government and all states provide penalties for bias crimes, the FBI gathers data on only those associated with race/ethnicity, religion, sexual orientation, or mental or physical disability. The number of bias crimes reported nationwide does not seem overwhelming, but we cautioned that many bias crimes likely go unreported to police. In addition, police agencies vary widely in the extent to which they enforce bias crime statutes or record bias crimes.

Stalking was sometimes referred to as the crime of the 1990s. The most recent research efforts give some attention to cyberstalking as well as the more traditional approaches such as following, sending mail, or telephoning victims. Researchers have proposed typologies of stalkers similar to the typologies that were proposed for serial killers and mass murderers. One very recent typology is that proposed by Beatty et al. (2002), who describe simple, love obsession, erotomania, and vengeance stalking. Although not violent in itself, stalking engenders fear—sometimes debilitating fear—in its victims. An undetermined percentage of stalkers do ultimately exhibit violent behavior. For the forensic psychologist, this is another illustration of the risk assessment enterprise to be discussed in Chapter 9 that is such an essential component of many clinical practices. We discussed recent efforts to distinguish between those stalkers who are likely to be violent and those who will cease their stalking behavior without harming their victims. At present, it appears that victims who are former intimate partners of the stalker are most at risk of being physically harmed. Past violent behavior does not appear to be a strong predictor of violence, but the research is somewhat inconsistent on this point and needs further attention.

CHAPTER 6

Psychology of Sexual Assault

Sex assaulters attack others for a wide variety of reasons. After three decades of research, it is clear that sexual assault is a multide-termined behavior committed by a heterogeneous group of offenders (Brown & Forth, 1997). Sexual gratification is often not the primary reason, whereas desire for power, control, and dominance frequently is. Addressing the heterogeneity of sexual offenders and their motives is critical if we are to identify effective strategies for offender management and treatment (Brown & Forth, 1997).

In this chapter, we provide a comprehensive summary of the incidence and complexity of sexual assault, the known characteristics and developmental histories of the various sex offenders, and the methods commonly used to assess and evaluate sex offenders. The effect of sexual assault on victims will be covered in Chapter 8, and the treatment of convicted sex offenders will be described in Chapter 12. This chapter will also cover typologies of sexual offenders that are often used by both law enforcement officials and mental health professionals. Typologies, which place people into categories or groupings, are an important first step in the understanding and management of sexual assaut. A typology is useful in classifying a wide assortment of behaviors, attitudes, motives, and beliefs into a manageable set of meaningful descriptions. It helps put order into an otherwise chaotic mass of observations, a process that enables research, assessment, prevention, treatment, and policy planning to take place. Nevertheless, typologies—though often appealing—are not perfect tools and must continually be subjected to revision and validation.

Definitions of Sexual Assault and Rape

Legal definitions of what constitutes a sexual offense vary widely from state to state. In a majority of states, the broad term *sexual assault* has replaced the term *rape* in the criminal statutes. **Rape** is a narrower term, referring to forced penetration in vaginal, anal, or oral regions. Sexual assault recognizes that victims may be violated in other ways as well. In addition, in an effort to include males as victims, the statutes are becoming increasingly gender neutral.

The definitions used in federal criminal law parallel the changes in definitions in many states. The Federal Criminal Code (Title 18, Chapter 109A, Sections 2241–2243) definition of sexual assault does not even use the term *rape* and does not require the victim to label the act as rape to meet the elements of the crime (Kilpatrick, Whalley, & Edmunds, 2002). Second, the federal code distinguishes between two types of sexual abuse on the basis of the degree of force or threat of force used: (1) aggravated sexual abuse and (2) sexual abuse.

Aggravated sexual abuse by force or threat of force is when a person "knowingly causes another person to engage in a sexual act . . . or attempts to do so by using force against the person, or by threatening or placing that person in fear that the person will be subjected to death, serious bodily injury, or kidnapping." The federal code also tries to take into consideration recent increases in the use of "date rape drugs" or "acquaintance rape drugs" by defining *aggravated sexual abuse by other means.* This occurs when a person knowingly renders another person unconscious and thereby engages in a sexual act with that other person. Aggravated sexual abuse by other means also occurs when a person administers to another person by force or threat of force, or without the knowledge or permission of that person, a drug, intoxicant, or similar substance and thereby (1) substantially impairs the ability of that person to appraise or control conduct and (2) engages in a sexual act with that person.

The Federal Criminal Code defines sexual abuse—as opposed to aggravated sexual abuse—in two ways:

- causing another person to engage in a sexual activity by threatening or placing that person in fear,
- engaging in a sexual act if that person is incapable of declining participation in or communicating unwillingness to engage in that sexual act.

Governmental Definitions

As we discussed in Chapter 4, the U.S. government has three major crime measures, each published in a separate document: the Uniform Crime Reports (UCR), the National Incident-Based Reporting System (NIBRS), and the National Crime Victimization Survey (NCVS). All three measures define sexual assault slightly differently. The UCR divides sexual offending into two categories: (1) forcible rape and (2) sexual offenses. The first is considered one of the eight index crimes for which crime rates and arrest data are gathered. According to the UCR, forcible rape is "the carnal knowledge of a female forcibly and against her will. Assaults or attempts to commit rape by force or threat of force are also included; however statutory rape (without force) and other sex offenses are excluded" (Federal Bureau of Investigation [FBI], 2002b, p. 29). Statutory rapes of female victims where no force is used and the victim is under the age of consent are categorized as other sex offenses. These are in a list of nonindex offenses for which only arrest data are collected. The UCR program counts each offense in which a female of any age is forcibly raped or on whom an assault to rape or attempt to rape is made. Of the total rapes reported for 2001, 90% were classified as rapes, and the remainder was categorized as attempts.

The UCR program does *not* recognize rape when males are the victims. These sexual assaults on males are classified as simple or aggravated assaults or sex offenses, depending on the nature of the crime and the extent of the injury. The UCR also does not tabulate cases in which the offender uses threats of *nonphysical* force to obtain sex, such as threatening a person with a loss of job or other punishment if this person does not comply. In recent years, however, a few state legislatures have broadened the definition of force and criminalized sex obtained by certain nonphysical forms of coercion (Kinports, 2002).

The relatively new NIBRS, also discussed in Chapters 4 and 8, has the potential to yield fairly detailed descriptions of sexual assaults reported by participating law enforcement agencies. The NIBRS divides crimes into two major categories: Group A and Group B. Group A contains the 46 most serious crimes, including sexual offenses, and Group B contains 11 of the less serious offenses, such as passing bad checks (see Box 8.4 in Chapter 8). The sex offenses in Group A are divided into two subcategories, forcible and nonforcible. The forcible offenses include forcible rape, forcible sodomy, sexual assault with an object, and forcible fondling. For these offenses, the NIBRS provides, among other things, the following:

- demographic information on all victims;
- levels of victim injury;
- victim's perceptions of offender's age, gender, race, and ethnicity;
- victim-offender relationship.

The NIBRS also collects information on the weapons used, location of the incident, and the demographics of the offender (if arrested). Like the UCR, the NIBRS is based on law enforcement data and does not include information on convictions.

As we discussed in Chapter 4, the National Crime Victimization Survey (NCVS) is a government-sponsored survey of victims of crime. In the NCVS, rape is defined as forced sexual intercourse in which the victim may be either male or female. Sexual assault—on the other hand—includes a wide range of victimizations involving attacks in which unwanted sexual contact occurs between the victim and the offenders. Threats and attempts to commit such offenses are included in the victimization data reported by the NCVS.

Many existing rape laws require that both force and lack of consent be proven before an individual can be convicted of rape. Traditionally, for example, a lack of resistance by the victim was interpreted as evidence of consent. Ironically, at the same time, rape victims were often advised not to resist because that would only anger the rapist even more. Although no jurisdiction still adheres to the requirement that the victim must have resisted "to the utmost," some state courts

continue to require some reasonable resistance unless the force exercised by the offender prevented the victim from resisting (Kinports, 2002). The issue of consent is a critical component in most cases involving rape or sexual assault because persons accused of these crimes who choose to go to trial often use consent as their defense when their alleged victim was an adult.

Statutory rape is the unlawful sexual intercourse with a female younger than the age of consent, which may be anywhere between 12 and 18, depending on the jurisdiction and state statute. Most states, however, use a cutoff point of age 16 or 18. The age limit appears to be an arbitrary legal cutoff considered to be the age at which the person has the cognitive and emotional maturity to give meaningful consent and understand the consequences. Therefore, the state is not required to prove that the intercourse was without the consent of the female, because she is presumed incapable of consent because of her young age. Moreover, mistake as to the victim's age is usually no defense. Kinports (2002) writes, "Although this crime was traditionally justified as a means of preserving an unmarried girl's economic value to her father, today it is seen as a way of protecting vulnerable children" (p. 737). Increasingly, many contemporary state statutes are becoming gender neutral, encompassing both boys and girls. Furthermore, there typically must be at least a 2-year span between the ages of the perpetrator and the victim.

Rape by fraud refers to the act of having sexual relations with a consenting adult female under fraudulent conditions. A frequently cited example is when a professional psychotherapist has sexual intercourse with a patient under the guise of "effective treatment."

Despite these broad and much-needed shifts in definition, *rape* and *sexual assault* are still used interchangeably in both law and research to describe crimes that involve unwanted and illegal sexual acts. This is especially true with official government documents, such as those published by the U.S. Department of Justice. Even there, *rape* is increasingly reserved for sexual acts that involve actual or threatened sexual penetration, whereas *sexual assault* refers to a wide range of sexual attacks, including rape. Put another way, rape is always sexual assault, but sexual assault is not always rape.

Mindful of the distinctions and changes in definitions and requirements, we will continue to use the term *rape* when it is clear that penetration is an issue. Otherwise, *sexual assault* will be used. In addition, our discussion of research studies and typologies will employ the terminology favored by the researchers who conducted and developed them.

Prevalence and Incidence of Rape and Other Sexual Assaults

National victimization surveys indicate that the vast majority of sexual assaults are never reported to law enforcement (Kilpatrick et al., 2002). Both the NCVS and data from nongovernmental sources support this observation. Nongovernmental surveys include the National Women's Study (NWS) (Kilpatrick, Edmunds, & Seymour, 1992), the National Violence Against Women Survey (NVAW) (Tjaden & Thoennes, 1998a), and the National Survey of Adolescents (NSA) (Kilpatrick & Saunders, 1997). According to the NCVS, only about one third of sexual assaults are reported to authorities. The NWS found that only 16% of rapes were reported to the police or other authorities, and the NSA discovered that only about 14% were reported. In addition, national studies also indicate that victims are reluctant to label the experiences as a sexual assault if the attacker is a spouse, boyfriend, or acquaintance (Acierno, Resnick, & Kilpatrick, 1997). Victims with disabilities are even less likely to report sexual assaults because of their social isolation and fear (Kilpatrick et al., 2002). Many of the assailants are family members or caretakers, and the victims fear loss of support or services if they report.

According to the UCR, 90,491 forcible rapes of females (females of any age are counted) were recorded during 2001 (FBI, 2002b). Based on that volume, 62.2 of every 100,000 females were

victims during the year. The rate of forcible rapes during the past 10 years has shown a discernible downward trend (see Figure 6.1).

For UCR purposes, an offense is "cleared" when at least one person is arrested and charged or when circumstances beyond the control of law enforcement preclude an arrest for a crime that has been solved. The latter would occur when a victim decides not to cooperate with police or a suspect dies before an arrest can be made. Nationally, 44.3% of rapes reported to police were cleared during 2001. However, it is important to emphasize that most rapes are not reported to police.

The NVAW survey reports that about 15% of the adult women in the United States have been raped sometime during their lives, and another 2.8% have been victims of attempted rape (Kilpatrick et al., 2002; Tjaden & Thoennes, 1998a). For adult men, lifetime prevalence estimates for sexual assault and attempted sexual assault were 2.1% and 0.9%, respectively. Survey research in the United States and Canada suggest that more than 50% of college women have been victims of some form of sexual assault (Morry & Winkler, 2001). The NWS found that about 13% of adult women had been victims of completed rape, and about 14% had been victims of other types of sexual assault. The NSA reports that an estimated 13% of female adolescents and 3.4% of male adolescents had been victims of sexual assault at some point.

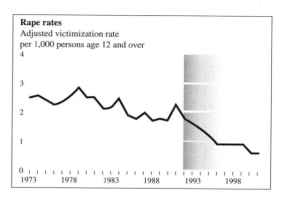

Figure 6.1   Forcible Rape Trends

Source: Bureau of Justice Statistics (2002b).

Date Rape

Date rape refers to a sexual assault that occurs within the context of a dating relationship. Date rapes appear to be far more common than originally supposed. Some researchers report that half of all rapes occur in dating situations (Madigan & Gamble, 1989). In many date rapes, the male often believes he is entitled to "payback" because he probably initiated the date, paid most of the expenses, and drove his vehicle. Hill and Fischer (2001) found in their study of male college students that "feelings of entitlement" appear to be a central feature in date rape behaviors and attitudes. In fact, feelings of entitlement may well be a key feature in other forms of sexual assault, including marital rape and incest. An understanding of the "entitlement" issue may significantly help in the development of date rape prevention, education, and intervention programs.

Under date rape conditions, it should be mentioned that the victim often blames herself for the attack and is often blamed by others for presumably arousing her date. Moreover, a sexual assault by a date or acquaintance may be more traumatizing than an assault by a stranger because of the implicit trust involved. The connection between alcohol use and date or acquaintance rape is strong. In more than half of sexual assaults involving dating partners, alcohol had been consumed by either one or both partners (Gross, Bennett, Sloan, Marx, & Jurgens, 2001). When the victim has been drinking, she is even more likely to blame herself for the attack.

Demographics of Men Who Rape

One of the most consistent demographic findings about rapists is that, as a group, they tend to be young. According to data reported in the UCR, for instance, nearly half of those arrested for forcible rape are younger than age 25, and more than 16% of those arrested are younger than age 18 (FBI, 2001). Another consistent finding is that *many* men convicted of rape manifest

a wide spectrum of antisocial behavior across their early life span. Warren, Hazelwood, and Reboussin (1991) report that in their sample of serial rapists, 71% were involved with shoplifting, 55% were assaultive to adults, 24% set fires, and 19% were violently cruel to animals during childhood and adolescence. Nearly 28% of convicted rapists released from prison are rearrested for a new violent crime within 3 years after release (Greenfeld, 1997). In addition, about 8% of these released rapists are arrested again for another charge of rape within that time frame. In fact, released rapists are more than 10 times as likely as nonrapists to be rearrested for rape, and those offenders who have served time for sexual assault are nearly 8 times as likely as those convicted of other crimes to be rearrested for a new sexual assault (Greenfeld, 1997).

In about 12% of the reported rapes, the offender used a firearm, 7% used a knife, and 80% involved the use of physical force only (Greenfeld, 1997). Murders classified as involving rape and other sex offenses are referred to as sexual assault murders. Sexual assault murders account for less than 1% of all homicides with known circumstances in the United States. Surprisingly, though, offenders younger than age 18 have accounted for more than 10% of the sexual assault murders that have taken place since 1976 (Greenfeld, 1997). A vast majority of the victims killed in sexual assaults are young White females killed by young White males. Twenty-five percent of the victims are younger than age 18, and 2% are younger than age 12. More than 80% of sexual assault murders are *intra*racial (victim and offender are of the same race or ethnic origin). And sexual assault murders are far more likely to involve strangers than rape alone or nonlethal sexual assault.

As a group, sex offenders appear to be deficient in social skills and intimacy and are often described as lonely (Marshall, 1996). Furthermore, child molesters, on average, appear to be more deficient in intimacy and are lonelier than rapists, who, in turn, appear to be lonelier and more lacking in intimacy than nonsex offenders (Marshall, 1996). Despite these generalizations, researchers know that sex offenders are not a homogeneous group. Several attempts have been made to capture their heterogeneity into categories or types. In the following sections, we will discuss the best known of these attempts to classify offenders.

Typologies of Men Who Rape

Classification systems, based on either personality traits or behavioral patterns of individuals, are called typologies, and they have been moderately successful in their ability to add to our understanding of criminal behavior. Chief among the typologies are those pertinent to men who rape. It is important to realize, however, that individuals do not always fit neatly into a particular type; they only approximate it. There are very few "walking textbooks." Underscoring this point, Don Gibbons (1988) wrote that classification systems or typologies generally consist

> of criminological foundations that assume that real life persons can be found in significant numbers who resemble the descriptions of offenders in the various typologies that have been put forth . . . researchers have often failed to uncover many point-for-point real life cases of these hypothesized types of offenders. (p. 9)

Another problem with typologies is that very few of them have been subjected to empirical verification or validation studies, and they sometimes encourage stereotypes of offenders (Schwartz, 1995). That is, typologies can promote a tendency for the public and professionals to jam people into their favorite categories without empirical support or thoughtful consideration of individual differences between offenders.

However, typologies can be very useful in organizing a vast array of behavioral patterns that would otherwise be a confusing muddle. They are also useful in correctional facilities for risk management, such as deciding where to place an inmate, or in treatment programming, such as deciding what particular treatment

technique or strategy might be most beneficial for an inmate or offender. The "acid test" of the usefulness of a typology, however, is its ability to estimate the risk of particular offenders to reoffend (Quinsey, 1986).

Many rape typologies have been suggested, including that used by the FBI (Hazelwood & Burgess, 1987), the Selkin typology (Selkin, 1975), the Nagayama-Hall typology (Nagayama-Hall, 1992), and the Nicholas Groth typology (Groth, 1979). The most empirically based typology, however, is the Massachusetts Treatment Center's typology, which has drawn and continues to draw considerable research attention.

The Massachusetts Treatment Center Rapist Typology

A group of researchers at the Massachusetts Treatment Center (MTC) (Cohen, Seghorn, & Calmas, 1969; Cohen, Garafalo, Boucher, & Seghorn, 1971; Knight & Prentky, 1987; Prentky & Knight, 1986) has developed an empirically based and useful typology based on the behavioral patterns of convicted rapists, including the appearance of aggressive and sexual patterns in the sexual assaults. It also provides an excellent framework for describing the psychological characteristics of rapists in general.

The MTC researchers believe that rape is a multidetermined behavior that can best be explained by models incorporating a multitude of dimensions. An empirically based typology that takes into account all possible categories of rape behavior is such a model. Originally, the researchers identified four categories of rapists: displaced aggressive, compensatory, sexual aggressive, and impulsive. These have been replaced with a new typology. The MTC classification system now identifies *four* major types based on the rapist's primary motivation (opportunistic, pervasively angry, sexual, vindictive) and *nine* subtypes (Knight et al., 1998; see Figure 6.2). The new system is called the Massachusetts Treatment Center Rapist Typology Version 3 (abbreviated MTC:R3) and has been subjected to extensive research by the MTC group as well as other researchers (Barbaree & Serin, 1993; Barbaree, Seto, Serin, Amos, & Preston, 1994; Harris, Rice, & Quinsey, 1994).

The nine discrete rape subtypes are differentiated on the basis of six variables that have been consistently found by clinicians and researchers to play an important role in the behavioral, emotional, and thought patterns of a wide array of rapists (and child molesters). Before covering the typologies themselves, we will discuss the six variables, which are as follows:

- Aggression
- Impulsivity
- Social competence
- Sexual fantasies
- Sadism
- Naive cognitions or beliefs

In a sense, these six variables form the "building blocks" for the development and ongoing revision of the MTC rape typology, and each should be described separately to get a deeper understanding of typology subtypes. It should be understood at the outset that some of these variables appear to be more prominent in some rapists than others.

Aggression

For our purposes here, aggression may be divided into two broad categories: (1) instrumental or strategic violence and (2) expressive aggression or nonstrategic violence (Prentky & Knight, 1991). The former represents the type of aggression used by rapists to gain victim compliance. There is usually no anger present in instrumental aggression, except in reaction to a victim's lack of cooperation or compliance. Expressive aggression, on the other hand, is used by rapists to hurt, humiliate, abuse, or degrade the victim in some way. This form of aggression goes way beyond simply obtaining victim compliance and is often extremely violent. Sexual desire may not even be the primary motivation for the attack. This instrumental-aggressive dichotomy does have

its limitations, however, as some rapists demonstrate a mixture of both. As Prentky and Knight (1991) point out, "Those rapists who intend only to force victim compliance are likely to vary widely in the amount of aggression evident in their offenses" (p. 647). It may depend on the extent of victim resistance, the level of alcohol or drugs ingested by the offender, the presence of other aggressors or victims, and the context in which the attack occurs. Furthermore, sometimes the expressive aggression is "sexualized," and sometimes it is not. However, the instrumental-expressive dichotomy does serve as a useful springboard for discussing most of the MTC subtypes.

Impulsivity

There is considerable research and clinical evidence that impulsivity is a significant factor in many sexual assaults and criminal behavior in general. Lifestyle impulsivity has been found to be a powerful predictor of recidivism and frequency of offending (Prentky & Knight, 1986, 1991). Some impulsive people seem to have an overpowering deficiency in self-control and continually revert to old behavioral patterns, regardless of the costs. Research has consistently found that lifestyle impulsivity emerges as one of the strongest and most meaningful ways to differentiate repetitive rapists and other repetitive sex offenders such as child molesters. It is also the major focus of many treatment programs designed to change the antisocial behavior of sex offenders. As noted by Prentky and Knight (1991), "Clinicians have long recognized the importance of impulsivity for relapse and have introduced self-control and impulsivity management modules into treatment" (p. 656).

Social Competence

Sexual offenders have often been described as having poor social and interpersonal skills, especially when dealing with the opposite sex (Prentky & Knight, 1991). The MTC researchers refer to this characteristic as social competence, a concept that plays an important role in developing the various subtypes of the MTC typology. This feature is especially prominent in the behavioral patterns of child molesters. There are also consistent research findings that rapists as a group are not assertive in their everyday relationships with others. It should be realized that social competence represents a wide range of different abilities, such as social assertiveness, communication skills, social problem solving, social comfort, and political savvy, and consequently should be understood as a complex skill that is developed within a variety of contexts.

Sexual Fantasies

Sexual fantasy refers to any mental imagery that is sexually arousing or erotic to the individual (Leitenberg & Henning, 1995). Many clinicians believe that sexual fantasy is a necessary precursor to deviant sexual behavior. As stated by Leitenberg and Henning (1995), "There seems to be little question that many men who commit sexual offenses frequently have sexually arousing fantasies about these acts and masturbate to these fantasies regularly and presumably more often than nonoffenders" (p. 487). In one clinical study of men who had been convicted of sexual homicide, approximately 80% had sexual fantasies related to sexually assaultive behavior (Burgess, Hartman, & Ressler, 1986), and the percentage appears to be even higher for serial sexual murders (Prentky et al., 1989). In fact, most treatment programs for sex offenders include a component designed to directly change sexual fantasies (Leitenberg & Henning, 1995). Some research has discovered that the content, frequency, and intensity of deviant sexual fantasies often differentiate between solo and serial sexual murderers (Prentky & Knight, 1991).

It should be noted that it is not unusual for people to have sexual fantasies that would be inappropriate, or even criminal, for them to act on. Briere and Runtz (1989) found that 21% of male college students in an anonymous survey admitted that children sometimes attracted them sexually, and 9% of the sample said they have sexual fantasies about children (Leitenberg & Henning, 1995). In a survey conducted by Malamuth (1981), 35% of male college students felt there was some likelihood that they would sexually assault if they could be sure of getting away with it. In another study, 60% of a group of 352 male undergraduates indicated that they might rape or force a female to perform sexual acts against her will if given the opportunity (Briere, Malamuth, & Ceniti, 1981). Nevertheless, research (e.g., Dean & Malamuth, 1997) suggests that although aggressive or violent sexual fantasies are common in some college males, the degree to which these fantasies translate into an actual sexual assault depends on the individual's empathy for others. More specifically, those men who are highly self-centered are more likely to be sexually aggressive and act out their sexual fantasies. "There is not evidence that sexual fantasies, by themselves, are either a sufficient or a necessary condition for committing a sexual offense" (Leitenberg & Henning, 1995, p. 488).

Sadism

"Typically, central to the definition of sadism is a pattern of extreme violence in the offense that has often focused on erogenous areas of the body and that may be considered bizarre or appear ritualized" (Prentky & Knight, 1991, p. 652). Sadism is illustrated by cruel and malicious acts that are enjoyed by and often sexually arousing to the offender. Sadistic rapists, compared to other types of rapists, tend to offend more frequently against victims who are close friends, intimates, or family (Prentky, Burgess, & Carter, 1986).

Naive Cognitions or Beliefs

Research indicates that offense-justifying attitudes are prevalent among males prone to rape and, to some extent, among the general male population as well. Similar to sexual fantasies, irrational attitudes and cognitive distortions usually are a major focus of most treatment programs for sex offenders.

Sexual socialization and social learning play very critical roles in the development of those who choose to sexually assault. Sexual behavior and attitudes toward women are acquired through the day-to-day contacts with family members, peers, entertainment models, and the media in general. Koss and Dinero (1988) found that sexually aggressive men expressed greater hostility toward women, frequently used alcohol, frequently viewed violent and degrading pornography, and were closely connected to peer groups that reinforced highly sexualized and dominating views of women. These same men were more likely to believe that force and coercion are legitimate ways to gain compliance in sexual relationships. Koss and Dinero conclude, "In short, the results provided support for the developmental sequence for sexual aggression in which early experiences and psychological characteristics establish conditions for sexual violence" (p. 144).

Research reveals that a majority of sexually aggressive men subscribe to attitudes and ideology that encourage men to be dominant, controlling, and powerful, whereas women are expected to be submissive, permissive, and compliant. Such an orientation seems to have a particularly strong disinhibitory effect on sexually aggressive men, encouraging them to interpret ambiguous behaviors of women as come-ons, to believe that women are not really offended by coercive sexual behaviors, and to perceive rape victims as desiring and deriving gratification from being sexually assaulted (Lipton, McDonel, & McFall, 1987).

Rape myths and misogynistic (hatred of women) attitudes appear to play a major role in sexual assault. Rape myths are "attitudes and beliefs that are generally false but widely and persistently held, and that serve to deny and justify male sexual aggression against women" (Lonsway & Fitzgerald, 1994, p. 134). Not all rapists tend to have these attitudes, however. Men who subscribe to these points of view hold more rape-supportive points of view (Good, Heppner, Hillenbrand-Gunn, & Wang, 1995) and date rape–supportive points of view (Hill & Fischer, 2001; Truman, Tokar, & Fischer, 1996). Researchers

have also explored the "macho personality constellation," which is characterized by having callous sexual attitudes, believing that violence is manly, and getting excitement from taking high risks (Hill & Fischer, 2001; Mosher & Anderson, 1986). Some sexually aggressive men also believe that women must be kept in their place—even if it means humiliating them—and the best way to achieve this world order is to assault them physically and sexually. The underlying cognitive framework that most sexually aggressive men seem to have is hostility toward women (Lonsway & Fitzgerald, 1995).

In his ongoing research on sexual aggression, Neil Malamuth and his colleagues have identified several characteristics that distinguish sexually aggressive males from their less aggressive counterparts. The more important characteristics include (1) an insecure, defensive, hypersensitive, and hostile-distrustful orientation toward women; (2) gratification from being able to control and dominate women; and (3) a strong tendency to misread cues from women (Malamuth, Linz, Heavey, Barnes, & Acker, 1995).

Malamuth and his associates (Malamuth, Heavey, & Linz, 1993; Malamuth, Sockloskie, Koss, & Tanaka, 1991) argue that sexually aggressive men have beliefs (or schema) that predispose them to regard women as untrustworthy. These men do not believe what women say or do, especially when it pertains to romantic or sexual interests. In short, these men are highly suspicious of women and perceive communication from women as having the opposite meaning of that intended. Malamuth et al. (1991) note that societies and subcultures that regard power, toughness, dominance, aggressiveness, and competitive selfishness as masculine qualities tend to breed men who are hostile to women and to the qualities associated with femininity, such as gentleness, empathy, and sensitivity. "The display of these traditionally feminine characteristics may signify to some men a loss of appropriate identity, whereas engaging in dominance and aggression, including the sexual arena, may reinforce the idea that they are 'real men'" (Malamuth et al., 1995, p. 354). For such men, sexual aggression may be a way to reaffirm their sense of masculinity, as advocated by that particular society or subculture.

Malamuth also has found that sexually aggressive men have information-processing deficits in their ability to separate seductive from friendly behavior or hostile from assertive behavior (Malamuth & Brown, 1994; Murphy, Coleman, & Haynes, 1986). For example, rapists are less accurate than nonrapists in reading women's cues in first date interactions (Lipton et al., 1987). This deficit is especially apparent when the woman's communication is direct, clear, and strong. If she protests too much, it means—to the sexually aggressive male—that she really means the opposite. To the sexually aggressive male, she is game-playing and attempting to be seductive by using assertiveness or aggression.

The misinterpretation of communication (both verbal and nonverbal) is not limited to the sexual assault context. It is often a key element found in highly aggressive and violent persons, including children. Kenneth Dodge and his associates, for example, discovered that highly aggressive children often have what he calls a **hostile attribution bias,** as described in Chapters 4 and 5. That is, children prone to high levels of aggression are more likely to interpret ambiguous actions of others as hostile and threatening than

their less aggressive peers (Dodge, 1993). They are apt to perceive aggression and attack where none was intended. Research has consistently shown that violent youth "typically define social problems in hostile ways, adopt hostile goals, and seek few additional facts, generate few alternative solutions, anticipate few consequences for aggression, and give higher priority to their aggressive solutions" (Eron & Slaby, 1994, p. 10). This information-processing deficiency may be the result of the lack of opportunity during early childhood to develop social and interpersonal skills for detecting correct cues from others.

MTC:R3

As described previously, the MTC:R3 rape typology consists of nine discrete rapists who are differentiated on the basis of the six variables already discussed. This section describes these nine types in more detail, and the typology is illustrated in Figure 6.2. Thus far, the research has focused almost exclusively on male rapists. Although a small percentage of reported rapes involve women as offenders, these women are almost invariably operating in partnership with a male offender. In recent years, though, some

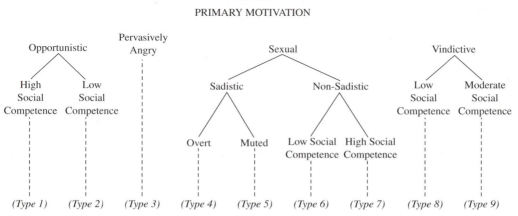

Figure 6.2   Breakdown of Four Categorizations of Rapist Type Into Nine Rapist Subtypes (MTC:R3)

Source: Knight et al. (1998). Copyright ©1998 by Sage Publications, Inc. Reprinted with permission by Sage Publications, Inc.

researchers are suggesting that the prevalence of independent female sexual offending has been underestimated, chiefly due to society's reluctance to accept that women sexually offend or that their offending is harmful to their victims (Becker, Hall, & Stinson, 2001). Thus, whereas our discussion of the MTC:R3 typology focuses on the male as perpetrator, we recognize that there are many unanswered questions about female offenders.

The Opportunistic Rapist (Types 1 and 2). The impulsive or **opportunistic rapist** engages in sexual assault simply because the opportunity to rape presents itself. Thus, this offender type is motivated more by contextual factors and opportunity than by any internally driven sexual fantasy (Prentky & Knight, 1991). The rape may occur within the context of some other antisocial act, such as a robbery or burglary. Alternately, the victim could be a woman encountered at a bar or party. The most prominent characteristic of these offenders is their impulsivity and lack of self-control, resembling those of an immature child. More important, this poor impulsive control leads to a pervasive and enduring lifestyle of impulsive and irresponsible behavior, frequently leading to an extensive criminal career. Thus, rape becomes only one of many antisocial behaviors in this person's repertoire.

The opportunistic rapist is not perceived to be "person oriented" and sees the victim only as a sexual object. He seems to have little interest in trying to arouse the victim and little concern for the victim's fear or discomfort. Opportunistic offenders consistently engage in troublesome acting-out behavior throughout their childhood, adolescence, and into adulthood. To be classified as an opportunistic rapist according to the MTC:R3, the offender must show the following:

- Callous indifference to the welfare and comfort of the victim
- Presence of no more force than is necessary to force the compliance of the victim (instrumental aggression). Any excessive force or aggression rules out this type.

- Evidence of adult impulsive behavior, such as frequent fighting, vandalism, and other impulsively driven antisocial behaviors

The MTC researchers have discovered that opportunistic rapists can be subdivided on the basis of their social competence and the developmental stage at which their high impulsivity is first noticed. The opportunistic offender who is high in social competence—a Type 1 rapist—manifests impulsivity in *adulthood*. The Type 2 rapist, on the other hand, is low in social competence and demonstrates impulsivity during *adolescence*.

The Pervasively Angry Rapist (Type 3). The **pervasively angry rapist** demonstrates a predominance of global and undifferentiated anger that pervades all areas of the offender's life. These rapists are angry at the world in general, and their anger is directed at both men and women. The acts reflect capricious and random violence directed at whoever gets in the way at the wrong time and wrong place (Prentky & Knight, 1991). When these men attack women, their violent and aggressive behaviors exhibit a minimum or total absence of sexual arousal. Their attacks are characterized by high levels of aggression, and they inflict considerable injury on their victims. Brown and Forth (1997) report that many psychopaths who sexually assault fall most often into the opportunistic or the pervasively angry categories.

The occupational history of the pervasively angry rapist is usually stable and often reveals some level of success. He perceives himself as athletic, strong, and masculine. More often than not, his occupation is a "masculine" one, such as truck driver, carpenter, mechanic, electrician, or plumber. His friends typically describe him as having a quick, violent temper (Holmes & Holmes, 2002). These offenders experienced chaotic and unstable childhoods and family life. Many of them were adopted or foster children who were often neglected or abused.

According to Knight and Prentky (1987), an offender must demonstrate the following characteristics during the attack to be classified as the pervasively angry type:

- Presence of a high degree of nonsexualized aggression or rage expressed through verbal and/or physical assault that clearly exceeds what is necessary to gain compliance of the victim (expressive aggression)
- Evidence of adolescent *and* adult unsocialized, antisocial behavior
- An attack that is usually unplanned and unpremeditated

So far, no particular subtypes have been identified for the pervasively angry rapist. Therefore, the pervasively angry rapist is referred to simply as Type 3.

The Sexually Motivated Rapist (Types 4 through 7). The motivation for the next four types is "sexual" in that their attacks are characterized by the presence of protracted sexual or sadistic fantasies that strongly influence the assaults. A discernible pattern of sexual preoccupation and fantasy is what all four have in common. The **sexually motivated rapist** is subdivided into sadistic or nonsadistic, and each itself is further subdivided (see Figure 6.2). Sadistic sexual offenders are either "overt" (Type 4) or "muted" (Type 5), depending on whether their sexual-aggressive acts are directly expressed in violent attacks (overt) or are only fantasized (muted). The muted offender's motive is the victim's fear or some violent fantasy that aids in his sexual arousal. That is, the victim's fear excites him, or he relies on some rehearsed sexual fantasy during the act to excite him. The overt sadistic rapist demonstrates *both* sexual and aggressive elements in his assault. In essence, the victim's actual (not fantasized) pain and discomfort are prerequisites for his sexual excitement. He believes his victims fundamentally "enjoy" being abused, forcefully raped, aggressively dominated, and controlled. Therefore, this type of rapist interprets the victim's resistance and struggle as a game, and the more the victim resists, the more excited and aggressive he becomes. At first, the attack may begin as attempts at seduction, but with increasing resistance from the victim, aggressive behaviors become increasingly prominent. On the other hand, rage or high levels of violence are precipitated in the offender when the victim, out of abject fear or helplessness, becomes passive and submissive, so it seems to be a no-win situation for the victim. In this context, in his eyes, the victim is no longer playing the "game" properly.

Overt sadistic rapists are frequently married, but they show little commitment to the marriage. Their backgrounds often are replete with antisocial behavior beginning during adolescence or before and ranging from truancy to rape murder. They have often had severe behavior problems in school, and throughout their lifetimes, they have displayed poor behavior control and a low frustration tolerance. They manifest consistently more paraphilias than the other types of rapists. **Paraphilias** are sexual disorders and deviations in which sexual arousal occurs almost exclusively in the context of inappropriate objects or individuals (Durand & Barlow, 2000). Examples include fetishism, voyeurism, sexual sadism, and sexual masochism.

On occasion, the Type 4 rapist engages in sexual sadism that is so extreme that the victim may be murdered. To qualify as an overt sadistic rapist, the offender must demonstrate the following:

- A level of aggression or violence that clearly exceeds what is necessary to force compliance of the victim
- Explicit, unambiguous evidence that aggression is sexually exciting and arousing to him. This can be illustrated either by descriptions that the offender derives sexual pleasure from injurious acts to the victim, or the injurious acts are focused on parts of the body that have sexual significance.

To qualify as a sadistic, muted rapist, on the other hand, the offender must demonstrate the following:

- Instrumental aggression or enough force to gain compliance
- Evidence that sexual fantasies of violence or the fear of the victim excite him

The Nonsadistic Offenders (Types 6 and 7). The **nonsadistic rapists** engage in a sexual attack because of an intense sexual arousal prompted by specific stimuli identified in the intended victim. Although rape is, by definition, clearly a violent act, aggression is not the significant feature in the attack of the sexually motivated, nonsadistic rapist. Rather, the fundamental motivation is the desire to prove sexual prowess and adequacy to the victim. This type is also known as the "power reassurance rapist" (Holmes & Holmes, 2002). These men live in a world of fantasy, oriented around themes of how victims will yield eagerly under attack, submit to pleasurable intercourse, and find their skill and performance so outstanding that the victims will plead for a return engagement. These rapists fantasize that they will at last be able to prove their masculinity and sexual competence to themselves and the victims. In their sexual assaults, these rapists are described as being highly sexually aroused and showing obvious disturbances of lack of control and cognitive-perceptual distortions of reality.

The victim of such a rapist is most often a stranger, but the rapist has probably watched and followed the victim for some time. Certain stimuli have drawn his attention and excited him. For instance, he may be attracted to college or professional women who normally would not be attracted to him. S. T. Holmes and R. M. Holmes (2002) report that nonsadistic, sexually motivated rapists prefer women who are approximately their own age and race, especially those residing in the same neighborhood or close to their place of employment. The attacks are often done at night, with a time interval between 7 and 15 days (Holmes & Holmes, 2002). If the victim physically resists his attack, the nonsadistic rapist is likely to flee from the scene. During the entire incident, there will be very low levels of aggressive behavior on his part. Sometimes, if he is successful, he may contact the victim at a later time to inquire about her well-being or even to ask for a date. Generally, this type of rapist confines his illegal activity to sexual assault and is not involved in other forms of antisocial behavior.

Assignment to the nonsadistic categories requires the following behavioral indicators:

- Presence of verbalizations aimed at self-reassurance and self-affirmation
- Behaviors that reflect, albeit in a distorted fashion, an attempt at establishing an amorous relationship with the victim
- Concerns for the victim's welfare, comfort, and enjoyment of the sexual experience

Research (e.g., Knight & Prentky, 1987; Knight et al., 1998) has shown that there may be at least two subtypes of nonsadistic, sexually motivated rapists, similar to the two subdivisions of the opportunistic rapist. One group may be described as quiet, shy, submissive, and socially inadequate. Although they are dependable workers, their poor social skills and resulting low self-esteem prevent them from succeeding at occupational advancement. This person is usually classified as low socially competent or Type 6. The second subtype may be more socially adaptable and competent and achieve more occupational advancement and professional development. This rapist is classified as highly socially competent (Type 7) (see Figure 6.2.).

The Vindictive Rapist (Types 8 and 9). In an effort to express their anger toward women, **vindictive rapists** use the act of rape to harm, humiliate, and degrade women. A violent sexual assault is, in their eyes, the most humiliating and dominating act possible. The victims are brutally assaulted and subjected to sadistic acts such as biting, cutting, or tearing of parts of the body. In most instances, the victims are complete strangers, although the victim may possess certain characteristics that attract the assailant's attention. Often, in addition to using physical abuse, this attacker will use a great deal of profanity and emotional abuse through threats. Resisting this particular rapist may engender more violence from him.

Although many of these rapists are married, their relationships with women are characterized by periodic irritation and violence, and they probably engage in domestic violence and wife abuse. These men generally perceive women as demanding, hostile, and unfaithful individuals who need to be dominated and controlled. They sometimes select their victim because they perceive something in her behavior or appearance that communicates assertiveness, independence, and professional activity. The assault usually follows some precipitating events involving a wife, girlfriend, or mother that he generalizes to all women in general. Upon arrest, the offender often attributes his offense to an "uncontrollable impulse" that he could not control. Like the opportunistic and nonsadistic rapists, the vindictive rapist can be subdivided into competence types, although they are low and moderate rather than low and high competence.

To qualify as a vindictive rapist, the following behaviors must be evident:

- Clear evidence, in verbalization or behavior, of the intent to demean, degrade, or humiliate the victim
- No evidence that the aggressive behavior is eroticized or that sexual pleasure is derived from the injurious acts
- The injurious acts are not focused on parts of the body that have sexual significance

Summary

Although human beings rarely fit neatly into typologies, the MTC rape typology is useful in understanding rape and helps in treatment and in the prediction of recidivism. It takes into consideration behavioral patterns, rather than simply personality traits, as well as the context within which the behavior patterns occur. However, the MTC typology needs refinement and reconstruction, a process the group has been pursuing for a number of years. Knight and Prentky (1990) conclude that "the MTC:R3 is a typological system that was developed to increase

understanding of the etiology of sexual offending and to help predict recidivism. It might be that an alternative typology or a variant of MTC:R3 can be developed to maximize detection" (p. 78).

The Groth Rapist Typology

Nicholas Groth (1979; Groth, Burgess, & Holmstrom, 1977) has proposed typologies for both rapists and child molesters that are somewhat similar to the MTC systems. We will cover the **Groth rape typology** in this section and the **Groth child molester typology** under the next section on the topic. Although the MTC:R3 was largely built on research and statistical analyses, the Groth typology has been largely clinically developed and has not been adequately tested for reliability and validity. Mental health workers, though, tend to like the Groth classification system because it is simple and more straightforward to use. In addition, many police investigators continue to use the system in the development of psychological profiles of sex offenders.

The Groth system is based on the *presumed* motivations and aims that underlie almost all rapes. According to Groth, rape is a "pseudosexual act" in which sex serves merely as a vehicle for the primary motivations of power and aggression. He asserts that "rape is never the result simply of sexual arousal that has no other opportunity for gratification. . . . Rape is always a symptom of some psychological dysfunction, either temporary and transient or chronic and repetitive" (Groth, 1979, p. 5). Rape, he says, "is always and foremost an aggressive act" (p. 12). On this basis, Groth divides rape behavior into three major categories: (1) anger rape, (2) power rape, and (3) sadistic rape.

In **anger rape**, the offender uses more physical force than necessary to gain compliance and engages in a variety of sexual acts that are degrading or humiliating to the female. He also expresses his contempt for the victim through abusive and profane language. Rape, for the anger rapist, is a violent act of conscious anger and rage toward women. According to Groth, sex is actually "dirty," offensive, and disgusting to the anger rapist, and this is the reason why he uses the sexual act to defile and degrade the victim. To illustrate, Groth (1979) quotes one rapist: "I wanted to knock the woman off her pedestal, and I felt rape was the worst thing I could do to her" (p. 14). Very often, his attacks are prompted by a previous conflict or humiliation by some significant woman in his life, such as a wife, supervisor, or mother. However, some anger rapists are also reacting to a recent upset that does not necessarily involve a woman, such as being rejected from military service, being fired, being burdened by financial debts, or being harassed by others. Considerable physical injury to the victim is common.

The offender in **power rape** seeks to establish power and control over his victim. Consequently, the amount of physical force and threat used will depend on the degree of submission shown by the victim. "I told her to undress and when she refused I struck her across the face to show her I meant business" (Groth, 1979, p. 26). The goal of the power rapist is sexual conquest, and he will try everything in his power to overcome any resistance. Sexual intercourse is his way of establishing his masculine identity, authority, potency, mastery, and domination as well as providing sexual gratification. According to Groth, the victim is sometimes kidnapped or held captive in some fashion, and she may be subjected to repeated sexual assaults over an extended period of time. However, the offender is often disappointed that the assault did not live up to his expectations and fantasies. "Everything was pleasurable in the fantasy, and there was acceptance, whereas in reality of the situation, it wasn't pleasurable, and the girl was scared, not turned on to me" (Groth, 1979, p. 27).

The third pattern of rape proposed by Groth is the **sadistic rape,** which includes both sexual and aggressive aspects. The sadistic rapist experiences sexual arousal and excitement at the victim's maltreatment, helplessness, and suffering. The assault may involve bondage and torture, and he often administers physical abuse to various parts of the victim's body. Prostitutes, women he considers promiscuous, or women representing symbols of something he wants to punish or destroy often incur the wrath of the sadistic rapist. The victim may be stalked, abducted, abused, and sometimes murdered.

Groth (1979) estimated that more than half of the offenders evaluated or treated by his agency (Connecticut Sex Offender Program) were power rapists, 40% were anger rapists, and only 5% were sadistic rapists. Interestingly, Groth asked convicted sex offenders to rate the sexual pleasure they had received from the rape on a scale from 1 (*little or none*) to 10 (*extremely satisfying*). Most of the offenders gave ratings of 3 or less, indicating low sexual pleasure from the act. In fact, Groth found that many men fail to have orgasms during the rape. Most reactions from all the sex offenders in the sample to the sexual aspects of the attack ranged from disappointment to disgust. Moreover, none of the offenders thought rape was more rewarding or gratifying sexually than consensual sex. Similar results have been reported by Warren, Reboussin, Hazelwood, and Wright (1989).

One of the major contributions of the Groth typology is that it questioned the notion that rapists are motivated largely by sexual desire or that rapists are all the same. However, although the descriptions of the offenders are intuitively appealing, empirical evidence in support of the reliability and validity of the typology is lacking. Very few research studies have examined the typology in recent years. Of the two major typologies, the MTC version is by far the more heavily researched and validated.

Pedophilia

Definitions of Pedophilia

Pedophilia, commonly known as "child molestation" or child sexual abuse, is defined in the *DSM-IV* as a condition in which, "over a period of at least 6 months, recurrent, intense sexually arousing fantasies, sexual urges, or behaviors involving sexual activity with a pre-pubescent child or children (generally age 13 years or younger)" occur (American Psychiatric Association, 1994, p. 528). The *DSM-IV* further speci-fies that some pedophiles are sexually attracted only to children (the exclusive type), whereas others are attracted sexually to both children and adults (nonexclusive type).

The term *pedophilia* is derived from the Greek words *pais*, meaning *child*, and *philein*, meaning *love*. If the child victim is the offender's relative—sometimes referred to as *intrafamilial* child molestation—the pedophilia is called **incest**. By far the largest group in this category is fathers who molest their sexually immature daughters or stepdaughters (Rice & Harris, 2002). *Extra-familial* child molestation, on the other hand, refers to sexual abuse from a person *outside* the family. However, the two categories probably overlap, perhaps to a large extent. Rice and Harris (2002), for example, report that a significant number of intrafamilial molesters have also offended outside the family.

Some mental health workers approach pedophilia by arguing that pedophilia and child molestation should mean two different things, with the former limited to fantasies of sexual attraction to children, whereas the latter refers to the act itself. In this section, however, we will continue to use the term *pedophilia* as advocated by the *DSM-IV*, which includes both fantasies and behaviors. In addition, the behaviors may range from touching to penetration.

A variety of other terms are also used to describe this behavior. Mental health workers may use the umbrella term *paraphilia*. The essen-tial features of paraphilia "are recurrent sexually arousing fantasies, sexual urges, or behaviors generally involving 1) nonhuman objects, 2) the suffering or humiliation of oneself or one's part-ner, or 3) children or other nonconsenting persons, that occur over a period of at least 6 months" (American Psychiatric Association,

1994, p. 522). Another term, *hebephilia*, is applied to men who are most attracted to pubescent or young adolescent children. However, the distinc-tion between hebephilia and pedophilia does not seem to be clinically meaningful and has yet to be demonstrated empirically as a distinct diagnostic category (Blanchard, Klassen, Dickey, Kuban, & Blak, 2001). *Teleiophilia* (from the Greek work *teleios*, meaning *full grown*) is sometimes used to denote men who have the normal erotic preference for physically mature persons but who occasionally molest children under certain circumstances, such as when the offender is intoxicated (Blanchard et al., 2001). However, their sexual interest in adults far exceeds their sexual interest in children.

Some Demographics of Child Molesters

Although there is considerable age variability, pedophiles tend to be older than those who rape, ranging between the ages of 36 and 40. Prentky, Knight, and Lee (1997) assert that the more an offender's sexual preference is limited to children, the less socially competent he is likely to be. In this context, social competence refers to the offender's strength and range of social and sexual relationships with adults. Many studies (e.g., Marshall, Barbaree, & Fernandez, 1995; Marshall & Mazzucco, 1995; Prentky et al., 1997) have continually documented the observation that pedophiles are inadequate socially, lack interpersonal skills, are underassertive, and have poor self-esteem.

Perhaps because of the extremely negative attitudes the public has toward child sexual abuse, pedophiles rarely take full responsibility for their actions. Many claim that they went blank, were too intoxicated to know what they were doing, could not help themselves, or did not know what came over them. Overall, they demonstrate a strong preference for attributing their behavior to external forces or motivating factors largely outside their personal control.

Few crimes are considered as despicable as the sexual abuse of children, and yet so little is understood about its causes, incidence, and reoffense risk (Prentky et al., 1997). Data on pedophilia are difficult to obtain because there are no central or national objective recording systems for tabulating sexual offenses against children. The available evidence suggests, though, that pedophilia is grossly underreported. Also, offenders may be arrested and prosecuted under a variety of statutes and for a variety of offenses, including child rape, aggravated assault, sodomy, incest, indecent exposure, and lewd and lascivious behavior. Although the UCR program lists arrests for sex offenses, it does not differentiate pedophilia from the mixture of other possible sexual offenses. In addition, arrests are reported for crimes against children, but not all crimes against children are sex offenses. Self-report surveys are somewhat more instructive. These surveys indicate that from a quarter to a third of all females and a tenth or more of all males in the United States have been sexually molested during childhood (Finkelhor & Lewis, 1988; Peters, Wyatt, & Finkelhor, 1986).

Similar to rapists, the classification, diagnosis, and assessment of child molesters are complicated by a high degree of variability among individuals in relation to personal characteristics, life experiences, criminal histories, and motives for offending (Prentky et al., 1997). "There is no single 'profile' that accurately describes or accounts for all child molesters" (Prentky et al., 1997, p. v). Perhaps the best way to provide a solid framework for any presentation on the complex nature of pedophilia and the offenders involved is through a discussion of two well-known typologies. Again they are the research-based (MTC:CM3) typology of the Massachusetts Research Center and the more clinically based Groth typology. Like the rapist typologies discussed earlier, these typologies have been formulated primarily with reference to male offenders. Women pedophiles, believed to be extremely rare, are not often subjected to research. As noted above, though, some researchers are questioning the earlier assumptions that women's sexual offenses are rare. According to Kaplan and Green (1995), between 4% and 25% of victims of child sexual abuse reported that their abusers were female. Becker et al. (2001) state that the available evidence to date suggests that female sex offenders are more prone to abuse female children than male children.

The MTC:CM3

Similar to their development of MTC:R3 for rape typing, the Massachusetts Treatment Center researchers (Cohen et al., 1969; Knight, 1989; Knight & Prentky, 1990; Knight, Rosenberg, & Schneider, 1985) have also developed one of the most useful typologies or empirically based classifications systems for pedophiles yet constructed. Called the **MTC:CM3** (Child Molesters, Revision 3), the system underscores the importance of viewing pedophilia as characterized by multiple behavioral patterns and intentions. The MTC:CM3 classifies child molesters according to variables on two basic dimensions or axes (see Figure 6.3). The first dimension focuses on the degree of fixation the offender has on children and the level of social competence demonstrated by the offender. The second dimension focuses on the amount of contact with children, the level of injury to the victim, and the amount of sadism manifested in the attack.

The First Dimension. The MTC researchers have distinguished four types of child molesters based on this dimension:

- High fixation, low social competence (Type 0)
- High fixation, high social competence (Type 1)
- Low fixation, low social competence (Type 2)
- Low fixation, high social competence (Type 3)

MTC:CM3

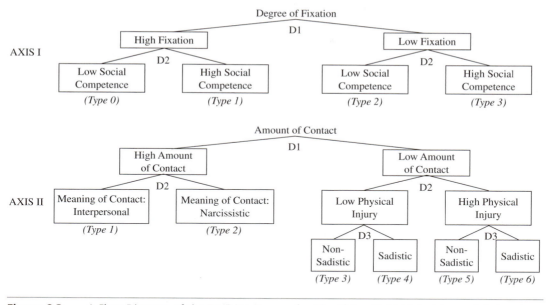

Figure 6.3   A Flow Diagram of the Decision Process for Classifying Child Molesters on Axis I and Axis II of the MTC:CM3 (MTC:CM)

Source: Knight et al. (1989, p. 8, Figure 1). Copyright ©1989 by Sage Publications, Inc. Reprinted with permission by Sage Publications, Inc.

The term *fixation* refers to the intensity of pedophilic interest or the degree to which the offender is focused on children as sexual objects. High fixation means that the offender demonstrates an exclusive and longstanding preference for children as sexual objects, whereas a low fixation connotes that children *and* adults can or have served as sexual objects. Social competence refers to the level of social and interpersonal skills, assertiveness, and self-esteem possessed by the offender. Low social competence signifies that the offender has inadequate social skills, is unassertive in dealing with adults, and demonstrates poor self-esteem. High social competence means the opposite.

The **Type 0** child molester displays a longstanding preference for children as both sexual and social companions. He has never been able to form a mature relationship with adult peers, male or female, and he is described by people who know him as socially immature, passive, timid, and dependent. He feels most comfortable with children. The Type 0 pedophile is rarely married and has a history of steady employment, although the type of work is often below his ability and intellectual capacity. Sexual contact with the child occurs after the two become fully acquainted through a number of social encounters. He rarely is aggressive or uses physical force and rarely engages in genital intercourse. The behavior is generally restricted to touching, fondling, or caressing the child. However, this pedophile is the most difficult to treat and is most likely to recidivate because he is not disturbed or troubled about his exclusive preference for children.

Type 1 is similar to Type 0 in his child molestation strategies but tends to be more socially competent in dealing with the world, has higher self-esteem, and usually has a good work history in line with his competence.

Type 2 child molesters have low fixation. They have had a fairly normal adolescence and good peer relationships and heterosexual experiences, but they later developed feelings of sexual inadequacy and self-doubt. These feelings of inadequacy were further exacerbated by failures in their occupational, social, or sexual lives. The Type 2 offender's background repeatedly includes alcohol abuse, divorce, and a poor employment history. Each pedophilial act is usually precipitated by a significant disappointment to the offender's sexual and social adequacy in interaction with either female or male peers. Unlike Types 0 and 1, the low fixated/low socially competent offender prefers victims who are strangers and who live outside his neighborhood or area. The victims are nearly always female, and he seeks genital sex with the victim. Unlike Types 0 and 1 child molesters, this offender often feels remorseful for his actions and is willing to change.

The Second Dimension. MTC researchers have also discovered that child molesters can be distinguished on the basis of how much daily contact they seek with children (see Figure 6.3). A high-contact offender has regular contact with children within both sexual and nonsexual contexts (Knight et al., 1989). These high-contact offenders often engage in occupations or recreational activities that bring them into frequent contact with children, such as bus driver, schoolteacher, Little League coach, or Boy Scout leader. The MTC research team identified two kinds of offenders who intentionally seek more extensive contact with children: (1) the *interpersonal* offender (Type 1), who seeks the frequent company of children for both social and sexual needs, and (2) the *narcissistic* offender (Type 2), who seeks the company of children primarily for sexual needs. The narcissistic offenders molest children they do not know, and their sexual acts with children are typically genitally oriented (Knight, 1989).

Another group of pedophiles includes low-contact seekers. In general, low-contact child molesters come into contact with children only

when they decide to sexually assault a child. Low-contact child molesters are subdivided into those who administer very little physical injury to their victims and those who administer high physical injury. Low physical injury is indicated by the absence of physical injury to the victim and the presence of such acts as pushing, shoving, slapping, holding, verbal threats, or other intimidation tactics. Low physical injury offenders are further classified into two types: (1) exploitative, nonsadistic offenders (called Type 3) and (2) muted or symbolic sadistic offenders (Type 4). The Type 3 offender uses no more aggression or violence than is necessary to obtain victim compliance. Type 4, on the other hand, engages in a variety of frightening, painful, or threatening acts, none of which causes significant physical injury to the child.

Finally, the MTC:CM3 classifies two types of child molesters who administer a high amount of physical injury to their victims: (1) the aggressive offender (Type 5) and (2) the sadistic offender (Type 6). High injury is characterized by hitting, punching, choking, sodomizing, or forcing the child to ingest disgusting things, such as urine or feces. The Type 5 offender is drawn to children for both aggressive and sexual reasons, but sadism is not the primary need. He is extremely angry about all things in his life and is generally violent toward people in his life, including children. The sadistic or Type 6 offender obtains sexual pleasure from the pain, fear, and physical harm he inflicts on the child. He exploits the child's vulnerability any way he can and attempts various strategies and ploys to get the child to comply. This pedophile does not care about the emotional or physical well-being of the victim and sees the child strictly as a sexual object. This offender usually has a long history of criminal and antisocial behavior. His relationships with peers are unpredictable, difficult, and stormy. He is unpleasant to be around, uncomfortable to work with, and generally moody and irritable. His very poor and abrasive interpersonal skills may be the principle reason he selects children as victims (Knight et al., 1985). This individual is very difficult to treat.

The aggressive-sadistic or Type 6 child molester is apt to have a long history of antisocial behavior and poor adjustment to his environments. Type 6 pedophiles most often prefer male children. Because the primary motive is to obtain sexual gratification without consideration for the victim, these offenders often assault the child viciously and sadistically. The more harm and pain inflicted, the more this individual becomes excited. Type 6 pedophiles are most often responsible for child abductions and murders by strangers. They are very difficult to treat, but, fortunately, they are also very rare. A well-known example of this offender would be John Wayne Gacy Jr., who sadistically murdered 33 teenage boys and young men and buried their bodies in the cellar of his suburban Chicago home.

The Groth Typology

Another often-cited typology that classifies child molesters is the one proposed by Nicholas Groth (1979; Groth & Burgess, 1977). Groth classifies child offenders on the basis of the longevity of the behavioral patterns and the offender's psychological aims. If the sexual preference for children has existed persistently since adolescence, he is classified an *immature* or *fixated* child molester. Like the MTC system's high fixation type, the fixated child molester has been sexually attracted to children throughout his life. Groth argues that this fixation is due to a lack of psychological development. On the other hand, if the child offender has managed to develop some normal aspects to his relationships with adults but turns to children for sexual comfort when stressed or when he experiences a blow to self-esteem, he is called a *regressed* child offender.

As mentioned above, Groth further subdivides child molesters on the basis of their intentions or psychological goals. He identifies two basic types: (1) sex pressure offenders and (2) sex force offenders. The sex pressure offender tries to entice the child into sexuality through persuasion or cajolement or to entrap the child by placing

him or her in a situation in which he or she feels indebted or obligated. Attractive gifts or "thoughtful" favors are the most common strategies. The sex force offender, on the other hand, uses threat of harm or brute physical force. The offender either intimidates the child by exploiting the child's helplessness, naïveté, or trust or simply physically overpowers the child.

Groth believes the sex force type can be subdivided into the *exploitative* type, who use the threat of force to overcome victim resistance, or the *sadistic* type, who derive great pleasure in harming the child. The exploitative offender employs verbal threats, restraint, manipulation, intimidation, and physical strength to overcome the child's resistance. His intent is not to physically harm the child but to obtain the child's compliance. According to Groth, the sadistic type eroticizes the pain he administers to the child. He uses more force than necessary to gain compliance and may even commit what some police investigators call a "lust murder." Therefore, the physical and psychological abuse is necessary for him to experience sexual excitement and gratification. Often, the child is beaten, choked, tortured, and violently sexually abused. Fortunately, this type of offender is very rare.

The Groth system has traditionally been the one most often used by police and federal law enforcement investigators, largely because it is intuitively appealing. In many ways, the Groth typology is similar to the MTC child molester classification system, although it has not been developed much beyond Groth's original formulation. Furthermore, and as pointed out by Heilbrun, Marczyk, and DeMatteo (2002), the Groth child molester typology remains speculative and continues to have very little empirical research to support it.

Juvenile Sex Offenders

According to the most recent FBI statistics (FBI, 2002b), about 16% of those arrested for forcible rape and 19% of those arrested for all other sex offenses (except prostitution) are younger than age 18. The NIBRS reports that 23% of sexual assault offenders are younger than age 18, and 77% are adults (Snyder, 2000). The extent of the offending may be underestimated because, for a variety of reasons, many (perhaps a majority) of juvenile sex offenders are unknown to the criminal justice system. Several studies do suggest, however, that at least 20% to 30% of rapes and 30% to 50% of child molestations may be committed by adolescents (Cellini, 1995). Most of the research on juvenile sex offenders has concentrated on adolescent males while neglecting preadolescent males and females and adolescent female sex offenders. Nevertheless, there are exceptions, as we will see shortly.

Juvenile male sex offenders represent a heterogeneous population and defy any unitary profile or simple description (Becker & Johnson, 2001). They come from all ethnic, racial, and socioeconomic groups. "However, what is known is that about 70% of adolescent sexual offenders come from two parent homes, most attend school and achieve average grades, and less than 4% suffer from major mental illness" (Becker & Johnson, 2001, p. 274). Further research indicates that the median age of juvenile sex offenders is between 14 and 15, more than 90% know their victims, and more than one third of the offenses involved the use of force (National Council of Juvenile and Family Court Judges, 1993). The victims are often substantially younger than the juvenile offender, are most often female (75%), and are usually relatives or acquaintances (Righthand & Welch, 2001). The median age of victims is 7 years old (National Council of Juvenile and Family Court Judges, 1993). Babysitting or some form of child care frequently provides the opportunity to offend, especially for female sex offenders.

Juvenile sex offenders frequently engage in a wide range of nonsexual criminal and antisocial behavior. They tend to shoplift, steal, set fires, bully, assault others (including adults), and are often cruel to animals. One study, for example, reported that more than one half of juvenile sex offenders were abnormally cruel to animals, including their own pets (Tingle, Barnard, Robbins, Newman, & Hutchinson, 1986).

Although most juvenile sex offenders attend school and achieve average grades, a significant number are truant, demonstrate behavioral problems, and have learning disabilities (Cellini, 1995). And although juvenile sex offenders are described as ranging from social outcasts to popular athletes and academically gifted students to tough delinquents (Cellini, 1995), research continually reveals that most juveniles with sexual behavioral problems have significant deficits in social competence and getting along with others (Becker, 1990; Knight & Prentky, 1993). As we found in Chapter 4 for life course–persistant (LCP) delinquents in general, inadequate interpersonal skills, poor peer relationships, and social isolation are among the social difficulties identified in these juveniles (Righthand & Welch, 2001).

The types of sexual offenses committed by juveniles vary widely, ranging from noncontact offenses (such as exhibitionism and voyeurism) to sexual penetration. About half of the contact offenses involve oral-genital contact or attempted or actual vaginal or anal penetration (Righthand & Welch, 2001). Juvenile sex offenders usually use more force when assaulting peers or adults than they do for younger children.

Many adult sex offenders began their sexual abusive behavior in their youth. Research studies report that 47% to 58% of adult sex offenders committed their first offense during adolescence or younger (Cellini, 1995; Cellini, Schwartz, & Readio, 1993).

Many experts and mental health professionals have made the point that a juvenile's own sexual victimization in childhood is a primary cause of later sex offending. Yet, such abusive experiences have not consistently been found to differ significantly from those of other juvenile offenders (Knight & Prentky, 1993; Spaccarelli, Bowden, Coatsworth, & Kim, 1997). We also must be careful not to assume that someone who was sexually abused as a child will then go on to abuse others.

In a recent British study, the researchers found that only 12% of the 224 boys who had been sexually abused as children later became sexually abusive themselves (Salter et al., 2003). Although the figure seems low and may reflect only the abuse that came to official attention, it does underscore the point that most children who are sexually abused do not become victimizers themselves.

The role of child maltreatment in the etiology of sex offending appears unclear and much more complicated than previously supposed (Prentky, Harris, Frizzell, & Righthand, 2000). There is some evidence, though, that abused children exhibit less empathy toward others than their nonabused peers, have trouble recognizing appropriate emotions in others, and have difficulty taking another person's perspective (Knight & Prentky, 1993). These themes we have seen before in the previous chapter, especially pertaining to psychopathy.

Female Juvenile Sex Offenders

According to the latest FBI statistics, juvenile females accounted for only 5.5% of all juveniles arrested for sex offenses (excluding forcible rape and prostitution) (FBI, 2001). Nevertheless, like adult female sexual offending, the prevalence of juvenile female sexual offending may be underestimated. Research on girls who have committed sex offenses has been relatively rare, and existing studies have been limited by small sample sizes and other methodological restrictions and problems (Becker et al., 2001; Righthand & Welch, 2001). Most of the available research has focused on adult female sexual offenders (Bumby & Bumby, 1997) and—as discussed above—that research itself is very limited. As Becker et al. (2001) observe, "Society in the past has been disbelieving in regards to the presence or potential threat of female sexual perpetrators" (p. 30). They add that the mental health professionals in routine clinical interviews rarely or never ask females about possible sexual aggression or paraphilias.

Fehrenbach and Monastersky (1988) report that most adolescent girls who sexually victimized young children did so while doing child care or babysitting. The victims of the 28 female sex offenders they studied were 12 years old or younger. The victims were mostly acquaintances (57%), followed by siblings (29%) and other relatives (14%). Mathews, Hunter, and Vuz (1997) provided data on 67 female adolescent offenders who ranged in age from 11 to 18. More than 90% of their victims were acquaintances or relatives. Each of the above two studies also found that a high percentage of the abusers (50% and 77.65%, respectively) themselves had a history of being sexually abused. Bumby and Bumby (1997) find that adolescent female sex offenders tend to be depressed, have a poor self-concept, have a suicide ideation, and have been victims of sexual abuse during childhood.

Conclusions and Future Directions

Becker and Johnson (2001) recommend that future clinical research on juvenile sex offending concentrate on the following four areas: (1) theory development that addresses the etiology of the behavior, (2) the development of classifications systems or typologies that encompass all juvenile ages and both genders, (3) further development of treatment interventions for different classifications of juvenile sexual offenders, and (4) treatment outcomes studies with long-term follow-ups.

Recidivism Rates of Sex Offenders

Recidivism refers to the repetition of criminal behavior. Usually, it is measured in four ways: (1) rearrest, (2) reconviction, (3) resentence to prison, and (4) return to prison with or without a new sentence (Langan & Levin, 2002). The observed rate of new sexual offenses among known sexual offenders is 10% to 15% after 4 or

5 years (Hanson, 2001; Hanson & Bussière, 1998). However, not all offenders reoffend at the same rate. As a group, child molesters commit a new but similar sexual offense at a higher rate than rapists. On the other hand, research suggests that rapists generally do not confine their repeat crimes to sexual offenses but engage in a wide variety of violent crimes, including violent sexual ones (Quinsey, Harris, Rice, & Cormier, 1998). Child molesters, on the other hand, tend to repeat their offenses of child sexual abuse and usually do not engage in other types of violent crimes.

Age Factors

A study by Karl Hanson (2001) confirms prior research that, on average, the rate of recidivism for rapists decreases with age. Hanson analyzed data from 10 follow-up studies of sex offenders released from prisons. He found important differences in recidivism risk according to both age and offense type. The highest risk age period for adult rapists was between 18 and 25 years, with a gradual decline in recidivism risk as the offender got older. Extrafamilial child molesters were far more likely to recidivate than either intrafamilial child molesters or rapists. The highest risk period for extrafamilial child molesters was between the ages of 25 and 35; moreover, there were only modest declines in their recidivism risk until after the age of 50 (Hanson, 2001). Intrafamilial child molesters, on the other hand, were at highest risk between the ages of 18 and 25 years of age, and they were the least likely of the three groups to recidivate, particularly after age 25.

Hanson (2001) notes that the age differential in recidivism between rapists and child molesters as a group might be attributable to a greater delay in the detection and prosecution of offenses against children than for offenses against adults. Another factor that may enter into the reported differences in age is that child molesters may be more skillful at avoiding detection.

Recidivism of Juvenile Sex Offenders

In general, research has found that the juvenile offender recidivism rate for sex offenses ranges between 2% and 14% (Reitzel, 2003; Rubinstein, Yeager, Goodstein, & Lewis, 1993; Sipe, Jensen, & Everett, 1998). Alexander (1999) reported an overall sexual recidivism rate (based on rearrest) of 7%, with juvenile rapists having the highest sexual reoffending rate of all juvenile sex offenders. More important, however, is the finding by some researchers (Alexander, 1999; Hunter & Becker, 1999) that juvenile sex offenders are less likely to reoffend than adult offenders.

Assessment of Sex Offenders

Assessment of sex offenders is an extremely challenging undertaking because of the heterogeneous and multidimensional nature of the persons who commit such crimes. Comprehensive assessment strategies include evaluations of the offender's needs (psychological, social, cognitive, and medical), family relationships, risk factors, and risk management considerations (Righthand & Welch, 2001). It should be noted that forensic psychologists assess sex offenders not only to decide on a treatment plan but also to gauge their likelihood of further offending. These **psychosexual evaluations** often are conducted at the request of judges, lawyers, parole officers, and other agents of the criminal justice system.

Clinical interviews are by far the most commonly used assessment procedure for evaluating sex offenders (Dougher, 1995). The assessment interview with sex offenders, however, is usually problematic because the sex offender has a strong tendency to deny or conceal his "true" thoughts, feelings, or deviant behaviors (Abel, Lawry, Karlstrom, Osborn, & Gillespie, 1994). Consequently, the information gathered is often unreliable and distorted and must be viewed with skepticism. It is important, therefore, that the clinician obtain as much collateral or outside information as possible during the assessment process to corroborate or supplement the interview material. Collateral information includes psychological and medical reports, previous statements made by the offender, police reports, arrest reports, and other information from those persons who know the offender (Dougher, 1995).

The use of various psychological tests for the assessment of sex offenders has a long history. These tests are primarily focused on identifying personality characteristics or developing a psychological profile of the offender. Usually, the tests are of the paper-and-pencil variety, where respondents answer "true" or "false" to items that ask about their thoughts, attitudes, and behaviors. Assessments based on psychological tests and inventories have largely focused on **risk assessment measures,** specifically the likelihood of recidivism or reoffense. These instruments are used in various jurisdictions to place sex offenders in risk tiers, which are then used in accord with community sexual offender notification regulations and civil commitment statutes (Heilbrun et al., 2002). For example, sex offender notification statutes typically require that low-risk offenders only register with police. In the case of high-risk offenders, it is expected both that they register and that police notify the community where they take up residence.

Many of the psychometric measures designed to measure sex offender characteristics have focused on measuring their attitudes toward women, sexual offending, and their own upbringing (Quinsey et al., 1998). Hanson and Harris (1998) posit that attitude measures can help in identifying which sex offenders are most likely to recidivate. In general, Hanson and Harris found that sexual recidivists, compared to nonrecidivists, showed little remorse or concern for their victims, believed that sexual crimes can be justified, believe that some women deserved to be raped, had attitudes that sexualized children, and were more likely to feel they were entitled to express their strong sexual drive. The recidivists tended to view themselves as being at little risk for committing new sexual offenses and took few precautions to avoid high-risk situations.

Although paper-and-pencil psychometric tests and questionnaires can be useful for assessing pertinent areas that may be related to sex offending, most are very limited in the depth and scope of their appraisal and should always be supplemented with other assessment strategies and information gathering. Furthermore, when the psychological tests and inventories are transparent—that is, it is clear to the respondent what is being asked—the clinician is faced with the same kind of denial, distortion, and dishonesty found in the interview process. Many personality inventories do have a "lie" scale, social desirability scale, and "test-taking attitude" scale designed to uncover some of the distortions and denials, but they still have their limitations.

After reviewing the research literature, Knight, Prentky, and Cerce (1994) concluded that "traditional measures of personality and psychopathology have yielded inconsistent results when administered to sexual offenders and have proven to be of limited utility with such offenders" (p. 91). Although there are several existing inventories for the assessment of sex offenders, the MTC group has been developing a comprehensive inventory that tries to assess all the domains of the MTC:R3 and MTC:CM3 classification systems (Knight & Cerce, 1999; Knight et al., 1994; Prentky & Edmunds, 1997). Called the Multidimensional Assessment of Sex and Aggression (MASA), it is a computerized, self-report inventory specifically designed for adult sex offenders. The inventory asks about attitudes and behavior in many areas of a person's life, including childhood experiences, family and social relationships, school and work experiences, alcohol and drug use, and sexual and aggressive behavior and fantasies (Righthand & Welch, 2001). The instrument also includes sophisticated methods for assessing distortions, random responding, and lying. A juvenile version is currently being developed and validated.

So far, the research finds that the MASA is a reliable inventory that has reasonable validity when it is administered to a *nondefensive, cooperative* sample. However, many practitioners would say this is unrealistic when working with sex offenders who have legitimate reasons for being guarded about what they say. It is in their best interest to present a socially desirable image. Consequently, one of the current limitations of the MASA—as with any personality or assessment measurement—is its limited ability to identify defensiveness or intentional distortion when reporting about one's own thoughts, believes, attitudes, emotions, and behavior. Nevertheless, as noted above, it has a method for detecting lying, so further work and revision of the MASA may solve this problem.

The Psychopathy Checklist series (discussed in Chapter 4) offers an alternative or a supplement to the MASA for evaluating risk and recidivism. Many sex offenders are not psychopaths, however. Currently, "there is no *specific test,* biological or psychological in origin, that can determine whether an individual has committed a specific sexual offense or predict possible recidivism" (Becker & Johnson, 2001, p. 274, emphasis added).

Assessing Deviant Sexual Arousal

The sexual interest of pedophiles can be detected by their physiological arousal to children. Similarly—if rape is at least partly committed for sexual gratification—highly aggressive and sadistic rapists should demonstrate arousal to aggressive and violent sexual stimuli that portray resisting and frightened victims. If rape is totally a violent act with no sexual arousal component, on the other hand, we have a different story.

Some researchers believe that the most objective way to measure deviant sexual arousal is to identify changes in penile size when the male is watching or listening to specific, deviant sexual stimuli. The method is called **phallometry.** "Phallometry measures a man's erectile responses while he watches or listens to various sexual stimuli chosen to represent those categories of behavior thought to be relevant to his offense" (Marshall, 1996, p. 163). The method was first

described by Freund (1963). The sexual stimuli most often used in phallometric methods are pictures depicting children or adults or audio-taped vignettes describing aggressive or nonaggressive sex between an adult and a child (Seto, Lalumière, & Blanchard, 2000). Although there is no broadly accepted standardized approach to phallometric assessment, the common practice is to expose the individual to stimuli classified as either deviant (e.g., exhibitions, peeping, sex with children, or forced sex) or appropriate (e.g., mutually consenting sex between adults). The examiner then calculates a ratio of the individual's relative arousal between these two classes of stimuli (Marshall, 1996).

Those who support phallometric assessment note that depictions of children elicit differential sexual arousal in child molesters compared with nonmolesters, same-sex molesters compared with opposite-sex molesters, and extrafamilial molesters compared with incest (intrafamilial) offenders (Prentky et al., 1997). Phallometric studies find that intrafamilial child molesters show far less sexual arousal (changes in penile volume) in response to children than do extrafamilial child molesters (Quinsey et al., 1998). In addition, phallometric tests reveal that extrafamilial child molesters prefer stories depicting sex with children to stories depicting sex with adults (Quinsey & Chaplin, 1988). Furthermore, child molesters who had physically injured their victims responded significantly more to children than to adults and more to coercive sex with children than did child molesters who did not attempt to physically injure their victims (Quinsey et al., 1998). Phallometric research has also discovered that those offenders who demonstrate discernible physiological arousal to stimuli of children are more likely to reoffend (Hanson & Bussière, 1998), although the relationship is not a strong one.

Phallometric assessment with various subtypes of rapists appears to be significantly less reliable than with child molesters, however (Schwartz, 1995). Most studies have shown that rapists are no more likely than nonrapists to show sexual arousal to specific, deviant stimuli. This would appear to provide strong support for the perspective that rape is essentially a violent act rather than a sexual act.

Under limited circumstances, phallometric tests can be valid and reliable, at least for pedophilia (Quinsey et al., 1998). Nevertheless, there are arguments against their use. Even child molesters can be skillful at faking their responses to sexual stimuli, especially those highly motivated to appear to have normal sexual preferences. Furthermore, the procedure itself has been challenged in a variety of legal contexts. Lawyers have argued, for example, that phallometric tests are humiliating, demeaning, and an invasion of privacy. Furthermore, some psychologists raise questions about the ethics of this approach, even when used solely for treatment purposes and even when the offender consents to the procedure. Ethics and legality aside, however, there is reason to be suspicious of phallometric assessment on a scientific basis as well. Marshall (1996) strongly questions the validity of phallometry in differentiating any sex offenders from nonoffenders because the differences are not observed consistently in most offenders.

Summary and Conclusions

Sex offending is of widespread concern in contemporary society. Statistics indicate that sexual victimization is a reality for many individuals, and it is well acknowledged that most such victimization does not come to official attention. Forensic psychologists are highly likely to come into contact with both offenders and victims. In this chapter, we covered the assessment tasks of psychologists in relation to sexual offending; sex offender treatment and work with victims will be covered in later chapters.

The terms *rape* and *sexual assault* are often used interchangeably, but we have made some distinction. *Sexual assault* is a broader term that covers a wide range of offenses, including rape. *Rape* is typically used to refer to sexual crimes

in which vaginal, anal, and sometimes oral penetration of the victim occurred. Increasingly, more state statutes are forgoing the term *rape*, however, to define instead forms and degrees of sexual assault (e.g., aggravated; sexual assault of a child; forcible sodomy). Research literature continues to report studies using the term *rape*, and offenders are routinely called rapists as opposed to sexual assaulters.

Statistics reporting on the incidence and prevalence of sexual offending often are not comparable, partly because of the differences in terminology. Nevertheless, it is possible to discern a variety of patterns. It appears, for example, that probably no more than one third of all sexual assaults are reported to authorities. Victims themselves may not label the attacks as rapes or as sexual assaults; when they do, they are often fearful of the consequences of revealing their victimization. Although the official rate of forcible rape has shown a downward trend, statistics and surveys about date rape, child sexual abuse, and juvenile sex offending indicate continuing cause for concern. Also of increasing interest is the topic of sexual offending by both adult and adolescent females. Whereas some studies in this area are available, they are often limited by their small sample sizes. By far, the greatest amount of research has focused on male offenders.

Research has indicated that men who rape often manifest a wide range of antisocial behavior in addition to their sexual offenses. Sex offenders as a group appear to be deficient in social skills and in their ability to maintain positive intimate relationships with others. A number of variables have also been found to play a key role in the behaviors, emotions, and thoughts of sex offenders. These include aggression, impulsivity, social competence, sexual fantasies, sadism, and naive beliefs, such as those demonstrated in a rapist's acceptance of society's "rape myths."

Nevertheless, sex offenders are not a homogeneous group. That very clear conclusion based on numerous research studies has led to the development of typologies or methods of classifying sex offenders for the purpose of both predicting deviant sexual behavior and providing treatment to offenders.

We reviewed two prominent typologies for both rapists and child molesters: the research-based typologies developed by the Massachusetts Treatment Center and the more clinically based typologies offered by Nicholas Groth. Mental health professionals as well as law enforcement and correctional officials are probably more familiar with the Groth typologies, but they are the least validated. The MTC rapist typology divides rapists according to one of four primary motivations: opportunistic, pervasively angry, sexual, and vindictive. Three of the four are further subdivided, resulting in nine rapist subtypes. The Groth typology identifies three forms of rape: anger, power, and sadistic rape.

Pedophilia—the clinical term for a condition in which recurrent sexually arousing fantasies, urges, or behaviors involving sexual activity with children occur—is both underreported and often difficult to treat. It is a challenge to obtain data on the prevalence of sexual abuse of children, and available evidence suggests that these behaviors are widely underreported. Both the MTC researchers and Groth have developed classification systems for child molesters, as they have for rapists. The MTC system classifies child molesters on two separate axes, one focusing on the offender's degree of fixation and the other on the amount of contact, level of injury, and extent of sadism demonstrated in the attack. Several radically different types of child molesters are especially difficult to treat. The first is the Type 0 offender, who has a longstanding and highly fixated preference for children as both sexual and social companions. Types 5 and 6, aggressive and sadistic offenders, inflict pain and physical harm on their victims, including harm that may result in death. Because of the nature of their crimes, they are unlikely to be included in treatment programs. Forensic psychologists who treat child molesters often do work with Type 0 offenders, however.

Groth's typology classifies offenders first on the basis of the longevity of their behavior patterns: They are immature (or fixated) or regressed. Groth also considers their psychological aims: They pressure or they force. Finally, offenders who force are subdivided into exploitative and sadistic types.

In recent years, researchers have been paying increasing attention to the problem of juvenile sex offenders. Statistics suggest that between 25% and 50% of sexual assaults may be perpetrated by adolescents. Although we must be guarded in accepting these figures, it is clear that juvenile sexual offending is of concern. As with adult offending, most of the research to date has been directed at males as perpetrators. Juvenile sex offenders are a heterogeneous group, and they frequently engage in a wide variety of nonsexual offending and exhibit behavioral problems. The typical juvenile sex offender has significant deficits in social competence, but again there are exceptions. It is important to point out that children who are sexually victimized do not necessary become sex offenders. However, it is likely that significant numbers of juvenile sex offenders—both male and female—were themselves victimized. Even so, the relationship between prior sexual victimization and juvenile sex offending is not clear and merits additional research before firm conclusions can be offered. The recommendations made by Becker and Johnson (2001) bear repeating. Theory development, typologies, additional treatment interventions for different classifications of juveniles, and evaluation research are all sorely needed.

Sex offender recidivism rates reflect the importance of preventing and treating the behaviors discussed in this chapter. Adult offenders show higher recidivism rates than juveniles, but these rates vary among offender types. Furthermore, not all reoffend at the same rate. Child molesters, for example, commit new offenses more often than rapists. Rapists, however, have been found to engage in other violent crimes in addition to rape.

The psychological assessment of sex offenders is a crucial task for forensic psychologists. Offenders are assessed not only for their amenability to treatment but also for their level of risk—or dangerousness—to society. An assessment may be performed, for example, to help a judge decide whether to incarcerate an offender or place him on probation. Risk assessment—as a role of the forensic psychologist—will be discussed again in Chapter 9. The Massachusetts Treatment Center has developed an assessment instrument to be used in tandem to its classification system. The Psychopathy Checklist series also may be used, but it is important to keep in mind that many sex offenders are not psychopaths. However, as Becker and Johnson (2001) stress, no specific test has been developed that can either determine that an individual has committed an offense or predict recidivism.

Some clinicians make use of phallometry to detect physiological arousal of child molesters and rapists. Presumably, once the objects of arousal are identified, treatment strategies are used to deprogram the offender. This assessment method has been more successful with child molesters than with rapists, but it is very controversial. Both legal and ethical objections have been raised. Essentially, however, phallometry is not considered by most clinicians to be a scientifically valid method that distinguishes sex offenders from nonoffenders.

PART IV

Victimology
and Victim Services

CHAPTER 7

Forensic Psychology and the Victims of Crime

We are all victims of crime. Whether or not we have been robbed, assaulted, deprived of our life savings or pension funds, or burglarized, we have all experienced the social and financial costs of crime. Even so-called "**victimless crimes**"—illegal drug use, prostitution, and illegal gambling—can be said to be harmful to society and leave victims in their wake. Many of us have experienced the fear of crime as well. It is not unusual to hear of women applying for permits to carry guns or sign up for self-defense classes following a string of sexual assaults in a small town or city, for example. In addition, many citizens are victimized by crime without being aware of it. Medical insurance fraud is a good example of this. How many beneficiaries of Medicare or Medicaid are able to review and monitor the statements submitted by medical practitioners on their behalf? It is estimated that health insurance fraud costs taxpayers millions of dollars annually.

When we speak of crime victims, however, we are most likely to be referring to individuals whose persons have been physically and/or emotionally harmed by crimes against themselves or their property. The U.S. government, which has been collecting victimization data for just over 30 years, focuses its efforts on crimes that are highlighted in the media—assaults, burglaries, robberies, larcenies—and rarely white-collar offenses or political crimes. Likewise, the forensic psychologist is far more likely to assess and treat the victim of rape, child abuse, attempted murder, or robbery than the victim of insider trading or illegal government surveillance. Moreover, when members of the public are asked about their fear of crime, they are more worried about child abduction than they are of credit card fraud, despite the relative rarity of the former and frequency of the latter. Child abduction is, of course, a serious, emotionally wrenching crime compared with fraud. Yet the person who is the victim of credit card fraud suffers both financial and emotional harm. The point made here is that victimization comes in many forms and touches people in numerous different ways. Although we may focus in this chapter on the forms of victimization most likely to be encountered by the forensic psychologist, the backdrop is victimization in its broadest sense.

Forensic psychologists will be increasingly employed as consultants, instructors, expert witnesses, evaluators, therapists, and service providers to victim service organizations in the coming years. Their help will be needed in many areas, including those involving victims of domestic violence, child abuse, elderly abuse, violent crime, and hate/bias crimes.

The chapter begins with an overview of the issues that forensic psychologists must deal with concerning victimization of people of diverse cultures and backgrounds, sexual orientation, disability, and religious preferences. We will then discuss victim rights and its ramifications. The greater part of the chapter, however, will focus on what is known about the victims of crime, the psychological impact of being victimized, and the various roles played by forensic psychologists in victim services.

Multiculturalism and Victimization

"Multiculturalism, in its broadest terms, not only is defined by race and ethnicity but also involves topics of gender, sexual orientation, and disability" (Bingham, Porché-Burke, James, Sue, & Vasquez, 2002, p. 75). Recognizing and respecting individual differences in culture, religious preference, sexual orientation, disabilities, and gender are important to sensitive and effective work with victims. Each person has his or her unique way of viewing the world through the lens of cultural and linguistic experiences. Currently, the racial/ethnic composition of the United States is approximately 72% White, 12% Black, and 11% Latino, but by the year 2030, it is estimated that the composition will be 60% White, 19% Latino, 13% Black, and 7% Asian (Ogawa & Belle, 2002). Native Americans are now recognized by the Bureau of Census to be represented by more than 500 separate nations

and tribes with 187 different languages (Ogawa & Belle, 2002). In addition, there are an estimated 2 to 3 million Arab Americans living in the United States, who represent perhaps one of the most misunderstood ethnic groups in this country today (Erickson & Al-Timini, 2001). They are also one of the most diverse ethnic groups in the United States in their cultural and linguistic backgrounds, political and religious beliefs, family structures and values, and acculturation to Western society (Erickson & Al-Timini, 2001). The exact number of Arab Americans is unknown because they are often reluctant to identify themselves for fear of possible negative social reactions, particularly in the wake of the terrorist attacks of September 11, 2001.

By the year 2050, it is projected that 50% of the U.S. population will consist of "ethnic minorities" (Bernal & Sharrón-Del-Río, 2001; Hall, 1997). The shift in racial/ethnic composition is projected to be more dramatic in some states, such as California and Texas, and will present enormous challenges to victim services providers, as well as to providers of other social services. The traditional Euro-American definition of the "healthy family" is culture bound and often not shared by multicultural families (Bingham et al., 2002). Members of immigrant families offer special challenges to psychologists who provide victim services because they are often afraid to ask for help due to language barriers, fear of deportation, and poor understanding of their rights in the community (Ogawa & Belle, 2002). If they are here temporarily or illegally, the challenges are multiplied.

> Once in the United States, undocumented aliens become easy prey for employment exploitation, consumer fraud, housing discrimination, and criminal victimization because assistance from government authorities is attached to the fear of deportation. There is an epidemic of sexual assaults, for example, committed upon undocumented Latinas. (Ogawa & Belle, 2002, p. 6)

Immigration status should not dictate whether individuals get protection from a society or receive victim services. Lest we forget, "almost 20 million international refugees throughout the world have been forced by extreme abuse of human rights to flee their home countries" (Gorman, 2001, p. 443). Many flee to this country. In recent years, the U.S. Immigration and Naturalization Service has authorized about 200,000 asylum cases, and another 90,000 illegal immigrants received amnesty permitting them to stay in the country (Gorman, 2001). Many of them have been abused and tortured in their home countries, and they are vulnerable to becoming victims of crime here. In working with refugees, promoting a sense of safety is an important task that requires a high degree of cross-cultural sensitivity.

Well-trained forensic psychologists must recognize that the traditional psychological concepts and theories used in assessment and treatment approaches were developed from predominately Euro-American contexts and may be limited in their application to racial and culturally diverse populations (Sue et al., 1999). Christine Iijima Hall (1997) has admonished that Euro-American psychology may become culturally obsolete if it is not revised to reflect a multicultural perspective. This revision, according to Hall, will require psychology to make "substantive revisions in its curriculum, training, research, and practice" (p. 642). Forensic psychologists should be especially attuned to the potential injustices and oppression that may result from monocultural psychology. Hall writes that "people of color and women have been misdiagnosed or mistreated by psychology for many decades" (p. 643). Even psychologists of color or those who are gay/lesbian/bisexual or from diverse backgrounds are not always knowledgeable about the psychological issues of other cultural groups or of their own groups. "Color, gender, and sexual orientation do not make people diversity experts" (Hall, 1997, p. 644). Although these challenges are crucial to all forensic settings, they are particularly important for

those who provide victim services in forensic settings. Without appreciation of their cultural backgrounds, some individuals become victims of crime, victims of the criminal justice system, and victims of the mental health professions that do not truly recognize their needs.

Victims With Disabilities

A neglected area in victimization research and practice is consideration of persons with disabilities. Victims in this instance extend not only to criminal victimization but also to discrimination and harassment at the workplace, as well as abuse and neglect in the home that falls short of criminal offending. Laws banning discrimination against persons with disabilities in work settings and public services open up new areas of opportunity for forensic psychologists.

> Psychologists may find opportunities to consult in the determination of reasonable workplace accommodation for persons with psychiatric, learning, and intellectual disabilities and to provide expert testimony in employment discrimination cases. Psychologists also have an essential role in evaluating neurological, learning, and psychological impairment and function as part of the process of determining reasonable accommodation for both students and employees with disabilities. (Gill, Kewman, & Brannon, 2003, p. 308)

Much of this recent activity in working with the disabled has been prompted by the Americans With Disabilities Act, implemented July 26, 1992. The act applies to public employers and private employers with 15 or more employees. It prohibits discrimination (a) in the hiring process; (b) regarding terms, conditions, and benefits of employment; and (c) in access to work-related amenities, facilities, and functions (Goodman-Delahunty, 2000). Employees who become victims of crime may suffer substantial, long-term psychological problems that may interfere or hamper their employment opportunities, advancement, and quality of life. The interested reader is encouraged to consult an article by Jane Goodman-Delahunty (2000), who identifies some common legal pitfalls for practitioners and forensic psychologists and provides suggestions of how to avoid these pitfalls when providing services to employers and/or employees with psychological impairments.

Approximately 15% to 20% of the U.S. population has some type of disability (Gill et al., 2003; Olkin & Pledger, 2003), broadly defined as a physical or mental condition that substantially limits one or more of the individual's major life activities. As a group, people with disabilities are older, poorer, less educated, and less employed than people without disabilities (Tyiska, 1998). Moreover, there are high probabilities that a large proportion of the disabled will become victims of crime, including physical and sexual abuse. In addition, they are often victims of harassment, discrimination, and emotional abuse. Many people with disabling conditions are especially vulnerable to victimization because of their real or perceived inability to fight or flee or to notify others (Tyiska, 1998). About 68% to 83% of women with developmental disabilities will be sexually assaulted in their lifetime, which represents a 50% higher rate than the rest of the population (Tyiska, 1998). In addition, people with developmental disabilities are more likely to be revictimized by the same person, and more than half never seek assistance from legal or treatment services (Pease & Frantz, 1994). Individuals with mental or psychological disorders are often subjects of harassment or abuse. And many persons become disabled because of repeated violent victimization.

It should be noted that disability is listed along with race, gender, age, sexual orientation, and other dimensions of human diversity in the "Ethical Principles of Psychologists and Code of Conduct" (American Psychological Association, 2002b). Psychologists working in forensic settings, therefore, may require specialized training and experience to be competent professionals in working with the disabled. In addition, the prevalence of severe disability is different among race and ethnicity groups. For example, in the population ages 16 to 64, 7.4% of Whites had severe disabilities compared to 12.7% Blacks, 11.7% American Indians, 9.1% of Hispanic/Latino origin, and 4.5% of Asians (Tyiska, 1998).

Victimization research on people with disabilities and the impact it has on their lives is desperately needed. Not everyone agrees, for example, that the victimization rates are substantially higher among people with disabilities. "Although the assertion that rates of all types of abuse are higher for children and adults with disabilities is legion in the literature, there is little to support this assertion, and rates found vary unbelievably from study to study" (Olkin & Pledger, 2003, p. 302). Psychology undergraduate and graduate programs lack courses and training on the disabled, and research interests and support are sparse (Olkin, 2002). Rhoda Olkin (2002) reports that graduate programs in clinical and counseling psychology offer very few disability courses, and when they do, they tend to be courses on "exceptional children," mental retardation and developmental disabilities, or learning disabilities and language disorders. In both the educational systems and in clinical practice, "persons with disabilities are administered tests without appropriate accommodations . . . and results are interpreted with norms that have excluded people with disabilities" (Olkin & Pledger, 2003, p. 302).

Protocols for first responders on how to serve crime victims with disabilities are also scarce, and those that do exist often have not been validated through well-executed research. Forensic psychologists could make substantial contributions in this neglected area through research and by providing service providers with the necessary education, training, and counseling to deal with this large and diverse population.

Empirically Supported Treatments and Multiculturalism

In 1995, the American Psychological Association's Division 12 (Society of Clinical Psychology) Task Force on Promotion and Dissemination of Psychological Procedures published its report on empirically validated treatments in *The Clinical Psychologist* (Task Force on Promotion and Dissemination of Psychological Procedures, 1995). The report included a list of psychotherapies originally labeled *empirically validated therapies*. The term would later be changed to **empirically supported treatments,** or ESTs (Bernal & Sharrón-Del-Río, 2001). The criteria used for determining each treatment's efficacy were adapted for those currently used by the Federal Drug Administration (Bernal & Sharrón-Del-Río, 2001; Beutler, 1998). The list has drawn considerable criticism and commentary, but the point here is that the list does not identify a single psychotherapy that has been shown to be effective with ethnic minorities or other diverse populations.

As emphasized by Bernal and Sharrón-Del-Río (2001), psychotherapy or psychological treatment is itself a cultural phenomenon, and culture plays a critical role in the treatment process. At the present time, "we know very little about efficacy of treatments for ethnic minorities" (Bernal & Sharrón-Del-Río, 2001, p. 333), despite the fact that ethnic minorities will make up more than 50% of the U.S. population in the next few decades. We simply do not have much information on the usefulness of culturally sensitive therapies. Unfortunately, forensic psychologists and other mental health professionals who provide training, counseling, and treatment to victims from diverse populations are generally without valid information for selecting the most effective approach in helping them. The topic also extends to treatment of other populations, such as persons jailed or imprisoned under correctional supervision in the community or held in a mental hospital. It is very clear that extensive research on the psychology of ethnic minorities is badly needed.

To the extent that a list of treatments are exported and marketed to other cultural groups without adequate evaluations and testing, we as researchers run the risk of engaging in false and misleading ways of thinking on the applicability of our limited knowledge of ESTs. . . . At minimum, efficacy and effectiveness research is needed with the primary ethnic minority groups (Black, Latinos and Latinas, Asian Americans, and Native Americans) and ideally with every cultural group, including large heterogeneous samples, to support the claims of generalization. (Bernal & Sharrón-Del-Río, 2001, p. 339)

Legal Rights of Victims

Crime victims' bills of rights have been enacted in all states, half of which provide for mandatory restitution unless compelling reasons to the contrary are stated on the record (Murray & O'Ran, 2002). In addition, at least 31 states have passed victims' rights constitutional amendments, and at least 10 of these provide for mandatory restitution (Murray & O'Ran, 2002). **Restitution** is a remedy for the recovery of some measure of economic and psychological wholeness. Restitution is an attempt to restore a victim's original financial, physical, or psychological position that existed prior to loss or injury. Undoubtedly, this is a laudable goal. However, crime victims have consistently reported their frustrations in obtaining adequate and timely restitution both from offenders and from public funds allocated for this purpose (Karmen, 2001).

There are two venues for justice that victims of crime can use. Criminal courts deal with that aspect of the justice system that determines guilt or innocence with reference to crime and metes out criminal sanctions (Gaboury & Edmunds,

2002). The civil justice system allows crime victims to seek civil remedies for the physical, financial, and psychological injuries they have suffered as a result of criminal acts, permitting vindication of their rights and recovery of financial reparations from the offenders (Gaboury & Edmunds, 2002).

Victims in Civil Courts

Civil litigation can be a complex, difficult, and expensive process. In recent years, crimes and other violations against women have been increasingly handled through the civil courts rather than the criminal courts. "As the public recognition of domestic violence, sexual assault, and sexual harassment become[s] better understood and recognized, victims are finding greater justice in civil courts" (Gaboury & Edmunds, 2002, chap. 5, p. 7). Very often, the courts look to forensic psychologists for evaluations of disability and treatment recommendations to provide guidance in determining the value that can be placed on the victim's injuries for the purposes of awarding damages. Compensation for the cost of psychotherapy can be one of the damages awarded.

Victims in the Criminal Courts

The criminal justice process, on the other hand, can be an intimidating and frustrating experience for victims of crime. From the moment some victims call police, they may find themselves faced with a spiral of events that is seemingly out of their control. They may perceive that police do not respond quickly enough, for example, and when police do arrive, victims may believe that police are not sensitive enough to the experience they suffered. Victims often find it difficult to understand why their property cannot be recovered or, if recovered, why it cannot be immediately returned. Victims of violent

crime are fearful that their aggressor will be released on bail; if convicted and imprisoned, they are fearful that he will be released on parole.

It is a reality in law that the Constitution of the United States protects the right of suspects and defendants but not the rights of victims. Criminal suspects do not have to speak with police, for example, and if they choose to do so, they are guaranteed the right to an attorney during police questioning. Defendants have the right to an attorney during every critical stage of the court proceedings, including arraignments, pretrial hearings, trials, and sentencing. Victims are not represented by lawyers unless they choose to hire a lawyer during a civil proceeding. Although it can be argued that the prosecutor is essentially the lawyer for the victim, the prosecutor is technically the lawyer for the government and may pay very little attention to the physical, financial, or emotional needs of victims. Victims often have to take time off from work or other obligations to appear in court, and when cases go to trial, they are subjected to the scrutiny of the media and grueling cross-examination in a courtroom in which they must be confronted by the defendant. As a result, victims have often complained that they are the forgotten component of the criminal justice process or are twice victimized—once when the crime first occurs and again when they encounter the criminal justice process.

Although the above reality strikes many citizens as unfair, it occurs because suspects and defendants have so much to lose from the criminal justice process, in which the awesome power of the state is brought to bear against the individual. A person accused of crime stands to lose his or her freedom, sometimes for life. Under the law, if we are ready to take away a person's freedom—in some cases even his or her life—we must "do it right" by providing the protections in accordance with the Constitution. The law does not plan to take away the freedom of the victim, and hence the victim's rights are not guaranteed in the Constitution.

This logic often does not convince victims or their advocates, however. In the 1970s, the nation saw a major trend in the direction of ensuring that victims, too, would have certain rights under the law. Thus, beginning in 1980, when Wisconsin passed the first "victims' bill of rights," states began to pass laws providing victims with certain statutory, if not constitutional, guarantees and protections. Congress, in the Victim and Witness Protection Act of 1982, enacted similar provisions into federal law. The Office for Victims of Crime (OVC) was created the following year. Throughout the 1980s, Congress passed a number of similar laws and funded programs designed to help victims. In addition, virtually every state fiscal budget now provides funding for victim advocates or victim assistants. These are professionals who serve as liaisons between the victim and the criminal court process. They perform a wide range of services aimed at informing victims of what they will encounter and offering support during this trying period.

Notification

Most states now have laws requiring that victims be notified at various stages during the criminal justice process. This is particularly true if a defendant charged with a violent crime against the victim is about to be released on bail or if a convicted offender is about to be released from jail or prison. Even if an offender will be out of prison for a limited time period, as in a work release program, the victim may be notified. Some states also require **notification** when a plea negotiation has been reached. Not surprisingly, all states require that victims be notified if an offender has escaped from prison.

Allocution

There are several decision-making points at which a victim's input may be accepted. The right of **allocution** is the right to speak out during

these proceedings. Chief among them are the bail hearing, the sentencing hearing, and the parole board hearing. At bail setting, victims are sometimes allowed to argue for a higher bail or, more commonly, to ask that the defendant be forbidden from contacting them. All states allow victims to speak out at sentencing hearings, either in person or in prepared written statements. Presentence reports—which are documents prepared by probation officers or other professionals to help judges reach sentencing decisions—typically include a victim impact statement. The person preparing the report interviews victims and obtains information about the extent of their suffering. A victim of an aggravated assault, for example, might describe being unable to sleep peacefully, recurring nightmares, expensive meetings with a psychiatrist, and his continuing fear of walking alone. When there is no presentence report, victims are allowed to present statements to the presiding judge or to appear in court and testify directly about what they have experienced. In death penalty cases, survivors of the victim are allowed to have the sentencing jury hear details about the suffering they have experienced (*Payne v. Tennessee*, 1991). A minority of states also allows victims to appear at parole board hearings to protest an offender's release.

Compensation

Although the physical and psychological impact of crime may be considered the most obvious aspect, the financial impact can also be devastating. "The financial losses incurred as a result of crime (unforeseen medical expenses, psychological counseling costs, and the need to replace stolen property) can be as debilitating as any other type of injury suffered by crime victims" (Gaboury & Edmunds, 2002, p. 2).

All 50 states, plus the District of Columbia, Puerto Rico, and Virgin Islands, have compensation programs that can pay for medical and counseling expenses, lost wages and support, funeral bills, and variety of other costs (Eddy & Edmunds, 2002). In some cases, the money is derived; in others, it comes from offenders themselves. An inmate may be earning money in a prison work program, for example, and a percentage of that income is allocated to the victim of the crime. It is also common for states to deny convicted offenders the right to profit from books they may write about their crimes. Called "Son of Sam" laws, after the infamous serial murderer David Berkowitz, who claimed he was controlled by the devil through a dog called "Sam," these laws sometimes redirect the income to the victim or to a victim's fund.

Despite the enactment of these laws, they do not seem to be working to the advantage of the great majority of victims. Research has indicated that only a small percentage of victims are even aware of their existence (Karmen, 2001; National Center for Victims of Crime, 1999). As noted earlier, victims also report that **compensation** takes time and is rarely provided in total. Notification, which places an added burden on agents of the criminal justice system, seems particularly problematic. It is often not clear who has the responsibility to keep the victim informed, and consequently, no one takes on this task. In communities with well-funded victims' advocates or victims' assistance programs, notification is more likely to occur. Likewise, most victims do not exercise their right of allocution at bail, sentencing, or parole hearings. When they do, the research is mixed with respect to their effectiveness, although results are slightly weighed in favor of having influenced parole decision makers. For example, several studies document that victims appearing before parole boards have been successful at delaying the offender's release (Karmen, 2001).

Victims are not typically successful at having sentences increased, however. After reviewing studies on the effect of victims' rights legislation, Karmen (2001) notes, "Even with all the new options, does institutionalized indifference toward the victims' plight still pervade the justice system? The answer seems to be a qualified 'yes,' according to some preliminary findings gathered from evaluation studies" (p. 317).

Shield Laws

Until the 1980s, victims of sexual assault were routinely asked about their own prior sexual activity in court. The passage of shield laws—so called because they protect victims from being asked about their sexual history—changed this common practice. All 50 states now have these laws. Before their passage, if the victim was sexually active, the jury was allowed to infer that the defendant was less responsible or not responsible at all. This was the case unless the victim was married. In that case, the jury was allowed to infer that the sexual assault was particular outrageous because the woman's husband was also victimized. The women's movement of the 1970s is widely credited for bringing attention to the fact that sexual assault is a crime of violence rather than a crime of passion. As an act of violence, sexual assault harms all victims, regardless of prior sexual activity or marital status. Thus, the perpetrator cannot be held less culpable because of the status of the victim. He can, however, be held more culpable, as in cases of sexual assault against children.

In the past, the law of sexual assault also required evidence that the victim had actively resisted her assaulter. Among the many myths about rape that circulated in society was the one that held that a person could not be raped if she fought off her attacker. At the same time, potential rape victims were often told not to resist: If they resisted, they would get hurt even more. Victims who were not bruised or had not left scratches, bite marks, or other markings on rape defendants were often assumed to have consented to the sexual activity. As a result of reform in rape law, judges now tell juries they may not infer consent just because there were no physical signs of a struggle.

Crime Victimization Data

Information about victimization in our society is best obtained from victims themselves. Persons who have been assaulted or burglarized can tell us when and where the crime occurred, whether they reported it to police, and the degree of physical and emotional harm they experienced, among many other things. These victimization statistics also help us understand the distribution of crime, including its geographical and temporal characteristics. Are certain regions of the country more "crime prone" than others, for example, or are certain months of the year more likely to see a reduction in crime? When victims know something about the person or persons who victimized them, victimization data also can provide information about those who commit crime.

The preeminent victimization survey in the United States is the **National Crime Victimization Survey (NCVS),** sponsored by the Bureau of Justice Statistics and conducted by the Bureau of Census. The NCVS reports the results of contacts with a large national sample of households (approximately 49,000) representing 101,000 persons older than age 12. On an annual basis, a member of the household is first asked whether anyone experienced crime during the previous 6 months. If the answer is yes, the victim is interviewed more extensively. The same households are recontacted every 6 months for a period of 3 years. The NCVS is currently designed to measure the extent to which households and individuals are victims of rape and other types of sexual assault, robbery, assault, burglary, motor vehicle theft, and larceny. The survey includes both crimes reported and not reported to the police. Consequently, there are differences between NCVS data and the FBI's Uniform Crime Report (UCR) data.

The NCVS was introduced in 1973 and was then known as the National Crime Survey (NCS). Until that time, the government's main measure of crime in the United States was the FBI's UCR, which reflected crimes that were known to police along with arrest data. Many

people—especially minorities and immigrants—do not report their victimizations to police, however. The NCS was developed to try to tap the "dark figure" of crime, or the crime that did not come to the attention of police. A victimization rate, expressed by the number of victimizations per 1,000 potential victims, is reported to the public. Developers of the NCS reasoned that some crime victims might be more willing to report their victimization to interviewers than to police. Furthermore, interviewers could probe and learn more about the effects of victimization. Over the years, these predictions have been borne out because victimization data continually indicate that, overall, at least half of all crimes are not reported to police. Not surprisingly, this figure varies according to specific crimes; reporting rates of auto theft, for example, are dramatically higher than reporting rates of sexual assault.

The NCS was revised in the 1980s and substantially redesigned in 1992, when its name was changed to the National Crime Victimization Survey (NCVS). Among the changes were questions asking victims how law enforcement officials responded when they reported their victimizations. Victims also were asked more details about the crime, including whether the perpetrator was under the influence of alcohol or illegal substances and what they were doing at the time of the crime (e.g., going to work, shopping). The redesign also included a more sensitive and comprehensive approach to asking victims about sexual assault (Karmen, 2001). In addition to household victimization, the Bureau of Justice Statistics also sponsors supplementary reports, such as surveys of school and workplace victimization and victimization of commercial establishments.

Ethnic/Minority Differences in Victimization

Recent NCVS data, tabulated by the Bureau of Justice Statistics (BJS) (Rennison, 2001, 2002),

---

BOX 7.1   Examples of Terms Used to Designate Hispanics/Latinos in the United States

---

Hispanic: refers collectively to all Spanish speakers and connotes a lineage or cultural heritage related to Spain.

Latino(a): Latino (male) or Latina (female) refers to people originating from or having a heritage related to Latin America. However, the term is commonly used to refer to all peoples who speak Spanish and Portuguese (such as Brazilians).

La Raza: refers to a designation acceptable to many Latino, Caribbean, Chicano, and Mexican Americans born in the United States or Latin America.

Americano(a): refers to Latinos living in the United States.

Mexican: a term used appropriately for Mexican citizens who visit or work in the United States.

Mexican American: refers to those individuals of Mexican descent who are U.S. citizens.

Chicano(a): a term used to describe Mexican Americans, although originally pejorative.

Nuyorican: refers to Puerto Ricans born in the continental United States, particularly New York City.

Rican: refers to the second- and third-generation Puerto Ricans on the U.S. mainland.

Caribeño(a): refers to the Latinos from the Caribbean.

Source: Comas-Díaz (2001).

---

provide information on the criminal victimization of five ethnic/minority or racial groups: White, Black, American Indian, Hispanic, and Asian. The American Indian classification is based on those NCVS respondents who identified themselves as persons of Indian, Eskimo, or Aleut descent. Asians were defined in this context as Japanese, Chinese, Korean, Asian Indian, Vietnamese, and Pacific Islander. Pacific Islander includes those persons who identified themselves as Filipino, Hawaiian, Guamian, Samoan, and other Asian. Respondents who identified themselves as Mexican American, Chicano, Mexican, Puerto Rican, Cuban, Central or South American, or other Spanish origins were classified as Hispanic. All the groups are extremely diverse, but the rapidly growing Hispanic/Latino group reflects perhaps the greatest diversity (see Box 7.1).

Because of this diversity, the BJS considered the "Hispanic" category as consisting of persons of any race in this tabulation. In other words, some Hispanics also report that they consider themselves White, Black, American Indian, or Asian, a point that needs to be considered when examining the statistical data on crime rates.

The most recent NCVS data (Rennison, 2001, 2002) show that American Indians experience aggravated assault, simple assault, rapes and sexual assaults, and other serious violent crimes at rates higher than those reported for Whites, Blacks, Asians, and Hispanics (see Table 7.1). The BJS data further suggest that, compared to the other ethnic/minority groups, American Indians are more likely to experience violence at the hands of other peoples besides their own (Chaiken, 1999). Bachman (1992) also discovered

Table 7.1   Rate of Violent Victimization by Type of Crime, Race, and Hispanic Origin, 2000

Rate of Victimizations Per 1,000	Hispanic	White	Black	American Indian	Asian
Total violent crime	27.9	26.5	34.1	52.3	8.4
Rape/sexual assault	0.6	1.1	1.5	7.7	0.2
Robbery	5.7	2.4	6.5	2.6	1.9
Aggravated assault	5.3	5.3	6.0	16.3	0.9
Simple assault	16.4	17.7	20.1	25.7	5.4

Source: Rennison (2002).

that American Indians have one of the highest suicide rates of all Americans, whereas Blacks have the lowest. She suggests that American Indians may live in a subculture that "tolerates" both external (homicide) and internal (suicide) acts of violence.

Asians experience overall violence, rape and sexual assault, aggravated assault, simple assault, and other serious violent crimes at rates lower than those reported for Whites, Blacks, Hispanics, or American Indians (Rennison, 2002). For decades, Blacks have consistently been disproportionately represented among homicide victims, especially Black males. Blacks are usually six times more likely than Whites and eight times more likely than persons of other races to be murdered (Rennison, 2001).

Studies have shown that approximately 70% of inner-city youth have been victimized by violent acts, including being threatened, chased, hit, beaten up, sexually assaulted, or attacked with knife or gun, and 85% of these youth report having witnessed violent acts (Kliewer, Lepore, Oskin, & Johnson, 1998). A survey of U.S. adults reveals that 43% had witnessed interpersonal violence, and 5% had a friend or relative die from homicide or suicide (Elliott, 1997; Hillbrand, 2001). Many children and youth (from ages 6 to 18) continually exposed to violence develop difficulty concentrating and learning, anxiety, fear, depression, and **posttraumatic stress disorder (PTSD)**.

Various kinds of violence have different kinds of impact on those individuals who experience and witness it. In other words, all violence is not the same. Violence between parents (interparental violence) may be more damaging to the psychological health of a young child than being beaten and chased at school. Furthermore, interparental violence in which weapons are used, such as guns and knives, may be more upsetting to children than those incidents not involving weapons (Jouriles et al., 1998). Approximately 25% of the victims of violent crime are injured, many of them severely (Simon, Mercy, & Perkins, 2001). Moreover, several studies have shown that the psychological impact of being a victim of violence differs from those of being a witness to violence (Shahinfar et al., 2001). Research also has found that adolescents who had been physically abused were more likely to be considered high risk to commit violent behavior themselves than those who had simply witnessed abuse (Shahinfar et al., 2001).

Psychological Effects of Criminal Victimization

Psychological Impact of Violence

A summary statement by the American Psychological Association's (1996) "Human Capital Initiative Report" begins this section well:

Violence harms its victims both physically and psychologically. It traumatizes victims, bystanders, and family members alike. It can trigger paralyzing anxiety and fear, long-lasting depression, or deep anger. Although a substantial amount of effort has been devoted to finding the best ways to treat violent offenders, little research has been conducted on the best ways to treat the victims of violence to minimize their psychological problems. Standard treatments for depression and anxiety may be inappropriate in these cases. Programs to treat victims have been shown to be most effective when they are delivered in natural locations, such as schools, community groups, health care environments, and when they are culturally relevant and age- and sex-specific. Therapies that are more specific to different types of victimization have yet to be developed. (p. 9)

The psychological impact of criminal violence on its victims is substantial and far-reaching. In fact, in many cases, the psychological trauma experienced by victims of crime may be more troubling to the victim than the physical injury or the loss of property. Psychological reactions to criminal victimization can range from mild to severe. Mild reactions to stress are characterized by a variety of symptoms, including minor sleep disturbances, irritability, worry, interpersonal strain, attention lapses, and the exacerbation of prior health problems (Markesteyn, 1992). Severe reactions, on the other hand, may include serious depression, anxiety disorders, alcohol and drug abuse problems, and thoughts or attempts at suicide (Walker & Kilpatrick, 2002). One of the most devastating and common reactions to criminal victimization is called *posttraumatic stress disorder*. Posttraumatic stress disorder, abbreviated PTSD, is so important in the understanding and treatment of criminal victimization that it will be worthwhile to discuss the symptoms and what is known about it in some detail.

Posttraumatic Stress Disorder (PTSD)

PTSD is a common psychological reaction to a highly disturbing, traumatic event, and it is usually characterized by recurrent, intrusive memories of the event. The memories tend to be vividly sensory, are experienced as relatively uncontrollable, and evoke extreme distress (Halligan, Michael, Clark, & Ehlers, 2003). According to the *DSM-IV,* PTSD is

the development of characteristic symptoms following exposure to extreme traumatic stress or involving direct personal experience of an event that involves actual or threatened death or serious injury, or other threat to one's physical integrity; or witnessing an event that involves death, injury, or threat to the physical integrity of another person; or learning about unexpected or violent death, serious harm, or threat of death or injury experienced by a family member or other close associate. (American Psychiatric Association, 1994, p. 424)

The precipitating event would be substantially distressing to almost anyone and is "usually experienced with intense fear, terror, and helplessness" (American Psychiatric Association, 1994, p. 424).

PTSD is diagnosed by a mental health professional when the biological, psychological, and social effects of trauma are severe enough to have impaired a victim's social and occupational functioning. PTSD may be either acute (duration of symptoms less than 3 months) or chronic (when symptoms last longer than 3 months), or the victim may show a delayed onset (when at least 6 months have passed between the traumatic event and the onset of symptoms). The usual course is for symptoms to be strongest soon after the event and then diminish over time. Symptoms may be more severe and longer lasting if the trauma is perceived by the victim as intentionally human made rather than an accident or a natural catastrophe. In other words, victims of violence such as rape, war, or a terrorist attack would be more likely to have long-lasting and more severe symptoms than those persons who experience a hurricane, earthquake, tornado, or an *accidental* plane crash.

PTSD symptoms include intense fear, helplessness, or horror. In addition, the victims continually reexperience the traumatic event in their thoughts and reactions, persistently avoid things that remind them of the incident, and have persistent symptoms of high levels of anxiety and stress that were not present before the trauma. The symptoms usually wax and wane, coming back and then going into remission for a time.

Surveys estimate that between 8% and 9% of all Americans adults suffer from PTSD (Kessler, Sonnega, Bromet, Hughes, & Nelson, 1995; Ozer, Best, Lipsey, & Weiss, 2003), although these figures may have changed since the terrorist attacks of September 11, 2001. Many Americans across the nation experienced considerable trauma after terrorists flew two airliners into the World Trade Center, killing more than 3,000 persons, and another airliner into the Pentagon. Still more were killed when passengers deflected a fourth plane that crashed into the ground in Pennsylvania. However, research done prior to the attacks on September 11 indicated that of the 50% to 60% of the U.S. population who are exposed to traumatic stress, only 5% to 10% develop PTSD (Ozer et al., 2003). These data suggest that people's reactions to stress are unique and different for each individual. It should be mentioned, however, that PTSD is underrecognized in routine clinical practice when PTSD symptoms are not the presenting complaint (Franklin, Sheeran, & Zimmerman, 2002).

The lifetime prevalence of PTSD for women is twice that for men (10.4% vs. 5.0%), according to a nationally representative sample of 5,877 people ages 15 to 45 years (Kessler et al., 1995). The prevalence of PTSD is high among immigrants and refugees in the United States, particularly those who immigrated because of war or political persecution and torture (Gorman, 2001;

Ozer et al., 2003). In a national survey of male and female Vietnam War veterans (Weiss et al., 1992), it was estimated that 30.9% of men and 26.0% of women met the diagnosis criteria for PTSD at some point since their service in Vietnam (Ozer et al., 2003).

About 20 years ago, Kilpatrick et al. (1985) conducted a random community survey of more than 2,000 adult women who had personally experienced such trauma as rape, sexual molestation, robbery, and aggravated assault. The women were asked—among other things— whether they had thoughts of suicide after the incident, attempted suicide, or had a "nervous breakdown." The results clearly indicated that rape caused the most psychological trauma, with 19% of the rape victims attempting suicide, 44% reporting suicide ideation at some point after the rape, and 16% saying that they had "a nervous breakdown." A comparison sample of women who had *not* been victims of any traumatic incidents reported the following: 2.2% made suicide attempts, 6.8% had suicide ideation, and 3.3% said they had nervous breakdowns in their lifetimes. Resnick, Kilpatrick, Dansky, Saunders, and Best (1993) found that 32% of rape victims met the criteria of PTSD at some point in their lives following the incident. Similarly, a study titled *Rape in America: A Report to the Nation* found that 31% of the women who had been raped developed symptoms that fully meet the criteria of PTSD (National Center for Victims of Crime, 1992). The same report indicates that rape victims are three times more likely than nonvictims to suffer major depression and four times more likely to show PTSD symptoms.

The psychological aftermath of exposure to traumatic life experiences is highly variable, with some persons adjusting well and others showing significant adverse emotional and psychological consequences of considerable duration (Marshall & Schell, 2002). Many researchers continue to search for an array of personal, social, and environmental factors that may contribute to PTSD. However, research on who is most susceptible to

PTSD is unclear. It is apparent, though, that social support is both a prevention factor before the person experiences trauma and a factor that helps the person recover faster after the trauma (Ozer et al., 2003).

The research literature suggests that psychological harm is not qualitatively dissimilar for victims of different criminal offenses but rather is a matter of degree (Markesteyn, 1992). That is, although the psychological reactions displayed by victims of sexual assault, robbery, burglary, and kidnapping vary in intensity, the nature of their distress is similar (Markesteyn, 1992). Markesteyn (1992) proposes, therefore, that in general, a victim's reactions and recovery may be mediated by three classes of variables: (1) victims' previctimization characteristics, (2) victims' postvictimization abilities to cope, and (3) factors related to the criminal event. Previctimization variables refer to such things as ethnic/minority background, religious or spiritual beliefs, socioeconomic status, gender, and age. Perhaps, as we noted above, one of the most important previctimization variables is the quality and availability of supportive relationships. Factors related to the criminal event include the degree of violence involved and the location of the crime (e.g., home or outside the home). Victims who are attacked in an environment they perceive as being "safe" have been shown to experience more negative reactions than those attacked in "unsafe" locations (Markesteyn, 1992). Postvictimization factors include the various coping mechanisms available to crime victims, such as where to place the blame, perceived control over their lives, and social and professional support. Fear of being revictimized is especially powerful as a postvictimization reaction. For example, mugging victims reported an increased sense of vulnerability and an extreme awareness of themselves as potential targets of another mugging. Robbery victims refrain from going out at night, change their place of employment, move to a new house, or acquire weapons for self-defense (Cohn, 1974). On the basis of an extensive research literature review, Markesteyn

(1992) concludes that "almost without exception, the research has demonstrated a correlation between the positive support people receive and their ability to adapt to and successfully overcome stressful life events" (p. 25). Victim services intervention appears to be especially critical.

Short-term psychological reactions to nondomestic assaults (robbery, aggravated and simple assaults) experienced by 40% of victims include anger, difficulty sleeping, uneasiness, confusion, bewilderment, denial, and fear (Markesteyn, 1992). The most serious reactions of depression, helplessness, loss of appetite, nausea, and malaise are reported by 20% to 40% of the victims. Most of these effects persist for up to 3 weeks. Three to 6 weeks later, approximately 15% of victims feel "very much" affected, and about 5% have lifelong reactions. Victims who do not receive support from others, especially professional intervention and treatment, are particularly at risk for developing subsequent psychological problems.

The impact of criminal violence extends beyond the direct victims, however. In 1997, 64% of Gallup poll respondents reported that they believe there is more crime than in previous years, despite the significant reductions in crime recorded nationally during the late 1990s (Walker & Kilpatrick, 2002). In an earlier poll (Kilpatrick, Seymour, & Boyle, 1991), 82% of the adults in the United States said they were personally very concerned about violent crime.

Homicide Victimization

On average, more than 21,000 people are murdered each year in the United States (Simon et al., 2001). Homicide victims represent the smallest proportion (.002%) of violent crime victims, but the psychological devastation experienced by survivors is enormous. Approximately 1 in every 10,000 Americans will become the victim of homicide during their lifetimes, a rate that has doubled since World War II (American Psychological Association, 1996). The nation's youth are especially vulnerable, with nearly 3 of every 10,000 young males likely to be victims of homicides prior to their 18th birthday (American Psychological Association, 1996). Murder rates of young minority males living in impoverished areas of large cities are much higher, with 1 in every 333 becoming victims of homicide before reaching the age of 25. The homicide rate of juveniles in the United States is very high compared to other countries. For instance, the U.S. rate is five times higher than the rate of the other 25 developed countries *combined* and nearly double the rate of the country with the next highest rate (Finkelhor & Ormrod, 2001b). In this country, minority children and youth are disproportionately affected: 52% of juvenile victims of homicide are non-White.

Homicides of young children are committed primarily by family members (71%), usually by "personal weapons" (such as hands and feet) to batter, strangle, or suffocate victims (Finkelhor & Ormrod, 2001b). Although victims include approximately equal numbers of boys and girls, offenders include a disproportionate number of women (Finkelhor & Ormrod, 2001b). Children at the highest risk for homicide are those younger than age 1. Usually, children in this age group are killed by relatives who do not want the child or believe they are ill-equipped to provide for the child. When young children (younger than 5 years of age) are killed by parents, it is usually as a result of the demands and constant attention they require. Two of the most common triggers of young child homicide are crying that will not stop and toileting accidents (U.S. Advisory Board on Child Abuse and Neglect, 1995). These fatalities appear to be more common in conditions of poverty and in families marked by divorce or absence of the father.

Middle childhood (ages 6–11) is a time when homicide risk is relatively low, whereas the risk of homicide for teenagers (ages 12–17) is high, remaining constant in recent years at 10% higher than the average homicide rate for all persons (Fox & Zawitz, 2001). Unlike homicides of children younger than age 12, relatively few homicides of teenagers (9%) are committed by family members.

As pointed out by Finkelhor and Ormrod (2001b), the actual homicide rate for young children may be higher than the statistics suggest. Homicides of young children are difficult to document because they can resemble deaths resulting from accidents and other causes. A child who dies from sudden infant death syndrome (SIDS) may be difficult to distinguish from one who has been smothered, or a child who has been intentionally dropped may have injuries similar to those who died from an accidental fall (Finkelhor & Ormrod, 2001b).

Relationship of the Offender to the Victim

Figure 7.1 shows the relationship of the victim to the offender, based on 2001 data reported by the FBI. As illustrated, about 13% of the homicides were a result of one family member killing another family member. Figure 7.1 also shows the number of victims killed within the family and other known relationships, with wife and acquaintance victims being the most common.

The term **covictim** is often used to emphasize the depth of the homicide's emotional impact.

> In the aftermath of the murder it is the co-victim who deals with the medical examiner, the criminal and juvenile system, and the media. The term co-victim may be expanded to any group or community that is touched by the murder: a classroom, a dormitory, a school, an office, or a neighborhood. Most of the individuals who make up these communities are wounded emotionally, spiritually, and psychologically by a murder, some more deeply than others. (Ellis & Lord, 2002, p. 2)

To be effective, victim service providers must be knowledgeable and carefully trained to deal with the wide range of reactions and

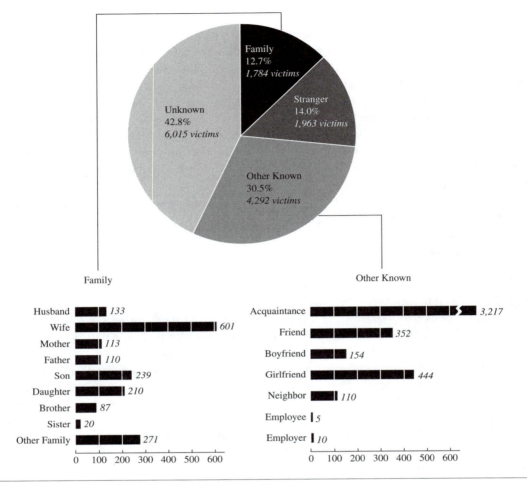

Figure 7.1   Relationship of Homicide Victims to Offenders

Note: Relationship is that of victim to offender. Figures are based on 14,054 murder victims for whom Supplementary Homicide Report data were received.

Source: Federal Bureau of Investigation (2002b).

needs of victims as well as the investigative and judicial processes involved in homicide cases. Competent, well-trained service providers are responsible and ethical professionals who recognize cultural diversity, understand the role that culture and ethnicity play with individuals and groups, and understand the socioeconomic and political factors that affect these groups (Hall, 1997). Covictims may respond to the notification of the death of their loved ones in a way that is compatible with their cultural/ethnic ways of dealing with death in combination with their psychological, emotional, and spiritual strengths.

Death Notification

Notification of family members of a death that resulted from violent crime is among the most challenging for professionals whose responsibility is to deliver the message (Ellis & Lord, 2002). The best available data indicate that nearly 2% of the adults in the U.S. population have lost an immediate family member due to criminal homicide (Amick-McMullan, Kilpatrick, & Resnick, 1991; Walker & Kilpatrick, 2002). It is also very often the most traumatic event in the lives of family members and loved ones. Not only is **death notification** highly stressful and intense, but the survivors have had no time to prepare psychologically. An inappropriate or poorly done notification can prolong survivors' grieving process and delay their recovery from the trauma for years. During notification and thereafter, the covictim needs may include (1) an opportunity for ventilation of emotion; (2) calm, reassuring authority; (3) restoration of control; and (4) preparation for what they need to do next (Ellis & Lord, 2002).

Forensic psychologists would most likely be involved in death notification by training and providing supportive counseling to police officers, mental health professionals, and death notification teams who are expected to provide the services to families and covictims of violent crime on a regular basis. There are several models for training death notifiers, but the best known and probably the most heavily relied on model was developed by Mothers Against Drunk Driving (MADD) (Ellis & Lord, 2002). Several other handbooks or manuals with training suggestions for death notification are also available. The U.S. Office for Victims of Crime (OVC), in cooperation with the National Sheriffs' Association, has prepared a handbook titled *First Response to Victims of Crime 2001* (Gillis, 2001), and the National Organization for Victim Assistance (1998) has published the second edition of the *Community Crisis Response Team Training Manual*. Chapter 6 of the manual is directly related to procedures and suggestions for death notification. Janice Lord (1997, 2001) has also been a leading expert in developing practices for death notification and has written several manuals or brochures for the OVC. In 1995, the OVC supported the MADD protocol in revising their death notification curriculum and tested it in seven sites (Ellis & Lord, 2002). Experienced death notifiers reported that their greatest unmet educational needs were the following:

- Specific details on how to deliver a notification
- How to manage immediate reactions of the family
- How to manage their own reactions
- General aspects of death notification

According to Ellis and Lord (2002), death notifiers should be sensitive, mature, positive, and calm persons who sincerely wish to become a notifier. Stressed, anxious individuals who lack confidence in delivering the message properly probably should not be selected as notifiers. Because death notification is a stressful event for all participants, burnout is a prominent danger for those professionals who are intimately involved on a regular basis. An important role for the psychologists in these situations is to provide support and counseling to the victim service providers and be watchful for burnout symptoms.

Reactions of Homicide Covictims

Family members exhibit a wide range of emotions when a loved one is murdered. The available research suggests that the reactions of survivors of homicidal death differ significantly from those of people who grieve the loss of a loved one who died nonviolently (Sprang, McNeil, & Wright, 1989). The process of mourning for families of murder victims lasts longer, is more intense, and is more complex (Markesteyn, 1992). The grief reactions of homicide survivors appear to be deeper, display rage and vengefulness more often, and result in longer lasting anxiety and phobic reactions (Amick-McMullen, Kilpatrick, Veronen, & Smith, 1989; Markesteyn, 1992). According to the available data, most (about 75%) display symptoms of PTSD during the initial stages of grief and mourning (Markesteyn, 1992).

Covictim reactions may be especially intense if the deceased was subjected to torture, sexual assault, or other intrusive, heinous acts (Ellis & Lord, 2002). Covictims often need to be reassured that the death was quick and painless and that suffering was minimal. "If the death was one of torture or of long duration, they may become emotionally fixated on what the victim must have felt and the terror experienced" (Ellis & Lord, 2002, chap. 12, p. 8). If the offender was of another racial/ethnic or other minority group, the covictim may develop a biased view of that particular group, which may have to be dealt with during counseling.

Hate or Bias Crime Victimization

The psychology of hate crimes and the trauma of discrimination have become increasingly important areas for forensic psychologists to address. Bias crimes often have long-term psychological and social repercussions that are extremely destructive to both the victims and their families (Seymour, Hook, & Grimes, 2002). Blacks still see racial discrimination and bias crimes to be dominant forces in their lives, despite the belief by White Americans that Black Americans are better off today than ever before (Dovidio, Gaertner, Kawakami, & Hodson, 2002). Contemporary racism is more subtle than the "traditional" racism that was blatant, extensive, and psychologically damaging, but it is still insidious.

In recent years, it has become apparent that sexual orientation bias has emerged as a dominant factor in hate crimes. Although difficult to verify, it is estimated that between 10% and 12% of the U.S. population may be gay or lesbian in their sexual orientation (Hall, 1997). Studies have consistently revealed that more than 90% of gay men and lesbians report some form of bias victimization. About half report they have been threatened with physical violence, and one fifth affirm they have been punched, kicked, or beaten because of their sexual orientation (Bernat, Cahoun, Adams, & Zeichner, 2001). The psychological effects of bias crimes based on sexual orientation may be more substantial than the effects of other nonbias crimes. For example, Herek,

Gillis, and Cogan (1999) report, on the basis of their national survey, that hate crime victimization is associated with greater psychological distress for both gay men and lesbians compared to victims of equally violent nonbias crimes. Preliminary research indicates that victims of bias crimes due to sexual orientation manifested more symptoms of depression, anger, anxiety, and posttraumatic stress than the nonbias crime victims.

Victims of hate/bias crimes experience not only physical injuries and/or property damage but also a sense of extreme vulnerability as members of a targeted group (Seymour et al., 2002). The social and psychological effects on the victims are considerable and long lasting. Seymour et al. (2002) conclude that hate or bias crime "is nothing less than an assassination of one's own sense of self" (p. 2).

Sexual Assault Victimization

Characteristics of the Victims

Age

Rape and sexual assault is primarily a crime against youth. The National Women's Study (Tjaden & Thoennes, 1998) reported the following data concerning the age of victims:

- 32% of sexual assaults occurred when the victim was between the ages of 11 and 17,
- 29% of all forcible rapes occurred when the victim was younger than age 11,
- 22% occurred between the ages 18 and 24,
- 7% occurred between ages 25 and 29,
- 6% occurred when the victim was older than 29 years old.

Additional data collected from the National Incident-Based Reporting System (NIBRS) add a more comprehensive picture. The NIBRS indicates that more than two thirds of all victims of sexual assault reported to law enforcement agencies were juveniles (younger than age 18)

Age distribution of victims of sexual assault
Rate per 1,000 victims

Age of victim

Figure 7.2   Age Distribution of Victims of
Sexual Assault

Source: Snyder (2000).

(Snyder, 2000). More than half of all juvenile victims were younger than age 12. More specifically, 33% of all victims of sexual assault reported to law enforcement were ages 12 through 17, and 34% were younger than age 12. Fourteen percent of victims were younger than age 5 (see Figure 7.2). In fact, for victims younger than age 12, 4-year-olds were at greatest risk of being sexually assaulted.

Juveniles were the largest majority of the victims of forcible fondling (84%), forcible sodomy (79%), and sexual assault with an object (75%), but they were the victims in less than half (46%) of forcible rapes (Snyder, 2000).

Although babysitters are responsible for a relatively small portion of the crimes against young children (4.2%), children at risk of physical assaults by babysitters are younger (ages 1–3) than those at risk of sex crimes (ages 3–5) (Finkelhor & Ormrod, 2001a). Males constitute the majority of sex-offending babysitters reported to the police (77%), whereas females make up the majority of physical assaulters (64%).

Gender

Overall, an estimated 91% of the victims of rape and sexual assault are female (Greenfeld, 1997). The NIBRS data on juvenile victims show that females were more than six times as likely as males to be victims of sexual assault (Snyder, 2000). Moreover, 89% of the victims younger than age 6 were female. The majority of juvenile victims of forcible sodomy (54%) were males, whereas young females were the large majority of victims in incidents of sexual assault with an object (87%) and forcible fondling (82%).

The child molester, or pedophile, is almost always male, but the victim may be of either gender. As mentioned in Chapter 6, however, researchers are beginning to question the assumption that females rarely commit sexual assaults against children (Becker et al., 2001). Heterosexual pedophilia—male adult with female child—appears to be the more common type, with available data suggesting that three quarters of male pedophiles choose female victims exclusively (Langevin, 1983; Lanyon, 1986). Homosexual pedophilia—adult male with male child—appears to be substantially less frequent, occurring in about 20% to 23% of the reported cases. A small minority of pedophiles prefers children of either gender.

Extent of Injury to Victims

Data on physical injury from sexual assault reveals that

- 70% of rape victims reported no physical injuries,
- 4% sustained serious physical injuries,
- 24% received minor physical injuries.

These data suggest that most victims will not exhibit overt physical evidence that most people believe is characteristic of violent sexual attacks. Unfortunately, many people who do see no clear evidence of physical injury will conclude that the victim must have consented. In addition, even though some attacks do not result in physical injury or death, sexual assaults inflict enormous psychological harm on victims, especially children.

Relationship of the Victim to the Offender

Rape

The legal scope of forcible rape has traditionally been confined to imposed sexual contact or assault of adolescent and adult females who are not related to the offender. In view of the fact that rape most often occurs between acquaintances, relatives, and spouses, this traditional definition is drastically outdated. Kilpatrick et al. (2002), for example, report compelling evidence that most rapes are of intimate partners and not strangers. Their data indicate that

- 24.4% of rapists were strangers,
- 21.9% were husbands or ex-husbands,
- 19.5% were boyfriends or ex-boyfriends,
- 9.8% were relatives,
- 14.6% were other nonrelatives, such as friends or neighbors.

Still, many people (including the victims themselves) do not define sexual attacks as rape unless the assailant is a stranger. Thus, if the victim is sexually assaulted by a husband, boyfriend, or a "date," she is unlikely to report the incident. Criminal justice officials and the general public frequently feel that marital or date rape is unimportant because they believe that it is less psychologically traumatic to the victim and more difficult to prove. Prosecutors, for example, admit they are reluctant to prosecute marital or date rape cases because of concerns that it is difficult to convince juries that husbands or boyfriends could be sexual assailants (Kilpatrick, Best, Saunders, & Veronen, 1988). However, available data suggest that more than 40% of the total rapes that occur may be committed by husbands or male friends (Kilpatrick et al., 1988).

Child Sexual Abuse

In most cases of child sexual abuse, the offender and the victim often know one another, often very well, and the crime frequently involves relatives (incest). Many victims are simply looking for affection, wanting only to be hugged or cuddled or to have human contact. The offender frequently misinterprets this behavior as a form of "seduction" and misgauges the amount of power he has over the child. Very often, the child may participate in the molestation primarily because he or she is too frightened to protest. Research indicates that pedophiles, on average, tend to have positive feelings toward their victims, generally perceiving them as willing participants, and frequently victimize children living in their immediate households (Miner, Day, & Nafpaktitis, 1989). In many cases, the sexual behavior between the offender and the same child has gone on for a sustained period of time.

Other Victim Characteristics

Approximately 90% of the time, the rape or sexual attack involves a single offender. The most common reason given by adult victims of rape or sexual assault for reporting the crime to the police was to prevent further crimes by the offender against them. The most common reason reported by the victim for *not* reporting the crime to the police was that it was considered a personal matter. Nationally, per capita rates of rape are found to be highest among residents ages 16 to 19, low-income residents, and urban residents (Greenfeld, 1997). There are no significant differences in the rate of rape or sexual assault among racial groups.

Juvenile victims were more likely to be victimized in a residence than adult victims (Snyder, 2000). The most common nonresident locations for sexual assaults of juveniles are roadways, fields/woods, schools, and hotels/motels. The weapons most commonly used in sexually assaulting juveniles were hands and fists, referred to as "personal weapons."

Psychological Impact of Sexual Assault

Sexual assault produces a wide range of psychological reactions in its victim. In some of the literature on sexual assaults, the woman "victim" is now often referred to as a "survivor," "a label that emphasizes her strength and avoids the connotation of passivity associated with the label of 'victim'" (Felson, 2002, p. 136). However, we will continue to use the more recognized *victim* in this context to emphasize the point that we are talking about *victimization* of all kinds in this chapter and discussing the many *victim* services available. In this text, all victims are survivors.

Sexual victimization usually provokes some type of reaction and physical, social, psychological, and, in the case of students, academic loss. After a sexual assault, some student victims have difficulty in concentrating, begin to miss classes, and fall behind in their school assignments. Some withdraw completely from high school or college. Furthermore, service providers and psychologists should be aware that many victims of sexual assault are often concerned about people finding out about the assault, such as family members (Kilpatrick et al., 2002).

Among the more common psychological reactions to sexual assault are PTSD, shame, helplessness, anger, and/or depression. The quality of life usually suffers as victims experience sleeplessness, nightmares, social isolation, flashbacks, and intense feelings of insecurity. Some research finds that 94% of rape victims met symptomatic criteria for PTSD shortly after the assault, and 47% continued to show symptoms of PTSD 3 months after the assault (Foa, Rothbaum, Riggs, & Murdock, 1991). In another study, 16.5% of rape victims showed PTSD symptoms 17 years after the assault (Kilpatrick, Saunders, Veronen, Best, & Von, 1987). Some of the mental health problems become life threatening in nature. Rape victims are 4 times more likely than noncrime victims to have contemplated suicide (Kilpatrick et al., 2002). Moreover, "rape victims were also 13 times more likely than noncrime victims to have

actually made a suicide attempt (13% vs. 1%)" (Kilpatrick et al., 2002, chap. 10, p. 15).

One controversial topic in the sexual assault literature is the concept of **rape trauma syndrome** (RTS). RTS was first introduced by researchers Ann Burgess and Lynda Holmstrom (1974) as a two-phase description of the commonly shared experiences of rape victims in the emergency room (Boeschen, Sales, & Koss, 1998). The description, or model, "consists of an 'acute' state of extreme fear and other emotional, physical, and psychological symptoms experienced immediately after a rape, and a second, 'reorganizational' phase of the more moderate and varied symptoms that appear in the course of recovery" (Boeschen et al., 1998, pp. 416–417). However, the RTS has been found to be problematic in the courtroom for a variety of reasons. One of its major problems is that the syndrome has not been supported by research (Frazier & Borgida, 1992). Although the original Burgess and Holmstrom study was important in raising awareness about the traumatic effects of sexual assault, "it was quite limited methodologically, and many of its results have not been replicated" (Frazier & Borgida, 1992, p. 299). Forensic psychologists (Boeschen et al., 1998; Frazier & Borgida, 1992) strongly recommend that PTSD replace RTS as more meaningful and research-based concept. For one thing, the term *PTSD* is viewed as less prejudicial than RTS because the former does not equate the symptoms exclusively with rape. Furthermore, PTSD is recognized as a well-received term by psychiatrists and psychologists and is found in the *DSM-IV* with distinct diagnostic criteria. Finally, a number of valid psychological measures and self-report inventories are available for PTSD.

Forensic psychologists and other psychologists working in forensic settings are often asked to do an assessment, provide treatment, or become an expert witness in sexual assault cases. The assessment may be done to evaluate the victim's claims, responses, and reactions, especially if they appear to be life threatening. The psychologist should be knowledgeable about the victim's cultural and ethnic background and how that culture perceives victims of sexual assault. A number of rating scales and psychological inventories are available to document the victim's level of trauma.

Expert testimony in the case might occur in a criminal or a civil case. A civil case may involve a victim suing an alleged attacker to recover damages or suing a third party for failing to provide adequate protection. A psychologist might testify in support of the victim's claim of severe emotional injuries, such as PTSD, which has led to the devastation of her (or his) social, occupational, and/or financial life.

Psychological Effects of Child Sexual Abuse

Child sexual abuse is the exploitation of a child or adolescent for another person's sexual and control gratification (Whitcomb, Hook, & Alexander, 2002). Research offers strong support for the assumption that sexual abuse in childhood (both violent and nonviolent) produces long-term psychological problems (Briere, 1988). Reports of severe depression, guilt, strong feelings of inferiority or inadequacy, substance abuse, suicidality, anxiety, sleep problems, and fears and phobias are common. Children may feel responsible for the abuse because no obvious force or threat was used by the adult, and only after the victims become adults do they realize that they were powerless to protect themselves.

The overwhelming evidence from both clinical and empirical studies is that most victims of sexual abuse are negatively affected by their experience (Haugaard & Reppucci, 1988). However, the long-term effects of child sexual abuse are unclear and appear to differ significantly from individual to individual. Although some victims apparently suffer no negative long-term consequences, studies with adults confirm the long-term effects of sexual abuse mentioned in the clinical literature for a majority of the victims (Browne & Finkelhor, 1986). For example, adults who were sexually victimized as children are more

likely to manifest depression, self-destructive behavior, anxiety, feelings of isolation and stigma, poor self-esteem, and substance abuse. A history of childhood sexual abuse is also associated with greater risk for mental health and adjustment problems in adulthood.

Studies suggest that sexual abuse by fathers or stepfathers may have a more negative impact than abuse by perpetrators outside the home (Browne & Finkelhor, 1986). Furthermore, the use of force or physical coercion in the assault usually results in more trauma for the child (Browne & Finkelhor, 1986). Experiences involving intercourse or attempted intercourse and genital contact by mouth also seem to be more troubling than acts involving touching of unclothed breasts or genitals. Penetration is especially traumatic for the young victim.

The child sexual abuse syndrome (CSAS) or **child sexual abuse accommodation syndrome (CSAAS),** originally proposed by Summit (1983), has received considerable attention in the literature. The syndrome is reserved for a cluster of behaviors that occur in children who have been victims of sexual abuse by a family member or by a trusted adult. According to Summit, children do not necessarily have an innate sense that sexual activity with an adult is wrong. However, if the sexual activity continues, the adults usually must pressure or threaten the child to prevent others from knowing about the activity. Often, the abuser presents these threats and pressures in such a way that the child is led to believe something terrible will happen (perhaps to a family member) if this "private" knowledge becomes known. Hence, the child is placed in the position of being responsible for the welfare of the family. The child also feels helpless to stop the activity. Thus, the child must "accommodate" these secrets into his or her daily living pattern.

However, there is still question whether the child sexual abuse syndrome actually exists. "At this point, professionals have not reached consensus on whether a syndrome exists that can detect child sexual abuse" (Myers, 1991, p. 82). Haugaard and Reppucci (1988) write, "The principal flaw with the notion of a specific syndrome is that no evidence indicates that it can discriminate between sexually abused children and those who have experienced other trauma" (pp. 177–178). Many of the behaviors listed by Summit (1983) may occur in any child who has experienced other types of trauma besides sexual abuse, although the behaviors usually do not demonstrate precocious sexual awareness. "As a result, one cannot reliably say that a child exhibiting a certain combination of behaviors has been sexually abused rather than, for instance, physically abused, neglected, or brought up by psychotic or antisocial parents" (Haugaard & Reppucci, 1988, p. 178).

Similar to rape trauma syndrome, child sexual abuse accommodation syndrome has questionable validity as a meaningful diagnosis or indicator of sexual abuse. On the other hand, children are highly vulnerable to PTSD, a more useful concept in describing the psychological impact of child sexual abuse (Whitcomb et al., 2002).

In child sexual abuse cases, the forensic psychologist may be asked to evaluate the child to determine if the allegations have foundation and, if they do, what level of trauma has been experienced. The forensic psychologist may also be asked to assess the competency of the child to testify in the case and may also help in preparing the child to testify. Finally, the psychologist may also be an expert witness in the case, such as testifying about the validity of the child's memory or level of understanding.

Property Crime Victimization

Research on the effects of victimization in property crimes is very limited. Consequently, we will only touch on the effects of burglary.

Psychological Impact of Burglary

According to the UCR, **burglary** is the unlawful entry of a structure, with or without force, with intent to commit a theft or other felony. According to the NCVS (Bureau of Justice Statistics, 2002b), approximately 4 million residences are burglarized each year. Although there is a considerable amount of information on burglary and how to prevent it, very little information is available for how most people react or adjust to this frequent crime.

Burglary is officially classified as a property crime, but it is also in many ways an interpersonal crime (Merry & Harsent, 2000). Many victims of burglary feel psychologically traumatized beyond the simple material loss. The invasion of the safety, privacy, and sanctity of the home can be discomforting and stressful, and a victim may take a long time to recover from the invasion. "It is a special place that is central to our daily lives, a place that is at the beginning and end of most our journeys; it is chosen and personalized" (Merry & Harsent, 2000, p. 36). Some victims describe burglary as a rape of their home, especially in cases when the burglar disturbed or damaged personal photographs, letters, and diaries. The distress levels tend to be more pronounced when the invasion extends to personal sectors of the home, such as bedrooms, closets, chests of drawers, bathrooms, and desks. Some victims, after being burglarized, install security systems, increase and improve the locks, buy "guard" dogs, or even move to new homes.

Some burglars also try to upset the members of the residence by leaving messages or items, vandalizing some personal items, or indicating they will be back. According to Merry and Harsent (2000), this aspect represents the "interpersonal dimension" of the crime. The emotional reactions of burglarized victims to these "signatures" often run the gamut from anger to fear and depression (Brown & Harris, 1989). It may well be that the victim's feelings of fear, vulnerability, or even anger are psychological reactions or "losses" that can be translated into psychological "gains" for the offender. Therefore, the burglar may gain materially as well as psychologically.

Most items stolen are never recovered, and if the property has unique or sentimental value for the victim, emotional reactions can be intense. It is not unusual for the victim or victims to become angry toward the police for their seeming lack of concern.

Summary and Conclusions

As we noted at the beginning of the chapter, forensic psychologists will be increasingly employed as consultants, instructors, expert witnesses, evaluators, therapists, and service providers to victim service organizations in the coming years. In the chapter, we explored some of the many areas in which their services will be most needed in the very near future. We described the well-trained forensic psychologist as being equipped with a deep appreciation for **multiculturalism** and the many diverse cultures she or he will work with. The knowledgeable forensic psychologist will also be capable of working with many victims with disabilities, a group that represents a very large, diverse, but underserved population in American society.

We learned that the many forms of psychotherapy are largely based on European, White values and beliefs and are in need of considerable revision if they are to be effective with ethnically and culturally diverse populations. We reviewed some highlights of victim rights, with an emphasis on victims who must deal with the criminal justice system.

Crime victimization data were covered briefly, focusing on some of the racial, ethnic/minority differences reported in the available victimization statistics. The psychological effects of criminal victimization, particularly violent victimization, were described in some detail.

PTSDs appear to be the most common psychological reactions to crime of all kinds, although the reactions are usually most intense and long lasting after a violent incident. The covictims of homicide incidents, especially when the dead victim is a family member, are especially devastated and probably never fully recover. Sexual assault also represents a highly traumatic event that is often followed by a wide range of psychological reactions and disorders, especially PTSD. Child sexual abuse is not only common, but the long-lasting psychological damage for some children will remain with them for the rest of their lives. However, the chapter also emphasizes that victims respond to trauma and disaster differently, with some coping extremely well while others struggle. Consequently, the existence of "textbook syndromes" as a direct result of victimization should be viewed cautiously and with the expectation that many—perhaps most—victims do not exhibit a set pattern of symptoms. Therefore, indications of rape trauma syndrome or child sexual abuse accommodation syndrome may not occur in most rape victims or sexually abused children.

Property crime victimization and its psychological consequences are unexplored areas. Thus, we could only briefly touch on the psychological effects of burglary victimization because it was one of the very few areas of property crime that has received any significant research. All crimes engender psychological effects and potential scars on their victims. Therefore, an area worth exploring for those forensic psychologists interested in doing research would be the psychological effects of property crime on its victims.

CHAPTER 8

Family Violence, Abuse, and Victimization

orensic psychologists and other clinicians working within forensic settings frequently encounter both perpetrators and victims of violence among and within families and between intimate acquaintances. The tasks they perform include doing assessments, consulting with legal authorities and social service providers, testifying in courts, and providing psychotherapy for victims as well as offenders. As will be seen throughout this chapter, family violence in all of its manifestations is found at all socioeconomic levels and spares no age, race, religion, or ethnic group.

The chapter begins with a discussion of the violence directed at spouses or other intimate partners, then moves to child abuse and the more serious physical forms of abuse, including infanticide, Munchausen syndrome by proxy, and shaken baby syndrome. Repressed and recovered memory is covered in some detail because this topic has received considerable attention in recent years, especially in cases involving child sexual abuse. It is one of the most controversial topics in psychology today. Child and juvenile abduction is presented as a special area that has

not received the professional attention it deserves. The chapter ends with another neglected topic, elder abuse. There is a rapidly growing demand for forensic geropsychologists throughout the country, and we will provide some of the career opportunities in that expanding discipline.

Intimate Partner Violence

The broad term **family violence** (also known as domestic or intrafamilial violence) refers to any assault, sexual assault, or other crime that results in the personal injury or death of one or more family or household member(s) by another who is or was residing in the same dwelling. It often occurs in intimate relationships, for instance, between current or former spouses, partners, or significant others. As such, it is more likely to be called *intimate partner violence,* a term that also encompasses violence in a relationship where the two individuals may not be living together (or have lived together). Approximately 13% of all homicides involve one family member killing another family member (Federal Bureau of Investigation

[FBI], 2002b). One third of female victims of homicide were slain by a husband or boyfriend, usually during an argument (see Table 8.1) (FBI, 2001, p. 27).

Whether referred to as domestic, family, intrafamilial, or intimate partner violence, it is found across all ethnic and racial groups and all socioeconomic classes. It occurs against people of all ages, cultures, and living conditions. However, there are major gender differences. In any given year, females are the victims in about 75% of murders by intimates and about 85% of the nonlethal intimate violence (Meuer, Seymour, & Wallace, 2002). Research also indicates that

violence directed at women is more likely to occur in homes characterized by poverty, communities with few resources, socially isolated immigrant families, and subcultures where there is greater acceptance of gender inequities (Walker, 1999).

The motivations for **intimate partner violence**—as they are for all forms of human violence—are highly variable, but the overriding motive of male offenders who abuse women is to establish or maintain power and control over them. When women use violence in domestic situations, it is most often for self-defense, in anticipation of violence, or in retaliation for violence perpetrated against them (Meuer et al.,

Table 8.1   Murder Circumstances, by Victim's Sex, 2001

Circumstances	Total Murder Victims	Male	Female	Unknown
Total	13,752	10,503	3,214	35
Felony type—total	2,279	1,813	464	2
Rape	59	4	55	0
Robbery	1,042	879	163	0
Burglary	73	49	24	0
Larceny-theft	16	13	3	0
Motor vehicle theft	20	13	7	0
Arson	70	38	31	1
Prostitution and criminalized vice	5	2	3	0
Other sex offenses	7	1	6	0
Narcotic drug laws	558	515	43	0
Gambling	3	3	0	0
Other—not specified	426	296	129	1
Suspected felony type	72	60	12	0
Other than felony type—total	6,948	5,088	1,854	6
Romantic triangle	118	87	31	0
Child killed by babysitter	37	19	18	0
Brawl due to influence of alcohol	151	136	15	0
Brawl due to influence of narcotics	118	99	18	1
Argument over money or property	194	172	22	0
Other arguments	3,544	2,519	1,023	2
Gangland killings	74	71	3	0
Juvenile gang killings	865	813	52	0
Institutional killings	8	8	0	0
Sniper attack	7	6	1	0
Other—not specified	1,832	1,158	671	3
Unknown	4,453	3,542	884	27

Source: Federal Bureau of Investigation (2002a).

2002). Many male abusers are serial abusers. That is, if they leave or are left by one victim, they quickly become involved with another partner whom they soon abuse. Furthermore, this cycle of violence or pattern of abuse is not easily broken, as we shall see.

The Typical Development of an Intimate Partner Violence Relationship

Meuer et al. (2002) outline the typical sequence that characterizes the pattern of such violence, which they refer to broadly as domestic violence. They identify nine stages. It should be noted that we use opposite-sex pronouns (he and she) in the illustrations below because heterosexual relationships are dominant in society. We also refer to the abuser as male because these are the most typical abusive relationships. However, intimate partner violence also occurs in same-sex relationships, a topic we will return to in the pages ahead.

During the *first stage* identified by Meuer et al. (2002), the relationship seems wonderful and intense, with the husband or partner taking an active interest in everything his spouse or partner does and everywhere she goes. He wants to be with her all the time, flatters her, confides in her, and proclaims he wants to spend the rest of his life with her. Many victims, Meuer et al. point out, mistake these obsessive and controlling behaviors as devotion to the relationship rather than recognizing them as red flags that may lead to an abuse relationship. *Stage 2* emerges when he begins to insist on knowing her whereabouts at all times, begins making decisions for her, and demands her loyalty to the relationship. He indicates he is in charge, he will make the rules, and he expects her to follow him and attend to his needs. During this stage, he also may begin to blame a former spouse or partner for the problems in a previous relationship, saying she had him arrested or unjustifiably obtained a restraining order against him. During *Stage 3*, she

becomes adjusted to the attention, jealousies, and control he displays. She makes a commitment to him—usually under his pressure—and convinces herself that she is happy to be with someone who cares so much for her. *Stage 4* is characterized by the beginning of excessive control through psychological and emotional abuse. He begins to demand control over things dealing with all phases of her life, including clothing, hairstyles, and how she should act. He becomes angry if she deviates from his requests. His actions communicate that she is unattractive or that her appearance is somehow faulty.

Stage 5 is characterized by the first incident of physical abuse. The victim will probably view the response as an aberration that will unlikely occur again. The abuser often says he is sorry and that it will never happen again. She accepts his apologies and explanation and may wonder what she did to prompt his behavior. In *Stage 6*, the psychological and physical abuse occur again. The victim will ask why he is repeating such behavior, and he will, in turn, blame the victim for prompting his abusive behavior because she is not meeting his expectations. He makes it clear that she is responsible for setting him off and that it will not happen again if she changes her ways. The victim at this stage begins to internalize the blame more completely. *Stage 7* occurs roughly simultaneously with Stage 6. Meuer et al. (2002) refer to this stage as the beginning of the isolation process. The abuser wants to know who she spends time with and either asks her to not see them again or forbids her to see them again. He further makes it difficult for her to see anyone and gets excessively suspicious if she has a good time with anyone but him. Eventually, she stops seeing people of whom he disapproves, and she becomes increasingly isolated.

As the relationship continues, she experiences considerable emotional conflict and confusion. This phase represents *Stage 8*. The abuser blames the victim, and the victim is confused about what is wrong. In *Stage 9*, the abuser increases his use of psychological threats and physical force to gain and maintain control and dominance. If she confronts him or threatens to leave him, he escalates his use of threats and force. The victim may eventually conclude that it is safer to stay in the relationship than to leave. She may feel she cannot make it on her own for a variety of reasons.

During the later stages, the abusive behavior is usually followed by promises that he will never do it again. As noted by Meuer and her colleagues (2002), most victims of intimate partner violence repeatedly attempt to leave the relationship but return when they believe they cannot overcome the obstacles of getting away from the abuser.

According to these researchers, leaving the relationship is not always the best approach and may increase the potential danger to the victim. Unfortunately, there is evidence that victims who attempt to leave are often stalked, harassed, and threatened on an ongoing basis. The stalking may occur even when a divorce is filed or granted. It was originally believed that if a battered woman could be persuaded to leave the abusive relationship, the violence would stop (Walker, 1999). Unfortunately, this has been found to be not the case in too many situations. In fact, "many batterers continue to harass, stalk, and harm the woman long after she has left him, sometimes resulting in someone's death" (Walker, 1999, p. 25). In many cases, most of reported injuries from domestic violence occur *after* the separation of the couple. Some evidence also suggests that women who leave their batterers are at a 75% greater risk of being killed by their batterers than those who stay (Wilson & Daly, 1993).

The above perspective—that leaving may not be the best thing—is strongly resisted by advocates of victims of intimate partner violence, who maintain that getting out of the relationship is still precisely what victims must do. However, society itself places obstacles in their path. For example, their economic options are limited, and deeply entrenched cultural norms hold them responsible for dealing with the violence against them (Dobash & Dobash, 2000). Community support is too often unavailable. If shelters, support groups, and a supportive law enforcement response were present, the odds of successfully

escaping an abusive situation would increase. In general, advocates maintain, the risk of staying is much greater than the risk of leaving. This is a complex issue and one not clearly resolved by the empirical data. However, it is probably fair to say that most forensic psychologists working with victims of abuse would be supportive of their efforts to leave but would also help them to identify the resources necessary to enable them to do that.

Psychological Characteristics of Batterers

Battering is a term often reserved for *physical violence* experienced in intimate relationships, either in a dating relationship, marriage or partnership, or separation and divorce. Some researchers use *battering* to represent the more serious and frequent abuse, including the more severe psychological abuse. Men who batter often deny, minimize, or blame their use of violence on others. In fact, the shoving, kicking, striking, hitting, or punching he does to the victim is often not seen by the batterer as abuse (Meuer et al., 2002). Rather, he justifies his behavior as being provoked, triggered, or in response to something done by the victim. In other words, he perceives his behavior as a natural and understandable reaction to frustration.

A strong predictor of whether a man will abuse his spouse or significant others appears to be whether he has experienced or witnessed violence in his own family while growing up (Meuer et al., 2002). Violence is learned behavior that is passed down from one generation to the next (Eron, Gentry, & Schlegel, 1994; Walker, 1999). Not all men from abusive or violent homes become abusers themselves. Those who do, compared to those who do not, are less capable of attachment to others, are more impulsive, are more lacking in social skills, and possess different attitudes toward women, the masculine role in the family, and violence. Some research has also indicated that many batterers have serious mental disorders in addition to their problems with power and control over women that encourage their use of violence (Dutton & Golant, 1995; Walker, 1999). It appears, therefore, that treatment programs that focus on both the batter's emotional problems and his misguided beliefs and values may help in the amelioration of domestic violence for those abusers who shows signs of psychopathology.

Several typologies of male batterers have been proposed in recent years. A well-validated typology of batterers would allow a systematic examination of how and why different men use violence against their wives and partners, as well as help design effective prevention and treatment strategies for dealing with them. After a thorough review of the research literature on batterers in domestic situations, Holtzworth-Munroe and Stuart (1994) were able to identify three types of male batterers that emerge with consistency in a variety of studies: (1) family only, (2) dysphoric/borderline, and (3) generally violent/antisocial. The typology is based on the severity and frequency of the marital violence, the generality of the violence (only within the family or outside the family), and the amount of emotional or mental dysfunction exhibited by the batterer.

Family-only batterers are typically not violent outside the family and engage in the least amount of severity and frequency of violence. Their violence tends to be periodic, primarily when stress and frustration reach a peak. However, they do not demonstrate discernible indications of severe mental disorders or psychopathology. In addition, they are least likely to have previous arrest records and alcohol problems and are most likely to apologize after the violence. Their major problems are being appropriately assertive in their relationships and their tendency to misinterpret social cues. Consequently, they have resorted to violence rather than appropriate nonviolent means to resolve conflicts with their partners. This group is estimated to constitute about 50% of the known batterers (Holtzworth-Munroe & Stuart, 1994).

Dysphoric/borderline batterers exhibit mental disorders and are psychologically disturbed and emotionally volatile. These individuals often engage in moderate to severe spousal abuse, including psychological and sexual abuse. Although this group's violence is mainly confined to the family, they may also exhibit some extrafamilial violence. Their anger is generalized and explosive in nature and is apt to become displayed anytime they become frustrated. The disturbed batterer also tends to have serious alcohol and drug abuse problems. It is estimated that this group comprises about 25% of the known batterers.

Generally violent/antisocial batterers are more likely to use weapons and more prone to inflict severe injury on wives, partners, and other family members, in addition to engaging in extrafamilial violence. They also are more likely to have an extensive history of contacts with police, arrests, and convictions. Generally violent batterers tend to be highly impulsive and explosive. Moreover, they exhibit serious problems with alcohol and drug abuse, and many show characteristics of psychopathy. Overall, they probably make up about 25% of the batterer group (Holtzworth-Munroe & Stuart, 1994).

Mental health professionals have made some progress in the treatment of batterers, both with programs in the community and in prison settings. However, researchers have not yet concluded that any specific approach to treating batterers is significantly more effective than others, assuming equivalent training of the providers and a comprehensive treatment strategy (American Psychological Association, 2003b). Most treatment programs include some form of cognitive-behavioral psychotherapy, although the specifics vary with the types of abuse for which the offender is being treated. Waltz, Babcock, Jacobson, and Gottman (2000) suggest that, generally, violent batterers and disturbed batterers are unlikely to benefit from short-term treatments focusing on anger management. According to Waltz et al., these approaches often assume—incorrectly—that the acquisition of anger control and attitude change are sufficient. However, a variety of broader, more complex issues may interfere with short-term treatment approaches. Long-term treatment strategies that concentrate on cognitive-behavioral and psychopathological issues are more likely to be effective. How effective these strategies are for psychopaths who are batterers remains an unfinished story. We simply do not have enough empirical study to know what works with this troubling group.

For family-only batterers, treatments that focus on violence, abusive behavior, and relationship problems are likely to be successful for these men because they appear to be more sensitive and empathic to the needs of others. One thing is clear, however. The form of treatment used by mental health professionals must address the offender's use of dominance and control, as well as the attitudes and cognitions that underlie his acts of violence.

Battered Woman Syndrome

Battered woman syndrome (BWS) is a term first used by psychologist Lenore Walker (1979). Walker identified the syndrome based on a volunteer sample of abused middle-class women. In her clinical practice, Walker observed a cluster of behavioral, cognitive, and emotional features that she believes are frequently found in women who have been battered and psychologically abused *over a period of time* by their partners. She later documented BWS more fully on the basis of extended interviews with 435 battered women (Walker, 1984). The core features she identified include feelings of learned helplessness (Seligman, 1975), the development of survival rather than escape skills (e.g., appeasing the batterer rather than planning to leave), low self-esteem, and feelings of depression. Currently, Walker considers BWS to be a subcategory of posttraumatic stress disorder (PTSD).

Walker, a leading but controversial expert on domestic abuse, contends that battering relationships generally follow a three-stage cycle of violence: (1) the tension-building phase, (2) the acute battering incident phase, and (3) the honeymoon or contrition phase. The cycle has similarities to the nine-stage sequence later proposed by Meuer et al. (2002) and discussed above. During the tension-building phase, there may be minor physical, emotional, or verbal abuse. During this phase, the victim often tries to placate her abuser but with only limited success. This initial phase is followed by the second phase, which is characterized by an escalation of serious physical violence and the inability of the woman to placate the batterer at all, no matter what she does. This acute battering phase is followed by the "honeymoon stage" (also referred to as the "loving and contrition stage"), in which the batterer expresses his regret for the assaultive behavior and vows to change his ways. He may send her flowers, give her gifts, and pay a great deal of attention to her. At some point, however, he communicates to her that the incident was her fault. Soon, the violence cycle is repeated.

According to Walker (1979), a woman qualifies for BWS when she has experienced the complete cycle at least *twice*. Walker further suggests (Walker, 1989) that the third stage of the cycle often disappears as the relationship continues to deteriorate over time and the violence increases. She argues that, over time, the tension-building phase becomes more common, whereas the contrition phase eventually drops out of the cycle completely. Unless some effective intervention takes place, when Stage 3 drops out, many battered women are in grave danger of becoming homicide victims.

Although Walker does admit that not all battered women report many of the features she describes, many researchers continue to challenge her general propositions on BWS (Levesque, 2001) and its scientific validity (see McMahon, 1999). Roger Levesque (2001) argues that one of the real dangers of indiscriminately applying the BWS label to all battered women is that it may mistakenly lead the public, lawmakers, and the courts to perceive women's positions in violent relationships to be essentially identical. As Levesque points out, cross-cultural analysis indicates that the abusive relationship dynamics found in U.S. studies on mainstream culture may not apply to other societies, cultures, or even subcultures within the United States. "Thus, different groups may experience maltreatment events differently, which may exacerbate the difficulties others face in situations that happen to garner the same label" (Levesque, 2001, p. 51).

The term *BWS* also portrays a stereotypical image of battered women as helpless, passive, or psychologically impaired, and the battering relationship is seen as matching a single, stereotypical pattern of all domestic violent cases (Dutton, 1996). In contrast to the expected stereotypical pattern of depression, helplessness, and passivity, many battered women demonstrate a wide range of behavioral patterns and emotions that often reflect survival skills and effective adaptations to a serious, life-threatening situation. Unfortunately, the BWS label undermines the enormous coping skills and psychological strength of many—if not most—battered women across a wide spectrum of cultural and social circumstances.

Evan Stark (2002) strongly recommends that psychologists and other mental health practitioners, when preparing forensic assessments and legal testimony for the courts, emphasize the *process* of unique coercive control used by some batterers, rather than focusing strictly on the generalized psychological trauma assumed to be experienced by all battered women. Stark argues that stressing the systematic use of the abuse, coercion, and control in a *particular* relationship and the harms associated with this complete domination is a more meaningful approach than simply trying to identify the psychological damage done to the victim. Many victims, he notes, do not exhibit clearly discernible clusters of psychological maladjustment, depression, and helplessness outlined in much of the literature, even though they may have been subjected to incredible amounts of coercion, domination, and abuse during a lengthy relationship. Furthermore,

Stark concludes from the extant research that most battered women experience neither the cycle of violence nor learned helplessness. Some experience a range of psychological and behavior problems that fall outside the purview of BWS, whereas others demonstrate virtually no mental health problems at all. Stark also cautions about a common misconception that the severity of domestic violence can be measured by those physical injuries and emotional disturbances that come to the attention of the police and medical personnel. These groups do not learn about the tyrannical control and low-level violence that, when administered chronically and over an extended period of time, severely affect the victim's quality of life. Nevertheless, the behaviors may not follow an identifiable syndrome.

A minority of victims of intimate partner violence kill their abusers; in fact, research consistently indicates that they are far more likely to be killed than to kill (Ogle, 2000). When they do kill, BWS has sometimes been used as a defense. Proponents of this approach argue that women suffering from BWS are in continuing fear of immediate and severe bodily harm (including death). Therefore, under the law of self-defense, they should be excused for killing an abusive partner. Although courts today are more likely to allow than to exclude such expert testimony (Slobogin, 1999) it does not guarantee that the defendant will be acquitted. Also, the term *battered women syndrome* is used by most courts today to refer to the "generic issue of battering rather than to Walker's specific formulation" (Stark, 2002, p. 227). BWS has become a legal catchall phrase to refer to all victims of domestic abuse if it can be established that they display any symptoms of distress. However, "courts that rely exclusively on the Walker model have discounted the credibility of victims who appear strategic or aggressive rather than 'helpless' or dependent, particularly if they are from income or ethnic groups stereotypically portrayed as aggressive" (Stark, 2002, p. 227). Accordingly, a victim who exhibits emotional and cognitive strength is suspect because she does not demonstrate the classic characteristics, and many may conclude that she should have been able to do something about the situation earlier and more effectively.

Same-Sex Domestic Violence

Researchers in recent years have given considerable attention to the issue of intimate partner violence between members of the same sex. As a general proposition, virtually all of the literature reviewed above applies in this context as well. For example, Potoczniak, Mourot, Crosbie-Burnett, and Potoczniak (2003) find some striking similarities in the research literature in the violence cycle and stages of abuse between same-sex domestic violence (SSDV) and opposite-sex domestic violence (OSDV). Similar to OSDV perpetrators, SSDV perpetrators blame their partners, are extremely controlling, and are highly self-focused. Many SSDV victims also follow many of the same characteristics described for OSDV victims. The major difference between OSDV and SSDV incidents appears to be how the community, police, medical personnel, and available helping programs respond to the victims.

Turrell (2000) investigated same-sex domestic violence among lesbians, gay women, and gay men (female participants were allowed to choose between the labels *lesbian* and *gay women*). Turrell discovered a sexual abuse prevalence rate of 13% for gay men, 11% for gay women, and 14% for lesbians in a past or present relationship. Of those who reported sexual abuse, other physical abuse was also common. Specifically, 44% of the gay men, 58% of the gay women, and 55% of the lesbians reported receiving physical abuse in a past or present relationship.

Potoczniak et al. (2003) point out, based on a study by Hill (2000), that gay, lesbian, and bisexual (GLB) persons involved in domestic violence are perceived by jurors as having a lower moral character than their heterosexual counterparts. In line with this type of reasoning, jurors feel also that rape committed against a GLB person by another GLB person is not as serious as a heterosexual rape and consequently should receive a less severe penalty in a judicial setting (Hill, 2000).

Research also suggests that female victims of same-sex domestic violence find help at different places than the female victims of opposite-sex domestic violence. For example, OSDV victims find domestic violence shelters more helpful than many other resources, whereas female victims of same-sex domestic violence reported these same shelters to be the *least* helpful (Potoczniak et al., 2003; Renzetti, 1992). Furthermore, SSDV female victims most often find friends the most helpful resources, followed by counselors and relatives. It is no surprise that SSDV female victims report that the police, attorneys, and medical professionals are generally *not* helpful. Interestingly, one of the very few studies that examined the help-seeking behaviors of gay male victims of SSDV (Merrill & Wolfe, 2000) found that many male victims not only sought help from friends and counselors but also found gay domestic violence programs very helpful (Potoczniak et al., 2003).

The Roles of the Forensic Psychologist in Domestic Violence

Forensic psychologists are often asked to do risk assessments of batterers at all stages of the criminal justice process, from pretrial assessment to sentencing to correctional release. They may be asked to be an expert witness during a civil or criminal trial. If the batterer is a defendant in a criminal case, the psychologist may be asked to assess his level of danger if released on bail before the next court appearance. In a criminal trial in which a defendant assaulted or killed an abusive partner, the defense may request the forensic psychologist to identify whether the defendant qualified for BWS or PTSD. During the jury selection process in criminal cases, the forensic psychologist may also be asked to evaluate the extent of myths about family violence within the jury pool or community. In civil matters, the psychologist may be asked to evaluate the family dynamics or parental suitability to help in custody decisions involving the children. And in many instances, forensic psychologists and other mental health professionals will provide crisis intervention or treatment consultation or provide the services themselves.

Forensic Assessment of Domestic Violence

Before engaging in any kind of assessment or treatment of domestic violence victims, the forensic psychologist must be keenly aware of the impact of cultural and lifestyle variables on the battered person's response to the abuse and her recovery (Dutton, 1992; Jackson, Petretic-Jackson, & Witte, 2002). For example, many cultural and social barriers impede help-seeking behavior for a wide spectrum of cultural groups. In some cultures, violence may even be condoned within the secrecy of the family, although there are currently worldwide attempts to change this tolerance (Kozu, 1999; McWhirter, 1999). For some minority women or immigrants, a language barrier makes it doubly hard to find help and support.

A multimodal approach is most often recommended for the assessment of battered victims and battering offenders. The term *multimodal* refers to the use of a combination of psychological instruments and information-gathering strategies, including open-ended interviews, structured interviews, questionnaires, and standard psychological measures. An open-ended interview allows people to respond "in their own words" or tell their "own story" with a minimum of redirection from the clinician. It allows considerable flexibility for the clinician to modify the goals, the questions, and the general flow of information from the person being interviewed. The structured interview involves a more standardized set of procedures and questions that lessen the clinician's freedom to redirect the information-gathering process. It normally asks specific, predetermined questions that restrict the evaluator's inquiries during the administration of the interview.

Assessment of Victim Reactions

Although the BWS is facing considerable opposition in the research community, there is support for the presence of PTSD symptoms in battered women, with rates ranging from 45% to 84% (Jackson et al., 2002). Several measures commonly used to assess the level of PTSD symptomatology are the PTSD Symptom Scale (Foa, Riggs, Dancu, & Rothbaum, 1993), the Posttraumatic Diagnostic Stress Scale (Foa, Cashman, Jaycox, & Perry, 1997), the Crime-Related Post-Traumatic Stress Disorder Scale (Saunders, Arata, & Kilpatrick, 1990), the Distressing Event Questionnaire (Kubany, Leisen, Kaplan, & Kelly, 2000), and the Traumatic Life Events Questionnaire (Kubany, Haynes, et al., 2000).

The forensic psychologist is likely to administer formal psychological tests and inventories or other appropriate psychological measures to determine whether any discernible changes in attitude, cognitive functioning, behavior, and emotions are a result of the abuse. In any forensic setting, documentation is critical at all phases of the assessment process. Documentation may include court records; police reports; mental health and medical records; investigative reports of friends, family, or neighbors or other witnesses; and related legal proceedings such as depositions, trial transcripts, and protection orders. The evaluator should be aware that "unconventional sources" might provide invaluable documentation (Stark, 2002). Unconventional sources include "date books, logbooks, telephone messages, diaries, letters (including threatening letters from partners), tapes, photographs, and other records" (Stark, 2002, p. 232).

The assessment of the family must also consider the age, social class, occupational status, level of acculturation, prior exposure to violence, normative approval of violence, family structure, and cultural coping strategies (Jackson et al., 2002; West, 1998). It is important for the clinician to also realize that the victim may have distorted beliefs that she is the cause of the abuse and is at a loss about what to do about it. Unfortunately, very little empirical research on the effectiveness of therapeutic interventions with battered women has been conducted (Petretic-Jackson, Witte, & Jackson, 2002).

Risk Assessment: Is the Victim Safe?

Another important task for the forensic psychologist during assessment is to determine the level of danger the victim may be in and/or the likelihood the battered victim may assault or kill his or her abuser. The one thing that all practitioners who work with family violence can agree on is that the ongoing safety of the victim must be considered first and foremost (Petretic-Jackson et al., 2002) (see Box 8.1). Failure to put this factor into the equation may result in the death or serious injury of one or more family members. One instrument that may be useful for predicting risk in family situations is the **Spousal Assault Risk Assessment (SARA)**, developed by Kropp, Hart, Webster, and Eaves (1998). The SARA is a 20-item checklist designed to screen for risk factors in individuals suspected of or being treated for spousal or family-related assault. It is used when a clinician wishes to determine the degree to which an individual poses a threat to his or her spouse, children, or other family members.

Another useful risk assessment measure is Danger Assessment (DA), developed by Jacquelyn Campbell (1995). The first part of the DA is designed to determine the severity and frequency of battering by presenting the victim with a calendar of the past year. He or she is then asked to mark the approximate dates when physically abusive events occurred and to rank the severity of the incident on a 1 to 5 scale (ranging from 1 = *low* to 5 = *use of weapon*). The second part of

the DA is a 15-item questionnaire requiring a yes or no response to each item. The items are intended to provide an overview of the range of tactics used by the batterer.

We have described only two instruments designed to assess risk in abuse situations. The topic of risk assessment and the measures used will be revisited in Chapters 9 through 12.

Necessary Training for Domestic Violence Assessment

Forensic psychologists and other mental health workers who deal with domestic violence and its victims should have special training that emphasizes that assault by an intimate partner is a unique form of violence that differs in important ways from other forms of violence. Although violence from strangers is often an isolated, one-time event, the type of violence found in domestic violence is an ongoing occurrence characterized by repetitive abuse from a once-trusted person over a long period of time. In short, domestic violence is a process that has incalculable cumulative effects over time. Moreover, the victim may feel trapped in the home or situation in which it occurs, often with no *perceived* hope for escape. "Because of marital commitments, financial ties, and child care, victims of intimate partner violence cannot as easily remove themselves from the situations as can victims of abuse by a nonintimate" (Petretic-Jackson et al., 2002, pp. 300–301). This perceived hopelessness may lead to depression and inhibiting feelings of helplessness for some victims, but—as noted above—many other victims handle the situation quite differently. Consequently, forensic psychologists and other clinicians must be prepared for the wide range of psychological symptoms and coping mechanisms that victims will display.

Intimate partner violence, as well as domestic violence in general, is also apt to engender a variety of reactions from psychologists, especially if they or someone close to them have personally experienced such violence. Working with victims of domestic abuse (both adults and children) is especially stressful, and when clinicians are exposed to trauma victims, it leads to a high incidence of professional burnout. The term **vicarious traumatization** has sometimes been used to describe the psychological distress that clinicians themselves experience as a result of working with traumatized victims (McCann & Pearlman, 1990; Petretic-Jackson et al., 2002).

Child Abuse

In 2001, an estimated 903,000 children were victims of maltreatment in the United States (U.S. Department of Health and Human Services, 2003). These statistics indicate that about 12 out of every 1,000 children are victims of maltreatment each year, a rate that has been fairly consistent over the past decade. The data also show that child protective service agencies received about 2,672,000 reports of *possible* maltreatment in 2001.

About 1,300 children die of maltreatment each year, a rate of 1.81 per 1,000 children in the United States, and most (75%) are children younger than age 3. About 50% of the children who die of maltreatment in the United States have already been referred to a child protection agency (National Resource Center on Child Sexual Abuse, 1996).

Types of Maltreatment

There are four major types of child maltreatment: (1) neglect, (2) physical abuse, (3) sexual abuse, and (4) emotional abuse. Neglect refers to failure to provide for a child's basic needs, such as lack of appropriate supervision or failure to provide necessary food, shelter, or medical care. Neglect may also include failure to educate a child or attend to special education or emotional needs. Physical abuse refers to anything that may cause physical injury as a result of punching, beating, kicking, biting, shaking, throwing,

stabbing, choking, burning, or hitting. Sexual abuse includes activities by a parent or caretaker such as sexual fondling, incest, rape, sodomy, indecent exposure, and commercial exploitation through prostitution or the production of pornographic materials. Emotional abuse refers to behavior that impairs a child's emotional development or sense of self-esteem or worth and may include such things as constant criticism or rejection.

According to the U.S. Department of Health and Human Services (DHHS) (2003), about two thirds of maltreatment victims experience neglect. About 19% are physically abused, and 10% are sexually abused. Only 8% reportedly are emotionally abused, a figure that probably is greatly underestimated. Boys and girls are about equally neglected or physically abused, but girls are four times more likely to experience sexual abuse. About one quarter of the victims experience more than one type of maltreatment. About 60% of children seen by a physician for a physical abuse injury will return with further inflicted injuries. Approximately 10% will eventually die from the continual abuse. About 10% of all children seen in emergency rooms have some form of nonaccidental injury. Although abusive injuries are seen in all socioeconomic levels, fatal cases of abuse are most common in the poorer segments of the population. Children of all races and ethnicities experience child abuse.

Pet and Child Abuse

Recent research has discovered that pet abuse often accompanies child abuse (Arkow, 1998). That is, adults who abuse their children also tend to abuse the family pet, which is usually a treasured companion of abused children. Abusers often threaten to harm or kill a pet to frighten a child into secrecy about the abuse, particularly about sexual abuse. A strong relationship also exists between pet cruelty and spousal abuse. In one study, more than half of the victims at a women's shelter reported that their pets had been harmed or killed by their partner and that they delayed coming to the shelter for fear of harm to their pets left at home (Ascione, 1997). A growing body of research also suggests that violent people often commit considerable cruelty against animals in general, particularly against pets and stray animals (Merz-Perez, Heide, & Silverman, 2001).

Dynamics of Family Violence

Abusive families tend to be socially isolated and lack an extended social network of family and friends for social, financial, and emotional support. The family situation is usually unstable, punctuated by stormy relationships between adults, an unwanted child, financial constraints, heavy alcohol or drug abuse, and/or feelings of being trapped with little way out. Male abusers tend to be impulsive, immature, frustrated persons who believe it is their right as "man of the household" to dominate the female. Males become especially abusive if they are forced into providing primary care while the woman works because they interpret this situation as a loss of self-esteem and their traditional masculine role. Female abusers tend to be overstressed, dominated, depressed, and frustrated. The precipitating event for the abuse tends to be the infant's or child's crying or a soiled diaper.

There are uncertainties concerning the relative contribution of child abuse to later psychopathology (Knapp & VandeCreek, 2000).

Little is known about the impact of mitigating factors, such as having otherwise positive parental figures, receiving an early treatment after the abuse, or having a robust personality or a strong social network. Similarly, more needs to be known about the impact of exacerbating factors, such as having otherwise destructive parental figures, receiving blame or no treatment after the abuse, having a fragile personality, or lacking a strong social network. (Knapp & VandeCreek, 2000, p. 370)

Infanticide, Neonaticide, and Filicide

An estimated 1,200 to 1,500 young children are murdered each year by a parent or other person (Emery & Laumann-Billings, 1998). According to the FBI, two thirds of the infants younger than 6 days old are murdered by their mothers, who are often young (younger than age 20) and unmarried (Finkelhor & Ormrod, 2001b).

Infanticide, although the term literally means the killing of an infant, has become the umbrella term for homicide of children up to 2 years of age. Because there are significant differences between mothers who commit infanticide within the first 24 hours after birth, two additional terms are often used in the research and clinical literature. Specifically, **neonaticide** refers to the killing of the newborn within the first 24 hours, whereas **filicide** refers to the killing of a child older than 24 hours (Resnick, 1970). Mothers who commit neonaticide tend to be young, unmarried women who deny or conceal their pregnancy, fearing the disapproval or rejection from their family and society (Dobson & Sales, 2000). Mothers who commit filicide tend to be older and married and often demonstrate symptoms of depression (Dobson & Sales, 2000). Mothers of the second group are most often in situations they perceive as hopeless and dire. They believe that killing the child is the only way to prevent the child's suffering or potential suffering living under adverse conditions.

Traditionally, women who kill their children have been viewed by the legal system (and the public) as very likely suffering from serious mental problems. Most often, the clinical diagnosis is "postpartum depression," a depressive episode believed to be brought on by childbirth. However, it is important to realize that three categories of mental reactions may be apparent after childbirth: postpartum blues, postpartum depression, and postpartum psychosis (Dobson & Sales, 2000). The most common is *postpartum blues,* characterized by crying, irritability, anxiety, confusion, and rapid mood changes.

Approximately 50% to 80% of women show some minor features of postpartum blues between 1 and 5 days after delivery (Durand & Barlow, 2000). The symptoms may last for a few hours to a few days and are clearly linked to childbirth. Rarely do the symptoms last more than 12 days. The connection between postpartum blues and infanticide has not been supported by the research literature. As noted by Dobson and Sales (2000),

This mental disturbance is unlikely to play a major causative role in either neonaticide or filicide, because it occurs too late to affect mental status in women who commit neonaticide, and because its duration of less than 10 days is too short to play a major role in filicide, which can at occur at any time during the 1st postpartum year. (p. 1105)

The second category, *postpartum depression,* occurs during the weeks and months following childbirth. The symptoms include depression, loss of appetite, sleep disturbances, fatigue, suicidal thoughts, disinterest in the newborn child, and a general loss of interest in life's activities. The woman with postpartum depression often feels guilty for being depressed when she should be happy about a new baby. The incidence rate among childbearing women ranges from 7% to 17% in North America (Dobson & Sales, 2000). However, in contrast to postpartum blues, postpartum depression does not appear to be directly connected to childbirth but is more a clinical form of depression that is present before childbirth and may be a recurring disorder across the life cycle of the woman. Although women with postpartum depression may commit infanticide, research finds that this not common after childbirth, and infanticide is not directly caused by it.

The third category of mental problems associated with the postpartum period is *postpartum psychosis,* a severe mental disorder that is rare, occurring in 1 out of every 1,000 women following delivery. Usually, the psychotic features are highly similar to the symptoms of serious bipolar depression and appear to be directly connected to childbirth. As noted by Dobson and Sales (2000), "A number of epidemiological studies have provided clear scientific evidence supporting the link between childbirth and postpartum psychosis" (p. 1106). Sometimes the psychosis is severe enough to lead to the mother's attempted suicide, together with an attempt to kill her baby (Kendall & Hammen, 1995). There is some documentation that many women (estimates range from 20% to 40%) who commit filicide are suffering from postpartum psychosis (Dobson & Sales, 2000).

Overall, few infanticides are committed by mothers who suffer depression, despair, or psychosis. Infant homicides can result from acts of omission, such as neglecting to watch the child in hazardous environment, or acts of commission, such as delivering a swift blow to silence a crying infant. In many instances, however, it is difficult to determine whether the infant's death is due to an accident, biological deficiency (such as physical immaturity and genetic malformations), carelessness, or an intentional act to murder. For example, sudden infant death syndrome (SIDS) is the number one cause of death in infants between the ages of 2 weeks and 1 year, although the risk is greatest between 2 and 4 months of age. It is estimated that 1 in every 350 live births will be a victim of SIDS. Unfortunately, the disorder is largely unpreventable and unpredictable, and currently there is no known cause or cure. The victims of SIDS are usually healthy, well-cared for babies with no previous history of disease or illness. The parent or caretaker often finds the baby dead in its crib, usually in a normal sleeping position. In some cases, there may be some bloody fluid around the mouth and nose and some discoloration of the face and extremities, but these signs are not evidence of foul play or abuse. Consequently, an accurate appraisal of the cause of death often requires a careful autopsy by a skilled medical examiner, scene investigation, and careful review of the statements provided by parents or caretakers. We must emphasize that the vast majority of SIDS deaths are not due to parental neglect or parental actions. However, in rare cases, infants as well as young children may be killed in such subtle ways that only a very careful forensic investigation can discover the cause and manner of the death.

Munchausen Syndrome by Proxy

Munchausen syndrome by proxy (MSBP) is a form of child abuse in which a parent (almost always the mother) *consistently* and *chronically* subjects a child to medical attention without any "true" medical condition or symptoms being present. MSBP was first applied to children by Money and Werleas (1976) and Meadow (1977). Prior to the mid-1970s, Munchausen syndrome was considered exclusively an adult disorder (Robins & Sesan, 1991). "Adult Munchausen is characterized by an adult's chronic and relentless pursuit of medical treatment, involving some combination of consciously self-inflicted injury and falsely reported symptomatology" (Robins & Sesan, 1991, p. 285). The term *Munchausen syndrome* was apparently coined by the London physician Richard Asher (1951) to describe patients who consistently produced false stories about themselves to receive needless medical examinations, operations, and treatments. Asher named the syndrome after Baron Von Munchausen, a distinguished German soldier and politician who was born in 1720 (Dowdell & Foster, 2000). Asher named the behavior after Von Munchausen because of the many fabricated stories of incredible travels and brave military exploits he would tell to friends and acquaintances, including his physicians (Raspe, 1944).

In Munchausen syndrome by proxy, the child's presenting symptoms are either falsified or directly induced *by the parent.* In fact, the term *by proxy* refers to the parent's dominating influence in the presentation of symptoms to the medical staff. The most common cluster of symptoms reported by the parent concerning the child's condition involves seizures, failure to thrive, vomiting, diarrhea, asthma/allergies, and infections (see, generally, Howarth & Lawson, 1995). Symptom inducement by the parent may include adding fat to stools in order to produce a laboratory abnormality, initiating starvation in the child, placing blood into the child's urine sample before lab testing, or injecting contaminating or toxic material intravenously into the child's bloodstream (Murray, 1997; Pearl, 1995).

MSBP cases are found in homes of all socioeconomic levels, and the victims are most often young children ranging in ages from 6 months to 8 years. Both sexes appear to be equally susceptible to being victimized. The term *serial MSBP* is reserved for those cases involving more than one child in the same family (Alexander, Smith, & Stevenson, 1990).

The case histories of MSBP cases commonly illustrate an "overinvolved" mother and an "emotionally distant" or physically absent father (Robins & Sesan, 1991). MSBP mothers are often described as "emotionally empty" and lonely and often have experienced significant emotional, physical, and sexual abuse during their own childhood and young adulthood (Robins & Sesan, 1991). The mother often appears to others as the ideal parent and comes across as very concerned, devoted, attentive, and loving. However, she is also seen as overprotective and obsessed with the child's illness (Brown, 1997; Voltz, 1995).

The offending mother is often sophisticated about medical conditions, has some fascination with medical procedures and diagnosis, and may even be a health professional herself. Suspicions that MSBP may be present should be entertained when the parent is unusually attentive to the child and is very reluctant to leave the child's side during a medical examination or treatment. This, though, can be said of many if not most parents. A better sign is when a child has a series of recurring medical conditions that do not respond to treatment or follow an unanticipated course that is persistent, puzzling, and unexplained. Another indicator is when laboratory findings or symptomatology are highly abnormal and discrepant with existing medical knowledge.

The extreme forms of this child abuse may lead to serious injury or death.

Although there have been many cases of MSBP reported in the literature, the prevalence or incidence of the problem is unknown, largely due to the difficulty of identifying actual illnesses as opposed to fabricated ones and the general lack of knowledge about this unusual form of child abuse. It should also be mentioned that there have been some reports that, in some cases, the "proxy" is a family pet (Tucker, 2002). In a survey sent to 1,000 veterinary surgeons asking them about nonaccident injuries in animals, a small number of the respondents believed that they had encountered MSBP perpetrated by some pet owners. In other words, some pet owners may deliberately hurt their pets to get sympathy and medical attention.

In most cases, child protection services are brought into play if the MSBP is suspected, and rarely are criminal charges filed unless the behavior has resulted in serious injury or the child has died. The psychologist may become involved at both the child protection and the prosecution stages of the case. If the parent is unwilling or unable to stop the behavior, the child may need to be removed from the home until effective intervention or some appropriate arrangement with the parent is accomplished.

Shaken Baby Syndrome

Another form of child abuse is called **shaken baby syndrome (SBS),** in which a parent or caretaker shakes a baby so hard that serious brain damage occurs. The brain damage can result in mental retardation, speech and learning disabilities, blindness, paralysis, seizures, hearing loss, or death. A baby's brain and blood vessels are very fragile and can be easily damaged by whiplash motions, such as shaking, jerking, and jolting. Their neck muscles are not strong enough to control head movements, and rapid movement of the head can result in the brain being damaged from banging against the skull wall.

SBS is difficult to diagnosis, unless a witness accurately describes the incident. Medical personnel report that many babies symptomatic of SBS are brought in for medical attention for a fall, difficulty breathing, seizures, vomiting, altered consciousness, or choking. The parent or caretaker may admit that he or she shook the baby in an effort to resuscitate it. To diagnose SBS, physicians will look for bleeding in the retina or retinal detachment, blood in the brain, and increased head size indicating excessive accumulation of fluid in the tissues of the brain. Fixed pupils, inactivity, and breathing problems may also be evident. Spinal cord damage and broken ribs may also be present, depending on how the baby was held during the shaking.

Although there are not complete statistics on the frequency of SBS, there is consensus that brain trauma is the leading killer of abused children (more than 50%) and that shaking is involved in many of these cases (Duhaime, Christian, Rorke, & Zimmerman, 1998; Showers, 1999; Smithey, 1998). Ellis and Lord (2002) estimate that 10% to 12% of all deaths related to abuse and neglect can be attributable to SBS. Furthermore, studies indicate that 70% to 80% of the perpetrators of SBS are male, and most often they are the parent of the child (Child Abuse Prevention Center, 1998; Ellis & Lord, 2002). The offender is usually in his early 20s (Showers, 1997). Both male and female babies are equally victimized, and SBS cuts across all socioeconomic levels. Frustration from a baby's incessant crying or eating and toileting problems is usually reported as the precipitating event leading to the severe shaking. Ignorance of the dangers of shaking a baby is typical, and the overwhelming majority of offenders have poor child-rearing skills (which may or may not be susceptible to improvement).

Repressed and Recovered Memories

Over the past three decades, one of the most controversial topics in forensic psychology has been the question of whether a "lost" memory of abuse or other crime can be recovered at a later time. The topic is often referred to as **repressed memory,** recovered memory, or, less frequently, false memory (to imply questionable validity of the reported memory itself).

The notion of repressed memories has been around at least since the time of Sigmund Freud (1915/1957) and probably has been discussed in some capacity throughout the history of humankind. Freud, though, was certainly the most influential in bringing the concept into the limelight. Freud wrote that "the essence of repression lies simply in the function of rejecting and keeping something out of consciousness" (p. 105). To minimize anxiety and fear, we supposedly push out of our awareness painful or extremely troubling memories, and it is assumed we do this unconsciously. Current clinical thinking broadens the term *repression* to include a wide range of cognitive processes.

> Repression refers to the psychological process of keeping something out of awareness because of unpleasant affect connected with it. The "something" may be a memory (or part of a memory), a fantasy, a thought, an idea, a feeling, a wish, an impulse, a connection, and so forth. (Karon & Widener, 1999, p. 625)

Repression may include loss of memory for the trauma (amnesia) in some individuals, the inability to lose memory or the retention of extremely detailed memory (hypermnesia) in others, and partial, fragmentary memory in still others.

According to Freud—and many contemporary clinicians—a repressed or submerged memory continues to linger in the unconscious until it is retrieved during psychotherapy or under certain other conditions, such as dream analysis, hypnosis, or some other "method of recovery." For many individuals, these repressed memories are never satisfactorily retrieved and may continue to raise havoc by causing psychological problems across their life spans—at least this is the position held by some clinicians. Many clinicians are convinced that they encounter many forms of repression—particularly memories of early childhood abuse—during their routine practice. On the other side of the ledger are cognitive scientists who question the frequency of "true" repression and the clinical assumptions of how or why it occurs.

The courts have had to face the issue of repressed memories in numerous cases in recent years. Adults who were allegedly the victims of abuse, especially sexual abuse, claim in civil or criminal trials that they had initially forgotten these traumatic experiences but eventually remembered them, usually with the help or guidance of therapists and often under hypnosis or some other "discovery" process. The courts refer to repressed-then-recovered memory as "delayed discovery." The alleged abuser, often the father or another family member, having been named, disclaims abuse, countering that the victim's memories are false and that they have been implanted by the psychotherapist, investigator, or evaluator (Partlett & Nurcombe, 1998). The accuracy of these recollections has been the center of the contentious debate of experts spanning nearly 30 years, as well as between the experts providing testimony in the courtroom.

It should be noted that criminal prosecutions for child or adult sexual abuse cannot be brought after the statute of limitations has expired (*Stogner v. California*, 2003). The statute of limitations is the legal time limit placed on the filing of criminal charges or a civil complaint. In criminal cases, it is typically 1 year after the event, except for murder, for which the time period does not expire. In recent years, however, many states have begun to extend their statute of limitations in recognition that it may take years for victims of sexual abuse to come forward—even when repressed memories are not at issue. Many court cases in which sexual abuse is alleged are civil in nature. The widely publicized priest abuse cases are a case in point. Sexual abuse allegations also occur with some frequency in child custody and visitation cases.

In both civil and criminal cases, the defense tries to call an expert witness to challenge the testimony offered by the prosecution's or the plaintiff's witness. The focus is usually on questioning the circumstances under which the original report was elicited and the interviewing methods of investigators or other involved professionals (Berliner, 1998). Some victims, under the repeated urging of their psychotherapists, often combined with discovery methods such as hypnosis, come to remember (often suddenly) that they were sexually abused by parents, siblings, relatives, and/or strangers. Convinced that these abuses are the core ingredient of their maladjustment or current difficulties or that their abusers should be punished, a significant number of these victims seek redress through the courts, primarily civil courts. Although these recovered memories may have foundations in some (perhaps many) cases, these claims must be evaluated very carefully by the forensic psychologist before proceeding to the legal arena. Lilienfeld and Loftus (1998) write, "The question of whether traumatic memories can be repressed for long periods of time (i.e., years or decades) and then suddenly recovered in intact form is perhaps the most controversial issue in clinical psychology today" (p. 471).

There are very few figures on how frequently repressed memory occurs in clinical practice. In one of the few studies conducted so far, Polusny and Follette (1996) reported that 72% of the psychologists whom they surveyed had *not* encountered a case of "repressed" memory in the past year, and 15% had seen only one repressed-memory case during that time.

Special Expert Panels on Repressed Memory

In an effort to clear up some of the controversy and debate on repressed or recovered memories, the American Psychological Association appointed a "working group" of researchers and clinicians to study the issue and arrive at some consensus on what is known and how to proceed. Called the American Psychological Association (APA) Working Group on Investigation of Memories of Childhood Abuse ("Final Conclusions," 1998), the panel of clinicians and researchers was able to come to the following five conclusions (p. 933):

1. Controversies regarding adult recollections should not be allowed to obscure the fact that child sexual abuse is a complex and pervasive problem in America that has historically gone unacknowledged.

2. Most people who were sexually abused as children remember all or part of what happened to them.

3. It is possible for memories of abuse that have been forgotten for a long time to be remembered.

4. It is also possible to construct convincing pseudo-memories for events that never occurred.

5. There are gaps in our knowledge about the processes that lead to accurate and inaccurate recollections of childhood abuse.

But there were far more important issues on which the APA Working Group could not agree, mostly concerning the nature of early memory of abuse and its recovery. Although the group clearly strove to find consensus, the debate between some clinicians and researchers apparently became heated and polarized, resulting in a special issue in the December 1998 edition of *Psychology, Public Policy, and Law* that presents both sides. In this section, we will focus on the dominant view generally accepted by the cognitive and developmental scientists, but we will also give some attention to other perspectives where appropriate.

Before we proceed, however, we should mention that a similar panel of experts on repressed or recovered memory met in the United Kingdom shortly before the APA group convened. The group, called the British Psychological Society's Working Party on Recovered Memories, was sponsored by the British Psychological Society (BPS) to publish a position statement on the phenomenon for the members of the BPS, the media, and the interested citizen. The final document, which took more than 10 months to be finalized, is commonly referred to as the BPS Report (see British Psychological Society, 1995). The conclusions of the BPS Report generally coincide closely with the conclusions of the APA Final Report described above (Davies, Morton, Mollon, & Robertson, 1998). For example,

> Like the BPS Report, the APA Final Report concluded that it was possible for memories of abuse that had been forgotten for a long time to be remembered, but that it was possible to construct convincing pseudomemories for events that never occurred. (Davies et al., 1998, p. 1080)

However, the authors of the BPS Report also concluded that the APA Working Group neglected some important research findings that should have been addressed. The British group, for instance, thought that the APA panel neglected to establish an agreed-on scientific framework on which to base their discussions. More specifically, "there appears to be little consensus over the relevant evidence and methods of proof. In the absence of such fundamentals, the temptation is to revert to a political framework, which is unproductive from the standpoint of advancing theory and practice" (Davies et al., 1998, p. 1080). But even more relevant to our discussion here is the observation by the British group that

> the Final [APA] Report contains little serious discussion as to how memory mechanisms might mediate such diverse effects: The cognitivists merely accuse the therapists of clinging to a scientifically unsupported view of repression, and the therapists look in turn to the recent work of Van der Kolk

(e.g., Van der Kolk & Fisler, 1995) as providing a rationale for a special and different form of memory associated with trauma. (Davies et al., 1998, p. 1080)

Because the topic of repressed memory is so important in forensic psychological practice and because it sets the stage for understanding memory processes in witness and expert testimony in the courtroom, we will pay special attention to the issue in this section. We begin by briefly outlining some of what research has revealed about human memory in general.

Research Sketches of Human Memory and Its Limitations

In its simplest terms, memory involves acquisition, storage, and retrieval. Acquisition, also called the encoding or input stage, is the initial step in the memory process and overlaps considerably with the sensory perceptual process. Sensory perception is the process of organizing and making sense of the information received from the senses, such as the eyes, ears, smell, taste, somatosensory receptors, and vestibular and kinesthetic senses. Memory storage, also called retention, is when information becomes "resident in memory" (Loftus, 1979). In the retrieval stage, the brain searches for the pertinent information and retrieves it, a process somewhat like searching for a document in a filing cabinet.

In any discussion of forensic matters and memory, it will be helpful to begin with four important points about memory made by three of the leading scientists in the area: Peter Ornstein, Stephen Ceci, and Elizabeth Loftus (Ornstein, Ceci, & Loftus, 1998a).

- Not everything gets into memory.
- What gets into memory may vary in strength.
- The status of information in memory changes in memory.

- Retrieval is not perfect (i.e., not all that is stored gets retrieved).

In reference to the first point, some experiences may not be recalled because they were not entered into memory in the first place. The human cognitive system is limited in its information-processing capacity and cannot simultaneously attend to everything going on in the environment. We have to be selective in what is noticed. Consequently, considerable information is never processed. Furthermore, information processing is influenced by prior knowledge and experience. In other words, to understand and interpret what is being experienced, the brain compares "new" material to "old" stored material. By analogy, the new material is fitted onto a "cognitive template" to see how it compares. How one "sees" the world is dictated to a large extent by "cognitive templates" that are already in place from previous experiences and knowledge.

Concerning the second point raised by Ornstein et al. (1998a), several factors may influence the strength and organization of the resulting memory "trace." In addition, strong memory traces may be readily retrieved, whereas weak traces may be more difficult to recover. The strength of the trace depends on such factors as the length of exposure to an event, the number of exposures, the age of the individual, and how significant or prominent the event is to the person. With increasing age (at least through young adulthood), there are corresponding changes in information-processing skills and the cognitive templates that have been developed from previous experiences.

The third point refers to what may happen once the information is stored and perhaps is one of the most important points concerning forensic issues. That is,

the memory trace can be altered during the course of the interval between the actual experience and a report of it. The passage of time, as well as a variety of intervening experiences, can influence strongly the strength and organization of stored information. (Ornstein et al., 1998a, p. 1028)

Apparently, due to the experiences of current events, humans continually alter and reconstruct their memory of past experiences rather than simply store past events permanently and unchangingly. Memory is not like a videotape camera that accurately stores events on film to be played back when necessary. And this alteration or "reconstructive process" is often done without the person's complete awareness. The individual is aware of the content of memory but is not usually aware of the transformations that have occurred during encoding, retention, and retrieval. The perspective that memory is continually vulnerable to revision is known as the **reconstructive theory of memory.** Overall, though, this reconstructive process probably does not *substantially* alter the *major* theme of the original memory for most people but does introduce a number of errors in *specific* descriptions of the event. For example, witnesses to a car accident may all report that two cars collided (as opposed to three trucks), but the specific details of the incident may vary considerably.

Moreover, "without reinstating events or experiences (e.g., through rehearsal, prompts, or visualizations), the strength of a memory trace decreases over time, and this trace decay combines with interferences in the delay interval to make access to stored information and successful retrieval more difficult" (Ornstein et al., 1998a, p. 1028). In young children, memory traces are often not as strong because children generally lack the requisite knowledge and experience to fully appreciate the event. Thus, they may undergo more rapid decay than the memory traces of older children. A growing body of research also indicates that young children (such as preschoolers) are usually more susceptible to the influences of misleading information received after the event than are older children and adults (Ceci & Bruck, 1993; Ceci, Ross, & Toglia, 1987; Ornstein et al., 1998a).

The fourth point refers to the common observation that not everything in memory can be retrieved all the time. Social pressures, stress, anxiety, information overload, and the low strength of the information itself are some of the many factors that may interfere with quick and immediate retrieval under certain conditions. People's names are especially difficult to retrieve for many people.

Many clinicians believe that memory for traumatic events may be encoded differently from memory for unremarkable events (Alpert, Brown, & Courtois, 1998). More specifically, some suggest that the enormous differences between normal resting states and high levels of arousal might result in changing the entire process of how memories are stored and retrieved. In the APA Working Group Report, as mentioned previously, the clinical group placed considerable reliance on the work of Van der Kolk and Fisler (1994, 1995) as evidence for memory repression. As pointed out by Davies and his colleagues (1998), Van der Kolk and Fisler did emphasize the difference between memories of traumatic events and memories of events that are merely stressful. More specifically, Van der Kolk and Fisler (1994) stated that traumatic memories may somehow be "frozen" in their original form and unmodified by further experience. Consequently, reliving these traumatic experiences can

be retraumatizing because retrieving them is actually like reexperiencing them. But note that this phenomenon refers to actively *avoiding* relieving the trauma, not *repressing* the event. If anything, Davies et al. note, Van der Kolk and Fisler are referring to state-dependent memory rather than repressed memory. **State-dependent memory** refers to the research findings that the things we experience in one emotional or physiological state—such as happiness, fear, or even intoxication—are sometimes easier to recall when we are again in that same state. (See Box 8.2 for more on this interesting phenomenon.) Although a person who does not like to revisit that same state of pain and trauma may avoid doing so as much as possible, it does not mean that person is *repressing* the memory, at least according to the typical clinical definition of repression.

In addition, the scientific evidence clearly indicates that memories from early infancy are highly unreliable, incomplete, and full of error. The phenomenon of infantile or childhood "amnesia" has long been noted by developmental psychologists (Dudycha & Dudycha, 1941). Infantile amnesia refers to the common observation that adults are usually unable to recall events that occurred before the age of around 3 years. According to the BPS Report (British Psychological Society, 1995), for instance, "nothing can be recalled accurately from before the first birthday

---

BOX 8.1 National Threat Assessment Center

The National Threat Assessment Center (NTAC), run by the U.S. Secret Service, was created to provide leadership and guidance to the emerging field of threat assessment. Specifically, the NTAC offers timely, realistic, useful, and effective advice to law enforcement and other professionals and organizations with responsibilities to investigate and/or prevent targeted violence.

Building on recent studies of U.S. assassins, attackers, and near-lethal approaches of public officials, the NTAC will develop and provide threat assessment training and conduct operational research relevant to public official, workplace, stalking/domestic, and school-based violence. In addition, the NTAC will offer its assistance to organizations interested in developing threat assessment programs.

Source: U.S. Secret Service, 2003. Available: www.secretservice.gov

and little from before the second. Poor memory from before the fourth birthday is normal" (p. 29). Most of us have little trouble remembering certain things that occurred when we were 7 years of age, such as a birthday party or a special occasion, but prior to that, things often become quite hazy. Even some things about our 7th birthday or other ordinary memories of early childhood may be nothing more than reconstructions based on stories told to us by parents or relatives (Knapp & VandeCreek, 2000, p. 367). However, scientists are not in complete agreement as to when this period of infantile amnesia ends for most children (Ornstein, Ceci, & Loftus, 1998b) or exactly why it occurs (Harley & Reese, 1999; see Box 8.3). Interestingly, Roseanne Barr, the well-known television sitcom star of the 1990s, claimed after therapy that she remembered her mother sexually abusing her when she was 6 months old (Ornstein et al., 1998b, p. 1001).

Claims and assertions of abuse during childhood are complicated by the fact that the very definition of abuse is culturally determined, and behaviors that would be taken by adults to be clear instances of abuse might not be viewed in a comparable fashion by children and vice versa (Ornstein et al., 1998b). For example, as Ornstein et al. (1998b) point out, circumcisions, insertions of anal suppositories, urinary catheterization, and other invasive medical procedures during the first few years of life may be perceived by the young child as "abusive."

Many practitioners believe that traumatized children are more likely to reenact traumatic events than to describe them verbally (Alpert et al., 1998). Although many children are unable

---

BOX 8.2 State-Dependent Learning

State dependence refers to the observation that a memory acquired in one state of consciousness cannot be recalled until the person returns to that same state of consciousness. Otherwise, the person will have great difficulty remembering the events if in a different psychological state. For example, if a person learns new material while under the influence of alcohol, he tends to recall it better if he is again under the influence of alcohol.

State-dependent learning was first described in 1784 but was not subjected to much scientific study until the 1960s (Eich, 1989; Schramke & Bauer, 1997). Early research concentrated on differences induced by drugs and alcohol, and then interest shifted to the effects of mood or emotional states on memory and learning. For example, research has discovered that negative events are recalled better when people are in a negative mood (Lewinsohn & Rosenbaum, 1987), and positive events are recalled better while in a positive mood (Ehrlichman & Halpern, 1988). Research now finds that state-dependent learning may be influenced by drugs, moods, levels of activation (e.g., anxiety levels), arousal (i.e., sleep and wakefulness), or environmental settings (i.e., where the memory was acquired) (Slot & Colpaert, 1999; Weingartner, Putnam, George, & Ragan, 1995). Pertaining to environmental settings, if you misplace your keys, trying to remember where you left them is often not as effective as physically retracing your steps in the actual environment. If a person hides money while intoxicated and forgets where the money was hidden, recall is likely to be enhanced by being similarly intoxicated and placed in the same environment.

The implications for forensic psychology are interesting. A person who witnessed a crime or traffic accident while under the influence may be better able to recall that incident if placed back into that same physiological or psychological state. In the case of environmental settings, it might be helpful if the witness also returns to the scene of the crime.

to give verbal descriptions of events that had taken place in their early years, they showed evidence of their memory in their behavior and play, where they reenacted the abuse events (Alpert et al., 1998). It is clear that children interpret and respond to trauma according to their developmental level and maturity, but description of the behavioral pattern in children has been limited. Terr (1991, 1994) developed a model (derived from clinical observations of hundreds of traumatized children) of two types of childhood trauma, each with corresponding memory encoding and retrieval. By her description, Type I trauma consists of sudden, external, single events that result in stereotyped symptoms of childhood PTSD along with detailed memories, but also with misperceptions and mistimings regarding characteristics of the events. Type II traumas are those that involve "long-standing or repeated exposure to extreme external events." According to Terr, memory loss is most common in this kind of trauma. However, as pointed out by Ornstein et al. (1998b), scientists who study memory have found that repetition enhances memory rather than diminishing it. "Research on memory with children and adults suggests that people are more likely to forget an isolated event than a series of repeated events, even though the repeated events may become blended into a typical script" (Ornstein et al., 1998b, p. 1000). "It is not useful to anyone to pretend that science has confirmed the existence of dubious claims such as that embodied in the Type I/Type II distinction" (Ornstein et al., 1998b, p. 1000).

Perhaps more troubling for the courts and to the psychological profession is that under certain circumstances, *false* memories of abuse can be created, often by psychotherapists or evaluators themselves. As reported by Roediger and Bergman (1998), "A substantial body of experimental evidence (buttressed by a long collection of anecdotal cases) shows that events that never happened can be vividly remembered, or that events can be remembered in ways quite different from the way they occurred" (p. 1102). Repeated suggestions, confrontations, or the use of highly

suggestive "memory recovery" techniques may cause the creation of memories that are not true (Knapp & VandeCreek, 2000). A growing literature further suggests that it is relatively easy to create pseudo-memories in some individuals, but it may be more difficult in others. "The available evidence makes clear that individuals who have been exposed to repeated suggestive techniques over long periods of time sometimes provide highly detailed and coherent narratives that happen to be false" (Ornstein et al., 1998a, p. 1045). Hypnosis as a memory recovery technique especially runs the risk of creating, distorting, or magnifying memories. At the very least, hypnosis as a discovery technique is considered by many forensic experts to be a very dangerous method of persuasion, if not indoctrination.

The tendency of clinicians to unintentionally engender symptoms or recollections in their patients is called the **iatrogenic effect** (*iatros* is the Greek word for *physician,* and *genic* refers to *cause*). In other words, clinicians who firmly believe in and are perceptually sensitive to certain symptoms as indicative of a specific disorder may, in effect, prompt the patient to think similarly. In this sense, certain therapists who are convinced that sexual abuse is the basic cause of many symptoms of maladjustment may have a strong propensity to look for and interpret a variety of behaviors as symptoms of sexual abuse. In effect, the clinician may encourage the reconstruction of memory in the patient to include accounts of sexual abuse that may have never occurred. In addition, the scientific research indicates that young children may be disproportionately vulnerable to suggestive influences, either during psychotherapy or more generally through daily living (Ceci & Bruck, 1993).

In summary, repressed memory of childhood abuse and its recovery by psychotherapists or through suggestions via self-help books or workshops should raise some red flags for further inquiry and reasonable evaluation and assessment by the forensic psychologist. We do not mean to imply that it could not happen—only that the overwhelming bulk of the research evidence suggests that if it does, it is probably full of error and will need further corroboration from independent sources and careful assessment. As asserted by two well-respected scientists, Roediger and Bergman (1998),

> Far more mysterious is how painful events, banished to an unconscious state for years though some mechanism of dissociation or repression, could be brought back to consciousness and recollected with great fidelity . . . no evidence from the voluminous literature on human memory makes us think this is possible. (p. 1095)

This is especially the case for adults who suddenly recollect from their "unconscious" traumatic events that happened 20 to 40 years previously.

The research clearly indicates that memories for emotional events are reasonably good and accurate, and very rarely are they repressed or forgotten (Roediger & Bergman, 1998). Many people have reported their memories for high-impact events with considerable accuracy, a phenomenon referred to as **flashbulb memory** (Brown & Kulick, 1977). You can probably remember what you were doing when you heard that two hijacked airliners crashed into the World Trade Center on September 11, 2001 or when you experienced some high-impact event during your childhood. People often feel that they remember with high accuracy even minor details of emotional events, such as earthquakes, tornadoes, and other natural disasters (Roediger & Bergman, 1998).

Roles of the Forensic Psychologist in Child Abuse Cases

In the past, clinicians rarely became involved in addressing forensic issues in child abuse before the cases were adjudicated (Melton et al., 1997). This has changed in recent years. Forensic psychologists are becoming involved much earlier in the process. Today, the forensic psychologist may assume the role of decision maker of the process

in its early phases and then be asked to return to the role of a "neutral" expert in the adjudication and disposition of the case (Melton et al., 1997). As decision maker, the clinician may be asked by a court to determine whether child abuse or neglect occurred and, if it did occur, what should be done about it. The second question requires immediate (emergency), short-term, and/or long-term predictions and decisions and is essentially a risk assessment determination (Melton et al., 1997). The second question focuses on the extent the child is in imminent danger. Early in the case, this might involve removing the child from the home for his or her protection.

It should be emphasized that many states are beginning to establish multidisciplinary teams for investigation, assessment, and intervention in child abuse or neglect cases. Consequently, the forensic psychologist rarely acts alone or without the expertise of other mental health professionals. Still, as pointed out by Melton et al. (1997), the forensic psychologist may be regarded as the team's sole expert in a variety of assessments and predictions.

The adjudication and disposition of the case refers primarily to the criminal proceedings against the alleged abuser. However, it may also occur in civil proceedings, such as custody hearings or hearings to decide whether visitation should be allowed. During adjudication, four issues that may involve the forensic psychologist are as follows:

1. What is the most appropriate procedure for taking a child's testimony?

2. Under what conditions is a child's out-of-court statement (hearsay) admissible?

3. Is the child competent enough to provide accurate testimony in abuse cases?

4. Did abuse or neglect occur, and who is responsible?

The first issue—which first emerged in sexual abuse cases—concerns identifying what special procedures would allow a child to testify without being under enormous duress in the presence of the defendant. Moreover, "the child is notoriously vulnerable while giving evidence against abusers, especially parents, when proof of the charge will result in separation. Many children are highly suggestible and subject to recantation when faced with the reality of parental separation" (Partlett & Nurcombe, 1998, p. 1260). These problems of recantation and suggestibility are especially troubling when accusations of abuse made during custody proceedings give one parent an advantage over the other.

In criminal cases, recent legal rules in many states limit the defendant's confrontation with the child by allowing, under special circumstances, the child's testimony to be taken through closed-circuit TV, courtroom closure, or in some other way. Thus, the jury can observe and hear the testimony and the cross-examination while the child's distress and the defendant's intimidation are presumably minimized. If such a limitation on the defendant's right to confront witnesses against him is to occur, it first requires an assessment of the emotional consequences of the child's "interaction with a particular adult in a specific context" (Melton et al., 1997, p. 458). In 1987, the U.S. Supreme Court (e.g., *Maryland v. Craig*, 1987) "opened the door to testimony by mental health professionals in hearings to determine whether there is a necessity for special procedures to protect particular child witnesses" (Melton et al., 1997, p. 458).

Clinicians who evaluate abused children are required to be skillful and sensitive to a wide range of factors. Budd, Felix, Poindexter, Naik-Polan, and Sloss (2002, p. 3) report that

> clinicians may be asked to assess the child's developmental or emotional functioning and needs, the effects of maltreatment on the child, the risk of harm should the child be united with his or her parents, the impact of separation from the biological family on the child's functioning, or the advantages and disadvantages of potential visitation or placement options. (p. 3)

In addition, the American Psychological Association's Committee on Professional Practice and Standards (1998) recommends the use of a multimethod, multisource, multisession assessment approach in the evaluation of abused children. As pointed out by Budd et al. (2002), the standards also encourage that the forensic psychologist be highly sensitive to and knowledgeable about the cultural, socioeconomic, and diversity issues relevant to the child's situation. Furthermore, the standards highly recommend that the forensic psychologist interpret his or her findings conservatively. That is, the psychologist should acknowledge the limitations of the assessment findings and refrain from stating opinions or recommendations that are not adequately supported by the data. It is also emphasized that the evaluator should focus on the child's strengths rather than only on her or his deficits (Budd et al., 2002).

Assessment of child abuse or child protection cases is very common, yet few surveys describe in detail current practice or which evaluation procedures are most useful. In their survey, Budd et al. (2002) found that psychologists conducted 90% of the evaluations of children in one urban juvenile court system. Unfortunately, many of the evaluations were not based on multisource, multisession information but were based on much more limited data. However, many of the evaluations did emphasize the strengths of the child.

In some cases, anatomically detailed dolls are used to help young children suspected of being sexually abused express themselves verbally on sexual topics. The practice of using them, however, has been questioned. Some experts (e.g., Bruck, Ceci, & Francoeur, 2000; Ceci & Bruck, 1993) contend that these dolls heighten the child's suggestibility and promote false stories. Others (e.g., Koocher et al., 1995) believe that, in the hands of well-trained professionals, they may be a useful communication tool, as long as they are used cautiously.

The expert testimony offered in child abuse cases is subject to the same legal rules as other forms of expert testimony (Berliner, 1998). "It must be relevant, not common knowledge; its value in helping prove the case cannot be outweighed by the potential for creating unfair prejudice; and it must be helpful to the trier of fact" (Berliner, 1998, p. 11). Because forensic psychologists have been increasingly asked to serve as expert witnesses in child abuse cases in recent years, they would be wise to become familiar with the general nature of the disputes and the current status of relevant knowledge. The courts have scrutinized expert testimony in child abuse cases more carefully and more thoroughly as the amount of such testimony has correspondingly increased. Furthermore, as we will find in Chapter 9, recent revisions in legal rules relating to the admission of expert testimony suggest that this scrutiny is apt to continue.

The psychologists may be asked in child abuse cases to provide expert testimony as substantive evidence or rehabilitative evidence (Berliner, 1998). An example of substantive evidence in this context revolves around professional opinions as to whether the child was abused or shares characteristics of abused children. An example of rehabilitative evidence would be testimony concerning the suitability of the child to tell his or her story. In other words, is the child credible, or is there an emotional or psychological problem that may hamper the veracity of the child's story or report?

> For example, if a child had exhibited reactions that were very unusual, such as severe dissociative symptoms, and these symptoms were used to discredit the child, the expert might properly explain the nature of dissociation and its possible association with a traumatic history. (Berliner, 1998, pp. 16–17)

In another situation, the psychologist may be asked to provide expert testimony for the defense, which seeks to discredit the child's testimony or to challenge it as being inconsistent with the reactions that would be expected if abuse actually occurred. Patterns of behaviors or "syndromes" do not automatically connote evidence of abuse, a fact that many courts and professionals have confused and misapplied. For example, the child sexual abuse accommodation syndrome (CSAAS) (Summit, 1983) does not necessarily verify that child sexual abuse occurred—nor did the originator of the term intend that the syndrome be applied that way (Berliner, 1998; Summit, 1992). In fact, because of the misapplication of the term, some courts have banned the term from being used at all (e.g., *Hellstrom v. Commonwealth*, 1992).

The American Psychological Association (1992, 2003a) has developed ethical codes for psychologists serving as expert witnesses. "Experts are expected to present scientific knowledge in complete and accurate fashion, prevent the misuse of research findings, not testify beyond their expertise, and resist the pressures to become partisans" (Berliner, 1998, p. 21). As Lucy Berliner (1998) points out, however, adhering to these standards can be exceedingly difficult in an adversarial context where forensic psychologists find the codes in conflict with the real-life pressures to become advocates instead of just witnesses, especially in child abuse cases.

Child Abduction

A person is guilty of **child abduction** (kidnapping) if he or she unlawfully leads, takes, entices, or detains a child under a specified age with intent to keep or conceal the child from its parent, guardian, or other person having lawful custody. Child abduction is relatively rare among violent crimes against children and juveniles. It makes up less that 2% of all violent crimes against juveniles reported to law enforcement (Finkelhor & Ormrod, 2000). Kidnapping is most often divided into three classifications based on the identity of the perpetrator: (1) family kidnapping (49%), (2) acquaintance kidnapping (27%), and (3) stranger kidnapping (24%). Most of the following data are drawn from the U.S. Department of Justice report, *Kidnapping of Juveniles,* prepared by Finkelhor and Ormrod (2000). The primary source of the data reported by Finkelhor and Ormrod came from the National Incidence-Based Reporting System (NIBRS) (see Box 8.4).

Family kidnapping is committed mostly by parents (80%), a phenomenon so common that it is labeled *parental abduction.* "Parental abduction encompasses a broad array of illegal behaviors that involve one parent taking, detaining, concealing, or enticing away his or her child from the parent having custodial access" (Wilson, 2001, p. 1). Parental abduction usually involves a child younger than age 6—most often around age 2. Both genders are equally victimized. The perpetrators are also evenly distributed (50%) between men and women. The abduction generally originates in the home.

Juveniles are more likely to be kidnapped by acquaintances than by complete strangers. Acquaintances are people they know but who are not family members. Acquaintance kidnapping most often involves a teenage female victim (72%). The perpetrator is often a juvenile himself (30%) and is frequently a boyfriend or former boyfriend (18%). The most common motives are to seek revenge for being spurned, to force a reconciliation, to commit a sexual assault, or to evade parents who want to break up the

---

BOX 8.3   Infantile Amnesia

What is your earliest memory? It is widely believed by psychologists that a vast majority of humans cannot recall events that occurred prior to age 3, a phenomenon called infantile amnesia. For some unknown reason, adult memory of childhood events appears to begin sometime after the 3rd or 4th birthday. Consequently, all those hours spent with a baby—rocking to sleep, playing, changing diapers, feeding, laughing, and cuddling—may be lost forever in the baby's mind. Childhood memories are fragile, but the common assumption is that *infant* memories are virtually nonexistent.

However, some recent research (Bauer, 1996) suggests that a baby may remember those events but in a different kind of "preverbal" memory. It appears that even infants in the first year of life are able to retain bits of information about unique episodes over time (Mandler, 1988, 1990), but because they do not possess language skills, they cannot put these experiences into words at a later time. Very young children often rely on forms of memory (e.g., kinesthetic memory) that do not depend on verbal processing to be cognitively stored.

Other factors probably also contribute to the difficulty to recall early childhood memories. Howe and Courage (1997) propose that childhood memories emerge as the cognitive self develops. The cognitive self is "a knowledge structure whose features serve to organize memories of experiences that happen to 'me'" (Howe & Crowe, 1997, p. 499). If the cognitive self is immature, the ability to recall remains disorganized and partly inaccessible. As children get older, the ability to maintain and organize information appears to increase. Other developmental aspects that probably affect childhood memory are the dramatic neurological and perceptual changes that occur during early childhood.

Whatever the mechanisms involved in early development, it appears that infants can "remember" events in nonverbal ways. It is possible, therefore, that certain smells, tastes, and auditory and visual environmental cues may bring some undefined, distant memory to us, but we tend to be unable to articulate from where or when. However, well-articulated claims by victims of child abuse, based on their early infancy memories, probably should be held suspect until other corroborating evidence is gathered.

relationship. In some instances, gang-related members kidnap other teenagers (whom they know) for intimidation, retaliation, or recruiting. A third type of acquaintance kidnapping involves family friends or employees (e.g., babysitters) who remove children from their home for the purpose of sexual assault or retaliation against the family. Acquaintance kidnapping victims suffer a higher rate of injury compared to the other forms of abduction, possibly because the victim is usually older and therefore more likely to resist the abduction. Another reason may be that intimidation, which often is associated with more physical force, is the primary motive in many of these abductions.

Stranger kidnapping victimizes more females than males (64% compared to 36%). Most stranger kidnappings victimize teenage and elementary school-age victims (57% and 32%, respectively). Preschoolers are rarely targeted. The perpetrator is predominately male (95%). About one out of five stranger kidnappings is associated with another violent crime, such as sexual assault in the case of girl victims and robbery in the case of boy victims. This is the type of kidnapping most likely to involve the use of a firearm. The location of stranger kidnapping is associated primarily with the outdoors (58%), such as streets, highways, parks, waterways, and other public areas. Finkelhor and Ormrod (2000) point out that, based on NIBRS data, school is usually *not* the location for child abductions, including family abductions.

The National Incidence Study of Missing, Abducted, Runaway and Throwaway Children (NISMART) (Finkelhor, Hotaling, & Sedlack, 1990; Johnston & Girdner, 2001) is a report describing the results of a nationwide telephone survey conducted in 1988. The study provided estimates of the number of family abductions to both domestic and international destinations nationwide. More important to our discussion here, the NISMART survey reports some of the common behavioral and psychological characteristics of parental abductors. The following characteristics were outlined by Johnston and Girdner (2001, p. 5):

- Abducting parents are likely to deny and dismiss the other parent's value to the child. They believe that they, more than anyone else, know what is best for their child. In some cases, the motivation to abduct may also be an attempt to protect the child from a parent who is perceived to be likely to molest, abuse, or neglect the child, which in some instances may be a legitimate concern.
- Abducting parents usually take very young children (the mean age is 2–3). Such children are easier to transport and conceal, are unlikely to protest verbally, and may be unable to tell others their name or provide other identifying information.
- Most abducting parents are likely to have a supportive social network of family, friends, or social communities that provide assistance and emotional and moral support. This pattern is especially prevalent when the abductor has no financial or emotional ties to the geographical area from which the child was taken.
- Most custody violators do not consider their actions illegal or morally wrong, even after the involvement of the district attorney's office.
- Mothers and fathers are equally likely to abduct their children, although at different times. Fathers tend to abduct before there is a child custody order in place, whereas mothers tend to abduct after the court has issued a formal custody decree.

Parental kidnappers who appear to be the most dangerous to the other parent and/or child manifest paranoid, irrational beliefs and delusions that do not dovetail with reality (Johnston & Girdner, 2001). This risk is especially high in those abductors who have a history of domestic violence, hospitalization for mental disorders, or serious substance abuse. They feel overwhelmed by their divorce and are convinced that their former partners have betrayed and exploited them. Revenge may emerge as a dominant motive for the abduction. Fortunately, this type of parental abductor is relatively rare. Interestingly, one study found that approximately 75% of male abductors and 25% of female abductors had exhibited violent behavior in the past (Greif & Hegar, 1993).

Psychological Impact of Abduction

The experience of abduction can be emotionally traumatic to both the child and the left-behind parent (Chiancone, 2001). The incident can be particularly damaging in cases in which force is used to carry out the abduction, the child is concealed, or the child is held for a long period of time. According to the NISMART survey, abductors use force in 14% of parental abductions and coercive threats in 17% (Chiancone, 2001; Finkelhor et al., 1990). The length of time separated from the left-behind parent is one of the major determinants of the emotional impact the incident has on the abducted child (Agopian, 1984). Children held for short periods (less than a few weeks) usually do not give up hope of being reunited with the other parent and do not suffer the emotional reactions found in long-term abductions (Chiancone, 2001). However, the story is different for those children who experience long-term abductions. In reference to the Agopian (1984) study, Chiancone (2001) writes,

> They [the children] were often deceived by the abducting parent and frequently moved to avoid being located. This nomadic, unstable lifestyle made it difficult for children to make friends and settle into school, if they attended at all. Over time, younger children could not easily remember the left-behind parent, which had serious repercussions when they were reunited. Older children felt angry and confused by the behavior of both parents—the abductor for keeping them away from the other parent and the left-behind parent for failing to rescue them. (p. 5)

Left-behind parents commonly experienced feelings of loss, rage, and impaired sleep, and more than half reported loneliness, fear, and/or severe depression. Social support and professional intervention are often important in helping them adjust to this traumatic experience.

One of the most dramatic cases of child abductions took place in 1976 when a California school bus carrying 26 children, ages 5 to 14, was commandeered at gunpoint by three kidnappers. The kidnappers were attempting to arrange a $5 million ransom. The bus was later found empty, covered with bamboo and brush in a drainage ditch. The victims—19 girls and 7 boys—were driven for 11 hours in two darkened vans before being entombed in a moving van buried in a rock quarry. They remained buried for 16 hours in an 8-by-16-foot space until two of the oldest boys and the bus driver managed to dig the group out.

All three kidnappers were eventually captured. On December 15, 1977, a California superior court judge found the trio guilty of three counts of kidnapping with bodily harm, a conviction that normally carries a mandatory sentence of life in prison without the possibility of parole. The kidnapping was eventually made into a made-for TV move titled *They've Taken Our Children: The Chowchilla Kidnapping*. Interestingly, the California Supreme Court refused to allow a suit by one of the kidnappers who claimed his role in the 1993 ABC docudrama had been distorted.

Psychiatrist Lenore C. Terr (1979, 1982, 1983) interviewed most of the victims and their parents 5 to 13 months after the kidnapping and again 4 years later. Virtually all the children suffered some short-term psychological effects, including sleep disorders, fear of being revictimized, and a variety of "unique" PTSD symptoms. Terr reported that the children, instead of demonstrating cognitive flashbacks, reexperienced the event through stereotyped, repetitive posttraumatic play (e.g., kidnapping games) that failed to diminish their anxiety about the abduction (McNally, 1991). One 5-year-old, for instance, began to bury her Barbie dolls, a process called behavioral reenactment. Many of the symptoms existed for some of the victims 4 or 5 years after the incident. The abduction underscores the short- and long-term psychological damage that often follows criminal victimization of many children.

Elder Abuse and Neglect

Approximately 2.5 million older Americans are victims of various kinds of abuse each year (National Center on Elder Abuse, 1999). **Elder abuse** is defined as the physical, financial, emotional, or psychological harm of an older adult, usually defined as age 65 or older (Marshall, Benton, & Brazier, 2000). Abandonment is usually included in the definition of neglect and is characterized by such things as desertion of an elder at a hospital, a nursing facility, or other similar institution or public place, such as a bus station. Financial abuse is also prevalent in cases of elder abuse. It refers to the illegal or improper use of an elder's funds, property, or assets. Sexual abuse, on the other hand, is relatively uncommon and refers to nonconsensual sexual contact of any kind with an elderly person.

The median age of elder abuse victims is 78 years (National Center on Elder Abuse, 1999). A majority of the victims are women (two out of three). Neglect—refusal, or failure, to fulfill any part of a person's obligations or duties to an elderly person—is the most common form of elder maltreatment in domestic settings,

representing 55% of the substantiated cases. Physical abuse accounts for another 15%, and financial or material exploitation accounts for 12% (National Center on Elder Abuse, 1999, p. 2).

Adult children are the most frequent abusers of the elderly (National Center on Elder Abuse, 1999). Other family members and spouses ranked as the next most likely abusers. Men tend to be the most likely perpetrators of elder mistreatment, although women are more likely to be involved in elder neglect (Administration on Aging, 1998). Most cases of elder abuse and neglect take place at home because most older Americans live at home rather than in nursing homes or institutions.

Because elder maltreatment is often subtle and provides few indications of clear or recognizable signs of the mistreatment, it is extremely difficult to say exactly how many cases there are in this country each year. It is estimated that only 1 out of 14 domestic elder abuse incidents comes to the attention of authorities (Pillemer & Finkelhor, 1988). The emotional or psychological abuse can range from name-calling or giving the "silent treatment" to intimidating and threatening the individual. It may also involve treating the older person like a child and isolating the person from family, friends, or regular activities. (See Box 8.5 on the growing field of geropsychology.)

BOX 8.4   National Incident-Based Reporting System

The U.S. Department of Justice is replacing its long-established Uniform Crime Reports (UCR) program with a more comprehensive National Incident-Based Reporting System (NIBRS). During the late 1970s, the law enforcement community called for the expanded use of the UCR and more detailed information on each criminal incident, in contrast to the straightforward statistics offered in the traditional UCR. In response to these concerns, the UCR reporting system was evaluated under federal contracts by Abt Associates of Cambridge, Massachusetts, which made a number of far-reaching recommendations for improvement. These recommendations formed the basis of the NIBRS under the support of the Uniform Federal Crime Reporting Act passed by the U.S. Congress in 1988. In this act, Congress required all federal law enforcement agencies, including those agencies within the Department of Defense, to collect and report more

(*Continued*)

BOX 8.4 (Continued)

complete data to the FBI on two categories of offenses: Group A, which includes 46 serious offense categories, such as arson, assault, homicide, fraud, embezzlement, larceny-theft, and sex offenses, and Group B, which includes 11 less serious offenses, such as passing bad checks, driving under the influence of alcohol, engaging in disorderly conduct, drunkenness, nonviolent family offenses, and liquor law violations. The NIBRS is designed to collect a wide range of information on victims, offenders, and circumstances for a wide variety of offenses.

Under the NIBRS, local law enforcement agencies are asked to compile information on crimes coming to their attention, and this information is then added together at the state and national levels. For a crime to be counted, it simply needs to be reported and investigated. In addition, another major difference between the UCR and the NIBRS is that the NIBRS records *every* crime that occurs during one incident, in contrast to the UCR, which only records the most serious crime. Presumably, the added information from Group A data will become an indispensable tool for law enforcement agencies and researchers because it will provide detailed data about when and where specific types of crime take place, what forms they take, and the characteristics of their victims and perpetrators. Because reporting agencies are expected to submit a brief account of each incident, the NIBRS data include the number of offenders, the number of victims, and/or multiple attributes (e.g., weapons, property loss, drugs, alcohol) for each crime. To date, data from this system are still in their infancy in terms of nationally representative information, and many agencies have been slow in linking into the system. The NIBRS has the promise of being the first explicitly computer-based and standardized reporting system in U.S. law enforcement, providing a rich source of data for researchers and policymakers.

Roles of the Forensic Psychologist in Elder Abuse

Melton and his colleagues (1997) posit that, for the forensic psychologist, the issues of elder abuse and neglect are closely related to child abuse cases in many respects. "Evaluators should address many of the same domains in dispositional evaluation, and they should be alert to many of the same potential problems and role confusion" (Melton et al., 1997, p. 479). Dispositional evaluation refers to an assessment of the attitudes, desires, and motivations of an individual. There are, however, two major differences between forensic evaluations for child abuse and elder abuse.

First, clinicians conducting dispositional evaluations in cases involving elders or other dependent adults need to be aware of the service alternatives for adults with disabilities, and they need to have a realistic view of the care needs that the victim presents. In that sense, the scope of an evaluation in an elder maltreatment case may have much in common with an evaluation for limited guardianship. (Melton et al., 1997, p. 479)

Guardianship refers to the appointment of authority over an individual's person or estate to another person when that individual is considered incapable of administering his or her own affairs. Guardianship can come in many forms, but the two that are most pertinent here are general and specific or special guardianship. As the name implies, a general guardian is one who has the general care and control of the person and the estate, whereas the specific guardian is one who has special or limited powers and duties with respect to the person. For example, the specific guardian may have the legal authority to make only certain treatment decisions,

---

BOX 8.5   Geropsychology: Meeting the Needs of Older Adults

The graying of the baby-boom generation and better quality health care have combined to make older adults the fastest growing age group. It is expected that persons older than age 65 will represent 20% of the population by 2030 (Qualls, Segal, Norman, Niederche, & Gallagher-Thompson, 2002).

Although society recognizes the desire of older adults to maintain their independence, concerns are often raised about their capacity to live alone. When they live in other settings—such as assisted living facilities or nursing homes—their well-being in such alternative living arrangements must be addressed.

Geropsychology is a specialty area devoted to the research, assessment, and treatment of older adults. Geropsychologists may be asked to evaluate an individual's competency or capacity to manage funds, make informed decisions about medical treatment, or draft legal documents, such as wills or real estate contracts. According to psychologists with expertise in this area, "A clinical assessment . . . in an older adult is an exacting task: It must be comprehensive, address a host of ethical and environmental issues, and address multiple co-morbidities" (Baker, Lichtenberg, & Moye, 1998, p. 151). Fortunately, the Department of Veterans Affairs (1996) has led the way in developing a helpful resource guide for geropsychologists for this purpose.

The treatment tasks of geropsychologists presume an understanding that older adults are different from young adults and have very unique mental health needs. In addition to diagnosable mental disorders such as depression or paranoia, they also may have cognitive impairments, including dementias that are associated with a variety of illnesses. Mentally healthy older adults often need emotional support when faced with crises such as the loss of a spouse or adult child, a debilitating physical illness, or a change in living situation.

The need for both assessment and treatment of older adults is expected to increase well into the 21st century, but questions are being raised about who will meet this demand (Qualls, 1998). According to Qualls (1998), three levels of specialization have been identified. **Generalists** will do limited work with older adults but have at least basic exposure to geropsychology. **Generalists with proficiency** will have achieved more in-depth study of aging and have a wider array of specialized skills. Qualls predicts that these practitioners will provide the majority of services to older adults. **Specialists** will operate at the expertise level. Having obtained advanced skills, they will conduct research and training, set standards and policies, and be responsible for generating new knowledge in the field.

Graduate training in psychology is rapidly recognizing the demand for geropsychological services, but not all programs even offer a course in aging. Readers interested in learning more about educational and career opportunities in this field are referred to Qualls's (1998) article as well as to APA Division 20 (Adult Development and Aging) and Division 12, Section II (Clinical Geropsychology).

---

whereas in other areas, the affected person is free to make other decisions. In other words, the guardian has limited authority.

The second major difference between child abuse and elder abuse evaluations is that the victim, unlike in child abuse or protection cases, is presumed to be competent until there is a legal determination otherwise. In addition, about one fourth of the complainants in the elder abuse cases are the victims themselves (Melton et al., 1997). Furthermore, there may be significant financial conflicts of interest, especially if the assigned caregivers are financially (and perhaps emotionally) dependent on the victim. Consequently, the clinician needs to be aware of and sensitive to the complicated relationships that may exist between the guardians and the victim.

Summary and Conclusions

Forensic psychologists are all too familiar with the results of violent victimization. When the perpetrator of the violence is a family member or an intimate partner, the effects are particularly devastating. Psychologists not only offer treatment to victims of violent crime but also evaluate them to assess the extent of their psychological injury. Results of those evaluations then may be used in civil or criminal proceedings. Psychologists also may evaluate or offer treatment to violent offenders, a topic that will be covered more fully in the chapters ahead. In this chapter, we have focused on the services provided to victims of violent crime, as well as the information that has been gathered on the nature and extent of the crime itself.

Family violence—as used in the title of this chapter—is a very broad term that encompasses each of the areas discussed. The term is not perfect. We have taken some liberty with it because much of the violence described in this chapter is not technically between family members. Nevertheless, no other term adequately covers each area discussed herein. Many researchers use the term *domestic violence,* which includes spouse or partner violence, sibling violence, child abuse within the home, and elder abuse—but it does not technically cover intimate partner violence when the partners do not reside in the same domicile.

Researchers have made considerable progress in their study of intimate partner violence. Whereas earlier studies focused primarily on female victims, often describing them as passive, depressed, and helpless, later research focused on

descriptions of the abuse relationship and features of the male batterer. Likewise, researchers have explored intimate partner violence between same-sex couples and between couples when the woman is the abuser. In the great majority of intimate partner abuse situations, however, the male is the abuser. We explored some of the issues faced by forensic psychologists who treat abusers and victims, as well as the challenges they face in expert testimony.

Child abuse is a continuing and disturbing problem. After reviewing statistics associated with this crime, we focused on the most severe forms, including infanticide, sexual abuse, and the little-researched Munchausen by proxy and shaken baby syndromes. Evaluations of children who have allegedly been sexually abused are among the most challenging for psychologists in forensic practice. A related area, alleged instances of child abuse in the distant past, has been extremely controversial for many psychologists. These cases often—but not inevitably—revolve around the issue of repressed or recovered memory. We presented the research associated with this topic as well as conclusions from both American and British working groups. Although the repressed memory issue is far from resolved— and it often pits research psychologists against clinicians—it is important to note that the empirical research to this point does not strongly support widespread forgotten memories. It is possible, though, that some victims of sexual assault do forget and do remember their victimization many years later.

The chapter ended with coverage of two areas that are underresearched by psychology, though not ignored by the law or by victim advocates. Child abduction and elder abuse have both received a good deal of public attention over the past two decades. Psychologists in forensic practice are likely to encounter these issues primarily in the treatment context, such as when providing services to the elderly or to the parent or parents who are left behind.

PART V

Psychology and the Courts

CHAPTER 9

Consulting and Testifying

The psychologist is a common sight in the courtroom today, both on the witness stand and, less frequently, sitting at the defense or prosecution table as a jury or trial consultant. Even when psychologists are not directly in the courtroom, their presence may be felt in the reports they have prepared or sworn statements they have made that are entered into the court record. Very early in the case, when attorneys are gathering information and preparing their trial strategy, a psychologist may be called to testify during a deposition. For example, lawyers for a plaintiff in an employment discrimination suit may depose the psychologist who administered and evaluated promotional exams. In a criminal case, the judge at a sentencing hearing may have access to a report detailing an offender's mental status based on a psychological assessment.

Psychology's entry into the courtroom did not come easily. Until the 1960s, psychiatrists were the only mental health experts recognized in many courts. Those courts that *did* welcome psychologists tended to limit their tasks to very specific areas, such as reporting on the results of intelligence or personality tests. Criminal courts were particularly reluctant to accept expert testimony from a nonmedical professional when a defendant's criminal responsibility or sanity was in question. Because mental disorder was considered a disease, the professional with a medical degree—the psychiatrist—was believed to be the appropriate expert. Although there were exceptions, for the most part, the courtroom was the province of the psychiatrist, not the psychologist.

In 1962, however, a federal appeals court in *Jenkins v. U.S.* ruled that the lack of a medical degree did not automatically disqualify psychologists from providing expert testimony on the issue of mental disorder. Jenkins had pleaded not guilty by reason of insanity to sexual assault charges. Interestingly, the judge at his trial had allowed psychologists to testify that he did not have the required mental state to be found responsible, but the judge then told the jury to disregard the psychologists' testimony. "A psychologist is not competent to give a medical opinion as to a mental disease or defect," the judge said. Jenkins was convicted, but he appealed his conviction claiming that the judge's jury instruction violated his right to due process. The American Psychological Association and the American Psychiatric Association both filed briefs with the federal court on behalf of their respective professions. Psychologists, of course, hoped that the court would support their entry as experts; psychiatrists hoped to preserve their near-exclusive reign.

The federal appeals court supported psychologists, ruling that a psychologist with proper credentials could indeed provide competent testimony on the issue of mental disorder. Gradually, after the *Jenkins* case, psychologists began to provide testimony not only on issues relating to mental disorder but also on a wide range of issues about which they were conducting research. For example, they provided data on subjects as diverse as the influence of pretrial publicity on juries, the effects of pornography on adolescents, and the influence of advertisements on consumers (Bartol & Bartol, 1999).

This chapter will offer many additional examples of psychologists working directly in courtroom settings, as well as behind the scenes at tasks relevant to the judicial process. Although most of us are familiar with the appearance of a courtroom either from personal experience or from media portrayals, knowledge of how courts are set up and how a case proceeds through various stages is less widespread. Therefore, the chapter begins with an overview of the structure and process in both criminal and civil courts.

Court Structure and Jurisdiction

In the United States, federal and state courts exist side by side, independent of one another, sometimes in the same geographical location. In most sizable cities, one can find municipal or county courts in one building and the federal court building not too far away. This **dual-court system** exists to recognize the unity of the nation as a whole, on one hand, and the sovereignty of the 50 individual states, on the other. Among their many functions, federal courts interpret and apply the U.S. Constitution and acts of Congress, settle disputes between states or citizens of different states, and deal with such specialized matters as bankruptcies, copyrights, and patents. Persons accused of violating federal criminal laws are also

processed in federal courts. State courts interpret and apply state constitutions and laws passed by state legislatures. They also settle disputes between citizens or between the government and citizens within the state. A group of taxpayers, for example, may challenge a state education-funding plan that increases the taxes of property owners living in certain communities. In recent years, much has been made of the overwhelming workload of federal courts. To ease this burden, state courts will sometimes settle disputes between citizens of different states, as long as the parties agree to have their case heard in a state rather than a federal court (Abraham, 1998).

All courts, federal and state, are either established under the U.S. Constitution or the constitutions of the various states or are created as needed by Congress or state legislatures. The constitution or the legislative enactment also specifies the court's **jurisdiction,** or authority. All courts have **subject-matter jurisdiction** and **geographical jurisdiction** as outlined in the law. For example, a family court may have authority over divorce, custody, adoption, and delinquency matters (subject-matter jurisdiction) in a given county within the state (geographical jurisdiction). Many courts have only **limited jurisdiction,** or limited authority, meaning that they can only settle small disputes or deal with preliminary issues in a major case. By contrast, courts of **general jurisdiction** have broad authority over a vast array of both simple and complex cases, both civil and criminal. **Appellate jurisdiction** refers to a court's authority to hear appeals from decisions of lower courts.

Courts present an often-confusing array of physical structures, terminology, and individuals with an equally confusing array of titles and roles. Some court proceedings are conducted at a table in the basement of a town hall at 10 p.m., whereas others are conducted in dignified, velvet-curtained surroundings. Increasingly today, more court proceedings—particularly at the early stages of a case—are conducted via closed-circuit television. A **defendant** being detained in jail, for example, may "appear" before a judge for a bail reduction hearing. However, the defendant is in the jail and the judge is in her or his courtroom 5 miles away. Via closed-circuit television, the judge may reduce the bail and communicate to the defendant the conditions under which he or she is being released.

The structure of the federal court system is actually quite simple. The federal courts may be divided into four basic levels, two trial court levels and two appeals or appellate levels. At the trial court levels are courts of limited jurisdiction (e.g., magistrate judge's courts) and general jurisdiction (U.S. district courts). At the appellate level are the intermediate courts of appeal for the various circuits and the court of last resort, the U.S. Supreme Court.

By contrast, state court structures can be quite complicated. No two state court systems are identical, leading to the often-made comment that we have 51 very different court systems in the United States: the federal system and the systems of each of the 50 states. Nonetheless, common features exist. Like the federal system, all states have trial and appellate courts, with the trial courts being divided into those of limited and general jurisdiction. At the very lowest level are courts overseen by a justice of the peace or a magistrate who presides over minor civil and criminal matters. This level also may include municipal courts—sometimes called traffic courts, night courts, or city courts. These lower courts are courts of limited jurisdiction and typically cannot conduct major civil trials or felony trials. At the next level are county courts, which have been called the "workhorse of the average judiciary" (Abraham, 1998, p. 155). County courts are courts of general jurisdiction, handling a wide range of both civil and criminal cases. Every state also has a court of last resort, which is the highest appellate court in that state, but not all have *intermediate* appeals courts. In addition, states often have a variety of **specialized courts,** which deal only with particular matters. Family courts, drug courts, mental health courts, and domestic violence courts are all examples of specialized courts. These courts are often of particular interest to psychologists because of the subject matter with which they deal. (See Box 9.1 for an illustration of a mental health court in operation.)

BOX 9.1   Mental Health Courts

On a cold winter evening, police in an urban area received a call from a priest who told them that a woman, armed with a knife, had broken into a church, pried open an offering box and taken coins, and was screaming and threatening to kill herself. Officers who had received special training in dealing with the mentally disordered arrived on the scene and succeeded in calming the woman, whom they had previously encountered on other occasions. She had a history of short-term commitments to a state mental hospital and was presently living with a relative, who was becoming increasingly frustrated in her attempts to offer the woman a safe living arrangement.

Under the law, the woman could have been charged with a number of offenses, including burglary, trespassing, resisting arrest, disturbing the peace, vandalism, and larceny-theft. She also could have been taken to the police station, booked, and held in jail overnight until a court appearance the following day. This pattern, in fact, had occurred on numerous previous occasions. Now, though, a mental health court had been established.

(Continued)

BOX 9.1 (Continued)

Police contacted a representative of the prosecutor's office; the woman was charged only with petty larceny and disturbing the peace and was held in a therapeutic unit attached to but separate from the local jail. Psychiatric staff screened her for suicidal tendencies, gave her stabilizing medication, and kept her under careful observation. An attorney who had many clients with mental disorders on his caseload was contacted and agreed to represent her.

Within 48 hours, the woman and her attorney appeared before the judge in a mental health court, which had few of the formalized features of the traditional courtroom. Although all of the key players were present (prosecutor, defense lawyer, judge, court clerk), the room was small and had few seats for observers. The defendant's relatives were in attendance. The judge's bench was actually a table at the same level as that of other participants, and the judge—who had undergone specialized training in dealing with the mentally disordered—spoke calmly and compassionately with the defendant. On the recommendation of a clinician, the judge ordered a temporary detainment for observation and evaluation in a local mental health facility that was not to exceed 7 days. At the end of the 7 days, the defendant returned to court, where the judge was ready to offer her a living accommodation in a group home, whose staff worked closely with the mental health court. The woman agreed to be placed on a community treatment order, which meant that she would have to be monitored and treated for her mental disorder while living in the group home. The prosecutor dismissed the criminal charges.

Mental health courts are a possible solution to the vexing problem of crime—typically minor crimes—committed by individuals with mental disorders. Although they operate in different ways, most of these courts involve an immediate screening by a mental health clinician or team, which then makes a treatment recommendation to the presiding judge. Although defendants or their guardians may have to consent to go to this specialized court, avoiding placement in a traditional jail setting is a strong incentive. Some mental health courts accept defendants only after they have pleaded guilty to a criminal offense. In that case, the judge orders mental health treatment as a condition of probation and carefully supervises the progress of this treatment. Psychologists or other mental health professionals associated with the court work cooperatively with the judge to follow the individual through his or her course of treatment.

Observers have expressed a range of concerns about mental health courts, with the subjective decision-making power of the judge being a major theme. In most mental health courts, clinicians screen clients and make recommendations, but it is the judge who decides whether the individual is making sufficient progress. Many mental health professionals believe this should be a clinical decision (Hasselbrack, 2001). Other observers have expressed concerns that judges want early intervention and efficient processing, but the mental health professional needs time to conduct an assessment that is accurate and complete (Goldkamp & Irons-Guynn, 2000). Still others are concerned that adequate resources are not made available to provide recommended treatment (Steadman, Davidson, & Brown, 2001).

Mental health courts and other specialized courts (e.g., drug courts, domestic violence courts) face numerous challenges and require more research attention before we can conclude under what conditions they are effective. Whether they will be able to fulfill their promise of offering meaningful services to criminal defendants with mental disorders remains to be seen. It is hoped that they will because they represent a creative and compassionate response to complex social problems.

The federal and state systems intersect when a case moves—or attempts to move—from the state court to the federal courts. Although there are a variety of ways in which this can happen, perhaps the most common is when an individual has lost his or her case after having exhausted all appeals in state courts. If a substantial federal question has been raised, the case may be heard in the federal courts. For example, when a state law is said to violate the U.S. Constitution, federal courts may ultimately decide whether it truly does. In 2003, in *Lawrence and Garner v. Texas*, the U.S. Supreme Court examined a state law that made it a crime for two individuals of the same sex to engage in certain intimate sexual conduct. The majority opinion held that this law violated the liberty interests guaranteed by the Constitution.

In deciding *Lawrence and Garner v. Texas*, the Court overruled an earlier case, *Bowers v. Hardwick* (1986), in which it had ruled a similar Georgia statute *not* unconstitutional. Five of the six Justices in the majority made it clear that they believed that earlier case was wrongly decided. The sixth Justice—Justice O'Connor—believed the Texas law was a violation of the Constitution's guarantee of equal protection under the law, but she saw a distinction with the earlier case and would not have overturned it. It should be noted that the Supreme Court has virtually unlimited discretion as to whether it will accept a case for review; on average, it agrees to hear only about 10% to 15% of the cases that come to its attention (Abraham, 1998). At least some of the Justices may have accepted the Texas case partially because of the opportunity it presented to overturn the earlier case.

Civil and Criminal Courts

The distinction between criminal and civil courts essentially refers to the type of case that is being heard. In large courthouses, certain rooms are set aside for civil cases and others for criminal cases. In small communities, however, the same courtroom may be used for criminal proceedings one day and a civil trial the next. Furthermore, the same judge may be presiding over all proceedings. The distinction between civil and criminal cases rests primarily on who brings the action and, to a lesser extent, the disputive versus punitive nature of a case. In a **civil case,** two or more parties (litigants) approach the legal system, often seeking resolution of a dispute. In the most common of civil actions, the **plaintiff** seeks relief or a remedy from the defendant, maintaining that he or she has been personally harmed. This relief or remedy could come in the form of a court injunction (an order to stop some practice), a protective order (such as an order to remain beyond a certain distance from an individual), or damages (a money award) for losses suffered. Although civil cases are normally between private individuals or organizations, governments also may be involved. For example, a state may file a civil action against an employer for allegedly discriminatory hiring practices, in violation of the state's antidiscrimination laws. A **criminal case,** on the other hand, involves an alleged violation of rules deemed so important that the breaking of these rules incurs society's formal punishment, which must be imposed by the criminal courts. In a criminal case, the government, represented by the prosecutor, brings the action against the individual.

Sometimes, the lines between civil and criminal cases are blurred. In most states, for example, if a juvenile is accused of committing a crime, he or she will most likely be brought to a juvenile or family court, which is considered a civil rather than a criminal setting. Juvenile courts are more informal and are typically closed to the public. However, they have aspects of criminal proceedings, such as the right to a lawyer and the opportunity to confront and cross-examine one's accuser and other witnesses. Disputes between private persons or organizations, such as breaches of contract, libel suits, or divorce actions, are clearly civil cases. Certain actions, however, can incur both civil and criminal penalties. The massive cases of Enron Corporation, Anderson Accounting Firm, and WorldCom in 2002 included alleged violations of both criminal and civil laws.

Despite media coverage suggesting the opposite, most cases reaching the courts are civil rather than criminal, and civil cases are often more complex. The backlog of civil disputes is very high, and the process of achieving settlement can be tedious. In addition, civil courts deal with extremely emotionally wrenching issues, including the personal disputes that occur among family members and intensely personal matters such as those requiring end-of-life and other medical decisions.

The Judicial Process

The judicial process consists of a series of steps or stages through which litigants proceed. In high-profile and/or complex cases, the process can be very lengthy, sometimes taking years to complete, especially in civil cases. In the 1990s, tobacco and asbestos litigation cases threatened to immobilize the courts. Even relatively simple cases can get bogged down in the courts, however. These delays can be problematic in both criminal and civil cases, for all parties involved, and for many different reasons. For example, in criminal cases, evidence deteriorates, and crime victims, as well as defendants, are held in abeyance. The defendant also may be confined in jail, unable to post bail. In civil cases, both plaintiffs and defendants have their lives on hold until the court proceedings have been terminated. On the other hand, delays also can be functional, as in encouraging a settlement, allowing more extensive investigation, or uncovering new witnesses who may come forward and help absolve an innocent defendant.

It is helpful to divide the judicial or court process in both criminal and civil cases into four broad stages: (1) pretrial, (2) trial, (3) disposition, and (4) appeals. Various court appearances and hearings can occur at each of these stages,

and there are many illustrations of what practicing psychologists can contribute. In the discussion below, we will emphasize those proceedings at each stage that are most likely to involve the assistance of the forensic psychologist. Unless otherwise specified, the discussion relates to both civil and criminal cases. In addition, although we describe a process that is typical in courts across the United States, the proceedings and what they are called may vary across jurisdictions.

The Pretrial Stage

The courts can become involved in a *criminal* case very early, when police contact a judge or a magistrate to obtain a warrant to search or to arrest a suspect. Most arrests and most searches do not require warrants, however, so a court's first contact with a criminal case is typically either at the initial appearance or at the arraignment. However, in the federal system and some states, the prosecutor must obtain an indictment from a grand jury very early in the process. The **grand jury** is a body of citizens that reviews the evidence provided by the prosecutor and decides whether there is sufficient evidence to indict (formally accuse) the individual.

The **initial appearance** occurs if an arrested individual is being held in jail rather than released or cited to appear in court at a later date. Detained individuals must appear before a judge or magistrate, usually within 24 hours, to ensure that there is legal ground to hold them.

Because jail detention can be an extremely stressful occurrence, detainees are screened for evidence of mental disorder or psychological crisis. Although jail officers or social caseworkers often perform this initial screening, a consulting psychologist or psychiatrist may be called in if a detainee appears to be in major psychological crisis. Some large jails have psychologists, psychiatrists, or other mental health professionals on staff, but the typical jail setting employs them on a contract or as-needed basis. As noted in Box 9.1, communities across the United States are experimenting with mental health courts to divert some suspects with apparent mental health problems away from traditional criminal courts. Similarly, suspects with apparent substance abuse problems or persons arrested in some domestic violence incidents may be diverted to drug or domestic violence courts.

The next pretrial step relevant to psychological practice is the **arraignment,** an open proceeding at which formal charges are read. At the arraignment, the presiding judge asks defendants if they understand the charges, informs them of their right to counsel, and asks them to enter pleas. At this point, it is not unusual for persons charged with minor offenses and even many felonies to plead guilty and receive an immediate fine or sentence. Others plead *nolo contendere,* indicating that they will not contest the charges but are not admitting their guilt. For purposes of the criminal law, a *nolo contendere* plea has the same effect as a guilty plea; that is, a conviction is entered on the record.

Since the 1990s, forensic psychologists and psychiatrists have given considerable attention to the issue of a person's competency to plead guilty. This is an important matter because approximately 90% of criminal defendants plead guilty at arraignment or change their not-guilty plea to guilty before a trial date (Neubauer, 2002). Another possible plea—one highly relevant to forensic psychology—is not guilty by reason of insanity (NGRI), which is actually a not-guilty plea accompanied by notice that insanity will be used as a *defense.* When an NGRI plea is being considered, the forensic psychologist or psychiatrist is typically asked to examine the defendant and determine whether an insanity defense could be supported. This evaluation—called a criminal responsibility (CR) or mental state at the time of the offense (MSO) evaluation—is usually requested and/or arranged by the defense lawyer. A separate inquiry, whether the defendant is competent to stand trial, may be conducted at the request of the defense lawyer, the prosecutor, or the presiding judge. Criminal responsibility and competency examinations will be covered in detail in Chapter 10.

The not-guilty plea sets the trial process in motion. The next step is one or more pretrial hearings, during which witnesses, arresting officers, and other parties may present evidence. Numerous decisions may be made during these pretrial hearings. They include whether evidence is admissible, whether a trial should be moved because of extensive pretrial publicity; whether a youth should be transferred to juvenile court, whether a defendant is competent to stand trial, or whether bail should be denied because of the alleged dangerousness of a defendant.

Forensic psychologists are involved extensively during the pretrial stage in both juvenile and adult criminal cases. In cases where a judge must decide whether a juvenile's case should be heard in criminal court or in juvenile court, psychologists frequently assess the juvenile and file a report (or testify) as to the juvenile's level of development and ability to be rehabilitated. As noted above, when the mental health of a defendant is in question, the psychologist is again called on to perform an assessment. If a defendant is subsequently determined not competent to stand trial, forensic psychologists may be involved in treating the defendant to restore competency. Defendants also may be evaluated with reference to their potential dangerousness or risk to the community if allowed free on bail pending their next court appearance.

The pretrial process in *civil* cases has parallels to the above but many differences as well. Those filing suits are called plaintiffs, and those being sued are defendants. The plaintiff's lawyer files a complaint outlining the alleged wrong and the desired remedy. The defendant is served with the complaint and is given a time limit in which to respond. As in criminal cases, there may be extensive negotiation between parties. In addition, there are pretrial conferences with the judge in an attempt to facilitate a settlement. In civil cases, forensic psychologists are more likely to be involved behind the scenes, consulting with one or the other attorney in the preparation of a case. A neuropsychologist, for example, may be asked to conduct a variety of tests on a plaintiff who is suing his employer for hazardous work conditions that resulted in a near-fatal accident and substantial injury to the brain.

The **discovery process** is an important component of the pretrial process in both criminal and civil cases. This requires each side to make available information at its disposal to the other side in the preparation of its case. The exact type of information to be made known is regulated by statute. For example, in virtually all states and the federal government, the prosecutor is expected to inform the defense lawyer about information that might exculpate the defendant. The defense lawyer, however, is not bound to inform the prosecutor of evidence that might inculpate her or his client. However, if the defendant plans to raise a defense based on mental state (e.g., insanity or duress), the defense lawyer may be required to share the contents of a court-ordered psychological evaluation with the prosecutor. It should be noted, though, that there is wide variation in state laws relating to the amount of information that the defendant is entitled to from the prosecutor.

As part of the discovery process, **depositions** may be required. These are proceedings during which potential witnesses, including expert witnesses, are questioned by attorneys for the opposing side, under oath and in the presence of a court reporter, although typically away from the courtroom. The deposition is part of the court record, and information obtained therein may well reappear at the trial. Forensic psychologists are advised to review the transcription of a deposition very carefully, in the event that clerical errors might appear (Hess, 1999).

The Trial Stage

In both criminal and civil cases, trials follow a similar pattern of stages. If it is to be a trial by jury (as opposed to a trial before only a judge, called a **bench trial or court trial**), the first step is to select jurors from a jury pool representative of the community. The process of selecting jurors from a pool for a particular trial is relevant to those forensic psychologists who serve as trial consultants to lawyers. In all jury trials, potential jurors are questioned by lawyers and sometimes by the presiding judge. This process, formally called the *voir dire,* is done to uncover bias and to attempt to produce an objective jury. In addition, the *voir dire* allows lawyers to select individuals whom they believe will be sympathetic to their case. When jury consultants are involved, they have often gathered information about potential jurors from public records or even from interviews with their acquaintances. The lawyer can then use this information in forming questions to ask of a potential juror. The consultant also may sit at the defense or prosecution table and make inferences based on a potential juror's nonverbal behavior or reaction to questions. These inferences are then communicated to the lawyer who has hired the consultant, and the lawyer must decide whether to "strike" the individual from the jury. We will discuss this aspect of jury consultation in more detail later in the chapter.

Lawyers have two avenues by which to strike or remove a potential juror. One, the **peremptory challenge,** allows the lawyer to reject a potential juror without stating a reason. Based on a "gut feeling" or on the recommendations of a consultant, a lawyer may decide that a given individual would not be receptive to the lawyer's side. The U.S. Supreme Court has placed some limitation on these challenges, ruling that they may not be exercised on the basis of race or gender (*Batson v. Kentucky,* 1986; *J.E.B. v. Alabama,* 1994). For example, a lawyer cannot remove all women from a jury because the lawyer believes women would not be sympathetic to his client. If the presiding judge suspects that this is being done, the judge must inquire into the lawyer's reasons to ensure that the peremptory challenge is not being used in a discriminatory fashion. The second avenue for striking a potential juror is the **challenge for cause.** Here, a specific reason for removing the individual is offered. For example, the potential juror may have a past relationship with one of the parties or may even be an outspoken advocate on a matter that is crucial to the

Department at 1-800-818-7243 and press "1."

If you'd like to learn more about this title, the availability of supplements, etc., feel free to contact our **Textbook Sales Department** at 1-800-818-7243 and dial in extension 7212, or e-mail us at *collegesales@sagepub.com*.

To get more information about our books and supplements, visit our Web sites at *www.sagepub.com* and *www.pineforge.com*.

Finally, we invite you to join our customer care program by filling out your personal profile at our Web site, *www.sagepub.com/profile*. By doing so, you'll receive timely information about new publications in your research and teaching areas, future desk and examination copies will be expedited to you, and we'll notify you occasionally via e-mail with news about our books and journals in your discipline.

Thanks so much for considering the enclosed title(s) for classroom use. Have a great Fall!

Sincerely,

The Marketing Team
SAGE Publications and Pine Forge Press

SAGE Publications
PINE FORGE PRESS

Complimentary
Review Materials

Dear Professor:

We've taken the initiative to send you the enclosed new title(s) from SAGE Publications or Pine Forge Press because our records indicate that you've taught a course in the past for which these materials may be relevant, and we're hoping that you'll consider our products for an upcoming term. In some cases, we may have noted that you've adopted a previous edition of this title, and we're sending you the latest revision.

If our records are incorrect, may we ask that you pass this copy along to another colleague in your department who may find it of more relevance to his/her courses?

case at hand. A potential juror who has already formed a strong opinion of the case is also apt to be removed "for cause."

During the presentation of evidence and cross-examination of witnesses, forensic psychologists who serve as trial consultants may continue to sit at the defense or prosecution table, conducting tasks similar to those performed during jury selection. Alternately, they may be working behind the scenes helping an attorney in ongoing case preparation, including the preparation of witnesses. The most visible role for psychologists during the trial is that of expert witness. These topics will be covered in some detail in the pages ahead.

The Disposition Stage

In a criminal case, when a judge or jury renders a verdict of not guilty, the case is over and the defendant is free to go. If the defendant is convicted, however, a decision must be made whether to incarcerate the individual and for how long and, in death penalty cases, whether to impose the ultimate penalty or an alternative life sentence. The role of the forensic psychologist at sentencing can be a critical one. In civil cases, when a verdict favors the plaintiff, a **judgment** is handed down, specifying the remedy to be borne

by the defendant. In deciding on a remedy, judges and juries often consider testimony relating to the psychological harm a plaintiff may have suffered. It should be noted also that the juvenile process—which is civil—also might involve a "sentence," which is called a **disposition** in juvenile courts. Here, psychologists may be asked to offer opinions on the type of rehabilitative strategies that could be used for a particular juvenile.

In many felony cases, sentencing judges have obtained a **presentence investigation** (PSI) report. This is a document that has been prepared by an agent of the criminal justice system (typically a probation officer) or by a private firm. The PSI is a social history that includes information about the offender's family background, employment history, level of education, substance abuse, criminal history, medical needs, and mental health history, among other factors. PSI reports often include a victim impact statement, which is a summary of what the victim suffered—both physically and emotionally—as a result of the crime. Psychologists who have examined the offender or the victim may submit a report that is appended to the document. Alternately, information obtained by psychologists may be included within the PSI itself. Care must be taken in communicating the results of psychological tests, however (see Box 9.2).

BOX 9.2 Releasing Test Data

Many practicing psychologists have on occasion struggled with the problem of whether to release scores or standings on tests to either clients or to others. Attorneys representing criminal defendants or representing plaintiffs or defendants in civil suits often request these data, and reports to courts often contain such information.

Standard 9.04 of the Ethical Principles of Psychologists and Code of Conduct (APA, 2002b) defines test data as "raw and scaled scores, client/patient responses to test questions or stimuli, and psychologists' notes and recordings concerning client/patient statements and behavior during an examination." The code presumes that data will be released if a patient or client signs a release form. Without such a release, psychologists provide test data only if required to do so by

(Continued)

BOX 9.2 (Continued)

---

law or court order. A clause in the code also permits psychologists to withhold data to protect persons from harm or to prevent misuse or misrepresentation of the data.

APA Ethics Director Stephen Behnke (2003) notes that the presumption of release is a change from the earlier code (APA, 1992), which presumed that raw test results or raw data would *not* be released to persons who were not qualified to use such information. Patients or clients could, however, receive such data "as appropriate," a condition that was left to the psychologist to determine. According to Behnke (2003), the change reflects a "trend in law and ethics that began over three decades ago, that of a greater emphasis on patient autonomy" (p. 71). Thus, in a sense, clients and patients are now more in charge of their test data.

This suggests that a psychologist who wishes to withhold test data from a client who requests it will have a heavier burden to meet to justify denying the request. On the other hand, the change may result in improved services to patients. If an individual wishes to release data, the psychologist who grants that request will presumably interpret the data, along with its limitations, very carefully to both the individual and to the recipient.

The Appellate Stage

Neither civil nor criminal cases necessarily end with the trial and disposition stages. Defendants who are losing parties have a variety of options for appealing their convictions, their sentences, or the judgments against them. A person convicted of a crime may appeal his or her conviction on a number of grounds, including errors made during the pretrial or trial stages or inadequate assistance of counsel. Likewise, sentences may be appealed for being disproportionate to the crime committed or on the basis of errors made during the sentencing hearing. The vast majority of criminal appeals are unsuccessful; roughly one out of eight criminal appellants wins on appeal (Neubauer, 2002). A "win" does not mean that the convicted person will be free, however. When appeals courts rule in favor of convicted offenders, they almost always order new trials, a resentencing, or a lower court review of the case consistent with the appellate court's decision. It should be noted that a prosecutor cannot appeal a not-guilty verdict (this would violate the Constitution's prohibition against double jeopardy), but he or she can appeal a sentence that is considered too lenient. This is very rarely done, however.

Appeals of civil cases often revolve around a defendant's appeal of a judgment or a jury award. In recent years, for example, defendants have been appealing large damage awards given to plaintiffs by civil juries, and some judges have reduced these awards. Judgments in civil cases also are notoriously difficult to enforce, and when defendants do not comply, plaintiffs must initiate further legal action. "The arduous process of litigation may prove to be only a preliminary step to the equally protracted travail of collecting the award" (Neubauer, 1997, p. 331).

The individual forensic psychologist has little to do with the appellate stage, although she or he may have considerable stake in the outcome. In some cases, the psychologist's role during the earlier stages of the case may itself be in question. During the 1980s, for example, many individuals convicted of child sexual abuse appealed their convictions on the basis that psychologists who had interviewed alleged victims unduly influenced their testimony. In 2003, a federal appellate court ruled that a new trial might be required in a double-murder case because a psychologist who testified at the original trial had misrepresented his credentials (Ewing, 2003). Interestingly, the appeals court indicated that the false credentials themselves were not the critical factor that would determine the need for a new trial; rather, the critical factor was whether the prosecutor knew or should have known that the testimony was perjured (Ewing, 2003).

Another way in which forensic psychologists are connected with the appellate stage is through the filing of **amicus curiae** (friend of the court) briefs. An amicus brief is a document filed by interested parties who did not participate directly in the trial but either have a stake in the outcome or have research knowledge to offer the appellate court (Saks, 1993). Amicus briefs are typically filed by organizations on behalf of their members. The American Psychological Association (APA), for example, has filed numerous briefs with state and federal appellate courts on topics such as involuntary civil commitment, homosexuality, professional licensing, child testimony in sexual assault cases, the forced medication of inmates, and the effects of employment discrimination. (Box 9.3 includes excerpts from the amicus curiae brief filed in a recent case. That case will be discussed again in Chapter 10.)

BOX 9.3   Amicus Curiae Brief—*Sell v. U.S.*

Sell, a former dentist, was charged with multiple counts of fraud. Ruled incompetent to stand trial and placed in a federal mental health facility for restoration to competency, Sell refused to take psychoactive medication. Lower courts determined that Sell was not a danger to himself or others. Prosecutors asked the Court to allow forced medication, in the interests of taking Sell to trial. The American Psychological Association filed an amicus curiae brief in which the following main arguments were outlined:

- Defendants charged with crime have a liberty interest in the control of their own body.
- When powerful drugs affecting brain chemistry are at issue, defendants also have an interest in their own thought processes.
- Antispychotic drugs may affect a defendant's courtroom demeanor and ability to communicate with his or her attorney.
- Trial courts should explore the possibility of less intrusive, nondrug treatment.
- If the court is persuaded that nondrug treatment would not be effective, the appropriateness of particular medications should be considered.
- However, trial courts should not *assume* that coercive administration of drugs would be appropriate.
- Trial courts should order the medication *only* if the specific medications proposed have a substantial likelihood of success in restoring the defendant to competence *and* if the likelihood of success outweighs the possible side effects.
- The trial court should be mindful of the characteristics of the defendant's specific disorder and of the medications under consideration.
- Although new drugs are available that are more easily tolerated by most patients, the trial court should not consider these panaceas. If professionals disagree about whether a defendant

(Continued)

BOX 9.3 (Continued)

with a particular disorder will respond to particular medications, the court should probe more deeply.

- If drug therapy is likely to succeed, the court should consider the potential for side effects and do everything it can to minimize them.
- Many antipsychotic drugs deaden a person's reactions, make him or her seem restless, or cloud a person's cognitions. If the drugs prejudice the defendant's fair trial rights, the defendant should not be tried in a medicated state.

Source: American Psychological Association (2002a); adapted from Amicus Curiae brief.

Appellate courts, of course, do not necessarily rule in accordance with the weight of the social science evidence. Two recent U.S. Supreme Court cases are illustrative. In one case, *Boy Scouts of America v. Dale* (2000), the APA submitted a brief that outlined a long line of research supporting equal treatment for gays and lesbians. For example, the brief cited the overwhelming social science research that gays and lesbians are no more likely to abuse children than are heterosexuals and are equally likely to form loving, long-term relationships with other adults. Nevertheless, the Court ruled that the Boy Scouts organization had a First Amendment right to exclude homosexuals from serving as Scoutmasters. Although the *Dale* case appears to conflict with the Court's most recent decision in *Lawrence and Garner v. Texas* (2003), there was a significant difference in that the state was punishing homosexuals for what the Court determined to be private consensual behavior within their home. In *Atkins v. Virginia* (2002), the APA brief was apparently more persuasive, although it was one of many that were filed with the Court. The case involved the execution of mentally retarded individuals; brief writers argued that, considering the decision-making abilities of persons whose mental development is below the normal range, it violated common standards of decency to put these individuals to death. In a 6–3 decision, the Supreme Court agreed, ruling that persons with an IQ below 70 who were so developmentally disabled that they could not perform for themselves the daily tasks of living could not be put to death.

Some time ago, Grisso and Saks (1991) urged psychologists not to be discouraged when appellate courts did not rule in line with social science evidence. The U.S. Supreme Court's expertise in constitutional analysis, as well as the numerous other sources of information available to the Justices, must be considered. Grisso and Saks maintained that the Court does not directly *reject* social science evidence but rather has often based its decisions on other grounds. *Boy Scouts v. Dale* is a case in point. The Court did not disagree with the points made by the APA and other groups that filed similar briefs. Rather, they found that, as a private organization, the Boy Scouts had a First Amendment freedom of association and thus could reject individuals for leadership positions based on their sexual orientation. Nevertheless, it can be very frustrating for forensic psychologists and researchers in other social scientists when appellate courts seem to ignore the social science evidence offered to them.

In this and the following two chapters, we will turn our attention to a discussion of specific tasks assumed by psychologists in their interaction with the civil and criminal courts. In this chapter, we discuss their work as trial consultants, both in preparation for the trial and during the trial itself, and their participation as expert witnesses.

Trial Consultation

Psychologists often consult with key players in the judicial process, particularly lawyers. There appears to be no shortage of tasks to perform, both before the trial and during the trial itself, and the work can be quite lucrative. Although members of other professions can and do serve as trial consultants (e.g., sociologists, economists, political scientists), the majority of trial consultants are psychologists (Strier, 1999). The two main areas in which they work are in jury selection and in assisting the lawyer during the trial process. Increasingly, however, consultants help attorneys at a variety of trial preparation tasks, such as preparing witnesses and making decisions about particular trial strategies (Boccaccini, 2002; Myers & Arena, 2001). For example, a lawyer might wonder what type of mental health professional to contact for the purpose of testifying about the effects of posttraumatic stress disorder. In her or his role as trial consultant, the psychologist would offer suggestions. (Box 9.4 provides an example of a "want ad" for a trial consultant.)

As noted earlier, the case that actually goes to trial is the exception. The great majority of both civil and criminal cases (often as many as 90%) are resolved through negotiation or mediation. Both parties wish to avoid the time, expense, and unpredictability of a protracted trial, and—in criminal cases—a defendant may decide to plead guilty to protect another person or in exchange for a lighter sentence. Recall from Chapter 3 that even persons who are not guilty sometime plead guilty, a reality that members of the public often have difficulty comprehending.

The cases that do go to trial are often high-profile cases in which the defendants (both criminal and civil) have a good deal to lose if the verdict does not come out in their favor. In the criminal context, they may be cases in which the defendant is truly innocent, despite the fact that probable cause to believe he or she committed the crime has been established. They may be death penalty cases or cases that would incur a long prison sentence. In the civil context, cases that go to trial may involve highly emotional situations in which one or both sides do not wish to compromise, such as litigation over

---

BOX 9.4   Help Wanted: Trial Consultant

DecisionQuest, a trial consulting firm based in California, advertises its services as a recognized leader in the field of trial consulting. It specializes in developing persuasive communication strategies for *Fortune* 1000 clients in both litigation and nonlitigation settings. It recently recruited for the following position:

Research Associate: trained at the PhD or master's level in an area of the social sciences. The position involves research design and analysis, strategic problem solving, and presenting strategies to clients.

The ad notes that candidates should expect to travel often and do applied research in settings across the United States. In addition, the firm works on many different projects at once and often under urgent deadlines. The work is difficult, the ad states, but rewarding.

Source: www.decisionquest.com

custody of dependent children or the contesting of a will. They also may be those in which a corporate defendant stands to lose millions of dollars or even faces corporate dissolution if found to be at fault. The highly litigated case against A. H. Robins corporation in the late 1970s and 1980s is a case in point (see Finley, 1996). Robins manufactured the Dalkon Shield, a birth control device that was subsequently found to produce numerous negative consequences (e.g., extreme bleeding, maiming, cramping, nausea, infections) for the women who used it. Women across the country sued Robins, and one jury, in Kansas, returned a $7.5 million punitive damages verdict against the company. Robins eventually filed for bankruptcy. Thus, when stakes are high, defendants (and occasionally prosecutors) with the financial means to do so are willing to assume considerable expense to hire experts to assist them in their jury selection and other trial preparation work.

Scientific Jury Selection

Scientific jury selection is the application of social science techniques in an effort to find a jury that will be favorably disposed toward one's case. This process may include attitude surveys within the community in an attempt to determine representative views on matters dealing with the upcoming case. Defense lawyers representing a corporate client being sued for illegally dumping hazardous wastes might want to know how members of the community in general view corporate crime. More important, what are the demographic profiles of persons who are friendly toward corporations? And what of the anti-corporation individual: What type of individual is most likely to be favorably disposed toward someone suing a large corporation? Trial consultants conduct surveys, set up focus groups, interview community members, or employ other research strategies to try to help predict who will likely be a good juror for their client. At the pretrial stage, lawyers are also concerned about

the effect of publicity that could be prejudicial to their client's case. Thus, trial consultants may be asked to conduct surveys of the community and collect evidence of negative publicity, which would support a motion for a change of venue (change in the location of the trial).

Witness Preparation

Trial consultants also help attorneys prepare witnesses and determine effective strategies for presenting evidence and persuading jurors (Myers & Arena, 2001). In preparing for the trial date, attorneys on each side of the conflict often meet with the witnesses they will be calling to the stand. This is done "to review, discuss, and sometimes modify the substance and delivery of their anticipated testimony" (Boccaccini, 2002, p. 161). In the case of lay witnesses who are not accustomed to a courtroom appearance, this prior meeting with lawyers (or sometimes with trial consultants) is considered an important step to avoid "surprises" in the testimony and to lessen the courtroom-related stress that witnesses may experience. Although attorneys are obviously concerned about the substance of a witness's testimony, they also are concerned about the presentation. The task of preparing witnesses may be shared with a trial consultant, part of whose task is to coach an individual in how to be a persuasive, confident witness.

On the basis of his review of the available literature on this topic, Boccaccini (2002) notes that **witness preparation** involves three broad components: witness education, attorney education, and modification of testimony delivery. Witness education orients the witness to the courtroom process and reviews with the witness his or her previous statements (e.g., to police or during pretrial depositions) to ensure that there will be no contradictions. Attorney education allows the lawyer to be totally familiar with the information held by the witness. The modification of testimony delivery involves coaching the witness in such behaviors as speaking, dressing, and responding to the judge or the cross-examining attorney. Very little is known about the actual strategies used in witness preparation or about the extent to which such preparation affects the final outcome of a court case.

Certain aspects of witness preparation are controversial because they may reinforce in the witness a memory that is actually quite weak. Recall our discussion in Chapter 3 of the police questioning of witnesses during a lineup; an initially uncertain witness can be led to be very certain by police statements that imply approval of his or her lineup identification. In similar fashion, rehearsal of one's testimony during witness preparation is likely to increase one's confidence in that testimony. Research on eyewitness testimony indicates that jurors are more likely to believe or find credible a witness who speaks clearly and appears highly confident (Penrod & Cutler, 1995).

Suggestive questioning by attorneys or trial consultants also might lead witnesses to recall details that they did not initially remember. "Objectively false but subjectively true testimony can be created when a witness's memory of an event is distorted during the course of witness preparation, leading them to give unknowingly false or misleading testimony" (Boccaccini, 2002, p. 166).

The *Voir Dire*

During the trial itself, trial consultants perform a different group of tasks. The first stage of the trial is the jury selection process, technically called the *voir dire*. This involves the questioning of potential jurors to best ensure a nonbiased jury. Here, the pretrial research done by the trial consultant is put to practical use, as lawyers attempt to remove from the jury persons who will not likely be sympathetic to their side and select those who would be. The consultant may suggest *voir dire* questions to lawyers and make inferences about prospective jurors based on

their responses or even on their nonverbal behavior (Strier, 1999).

Also during the trial, a "shadow jury" may have been set up. These are individuals similar in demographics to persons who are serving on the actual jury. The trial consultant keeps in close touch with the shadow jurors, noting, for example, their reactions to the evidence as it being presented as well as to the tactics and strategies of the respective lawyers. Information from the shadow jury can then be transmitted to the trial consultant's client. During the trial, the trial consultant also may suggest questions or strategies to the lawyer.

The efficacy of such trial consulting has yet to be demonstrated scientifically, although there are anecdotal accounts of its success in major trials. Defense lawyers in a number of politically related trials in the 1960s and 1970s, for example, credited jury consultants in helping them select jurors when their clients were acquitted. Since that time, defense teams in a number of other high-profile cases that ended in acquittals (e.g., the O. J. Simpson case) have hired consultants. Although their help in selecting jurors may have contributed to the overall success of the defense in these cases, numerous other factors are relevant. Defendants able to afford trial consultants, for example, are also able to afford lawyers who can devote their full attention to the case, in contrast to less economically advantaged defendants. This raises concerns about the fairness of using consultants. In politically charged trials, when the individual defendants themselves do not have the financial resources to hire consultants, supportive interest groups may provide funds for the consultants. However, the average criminal defendant or the average litigant in a civil suit is usually unable to afford such services.

Trial Consultation: The Main Concerns

Research psychologists tend to be very skeptical of trial consulting, particularly as it attempts to select jurors sympathetic to one's case. As mentioned above, some aspects of witness preparation also raise concern. With respect to scientific jury selection, comments by Ellsworth and Reifman (2000) are representative: "Jury researchers have searched in vain for individual differences—race, gender, class, attitudes, or personality—that reliably predict a person's verdict and have almost always come up empty handed" (p. 795). In a similar vein, law professor John Conley (2000) expressed wonderment "at the vast sums of money that lawyers and clients expend on jury-selection 'experts' who purport to produce psychological profiles of 'ideal' jurors for particular cases" (p. 823).

The lack of oversight of trial consulting has also been noted. As Strier (1999) observed, both profit and nonprofit trial consulting can now be found online, but whether online or not, it is largely unregulated. "There are no state licensing requirements, nor is there any binding or meaningful code of professional ethics" (Strier, 1999, p. 96). Myers and Arena (2001), acknowledging the legitimacy of Strier's concerns, nevertheless are supportive of trial consultation. Psychologists, they believe, can help to restore the balance in the presently unbalanced scales of justice. They agree, though, that better standards in training and methodology are needed if the field is to advance.

Expert Testimony

In addition to working behind the scenes or sitting in the courtroom as trial consultants, psychologists also may be found on the witness stand, testifying as expert witnesses in a wide range of cases. This very visible role has produced extensive research and commentary and has been the subject of three significant Supreme Court decisions over the past decade. Together, the three decisions (*Daubert v. Merrill Dow Pharmaceuticals, Inc.*, 1993; *General Electric Co. v. Joiner*, 1997; *Kumho Tire Co. v. Carmichael*, 1999) articulate the standard to be applied by federal courts in deciding whether expert testimony

should be admitted if it is challenged by the opposing lawyer. By the end of the 20th century, 30 states also had adopted a standard identical to or closely related to *Daubert* (Parry & Drogan, 2000). We will discuss this in more detail shortly.

Expert testimony may occur in a variety of pretrial hearings, during both civil and criminal trials or delinquency proceedings or during sentencing or disposition hearings. In each of these contexts, the role of the expert witness is to help the judge or the jury in making decisions on matters that are beyond the knowledge of the typical layperson. Most jurors and judges, for example, are not versed in neurology and the fine workings of the brain. Thus, a neuropsychologist may be called to testify about the effects of physical trauma—such as a severe head injury—on brain functioning. Likewise, most jurors and judges are unfamiliar with the psychological effects of ongoing physical abuse or experiencing a highly traumatic event such as a rape or a kidnapping. Psychologists also have valuable information to convey to courts relative to eyewitness identification, pretrial publicity, human perception and memory, the credibility of child witnesses, or the effect of divorce on children.

Clinical psychologists are also frequently called to testify about the results of evaluations they have conducted. In the criminal context, for example, psychologists frequently conduct court-ordered evaluations of a defendant's competency to stand trial or of his or her mental state at the time of the crime. In these situations, the psychologist will submit a written report to the judge and the attorneys. If the parties do not agree with the psychologist's conclusions, or if the judge wishes additional information or clarification, the psychologist may then be called to testify. In highly litigated cases—such as in a serious, violent crime or a custody dispute—another clinician may be called to testify as well. This resulting "battle of the experts" is often disparaged: "If you look hard enough, you'll find a 'so-called expert' willing to testify to anything."

Research with mock juries suggests that the response to expert testimony is lukewarm or guarded, rather than wholeheartedly supportive (Nietzel, McCarthy, & Kerr, 1999), and that clinical testimony is favored more than the research-based testimony provided by academicians (Krauss & Sales, 2001). In a survey of 488 adult residents in one state, Boccaccini and Brodsky (2002) found that the public was far more likely to believe expert witnesses who worked with patients rather than those who engaged in academic activities. Respondents also were more likely to believe experts who received no payment for testifying, and there was some preference for those who came from the community. Expert testimony will be covered again in the next two chapters. For the present, it is important to look at issues that are common to all such testimony.

Expert Certification

To qualify as an expert witness, a psychologist must first establish her or his credentials, including the requisite advanced degree, licensing or certification if relevant, and research or practical experience in areas about which she or he is testifying. As mentioned at the beginning of this chapter, until the mid-20th century, courts were divided over whether psychologists were competent to testify on mental health issues, so the typical expert on issues such as insanity, competency to stand trial, dangerousness, or amenability to treatment was a psychiatrist. In *Jenkins v. United States* (1962), however, an influential federal appellate court acknowledged that psychologists as well as psychiatrists could qualify as expert witnesses. In each case, it is left to the discretion of the trial judge to accept or reject an individual's qualifications as an expert, subject to review by appellate courts. However, in some states, the statutes require specific credentials or licensing to perform some of the evaluations and subsequently testify in court proceedings.

The expert's credentials may be critical to the final outcome of the case. In the double-murder case mentioned earlier in the chapter, where two young people were shot in their car by a

classmate, a psychologist who testified for the prosecution falsified his credentials and testified about a supposed "syndrome" that no one else had ever heard of (Ewing, 2003). It is not clear at this point whether the prosecutor knew or should have known of the misrepresentation—recall that the appeals court sent the case back for clarification on that issue. According to Ewing (2003), the case illustrates a new concern among forensic psychologists:

This has recently become an issue within the field of forensic psychology—to what extent are some psychologists presenting credentials in court purchased from vanity or mail-order boards (credentials sold with little or no scrutiny of credentials or competence) to pad their credentials? (p. 84)

Ewing cautions lawyers who call on expert witnesses to carefully vet their résumés before putting them on the stand. Unfortunately, incidents such as that described above damage the reputation of psychology as a whole and erode public confidence in both law and mental health professionals.

Legal Standards for the Admission of Scientific Evidence

Even though an expert has the professional background to qualify for certification as an expert witness, it is possible that the presiding judge will not allow the evidence the expert has to offer. Under federal law and the law of the states that have adopted similar standards, if the opposing lawyer challenges the introduction of the evidence, the judge must decide whether the evidence is reliable, legally sufficient, and relevant to the case at hand. This was the standard for federal courts announced by the U.S. Supreme Court in its 1993 decision, *Daubert v. Merrill Dow Pharmaceuticals, Inc.* The *Daubert* rule replaced an earlier standard (announced in *Frye v. U.S.*, 1923), which was loosely known as the "general acceptance" rule. According to that earlier standard, the expert's evidence must have been gathered using scientific techniques that had reached a general acceptance in the science field. Once that standard had been met, all relevant testimony would be admissible.

Over the years, the *Frye* standard lost favor because—among other things—it was considered to be too stringent, presenting an obstacle to the introduction of evidence that had not yet reached "general acceptance." For example, evidence of battered woman syndrome or evidence obtained through hypnosis might be too controversial to be considered widely accepted by mental health practitioners. In the Federal Rules of Evidence, adopted in 1975, Congress provided a different standard. The pertinent rule, Rule 702, did not require general acceptance, but it did require that evidence be relevant and reliable. Even relevant information could be excluded, however, if it would serve to prejudice the jury. In *Daubert,* the Supreme Court supported the standard set by the Rules of Evidence. It did not completely denigrate the "general acceptance" criterion, however. Rather, it announced that general acceptance by the scientific community could be taken into consideration in deciding whether evidence was reliable. General acceptance should not, however, be a *necessary* condition. Although this may appear to be a more liberal standard, some research indicates it has had the opposite effect, as we will see below.

The *Daubert* **standard** makes the judge a gatekeeper who must evaluate evidence—including the testimony of a mental health practitioner—and decide whether it should be admitted. In a later case, *General Electric Co. v. Joiner* (1997), the Supreme Court made it clear that it would not second-guess judges unless they clearly abused their discretion in allowing or not allowing testimony. According to the Court, the trial court judge in the *Joiner* case had conducted a careful review of the scientific information that would have been offered by four different experts before concluding that it should not be admitted. Following that case, some commentators have

suggested that the psychologist or other expert must take care to explain carefully to judges how and why their information is reliable and relevant. In other words, the testimony evaluated by the judge in the *Joiner* case may have been based on good science, but the experts may not have explained their work adequately.

In *Kumho Tire Co. Ltd. v. Carmichael* (1999), the Supreme Court ruled that *all* expert testimony—whether it is based on scientific, clinical, or technical knowledge—is subject to the same *Daubert* standard of relevance and reliability. Thus, clinical psychologists are clearly held to the same standard, something that was not clear until the Court's ruling in the *Kumho* case. As Otto and Heilbrun (2002) have noted, the mantle of science has been placed over the shoulders of practitioners as well as researchers.

Although state courts are free to adopt their own rules of evidence, in practice, many use federal rules as a model. As noted earlier, approximately 30 states use *Daubert*-like criteria for the admission of scientific evidence. Some courts already have seen the *Daubert* trilogy (as the three cases have come to be called) as an invitation to give very careful scrutiny to a variety of psychological tests used by clinicians in their assessment practices. In addition, the professional literature has hosted spirited debates over the relevance and reliability of these measures. The debate between supporters and critics of the Rorschach Comprehensive System (RCS) is one of the most contentious. First published in 1974, it is believed to be the most frequently used approach to scoring the Rorschach (Grove & Barden, 1999; Weiner, 2001). The Rorschach is a projective test known to the lay public as the "inkblot test." Grove and Barden (1999; Grove, Barden, Garb, & Lilienfeld, 2002) have fueled the debate with their scathing indictment of the RCS. They argue that, based on its lack of relevance and reliability, expert testimony based on results using the RCS should not be admitted into courts. Wood and his colleagues (Wood, Nezworski, Stejskal, & McKinzey, 2001) summarized succinctly the limitations of the RCS that make it vulnerable to challenge by well-informed attorneys. On the other hand, supporters of the RCS (e.g., Hamel, Gallagher, & Soares, 2001; Ritzler, Erard, & Pettigrew, 2002a, 2002b; Weiner, 2000) have taken up the gauntlet, arguing that the scoring system is indeed valid and reliable and meets *Daubert* criteria for admission into court. To some extent—but not exclusively—the controversy reflects a split between the scientific community and the clinical community, although this is not to suggest that clinicians are not also scientists. Nevertheless, criticism of the RCS typically comes from those identified *predominantly* as researchers, whereas support comes from those identified *primarily* as clinicians. Similar researcher-practitioner splits have been encountered relevant to assessments in other contexts, such as child custody evaluations, repressed memory, hypnosis, and use of the polygraph (Otto & Heilbrun, 2002).

In spite of the above discussion, it is important to emphasize that a judge will not conduct a review of the relevance and reliability of the expert's testimony in all cases. Judges apply the *Daubert* standard only when an attorney challenges the *introduction* of the evidence. Shuman and Sales (2001) note that,

> like most other rules of evidence, *Daubert* relies on trial lawyers to identify issues of admissibility (e.g., the reliability of the expert testimony) and choose whether to raise them before the trial judge, to present on issues of credibility to the jury, or to ignore these issues. (p. 71)

Shuman and Sales (2001) add that a lawyer may not recognize that certain expert testimony is based on unreliable methods; alternately, the methods used by the lawyer's own expert may be just as faulty. In neither case would the lawyer be likely to challenge the opposing expert. In still another scenario, the lawyer may wait until the opposing expert is on the witness stand and within view of the jury before questioning the credibility of the information. Finally, pretrial

Daubert motions cost money, take up court time, and require judges and lawyers to master science as well as the law. For all of the above reasons, they are not likely to become enthusiastically embraced in the nation's courtrooms (Shuman & Sales, 2001).

However, a review of civil cases in federal district courts indicates that judges do appear to be excluding more scientific evidence than ever before in the wake of *Daubert*. Dixon and Gill (2002) reviewed a sample of federal civil cases between 1980 and 1999 in which expert testimony was offered. The experts represented a variety of fields, including health care and medicine, engineering and technology, the physical sciences, the social and behavioral sciences, and business, law, and public administration. The researchers found significant changes after the Court announced its decision. For example, specifically referring to the social and behavioral sciences, judges rejected expert testimony as unreliable in 43% of the cases over a 10-year period prior to *Daubert*. After the *Daubert* decision, they rejected testimony in 61% of the cases between 1995 and 1997. Interestingly, in the 2-year period from 1997 to 1999, the rejection rate went down to 47%, suggesting the possibility that experts might have been better prepared to address the reliability of their finding.

The study also revealed that general acceptance of the evidence by others in the profession was no longer sufficient for the admission of expert evidence. However, *lack* of general acceptance was a barrier to admission. In other words, it had not become easier for novel or unusual evidence to be accepted. Dixon and Gill (2002) concluded that, since *Daubert*, federal judges—at least in civil trials—have heeded the instructions of the Supreme Court and have increasingly acted as gatekeepers for reliability and relevance.

The evidence suggests that since *Daubert*, judges have examined the reliability of expert evidence more closely and have found more evidence unreliable as a result. Our analysis, however, does not allow us to conclude whether this increased scrutiny resulted in better outcomes. (Dixon & Gill, 2002, p. 269)

In other words, from the results of their study, Dixon and Gill (2002) could not say that the excluded evidence should have been admitted (or that admitted evidence should have been excluded). They did suggest, though, that judges might not be knowledgeable enough about scientific methodology to make informed and accurate determinations. One way to evaluate this, they added, would be to assemble an independent panel of experts to review evidence offered in court cases and compare the panel's assessment of that evidence to the judge's decisions.

Since the *Daubert* decision, considerable research and commentary has addressed the Court's assumption that judges, who rarely have a scientific background, would be able to evaluate scientific evidence. Kovera, Russano, and McAuliff (2002) maintain that most judges and most jurors are similar in their ability to identify flawed expert evidence because neither has received formal training in the scientific method. They further maintain that such individuals cannot differentiate between valid and flawed research. Jurors, as the research has consistently indicated, are highly unlikely to be able to distinguish the flawed research, even when an opposing expert highlights these flaws (Cutler & Penrod, 1995; Cutler, Penrod, & Dexter, 1989). Neither jurors, nor judges, nor lawyers typically can understand the importance of control groups or appreciate the relative merits of small and large sample sizes (Kovera et al., 2002).

Kovera and her colleagues (Kovera & McAuliff, 2000; Kovera et al., 2002) asked judges and attorneys to evaluate studies that represented four methodological variations: a valid study, a study that was missing a control group, a study that contained a confound, and a study that used a nonblind confederate. Judges were asked whether they would admit the evidence; lawyers were asked whether they would file a motion to exclude it. Judges admitted flawed research at the same rates as they admitted valid testimony. When attorneys wanted evidence excluded (which was almost invariably), it had no relationship to their perceptions of the scientific reliability of the evidence. Kovera and her colleagues conclude that it remains likely that some "junk science" will make its way into the courtroom and that some valid evidence will be excluded.

Although the fallout from the *Daubert* decision continues to be investigated, expert witnesses continue to face other challenges in the courtroom. As many commentators have remarked, testifying in court is not an exercise for the faint of heart. Expert witnesses—just like lay witnesses—face the possibility of being subjected to grueling cross-examination. Even very low-profile trials or pretrial proceedings can produce anxiety for the expert being subjected to sharp cross-examination. Some experts also struggle with their concerns about confidentiality, "ultimate opinion" testimony, and the prediction of dangerousness or assessment of risk. We will discuss each of these hurdles below, beginning with the problem of confidentiality.

The Confidentiality Issue

The obligation to maintain confidentiality in the patient-therapist relationship is fundamental. In the courtroom setting, though, confidentiality is not absolute. When clinicians have been asked by the court to evaluate a defendant, the results of that evaluation are shared among the judge and the lawyers. In these situations, the clinician's client is the court, not the individual being examined. The evaluation also may be discussed in the open courtroom if the clinician is called to the stand. In such cases, persons who have been evaluated have been warned of the limits of confidentiality at the outset of the evaluation. As noted in Box 9.2, even the confidentiality of test data is not guaranteed if the client signs a release or if the court orders it released.

Under the "Specialty Guidelines for Forensic Psychologists" (Committee on Ethical Guidelines for Forensic Psychologists, 1991), clinicians are advised to inform the individual of the nature and purpose of an evaluation, as well as who will be receiving a report. They also should ensure that the individual is informed of his or her legal rights.

> If the person [being assessed] is not the client, the psychologist owes no duty of confidentiality to that person; but, because of the requirement of informed consent, must make the fact known to the person being assessed that the information to be obtained is not confidential. (Ogloff, 1999, p. 411)

Nonetheless, even if notified of the limits of confidentiality, the individual in reality has little choice in submitting to the evaluation if he or she has not requested it (Perlin, 1991). In addition, the individual may suffer harm as a result of the psychologist's participation in the evaluation process (Perlin, 1991).

When it is not evaluation but rather psychotherapy or treatment that is at issue, all courts recognize the patient-therapist privilege, although it is not absolute. The U.S. Supreme Court, for example, has firmly endorsed confidentiality in federal courts (*Jaffe v. Redmond*, 1996). Redmond was a police officer who shot and killed an allegedly armed suspect whom she believed was about to kill another individual. The suspect's family sued, maintaining that he was not armed and that Officer Redmond had used excessive force, a civil rights violation. When the plaintiffs learned that Redmond had attended counseling sessions with a psychiatric social worker after the shooting, they subpoenaed the social worker, who confirmed that the officer had been a patient. However, the social worker refused to answer specific questions about treatment. The judge in the cases refused to recognize a therapist-patient privilege and informed the jury that they were entitled to presume that the testimony would have been damaging to Redmond's case. The jury found for the plaintiffs, but the Seventh Circuit Court of Appeals threw out the verdict.

In its 7–3 decision, the U.S. Supreme Court affirmed the appeals court's decision. The Justices not only recognized the importance of the psychotherapist-patient privileged communication but also placed licensed social workers under this protective cloak. The Court did not consider the privilege absolute—or totally protected under all conditions—but did not specify when it would *not* apply. It is likely, however, that restrictions of the psychotherapist-patient privilege in federal courts would be similar to those in states. For example, the privilege generally does not apply when patients voluntarily introduce their mental health into evidence. Confidentiality also is not protected when a patient sues the therapist, because the therapist is entitled to use otherwise privileged information to defend himself or herself (Ogloff, 1999).

The law places other limits on confidentiality that do not directly affect courtroom testimony. For example, in many states, clinicians have a **duty to warn or protect** third parties who may be in danger from a patient who has threatened their lives. The duty to warn or protect is referred to as the *Tarasoff* requirement, named after a court ruling. The specific requirements vary by state, which is why it is alternately called a duty to warn and a duty to protect. In some states, for example, therapists are expected to notify the threatened individual directly (warn), whereas in other states, therapists can meet the requirement by contacting law enforcement authorities or by taking active steps to have their patient institutionalized (protect). In those states with duty to warn or duty to protect legislation, psychologists who fail in this duty are subject to being sued civilly by victims who suffer harm at the hands of their clients. In all states, practitioners also are required by law to report evidence of child abuse (and, in some cases, elder or other abuse) encountered in their practice to appropriate parties, which may include law enforcement or social service agencies. Although many clinicians say they can live within the spirit of *Tarasoff* and other reporting requirements, others have been critical of the violation of trust that these requirements engender.

Ultimate Issue or Ultimate Opinion Testimony

The testimony provided by expert witnesses is different from that provided by lay witnesses. Recall that a main role of the expert is to assist triers of fact (judges and juries) in matters about which they would not otherwise be knowledgeable. In most jurisdictions, *lay* witnesses can testify only to events that they have actually seen or heard firsthand. Their opinions and inferences are generally not admissible. *Expert* witnesses, on the other hand, testify to facts they have observed directly, to tests they may have conducted, and to the research evidence in their field. Moreover, the opinions and inferences of experts not only are admissible but are also often sought by the courts.

Currently, there is considerable debate among mental health professionals about the wisdom of offering an opinion on the "**ultimate issue.**" The ultimate issue is the final question that must be decided by the court. For example, should the expert provide an opinion about whether the defendant was indeed insane (and therefore not responsible) at the time of his crime? Should the expert recommend which parent should be awarded custody? Should the expert opine that a defendant is competent to be executed? Should the expert recommend that a juvenile's case be transferred to criminal court? It is quite clear that courts frequently request and hope for such opinions (Melton et al., 1997; Redding, Floyd, & Hawk, 2001; Slobogin, 1999). In one study, despite a statutory prohibition on ultimate opinion testimony in insanity cases, judges and prosecutors indicated a strong desire for clinical opinion (Redding et al., 2001). Defense attorneys were less likely to support this.

Those who oppose ultimate issue testimony (e.g., Melton et al., 1997) believe—among other things—that it is highly subject to error. The expert may misunderstand the law, may apply hidden value judgments, or may believe a particular outcome is best for an individual, even if legal criteria are not met. A clinical psychologist, for example, may truly believe that an individual needs to be placed in a secure mental health facility and treated for a serious mental disorder, even if the person does not technically meet the criteria for institutionalization. Thus, the psychologist might offer the opinion that the individual is not competent to stand trial, knowing that if the individual is ruled incompetent, he or she will most likely be sent to a mental hospital and will receive some treatment.

Opponents of ultimate issue testimony also fear the undue influence of the expert on the fact finder. They stress that decisions such as whether an individual was insane at the time of the crime or whether a father or a mother should be awarded custody of a minor child are legal decisions. Asking the expert to express her or his opinion suggests that great weight will be placed on that opinion, when in fact the decision must be made by a judge or a jury and must be based on legal factors.

There is partial research support for the assumption of undue influence. Research suggests that the expert's opinion heavily influences judges in *pretrial* situations but not judges or juries at the *trial* stage. On issues such as competency to stand trial or the dangerousness of a defendant (warranting a denial of bail), the influence of the expert is substantial (Melton et al., 1997). Trial jurors, however, do not seem to be unduly dictated by the opinions of experts (Nietzel et al., 1999). This may be because opposing experts and aggressive cross-examination are more likely in a trial situation than in a pretrial. Furthermore, jurors perceive experts as "hired guns" who would not be placed on the stand if their opinions did not support the side that called them. Jurors do listen to expert testimony, but "the effect is modest and leaves opportunity for both foes and fans of ultimate opinion testimony to find support for their positions" (Nietzel et al., 1999, p. 41).

Those who favor testimony on the ultimate issue (e.g., Rogers & Ewing, 1989) argue that judges often depend on it and that such testimony can be carefully controlled, particularly by means of effective cross-examination. They note also that judges and lawyers are becoming increasingly sophisticated about possible sources of error in an expert's opinion; to believe otherwise is to insult their intelligence. Furthermore, in pretrial situations in both criminal and civil cases, judges typically ask an opinion of the clinician who has been appointed by the court and who is acceptable to both parties. These court officers have come to value and trust the professional's opinion as a result of having him or her involved in past cases.

Reflecting the lack of consensus on this matter, the American Psychological Association has not taken a stand on whether ultimate issue testimony should be provided, even when courts request it. The 1994 "Guidelines for Child Custody Evaluations in Divorce Proceedings" (American Psychological Association, 1994), for example, specifically refer to the lack of consensus. Guideline 14 notes that psychologists "are obligated to be aware of the arguments on both sides of this issue and to be able to explain the logic of their own practice." The guideline further states that, if they choose to make a custody recommendation, the recommendation should be derived from sound psychological data and based on the best interests of the child. Furthermore, they should guard against "relying on their own biases or unsupported beliefs in rendering opinions in particular cases." Likewise, the "Specialty Guidelines for Forensic Psychologists" (Committee on Ethical Guidelines for Forensic Psychologists, 1991) neither encourage nor discourage ultimate issue testimony. They note only that "professional observations, inferences, and conclusions must be distinguished from legal facts, opinions, and conclusions."

Surviving the Witness Stand

Courtroom testimony can be a stressful experience, even for those who appear in court on a regular basis. Cross-examination by an opposing attorney is particularly discomfiting. Forensic psychologists, like other expert witnesses, may enter the courtroom totally confident in their professional knowledge and the evidence they are about to present. However, faced with the grueling questions of a legal adversary and frustrated with legal rules of evidence that limit their testimony, they may wish for a very quick end to a painful experience.

Nevertheless, numerous forensic psychologists have learned to negotiate the landscape of the courtroom and have developed the skills needed both to provide the court with specialized knowledge and to respond to cross-examination in a calm, professional matter (see Box 9.5). This is crucial, because it is not unusual for cross-examining attorneys to berate or insult experts, their field of study, or methods used in their research. The professional literature contains ample advice for psychologists preparing to testify as expert witnesses. Poythress (1979), for example, recommends that the psychologist observe other expert witnesses and, if possible, participate in mock trial situations. He also recommends specific course work or field placements in forensic settings. Today, most forensic psychology graduate programs offer courses or workshops on testifying in court.

Others have offered advice not only for the witness stand but also for a wide range of meetings and proceedings that are part of the trial preparation process (e.g., Heilbrun, 2001; Heilbrun et al., 2002; Hess, 1999). Expert witnesses are urged to establish a communicative relationship with the attorney who has called them early in the legal process so that each side will know what can realistically be expected from the other.

> Some attorneys stereotypically view psychologists as soft thinkers, lacking in discipline, while psychologists often regard attorneys as narrowly focused, rigid, and inflexible. These stereotypes result from a failure to understand the other's professional needs at the outset of the consultation. (Singer & Nievod, 1987, p. 530)

BOX 9.5   Rules for Testifying

Psychologists are provided with a wealth of advice about how to approach the witness stand in both criminal and civil cases. For example, Barsky and Gould (2002, pp. 109–118) propose the following 10 rules, regardless of who is asking the questions:

1. Tell the truth, the whole truth, and nothing but the truth.

2. Convey professionalism.

3. Respect the formalities of the tribunal.

4. Speak slowly, loudly, and without hesitation.

5. Provide clear and concise answers.

6. Let the attorney lead the questions.

7. Just the facts, Ma'am/Sir.

8. Keep your composure.

9. Maintain eye contact.

10. Use notes to refresh your memory.

Pretrial *preparation* is essential, and psychologists should not allow themselves to be persuaded to enter the courtroom without advance notice and sufficient preparation time (Singer & Nievod, 1987). They are advised to gather information carefully, pay attention to details of the case and the legal issues involved, remain impartial, and keep clear, organized notes (Chappelle & Rosengren, 2001). It should never be assumed that notes, correspondence, and tape recordings would never be made available to attorneys for both sides under the rules of discovery. At some point in the proceedings, considering *Daubert* and other relevant cases, either the judge or the opposing attorney is likely to inquire whether the techniques or theories on which the expert is relying have been scientifically evaluated. The error rate is also important. Thus, in the process of preparing his or her testimony, the expert witness must take care to address these questions.

Expert witnesses are also advised to pay particular attention to their nonverbal behavior in the courtroom. Any behaviors that suggest arrogance, confusion, hostility, or anxiety are to be avoided. Chappelle and Rosengren (2001), reviewing the recent literature on expert testimony, note that the need to maintain composure is a theme in this literature. The knowledge offered by the expert is more likely to be accepted by judge and jury if the expert projects a professional, confident, and respectful persona. Experts also must recognize that attorneys will try to get them rattled or agitated and must resist becoming so. Chappelle and Rosengren even suggest anti-anxiety medication or other pharmaceutical agents to help the expert remain calm, if necessary. They caution, however, that these have the potential of interfering with one's cognitive abilities.

Psychologists are often advised to read Ziskin and Faust's (1994) *Coping With Psychiatric and Psychological Testimony*. The authors are critical of psychological and psychiatric testing, research, and diagnosis, and their book is on many an attorney's reading list. "Their express purpose is to embarrass mental health professionals out of the courtroom" (Hess, 1999, p. 551).

The Assessment of Risk

Forensic psychologists are very often asked to predict the likelihood that a particular individual will be "dangerous" to self or to society. This question becomes relevant when courts decide whether to release a person on bail, whether to place a mentally disordered individual in a psychiatric treatment facility against his or her will, or whether to hold a juvenile in a secure setting. Although *dangerousness* typically refers to violent or aggressive behavior, a wide range of behavior is included under that rubric. For example, threatening to harm someone, setting a barn on fire, attempting suicide, and assaulting one's neighbor could all be considered violent behaviors, even though only one results in actual injury to another individual. Can psychologists or any other clinicians predict such behavior with any degree of confidence?

Some clinicians—called to testify in criminal and juvenile courts during the last quarter of the 20th century—have been quick to say that they can. "On a scale of 1 to 10, with 10 being the most dangerous, this person is an 11," one psychiatrist was fond of saying. Others made statements such as, "For his own good, this juvenile must be locked up; he will definitely commit more crime if not institutionalized." These types of predictions were cited in court cases (e.g., *Barefoot v. Estelle,* 1983) in which individuals challenged their bail denials, their sentences, or their confinements. For the most part, courts have allowed clinicians to make predictions but have also acknowledged their fallibility. In a juvenile case, *Schall v. Martin* (1984), for example, the U.S. Supreme Court recognized that predictions of behavior were imperfect and fraught with error but ruled nevertheless that they had a place in the law. The case involved juveniles who were held in secure detention prior to their delinquency hearings, partly because there was a serious risk that they would commit more illegal activity if allowed to remain free.

Today, many forensic psychologists are careful to point out the fallibility of behavioral prediction. Although they acknowledge that prediction is an important aspect of the services they provide to courts and other institutions, they are carefully guarded in their conclusions. When it comes to predicting violence, many now prefer the terms *risk assessments* or *threat assessments* rather than *prediction of dangerousness. Risk* or *threat assessment* communicates the important point that in their evaluation, psychologists are providing courts or other agencies with a probability statement that a given individual will behave in an inappropriate manner. The probability assessment may be based on clinical judgment or on certain "predictor variables" that are in the individual's background. For example, past violent behavior, age, lack of adequate system of social supports, alcohol or other substance abuse, and a history of serious mental disorder together are good indicators that a person is likely to be violent once again (Monahan, 1996).

Communication of Risk

The communication of risk to courts and other agencies that have requested **risk assessments** has become a topic of considerable interest in the forensic psychological literature (Heilbrun, O'Neill, Strohman, Bowman, & Philipson, 2000; Monahan & Steadman, 1996). Some have noted that the professional literature is rich in theoretical and empirical work on risk assessment, but it contains little information on how to communicate risk to those who have requested risk assessments (Borum, 1996; Heilbrun et al., 2000).

Monahan and Steadman (1996) drew an analogy between the psychologist's violence risk assessment task and weather forecasting. They note that weather forecasters provide not only risk levels of severe weather but also prescriptive statements indicating the need for further information and the strategies that should be taken to manage the risk. Thus, a hurricane "prediction" would include the likelihood of this happening and under what conditions, as well as steps to be taken in preparation to cope with the event. Likewise, the psychologist communicating a risk assessment should not only provide an assessment of the level of risk (e.g., high, moderate, low, or gradients in between) but also carefully specify the risk factors in a particular case and suggest interventions that might be taken to reduce the risk.

Some studies have investigated the preferred approaches taken by psychologists, psychiatrists, and other clinical professions in communicating the results of their risk assessments. Numerical probabilities, for example, are often avoided, even though the data on which the assessment was based were actuarial in nature (Heilbrun, Philipson, Berman, & Warren, 1999; Lidz, Mulvey, & Gardner, 1993). Numerical estimates—for example, "there's a 65% chance this person will be violent after release" or "on a scale of 1 to 10, he's a 9"—appear too definitive. The assessment enterprise itself is anything but definitive.

Kirk Heilbrun and his colleagues (Heilbrun et al., 2000) were interested in studying the preferred mode of risk communication among a sample of clinicians. They analyzed responses to vignettes that had been mailed to 28 psychiatrists, 41 psychologists, and 2 sociologists, all of whom had expertise in violence risk assessment, with a mean of 23 years of postdegree experience. To analyze the data, the researchers grouped the sociologists with the psychologists.

The most highly valued form of communication among both groups was "risk management oriented." That is, all clinicians expressed a strong preference for both identifying the risk factors and specifying the interventions that could reduce the risk. The next preferred form of communication varied according to professional affiliation. Psychologists preferred a predictive approach, specifying risk level (e.g., high, medium, low), whereas psychiatrists preferred a descriptive approach in which they would simply

state information about the examinee (e.g., history of violence or not psychopathic). The form of communication least used by both groups was the percentage probability (e.g., there is a 40% likelihood that Mr. X will commit a violent act). The preference for risk management strategy was especially evident in those vignettes that suggested that the individual had a high potential for violence. In other words, the clinicians probably felt they should suggest something that could be done to try to prevent more violence. The percentage of time spent in practice compared with time spent in research was also related to the preferred mode of communication. Clinicians who spent more time in practice were more likely than their research-oriented colleagues to prefer the risk management approach.

According to Heilbrun et al. (2000), the study represents an initial effort to identify practice standards among those who are conducting risk assessments. They were encouraged to learn that disciplinary differences did not translate significantly to differences in preferred communication approach. Both groups strongly resisted making "dangerousness" predictions and specifying numerical probabilities that individuals would act violently. It is important to note that the vignettes used in the above study covered risk assessment in a variety of contexts (e.g., bail denial, civil commitment, parole decision making). Future researchers may be interested in expanding this work to explore whether preferred modes of communication vary according to context as well as the perceived risk levels identified in this study.

Regardless of the context, though, psychologists should avoid dogmatic and definitive statements and should specify the conditions under which the behavior is likely to occur. The consistency of human behavior varies across situations; a person may display highly aggressive behavior in one context but be very docile in others. Most domestic abusers, for example, do not display in their workplaces or in their social situations the violent behavior they display in the home. Finally, when possible, psychologists should offer proscriptive measures that might be taken to avert the violence. This may include strategies to help the individual avoid situations that have led to problem behavior, such as staying away from bars or stores selling pornographic materials. In addition, as Heilbrun et al. (2002) note, "Monitoring has been empirically demonstrated to lower an individual's risk for engaging in violent or antisocial behavior" (p. 462). The forensic psychologist offering a risk assessment may recommend that the individual be kept under close supervision in the community.

Risk Assessment Instruments

A variety of instruments are available to psychologists engaged in the risk assessment enterprise (see Box 10.5 in the following chapter). These tests often are based on actuarial or statistical data, rather than clinical impressions. They are designed by gathering information on a large group of individuals within a target population (e.g., paroled offenders or patients in a mental institution). On the basis of data from that group, the researcher identifies key variables (predictor variables) that are associated with the behavior of concern (e.g., violence). People are then rated on the number of these variables they have in their present lives or backgrounds. An individual with a score below the cutoff for a particular risk assessment instrument would be judged as being at a high risk of offending. Although the empirical literature has consistently supported the superiority of **actuarial data** over clinical data in predictions of human behavior, some forensic psychologists are not comfortable with the use of risk assessments to the exclusion of clinical factors. Heilbrun et al. (2002, p. 478) summarize their concerns as follows. Actuarial instruments, they say,

- focus on a small number of factors and may ignore important factors that are idiosyncratic to the case at hand (e.g., recent legal or medical problems);

- are passive predictors, focusing primarily on relatively static variables, such as demographics and criminal history;
- may include risk factors that are unacceptable on legal grounds, such as race or sex, and may ignore risk factors that have unknown validity but are logical to consider (such as threats of violence);
- have been developed to predict a specific outcome over a specific period of time in a specific population, and they may not generalize to other contexts;
- have a restricted definition of violence risk and cannot address the nature of the violence, its duration, its severity or frequency, or how soon it may occur.

Heilbrun et al. (2002) add that clinicians themselves—unless they are sufficiently schooled in psychometric theory—may tend to overuse or underuse the actuarial instruments. Although acknowledging the value of risk assessment instruments, they also caution forensic psychologists not to undermine the role of clinical judgment in their assessments of risk. Nevertheless, "the problem with the judgment-based approaches is that they are inherently speculative" (p. 478).

Others have noted (e.g., Doren, 2002) that clinical examiners often adjust the scores on risk assessment instruments upward or downward to incorporate data that might not be covered by the instrument. As an example, a psychologist might increase the risk level if the individual has experienced a recent, highly stressful event that the psychologist believes might affect his or her judgment and lead this person to be aggressive or violent. Campbell (2003) observes—based on the research in this area—that upward or downward adjustments do not improve the quality of the prediction. We will discuss risk assessment again in Chapter 10. For the time being, it is important to be aware that neither risk assessment instruments nor clinical judgment are perfect predictors of human behavior.

The clinical-actuarial debate also extends to the issue of which type of testimony is preferred by judges and juries. It is often reported in the literature that courts are more favorably disposed to information that comes from clinical data than from actuarial or statistical data (e.g., Krauss & Sales, 2001; Melton et al., 1997). Studies with mock jurors—a common approach in jury research—also indicate that jurors underuse or misunderstand statistical data (Cunningham & Reidy, 1999; Smith, Penrod, Otto, & Park, 1996). However, the *actual effect* of expert testimony (regardless of the form) on jury verdicts is assumed rather than documented, and as we noted earlier in the chapter, some research suggests it may not be that significant (Nietzel et al., 1999). In addition, a study involving risk assessment with sexually violent predators indicated that jurors did not value one form of testimony (clinical or actuarial) over the other (Guy & Edens, 2003).

Summary and Conclusions

The main purpose of this chapter has been to introduce the structure and process in criminal and civil courts along with some of the specific tasks performed by forensic psychologists in those settings. After reviewing court structure and discussing basic concepts relating to criminal and civil cases, we provided illustrations of the work psychologists do at each of the major stages of the court process. In the next two chapters, these court-related tasks will be described in greater detail.

A major undertaking for forensic psychologists is to serve as expert witnesses in both criminal and civil courts. It is now clear that all experts—from the physical, behavioral, and social sciences, as well as those representing medicine, law, and business—fall under the mantle of science identified in the *Daubert* case, at least in federal courts. Courts in most states also have adopted *Daubert* or highly similar standards as well. We discussed the reliability and relevance requirements associated with that case and some of the research on its effect. It appears that, since

Daubert, many judges are scrutinizing and rejecting expert testimony more than before. Although there are concerns that *Daubert* will allow more "junk science" to be admitted into courts, the evidence thus far does not indicate that this is happening. It is also not clear how much "good science" is rejected because judges are unable to evaluate it properly. More research addressing how well judges are performing their gatekeeper function is needed before conclusions can be reached on this issue.

The present chapter also covers issues that cause some psychologists to pause before agreeing to participate in court proceedings. Some psychologists are not comfortable divulging information that in other contexts would be confidential, even though they are allowed (and sometimes required) to do so by the law. When psychologists are asked to conduct an evaluation, the client is often not the individual being evaluated but the court. In that case, copies of the psychologist's report are sent to court as well as to attorneys on both sides of the case.

The patient-therapist relationship is different from the relationship between the examiner and the person being evaluated. Courts have respected patient-therapist confidentiality, but even that may give way in certain situations when balanced against other interests. In many jurisdictions, for example, therapists have a duty to warn or to protect when their clients have made serious physical threats against an identified third party. The patient-therapist privilege also gives way when a patient sues a therapist.

Some forensic psychologists also resist being pressed for an opinion on legal matters or being subjected to grueling cross-examination by an opposing lawyer. Yet each of these is a routine occurrence in courtroom appearances. Judges often want to know the psychologist's conclusion as to whether an individual is competent to stand trial, whether someone is insane, or who would be the better of two parents. Technically, these are legal issues—the "ultimate" issues to be decided by the court, not the psychologist. Although some forensic psychologists are willing to express these opinions, others find them out of their purview.

The communication of risk is another area that presents ethical concerns to many psychologists. Many psychologists today prefer to engage in the enterprise of "risk assessment" rather than the "prediction of dangerousness." Given the fallibility of predictions of dangerous behavior, it is important that the legal system refrain from pressing psychologists for definitive answers as to whether a given individual "will" be violent, although we are optimistic that the great majority of psychologists would resist such pressure. In assessing risk, many psychologists provide the courts with probabilities that a given individual will engage in antisocial behavior, or indicate the level of risk, and they are careful to note the limitations of their data. In addition, research indicates that mental health practitioners also try to offer strategies for managing the risk whenever possible. The communication of risk also may be based on clinical findings, such as deductions made from information obtained in a clinical interview or on the basis of performance on personality or projective tests. Many forensic psychologists today incorporate both clinical and actuarial data in their reports and in their testimony. The themes introduced in this chapter will be developed in the following two, where we describe in greater detail the contributions made to both criminal and civil courts.

CHAPTER 10

Consulting With Criminal Courts

Charles Sell, once a practicing dentist, was charged with multiple counts of fraud. Sell had a history of mental illness that included an incident in which he called police to report a leopard boarding a bus. After a psychiatric evaluation, Sell was found competent to stand trial. In an initial appearance, Sell was out of control, used personal insults, and spat in the judge's face. He was examined again for competence and ruled incompetent. Staff at the federal medical center where he was held recommended that he take psychoactive medication, but Sell refused.

Andrea Yates drowned her children in a bathtub in 2001. Mental health professionals who examined her reported that she had a history of mental illness, including severe postpartum psychosis. Yates was found competent to stand trial and was then tried for murder. She pled not guilty by reason of insanity, but a jury did not find her insane and convicted her in the deaths of her children. She is now serving her sentence in a Texas prison.

Albert Crowel was convicted of his third driving-while-intoxicated offense. At the time of the incident, he was driving with a suspended license. He had a 6-year history of substance abuse but had never received treatment for this problem. He also had been convicted of domestic assault, for which he had served a 2-year prison term. In prison, he had participated in a program for violent offenders and had been a model prisoner. At his sentencing hearing, the defense lawyer called to the stand a forensic psychologist who had examined Crowel and concluded that he would be a good candidate for a substance abuse program that was available in the community, on an outpatient basis. The psychologist also reported that he was a very low risk of further violence.

The above three scenarios, reporting on actual court cases, illustrate some of the most common **forensic mental health assessments (FMHAs)** conducted by psychologists and psychiatrists consulting with criminal courts. By far, the most frequent is the assessment of competency to stand trial, also called adjudicative competence. It is estimated that some 60,000 criminal defendants are evaluated for this purpose every year (Bonnie & Grisso, 2000). Sanity evaluations—also called criminal responsibility (CR) or mental state at the time of the offense

(MSO) evaluations—are less frequent, although they are often combined with evaluations of competency to stand trial. Likewise, psychological and psychiatric input is the exception, rather than the rule, at sentencing, although it often does occur, particularly when a death sentence is a possibility.

The chapter will be devoted primarily to these three areas: competency, insanity, and sentencing. Throughout the chapter, we will be referring to the forensic psychologist, but it is important to remind readers that forensic examiners are often psychiatrists and psychiatric social workers as well. In addition, we will cover the controversy surrounding the civil commitment of sexual predators after they have served their criminal sentences, a topic that reminds us of the interrelationship between criminal and civil courts. It should be noted that an important service provided by forensic psychologists—the assessment of victims of crime—was covered in Chapters 7 and 8. Before beginning with the main material, though, we will discuss a less traveled area, the bail denial process.

Preventive Detention

Because criminal defendants are considered to be innocent until proven guilty in a court of law, there is a presumption that they will be free pending their trial or the final resolution of their case. At their initial appearance or their arraignment, the law allows judges and magistrates to set bail to ensure that the defendant will return to court for the next scheduled hearing in the case. Research has consistently shown that the great majority of defendants who are released on bail do return to court (Neubauer, 2002).

The U.S. Constitution does not guarantee a right to bail; it only specifies that the bail must not be excessive (*U.S. v. Salerno,* 1987). Thus, some defendants are denied bail on the basis of their dangerousness. In most jurisdictions, if an individual is charged with a capital crime (one that carries a possible life sentence or a sentence

of death), dangerousness is presumed and bail is usually (but not invariably) denied. However, for a number of violent crimes that are not capital crimes, prosecutors also may ask the judge to deny bail. A request like this is not unusual in domestic violence situations, such as when a woman expresses intense fear that the person who allegedly assaulted her will be released prior to trial. In these cases, defendants are entitled to a hearing on the issue of their dangerousness before the presiding judge can deny bail. At the hearing, the prosecutor presents evidence of the defendant's dangerousness, and the defense lawyer refutes that evidence by cross-examining the prosecution's witnesses and presenting evidence and witnesses in the defendant's favor.

Forensic psychologists, then, may be asked to "predict the dangerousness" of the defendant charged with the violent crime. As we noted in the previous chapter, the preferred term in the psychological literature is *risk assessment.* In addition to conducting such an assessment and filing a written report, the psychologist may be called to testify during the bail hearing. Risk assessments conducted for bail decision-making purposes are very similar to risk assessments conducted for other release decisions in the criminal justice process. For example, at sentencing, judges often must decide whether to place an offender on probation or send him or her to prison. A risk assessment may also occur when an imprisoned offender has become eligible for parole or early release. Because sentencing will be discussed later in the chapter, we will defer the discussion of risk assessment until that point.

Criminal Competencies

We began this chapter with an illustration of competency to stand trial. It should be noted, however, that although courts and statutes continue to use the term *competency to stand trial,* the psychological research literature is increasingly replacing the term with *adjudicative competence* (e.g., Mumley, Tillbrook, & Grisso, 2003;

Nicholson & Norwood, 2000). This is in response to the theory proposed by Richard Bonnie (1992), who suggests that competency to stand trial must involve both "competency to proceed" and "decisional competency." As Bonnie has stated, courts thus far have focused almost exclusively on the competence to proceed without thoroughly taking into account the complex decisional abilities that are required of defendants in a wide variety of contexts. Bonnie and others (e.g., Mumley et al., 2003) urge psychologists evaluating defendants to consider these abilities very carefully. Thus, the term **adjudicative competence** is increasingly being used in the literature to recognize Bonnie's important contribution (Mumley et al., 2003).

The term *adjudicative competence* also is broad enough to subsume a wide range of abilities defendants are expected to possess. For example, if defendants waive their rights to lawyers, the law says they must be competent to do so. If they plead guilty to a crime—and thereby waive their right to a jury trial with all of the due process protections that a trial entails—they must be competent to do so. It is estimated that 90% of criminal defendants plead guilty rather than going to trial.

Criminal defendants have much to lose in the face of criminal prosecution (e.g., their freedom and sometimes their lives). Therefore, the law guarantees them a number of due process protections, including the right to a lawyer during custodial interrogation, the right to a lawyer at every critical state of the criminal proceedings, and the right to a jury trial in most felony and some misdemeanor cases. Again, if they waive these rights, they are supposed to be competent to do so. The courts have determined that a waiver of constitutional rights must be knowing, intelligent, and valid.

Legal Standard for Competency

Due process also requires that defendants not be tried if they do not have a sufficient present ability to help their attorneys and a rational and functional understanding of the proceedings against them. This is the two-pronged standard for competency to stand trial that was announced by the U.S. Supreme Court in the 1960 case *Dusky v. U.S.* and has been adopted in most states. However, many clinicians have pointed out that the law does not give enough attention to the *level* of competency required in a particular case (e.g., Brakel, 2003; Roesch, Zapf, Golding, & Skeem, 1999). That is, a defendant might meet the standard for competency if charged with retail theft in a straightforward case. The same defendant, charged with manslaughter and facing what is expected to be a protracted trial, might not meet the standard.

The Supreme Court has ruled (*Godinez v. Moran*, 1993) that the *Dusky* standards apply to guilty pleas as well; that is, defendants pleading guilty must have a rational understanding of the court process. Again, some mental health professionals believe that this "one size fits all" approach leaves much to be desired. Guilty pleas, they argue, should be scrutinized very carefully because of their implications. The waiver of a number of constitutional rights that a guilty plea entails requires decisional competence that many defendants simply do not have.

It is not altogether clear whether the unitary standard announced in the *Moran* case applies to proceedings before arraignment or after the verdict (Perlin, 2003). Waivers—and the question of competency—can occur during the police interrogation stage, while police are conducting searches, during lineups, at a sentencing hearing, at a hearing on the revocation of probation or parole, or during the appeals process, for example. The Supreme Court's opinion did not touch on these, although the concurring opinion of Justice Kennedy suggested that the *Godinez* rule might possibly not apply in these pretrial and after-verdict situations (Perlin, 2003).

In some criminal cases, defendants choose to waive the right to an attorney and to represent themselves. Alternately, some defendants choose to ignore the advice of their attorneys and proceed with a defense that the attorney believes is not in their best interest. Two high-profile criminal cases in the 1990s led many scholars to question the wisdom of allowing criminal defendants who were presumably mentally disordered to take each of these approaches (e.g., Litwack, 2003; Slobogin & Mashburn, 2000). Theodore Kaczynski (the Unabomber) was an apparently delusional defendant who rejected the advice of his attorney to plead not guilty by reason of insanity. He subsequently pleaded guilty and avoided a death sentence. Colin Ferguson, who opened fire on a Long Island commuter train, killed six people, and injured many others, was allowed to waive his right to a lawyer and represent himself during his trial.

Many scholars and observers believe that the trial of Colin Ferguson was an embarrassment to our system of justice (Perlin, 1996). Some argue that he was not competent to stand trial; others argue that he was competent to stand trial but not competent to defend himself. Ferguson was evaluated by two psychologists who found him educated and articulate but suffering from paranoid personality disorder (Slobogin & Mashburn, 2000). Nevertheless, they believed he was competent to stand trial under the *Dusky* standard, and the judge agreed. Ferguson rejected the advice of his attorney that he plead not guilty by reason of insanity, insisted on defending himself, and was allowed to do so.

"Ferguson proceeded to represent himself in a fashion that observers unanimously considered bizarre" (Slobogin & Mashburn, 2000, p. 1608). During the trial, he made rambling statements, proposed conspiracy theories, and tried to call President Clinton as a witness. Critics of that trial process (e.g., Perlin, 1996; Slobogin & Mashburn, 2000) believe he was not competent to reject an insanity defense and should not have been allowed to represent himself, although others disagree (e.g., Litwack, 2003). Ferguson is presently incarcerated in the New York prison system, serving life sentences.

The Byron Keith Cooper case provides another sobering illustration (*Cooper v. Oklahoma*, 1996). Cooper was originally ruled incompetent to stand trial (IST), was treated in a mental institution for 3 months, and then was found competent. His behavior during the competency hearing and the trial was bizarre at best. He refused to wear civilian clothes during his trial, claiming that these clothes were burning him, so he wore prison overalls. He crouched in a fetal position and talked to himself during much of the trial. However, the state of Oklahoma required **clear and convincing proof** of a defendant's incompetence, and the judge in the case concluded that Cooper had not met that burden (see Box 10.1 for a review of burdens of proof).

BOX 10.1 Burdens of Proof

In adversary proceedings, the final legal decision requires that proof be established at a specified level.

Beyond a Reasonable Doubt

This is the standard of proof required in all criminal proceedings as well as delinquency proceedings when a juvenile is charged with a crime. It is proof that is just short of absolute certainty. "In evidence means fully satisfied, entirely convinced, satisfied to a moral certainty" (H. C. Black, 1990).

Clear and Convincing Proof

This is the standard required in some civil proceedings, such as when the state wishes to commit an individual to a mental hospital against his or her will. It is an intermediate standard, resulting in

(Continued)

BOX 10.1 (Continued)

"reasonable certainty of the truth of the ultimate fact in controversy. . . . Clear and convincing proof will be shown where the truth of the facts asserted is highly probable" (H. C. Black, 1990).

Preponderance of the Evidence

This is proof that one side has more evidence in its favor than the other. It is "evidence which is of greater weight or more convincing than the evidence which is offered in opposition to it; that is, evidence which as a whole shows that the fact sought to be proved is more probable than not" (H. C. Black, 1990). It is the standard required in most civil suits and may be relevant to criminal proceedings as well. For example, when states require criminal defendants to prove they are incompetent to stand trial, they cannot require this by a standard more demanding than the preponderance of the evidence.

The Supreme Court ruled that states could require defendants to prove their incompetence by a **preponderance of the evidence** but no more than that.

Questions about a defendant's adjudicative competence can arise at many different stages of the criminal process. In Bryan Cooper's case, questions were raised five different times, the last time at his sentencing hearing. In the Sell case that highlighted the opening of this chapter, Sell was originally evaluated, found competent, then evaluated again and found incompetent. In addition, an unknown number of criminal defendants are reevaluated over a period of years because they are charged with additional crimes. In virtually every state, certain defendants charged with misdemeanors or lesser felonies are well known to both the judicial system and the mental health system. They continually appear before the court, are sent for competency evaluation, are found incompetent (or competent), are hospitalized (or not), have charges dropped (or plead guilty), spend time on probation (or in jail), and go forth into the community until their next criminal charge. The mental health courts described in Chapter 9 are intended to prevent the perpetuation of this revolving door process by diverting nonviolent mentally disordered individuals from the criminal process and providing community supervision and meaningful treatment.

Evaluating Adjudicative Competence

Forensic psychologists may evaluate defendants for adjudicative competence in a number of different settings. For example, a brief competency screening may be carried out very early in criminal processing while the defendant is being held in jail. Defendants also may be evaluated in the community, on an outpatient basis, while on pretrial release. Although such outpatient evaluations are on the increase (Roesch et al., 1999), many defendants are evaluated while hospitalized in a public mental facility. In fact, most states either permit or require hospitalization for both the evaluation of competence and the treatment to restore competence (Miller, 2003). Outpatient *evaluation* is far more common than outpatient *treatment*, however.

It should be noted that the persons referred for competency evaluations tend to be those with a past history or presenting signs of mental disorders. The typical evaluation is conducted when defendants are deemed mentally disordered, such as schizophrenic or psychotic (Mumley et al.,

2003). Therefore, competency evaluations often are prompted by a defendant's past history of psychiatric care, institutionalization, bizarre behavior at arrest, or attempt to commit suicide while held in detention. On the other hand, mental retardation, emotional distress, or even advancing age might lead to questions about a defendant's competence. For example, a defendant charged with vehicular homicide might be so distraught over the incident that she is unable to meet the standard for adjudicative competence. In such situations, the individual is less likely to require hospitalization during the evaluation process.

The request for an evaluation may come directly from the defense attorney or from the court. It is important for psychologists to note the difference. When the defense requests and pays for the evaluation, the client is the person being examined and the report goes to his or her representative, the defense attorney. Depending on the evaluation's results, the attorney may or may not share the report with the prosecutor. When the evaluation is court ordered, even if ordered at the request of the defense attorney, the client is the court. Motions for court-ordered examinations may be made by the defense attorney (whose client is unable to pay for a private evaluation), the prosecutor, or the judge. The examiner should expect that the report of a court-ordered evaluation will be shared among all parties.

Research indicates that most competency evaluations are court ordered and that no more than one evaluation is performed (Melton et al., 1997). In other words, "competing" evaluations are not the norm. Furthermore, judges almost always accept the recommendation of clinicians conducting the evaluation (Cruise & Rogers, 1998; Melton et al., 1997). Some researchers report agreement rates well over 90% (Cruise & Rogers, 1998; Zapf, Hubbard, Galloway, Cox, & Ronan, 2002). In at least this pretrial context, therefore, clinicians seem to have considerable influence on the courts. However, competency evaluations, like many other forensic mental health assessments, raise the "ultimate issue" question discussed in Chapter 9. Competency is a legal issue, not a clinical issue, and there continues to be debate over whether a psychologist should express an opinion as to whether the defendant is competent to stand trial.

As in all forensic mental health evaluations, the assessment of adjudicative competence should begin with a notice to the person being evaluated of the limits of confidentiality and the purpose of the evaluation (see Box 10.2 for a list of factors common to all evaluations). As noted above, unless the psychologist is hired directly by the defense attorney for an appraisal of his or her client's competency and general mental status,

---

BOX 10.2 Common Aspects of FMHAs

Although forensic mental health assessments (FMHAs) are conducted for a wide variety of reasons, they have at least the following features in common:

- Before meeting with the person being assessed, the examiner should

  Understand the purpose of the referral

  Decline to conduct the evaluation if there is a conflict of interest or if the examiner has ethical or moral objections to participating

  Gather background information and records when available

(Continued)

BOX 10.2 (Continued)

Be knowledgeable about the law relative to the assessment

Clarify and agree on the time and method of payment

Clarify when a report is needed and to whom it should be submitted

- Before conducting the evaluation, the examiner should

Explain its purpose to the person being evaluated

Stress that this is not a treatment relationship

Explain the limits to confidentiality

Warn the examinee of the possible uses of the examination

Tell the examinee who will be getting copies of the report

Obtain the examinee's written consent, if consent is needed

- The examiner's written report should

Be clearly written and free of slang or excessive "jargon"

Be submitted within a reasonable time after the evaluation has been completed

State the purpose of the report, identify the legal issues, and who requested the report

Specify documents reviewed and any tests/inventories that were administered

State clearly the basis for any conclusions reached

Be submitted with an awareness that a variety of individuals will see the report

---

the competency report will be shared among the attorneys and the presiding judge. For this reason, examiners are often reminded to carefully limit the report to the defendant's present status and not include information that might provide details about the crime itself (Grisso, 1988; Roesch et al., 1999).

Examiners are also warned about avoiding the **dual relationship** of evaluator and treatment provider. In fact, both ethical standards and specialty guidelines frown upon this for a number of reasons (see Box 10.3). If a psychologist has been seeing the defendant in a therapist-patient relationship or has any other prior relationship with the defendant, the psychologist should not examine the defendant for adjudicative competence.

The examination process itself varies widely according to the examiner's training and theoretical orientation. As Cruise and Rogers (1998) stated, "There is no clear consensus on a standard of practice for competency evaluations" (p. 44). Some examiners conduct only a clinical interview, whereas others conduct an interview and administer a variety of projective and/or objective tests. Other examiners file a generic report that includes behavioral observations of the defendant and extensive background information.

BOX 10.3 Avoiding Multiple Relationships

Standard 3.05 of the Ethical Principles of Psychologists and Code of Conduct (APA, 2002) warns psychologists to avoid engaging in multiple relationships. These relationships can occur, for example, "when a psychologist is in a professional role with a person and (1) at the same time is in another role with the same person." Thus, when a psychologist takes on two different roles in a single case, such as the role of evaluator and the role of therapist, this is an example of a multiple relationship. Multiple relationships also extend to relationships with persons who are closely related to the person with whom the psychologist has a professional relationship.

Standard 3.05 indicates, though, that not all multiple relationships are unethical:

A psychologist refrains from entering into a multiple relationship *if the multiple relationship could reasonably be expected to impair the psychologist's objectivity, competence, or effectiveness in performing his or her functions as a psychologist, or otherwise risks exploitation or harm to the person with whom the professional relationship exists.* (Emphasis added)

Thus, the individual practitioner must exercise his or her judgment regarding whether the multiple relationship will harm the individual. Some clinicians strongly believe that forensic assessments should not be conducted if the psychologist has *any* prior contact with key parties in a case (e.g., in a criminal case, a defendant, a victim, or their relatives). Less objectionable but still questionable is the assessment of an individual who might eventually become a client. For example, some believe a clinician should not conduct an assessment of an offender's amenability to sex offender treatment if the clinician will likely be asked to provide that treatment. However, this may be very impractical in communities where a range of treatment providers does not exist.

Heilbrun et al. (2002, pp. 387–388) summarize problems associated with child custody evaluations when there was a prior treatment relationship with one or more family members. These problems could apply to any other context in which the examiner takes on the dual role of treatment provider and evaluator:

- Because of existing preconceptions, the evaluator's impartiality is reduced.
- Serving as an evaluator will interfere with subsequent treatment effectiveness.
- The clinician will have to change from a supportive and empathic treatment role to an impartial and skeptical evaluator role.
- The person evaluated would have to revise his or her understanding of the nature of the service provided by the clinician and the limits of confidentiality.
- Because of the treatment relationship, the person evaluated may feel betrayed if the clinician's recommendation is unfavorable.

Traditionally, competency evaluations tended to include a good deal of information that was irrelevant to the issue of whether the defendant was competent to stand trial (Grisso, 1988). In recent years, with more guidance provided to clinicians, misconceptions about competency evaluations have lessened, and reports have improved in quality (Roesch et al., 1999).

Competency Assessment Instruments

Over the past 20 years, researchers have developed and attempted to validate a variety of instruments for the assessment of competency to stand trial. Some are screening instruments generally taking under 30 minutes to administer, whereas others are more elaborate instruments based on both interviewing and test administration. Also available is a computer-assisted tool—the CADCOMP (Computer-Assisted Competence Assessment Tool)—that is heavily based on the defendant's self-reports of his or her background, legal knowledge, and behaviors (Barnard et al., 1991). Zapf and Viljoen (2003) have provided a recent review of these assessment instruments. Although we do not provide a comprehensive review here, we will discuss a few for illustrative purposes.

The **Competency Screening Test** (Laboratory of Community Psychiatry, 1974) is a sentence completion test that is intended to provide a quick assessment of a defendant's competency to stand trial. The test taps the defendant's knowledge about the role of the lawyer and the rudiments of the court process. For example, defendants are asked to complete the following: "When a jury hears my case, they will. . . ." If defendants score below a certain level, they are evaluated more completely. The test's main advantage is the ability to screen out quickly the obviously competent defendants. According to Roesch et al. (1999), the test has a high false-positive rate (53.3%), identifying many competent defendants as incompetent. Because persons so identified in a screening test are likely to be hospitalized for further evaluation, this presents a significant deprivation of liberty for the defendant who would otherwise be free on bail. On the other hand, some defendants unable to post bail might prefer the security of a hospital to the chaos and crowded conditions of some jails. Nevertheless, hospitalization is no bargain.

The **Georgia Court Competency Test** (GCCT) and its Minnesota State Hospital revisions (GCCT-MSH) have received mixed reviews. These are short tests—17 and 21 items, respectively—that some examiners prefer to use primarily as a screening mechanism. The GCCT apparently has good internal consistency and interrater reliability, and it has a promising screen for malingering or feigning incompetence (Gothard, Rogers, & Sewell, 1995). However, it has been criticized for its lack of addressing decisional competency (Zapf & Viljoen, 2003).

The MacArthur Foundation Research Network on Mental Health and the Law initially developed the MacArthur Structured Assessment of the Competencies of Criminal Defendants (MacSAC-CD) (Hoge et al., 1997). This was a rather cumbersome research tool that led to a shorter instrument, the **MacArthur Competency Assessment Tool—Criminal Adjudication (MacCAT-CA)**, containing 22 items. Defendants are provided with a vignette describing a situation in which a person is charged with a crime. They are also asked questions about their own situation. Although fairly new, the MacCAT-CA has received good reviews as being superior to other assessment instruments (Cruise & Rogers, 1998; Zapf & Viljoen, 2003). The late Robert Nicholson (1999) believed that it represented "a major contribution to the assessment of adjudicative competence" (p. 150).

Despite the continuing development of forensic assessment instruments, they do not appear to be widely used in forensic practice. A study by Borum and Grisso (1995) indicated that 36% of psychologists in their sample never use such forensic assessment instruments, whereas 40% use them almost always or frequently. Competency assessment instruments are used more frequently than instruments to assess criminal responsibility at the time of offense (insanity), however.

Assessment of Malingering

Virtually every type of forensic mental health assessment requires some appraisal of possible **malingering** (or faking) on the part of the person being evaluated. For a variety of reasons, criminal defendants may pretend they have symptoms of a serious disorder when they actually do not. Rogers (1997) has described malingering as a response style in which the individual consciously fabricates or grossly exaggerates his or her symptoms. He observes that this is understandable in the light of the individual's situation. The obvious example is the offender who pretends to be mentally ill, believing that the judge is less likely to sentence him to prison. In the competency context, a defendant may pretend to have symptoms of a mental disorder to postpone the trial or avoid going to trial altogether. Although we discuss malingering in this chapter, it should not be assumed that this problem is limited to the criminal context. As we will note in Chapter 11, individuals being assessed in civil cases may be equally motivated to feign symptoms.

Forensic psychologists have at their disposal a variety of validated tests for detecting malingering. The Structured Interview of Reported Symptoms (Rogers, 1992) is a well-regarded instrument for detecting the malingering of psychotic symptoms. Another example is the Test of Memory Malingering (Tombaugh, 1997). In addition, some commonly used psychological tests, such as the Minnesota Multiphasic Personality Inventory (MMPI-2) and the Millon Clinical Multiaxial Inventory—III (Millon, 1994), as well as some forensic assessment instruments (e.g., the **Rogers Criminal Responsibility Assessment Scales [R-CRAS]**), also have power to detect malingering. There is, though, no foolproof way to detect malingering (Butcher & Miller, 1999). As Heilbrun et al. (2002) note, it is important for the clinician to use multiple measures rather than one or two tests to assess this.

Restoration to Competence

Research indicates that approximately 15% to 20% of defendants referred for competency evaluations are ultimately found incompetent. Persons found incompetent tend to be those with a history of institutional treatment and/or diagnosis of a serious mental disorder. Research also suggests that a clinical diagnosis, when included in a competency evaluation report, is a strong predictor of a finding of incompetence (Cochrane, Grisso, & Frederick, 2001). Interestingly, forensic examiners are often advised not to include diagnoses in their reports (Golding & Roesch, 1987; Grisso, 1986). The diagnosis may not be accurate, and even if it is, it is subject to misinterpretation on the part of persons not trained as mental health practitioners.

The majority of persons found incompetent to stand trial are those suffering from schizophrenia and psychotic symptoms (Morse, 2003). Although mental disorder seems to be a requirement for most incompetency determinations, mental disorder itself—even serious mental disorder—is not sufficient. Recall the case of Andrea Yates mentioned at the beginning of the chapter. Once an individual has been found IST, efforts are made to restore the person to competence to bring him or her to trial. Clinicians typically are asked to make some assessment of the likelihood that an individual will be restored to competency. If restoration is highly unlikely, the state must decide whether to drop the criminal charges and, if necessary, initiate **involuntary civil commitment** proceedings. (These will be discussed in Chapter 11.)

Every state has its examples of defendants who were found incompetent to stand trial and who are held in institutions for seemingly very lengthy periods (see Box 10.4 for an example). The U.S. Supreme Court did place a limit on this practice, ruling in *Jackson v. Indiana* (1972) that incompetent defendants could not be held indefinitely if there was no likelihood that they would be restored. In most states, periodic hearings are held to assess an incompetent defendant's status; defendants are kept institutionalized as long as some progress is being made. Some states do not allow incompetent defendants to be held for longer than the maximum sentence they would have served had they been convicted. Research suggests that the average period for inpatient

---

BOX 10.4 When Restoration Fails

In 1991, L. O. (not the real initials) allegedly walked into an Eveready battery plant in a small city and opened fire, killing the plant supervisor and wounding two employees. Found incompetent to stand trial, she was hospitalized in a state mental institution for competency restoration.

Twelve years later, at age 41, she remains hospitalized in a security ward where, at times, she has been the only woman. Psychiatrists at the hospital have diagnosed her as a paranoid schizophrenic who is subject to hallucinations and delusions. She routinely refuses to participate in therapy sessions and to take medication prescribed by psychiatrists. However, she has apparently had medication administered against her will when she became agitated and threatened to kill those around her (Crabtree, 2003).

According to L. O., computer hackers are attempting to take control of the world. The primary culprits are two individuals she met in grade school who now control her thoughts and actions. "I know it sounds strange and bizarre, but so did cloning 20 years ago," she told the court during her most recent appearance. She periodically writes letters to her therapists, the media, politicians, the FBI, and the CIA to warn them of the conspiracy that she is convinced is afoot.

When it became apparent that there was no progress toward restoring L. O. to competency, the state dropped charges against her without prejudice, meaning that charges could be reintroduced if she were ever to regain competency. However, she remains institutionalized on the basis of her dangerousness to herself and others. Under state statutes, her involuntary commitment is subject to annual review.

In her latest court appearance, L. O. told the court she was not "crazy." According to a newspaper report of the hearing (Crabtree, 2003), she said that she was not now nor has ever been mentally ill. Rather, her mind has been controlled by the two above-mentioned childhood friends who are terrorists without "compassion or conscience" and who use an elaborate computer system to program her and other victims.

---

treatment is 6 months, but many defendants are held for much longer periods (Miller, 2003).

Restoration of competence need not be done in an institution. Like competency evaluations, treatment for incompetent defendants can be provided in community settings. In fact, many legal commentators as well as clinical practitioners believe that outpatient treatment rather than institutionalization should be made available to more defendants found IST (Miller, 2003; Roesch et al., 1999). R. D. Miller (2003) surveyed mental health program directors across the United States and found that, though outpatient *evaluation* was on the increase, outpatient *treatment* to restore competence was rare. "Despite the availability of outpatient treatment, few states utilize it very often" (Miller, 2003, p. 384).

Eighteen states *required* the hospitalization of incompetent defendants and 21 *permitted* it, but without specific criteria for doing so. In 5 states, incompetent defendants had to meet civil commitment criteria before they could be hospitalized. In 21 states, there were no effective time limits on hospitalization, whereas in 11 states, the limit was between 1 and 5 years.

R. D. Miller (2003) notes that the length of stay for forensic patients—such as those found incompetent to stand trial or not guilty by reason of insanity—is measured in months or years, but the length of stay for nonforensic civil patients is measured in days or weeks. Thus, although most states have made significant progress in "de-institutionalizing" those with mental disorders, the liberty interests of forensic populations remain unacknowledged. Although conceding that some defendants clearly need hospitalization for both evaluation and—if found incompetent—for treatment, Miller notes that hospitalization is overused. "For defendants who have demonstrated their ability to remain safely in the community before determination of their competence, there is little justification for hospitalization" (Miller, 2003, p. 386).

According to Roesch et al. (1999), "The disposition of incompetent defendants is perhaps the most problematic area of the competency procedures" (p. 333). Many researchers have observed that, although **restoration to competency** is the intent, IST defendants are rarely treated differently than other hospitalized populations (Siegel & Elwork, 1990). For the IST defendant, however, restoration should focus not only on his or her decisional capacities but also on his or her understanding of the criminal process. In other words, depending on the defendant's individual situation, restoration may require education about the legal system. To illustrate, we will use the example of a defendant who is mentally retarded and has been found incompetent to stand trial.

In recent years, much attention has been given to the plight of individuals with mental retardation who are arrested and processed by the criminal justice system. Mental retardation does not guarantee that an individual will not be held responsible for a crime; indeed, prisons and jails in the United States are believed to hold a substantial number of convicted offenders with this mental disability. However, when individuals with mental retardation are found incompetent to stand trial, restoration is unlikely to occur because mental retardation is a chronic condition. Anderson and Hewitt (2002) reported on an education program in Missouri that specifically addressed the restoration needs of defendants with mental retardation. The program consisted of a series of classes in which defendants learned about the legal system and participated in role-playing activities. The competency training had very little success, with only one

third of all defendants restored to competency. The defendant's IQ contributed to the outcome, but the IQ score was just short of reaching statistical significance. According to the researchers, "Persons with certain levels of MR [mental retardation] may inherently lack the skills needed to actively participate in trial proceedings. Abilities such as abstract reasoning, decision-making, and so forth are not only difficult to teach but are extremely difficult to learn" (Anderson & Hewitt, 2002, p. 349). Once again, this speaks to the importance of mental health courts and their ability to divert some individuals from the criminal process.

Although states vary in their approaches to restoring competency, the most common means of doing this appears to be through medication (Roesch et al., 1999). Psychoactive drugs are widely administered in the efforts to restore competency. In fact, in the study mentioned above, Anderson and Hewitt (2002) noted that—before a special program was initiated—defendants with mental retardation had been treated with **psychoactive medication** just like other IST defendants. In recent years, the involuntary administration of these drugs has received considerable national attention. Both a high-profile case involving the alleged shooter of capitol police officers and the recently announced Supreme Court case *Sell v. U.S.* (2003) revolved around this issue.

Drugs and the Incompetent Defendant

Antipsychotic or psychoactive drugs have improved significantly in effectiveness, but they still may produce unwanted side effects, including nausea, headaches, loss of creativity, inability to express emotions, and lethargy in some individuals. As we noted at the beginning of this chapter, Charles Sell refused to take antipsychotic medication that was intended to make him competent to stand trial. (Sell had previously taken antipsychotic medication during an earlier period of hospitalization.) Sell's case proceeded through a number of administrative and court hearings. Staff at the federal medical facility, as well as a federal magistrate, determined that Sell was dangerous to others and therefore required involuntary medication. Sell had apparently become infatuated with a nurse and had inappropriately accosted her, though had not physically harmed her. A district court judge and the 8th Circuit Court of Appeals both ordered the medication on different grounds. These courts did not consider him dangerous but did approve the forced medication to render him competent to stand trial.

In 2003, the U.S. Supreme Court sent the case back for further inquiry (*Sell v. U.S.*, 2003). According to the Justices, Sell's dangerousness had not been established, a fact that had been noted by the federal district court and the court of appeals. However, those lower courts had not sufficiently reviewed the possible trial-related risks and side effects of the medication. "Whether a particular drug will tend to sedate a defendant, interfere with communication with counsel, prevent rapid reaction to trial developments, or diminish the ability to express emotions are matters important in determining the permissibility of medication to restore competence," the Court said.

Sell's alleged crimes (Medicaid fraud, mail fraud, and money laundering) were not violent. The crimes allegedly committed by Rusty Weston, the shooting death of two capitol police officers and the wounding of two others in the summer of 1998, were. Like Sell, Weston had a history of mental disorder that included serious delusional symptoms. Like Sell, he was found incompetent to stand trial and, like Sell, resisted taking the medication that was intended to restore him to competence. He languished in federal detention for 3 years, unmedicated, while his lawyers argued before various courts that he should not be forced to take medication against his will. In July 2001, a federal court of appeals ruled that the government's strong interest in bringing this defendant to trial overrode his right to remain free of psychoactive drugs. The Supreme Court refused to hear the case, leaving the decision of the lower court standing.

Although some might wonder if the Court would rule differently today, in light of its decision in the *Sell* case, there are distinguishing features. Weston's alleged crime, the nature of his illness, and his past violent behavior all suggest that he is a probable threat to others. Furthermore, the crime of which he is charged—murder—is a capitol offense, one that the government has a strong interest in prosecuting. More important, though, the court in Weston's case carefully considered the side effects of the medication and was careful to note that heightened scrutiny was required before forcing medication on incompetent defendants.

The medication controversy extends to the trial process itself. Although defendants often respond well enough to medication to render them competent to stand trial, continual medication during the trial itself is often, if not invariably, warranted. In other words, to remain competent, the defendant must continue to be medicated. Yet the medication itself may affect the defendant's ability to participate in the proceedings, as the Supreme Court observed in the *Sell* case. Medication also creates an interesting conundrum for defendants who have raised an insanity defense. We will return to this issue below, after introducing the concept of insanity and its assessment.

Insanity

A person cannot be held responsible for a crime if he or she did not possess the "guilty mind" that is required at the time the criminal act was committed. The law recognizes a number of situations under which the guilty mind is absent. For example, if a person acts in self-defense, believing she or he is in imminent danger of grave bodily harm, that person will not be held responsible provided a judge or a jury agrees with her or his perceptions. Likewise, if a defendant charged with sexual assault can convince a judge or jury that the alleged victim consented to the sexual activity, he or she will not be held responsible. When it is mental disorder that robs the individual of a guilty mind, the law refers to this as **insanity.**

The distinction between insanity and competency to stand trial is crucial. Competency refers to one's mental state *at the time of the criminal justice proceedings* (e.g., waiving the right to a lawyer, pleading guilty, standing trial). Sanity (or criminal responsibility) refers to mental state *at the time of the crime.* It is possible for a person to be insane yet competent to stand trial or sane but incompetent. Obviously, it is also possible for people to be both insane and incompetent or sane and competent. Furthermore, in contrast to competency to stand trial, where the *Dusky* standard is universal, there is no uniform standard for determining insanity. Federal courts and state courts use a variety of "tests" for this purpose, a common one being knowledge of the difference between right and wrong. In some states, even if a person knows the difference between right and wrong, the evidence of an inability to conform his or her conduct to the requirements of the law will suffice. For example, in these states a person who— as the result of a mental disorder—is compelled by "voices" to kill his victim could be excused.

Over the past 20 years, changes in the federal law as well as the law in numerous states have made it more difficult for defendants pleading not guilty by reason of insanity to win acquittal. Ways in which this has been done include the following:

- The federal government and some states now no longer allow defendants to claim they could not control their behavior; if they knew the difference between right and wrong, they can still be held responsible.
- The federal government and most states now require defendants to prove their insanity by a preponderance of the evidence.
- A minority of states abolished the insanity defense.

- In federal courts and in some states, forensic examiners are not allowed to express an ultimate opinion on whether the defendant was insane.

Interestingly, research indicates that juries sitting on cases involving the insanity defense very rarely apply the tests for insanity, so changes in the tests may not be that significant. Rather, insanity cases appear to be decided more on moral grounds or on what jurors believe is the "right" outcome in a given situation. There are clearly exceptions, though. John Hinckley was tried in the attempted assassination of President Ronald Reagan and the shooting of his press secretary, Jim Brady, in 1980. The federal jury applied the federal standard that was in effect at that point in time, and it found Hinckley not guilty by reason of insanity.

It should be noted that cases in which defendants actually plead not guilty by reason of insanity are rare, comprising a mere 1% to 3% of all criminal cases (Golding et al., 1999). Furthermore, despite media publicity surrounding the insanity defense—one commentator (Perlin, 2003, p. 297) has referred to it as the "media darling"—the defense is usually not successful. Like Andrea Yates, most defendants who argue that they were not criminally responsible are found guilty.

The rates of acquittal vary widely by jurisdiction, though. Some multistate surveys have found acquittal rates of 20% to 25% (Cirincione, Steadman, & McGreevy, 1995). Although a "success" rate of one in four may surprise some observers, acquittal does not bring freedom to NGRI defendants. The defense may be used in both misdemeanor and felony cases, and it is sometimes used to obtain treatment for an individual who might not otherwise qualify for civil commitment. Consider the following example, based on facts from an actual case.

A person who is mentally disordered breaks into a home to obtain shelter for the night (breaking and entering). Because he is not a danger to himself or others, nor is he gravely disabled, he would not be eligible for involuntary hospitalization. Charged with a crime, though, he may be referred for a competency evaluation. The evaluation allows his hospitalization for at least a temporary period, which may be sufficient to stabilize his mental disorder. Returned to court, he is found competent, but his attorney wonders whether a defense of not guilty by reason of insanity could be supported. The defendant is returned to the hospital for another evaluation, which concludes that such a defense could indeed be supported. The prosecutor and defense attorney stipulate to the report (accept its findings), and the judge enters a not-guilty verdict. The acquitted individual then may be returned to the hospital for more treatment. Such "backdoor" commitments are believed to be common in many communities where community mental health services and resources for the mentally disordered are not available.

In approximately 12 states, an alternative verdict of **guilty but mentally ill** can be returned. This interesting but troubling verdict form allows judges and jurors a middle ground, supposedly reconciling their belief that the defendant "did it" with their belief that he or she "needs help." It makes little difference in the life of the person who obtains this verdict, however. Defendants found guilty but mentally ill are still sent to prison and are no more likely to receive specialized treatment for their disorder than other imprisoned offenders (Borum & Fulero, 1999; Bumby, 1993).

Assessment of Criminal Responsibility

The evaluation of a defendant's criminal responsibility at the time of the crime is widely recognized by clinicians as an extremely complex one. Note that it is, by definition, retrospective. The clinician must look back and attempt to gain some understanding of the defendant's state of mind at the crucial point in the past when the crime was committed. This may be weeks or even months after the event itself. According to

Golding et al. (1999), the clinician must determine whether and what sort of disturbances existed at the behavioral, volitional, and cognitive levels and clarify how those disturbances relate to the criminal act. Melton et al. (1997) have likened the clinician's role to that of an investigative reporter, who gathers information and documents from a wide variety of sources. Likewise, Shapiro (1999) notes that in addition to a clinical interview, the evaluator should obtain copies of police reports, hospital records, statements of witnesses, any past psychological tests, and employment records, if possible.

All of the cautions mentioned in our discussion of competency evaluations (and the principles in Box 10.2) apply here as well. One point on which clinicians seem to lack consensus, though, is the appropriateness of conducting **dual-purpose evaluations.** It is not unusual for clinicians to conduct evaluations of a defendant's competency to stand trial and criminal responsibility at the same time. In fact, statutes in many states encourage this practice. Judges will frequently order both a competency evaluation and a **criminal responsibility evaluation** "to see whether an insanity defense could be supported." In one study (Warren, Fitch, Dietz, & Rosenfeld, 1991), 47% of competency evaluations also addressed questions of sanity. Although this seems like an efficient and cost-saving practice, it poses problems, and some scholars have been extremely critical of the process (e.g., Roesch et al., 1999). They emphasize that competency and criminal responsibility are very separate issues requiring separate determinations. According to Roesch et al. (1999, p. 343), it is "cognitively almost impossible" for a judge to keep them distinct when the reports are combined. In addition, an evaluation of criminal responsibility is likely to include a good amount of background information that should be irrelevant to the limited question of whether the defendant is competent to stand trial.

Clinicians have access to forensic assessment instruments similar to those discussed in the competency evaluation process to help in their CR evaluations. By far, the most dominant one is the R-CRAS, developed by Richard Rogers (1984). Defendants are rated on a number of characteristics, including psychopathology, reliability of their report of the crime, organicity, cognitive control, and behavioral control. Rogers has used a quantitative approach and notes that the R-CRAS has been validated through a series of empirical studies (Rogers & Sewell, 1999; Rogers & Shuman, 1999).

The use of instruments for assessment of criminal responsibility may be on less solid ground than the use of instruments to assess competency (Grisso, 1996; Nicholson, 1999). Far more research has been conducted with competency assessment, and the *Dusky* standard has remained relatively stable through the years. As we noted earlier, the MacCAT-CA in particular shows promise as an instrument that will take competency assessment to a higher level. Thus far, with the exception of the R-CRAS, no comparable well-regarded instrument is available for sanity evaluations. In light of their complexity and the wide range of information that must be obtained in these assessments, however, development of additional instruments may not be warranted.

Insanity Trials

Once a defense attorney has received a clinician's report suggesting that an insanity defense could be supported, the attorney hopes for a verdict that his or her client is not guilty by reason of insanity. As in the competency context, this is a legal decision, not a clinical decision, and it is one that must be rendered by a judge or a jury. Research indicates that judges are far more sympathetic to the insanity defense than are juries, so a bench trial is more likely to result in a not-guilty verdict than a jury trial (Callahan, Steadman, McGreevy, & Robbins, 1991). Juries also have been found to have many negative attitudes toward, as well as misconceptions about, the insanity defense (Bailis, Darley, Waxman, & Robinson, 1995; Golding et al., 1999; Perlin, 1994).

The most difficult insanity cases are those in which defendants are charged with serious crimes and go to trial. A critical issue that has emerged in recent years pertains to the case of the medicated defendant. As we noted earlier, defendants found incompetent to stand trial are typically given psychoactive medications to restore them to competency. However, to maintain trial competency, defendants may need continued medication. Thus, during their trials, juries see them in a calm, often emotionless state that is far different from the mental state they claim they were in at the time of the crime. Recall that the Supreme Court expressed some concern about this in the *Sell* case. In an earlier case, the Court had ruled that defendants claiming an insanity defense have a right to be seen by a judge or jury in their natural, unmedicated state (*Riggins v. Nevada,* 1992).

Treatment of Defendants Found Not Guilty by Reason of Insanity

When a defendant is found not guilty by reason of insanity, he or she will rarely be free to go. All states and the federal government allow a period of civil commitment in a mental institution or, less frequently, on an outpatient basis. In practice, hospitalization is the most common outcome of a finding of not guilty by reason of insanity, and in practice, numerous individuals found NGRI are hospitalized for longer than the time they would have served had they been convicted (Golding et al., 1999).

Civil commitment cannot be automatic, however. A hearing must be held to document that the individual continues to be mentally disordered, in need of treatment, and a danger to self or others. Nor can commitment be indeterminate, without periodic reviews of the need for commitment. Most states require NGRI patients to prove they are no longer mentally ill and dangerous to be released. However, an individual cannot be held solely based on dangerousness if there is no longer evidence of mental illness (*Foucha v. Louisiana,* 1992). The exception may be the case of sexually violent predators, whom we will discuss later in the chapter.

Recall that persons found incompetent to stand trial are hospitalized with the goal of being restored to competence, so that the legal process may continue. Especially in serious cases, the state has a strong interest in bringing them to trial. In the case of persons found NGRI, the state cannot retry them—this would be an example of double jeopardy, which is in violation of the Constitution. Thus, if they are institutionalized, they receive treatment that is usually indistinguishable from the treatment received by other hospitalized patients. In recent years, some states have crafted programs that are particularly directed at persons found NGRI, both in forensic hospitals and in community settings. Furthermore, aware that many insanity acquittees have "significant lifelong psychopathological difficulties" (Golding et al., 1999, p. 397), some states discharge individuals on a conditional basis and provide follow-up and monitoring services in the community. We will discuss outpatient commitment for a variety of individuals in more detail in the following chapter.

Sentencing Evaluations

Criminal sentencing in the United States went through a period of "reform" during the last quarter of the 20th century. Until that time, sentencing was primarily indeterminate, with offenders being sent to prison for a range of years (e.g., 5 to 10). Indeterminate sentencing was based on a rehabilitative model of corrections; it was assumed that prisoners would be provided with rehabilitative services while in prison and that they would be released when they had made sufficient progress. Alternately, offenders could be placed on probation to serve their sentences in the community, but again with the assumption that rehabilitation would be offered. The psychologist or psychiatrist might be asked to evaluate the offender and offer a recommendation for treatment, which would then be forwarded to correctional officials.

Although rehabilitation remains an important consideration, it is no longer the dominant consideration in the sentencing schemes of the federal government or approximately 15 states today. These jurisdictions have adopted determinate sentencing, which attempts to make the punishment fit the crime and have an offender serve the sentence he or she supposedly deserves, regardless of individual characteristics and the extent to which rehabilitation is accomplished. The sentencing discretion provided to the judge in these states is usually quite limited; judges are usually provided with guidelines that take into consideration the seriousness of the crime and the individual's prior record in determining the appropriate sentence. Additional factors—such as the offender's age or the extent to which he or she might be a good candidate for a particular program—are not taken into account at sentencing. For this reason, the psychologist's role at recommending rehabilitation strategies has been diminished in these states.

In determinate sentencing states, though, courts may consider evidence of diminished mental capacity or extreme emotional distress and may reduce the sentence that would otherwise be imposed. In addition, psychologists may be called on to assess risk. In short, sentencing evaluations today may focus on treatment needs, the offender's culpability, or future dangerousness (Melton et al., 1997).

Regardless of whether the jurisdiction has determinate or indeterminate sentencing, the forensic psychologist might be called in to assess an offender's *competency* to be sentenced, however. There is very little literature on this as a separate competency assessment, and we have virtually no information on how often it occurs.

In those states where indeterminate sentencing is still in effect, the psychologist may still play a crucial role. The defense attorney is the legal practitioner who is most likely to contact the clinician. The attorney is attempting, in this context, to craft the best sentencing package for his or her client. Thus, a lawyer trying to keep his or her client in the community rather than imprisoned might offer to the court a report from a forensic psychologist suggesting that the client would likely benefit from substance abuse treatment, which is only intermittently available in the state prison system.

Risk Assessment

Clinicians are now being called in frequently to assess the offender's dangerousness to society. As we noted at the beginning of the chapter, such risk assessments may occur very early in the criminal justice process, when a decision is being made whether to deny bail to a defendant who has been charged with a violent crime and would allegedly be dangerous if released.

As noted throughout this book, many clinicians today see their task as one of assessing risk rather than predicting dangerousness. This is to emphasize that human behavior, including that which is violent, cannot be comfortably predicted. Rather, the best a clinician can do is assess probabilities based on a variety of factors in the individual's unique situation. Risk assessments are useful to the courts in deciding whether an individual should remain in the community.

Heilbrun et al. (2002) emphasize the importance of clarifying the purpose of the risk assessment, as in all forensic mental health assessments.

They note that the clinician must ascertain "whether the purpose . . . is to predict future behavior (e.g., provide a classification of risk or a probability of the likelihood of future violence), to identify risk factors and include recommendations for reducing risk, or both" (p. 461). They add that if the purpose is one but not the other, it may not be appropriate to address the other. We might illustrate this with the following example. A lawyer requesting a risk assessment prior to representing his or her client at a sentencing hearing may be interested only in an identification of risk factors and strategies for reducing risk in the hope that the judge will agree to place the convicted individual on probation. To include a statement that the individual has an extremely high probability of reoffending would be problematic for the client.

Instruments for assessing risk are more widely available and empirically supported than are instruments for assessing the reduction of risk, or the second question referred to above (Heilbrun et al., 2002). Yet, even though researchers have developed empirically sound instruments for assessing risk, even the most well known (e.g., the Violence Risk Appraisal Guide [VRAG], the Historical/Clinical/Risk Management Scale [HCR-20], and the Iterative Classification Tree [ICT]) have their limitations. (These instruments are discussed in Box 10.5).

BOX 10.5 Risk Assessment Instruments

The risk assessment enterprise includes a variety of instruments that researchers have designed specifically to assess risk of violence among certain populations. As noted in the chapter, there is no perfect test for predicting that a person will or will not engage in violent or other antisocial behavior. Nevertheless, some of the more promising instruments and guidelines are the following:

HCR-20 (Webster, Harris, Rice, Cormier, & Quinsey, 1994). The Historical/Clinical/Risk Management Scale is a 20-item instrument that includes items based on a person's background (historical), attitudes or mental disorders (clinical), and external risk factors (R), such as housing or family support. It assesses violence risk among persons with serious psychiatric or personality disorders.

Iterative Classification Tree (Monahan, Bonnie, et al., 2001). Developed on psychiatric patients, the Iterative Classification Tree (ICT) is a yes/no flowchart that takes into consideration

(Continued)

BOX 10.5 (Continued)

---

both clinical observations and variables traditionally associated with a prediction of violence. It is particularly effective at identifying those individuals at high risk and low risk of offending.

SARA (Kropp & Hart, 2000). The Spousal Assault Risk Assessment (SARA) guide assesses an individual's risk of committing violence against a spouse or intimate partner. It may be used in situations when a release decision is being considered (such as bail or parole). It assesses risk factors relating to psychosocial adjustment (such as employment or relationship problems) as well as the seriousness of criminal offenses.

VRAG (Harris, Rice, & Quinsey, 1993). The Violence Risk Appraisal Guide (VRAG) is based on 12 variables, including such background variables as alcohol abuse and elementary school maladjustment, as well as present mental status, such as schizophrenia and symptoms of psychopathy. It assesses the risk of violence in the community over a relatively long period (e.g., average is 7 years).

Researchers have also developed instruments designed to assess risk among sex offenders. These instruments are less widely accepted, primarily because they have not yet been subjected to extensive empirical research. The most common are the Minnesota Sex Offender Screening Tool—Revised (Mn-SOST-R) (Epperson, Kaul, & Hesselton, 1998), the Static-99 (Hanson & Thornton, 2000), and the Registrant Risk Assessment Scale (Ferguson, Eidelson, & Witt, 1998), which was developed in New Jersey to evaluate and place sex offenders into risk tiers for sex offender registration purposes.

If they were developed on different populations, or predict outcomes that are different from what is being assessed in the immediate case, or use an outcome period that is not applicable, then they might not be particularly useful in that case. (Heilbrun et al., 2002, p. 461)

Readers should also recall the limitations of actuarial risk assessment, as discussed in Chapter 9.

For purposes of assessing change in risk *level,* Heilbrun et al. (2002) recommend a number of strategies, even if instruments are not widely available. They suggest, for example, assessing the dynamic risk factors that were in operation at the time of the individual's violent act and determining whether they still exist. For example, at the time of the alleged assault, the individual had just lost his job; he has since gained new employment. "Protective factors" that may have inhibited violence in the past should also be assessed to see if they are still in place. An example of a protective factor would be a child who looks up to the individual and for whom he is responsible. Heilbrun et al. also recommend close observation of an individual's behavior, modification of the environment that may be conducive to violent behavior, and an assessment of the impact on monitoring, "which has been empirically demonstrated to lower an individual's risk for engaging in violent behavior" (p. 462).

Capital Sentencing

Risk assessments are useful to courts in the 38 death penalty states, as well as the federal government and the military, where the decision between life and death may revolve around the extent to which the individual is a danger to society. Some psychologists have strong moral objections to participating in any phase of a death penalty case, with particular antipathy toward assessing risk at the sentencing stage.

Many also do not choose to participate in assessments of competency for execution, which occur later in the criminal process, as the execution date is approaching. Evaluations of competency to be executed will be discussed in Chapter 12.

Risk assessment is not the only function of the psychologist at **capital sentencing,** however. The psychologist also may be asked to provide a more general evaluation of the offender's psychological functioning to learn whether there is anything that might mitigate, or lessen, the offender's culpability for the crime. In all death sentencing, juries must take into consideration any **mitigating factors**—or factors that might lessen the offender's responsibility. The type of factors accepted as mitigating varies according to jurisdiction. Neuropsychological deficits and a childhood marred by serious and systematic abuse are examples of mitigating factors in many states.

According to Heilbrun et al. (2002), "Capital sentencing evaluations are among the most detailed and demanding forensic assessments that are performed" (p. 116). The clinician is called in to provide a broad-based report that will presumably assist in determining whether a person convicted of a capital crime should be sentenced to death. Many capital sentencing evaluations are conducted at the request of the defense attorney, who wants information that can be used in making arguments before the jury.

On the other hand, jurors in most states also review **aggravating factors,** or those factors that make the situation worse for the offender. An aggravating factor, for example, is the high probability that the offender is a continuing danger to society; another is evidence that the victim was slowly tortured to death. Thus, although defense attorneys, in requesting sentencing evaluations, are looking for evidence of mitigation that they can present to the sentencing jury, prosecutors are looking for evidence that the offender is a continuing danger. In many cases, the clinician conducting the evaluation will also be called to the stand.

This aspect of capital sentencing is particularly controversial, and it may create ethical

problems for some psychologists. Recall in our discussion of the criminal psychopath in Chapter 4 that some researchers have suggested that the psychopath designation should not be used at this phase of the criminal process. Psychopaths are widely believed to be cold, unfeeling, nonresponsive to treatment, and, of course, dangerous.

During the sentencing phase of the case, which must be separate from the trial phase, jurors hear testimony from forensic psychiatrists or psychologists as to the likelihood that this individual will continue to be dangerous if not put to death. These predictions of dangerous, like other risk assessments, may be based on clinical or actuarial data.

In light of a long line of research documenting the deficiencies of clinical predictions of dangerousness, many forensic examiners are reluctant to rely on clinical impressions alone (Heilbrun et al., 2002). Nevertheless, as we noted in this and earlier chapters, actuarial or statistical data are not foolproof, either. In the death penalty context, actuarial data may be especially suspect. Cunningham and Reidy (1998, 1999) have brought attention to a problem dealing with the base rate, which is the fundamental group statistic in risk assessment. The base rate of murderers, they say, does not justify a prediction of dangerousness in death penalty cases. As a group, convicted murderers are neither violent in prison nor violent if released on parole. Other research has reached similar conclusions (Bohm, 1999).

In sum, the role of the forensic psychologist at capital sentencing is both crucial for obtaining possible evidence in mitigation and controversial for its contribution to the jury's prediction of dangerousness. Cases in which the death penalty is a possible outcome are unique. As the U.S. Supreme Court has so frequently observed in its death penalty opinions, death is different, and there is a bright line separating capital from noncapital cases. In *Furman v. Georgia* (1972), where the "death is different" principle was first expressed, the Court noted that death is "an unusually severe punishment, unusual in its pain, in its finality, and in its enormity." The bright line that separates death penalty cases from those in which death is not a possible outcome is one that many psychologists prefer not to cross. Yet others believe that they are in a unique position to document the existence of mitigating factors that may spare a convicted offender the death sentence.

Sex Offender Sentencing

As we discussed in Chapter 6, psychologists have conducted extensive research on the nature, causes, and treatment of sexual offending. Because of their expertise, psychologists are often asked to provide assessments of convicted sex offenders to help courts decide on a just punishment. In many jurisdictions, these evaluations are known as "psychosexual assessments." They are typically very broad based, with the psychologist providing a wealth of background information, test results, observations, and, in some cases, risk assessments. Psychosexual assessments also typically include recommendations for treatment and for managing any risk believed to be posed by the offender. For example, if an offender will almost assuredly be sent to prison, the evaluator may indicate that he is a good candidate for a sex offender treatment program known to be available in the prison system. For an offender who may be placed on probation, the evaluator might suggest that the supervising probation officer pay close attention to his employment status because he was particularly vulnerable to committing offenses during periods in which he was laid off from work.

There are unique problems associated with sex offender evaluations. Because of the nature of these offenses, some clinicians prefer to avoid them altogether or limit their involvement. Goldstein (2002b) has described a decision to call a temporary halt to some sex offender evaluations:

Several years ago, within a period of 2 months, I conducted three independent sentencing evaluations of men accused of molesting young children. By the end of the third evaluation, I began to feel anger and disgust over what appeared to be their consistent attempts to rationalize their actions and blame their young victims (statements consistent with research on this topic). In light of my feelings about these crimes, I decided to take a "sabbatical" from cases involving sexual abuse of children. (p. 151)

Goldstein added that he eventually returned to the evaluation of such cases because the cumulative effects of the three cases had diminished.

Heilbrun et al. (2002) warn clinicians to be very careful in using some of the typologies discussed in Chapter 6 to classify sex offenders in their reports to the courts. Although the typologies may be useful in clinical practice and may be intuitively appealing, few have received empirical support. Typologies also offer convenient and catchy "labels" that may follow an offender throughout his prison career, again with little validity. An offender tagged by professionals as a "sadistic rapist" or a "fixated child molester" may encounter adjustment problems in prison over and above the problems faced by inmates with more innocuous or "normal" labels—burglar, killer, or even rapist. In addition, the typologies may unjustly confine an offender to a higher security level than is warranted or limit his opportunity for participation in work programs or for early release.

According to Heilbrun et al. (2002), more promising than typologies are the risk assessment scales that have been developed specifically for sex offenders (see Box 10.5). As with other risk assessment instruments, though, care must be taken to choose the appropriate instrument and to be sure it is used in combination with other methods of assessment. T. W. Campbell (2003) is extremely critical of the use of these actuarial risk assessments for sex offenders as a whole, but particularly the Rapid Risk Assessment for Sex Offender Recidivism (RRASOR) and the Static-99. He notes that both instruments have been determined to be moderately accurate instruments for identifying risk. "When using the RRASOR and Static-99 in legal proceedings, however, terms such as 'moderately accurate' are obviously ambiguous" (Campbell, 2003, p. 269). Campbell believes it is incumbent on psychologists who use these tests to communicate carefully their limitations to the courts. "There is no shame in psychologists candidly acknowledging the limits of our expertise" (Campbell, 2003, p. 277).

It is widely recognized that clinicians often adjust the scores on actuarial risk assessments upward or downward in an effort to compensate for their limitations (Doren, 2002; Hanson & Bussière, 1998). Even adjusting the scores in an effort to limit false-positive or false-negative predictions will not ensure a valid measure, Campbell (2003) argues. Studies of the methods clinicians use to adjust scores indicate that these adjustments often have nothing to do with recidivism, and the accuracy of the test is diluted. For example, clinicians may rely on the results of a past risk assessment or on their own individual biases (Campbell, 2003, p. 277).

It should be emphasized that both the ethical code of the American Psychological Association (1992, 2002b) and the "Specialty Guidelines for Forensic Psychologists" (Committee on Ethical Guidelines for Forensic Psychologists, 1991) make it clear that psychologists should use validated instruments. Furthermore, they should acknowledge the limitations of the instruments they do use and should communicate their findings in a manner that will promote understanding and avoid deception.

Civil Commitment of Sexually Violent Predators

In the 1980s and 1990s, legislators in many states passed laws and funded programs that were designed to address the many problems associated with sex offending. Most of us are familiar with variants of these laws or programs that are named after the victims of heinous offenses (e.g.,

Megan's Law or the Amber Alert). As a group, these legislative enactments provide resources for police in the prevention of sex offending as well as services for victims and their relatives. Many of the laws also provide for registration of sex offenders after they have been released from prison and, in some instances, community notification. Today, names of registered sex offenders are widely dispersed on the Internet.

A less widely publicized practice is the commitment of dangerous sex offenders to mental institutions for indeterminate periods, against their will, after they have completed their prison sentences. In some states, the law also allows persons charged with violent sex offenses to be detained in mental institutions rather than in jails. Approximately 16 states have such provisions, cumulatively known as sexually violent predator (SVP) statutes. Estimates of the number of individuals detained or committed under these laws range from 1,300 to 2,209 (La Fond, 2003). Janus and Walbek (2000) note that these commitment schemes are exceedingly expensive, with the annual cost per patient ranging from $60,000 to $180,000. This does not include cost of commitment proceedings or capital costs for constructing needed facilities.

Numerous legal, ethical, and practical issues have been raised about this practice. However, the U.S. Supreme Court has allowed it, provided the offender has a history of sexually violent conduct, a current mental disorder or abnormality, a risk of future sexually violent conduct, and a mental disorder or abnormality that is connected to the conduct (*Kansas v. Hendricks,* 1997). In *Kansas v. Crane* (2002), the Court added that the state also had to prove that the individual had *some inability* to control his behavior. (The Kansas Supreme Court had ruled that the individual had to be found *unable to control* his dangerous behavior; the federal Court ruled that this was too heavy a burden for the state to bear.) The forensic psychologist or psychiatrist may be called in to assess any or all of these components.

Although the involuntary civil commitment of SVPs technically comes under the purview of civil law, it is so closely related to the criminal justice process and to the risk assessment instruments discussed above that we cover the topic here. In the following chapter, civil commitment of other individuals will be discussed.

Forensic psychologists may face a number of dilemmas relative to the assessment of sexually violent predators. The usual concerns about the assessment of risk, including the use of specialized instruments for use with sexual offenders, must be considered. Although progress has been made on risk assessment in a number of contexts, the enterprise is by no means on solid empirical ground. This is an important point to make in all legal contexts, but when it comes to sexually violent predators, there are additional ethical considerations. Because of the nature of this crime, courts are highly likely to err on the side of caution and to accept any documentation provided by the clinician; the high numbers of offenders who have been committed under these statutes suggest that commitment is not difficult to achieve.

It is also important to note that commitment does not require evidence of a recognized mental disorder; mental "abnormality" is sufficient. Researchers have found that many sex offenders do not suffer from mental disorder or mental illness. Nevertheless, the statutes often allow them to be civilly committed. In an analysis of sex offender commitment in Minnesota, Janus and Walbek (2000) learned that more than half of the 99 men in the study for whom diagnostic information was available had not been diagnosed with a sexual deviation disorder. Although other diagnoses were present (e.g., dementia, 2%; antisocial personality disorder, 26%; substance abuse or dependency, 52%), 10% had no diagnosis other than substance abuse or dependency. It should be noted that the civil commitment of persons other than SVPs requires a diagnosis of mental disorder or illness; a substance abuse or dependency diagnosis would not qualify.

An additional concern expressed in the literature is the possible lack of treatment that accompanies SVP commitment (Janus, 2000; Wood, Grossman, & Fichtner, 2000). Although the statutes typically include a provision that treatment will be offered if available, most statutes do not guarantee that this will occur. "Nevertheless, many states claim that sex offender commitments are aimed at treatment, and that they are providing effective—or at least state of the art—treatment" (Janus & Walbek, 2000, p. 347).

Critics of these commitment statutes maintain that they are really being used to extend punishment rather than provide treatment (La Fond, 2000). In other words, treatment is a secondary purpose. It should be noted also that not all sex offenders are mentally disordered to begin with, as Janus and Walbek's (2000) Minnesota study confirms. In fact, some researchers maintain that most are not. "The absence of a major mental disorder unique to offenders who commit sex crimes suggests that mental health treatment for most sex offenders needs to be questioned" (Simon, 2000, p. 295).

Still another concern is that sex offender commitment seems to result in very lengthy confinement. Recall from earlier in the chapter that the confinement of persons to civil mental institutions for nonforensic purposes is more likely to be measured in terms of days or weeks, whereas forensic populations are measured in terms of months or even years. Janus and Walbek (2000) observed that committed sex offenders almost never get released. "As a practical matter, the burden of proof to support discharge is a heavy one" (Janus & Walbek, 2000, p. 346). This is illustrative of an observation that has frequently been made about sex offenders. "Historically, sex offenders have been singled out for differential treatment by the legal and mental health systems" (Simon, 2000, p. 275).

In light of some of the above concerns, La Fond (2003) has advanced an interesting but undoubtedly controversial argument for outpatient commitment for violent sexual predators. Some SVPs, he believes, could benefit by initial outpatient treatment, whereas others could benefit by outpatient commitment as a transitional measure after institutionalization. La Fond refers to the consensus among treatment providers that persons who are enrolled in sex offender treatment programs within a secure facility should be followed up in the community to achieve maximum treatment outcomes. Thus, for those SVPs who get treated within the prison or the mental institution, outpatient commitment would provide continuing supervision and treatment upon release. Yet, **sexually violent predator statutes** in most of the states that have them do not provide for such outpatient commitment. When they do, there is very little evidence that it is used (La Fond, 2003).

The above are only some of the many issues that have been raised about the wisdom and ethics of involuntary civil commitment for sexually violent predators. Psychologists are likely to be involved in both the assessment and the treatment (if provided) of sexual offenders. Some evaluators may assume, when conducting risk assessments, that treatment will be provided once the individual is civilly committed. As we have seen, this is not necessarily the case. In addition, as we will discuss again in Chapter 12, the *effectiveness* of sex offender treatment programs is still very much in question. Although the forensic psychologist does not set social policy, he or she should be aware of the research and the growing controversy in this matter.

Summary and Conclusions

This chapter has reviewed a wide variety of tasks performed by forensic psychologists in their interaction with criminal courts. The available research suggests that the dominant tasks revolve around the various competencies that criminal defendants must possess to participate in criminal proceedings. Competency to stand trial, competency to waive the right to a lawyer, competency to plead guilty, and competency to be sentenced are examples. Recently, the psychological literature has begun to adopt the term *adjudicative competence* to embrace all of these separate competencies. Adjudicative competence—as

conceived by Richard Bonnie—also includes the important aspects of being able to communicate effectively with one's attorney and making decisions across a wide range of contexts.

There appears to be no consensus about how competency evaluations should be conducted, although most guidelines and publications indicate that the traditional clinical interview does not suffice. Although some psychologists administer traditional psychological tests, instruments specifically designed to measure competency are becoming more widely available. Among the most promising is the MacCAT-CA, developed by researchers from the MacArthur Foundation. The results of the competency evaluation appear to have a significant effect on a judge's decision, with judges almost always agreeing with recommendations offered by the examiner.

Psychologists also conduct sanity evaluations, more formally known as assessments of criminal responsibility or mental state at the time of the offense. These evaluations are widely considered to be far more complex than most evaluations of adjudicative competence—but there are exceptions. The assessment of criminal responsibility requires the collection of a large amount of background data, interviews with the defendant, and contacts with other individuals who may be able to provide insight into the defendant's state of mind when the crime was committed. The Rogers Criminal Responsibility Scale (R-CRAS) is the dominant instrument available for this purpose, though—like the competency assessment instruments—it is not universally used.

A controversial topic relating to both competency and insanity is the administrative of psychoactive medication against an individual's will. Medication is the dominant way of treating incompetent defendants to render them competent to stand trial. However, medicated defendants may suffer a variety of side effects, some of which may interfere with their capacity to participate in the trial process. The U.S. Supreme Court has indicated that extreme care must be taken before medicating defendants against their will to restore them to competency. In the case of a nondangerous defendant charged with a nonviolent offense, the Court disallowed the forced medication because the lower courts had not sufficiently considered its side effects. However, the Court refused to hear the case—and thus allowed the involuntary medication—of an incompetent defendant who was charged with a serious violent crime and was determined to be dangerous. The Court has ruled, though, that defendants have a right not to be medicated during their trials if they are pleading not guilty by reason of insanity and want jurors to see them in their natural, nonmedicated state.

Psychologists also consult with criminal courts as judges are preparing to sentence an offender. These sentencing evaluations are conducted primarily to determine whether the offender would be a good candidate for a particular rehabilitative approach, such as substance abuse treatment or a violent offender program. Sentencing evaluations also may involve assessments of risk, however, because courts are often interested in an appraisal of the convicted offender's dangerousness. Risk assessment remains an imperfect enterprise, but a variety of valid instruments are available for this purpose. We reviewed some of the major concerns surrounding risk assessment of special populations, such as sex offenders and defendants convicted of capital crime and facing a possible death sentence.

The chapter ended with a discussion of sexually violent predators and their indeterminate commitment to civil mental institutions. Approximately 15 states now allow such a commitment, provided that the offender is dangerous and has a mental disorder or some mental abnormality—a very broad term that has been criticized by many scholars. Although statutes often indicate that treatment will be provided, it is widely suspected that the primary intention of these statutes is to keep sexual predators incapacitated.

CHAPTER 11

Consulting With Civil Courts

The criminal courts discussed in Chapter 10 tend to get the most public and media attention, but the courts that are the subject of this chapter are noteworthy for different reasons. The average citizen is far more likely to come into contact with a civil court than a criminal court. Claims of breach of contract, sexual harassment, libel, invasions of privacy, age discrimination, and medical malpractice are all brought before the civil courts. These courts settle property disputes and adjudicate contested wills. Judges and juries decide such highly emotional issues as who will obtain custody of minor children, whether an individual is competent to make decisions about medical treatment, and the extent to which a victim of discrimination suffered emotional distress. They declare juveniles delinquent and allow persons to be committed to mental institutions against their will. In some of the most highly litigated cases in recent years, civil courts have dealt with numerous suits against corporations, such as the tobacco and asbestos cases of the past 20 years.

Not surprisingly, forensic psychologists have been extensively involved in this arena and in virtually every form of litigation mentioned above. Because of the wide array of issues that reach the civil courts, it is impossible to present a comprehensive review of the work of forensic psychologists in one chapter. Instead, we will represent their work by focusing on select activities. First, we discuss consultation with juvenile courts, which are sometimes referred to as "quasi-civil" because they have many features of criminal courts. Then we will cover family and probate courts, where issues involving divorce, child custody, child neglect, civil commitments, and competency to make medical decisions may be decided. Finally, we review disputes in civil courts involving personal injury (mental and physical) and discrimination. Please remember that each state—as well as the federal government—has its unique way of organizing and naming its courts and determining their jurisdiction. In many states today, for example, juvenile delinquency proceedings take place within the family court, not in a separate juvenile court. Likewise, custody may be litigated in probate, family, or courts labeled "superior courts" in some states. Civil commitment proceedings may occur in mental health courts, probate courts, family courts, or in the nonspecialized district or county courts. Therefore, although we divide the material to follow into sections, students should be aware that considerable overlapping could occur.

Juvenile Courts

The juvenile justice system provides numerous opportunities for the forensic psychologist. Various statistics indicate that juveniles today are more likely to come into contact with police, courts, and correctional facilities than at any other time in history. Arrest data reveal that police take into custody some 2.5 million juveniles every year. In 1998, 1.8 million delinquency **petitions** were filed with juvenile courts (Sickmund, 2003). Also in 1998, 327,700 juveniles were being held in juvenile detention facilities prior to adjudication (Puzzanchera, Stahl, Finnegan, Tierney, & Snyder, 2003) and 176,700 were held in residential treatment facilities (Sickmund, 2003). An unknown number of juveniles, chiefly between the ages of 14 and 18 (but sometimes younger) are tried in criminal rather than juvenile courts. Nevertheless, the juvenile crime rate—which began to rise quite dramatically in the 1980s—has been stabilizing, suggesting that juveniles today are not significantly more likely than in the past to commit crimes, particularly serious crimes. In the late 1990s, for example, the arrest rate for violent juvenile crime dropped 9%; the juvenile homicide rate dropped 31% (Howell, 1998). However, public officials, clinicians, and legal and social service professionals alike are concerned about the still-disturbing patterns of juvenile crime, particularly substance abuse, violence, and sex offending.

Juvenile courts may exist as separate entities or may be part of a broader "family court" system. Regardless of how these courts are structured, judges, lawyers, and social service representatives consult with forensic psychologists for a wide variety of reasons. A defense lawyer may want an appraisal of her or his client's adjudicative competence or an assessment of the client's overall intellectual functioning. When juveniles waive their constitutional rights, such as the right to remain silent or the right to a lawyer during police interrogation, judges (and defense lawyers) often want to know whether the juveniles possessed the necessary cognitive skills to make such a waiver. Psychological assessments may be sought to determine whether a youth is a threat to society or is amenable to rehabilitation. In addition to this, juvenile court judges as well as lawyers often want to know whether treatment is available to meet the needs of a given young offender, along with the cost of such treatment and the probability that it will be effective. (Box 11.1 contains a "help wanted" ad for a forensic psychologist in a juvenile court clinic.)

BOX 11.1 Wanted: Forensic Psychologist for Juvenile Court

The following ad is typical of many that appear periodically in the professional literature:

The Juvenile Court Clinic . . . is seeking full-time licensed psychologists to conduct court-ordered child protection and juvenile justice forensic evaluations. These include the assessment of parents, adolescents, and children involved in juvenile court proceedings through clinical interviews, collateral contacts, record review, psychological testing, and parent-child observations. Responsibilities include supervising master's-level staff and preparing materials for national dissemination. This position also includes supervising graduate students and training judges and lawyers in using and acquiring clinical information.

Minimum requirements include a doctorate in clinical psychology from an accredited program, an accredited predoctoral internship, and licensure. Specialized forensic training is preferred but not required. The ideal candidate will possess sound assessment skills, strong writing skills, and extensive experience working with adolescents and/or parents involved in court proceedings, particularly in urban settings. Minorities and bilingual applicants are encouraged to apply.

In addition to the above assessment tasks, forensic psychologists are called on to offer treatment to juveniles, both within juvenile facilities and in community settings. In this chapter, we will discuss psychological involvement at the early stages of the juvenile process, up to and including the adjudication of delinquency. A separate chapter—Chapter 13—is devoted to juvenile corrections. In that chapter, we will cover a variety of rehabilitation programs and treatment strategies for dealing with delinquent youth.

Historical Background

It is important for forensic psychologists working with the juvenile justice system to be aware of its history. Many concerned advocates for juveniles today fear that problems very similar to the problems of old have reoccurred or, in some cases, never really disappeared. Furthermore, the history of the juvenile court is also very much the history of family courts because separate courts with exclusive jurisdiction over family matters did not emerge in most states until the last quarter of the 20th century.

Slightly over 100 years ago, in 1899, the first juvenile court was established in the United States, in the state of Illinois. A broad group of social activists had influenced the Illinois legislature to establish a judicial system for children that was to be separate from that faced by adults. Children were presumed to be in need of protection, less accountable for their offenses than adults, and more amenable to rehabilitation once

they had strayed. Furthermore, many children were neglected by their parents or guardians and required the intervention of the state for their own best interest. Thus, the first juvenile court was intended to serve the needs of all children who needed supervision, including those who violated the law. Other states followed Illinois's lead, and by 1925, all but two states (Maine and Wyoming) had established similar courts with exclusive jurisdiction over minors, usually defined as children younger than age 18 (Bartol & Bartol, 1998; Tappan, 1949).

The courts were strongly based on a *parens patriae* rationale. The doctrine of *parens patriae*, first applied to children in a Pennsylvania case (*ex parte Crouse*, 1838), gives the state the power to intervene in a child's life, even over the objections of the parents, because such intervention is presumed to be in the best interest of the child. The doctrine has survived and remains a strong component of much juvenile law today, although the law is also very oriented toward recognizing the legal rights of juveniles, at least in principle.

Prior to the establishment of the juvenile courts, children who allegedly broke the law were handled through the social service system or were taken before criminal courts. In the mid-19th century, the nation's largest cities had **Houses of Refuge,** which were institutional settings presumably intended to protect, nurture, and educate neglected and/or wayward children. Children who were sent to Houses of Refuge were poor and/or homeless, were considered incorrigible, or had committed usually minor law violations—or some combination of the above. Houses of Refuge in the 19th century—with some exceptions—very rapidly earned the reputation of being emotionally cold facilities that often exploited their young charges by contracting their domestic and manual labor to households in the community (Bernard, 1992).

Young offenders who were processed in criminal courts were allowed to remain in the community if they stayed out of trouble. This is similar to the probation of today, but there were few probation officers available to monitor behavior and offer support and guidance as needed. The early probation officers were volunteers or police officers assigned to this special duty (Cromwell, Killinger, Kerper, & Walker, 1985). It was not until the end of the 19th century that states began to authorize probation and provide funds for probation officers on a systematic basis. Before that time, probationary status was available only in areas where volunteers or police were available. Many young offenders, then, were sentenced by criminal courts to serve time in prisons or reformatories. The latter were intended primarily for first-time offenders. Their purpose was to give these offenders a second chance, offering them education and discipline in preparation for a law-abiding life. Like the Houses of Refuge, many of those reformatories were criticized for abusing young offenders, ruling by fear, and not delivering on their promise to provide education and rehabilitation (Bernard, 1992; Johnson, 1996).

When we consider the above problems, the motives of those who fought for the establishment of a separate court for juveniles appear noble. Few will disagree that children need more protection than do adults and that children, on the whole, are less cognitively and emotionally mature than most adults. On the other hand, once they reach adolescence, their abilities to make decisions and their emotional maturity vary widely. Indeed, the competence of adolescents to make decisions in their own interests is a hot topic in child development research today (see, generally, Grisso & Schwartz, 2000). Children and adolescents are also vulnerable to exploitation. Institutional settings that degrade, humiliate, fail to educate, and fail to nurture the young cannot protect or rehabilitate them. In addition, few will disagree that some children are neglected and physically abused in their own homes and require the intervention of a protective state. At the end of the 19th century, then, a separate court with the mandate of focusing exclusively on the needs of children seemed to be a major improvement over what had been occurring.

However, some scholars have strongly questioned the actions of those who worked to establish these juvenile courts, suggesting that they were primarily motivated by their desire to control the children of the poor, who were considered all too visible reminders of growing inequality in society (Platt, 1969). Poor children were considered offensive ruffians, spending too much time on the streets and threatening the comfortable lifestyles of those who were more privileged. Thomas Bernard (1992) suggests that social reformers were first and foremost interested in bringing about social change. However, they gave up their efforts to improve social conditions that produce crime and reverted instead to trying to "fix" children and their families.

> Eventually, social workers stopped trying to change the rich and powerful and started trying to change the poor and powerless. The seeds of both casework and social reform had been present at the beginning of the juvenile court, but only the seeds of casework sprouted and grew. The seeds of social reform withered and died. (Bernard, 1992, p. 102)

The juvenile courts clearly were trying to change children and their families, but it is highly questionable whether they were effective. Until the 1960s, they operated very informally, and judges and other court officers had very broad discretion over the lives of juveniles. The courts were supposedly intended to help juveniles, preferably within the community and within their own homes. Proceedings were informal and closed to the public, and all aspects of the juvenile's life were subjected to inquiry by the court. Psychiatrists and psychologists working in child guidance clinics provided judges with cognitive and personality test results and offered recommendations based on their interviews with the child and family members (Rothman, 1980).

Gradually, despite the allegedly good intentions of the founders of the juvenile court movement, the courts gained the reputation of being authoritarian, imposing unreasonable expectations on juveniles and their families, particularly the economically disadvantaged. When these expectations were not met, juvenile judges were not averse to sending juveniles to secure training schools, where they encountered punitive treatment rather than effective rehabilitation. These decisions to institutionalize were routinely made with little attention to due process of the law; juveniles in most courts did not have the assistance of lawyers, nor did they have reasonable opportunity to confront the witnesses against them or to challenge the actions of court officials. Juvenile courts also routinely urged—and in some cases required—juveniles to confess their offenses. When juvenile court judges believed that the juveniles were not appropriate for juvenile court, they would transfer them to criminal court, where they would presumably be treated the same as adults.

Supreme Court Decisions

Two U.S. Supreme Court cases in the 1960s signaled a need to change procedures in juvenile court. One—*Kent v. U.S.* (1966)—required that a judge hold a hearing before transferring a juvenile to adult court. At that hearing, the juvenile had a constitutional right to have the assistance of an attorney and to challenge the transfer. The Court also suggested factors that judges could consider in deciding whether the transfer was appropriate. These included the child's age, the seriousness of the crime, prior record with the juvenile court, the prospect of rehabilitation if

kept in the juvenile system, the likelihood of being rehabilitated if transferred to criminal court, and the threat to the security of the community if not transferred. The Supreme Court opinion in *Kent* also presents a scathing indictment of the juvenile court system as it operated at that time, serving as a precursor of the case that would follow.

The following year, in a landmark juvenile case (*In re Gault*, 1967), the Supreme Court dramatically altered procedures associated with delinquency hearings. Gerald Gault had been taken into custody by police, taken to the police station, and subjected to two hearings before a judge who ultimately adjudicated him delinquent and sent him to a juvenile training school, where he could have been kept until his 21st birthday. Gerald was 15 years old at the time of his offense. His crime? He had placed an obscene phone call to his next-door neighbor. Although his parents were present at the delinquency hearing, Gerald was not represented by counsel, and his alleged victim did not appear in court to testify against him.

In a lengthy opinion that traced the history of the juvenile court in the United States, the Supreme Court noted that Gerald Gault, like Morris Kent before him, had been subjected to proceedings that could only be characterized as "a Kangaroo court." The Court therefore ruled that juveniles facing delinquency proceedings and possible institutionalization had, at a minimum, the following constitutional rights:

- Right to written notice of the charges against them
- Right to confront and cross-examine witnesses against them
- Privilege against self-incrimination
- Right to the assistance of a lawyer in their defense

Although *In re Gault* was a landmark decision widely hailed by children's rights advocates, it should not be assumed that it cured all of the ills of juvenile courts. Just over 20 years after the

Gault case, Barry Feld (1988) reported research that fewer than half of all juveniles were represented by lawyers in delinquency proceedings. Other research across 15 states suggests higher rates of representation, 65% to 97% depending on the jurisdiction. Nevertheless, even with a lawyer, there is some question as to whether juveniles can participate *effectively* in their defense.

When juveniles are *not* represented by lawyers, it is likely that they waived that constitutional right. In some cases, this was done on the advice of parents or other authority figures. Juveniles also have a constitutional right to a lawyer during custodial interrogation, but most juveniles speak to police without a lawyer present (Grisso, 1998). Thus, the validity of waivers—that is, whether the juveniles understood the consequences of giving up this right—is another topic of great interest to researchers.

Against this historical backdrop, we now turn to the specific tasks that are performed by forensic psychologists in consultation with the juvenile courts.

Juvenile Assessment: An Overview

As we noted in Chapter 10, assessment is an essential component of the daily professional life of the forensic psychologist. Also called psychological evaluation, assessment refers to all the techniques used to measure and evaluate an individual's past, present, or future psychological status. It may be considered "the act of determining the nature and causes of a client's problem" (Lewis, Dana, & Blevins, 1994, p. 71). Thus, interviews, observations, and reviews of records and other documents are all part of the assessment process. The forensic psychologist also will administer a variety of tests to measure cognitive abilities and personality attributes of the juvenile.

The assessment typically but not invariably will include phone or in-person interviews with relevant adults, including family members, and peers. Some forensic psychologists recommend observing the juvenile in a natural setting (e.g., in school, with parents and siblings at home) if possible. Although some forensic psychologists urge very wide-ranging assessment, others believe assessments should be limited in scope and should address only the referral question (e.g., did this juvenile possess the necessary cognitive ability to waive his or her right to a lawyer?). Because there are no clinical requirements and few legal restrictions (in most jurisdictions) associated with these assessments, the specific approach taken is left to the individual clinician. There is, however, a wealth of information in the form of handbooks, guidelines, and research studies that offers suggestions to clinicians (e.g., American Psychological Association [APA], 1996; Grisso, 1998; Melton et al., 1997).

The clinical literature advises forensic psychologists to be extremely cautious in assessing juveniles if their practice has been limited primarily to adults. "It is possible to conduct a seemingly competent evaluation but fail to obtain the data necessary to construct a complete picture of the developmental and familial context for the youth's clinical presentation and delinquent behavior" (Heilbrun et al., 2002, p. 187). Heilbrun et al. (2002) add that normal adolescent defensiveness and mistrust may make them appear cold and remorseless. Children of ethnic and racial groups that have experienced discrimination in society may be distrustful of authority figures, including the mental health professionals evaluating them. Adolescents as a group also may be reluctant to disclose embarrassing information that may actually help in their defense. An example is the fact that they were sexually abused by the individual they are charged with assaulting. Examiners also must be alert to the possibility of serious psychopathology, which can be overlooked in adolescents by clinicians accustomed to the symptomatology and clinical presentations of adults (Heilbrun et al., 2002).

Although assessment is an essential component of treatment, treatment does not necessarily accompany assessment. In fact, in this and many other contexts, psychologists are warned to avoid dual roles of evaluator and treatment provider (see Box 10.3 in the previous chapter). Because of this distinction between assessment and treatment, we discuss them as separate tasks and in separate chapters. (Treatment of juveniles is covered in Chapter 13.) Nevertheless, clinicians are often advised to include recommendations for treatment in assessment reports, if such treatment is known to be available (Grisso, 1998).

Assessment of Competence to Waive *Miranda* Rights

There is good evidence that many juveniles cannot understand their constitutional rights (Grisso & Schwartz, 2000). Psychologists who evaluate them must be knowledgeable not only about the law but also about adolescent development and decision making (Grisso, 1998; Heilbrun et al., 2002). Like adults, juveniles have a constitutional right not to incriminate themselves during their dealings with the criminal justice system. Juveniles do not have to answer questions posed by police while in custody (*Miranda v. Arizona,* 1966; *Fare v. Michael C.,* 1979). In addition, they do not have to take the stand during a delinquency proceeding (*In re Gault,* 1967). Closely associated with this privilege against self-incrimination is the right to an attorney. The above cases also established that juveniles have a right to have an attorney present during custodial interrogation and have a right to the assistance of counsel in delinquency proceedings.

In reality, many if not most juveniles waive these constitutional rights, as do many adults. The police questioning of juveniles who have been taken into custody is far more likely to occur solely in the presence of a parent or legal guardian than in the presence of an attorney. Research suggests strongly that these adults often encourage the juveniles to cooperate with police, answer their questions, and confess to their offenses. "At the time of their children's arrests, many parents themselves are anxious, fearful, or confused

during the police encounter. Others are angry at the youth and contribute to the coercive pressure of the interrogation" (Grisso, 1998, p. 44).

Under the law, a waiver is a valid one if it is made willingly, knowingly, and intelligently. At what age can the average juvenile meet this standard? Moreover, even if the average juvenile can meet the standard, what about *this* juvenile who is being confronted by police under stressful conditions? In *Fare v. Michael C.* (1979), the Supreme Court noted that a juvenile's waiver of the right to a lawyer before being questioned by police while in their custody (custodial interrogation) should be given very careful scrutiny if it comes to court attention. Thus, when defense attorneys challenge these waivers or when judges themselves decide there is reason to question their validity, forensic psychologists are called in to evaluate the juveniles' cognitive development and the extent to which they understood what they were doing.

Psychologist Thomas Grisso is a leading expert in adolescent development, the legal rights of juveniles, and a variety of forensic assessments. Early research by Grisso (1981) found that most juveniles age 14 and younger did not understand the meaning of the *Miranda* warning, nor the implications if they chose to waive their rights. Juveniles who were slightly older— 15 and 16—had similar difficulty if they were of below average intelligence. Most recently, Redlich, Silverman, and Steiner (2003) found that age and suggestibility were strong predictors of *Miranda* competence. Interestingly, juveniles who had frequent contacts with police, though not significantly less likely to comprehend their **Miranda rights** than those without frequent contact, had much more trouble understanding the vocabulary used in *Miranda* warnings (e.g., consult, interrogation). It should be noted that, in some states, a simplified version of the warnings is given to juveniles (see Box 11.2).

Grisso (1998) recommends three standardized instruments that may be helpful to the clinician in performing this assessment. The first is the Comprehension of Miranda Rights (CMR)

BOX 11.2 A *Miranda* Warning for Juveniles

In most states, police officers have no legal obligation to inform juveniles of their *Miranda* rights differently than they inform adults. However, if juveniles waive their constitutional rights after being warned, the validity of this waiver is subject to judicial review. Some judges scrutinize juvenile waivers very carefully. Consequently, some police departments—as a matter of policy—take particular care before interrogating juveniles.

Here is an illustration of one police department's attempt to fashion a *Miranda* warning specifically for use with juvenile suspects.

Miranda warning given by: *(officer's name)* at: *(time and date)*

1. You do not have to talk to me if you do not want to. If you decide to talk to me, you can stop at any time.

2. Anything you do tell me may be used against you in a court of law.

3. You can talk with an attorney and have him or her with you, now, or at any time while we are discussing this incident.

4. If you, or your parents/guardians, cannot afford an attorney, you can, if you want, be represented by the public defender at no cost to you or your family.

Do you understand your rights? _____

Having these rights in mind, do you wish to talk to me now? _____

Signature of Juvenile _____

Signature of Witness _____

---

and its offshoots. (These are the Comprehension of Miranda Rights—Recognition [CMR-R], the Comprehension of Miranda Vocabulary [CMV], and Function of Rights in Interrogation [FRI].) The second type of standardized instrument is any standardized test of cognitive ability. The third is personality inventories. Grisso also recommends a review of school, mental health, and juvenile court records, when available, as well as interviews with parents or caretakers along with the youth himself or herself. In other words, Grisso recommends conducting a very extensive assessment in an effort to determine whether the youth provided a valid waiver of the right to an attorney during custodial interrogation.

False Confessions

In addition to evidence that juveniles have trouble understanding their constitutional rights, there is evidence that they sometimes confess to crimes they did not commit. Recall our discussion of the research on this topic in Chapter 2 (e.g., Kassin, 1997; Kassin & Kiechel, 1996; Richardson, Gudjonsson, & Kelly, 1995). A false confession may occur for a wide range of reasons, some of which relate to psychological tactics used by police. For example, police may deceive a suspect into thinking they have evidence that they do not actually have, or they may befriend the suspect into thinking they are his or her only link to freedom. A juvenile eager to go home, or a juvenile who wants to protect a family member or friend, may decide to tell police what they want to hear. An evaluating clinician clearly should be alert to this possibility.

It should come as no surprise that juveniles may be particularly susceptible to making false confessions. Redlich and Goodman (2003) examined the suggestibility of three different age groups (12- and 13-year-olds, 15- and 16-year-olds, and 18- to 26-year-olds) in an experimental situation similar to many used in the false confession research (e.g., Kassin, 1997). Participants were given a computer task and told to not press a particular key. They were then told that they had pressed it when they really had not. In some experimental situations, the experimenter provides participants with "false evidence" that they pressed the key. Researchers then tabulate the number of "false confessions" and try to determine what, in addition to age, distinguishes participants who "admit" to something they did not actually do from those who do not.

Redlich and Goodman (2003) examined whether (a) scores on the Gudjonsson Suggestibility Scale (GSS) and (b) the presentation of false evidence would predict and facilitate a false confession. The GSS is an instrument designed to measure the extent to which individuals are susceptible to being influenced by others. Results indicated that 69% of all participants falsely confessed or complied, 39% internalized (believed they had pressed the forbidden key), and 4% confabulated (made up details about their behavior during the study). However, significant age differences emerged. For the mid-level age group (15- and 16-year-olds), false confessions occurred particularly when false evidence was presented. The youngest age group falsely confessed both when false evidence was presented and when it was not. In general, the two youngest age groups were more likely to say they had done something wrong than were the young adults. With respect to individual differences, scores on the GSS predicted compliance (admitting to the "offense") but not internalization or confabulation.

Research on the psychology of false confessions is still in its infancy (or perhaps its early childhood), and its ecological validity is questionable. Ecological validity refers to whether results obtained in a laboratory setting can be applied to the natural environment as well as whether events in the natural environment can be adequately represented in the laboratory. "It is ethically problematic to accuse someone of an actual crime in the laboratory" (Redlich & Goodman, 2003, p. 154). Nevertheless, there is reason to be concerned about what are widely accepted police interrogation processes, particularly when it comes to juveniles. Police interrogation involves intimidating authority figures and a high level of stress, both of which have been demonstrated in other social psychology experiments to elicit compliance (e.g., Milgram, 1974). The present study suggests that juveniles are significantly more susceptible to this influence than are young adults, although all age groups are affected.

Evaluating Adjudicative Competence

Juveniles whose cases are heard in criminal courts must, like adults, be competent to stand trial. Otherwise, the trial of an incompetent defendant violates due process of the law (*Drope v. Missouri*, 1975; *Dusky v. U.S.*, 1960). When a juvenile's case is heard in criminal court, competency to stand trial—if it is raised—is measured in accordance with the *Dusky* standard discussed in Chapter 10. Recall from that chapter that the standard for competency to stand trial is a sufficient present ability to consult with one's lawyer and a rational and factual understanding of the proceedings. Although most courts have not set a separate standard for juveniles, the *Dusky* standard is altered in some jurisdictions to inquire more carefully into the juvenile's decision-making abilities (Oberlander, Goldstein, & Ho, 2001).

This is a good move because many developmental psychologists and legal advocates for children believe that adjudicative competence in juveniles and adults is not identical. Even if a juvenile is knowledgeable about the role of the attorney and able to understand the charges, he or she may not be an *effective* participant in these proceedings. According to Richard Bonnie (1992), effective participation requires an ability to make decisions, weigh alternatives, and understand consequences—abilities he referred to as "decisional competency."

Juveniles may be particularly at a disadvantage when it comes to **decisional competency.** Although adults also may have deficits related to effective participation, juveniles—given their stage of development—are more likely to have these deficits and are thus at greater jeopardy. In addition, those juveniles who come before the juvenile courts are even more likely than other juveniles to be mentally retarded, mentally disordered, or emotionally or socially immature. The problem does not disappear if the juveniles are transferred to criminal court. In fact, it might be even greater because criminal court judges are not attuned to the needs of juveniles, having dealt with the legal question of competency primarily with adult defendants.

Competency to stand trial—or adjudicative competence—in the *juvenile* court emerged as an issue only since the early 1990s. At this point, statutes or case law in about half the states *require* an inquiry into adjudicative competency in juvenile courts. In the remaining states, the competency inquiry is raised on a case-by-case basis.

MacArthur Juvenile Competence Study

In an effort to shed some light on the juvenile competency question, the MacArthur Research Network began gathering data in 1999 for a multisite study of adjudicative competence in juveniles. Major questions addressed by the research were the following (see the **MacArthur Juvenile Competence Study** home page at www.mac-adoldev-juvjustice.org):

- Compared to adults in the criminal justice system, do youth in the juvenile justice system more often manifest deficits in abilities related to adjudicative competence?
- If so, on what abilities are these differences most apparent, and how are those abilities related to development?
- What types of youth are at greatest risk of adjudicative incompetence due to developmental immaturity? Might developmental immaturity interact with mental disorders to create increased risks of deficits in abilities related to adjudicative incompetence? Is there an age below which incompetence to stand trial should be presumed?
- What methods could clinicians and courts use to identify youth who are seriously deficient in abilities related to adjudicative competence?

In the first phase of the above study, Grisso et al. (2003) compared abilities of 927 adolescents in juvenile detention facilities and community settings and 466 young adults (ages 18–24) in jails and community settings in Philadelphia, Los Angeles, northern and eastern Virginia, and northern Florida. In addition to a standard battery of tests and record reviews, the groups were asked to respond to vignettes and were administered the MacArthur Competence Assessment Tool—Criminal Adjudication (MacCAT-CA) and a newly developed MacArthur Judgment Evaluation. The two youngest adolescent groups (ages 11–13 and 14–15) were three times and two times (respectively) as likely as the young adults to be seriously impaired in competence-relevant abilities. The 16- and 17-year-old juveniles did not differ from the young adults.

In addition to age, intelligence was also a predictor of poor performance. Gender, ethnicity, socioeconomic background, prior experience with the legal system, and symptoms of mental health problems were not predictors (although few individuals with serious mental health problems were included in the sample). The adolescents also tended to make choices that reflected compliance with authority and psychosocial immaturity. Grisso and his colleagues (2003) recommend that legal standards recognize immaturity as a potential predicate of incompetence to stand trial. They recommend also that states rethink transferring juveniles age 13 and younger to criminal courts, given the high proportion of youth in that age group who were considered significantly impaired (about 30% total, but more than half of those with below-average intelligence).

The Lawyer-Client Relationship

In a separately published study, Schmidt, Reppucci, and Woolard (2003) reported on 203 juveniles and 110 adults who were given vignettes relating to attorney-client issues. In the vignette, an individual was charged with a robbery, and the respondents were asked a variety of questions as to what the defendant should do. Age had a significant effect on responses to the vignettes. Juveniles were more likely to say the defendant should deny guilt to his lawyer, less likely to recommend that he should communicate honestly, and more likely to be influenced by short-term consequences as opposed to long-term consequences. Juveniles who had previously been detained within the juvenile justice system were even more distrustful of defense attorneys than juveniles who had had less or no experience with the system. However, juveniles previously charged with property offenses (and presumably aware that lawyers had been helpful) were trustful. Black, Latino, and Asian juveniles were more distrustful than Whites.

Schmidt et al. (2003) believe that the results of their study highlight the importance of taking developmental differences into consideration when considering the attorney-client relationship. Together with other researchers (e.g., Buss, 2000; Tobey, Grisso, & Schwartz, 2000), they recommend that lawyers receive training in developmental issues relating to children and adolescents and guidance in how to effectively

represent young clients, based on knowledge from developmental psychology. In a similar vein, clinicians conducting evaluations of adjudicative competency in juveniles are advised to gather information about the attorney-client relationship, including, if possible, an interview with the juvenile's attorney (e.g., Barnum, 2000). As Grisso (1999) has observed, a juvenile may be highly capable cognitively but may still be reluctant to accept that an adult such as a public defender is working for him or her and in this juvenile's best interests.

A recent study exploring the relationship between juveniles and their lawyers provides a somewhat different—but certainly not optimistic—view. Pierce and Brodsky (2002) recruited 163 male juveniles and young adults with experience in the juvenile or criminal justice system. Participants were in residential facilities, a group home, or a day diversion program. On measures of *trust* (in lawyers, in others, or in authority), there were no significant age differences. However, there was pervasive distrust in lawyers within the group. Significant differences in *understanding the role of counsel* emerged as a function of age, with juveniles ages 12 to 14 years (the youngest group in the study) demonstrating the least understanding. In addition, those youth who were least trustful of attorneys, regardless of age level, were also the ones who demonstrated the least understanding of attorney roles. Cognitive abilities were also negatively correlated with both trust and understanding. In other words, the less cognitively developed the youth, the more distrustful of lawyers and the more lacking in understanding their function. Black participants were less trusting and understanding than White participants, even when intellectual functioning was controlled. However, Blacks with higher intellectual functioning were less trustful than Whites with higher intellectual functioning, a finding that Pierce and Brodsky interpreted as "justified cynicism regarding the treatment of Black individuals in this society" (p. 104). Once again, psychologists evaluating the competency of juveniles to participate in court proceedings should take into account not only developmental and cognitive differences but also cultural differences.

Complicating the matter of juveniles effectively helping their lawyers is the reality that some lawyers in juvenile court do not provide the zealous advocacy that they provide for adults in criminal courts. Barry Feld (2000) points out that many well-meaning attorneys truly believe it is in their client's best interests to be adjudicated delinquent and receive treatment. As Feld notes—and as we will discuss in Chapter 13—the efficacy of many treatment programs is questionable. On the other hand, successful programs do exist. Forensic psychologists consulting with defense attorneys should be aware of the evaluation literature and should advise lawyers to advocate for a disposition "package" for their clients that would be the most likely to achieve rehabilitation.

If the lawyer is inclined to recommend a plea bargain, psychologist Richard Barnum (2000) recommends that examining clinicians determine the extent to which the juvenile is willing to undergo the treatment that will likely accompany it. Plea negotiation is increasingly common in the juvenile system, just as it is in criminal courts. Yet, developmentally, youth are far less likely than adults to understand the stakes and ramifications of admitting guilt. There are both risks and benefits. For example, although juvenile probation will allow the youth to remain in the community, it may require a lengthy period of supervision and frequent, unannounced home visits. "Whether the juvenile actually understands what may be involved in elaborate probation agreements and treatment contracts, may be critical issues in determining his competence to take part in a negotiated solution" (Barnum, 2000, p. 196). Barnum also notes that, even though the juvenile court may be rehabilitative, the loss of liberty involved may be far greater than the juvenile would receive for the same offense in criminal court. Recall the *Gault* case, in which the juvenile faced a 6-year confinement for making an obscene phone call.

Finally, in evaluating adjudicative competency, clinicians are advised to evaluate the juvenile-parent relationship and assess how well the parent or guardian understands the juvenile's capacities and needs. Barnum (2000) notes that this can be a cumbersome process but adds, "When there is doubt about the juvenile defendant's autonomous competence, it is appropriate to examine the parent's ability to provide appropriate support and advice to make up for the youth's deficits" (p. 213).

There is less agreement in the literature on whether specific treatment recommendations should be made or on whether clinicians should express an ultimate issue opinion: Is this juvenile competent to stand trial (or participate in juvenile proceedings)? Barnum (2000) considers it unethical for clinicians to express an ultimate legal opinion, even though courts may press for them. He does not, however, believe it problematic for the clinician to provide treatment recommendations—but they should be phrased in a conditional way—for example, "If the defendant is found incompetent . . ." or "If the defendant is found competent and adjudicated delinquent. . . ." "Having carefully avoided offering an opinion as to the ultimate opinion of competence, the consultant may introduce new confusion if she offers a clinical recommendation that is available only to an adjudicated delinquent" (Barnum, 2000, p. 220). Barnum believes that if treatment recommendations are made, the clinicians must be careful to distinguish between those recommendations aimed at establishing competence and those aimed at overall clinical care.

Amenability to Rehabilitation

The decision as to whether a juvenile is likely to benefit from rehabilitative services and what types of services are most promising may be made at several points during juvenile justice processing. In addition, **amenability to rehabilitation** commonly takes into consideration a juvenile's present treatment needs. Two contexts in which courts request these evaluations are the judicial waiver decision and the disposition decision.

Waiver Decisions

Judges in both criminal and juvenile courts are often faced with the decision whether to transfer jurisdiction of juveniles, or "waive" a juvenile to the other court. Most **judicial waivers** are made at the request of prosecutors who want to prosecute juveniles in adult courts. In making the transfer decision, judges consider factors such as those recommended by the U.S. Supreme Court in *Kent v. U.S.* (1966).

The transfer by judges is only one of several possible forms of waiver. A great number of juveniles are tried in criminal courts as a result of **legislative waiver,** also called **statutory exclusion** or **waiver by statute.** These are waivers whereby the legislative branch has ordained that juveniles of specified ages will have their cases heard in criminal courts when charged with specific crimes. For example, in the great majority of states, a 15-year-old charged with murder will automatically be tried in criminal court. (A criminal court judge may transfer his or her case to juvenile court, but this very rarely occurs.) Still another form of waiver, **prosecutorial waiver,** gives prosecutors the authority to decide whether the case will be taken to juvenile court or criminal court. Most state statutes allow some combination of these waivers, depending on the age of the juvenile and the seriousness of the offense. Opponents of waivers argue that they are overused and unjustifiably consign too many adolescents to the adult system, where the emphasis is on punishment more than on rehabilitation (Bishop, 2000).

Even when juveniles have been transferred to criminal courts, however, an amenability for rehabilitation evaluation may be requested. A defense attorney, for example, may desire such an assessment for help during the plea negotiation process or during the sentencing phase, if her or his client is convicted.

It should be noted that there is considerable controversy about the issue of trying juveniles in criminal courts, a phenomenon that has increased steadily in recent years. All but one state (Nebraska), along with the District of Columbia, enacted or expanded transfer provisions between 1992 and 1999 (Sickmund, 2003). Juveniles being considered for transfer to criminal court have a good deal to lose. Prosecution in criminal court involves public proceedings, a criminal record if found guilty, and possible incarceration in an adult prison. A juvenile who is considered an unlikely candidate for rehabilitation in the juvenile system is not likely to get rehabilitative services once transferred to adult settings. Research has also documented that juveniles charged with serious crimes in criminal courts and juveniles facing property offenses in juvenile courts both get harsh dispositions (Podkopacz & Feld, 1996). The most recent data also indicate that juveniles prosecuted in adult courts may or may not receive harsher sanctions than adults (Sickmund, 2003). For example, juvenile defendants convicted of burglary, larceny, or weapons offenses were more likely to be sentenced to prison than were adults convicted of the same offenses; juvenile defendants convicted of murder or weapons offenses also received longer prison terms than adults. However, those convicted of sexual assault, burglary, or drug offenses received shorter prison terms than adults.

Disposition

Disposition is the equivalent of sentencing in the adult context. (See Box 11.3 for other terms relating to juvenile justice processing.) Once a juvenile has been adjudicated a delinquent in a delinquency hearing, the judge chooses from a variety of disposition alternatives, ranging from community-based services to confinement in a secure facility. In most jurisdictions, juvenile judges themselves do not choose among a variety of community alternatives, however. The judges place juveniles in the custody of juvenile justice officials (e.g., a juvenile correctional agency or a department of human services), who determine the best program approach for each juvenile. Placement

BOX 11.3 Common Terms in Juvenile Courts

Intake

The juvenile's first contact with the juvenile system following police custody. Here a decision is made whether to dismiss the case, handle it informally, or refer it formally to juvenile court. About half of all cases are handled informally. This may include referral to a social service agency, informal probation, or even the payment of some fines or voluntary restitution.

Intake workers also decide whether a juvenile should be detained, though a judge must review the detention, typically within 48 hours. Intake officers may be probation officers, social workers, or representatives from the prosecutor's office.

Diversion

The process of steering youth away from court and referring them to a structured program. The decision to refer a youth to diversion is usually made by intake workers or by prosecutors. Diversion programs vary widely, usually requiring youth to admit their actions, sign contracts, and agree to certain conditions (e.g., perform community service). Some diversion programs include teen courts, where juveniles are "judged" and "sentenced" by peers.

Delinquency Petition

This is the formal document prepared by the prosecutor that states the allegations against the juvenile and asks the juvenile court to adjudicate the juvenile a delinquent.

Preventive Detention

Juveniles may be detained securely to prevent them from committing additional offenses. Although an intake worker may make the initial detention decision, a judge or magistrate must review the need for continued detention. Juvenile courts often use detention as an opportunity to order psychological evaluations and other tests.

Waiver Petition

The prosecutor's request that the juvenile's case be transferred to criminal court.

Delinquency Hearing (or Adjudicatory Hearing)

The equivalent of a trial in criminal court. Like adults, the juvenile has a right to have a lawyer, to confront and cross-examine witnesses, and to remain silent. The prosecutor must prove all elements of the offense beyond a reasonable doubt. However, the juvenile does not have a constitutional right to a trial by jury.

Blended Sentencing

In approximately half the states, both juvenile and criminal courts are allowed to impose juvenile and/or adult sanctions on certain juveniles (usually dependent on ages of juveniles and crime charged).

Aftercare

The equivalent of adult parole. This involves supervision of the juvenile after release from some form of residential treatment.

---

in a secure facility, however, must be made by a juvenile court. In either case—community setting or institution—psychological assessment may occur later in the process rather than in consultation with the juvenile court. Juvenile correctional officials may want help deciding on a programmatic approach for a particular juvenile. A juvenile probation officer, for example, may wonder whether a boy on her caseload is a good candidate for a substance abuse program in the community. We will discuss these assessments again in Chapter 13.

The extent to which psychologists actually do consult with the juvenile courts for amenability to rehabilitation evaluations varies by jurisdiction. It appears that they are used more prior to judicial waivers than prior to disposition. For example, Podkopacz and Feld (1996) found that court psychologists had examined and filed reports on 46% of juveniles facing transfer proceedings in their Minnesota sample, with percentages increasing in later years (63% in 1991 and 57% in 1992). By comparison, Hecker and Steinberg (2002) found that only 2% to 3% of juvenile cases in the jurisdiction they studied were referred for psychological assessment *prior to disposition.* A slightly higher percentage (10%–15%) was referred for screening, as opposed to full assessment. (It is possible, though, that the records of juveniles not referred contained psychological reports of evaluations that had been conducted earlier in the juvenile process.) It should be noted that in both of the

above studies, the recommendations of the clinicians carried heavy weight with judges.

Conducting the Evaluation

A number of manuals and suggestions are available for psychologists conducting psychological evaluations relating to transfer and disposition decisions (e.g., Grisso, 1998; Melton et al., 1997). As Hecker and Steinberg (2002) note, however, "an empirically validated 'gold standard' for the predisposition evaluation of juvenile offenders remains elusive" (p. 300). Psychologists are typically advised to review the juvenile's files, including school, social service, and juvenile court records. In addition, they are advised to obtain information about family history and substance use and abuse, as well as assess intellectual, academic, personality, and vocational functioning, using a range of possible measures. Furthermore, although most juvenile offenders are not seriously emotionally disturbed, mental health needs are common. Juveniles in correctional facilities, for example, are believed to have mental health needs ranging from conduct disorders to severe depression and suicidal tendencies (LeCroy, Stevenson, & MacNeil, 2001). Developmental disabilities and cognitive impairment also plague both institutionalized juveniles and those under community supervision (Day & Berney, 2001). Many juvenile offenders also are substance abusers, often with significant chemical dependency problems, and many others are sex offenders. The psychologist assessing juveniles, therefore, should be aware of the range of treatment and rehabilitation services available, both in the community and within institutional settings.

Many psychologists are concerned about the possible negative effects of labeling juveniles. Of particular concern are those labels that suggest that prospects for change are not good. In recent years, for example, as we discussed in Chapter 4, juvenile psychopathy has received considerable research attention. It has prompted the development of a special version of Hare's Psychopathy Checklist, the Psychopathy Checklist: Youth Version (PCL:YV) (Forth et al., 1997). Some researchers have argued, though, that it is premature to place this pessimistic label on juveniles who may possess psychopathic characteristics that they may well outgrow (Edens, Skeem, et al., 2001; Seagrave & Grisso, 2002). Edens, Skeem, et al. (2001) also suggest that labeling adolescents this way may violate the two ethical principles of social responsibility and do no harm. There is also concern that labeling a juvenile a psychopath in an amenability for rehabilitation evaluation will almost assuredly guarantee that he or she will be transferred to criminal court.

Another pessimistic label that might be problematic is *life-course-persistent offender* (LCP), in accordance with Moffitt's (1993a) adolescent-limited (AL)-LCP dichotomy. Diagnostic categories in the *DSM-IV-TR* (American Psychiatric Association, 2000) (e.g., attention-deficit hyperactivity disorder [ADHD], conduct disorder) are problematic if the individuals working with the juvenile after the assessment do not understand their limitations as well as their significance. Labels that make their way into files of juveniles in correctional facilities or community programs may be as damaging as labels that make their way into school files of nondelinquent children.

Hecker and Steinberg (2002) appraised the quality of psychological evaluations submitted to juvenile courts prior to disposition as well as the effect of the reports on judges' decision making.

They reviewed 172 predisposition reports submitted to juvenile courts in Philadelphia between 1992 and 1996 by four independent practitioners, who were licensed psychologists in Pennsylvania.

Findings included the following:

- A vast majority of the assessments included a standardized measure of intellectual functioning, but few included a standardized personality measure; instead, projective tests were typically administered for measuring personality.
- There were no statistically significant individual differences in either judges' acceptance/rejection of recommendations or among clinicians in whether their recommendations were accepted or rejected.
- A high percentage of recommendations were accepted; in fact, recommendations were fully rejected in only 8 of the 172 cases.
- Many reports lacked information about the juvenile's mental health, criminal, or substance abuse history, all of which the researchers considered crucial information because of their links to recidivism.
- Judges were most likely to accept recommendations if the reports included information about mental health, regardless of the quality of this information. This was troubling to the researchers, who believed that reports did not include sufficient detail in this area, as noted above.

Hecker and Steinberg (2002) emphasized that their study may not be representative of other jurisdictions, considering the small number of judges and clinicians as well as the small number of cases in their sample. Nevertheless, they described a useful coding scheme by which researchers might evaluate predisposition reports, along with their impact on judicial decisions, in other jurisdictions.

In sum, research on amenability to rehabilitation evaluations suggests that they vary widely in quality, despite the fact that there is consensus on what should be included in the evaluation reports. Most sources recommend comprehensive evaluations that will assess the juvenile's family background; determine developmental, cognitive, and emotional functioning; and identify promising treatment options. Evaluators are advised to avoid labels that might be pessimistic and suggest that there is little hope for the juvenile. As Grisso (1998) has noted, a pessimistic report may become a self-fulfilling prophecy if the rehabilitation staff becomes discouraged. "Reservations about the prospect for change . . . should always be coupled with suggestions to staff that might increase the prospects" (p. 192).

Family and Probate Courts

As noted in Chapter 9, states are increasingly establishing specialized courts to deal with a very wide range of civil and criminal matters, such as mental health, drug, and family-related issues. Family courts are a good example of this trend, having jurisdiction over virtually all matters pertaining to the family, including delinquency matters. Thus, in many states, the juvenile courts discussed in the previous section are actually a subset of family courts. Probate courts, though also specialized, have a longer history. These are the courts that have general powers over wills and administration of estates. In some states,

they can appoint guardians and approve the adoption of minors (Black, 1990).

Both family and probate courts deal with some of the most emotionally charged and contentious issues in society. In most states, family courts are the venue for litigating divorce proceedings and making custody decisions, although these proceedings also may occur in courts of general jurisdiction (e.g., superior courts or district courts, depending on the state). Family courts also have the power to remove neglected and abused children from their homes and place them into temporary custody of the state, as well as the power to revoke parental rights permanently. In states where minors must notify a parent and obtain parental consent before obtaining an abortion, family courts can override that requirement in the best interest of the girl seeking the abortion. In domestic violence situations, family court may be the place where a victim seeks a temporary or permanent restraining order against an abuser. Adoptions are finalized in family or probate courts. Similarly, contested wills, decisions about competency to make medical decisions, and involuntary commitments to mental institutions come under the jurisdiction of some—but not all—family and/or probate courts. In light of the powers listed above, it is not surprising that psychologists and other mental health professionals play a role in the day-to-day operation of these courts and that family forensic psychology is a rapidly developing specialization (see Box 11.4).

BOX 11.4 Family Forensic Psychology

In June 2003, the *Journal of Family Psychology* published a special issue devoted to the intersection of family psychology and family law. According to the editors of this special issue, its primary goal was "to introduce readers to new and emerging opportunities for research and practice in the areas where family psychology and family law overlap" (Grossman & Okun, 2003, p. 163).

Family psychologists—whether clinicians or researchers—have extensive knowledge about human development and systems theories. Forensic psychologists have knowledge and expertise

---

(Continued)

BOX 11.4 (Continued)

---

in assessment and consultation with courts and legal professionals. They also know legal theories and procedures that relate to clinical practice and have experience at providing expert testimony. Family forensic psychologists, then, represent a combination of the knowledge and skills of forensic psychologists and family psychologists.

Grossman and Okun (2003) define family forensic psychology as

the study of families, members of family units, organizations, and larger systems from a family systems perspective in assessment and intervention regarding interaction with the legal system. Among the areas that assessment and intervention include are prevention, education, evaluation, various forms of conflict resolution, treatment, and outcome assessment. Family forensic psychologists provide expertise to the legal system. (p. 166)

Family forensic psychology can make contributions in all of the following areas: adoption; divorce, child custody, and visitation; conflict resolution and mediation; juvenile justice; assessment of parental fitness (e.g., when parents have a psychiatric diagnosis); termination of parental rights; elder law and estate planning; child-parent relationships when parents are imprisoned; guardianship; reproductive rights and technologies; and family violence. Because all of these issues are increasingly being adjudicated in family courts and other specialized courts, family forensic psychologists should continue to be in high demand.

Child Custody Evaluations

Among the most contentious areas faced by family courts are those involving divorce and child custody, most particularly when custody is contested. Although it is estimated that children are involved in about 40% of divorces (Horvath, Logan, & Walker, 2002), the majority of these do not require a custody decision by the court. Instead, custody is not contested because parents, alone or with the help of a mediator, have agreed on a mutually satisfactory custody arrangement. Studies suggest that courts make decisions in 6% to 20% of all divorce cases (Melton et al., 1997). When courts do make decisions, however, they turn to mental health professionals. Research suggests that psychologists are the most frequent examiners (Mason & Quirk, 1997), but they are also apparently highly paid compared with other examiners, such as social workers. Bow and Quinnell (2001) reported that the average charge for a custody

evaluation performed by a licensed psychologist in private practice was $3,335. Thus, many courts use mental health practitioners who are associated with public court service agencies, such as master's-level psychologists or clinical social workers (Horvath et al., 2002).

At the outset, we must acknowledge that individuals other than the child's biological or adoptive parents may seek custody of minor children. In fact, over the past decade, family courts have seen an unprecedented explosion in both custody and visitation requests from stepparents, grandparents, other relatives, gay and lesbian partners of deceased biological or adoptive parents, cohabiting but nonmarried parents who have split up, family friends, and surrogate mothers (Grossman & Okun, 2003). Although legal parents clearly have both constitutional and civil rights to be involved in their children's lives, the rights of other individuals, including grandparents, are not universally well defined. The U.S. Supreme Court has denied grandparents a constitutional right to see their grandchild over the objection of the child's competent mother (*Troxel v. Granville,* 2000). However, in that case, the mother had not totally deprived the grandparents of visitation privileges but had refused to allow more than one visit every month. Thus, although the decision did not represent a victory for grandparents, it is unclear what would have been decided had the mother refused to allow *any* visits. Psychological researchers are just beginning to discuss and explore the implications of custody evaluations and visitation requests.

Child Custody Standards

Historically, courts have relied on a number of different standards for determining child custody. The primary standard was the **tender years doctrine,** in which it was presumed that the children, particularly girls and very young children, were best left in the care of the mother. An early appellate case (*People v. Hickey,* 1889) suggested that even if the father was without blame, he had an "inability to bestow on [the child] that tender care which nature requires, and which it is the peculiar province of the mother to supply" (Einhorn, 1986, p. 128). Today, the tender years doctrine has given way in most states to a standard that does not presume that either parent is naturally better than the other but rather looks at what is in the **best interest of the child (BICS).**

Krauss and Sales (2000) maintain that the dominant best interest of the child standard should be replaced by a **least detrimental alternative** standard. They argue that psychological knowledge, in its present state, cannot determine which custody arrangement is truly in the child's best interest. At best, psychological knowledge can help in identifying which arrangement would do the least harm. Psychological assessment instruments, according to Krauss and Sales, tend to be pathology focused, identifying deficits more than strengths. In that sense, a custody evaluation would be more efficient at "screening

out" the custody arrangement that would create problems for the child rather than making a determination that one parent would be better than the other. Interestingly, representatives of **family forensic psychology** suggest that the legal principle should be the best interests of the child *in relation to the family* (Grossman & Okun, 2003).

Deciding what is in the best interest of the child sounds sensible, but the process of arriving at that determination remains highly subjective and controversial. A number of researchers have noted that custody evaluations—compared with other psychological services—are disproportionately associated with ethical problems and complaints to state licensing boards (Bow & Quinnell, 2001; Kirkland & Kirkland, 2001). The APA (1994) has published a list of 16 guidelines for child custody evaluation, which focus on the purpose of the evaluation, the competence needed by the psychologist, and specific recommended procedures, such as using multiple methods of data gathering and clarifying financial arrangements. The guidelines are recommendations and suggestions that are aspirational rather than mandatory. By comparison, APA *standards* are mandatory and may be accompanied by an enforcement mechanism (APA, 1993). The Ethical Principles and Code of Conduct of the APA (2002) is an illustration of standards as opposed to guidelines.

Like competency to stand trial and criminal responsibility evaluations, custody evaluations also raise the "ultimate issue" question that was introduced in Chapter 9. Should examiners make a recommendation as to which parent should be given custody of the child? The APA guidelines do not take a position on this beyond advising psychologists to be aware of both sides of the ultimate issue controversy and to be aware of their own biases in making custody recommendations. This caveat is particularly relevant when we consider the changing definitions of family that go beyond the traditional definition of individuals related by blood or marriage.

Methods of Evaluation in Child Custody Cases

Several studies have examined the methods used by psychologists in conducting custody evaluations (e.g., Ackerman & Ackerman, 1997; Bow & Quinnell, 2001; Keilin & Bloom, 1986; LaFortune & Carpenter, 1998). These studies suggest that evaluators progressed from relying almost exclusively on interview data (Keilin & Bloom, 1986) to using a wide range of assessment measures, including tests developed specifically for custody evaluations (Bow & Quinnell, 2001). However, it should be noted that these tests themselves have been criticized by some psychologists for not being grounded in sufficient research before being used in practice (Krauss & Sales, 2000; Otto & Heilbrun, 2002).

In their survey of 198 psychologists in 38 states, Bow and Quinnell (2001) found that psychologists were testing parents more and children less. In other words, they made greater use of parent rating scales and parenting inventories and less use of cognitive and personality tests for children. According to their own reports, psychologists were following the APA (1993) guidelines by using multiple methods of data collection and attending seminars and workshops to gain more expertise at this task. Although Bow and Quinnell identified problem areas relating to ethical issues, they concluded that psychologists seemed to be doing a better job of conducting custody evaluations than early studies indicated. Interestingly, almost all respondents (94%) provided a recommendation to the court as to which parent should gain custody. As we noted above, the guidelines do not take a position on this issue.

Horvath et al. (2002) used a different methodology to research custody evaluation procedures—a method that, it is hoped, will be adopted by other researchers in different jurisdictions. Rather than asking psychologists to report their own practices, Horvath et al. performed a content analysis of evaluations in 60% of custody cases decided in one court over a 2-year period. (**Content analysis** is a technique in which the researcher carefully examines the content of documents to discover common elements.) A total of 102 evaluation reports were examined. The evaluators represented a variety of professionals, including social workers, child protective service investigators, and clinical, counseling, and educational psychologists. Both private and court-appointed evaluators were represented in the sample.

Horvath et al. (2002) found that there was considerable variability in the contents of the reports and in methods of the evaluations, leading them to the conclusion that there was no standardized approach for conducting custody evaluations. More disturbingly, though, the researchers found that parent interviews often failed to address variables that would seem critical to custody determination.

> In particular, evaluators frequently neglected assessment of domestic violence and child abuse, adequate assessment of parenting skills, assessment of health status, and formal psychological testing. . . . It is also noteworthy that approximately 40% of the evaluations relied on only two methods of assessment to determine a custody arrangement. (p. 7)

Some differences emerged across professionals and between private and public evaluators. For example, private evaluators were more likely to include formal psychological testing of both parents and children. MSWs (masters in social work) were more likely to include home visits. None of the educational psychologists included parent-child observations in their reports, whereas 62.5% of the MSWs and 76.2% of the clinical and counseling psychologists included these observations.

The content analysis confirmed information derived from self-report studies (e.g., Bow & Quinnell, 2001; LaFortune & Carpenter, 1998) that examiners almost always offer custody and visitation recommendations (only 8 of the 102 evaluations did not include these). Horvath et al. (2002)

were able to compare the recommendations to the final decision. The final determination was exactly as evaluators recommended in 27.3% of the cases and similar to the recommendations but with a few modifications in 63.6% of the cases. It appears, therefore, that the examiner's opinion carries considerable weight in crafting the final custody and visitation arrangements. Considering the problems identified by these researchers in the reports they examined, this is a sobering fact. Horvath et al. recommend that continuing efforts should be made to developing a standard of practice so that, at the least, custody evaluations will contain information that is essential to deciding what is in the best interest of the child.

Visitation Risk Assessments

Closely related to the custody issue is the issue of visitation, and visitation recommendations are almost invariably included in custody assessments. Ideally, children should have access to both parents, and each parent also has the right to be involved in his or her child's lives. However, it is not uncommon for a custodial parent to challenge or request a change in the visitation rights of the noncustodial parent. This usually occurs under the premise that the noncustodial parent is emotionally or physically damaging the child—or presents a strong risk of inflicting such harm. Consequently—in addition to custody evaluations—psychologists and other mental health practitioners are sometimes asked to conduct "visitation risk assessments" to help courts decide whether visitation rights should be limited or abrogated completely. For example, on the basis of such an assessment, the family court judge may decide to require that all visits be supervised by the child's social service caseworker or by a court-appointed guardian.

The psychologist conducting the visitation risk assessment ideally interviews both parents and, depending on the circumstances, may also interview the child. The psychologist's role is to determine whether there is evidence of a

psychological problem or behavior pattern that would likely lead to inappropriate and potentially harmful interactions between parent and child. Like the custody evaluations discussed above, there is no "standard of practice" for visitation risk assessments. However, there is more research available on custody evaluations than visitation risk assessments.

Research on Custody Arrangements

Psychologists and other mental health practitioners conducting custody evaluations should be aware of the vast store of research on the effects of divorce and custody arrangements (e.g., Bricklin & Elliott, 1995; Johnston, 1995; Maccoby, Buchanan, Mnookin, & Dornsbusch, 1993; Wallerstein, 1989). However, sifting through this research can become an exercise in frustration because—as Krauss and Sales (2000) have noted, methodologically sound studies have reached different conclusions. Particularly equivocal has been research comparing joint custody to sole custody arrangements (e.g., Bauserman, 2002; Gunnoe & Braver, 2001), leading to conclusions that no one arrangement is clearly superior to the other. Numerous factors have been found to play a part in a child's adjustment to divorce and custody arrangements, including—but not limited to—the child's age, gender, hostility between parents, parenting skills, the quality of the parent-child relationship, and emotional and physical health of the parents. These factors should be taken into consideration when performing custody evaluations, but examiners should be careful not to generalize from the group data reported to what is in the best interest of the particular child or children involved in the presenting case.

Decisional Competency

Psychologists, as well as other clinicians, may be asked to evaluate whether an individual was or is capable of making a critical decision in his or her best interest. Persons who have reached adulthood are presumed to be capable of making these decisions. Likewise, they are expected to take responsibility for decisions that resulted in disastrous consequences. This decisional autonomy extends to such areas as consenting to medical treatment, joining a cult, engaging in a business contract, enlisting in the military, drafting a will, refusing medication or life-prolonging treatment, or consenting to participate in psychological or medical research. The presumption that one is capable of making decisions can be overcome if it can be demonstrated to the satisfaction of a court that the person was not mentally or physically competent at the time the decision was made (or is being considered). In most jurisdictions, the burden of proof in these situations is preponderance of the evidence, but some jurisdictions require clear and convincing evidence, which is a higher standard (see Box 10.1 in the previous chapter for a review of the burdens of proof). When a court determines that an individual is or was not competent, it invalidates a decision that was made (e.g., the terms of a will or a decision to forgo medical treatment). If the person is still alive, the court will usually appoint a guardian to decide what is in the person's best interest.

Testamentary Capacity

One decision that is frequently challenged—though not successfully—is the competence to make a will, called **testamentary capacity.** In most states, this would come under the purview of a probate court. As Slovenko (1999) has noted, making a will actually requires only minimal competency and is an easy task. The law requires only that one be "of sound mind" when making a will. Specific requirements are that individuals (1) know they are making a will, (2) know the nature and extent of their property, (3) know the objects of their bounty, and (4) know how their property is being divided (Melton et al., 1997). As

Melton et al. (1997) point out, it is possible for someone to be forgetful, addicted to narcotics or alcohol, mentally disordered, and/or have a low threshold of cognitive functioning yet still be capable of making a will. The evaluation of testamentary capacity is usually retrospective, such that it requires the evaluator to interview those who knew the individual, review any available records, and draw inferences about the individual's mental state at the time the will was formulated. In many respects, it is similar to the psychological autopsy discussed in Chapter 3, although far less detailed. However, in some situations, lawyers advise their clients to be evaluated for testamentary capacity at the time they execute their wills. Psychological assessment would especially be warranted if the individual exhibits signs of dementia, has a mental disorder that includes periods of cognitive incapacity, or has some mental retardation.

Competence to Consent to Treatment

Perhaps even more frequent than evaluations of testamentary capacity are evaluations of a person's competence to make decisions regarding medical and psychological treatment. These decisions require informed consent, a principle we covered in the previous chapter in our discussion of psychological assessments of competency to stand trial and mental state at the time of the offense. Recall that elements of this informed consent are disclosure, competency, and voluntariness. In other words, the individuals must be told of the possible consequences of the treatment, must be mentally capable of understanding what they are consenting to, and must be doing so of their own free will, without coercion. Each of these three elements is scrutinized separately by courts when questions of informed consent come before them. Interestingly, research suggests that disclosure is particularly problematic. "The most general thing that can be said about disclosure in health and mental health settings is that there is rarely adherence to the spirit of informed consent" (Melton et al., 1997, p. 352). Melton et al. note that consent forms are lengthy and beyond comprehension, patients often lack information about alternative treatments, and negative information (e.g., about side effects) is often omitted. A variety of explanations are offered for this failure to adhere to the spirit of disclosure requirements. For example, treatment providers may wish to protect their patients from excessive worry, or they may fear that they themselves will appear professionally weak by not knowing precisely how the patient will react to the treatment. Obviously, the quality of disclosure is an important component in a subsequent evaluation of consent to treatment. That is, if the individual did not receive sufficient information about treatment alternatives or about the risks associated with the treatment, the consent was not informed.

Measure of Competence to Consent to Treatment

The competence of mentally disturbed individuals to consent to treatment has been studied extensively by researchers associated with the MacArthur Foundation (e.g., Appelbaum & Grisso, 1995; Grisso, Appelbaum, Mulvey, & Fletcher, 1995). Their research has, in turn, been the subject of considerable scholarly comment (see, generally, Winick, 1996). The MacArthur Competence Study (Appelbaum & Grisso, 1995) assessed and compared decision-making competence in three groups: persons hospitalized with serious mental illness, persons hospitalized with medical illness, and community volunteers who were not patients. Despite some decision-making deficits, those hospitalized with mental illness were still capable of making decisions, as reflected on measures of decision-making ability. The exceptions were patients with schizophrenia who had severe psychiatric symptoms; nevertheless, the majority of patients with schizophrenia still performed adequately. Hospitalized patients with depression demonstrated intermediate

levels of decision making. The MacArthur researchers developed a tool—the **MacArthur Competence Assessment Tool—Treatment (MacCAT-T)** for use by clinicians who evaluate treatment competence. The interview format allows clinicians to test decision-making competence in four areas: ability to state a choice, ability to understand relevant information, ability to appreciate the nature of one's own situation, and ability to reason with the information provided.

Although the MacCAT-T has received favorable reviews (e.g., Winick, 1996), some researchers and scholars have issued cautionary notes. Kirk and Bersoff (1996) suggest that the instrument sets too low a standard for decision-making competence, focusing as it does on competencies rather than disabilities. In other words, under the instrument, too many individuals would be found to make competent decisions in their best interest, and their decisional disabilities would be overlooked. Stefan (1996) made a compelling argument that the MacCAT-T is not sufficiently sensitive to race, class, and gender differences in the determination of incompetence.

Kapp and Mossman (1996) believe there are inherent problems in any attempt to construct a universal test of decisional capacity to make medical choices. Although the MacArthur group clearly warned that their measures were still in the experimental stage, Kapp and Mossman expressed concern that clinicians will rush too quickly to adopt the competency assessment tool and that courts will accept it too readily. They note also that numerous other instruments are currently available to assess competency, many of which are accompanied by research testing their validity (e.g., the Mini-Mental State Examination [MMSE], the Geriatric Depression Scale, the Alzheimer's Disease Assessment Scale). Kapp and Mossman believe it is far more useful to develop a *process* than a universal test (or capacimeter) for evaluating competency to consent to treatment. "What is needed . . . is a credible process for collecting, critically examining, and drawing up usable guidelines from our extensive research and practice experience" (Kapp & Mossman, 1996,

p. 95). Critiques such as these highlight the need for forensic psychologists evaluating competency matters to exercise judgment in their approach and in communicating their findings to legal decision makers.

Incapacitation: Special Condition

Another decisional competency area that has been controversial involves persons who are comatose and/or cognitively incapacitated and in a permanent vegetative state. Obviously, they cannot make decisions in their best interest. However, if their wishes are known, they will generally (although not invariably) be honored. The tragic case of two young women, Karen Ann Quinlan and Nancy Cruzan, brought this issue directly to the Supreme Court. Injured in an automobile accident, Quinlan remained comatose and on life support systems with physicians giving no hope to her parents that she would ever be revived. The Supreme Court in that case (*In re Quinlan,* 1976) ruled that the wishes of a comatose person should be honored if she had made it perfectly clear what she would want in the event that she should become incompetent. Shortly thereafter, in the Cruzan case, the Court ruled that a guardian for a person in a permanent vegetative state could terminate life-sustaining procedures with clear evidence that the person would have wanted this (*Cruzan v. Director, Missouri Department of Health,* 1990). Together,

these two cases prompted many people to prepare **advanced directives** should they become physically incapacitated. In some cases, family members or other interested parties challenge these advanced directives, maintaining that the incapacitated person was not mentally competent at the time he or she formulated them. In these situations, the forensic clinician is asked to make an assessment similar to that involved in testamentary capacity. In recent years, advanced directives for mental health care are also being promoted, in the event that a person should become psychologically incapacitated (Monahan, Bonnie, et al., 2001; Stavis, 1999). In other words, individuals with mental disorders are urged—in their stable and lucid periods—to make it clear that they would (or would not) accept certain interventions, such as psychoactive medication, if they became too mentally disordered to make autonomous decisions at some point in time.

Although the Supreme Court has made it clear that competent individuals have a constitutional right to refuse life-prolonging treatment, it has not thus far supported the idea of aggressively hastening one's death. Thus far, it has been left to states to craft their own legal rules in this matter. Only one state, Oregon, allows terminally ill individuals to request and physicians to administer medication that will help them die. This has spurred the need for a new form of psychological assessment, the evaluation of competency to make decisions that will hasten one's death (see Box 11.5).

BOX 11.5 Hastened Death: The Psychologist's Role

The issue of physician-assisted suicide is certainly one of the most controversial in today's society. By now, the law is very clear that competent individuals have the right to forgo medical treatment. Most states, for example, allow the withdrawal of life support if it is demonstrated that this is what the individual wants or would want if he or she were able to make a decision. However, only one state, Oregon, allows physicians to prescribe medication that would hasten death at the request of a competent, terminally ill individual.

Under Oregon's "Death with Dignity Act," a mentally competent adult with less than 6 months to live may ask her or his physician for such medication. Under the law, the patient must be fully informed of the progress of the illness as well as the safeguards in place to prevent a rash decision and improve the quality of end-of-life care. Two physicians must review and approve of the request. If one or both physicians suspect the individual is not mentally competent, a psychiatrist or psychologist is brought in to conduct an evaluation.

Hastened death evaluations are beginning to be discussed in the forensic psychology literature, along with proposed guidelines for conducting them (e.g., Allen & Shuster, 2002; Werth, Benjamin, & Farrenkopf, 2000). Other states may well follow Oregon's lead and adopt similar statutes, in which case increasingly more clinicians will be asked to participate in the hastened death process. Although opponents of these laws say they undermine the value of life, supporters say they recognize the dignity and privacy of the individual who does not wish to postpone the inevitable death he or she faces in the near future.

Involuntary Civil Commitment

Closely related to competency to consent to treatment is the issue of hospitalizing individuals for psychological/psychiatric treatment against their will. Every state allows such commitment, both on emergency and extended bases. The typical statute allows an emergency commitment of 3 to 10 days and an extended commitment for a 3- to 6-month period subject to recommitment proceedings. Although standards vary somewhat depending on the state, the party seeking the commitment always has to prove by at least clear and convincing evidence that the individual is mentally ill and in need of treatment (*Addington v. Texas,* 1979). Furthermore, the individual must be a danger to self or others *or* so gravely disabled that this person is unable to meet his or her basic needs. It should be noted that, although individuals have a right to legal representation at commitment hearings, there is evidence that lawyers actually function paternalistically instead of advocating for the legal rights of their clients (Perlin & Dorfman, 1996). This is not unlike the situation of lawyers representing juveniles in delinquency proceedings, when they believe it is in the juvenile's interest to obtain treatment rather than aggressively forcing the state to prove the juvenile's guilt beyond a reasonable doubt.

An extremely controversial area in involuntary commitment is the civil commitment of sexual predators. Less controversial, but still of concern, is the civil commitment of persons found not guilty by reason of insanity. Both of these topics were addressed in the previous chapter and will not be revisited here.

The Supreme Court has ruled that persons who are seriously mentally disordered are unable to consent "voluntarily" to being institutionalized (*Zinermon v. Burch,* 1990). Burch, a mentally disordered individual who was found wandering along a highway in a highly disoriented condition, had signed forms voluntarily admitting himself into a mental institution. He later attempted to rescind his agreement. The Supreme Court declared his original admission invalid because, in his severely mentally disordered state, he could not have validly consented. Accordingly, persons who are unable to make competent decisions must be admitted to mental institutions via the involuntary commitment route described above (Slovenko, 1999).

Outpatient Civil Commitment

Civil commitment also can be achieved on an outpatient basis—in fact, statutes often require this least restrictive alternative if it can reasonably be provided. Courts are empowered to issue **"outpatient treatment orders"** or "orders of nonhospitalization." These orders typically require that the individual live in his or her own home or alternative group or foster home and comply with a medication regimen. Outpatient civil commitment has been a hot topic in the research literature, probably surpassing interest in institutional confinement (see, generally, Winick & Kress, 2003b).

Until recently, most states required that an outpatient order be based on showing that the individual was both mentally disordered and dangerous to self or others. Some states are now beginning to allow outpatient orders without the dangerousness component. Called **preventive outpatient treatment,** this approach allows the state to intervene before the individual's condition becomes worse. "The new broadened criteria still require mental illness, but instead of the dangerousness standard, they require a need for treatment to prevent further deterioration that would predictably lead to dangerousness based on the individual's illness history" (Hiday, 2003, p. 11). Hiday adds that the person must be judged unable to seek or comply with treatment voluntarily. In addition, like the outpatient orders based on a dangerousness standard, it must be determined that the individual can survive safely in the community with available supervision (Hiday, 2003).

Schopp (2003) has provided an additional description of outpatient civil commitment that helps clarify the situations under which it occurs. He notes that outpatient commitment can take three forms. First, persons who were institutionalized under civil commitment statutes requiring mental disorder and the dangerousness standard are conditionally released to the community; if they fail to meet the conditions of their release, they are subject to being returned to the institution. Second, persons who are eligible for institutional confinement under the civil commitment statutes are placed on an alternative mandatory treatment status in the community. Third, persons who would not qualify under the dangerousness standard but who are considered to need treatment to prevent further deterioration are assigned to preventive commitment.

Researchers are continuing to explore the effectiveness of involuntary outpatient treatment, which is increasingly being used in all three forms described by Schopp (2003). The main questions revolve around whether individuals can be "coerced" to get better; in other words, does treatment "work" if a person is forced to get it? In reviewing this literature, Hiday (2003) notes that early studies almost invariably found positive outcomes on a number of factors. For example, patients ordered to outpatient treatment had lower rehospitalization rates, better compliance with medication and other treatment, and generally better adjustment in the community than comparison groups of patients, such as those who were discharged without outpatient orders. Hiday also reports on a second generation of research conducted in North Carolina (Swartz, Swanson, & Hiday, 2001) and New York City (Steadman, Gounis, & Dennis, 2001) that is more empirically based, including random assignment to outpatient commitment and nonoutpatient commitment groups. Both groups received mental health and social services in the community. The North Carolina study again found that patients under outpatient orders had significantly more positive outcomes than those not under these orders. The New York study, though, found no significant differences, a finding that Hiday attributes to technical problems in the research. She notes that, despite the study's conclusions, New York State's Department of Mental Health remains supportive of outpatient commitment and reports positive outcomes for patients under those orders—including declines in harmful behavior and homelessness and an increase in medication compliance.

Not everyone is supportive of outpatient commitment, however, particularly when it is not based on dangerousness criteria. Civil libertarians have argued that such preventive commitment raises many legal questions without ensuring that effective treatment will be provided (e.g., Winick, 2003). Persons who would otherwise not qualify for civil commitment are forced to take medications and comply with other treatment regimens against their will. This, they say, is a dangerous expansion of the already overwhelming power of the state. The New York study, which reported no differences between those subjected to mandatory treatment and those who were not, provides additional support for this perspective—if forced treatment is no better than voluntary treatment, why force treatment? Such debates among reasonable people have a long history in the literature on civil commitment and will not likely be resolved in the near future.

It is also important to note that the research supportive of any form of outpatient commitment generally indicates that such treatment is effective only if it continues for a period of at least 6 months and is accompanied by the provision of intensive services (Winick & Kress, 2003a). Thus, forensic psychologists who are providing treatment to patients under such orders should be aware of the need to sustain these services.

Role of Forensic Psychologists

Regardless of the nature of the involuntary commitment (inpatient or outpatient and its variations), the assessment skills of forensic psychologists are required to help determine whether the individual meets the standards for commitment. If a showing of dangerousness is required, the psychologist again engages in the risk assessment enterprise we have discussed in the two previous chapters. Melton et al. (1997) warn that this is an area where clinicians must exercise extreme caution, considering the inadequate legal representation provided to so many individuals and the potential loss of freedom they are encountering. Demonstrating the presence of mental illness and determining treatment needs of the individual are probably the easier of the clinician's tasks. The accompanying assessment of dangerousness (or risk) is more formidable. All of the cautions about risk assessment referred to in the past two chapters should be recalled here as well.

The individual's potential for dangerousness to self involves an assessment of suicide risk. Clinicians should be informed about general research on demographics of suicide (e.g., males at higher risk, married persons at lower risk) as well as the individual's own clinical history. Interviews with the individual also may uncover suicide ideation, or fantasies of killing oneself. Both the frequency and intensity of such ideations should be considered. However, as Melton et al. (1997) note, the track record of mental health professionals at predicting suicide is very poor. They urge clinicians to refer to the person's risk compared with others in the population rather than state that he or she is a danger to himself or herself.

Other Civil Disputes

It has become commonplace to state that we are a litigious society, seeking redress through the courts for a wide range of alleged wrongs done to us by others. There are a variety of ways in which we may approach the civil courts, including—but not limited to—a civil rights claim, a claim of a breach of contract, intellectual property (e.g., a patent case), a prisoner case, or a labor case (e.g., unfair labor practices). The most common civil suit is the **tort,** which is the legal term for a civil wrong in which a plaintiff alleges some negligence on the part of the defendant. Courts consider torts on such matters as defamation, invasion of privacy, toxic harm, and personal injury, to name but a few. The redress sought is typically some form of financial compensation. To be awarded damages, though, the plaintiff must be able to demonstrate some physical harm or mental injury as a result of the actions of the defendant. Mental injury may also be referred to as emotional distress, emotional harm, or psychic trauma. Although courts were initially reluctant to accept these claims of mental injury, they have become far more commonplace, "at least in part because of an increased willingness by courts to accept diagnosis and prognosis as legitimate skills" (Melton et al., 1997, p. 374). A plaintiff alleging emotional distress is subject to being evaluated not only by a clinician contacted by his or her lawyer but also by a clinician hired by the defendant. In the usual case, the plaintiff hires the psychologist.

Psychologists also may be called as expert witnesses in these civil suits to testify more generally on the effects of the alleged wrong, without examining the plaintiff. For example, in a civil suit alleging discrimination on the basis of gender—a civil rights violation—a psychologist with research expertise on gender stereotyping may be called as an expert witness. As we noted in Chapter 9, researchers continue to examine the effects of the *Daubert* standard. Thus far, it appears that judges—particularly federal judges—are scrutinizing expert testimony more carefully and are rejecting more such testimony than they were in the years before the *Daubert* decision (see, generally, Studebaker & Goodman-Delahunty, 2002). How well judges are performing this gatekeeping function has yet to be determined, however (Dixon & Gill, 2002). It is interesting to note, though, that psychologists appear to be expert witnesses in a relatively small number of civil trials compared with other medical and mental health professionals. For example, Krafka, Dunn, Johnson, Cecil, and Miletich (2002) obtained information on 297 federal civil trials in 1998, involving 1,281 expert witnesses. Clinical psychologists comprised 3.4% of the total medical/mental health experts, and other medical/mental health experts (including research psychologists) comprised 14.8% of the total.

In the following section, we will discuss two additional areas in which forensic psychologists consult with civil courts. In both cases, psychologists will be asked to evaluate claims of mental harm, often as the result of another individual's behavior.

Sexual Harassment

Sexual harassment may be broadly defined as unwelcome sexual advances, requests for sexual favors, and other verbal or physical conduct of a sexual nature (Hellkamp & Lewis, 1995; Till, 1980). Civil claims of sexual harassment arise most frequently in employment and educational contexts, where harassment qualifies as discrimination in violation of Title VII of the Civil Rights Acts of 1971. The Supreme Court has recognized two primary forms of sexual harassment: *quid pro quo* and hostile environment (*Meritor Savings Bank v. Vinson*, 1986). In *quid pro quo* harassment, the offender uses his or her position of power to obtain sexual favors in exchange for something of presumed value to the victim. For example, a supervisor promises a promotion if the victim sleeps with him or punishes the victim who refuses his advances by recommending a demotion. In hostile-environment harassment, the offender's actions have created an unacceptably negative environment that has made it difficult for normal work or social interaction to occur. In this second category, the offender may be a coworker or a supervisor.

To qualify as hostile-environment harassment, the behavior must be more than irritating or mildly offensive. It must be severe and pervasive, so much so that it alters conditions of the victim's employment (*Harris v. Forklift Systems, Inc.*, 1993). The conduct also must be objectively offensive—or offensive to a reasonable person—not just subjectively offensive to the plaintiff (*Harris v. Forklift Systems, Inc.*, 1993). Some courts prefer a "reasonable woman" standard on the premise that men might not understand the effects of sexual harassment on women. Still other courts use a "reasonable victim" standard, which recognizes that both women and men suffer from the effects of sexual harassment, though women are most likely to be victims of this form of discrimination. In a review of the legal standards applied in sexual harassment cases, Goodman-Delahunty (1999a) maintains that the reasonable victim standard avoids gender bias and is most reflective of the spirit of sexual harassment law. Finally, although plaintiffs typically seek compensation for mental anguish and pain and suffering (e.g., anger, anxiety, loss of self-esteem, fear, and/or feelings of humiliation), extensive psychological harm need not be demonstrated for a plaintiff to prevail (*Harris v. Forklift Systems, Inc.*, 1993). In other words, the Supreme Court has recognized that some victims of sexual harassment may experience its negative effects without also experiencing debilitating psychological deterioration.

Forensic psychologists have a variety of tasks to perform relating to sexual harassment. They may consult with employers in setting up educational programs on the topic, including providing information on the effects on victims. They may also offer counseling services to victims of harassment. In the present chapter, we discuss their role in civil suits. Either side—plaintiff or defendant—might hire a forensic psychologist to evaluate the claims of emotional distress made by the plaintiff. The psychologist is also asked to address the question of whether the particular behavior of the defendant, if it did occur, could reasonably lead to the mental injury experienced by the plaintiff. In these examinations, the evaluator is asked not only to document the disorder but also to eliminate other possible sources that are unrelated to the alleged harassment. Both clinical and research psychologists also might be called as expert witnesses to testify on gender stereotyping or on the general psychological effects of sexual harassment. In the sexual harassment context as well as other contexts (e.g., custody evaluations), psychologists are warned to avoid dual relationships in which they both serve as evaluators or expert witnesses *and* offer treatment (Heilbrun et al., 2002; Hellkamp & Lewis, 1995; see Box 10.3 in the previous chapter).

In sexual harassment suits, the alleged victim may be compelled to undergo a psychological or psychiatric evaluation at the request of the defendant. Recall that we mentioned above that sexual harassment suits do not necessarily involve mental injury evaluations. Compelled examinations occur when the plaintiff claims any more than ordinary distress as a result of the harassment. For example, she may claim that the actions of the defendant not only were irritating or embarrassing but also caused a mental disorder, such as a major depressive disorder (Kovera & Cass, 2002). In compelled evaluations, the defendant asks the court to order an evaluation by a clinician contacted by his or her attorney. The defendant must show good cause for why the plaintiff should undergo it. Kovera and Cass (2002) note that courts tend to deny motions for a compelled examination if the disorder occurred in the past rather than being current. Furthermore, "simply claiming emotional damages does not put one's mental health into controversy and thus does not warrant a compelled mental health examination" (Kovera & Cass, 2002, p. 99). Rather, motions are more likely to be granted if the plaintiff meets a number of criteria, such as claiming *severe* disorder and signifying intent to put forth her or his own expert to substantiate any claims. A compelled evaluation is likely to open the way for a psychologist to gain information about sexual history, including sexual abuse, and this information is then made available to the opposing party. Shortly, we will explain why this is so controversial. As in all evaluations, then, it is critical that the examining clinician inform the person being evaluated of the potential use of the report.

Psychological Measures of Sexual Harassment

The dominant instrument for assessing sexual harassment is the **Sexual Experiences Questionnaire (SEQ)** (Fitzgerald & Shullman, 1985). It is recognized as "the most theoretically and psychometrically sophisticated instrument available for assessing incidence and prevalence of sexual harassment" (Cortina, 2001, p. 165). The SEQ lists 29 specific behaviors and asks respondents whether they have ever experienced them on a scale of *never* to *often*. Five types of harassment are measured: gender harassment, seductive behavior, sexual bribery, sexual coercion, and sexual imposition.

As with the great majority of instruments described in this text, the SEQ was developed from research focusing almost exclusively on White participants. Although acknowledging the usefulness of the SEQ, several researchers have noted that research on sexual harassment does not sufficiently take into consideration differences in ethnic and cultural norms that might affect non-White victims. Adams (1997) argued persuasively that sexual harassment of Blacks is reflective of both sex and race discrimination and that it perpetuates both gender and racial stereotypes. Cortina (2001) notes that Latinas might be more likely than non-Latinas to take offense at unwanted sex-related behavior in the workplace because of cultural norms emphasizing respect, dignity, and harmony in in-group relations. On the other hand, those Latinas who emigrated from countries where sexual harassment is more accepted might interpret fewer of the behaviors on the SEQ as harassing behaviors. After conducting focus group interviews with Latina working women, Cortina added new items to the SEQ (SEQ-L) to assess behaviors that were particularly relevant to Latina experiences. For example, focus group interviews suggested that the Latina women were offended by being addressed informally in Spanish when a more formal mode of address was expected and by being called Spanish pet names. They were also offended when someone stood too close or expected them to behave in certain ways *because of their ethnicity* (e.g., as a Latina woman, she was expected to wear sexy clothes). None of these behaviors were included in the original SEQ.

We have only touched the surface of the rapidly developing research on ethnic and race differences in attitudes and responses to sexual harassment. Clearly, though, it is incumbent on forensic psychologists working with culturally diverse groups to be aware of these findings and to be sensitive to between-group differences.

In addition to administering the SEQ, forensic psychologists might use a variety of assessment techniques, ranging from the clinical interview to personality measures. Scales such as the Self-Efficacy Scale (SES) (Scherer et al., 1982), the Impact of Events Scale (IES) (Horowitz, Wilner, & Alvarez, 1979), and the Attitudes Toward Women Scale (AWS) (Spence & Helmreich, 1978) may also be administered.

Private Life Issues in Sexual Harassment Cases

One controversial aspect of sexual harassment suits involves the private life of the victim, particularly her sexual history. Some defendants have argued that a plaintiff who has an active sex life with multiple partners is unlikely to be offended by their behavior, despite the fact that research does not support this assumption (Kovera & Cass, 2002). Although many states have passed "rape shield laws" to protect victims of rape from having their sexual history exposed in court, such protections are rarely available to plaintiffs in sexual harassment suits if their history is part of the psychological record (Kovera & Cass, 2002). Thus, when psychologists evaluate plaintiffs in sexual harassment suits, particularly when the examination is a compelled one, they should be aware that information about the plaintiff's sexual past could be appropriated by the defense and used to its advantage. This is not to suggest that defendants in sexual harassment suits should not have resources to defend themselves against false claims; rather, it is to emphasize that anyone, regardless of sexual history, can be subjected to hostile environments and unwelcome sexual advances.

Defendants also have argued that victims who were prior victims of sexual assault and/or domestic violence might be hypersensitive to social situations involving sexual overtones. This hypersensitivity, they say, results in an aversion to even the most benign interactions. Some psychologists agree, maintaining that prior abuse alters the perceptions of victims and leaves them susceptible to revictimization as adults. In arguing against this perspective, other researchers point out that there is no empirical evidence that many victims of sexual harassment were victims of past abuse (Fitzgerald, Buchanan, Collinsworth, Magley, & Ramos, 1999). Furthermore, even if they were victims of such abuse, reviews of the literature (e.g., Stockdale, O'Connor, Gutek, & Geer, 2002) indicate that there is no strong and consistent relationship between past victimization and attitudes and perceptions about sexual harassment, although some studies do show a relationship. Stockdale et al. (2002) conducted a series of studies in which participants were provided with written scenarios or videos of a sexual harassment case. Those who reported prior abuse did not differ significantly from those who did not in their perceptions of the validity of the claim. Stockdale et al. concluded that, on the basis of the available research, it is unwarranted to make assumptions about plaintiffs or jurors in sexual harassment cases who may have experienced prior sexual abuse. This research is obviously of import to forensic psychologists, particularly those who interview plaintiffs or help attorneys select jurors in sexual harassment cases.

Employment Compensation and Personal Injury Claims

Employment compensation laws were passed to avoid extensive tort actions on the part of employees who were injured in the course of their work. In passing these laws, Congress and state legislatures also recognized the formidable task faced by the injured worker pitted against his or her powerful employer. Under tort law, the employee would have to prove some fault on the part of the employer. This was a long, involved process that rarely resulted in a successful claim and often left the worker and/or the family in poverty (Melton et al., 1997). Under the employment compensation system, employers agree to insure their workers, and workers agree not to

seek the greater compensation that they might possibly achieve if they filed a civil suit and succeeded in proving some negligence on the part of the employer.

Although **employment compensation claims** involve physical injuries, psychic injury or emotional distress is also typically asserted. To use a hypothetical example, Jason is employed by a roofing company that often repairs roofs that were damaged by severe weather conditions. While replacing shingles on a roof that is three stories high, Jason is caught by a wind gust and swept off the roof, suffering extensive back injuries. In addition to this physical injury, Jason claims extreme emotional distress that includes fear of heights manifested in an inability to climb ladders, take escalators, or accompany his 10-year-old son on a skiing chairlift. Note that Jason is not claiming that his employer was at fault for dispatching him to repair the roof on a high-wind day. He is merely stating that he should be compensated for his lost wages, the physical and neurological effects of the fall (e.g., debilitating back pain, recurring headaches), and the life changes necessitated by his fear of heights.

Evaluations of mental injury—both psychological and neurological harm—also occur in a wide variety of personal injury litigation that is not necessarily employment related. For example, mental health is included in "pain and suffering" and "emotional distress" claims by individuals who were injured in car accidents, in a fall in a neighbor's yard, or by a cup of excessively hot coffee served by a fast-food chain. Plaintiffs also claim psychological and neurological harm from exposure to environmental contaminants or from defective products.

Melton et al. (1997) state that evaluations of mental injury have many similarities to the inquiry into the mental state at the time of the offense (MSO), which we covered in Chapter 10. Like MSO evaluations, they are retrospective and complex. However, mental injury evaluations are also prospective, in the sense they must make some judgment about the plaintiff's future functioning: Will the plaintiff be able to function as he or she functioned prior to the claim? In the case of employment compensation claims, what is the extent of the loss in earning capacity suffered by the plaintiff?

As in other mental injury claims, the forensic psychologist is advised to gather an extensive store of information in an attempt to compare the past and present functioning of the individual as well as project into the future. If the injury is work related, all information pertinent to the workplace is relevant to the inquiry. Melton et al. (1997) point out that personality inventories are helpful, particularly if they can be compared with inventories taken before the injury occurred. In addition, they remind the psychologist to investigate the extent of physical injury, using neurological tests if needed, in addition to mental injury. Furthermore, the evaluator should be attuned to the possibility of posttraumatic stress disorder.

In a summary article on personality assessment in personal injury litigation, Butcher and Miller (1999) suggest that the Minnesota Multiphasic Personality Inventory (MMPI-2) is superior to any other specific inventories because it can be interpreted objectively and can differentiate between persons with mental health problems and those who are not psychologically disturbed. They caution, however, that a psychological test cannot determine whether a person's physical injuries are based on organic conditions or derive from personality factors. And, of course, without the results of a test administered prior to the injury, the forensic psychologist cannot assess how the individual's preinjury personality might influence his or her current functioning. The psychologist can, though, "provide indication of the severity and long-term stability of the individual's problems" (Butcher & Miller, 1999, p. 110).

As we noted in the previous chapter, malingering and the exaggeration of symptoms have received considerable attention in the research literature (e.g., Gothard et al., 1995; Mossman, 2003; Rogers, 1997). In all mental injury evaluations, psychologists and other clinicians must be concerned about the possibility that the individual being evaluated is "faking" the symptoms he or she is claiming or presenting them as being much worse than they are. Butcher and Miller (1999) emphasize that there is no foolproof way to assess malingering, although the MMPI-2 appears to have valid indicators. Continued research is needed, however, before firm conclusions can be drawn.

Butcher and Miller (1999) also advise the evaluator to be extremely conscious of the role of the individual's lawyer. "One of the most problematic factors encountered in forensic assessment is the tendency of many attorneys to guide their clients through a desired strategy for responding to psychological test items" (Butcher & Miller, 1999, p. 110). They advise clinicians to try to determine whether the individual has been "coached" by the lawyer and the extent and nature of the coaching. Basically, the individual should be asked what he or she has been told. The final report should reflect how this coaching might have affected the results of the examination.

After a comprehensive discussion of mental injury evaluations, Melton et al. (1997, p. 381) conclude with three general points about communicating with the courts relevant to these assessments. First, they urge clinicians to not rely overly on diagnoses because these will not explain why a particular individual reacted in a particular way to the particular events. Second, they emphasize that a longitudinal history of the impairment, its treatments, and efforts at rehabilitation is necessary. Third, they maintain that conclusory information should be avoided. Clinicians should provide descriptive reports of their findings but allow the legal decision makers to decide the critical legal question of whether the plaintiff should be compensated.

Summary and Conclusions

As we have so often stated throughout this book, there is no shortage of tasks for forensic psychologists to perform in a given context. Consultation with the civil courts is no exception. In this chapter, we have attempted to provide a representative sampling, but several areas were left untouched or barely addressed. For example, forensic psychologists participate in a wide variety of personal injury litigation and disability evaluations other than the employment compensation claims that were highlighted here. Likewise, they participate in discrimination suits other than sexual harassment, such as race, age, disability, and gender discrimination in both employment and nonemployment situations. They perform assessments of families and of children at risk in child protection proceedings. They evaluate children who have allegedly been sexually abused and whose parents wish to file civil charges against the alleged perpetrators. These and numerous other areas have contributed to making forensic psychology the exciting and growing field that it is.

Consultation with the juvenile courts is an area that has been heavily researched; consequently, we covered this in some detail. Traditionally rehabilitation oriented, the juvenile courts today resemble criminal courts in many ways, although rehabilitation is still a primary focus. Psychologists have a major role to play in assessing the extent to which juveniles are amenable to rehabilitation—but just as important, it is incumbent on them to avoid pessimism, to be aware of available programs, and to suggest alternative approaches. Negative—and possibly invalid—labels should be avoided because these labels may consign juveniles to criminal courts or encourage staffs of juvenile facilities to expend less energy on juveniles who may be perceived as hopeless.

Psychologists also have an important role to play in assessing whether juveniles understood the consequences of waiving their constitutional rights. The adjudicative competence of juveniles is heavily researched, with recent studies suggesting that juveniles as a group have considerable deficiency in both understanding their rights and participating in juvenile proceedings. With this

knowledge, it is critical for forensic psychologists to pay attention to the lawyer-juvenile relationship, as well as the parent-child relationship, in juvenile cases.

Child custody evaluations are among the most controversial for forensic psychologists. They are emotionally laden, have engendered ethics complaints, and raise numerous questions as to what is the proper standard for making custody decisions. A major concern in this area is the instruments that are sometimes used to assess parental abilities because few have been submitted to empirical validation. Furthermore, because there is no one clearly identified preferred custody arrangement, psychologists must be cautious about research that suggests one form of custody is superior to the other.

We covered a variety of contexts in which decisional competencies might be assessed. Chief among these is the competency to make medical and legal decisions. Of particular concern, however, is the problem encountered when individuals are incapacitated and unable to make decisions in their own interest. A different problem relates to an individual's decision to hasten his or her death. Oregon has pioneered legislation allowing individuals to request the assistance of physicians in this matter, an approach that has prompted the need for psychological evaluations of whether the individual is mentally competent to request such assistance.

We ended the chapter with discussion of research and issues relating to sexual harassment and mental injury claims. Evaluations of persons who bring sexual harassment claims—particularly compelled evaluations—should be done with extreme caution. Fortunately, a number of inventories, including the well-regarded SEQ, are available. They are just beginning to address the perceptions and experiences of different cultural groups, however. Furthermore, a controversial aspect of sexual harassment evaluations is the relevance of information about the private life of the person who has allegedly been harassed.

The chapter included considerable discussion of **involuntary civil commitment,** most particularly commitment to outpatient treatment. This form of commitment is increasing in virtually every state, but it raises important questions about the civil liberties of individuals who would otherwise not be eligible for institutional confinement. Many forensic psychologists are supportive of this form of commitment, primarily because it allows individuals to receive needed treatment in a community setting. Thus far, research on treatment effectiveness has demonstrated positive results, particularly if the treatment continues beyond a 6-month period and is accompanied by intensive services.

PART VI

Correctional Psychology

CHAPTER 12

Correctional Psychology in Adult Settings

orrections today is a high-profile, complex operation that consumes very large portions of the operating budgets of the federal government and virtually all states. At the beginning of the 21st century, approximately 1 in 32 adults in the United States was under some form of correctional supervision (Bureau of Justice Statistics, 2002a). The majority of these (approximately two thirds) were under community supervision, which includes probation, parole, and their many variants. House arrest, electronic monitoring, halfway houses for newly released offenders, day reporting, and intensive supervision are examples of sanctions included under the term *community corrections*. About 22% of all adults under correctional supervision were being held in prisons, and about 11% were held in jails. These figures, representing more than 2 million persons, also represent a tripling of the rate of incarceration since 1980.

In this chapter, we will focus on the services offered by forensic psychologists to the wide variety of individuals under correctional supervision, particularly in prisons and jails. The chapter begins with this institutional focus, providing an overview of key concepts and the legal rights of inmates that are pertinent to psychological concepts. We then examine the assessment and treatment roles of correctional psychologists as well as aspects of the prison and jail environments that present obstacles to effective treatment. By far the greater research attention is paid to the work of psychologists who work in institutional settings, yet forensic psychologists as a group are more likely to come into contact with persons under community supervision than inmates within correctional facilities. During the latter part of the chapter, therefore, we will focus on **community corrections** and the contributions of forensic psychologists in that realm.

Institutional Corrections

The United States has the highest **incarceration rate** of any industrialized country, with the numbers of inmates behind bars having increased steadily over the past quarter century. The greatest population increase has occurred in the federal prison system (Bureau of Justice Statistics, 2002a) and is believed to be largely due to the nation's "war on drugs," whereby **mandatory sentences** have been in effect for individuals convicted of drug offenses. However, rising incarceration rates also have been observed in virtually every state, even during periods of declining crime rates. Consequently, by the end of the 20th century, every state was facing over-crowding in at least one, and typically more, of its correctional facilities.

The crimes for which offenders are incarcer-ated are not only those considered the most heinous. In state prisons, 51% of all offenders were serving time for violent offenses, 20% for drug offenses, 15% for public-order offenses, and 14% for property offenses, such as burglary or larceny (Bureau of Justice Statistics, 2002a). In contrast to what we might expect from media coverage, robbery—not homicide—accounted for the great majority of the violent offenses. Although robbery is a serious crime and its effect on the victim should not be discounted, it does not necessarily include the *use* of force. The tak-ing of property through *threat* of force—such as a weapon shown to the victim—is sufficient to classify a crime as a robbery. The point made here is that even the 51% of offenders serving time for violent offenses did not necessarily cause physical harm to their victims.

Women, compared with men, are even less likely to be incarcerated for violent offenses. Yet, since 1990, the number of female prisoners has increased 108% (compared with a male increase of 77%) (Bureau of Justice Statistics, 2001a). Researchers attribute these increases primarily to rising drug crimes among women.

Despite the rising incarceration rate, impris-onment does not seem to deter or rehabilitate a substantial number of offenders. Research on **recidivism**—typically measured by new arrests, new convictions, or sometimes by self-report data—is not encouraging. A recent government survey of persons released from prison in 15 states found that, over a 3-year period, a very high number were rearrested, particularly those who had been imprisoned for property offenses. For example, 78.8% of motor vehicle thieves,

77.4% of those who possessed or sold stolen property, 74.6% of larcenists, and 74% of burglars were rearrested within 3 years (Bureau of Justice Statistics, 2002c). Although these data suggest that neither the imprisonment itself nor programs offered to inmates had a positive effect on those who reoffended, recidivism data must be interpreted very cautiously.

An arrest does not necessarily mean that an individual has indeed committed an offense. Even if he or she has, however, it does not mean that a former offender has not benefited in other ways from the rehabilitation programs offered in a correctional setting. Nevertheless, recidivism statistics such as those reported above lead some observers to question whether incarceration is the best route to take in dealing with the problem of crime and others to question whether rehabil-itation is a realistic goal. Furthermore, many legal scholars and researchers in the social sciences are concerned about the disproportionate confine-ment of the poor and racial or ethnic minorities. The conditions within many prisons, including overcrowding and violence within the facility, provide further cause for concern. Although few scholars advocate the total abolition of jails and prisons, there are increasing calls for alter-natives to incarceration, especially for nonviolent offenders.

Forensic psychologists working in **institu-tional corrections,** then, must find ways to do their work within a system that is placed in the position of justifying its operations. The public wants its prisons but is resentful of the fiscal costs. And although public opinion surveys sug-gest continuing support for rehabilitation, indi-viduals working in corrections have learned that rehabilitation-oriented programs are the first to go when budgets need to be cut. Even with scaled-down programming, it is not unusual for the corrections budget to consume a greater share of state coffers than the education budget. Indeed, college students are often appalled to learn that their own hefty yearly tuition fee may be smaller than the cost of maintaining an inmate in prison for a year.

The psychologist in a correctional setting also must work in an environment that often diminishes the likelihood of therapeutic success. Inmates get transferred to other prisons, correctional officers may not support the psychologist's role, administrators may cut their budgets, there is little time to conduct research, and the limitations on confidentiality suggest to inmates that psychologists are representatives of the prison administration, not advocates for their own interests. We will cover these and other issues later in the chapter. For the time being, it is important to note that the recently updated standards developed by the American Association for Correctional Psychology (AACP, 2000) recognize the challenges presented by prison and jail environments. The AACP has published 66 standards intended to offer direction and support to practitioners. Box 12.1 contains a list of topics covered in the standards, and we will refer to them

---

BOX 12.1 AACP Standards

The American Association for Correctional Psychology (AACP) has developed a set of standards that provide the minimum acceptable levels for psychological services offered to offenders held in local, state, or federal facilities, as well as in the community (Standards Committee, 2000). Below are examples of topics and subtopics covered in the standards. Interested readers are advised to read the original standards, which include a discussion section explaining the rationale behind each one.

Roles and Services: Appropriate roles include but are not limited to consultation to correctional administration for mental health program design; psychological screening of security staff employed in specialized mental health units; classification for mental health program assignments; training of staff; assessment, diagnosis, and treatment of mental illness; crisis intervention; and advocacy for and evaluation of mental health programs and services.

Staffing requirements: At least one person responsible for psychological services in the facility has a doctoral degree that is primarily psychological in nature, is licensed/certified, and has training/experience in correctional psychology.

Documentation: All services and mental health information will be documented and/or maintained in a file specific to the offender in compliance with current professional and legal standards and guidelines.

Limits of confidentiality: Inmates will be informed both verbally and in writing of the limits of confidentiality as well as legally and administratively mandated duties to warn.

Informed consent: All screenings, assessments, treatments, and procedures shall be preceded by an informed consent procedure.

Employer and ethical/practice standards conflicts: There is a documented policy for the resolution of conflicts between the facility and the psychological services staff.

(Continued)

Screening/evaluation: All screening is performed only by psychological staff or facility staff trained by them. At no time are psychological data made available to inmate workers (this includes filing).

Inmate treatment: Diagnostic and treatment services are provided to inmates of the facility; those needing emergency evaluation and/or treatment are housed in a specially designated area with close supervision by staff or trained volunteers and with sufficient security.

In-service training: Written procedures provide for the training of facility and community staff (e.g., in recognizing psychological emergency situations and in procedures for making referrals to psychological services).

Research: Psychological services staff are encouraged to conduct applied and/or basic research to improve the delivery of psychological services.

throughout the chapter. In addition, psychologists working in corrections are expected to conform to the ethical code of the American Psychological Association (APA), which was most recently revised in 2003 (APA, 2003a). In addition, forensic psychologists are provided with a set of specialty guidelines that do not have the force of the ethics code but do serve to provide suggestions for practice. Finally, psychologists must be aware of all relevant state and federal laws and regulations. Interestingly, a recent review of standards for conducting *research* in prisons suggests that the new APA Code of Conduct has deleted sections relevant to prison research, including (1) a section pertaining to compliance with state and federal laws and (2) a section referring to the dignity and welfare of research participants (Kalmbach & Lyons, 2003).

Overview of Correctional Facilities

Persons detained, accused, and convicted, when not allowed to remain in their own homes, are housed in three types of facilities: jails, prisons, and community-based facilities. **Jails** are operated by local governments to hold persons temporarily detained, held for lack of bail while awaiting trial or other court proceedings, or

sentenced to confinement after having been convicted of a misdemeanor. **Prisons** are facilities operated by the federal government and all states for persons convicted of felonies and sentenced to terms of more than 1 year. **Community-based facilities** are less secure institutions, such as halfway houses or transition homes, typically intended as **intermediate sanctions** for offenders deemed to need less security than would be provided in jails or prisons but more than would be available in their own homes. Community-based facilities will be discussed later in the chapter.

On any given day, approximately half of the individuals held in jails are innocent; they are detainees, not convicted of the crime of which they are accused. Approximately another half is serving short-term sentences for misdemeanor offenses.

The proportion of detainees and sentenced misdemeanants varies widely by jurisdiction, though. In some facilities, up to 70% of the population comprises **pretrial detainees** who were unable to afford bail or who were denied bail because they were considered dangerous. Jails also may house a wide variety of individuals awaiting transfer to prison, to a mental institution, to another state, to a juvenile facility, or to a military detention facility, though such individuals usually make up a small portion (rarely more than 5%) of the jail population. In effect, though, jails hold a collection of persons at various stages of criminal, civil, or military justice processing. In some communities, jails also serve as temporary overnight shelters for individuals whom police arrest on minor charges, believing they need a safe haven.

In the federal system, pretrial detainees are held in **detention centers.** When space in federal detention centers is not available, persons accused of federal crimes or awaiting sentencing are detained in state or local jails. In fact, about two thirds of federal detainees are held in these state or local facilities (Clear & Cole, 2000). Federal detention centers have been heavily publicized since September 11, 2001, because the government has held an as-yet-undetermined number of individuals for questioning about possible terrorist involvement. "Makeshift" detention centers were opened, and numerous individuals were turned over to Immigration and Naturalization Services (INS) and deported after secret deportation proceedings before immigration judges. In addition, numerous persons identified by the government as terror suspects were being held at Camp Delta, the detention compound at Guantanamo Bay in Cuba. Civil libertarians have been highly critical of the detentions and deportations, primarily because they occurred in closed proceedings and with minimum due process protections. Moreover, in light of rises in suicide attempts at Guantanamo, human rights organizations have expressed concerns about both conditions of confinement and methods of interrogation. In November 2003, the U.S. Supreme Court announced that it would hear an appeal on behalf of these detainees.

Prisons, operated by states or by the federal government, hold only persons convicted of felonies. They are classified by the level of security maintained over the inmates: maximum, medium, and minimum, with sometimes gradients in between these three main alternatives. Different custody levels are also found within as well as among prisons. Thus, an inmate may be kept in close custody in a medium-security prison for disciplinary reasons, and an inmate in

a maximum-security prison may have attained "trustee" status, requiring minimal custody.

In the 1990s, **super-max prisons** were introduced in the federal government and approximately 41 states. These are extremely high-security facilities (or units within a maximum-security prison) supposedly intended to hold the most troublesome, violent inmates. As we will see later in the chapter, however, numerous concerns have been raised about these facilities. Prison systems also may include specialized facilities, such as work camps, classification centers, and units for inmates with mental disorders. Boot camps, prison farms, forestry centers, and ranches for young offenders who have committed primarily nonviolent crimes are other examples of specialized facilities.

In six states—Alaska, Connecticut, Delaware, Hawaii, Rhode Island, and Vermont—jails are under the control of the state rather than local government, and jail/prison functions are combined. Thus, detainees and sentenced offenders—both misdemeanants and felons—may be kept within the same facility, though they may be placed in separate housing units. A typical approach in these "mixed systems" is to have one or two facilities designated as maximum security, whereas the balance are medium- or minimum-security facilities capable of housing persons accused of crime as well as those who have been convicted and sentenced.

The federal prison system is highly organized and centralized under the **Federal Bureau of Prisons (BOP).** It consists of a network of facilities that are called penitentiaries, correctional institutions, prison camps, and halfway houses, as well as the detention centers referred to above. They are located on a continuum of five security levels: minimum, low, medium, high, and administrative. The nation's one federal super-max facility, located in Colorado, is classified at the administrative level. (See Box 12.2 on career opportunities for psychologists in the BOP.)

In addition to the features summarized above, jails and prisons can be contrasted on an important point that affects the work of psychologists. Prisons are far more likely than jails to offer

---

BOX 12.2   Career Opportunities in the Federal Bureau of Prisons

---

Employment opportunities in the Federal Bureau of Prisons (BOP) are expected to increase in light of projected increases in the number of inmates. Psychologists in this setting have doctorate degrees, with about 60% of those employed having completed internships in federal prisons.

Psychologists in the BOP are autonomous. They are the main providers of mental health services and—in contrast to psychologists in some state prisons systems and mental hospitals—are not under the supervision of psychiatrists. Staff psychologists have the opportunity to be involved in the following:

- Forensic evaluations for the federal courts
- Psychological evaluations of candidates for the witness protection program
- Hostage negotiation training
- Drug abuse treatment programs
- Suicide prevention program
- Crisis intervention response team for trauma victims
- Predoctoral internship training program
- Employee assistant program
- Inpatient mental health program
- Staff training
- Research

Entry-level positions, for those who have just completed their doctorates, are at the GS-11 salary level but are automatically upgraded after successful completion of the first year. An annual continuing education stipend—currently $10,000—is guaranteed. Other benefits include the Federal Employee Retirement System, which, among other things, provides an attractive pension plan and allows retirement after 20 years provided an individual has reached age 50.

Source: U.S. Bureau of Prisons, www.bop.gov

---

programs, including recreation, work programs, substance abuse treatment, and a variety of rehabilitative programs. This can be attributed to several factors. First, because a jail stay is relatively short, inmates are less likely to benefit from meaningful programming. Second, most jails are operated by local governments and do not have funds available for much beyond their custodial function. Third, most jails are operated by law enforcement professionals, such as county sheriffs, rather than corrections professionals. The law enforcement community is not trained to provide services to offenders or alleged offenders; it is trained to enforce the law, protect the public, and provide service to the community. Programming for detainees and inmates is not considered a priority. Nevertheless, there are exceptions, and programming can be found in many jails nationwide. Short-term programs, such as those aimed at substance abuse, domestic violence, and prevention of disease, are examples. Furthermore, a professional organization—the American Jail Association—publishes standards for operating jails that include training staff and offering a variety of services to detainees and inmates.

Although psychologists are less likely to be involved in treatment programs in jails than in prisons, their *assessment* and *crisis intervention* services are often more in demand in these short-term settings. Some pretrial detainees, for example, need to be assessed for their competency to stand trial and the variety of other competencies that were discussed in Chapter 10. Whether or not competencies are in question, pretrial detainees are often confused, frightened, and worried about their social, legal, and financial status. In a confusing, noisy, often crowded environment, detainees may experience "entry shock" (Gibbs, 1992). This is particularly—but not exclusively—a problem for persons being held in jail for the first time. Suicide is the leading cause of death in jails (Clear & Cole, 2000). Research also documents that suicide rates are higher in jail than in prison; some estimates are at least five times higher (Cohen, 1998; Steadman, McCarty, & Morrissey, 1989). Although screening for suicide risk is typically done by nonpsychological staff upon a detainee's or inmate's entry into the facility, mental health professionals are needed to do a more comprehensive assessment and to offer treatment to individuals who are at risk of taking their own lives. Ironically, however, jails are much less likely than prisons to have well-developed mental health services available to inmates (Steadman & Veysey, 1997). It is for this reason that many communities have now begun to experiment with the mental health courts that were highlighted in Box 9.1 in Chapter 9.

Correctional facilities—both jails and prisons—can be violent, noisy, disorganized, demeaning places that promote isolation, helplessness, and subservience through the use of overwhelming power, often through fear. Although this is particularly true of large, urban jails and maximum-security prisons, there are clearly exceptions. Furthermore, correctional professionals maintain that both jails and prisons also can be operated in a humane fashion and can achieve society's dual hope of protecting the public from crime and rehabilitating offenders.

Legal Rights of Inmates

It is a well-established principle in law that inmates do not lose their constitutional rights at the prison gate. In a great number of U.S. Supreme Court decisions, especially during the 1960s and 1970s, the Court specified minimum rights that were guaranteed to inmates under the Constitution. The cases decided by the Court involved procedures, practices, and conditions of confinement in jails and prisons. In addition to federal constitutional protections, inmates also may have rights that are guaranteed under their state constitutions or under both federal and state statutes. In this section, we will summarize the key doctrines that are most relevant to psychologists consulting with correctional systems or offering direct services to inmates. This will, of necessity, omit legal protections that are important to inmates but are at most peripheral to the professional concerns of psychologists. For example, inmates have a constitutional right to receive mail (although it may be censored) and a constitutional right to observe religious practices (including dietary practices) unless those interfere with institutional security or create excessive economic burdens. Readers are referred to the excellent treatises of Cohen (1998, 2000, 2003) and Palmer and Palmer (1999) for comprehensive coverage of correctional law that encompasses many areas not to be discussed here.

The principles to be discussed below have been announced in cases involving prisoners, but they also apply to those serving jail sentences. For this reason, we are using the term *inmate* throughout this chapter as a more generic term to cover both groups. The rights of pretrial *detainees*, however, are somewhat different because they have not been convicted of crime. Nevertheless, in the name of institutional security, detainees can be subjected to many of the same conditions as sentenced misdemeanants, as will be noted shortly.

Right to Treatment

A right closely aligned with the interests of psychologists is the constitutional right of the inmate to receive adequate medical treatment. Although the leading case on this matter (*Estelle v. Gamble*, 1976) involved treatment for a variety of physical ailments, it has widely been interpreted to include psychological or psychiatric assistance for serious mental disorders. To deprive the inmate of needed medical care violates the Eighth Amendment ban on cruel and unusual punishment. The question naturally arises, "What is 'adequate' medical treatment?" Inmates clearly do not have a right to "state-of-the art" treatment or therapy. In fact, in the *Gamble* case, even failure to obtain an X-ray of an inmate's lower back was not considered inadequate treatment. Although the Supreme Court in that case made it clear that inmates had a **right to treatment,** it did not second-guess the judgment of medical professionals who did not order the X-ray.

Gamble, a Texas inmate, was on a prison work assignment when a bale of cotton that he was loading on a truck fell on him. There followed 3 months of repetitive visits to prison medical staff, during which he was provided with muscle relaxants and other medications. By the end of this time period, he had received numerous different medications, blood tests, and blood pressure measurements, along with cell passes permitting him to stay in his cell. At one point, a prescription was not filled for 4 days because the staff had lost it. Eventually, he refused to work, saying that his pain was not dissipating, and he was brought before a prison disciplinary committee and then placed in solitary confinement as punishment. While in solitary, he asked to see a doctor for chest pains; a medical assistant saw him 12 hours later and hospitalized him.

Estelle v. Gamble (1976) is an important case because it not only clearly stated that inmates

had a constitutional right to medical treatment but also set the standard for deciding whether the Constitution had been violated. Inmates alleging such a violation would have to prove that prison officials were "deliberately indifferent" to their serious medical needs. Simple "negligence" would not be enough to amount to a constitutional violation (although negligence would be sufficient under some *state* laws). In a later case, *Farmer v. Brennan* (1994), the Court said that a prison official would not be liable unless that official both knew of and disregarded an excessive risk to an inmate's health and safety. The Court added that if an official *should have known* of a substantial risk but did not, the official's failure to alleviate the risk did *not* constitute cruel and unusual punishment.

Applied in the context of psychological treatment, it is clear that inmates should be offered treatment at least for their serious mental disorders, including psychoses, clinical depression, and schizophrenia. The AACP (2000) standards do not distinguish between serious and milder disorders, suggesting that mental health treatment should be available for *all* mental disturbances. Moreover, the standards indicate that it is generally inappropriate for inmates needing acute, chronic, or convalescent mental health care to be treated in jails and prisons. Rather, they should be transferred to facilities specifically for these purposes.

In reality, both jails and prisons hold substantial numbers of individuals with severe disorders. The lack of adequate mental health care in jails and prisons across the United States is widely acknowledged by commentators and courts alike (Cohen, 2000; Heilbrun & Griffin, 1999; Morris, Steadman, & Veysey, 1997). Although specialized treatment exists for forensic populations, a great number of individuals with mental disorders continue to languish in jails and prisons without adequate psychological intervention. It has been estimated that 16% of all prison inmates and 10% of jail detainees and inmates are in need of treatment for mental disorder (Ditton, 1999). In some jurisdictions, services are provided to fewer than

25% of the inmates requiring them (*Feliciano v. Gonzales,* 1998). Studies also indicate that the need among female inmates is even greater than among males (Clear & Cole, 2000). This estimate is somewhat confounded by the fact that women, compared with men, may be more likely to self-disclose their need for mental health services. The adequacy of medical services, including both physical and mental health, is a frequent point of litigation in class action suits brought by incarcerated individuals. (A class action suit is one brought on behalf of a group of people who have all allegedly been harmed by the actions of a defendant.) Interestingly, although there is a right to treatment for physical and mental disorders, there is no right to treatment for alcoholism or other substance abuse, as we will discuss shortly. These programs fall under the rubric of rehabilitation rather than medical treatment.

Right to Refuse Treatment

Although inmates have a right to treatment, they cannot be forced to participate in treatment programs. This applies to both physical and psychological treatment. However, if the state has a very strong interest in seeing the inmate's behavior changed, some leeway exists. In a recent Supreme Court case, *McKune v. Lile* (2002), the Court allowed prison officials to effectively punish an inmate for refusing to participate in a program, even though the state argued—and the Court agreed—that it was not acting punitively. Lile was a convicted rapist within 2 years of completing his sentence and being released. The state had a strong interest in enrolling him in a sex offender treatment program that required him to disclose his history of offending, but it did not guarantee that the information would be privileged. Lile—apparently concerned that disclosing information could lead to future prosecution for crimes he had not previously been accused of—refused to participate. Prison officials told him that his refusal could lead to him being transferred to a more dangerous prison. In

addition, they threatened to curtail a number of privileges, including canteen access and certain work activities. Lile then argued that he was essentially being forced to incriminate himself. In a close decision, a majority of five Justices did not agree. Thus, although inmates still may not be forced to participate in a treatment program, they can be persuaded to do so with threatened loss of privileges, provided that the state's interest in rehabilitation is high, as it was in this case.

In a similar fashion, inmates have a right to refuse medication, but this right can be overridden. Obviously, inmates cannot refuse treatment for a communicable disease, such as tuberculosis, that poses a risk to the prison population. Perhaps less obviously, the preservation of life may be given more weight than the inmate's own wishes. In a 1995 case, for example, an inmate with diabetes was forced to submit to monitoring of his blood sugar and to take insulin or other medications if ordered to by physicians (*North Dakota ex rel. Schuetzle v. Vogel,* 1995). On the other hand, a quadriplegic inmate who wished to die a dignified death was allowed by courts in California to reject force-feeding and other painful medical intervention (*Thor v. Superior Court,* 1993). One could argue that, had the diabetic inmate been allowed to have his way, the prison system would have been faced with significant medical costs resulting from complications associated with his disease. The quadriplegic inmate presented no such economic threats. The cases were not decided on the economic issue, however, but rather on the right of competent individuals to self-determination of their medical needs balanced against the state's interest in preserving life.

The U.S. Supreme Court has issued one decision on the right of inmates to refuse treatment in the form of psychoactive drugs (*Washington v. Harper,* 1990). In Washington state, felons with severe mental disorders were housed in a special unit within the prison system. Antipsychotic drugs were frequently used to control disruptive behavior. If an inmate refused to be treated with these medications, he was allowed to challenge the treatment in an administrative hearing before a three-person panel comprising a psychologist, a psychiatrist, and a member of the prison administration. Harper and other inmates wanted judicial review, before an independent court, rather than administrative review. They also wished to be afforded a right to counsel, rather than the lay adviser allowed in the administrative hearing. The Supreme Court, in a 6–3 ruling, however, found no fault with the procedure in use. Essentially, prison officials can give an inmate psychoactive drugs against his or her will, but it must be determined in an administrative hearing that such medication is necessary to control the inmate's disruptive behavior. It is important to note, though, that state statutes may be even more restrictive than this, prohibiting medication that might be more for the convenience of the staff than truly medically necessary.

Courts have also begun to address the issue of forcing an inmate to take medication to render him or her competent to be executed. In 1986, in *Ford v. Wainwright*, the U.S. Supreme Court ruled that executing a death row inmate who was "insane"—or too mentally disordered to appreciate what was happening to him—violated the Constitution. Since that ruling, many forensic psychologists and forensic psychiatrists have been troubled. Some psychologists resist participating in evaluations of an inmate's **competency to be executed,** knowing that their recommendation could facilitate the inmate's death. Some psychiatrists—who have the authority to prescribe medication—have not wanted to prescribe psychoactive medication that would stabilize the inmate enough to allow him or her to be put to death. Furthermore, lawyers representing these death row inmates argued that they should have a right to refuse the medication. In February 2003, a federal appeals court became the first federal court to rule that death row inmates do *not* have such a right.

Right to Rehabilitation

People are often surprised to learn that, although there is a right to *treatment* for physical and mental disorders, an inmate has no constitutional right to **rehabilitation** in correctional settings. In this context, rehabilitation refers to a variety of programs that presumably should increase the likelihood that the inmate will not reoffend upon release from prison. In a wide range of cases, inmates have asked the courts to grant them constitutional rights to participate in substance abuse programs, job training programs, educational programs, and programs for violent offenders, among many others. They have consistently been rejected. This is not to say that such programs should not exist. In fact, "It is clear . . . that a penal system cannot be operated in such a manner that it impedes the ability of inmates to attempt their own rehabilitation, or simply to avoid physical, mental, or social deterioration" (Palmer & Palmer, 1999, p. 221). Thus, lack of *any* meaningful rehabilitative opportunities, particularly within a prison system, would be regarded with suspicion by the courts. The key principle is that individual prisoners do not have a constitutional right to participate in any particular program. Corrections officials are given the discretion to decide who will be assigned to these programs.

Prison Transfers

Inmates have no constitutional right to be held in a specific facility, including one in their home state or close to their family. In many prison systems, it is not unusual for prisoners to be moved from one facility to another, often with little or no notice. During the 1990s, some states experiencing prison overcrowding sent inmates to out-of-state facilities, both public and private, and courts generally upheld the policies. Transfers are typically made not only to manage space but also to break up gangs or to send a prisoner to a more or less restrictive setting. Likewise, corrections officials have broad leeway to assign inmates to various security levels within a facility or to assign them to special treatment programs. Generally, courts have upheld these classification decisions of prison officials unless they are demonstrated to be arbitrary, abusive, capricious, or discriminatory on racial or religious grounds. In addition, if inmates are assigned a special status that would limit substantially their eligibility for parole, work release, or furlough programs, some due process protections are afforded them under many state laws. For example, they may have a right to appear before a neutral decision maker (Palmer & Palmer, 1999). Neutral decision makers, though, are almost invariably within the institution, rather than outside judicial or administrative forums.

The one type of **prison transfer** that has constitutional implications is the transfer to a civil mental institution. Inmates with mental disorders who are facing a transfer to a mental health facility outside of the prison system are entitled to a hearing before this occurs (*Vitek v. Jones*, 1980). Such a transfer, according to the Supreme Court, represents a significant deprivation of liberty, specifically because of the stigma of being in a mental institution and the lack of opportunity to earn good time credits while institutionalized. Therefore, the Court required a variety of due process protections. They include (a) a written notice to the inmate, (b) a hearing at which clear and convincing evidence of the inmate's mental disorder and dangerousness is provided, (c) an independent decision maker, (d) testimony of witnesses on both sides, and (e) qualified assistance for the inmate (though not necessarily a lawyer). In reality, transfers to mental institutions are rarely challenged (Cohen, 2000). Furthermore, inmates with mental disorders, when transferred, are usually sent to a mental health unit or facility within the prison system. Because it is not clear whether such transfers require hearings such as those outlined in the *Vitek* case, prison systems sometimes provide them as a matter of policy if the inmate protests the transfer. In addition, the AACP (2000) standards assume that hearings are required: "This requirement is not obviated by the receiving institution being in the same jurisdiction or the special management unit being within the same correctional facility" (Standard 42, Discussion).

Inmates With Mental Disorders

A number of court cases, including U.S. Supreme Court cases, have addressed special situations encountered by mentally disordered inmates in the nation's prisons. As noted above, inmates with serious mental disorders have a right to treatment under the disease model recognized in *Estelle v. Gamble* (1976). Although they may be able to refuse treatment, this refusal can be overridden if it shown that the inmate is disordered and dangerous to self or others (*Washington v. Harper*, 1990). In addition, as we saw above, courts are beginning to allow the forced medication of prisoners who, without the medication, would be incompetent to be executed. We will discuss the assessment of competency to be executed again later in the chapter.

The segregation of inmates with mental disorders raises many legal questions. Courts have allowed severely disturbed inmates to be placed in stripped-down observation cells—sometimes referred to as "safe cells"—for their own protection. They may be kept under extremely stark conditions while awaiting transfer to a treatment facility or until they can be stabilized with appropriate medication, but there are limitations on this type of confinement. A suit against the New York Department of Corrections (*Perri v. Coughlin*, 1999) is illustrative. Perri was an extremely disruptive, severely disordered inmate in the New York state prison system. He was held in an observational cell on three separate occasions, for a total of 108 days. The cell contained only a sink and toilet, and a brightly glaring light was on 24 hours a day. He had no clothes or blankets and had to sleep naked on the floor. The observational unit provided no opportunity for exercise, recreation, or group therapy. The lengthy confinement, coupled with failure to provide treatment, led to the court's decision to hold the New State Department of Corrections liable for damages (Cohen, 2000).

Privacy and Confidentiality

Inmates have very little right to privacy in prison or jail settings. Despite the fact that inmates often call their cells their "houses" or "homes," the law does not treat them this way. In the leading case on this issue, *Hudson v. Palmer* (1984), the Court gave corrections officials wide leeway in conducting unannounced cell searches out of the presence of inmates. Prisoners had asked to be allowed to be present when the cell searches were conducted, arguing that their property—including objects having sentimental value—was sometimes destroyed or was missing after these searches. Although not condoning malicious destruction of property, the Court majority nevertheless left these searches to the discretion of prison officials, in the name of maintaining institutional security.

Some state and lower federal courts have given inmates a right to privacy with respect to supervision by correctional officers of the opposite sex. Female inmates have a right not to be observed by male correctional officers while showering or toileting and vice versa. Body cavity searches by opposite-sex correctional officers also have been prohibited. These searches, generally visual in nature, may be conducted after contact visits with someone from the outside. They also may be conducted during routine searches for contraband.

Confidentiality of psychological records is a topic of more direct concern to the forensic psychologist. Psychologists have an ethical obligation to preserve inmate confidentiality to the maximum extent possible. The AACP (2000) standards indicate that nonpsychological staff should have access to confidential information only on a "need to know" basis and that psychological staff should supervise such releases and interpret information. Standard 28 specifies clearly that inmate workers should never have the

responsibility for test administration, scoring, or the filing of psychological data. Interestingly, courts have not provided inmates with a constitutional right to privacy in their records, though corrections officials can be held liable for disseminating information about an inmate that results in his or her being a target of violence by other inmates (Palmer & Palmer, 1999). Courts also have not considered it a constitutional violation when inmate clerks are involved in the filing of medical records. In fact, in some facilities, the "records room" is considered a choice work assignment by inmates because it provides access to information, "one of the most sought-after commodities in prison" (Clear & Cole, 2000, p. 338). "The contents of inmates' files are confidential, but it is hard to prevent the records room clerk from sneaking a look—or from trading the information for goods or favors" (Clear & Cole, 2000, pp. 338–339). Although psychological and other medical records should be kept separate from the inmate's history, parole dates, work assignments, and other information, there is no guarantee that some aspect of these psychological and medical records will not make it into the inmate's general file.

In the event that third parties within or outside the facility are provided with psychological information, release of confidential information forms should be completed by inmates and kept in the files. The standards also make it clear that inmates should be informed verbally and in writing of limits of confidentiality. For example, if a psychologist is made aware of an escape plan or of a plan to harm another inmate, she or he is obliged to notify prison officials. In addition, psychologists should obtain informed consent forms from inmates before conducting an assessment or initiating treatment.

Interestingly, even more basic than confidentiality is the actual *adequacy* of the records. Despite the fact that lower courts have made it clear that adequate records are prerequisite to continuity of care (Cohen, 1998), there is widespread concern about poor record keeping in many correctional facilities. According to Cohen

(1998), a lawyer and a scholar of correctional law,

> In my own work encompassing a large number of prisons, I would say that broadly deficient mental health records is the most consistently encountered problem I uncover. . . . What may be surprising is that even in relatively sophisticated systems, the mental health records are sometimes so deficient that there often is no treatment plan or only an old one that has not been changed or updated; what is there is illegible; there is no medical history or a clinically inadequate one; treatment recommendations are sparse or nonexistent; and there are no follow-up or progress notes. (pp. 10–12)

He adds that "decent treatment" may in fact be occurring in some cases, but this would not be evident from the files.

The limits on confidentiality and requirements for informed consent are problematic to many psychologists who are considering work in correctional settings. According to the AACP (2000), "The correctional psychologist works *with* the offender, but *for* the department, facility, or agency, and must be able to differentiate and balance the ethical/legal obligations owed to the correctional organization or agency and the community and the offender client" (Standard 20, Discussion). This can be difficult for the psychologist who is accustomed to working both for and with the same client. Furthermore, some psychologists are concerned that some inmates who "consent" to assessment and treatment do so because they believe they have no choice.

Solitary Confinement

Inmates may be isolated from the general jail or prison population for a variety of reasons. We referred above to the isolation of those with mental disorders in observation cells. In addition, inmates may be placed in **disciplinary segregation,** as punishment for violation of rules, or in **protective custody,** to keep them away from other inmates who may prey on them. Super-max or ultra-max facilities hold large numbers of allegedly violent and recalcitrant inmates in **administrative segregation** for years at a time. Courts have allowed corrections officials to segregate inmates but have placed some restrictions on the duration and the conditions of the confinement, particularly in the case of disciplinary segregation.

Conditions of segregation have been monitored more carefully than *duration* by the courts, though they are often considered in relation to the duration. Thus, placement in a stark cell with no opportunity to shower for 48 hours is not legally problematic; placement in the same cell and under the same conditions for 2 weeks would be. Hygiene, nutrition, the physical condition of the cell, and the physical condition of the inmate are all taken into consideration. "It is clear that there is not yet a minimum standard set on the number of days or other conditions that will constitute cruel and unusual punishment in punitive isolation in every situation" (Palmer & Palmer, 1999, p. 80). Thus, although psychologists may be concerned about the effects of isolation on the mental state of the inmate, and although inmates have argued unsuccessfully that isolation is per se cruel and unusual, the courts have placed limits on only the most egregious of situations.

Few limitations have been placed on the duration of protective custody or administration segregation, but again conditions may be scrutinized. The Supreme Court has yet to hear a case involving conditions of confinement in "super-max" facilities, but lower courts have weighed in on this issue. In super-max facilities, inmates are held in cells for 24 hours a day, with the exception of a brief (up to 1 hour) exercise period, usually in a secluded space. They have no contact with other inmates. Food is brought to their cells by guards.

A lower federal court (*Madrid v. Gomez,* 1995) has made it clear that the above conditions are particularly harmful to inmates who are at psychological risk or are presently mentally disordered. Reviewing conditions in the secure housing unit (SHU) at Pelican Bay State Prison in California, the court found that the following violated the Constitution's prohibition against cruel and unusual punishment: a pattern of excessive force by correctional officers within the facility, the lack of adequate provision of medical and mental health care, and the holding of inmates with mental illness in the SHU.

Nevertheless, the court did not find a constitutional violation in the SHU for *stable* inmates:

> Conditions in the SHU may well hover on the edge of what is humanly tolerable for those with normal resilience, particularly when endured for extended periods of time. They do not, however, violate exacting Eighth Amendment standards, except for the specific population subgroups [the mentally ill] identified in this opinion.

Pretrial Detainees

Under the law, persons accused of crime and held in jails or detention centers may not be punished. They are considered to be innocent unless and until they are proven guilty. Thus, a detainee cannot be placed in disciplinary segregation and lose good time credits because he or she is not serving time. However, courts allow detainees to be placed in highly restrictive conditions and to suffer significant invasions of privacy in the name of institutional security. In addition, a detainee can be placed in isolation for violating the rules of the facility. In the landmark U.S. Supreme Court case on this issue, *Bell v. Wolfish* (1979), detainees in a federal facility challenged a number of actions taken by administrators in the name of institutional security. For example, they were placed in two-person rooms and sometimes in makeshift accommodations due to overcrowding. They were not allowed to stand and watch if their rooms were searched. They were not allowed to receive packages containing food items

or personal items from outside the institution. The facility had a "publishers only" rule, whereby books and magazines had to come directly from the publisher. Finally, they were submitted to visual body cavity searches after contact visits. In a 6–3 decision, the U.S. Supreme Court ruled that these were not punitive conditions and were justified in the name of institutional security.

In addition to the constitutional protections discussed above, inmates may have certain rights under their state constitutions or laws passed by state legislatures. In some states, for example, inmates have a right to vote in national elections; there is no such constitutional right. Confidentiality of records, rights to participate in rehabilitation programs, and visitation rights are all areas that vary widely from state to state. The psychologist working in a correctional setting, then, must be aware not only of the constitutional principles but also of the law specific to his or her own state.

Correctional Psychologists

Correctional psychologists are sometimes distinguished from psychologists working in correctional facilities. The correctional psychologist typically has "specific academic and/or program training in correctional philosophy, systems, offender management, forensic report writing, treatment aimed at reducing recidivism, and outcome research" (Althouse, 2000, p. 436). Many—if not most—psychologists working in corrections do not have this specific background. Furthermore, not all psychologists hold doctorates, whether PhDs or PsyDs. Although it is estimated that more than 90% of psychologists working in the Federal Bureau of Prisons hold doctorates, it appears that those working in state prisons and local jails are more likely than not to hold master's degrees or certificates of advanced study. Nevertheless, psychologists at all levels clearly offer valuable services to corrections. For our purposes, therefore, we use the terms *correctional psychologist* and *psychologist working in corrections* interchangeably. This is consistent with the AACP (2000) standards, which note that the same level of professional practice is needed irrespective of the training level or educational background of the service provider.

Estimates of the number of psychologists working in correctional settings vary widely, partly because available surveys do not always include the many settings in which they can be found. According to Boothby and Clements (2000), more recent estimates indicate that more than 2,000 psychologists are now employed. In addition, some surveys count only those psychologists who work full-time within correctional systems. Other surveys maintain the distinction between *correctional psychologist* and *psychologist working in corrections* and count only the former. Memberships in professional organizations do not provide definitive answers because many psychologists who would be eligible for membership do not join these organizations.

Boothby and Clements (2000) conducted an extensive survey of 830 psychologists working in state and federal prisons across the United States. The great majority—88%—worked in the prisons full-time, whereas 12% provided services on a contractual basis. The survey did not include those working in jails or in juvenile facilities. Of their sample, 59% held doctorates and 37% were master's-level graduates. All psychologists working in federal prisons had doctorates, whereas state prisons employed master's- and doctoral-level psychologists about equally. An overwhelming majority of the psychologists (92%) identified themselves as Caucasian, and 62% were male and 38% female. The psychologists tended to work exclusively with one or the other gender. Thus, 82% worked only with male offenders, 8% only with female offenders, and 10% with both. The prison population itself comprises approximately 93% males and 7% females.

For some psychologists, a limitation of working in correctional settings is the amount of time they are able to allocate for research. Psychologists in the Boothby and Clements (2000) study reported that research endeavors occupied approximately 2% of their time. The AACP (2000) standards recognize the difficulty of setting aside time for research due to the increasing demand for psychological services. Nevertheless, Standard 64 encourages applied and/or basic research, and its discussion section recommends that full-time psychologists be engaged in "at least one evaluation project having practical relevance for correctional psychology" (Standard 64, Discussion).

In a follow-up study, Boothby and Clements (2002) reported on the job satisfaction of the psychologists in their survey. Satisfaction was measured on 18 job dimensions, including such items as opportunity for advancement, job security, salary, clear definition of roles, access to and influence on decision making, and safety. Overall, the psychologists were "moderately satisfied." They were most satisfied with safety, job security, and relationships with clients, and they were least satisfied with opportunities for advancement and professional atmosphere. The respondents were also asked to rate the importance of these 18 dimensions. All dimensions but one (job status or prestige) received average ratings of 3 or above on a 5-point scale, indicating that all of the 18 dimensions were important. However, the most important were autonomy, personally meaningful work, and achievement (although recognition of such achievement was not that important). Not surprisingly, salaries and the number of inmates in a facility were also correlated with job satisfaction, with high salaries and crowded conditions having opposite effects. Demographic variables such as age and gender were unrelated to job satisfaction. Correctional psychologists working in federal prisons were significantly more satisfied than those working in state systems on 8 of the 18 dimensions. These were opportunity for advancement, appropriate level of responsibility, job security, salary, achievement or success in job, status/prestige of job, professional atmosphere, and safety. Boothby and Clements concluded their report with a discussion of the implications for recruiting and retaining psychologists for work in correctional settings. (See Box 12.3 for examples of job ads for correctional psychologists.)

BOX 12.3   Help Wanted: Correctional Psychologist

The following are employment ads representative of attempts to recruit psychologists for state prison systems or other divisions of correctional services:

Prison Health Services has an exciting full-time career opportunity for a PhD-level psychologist. Responsibilities will include overseeing the care of acute and chronic mental health patients in a 60-bed mental health unit with an adult male population. Corrections experience is preferred. We offer excellent compensation, a complete benefits package, and flexible scheduling.

National behavioral health care agency seeks well-rounded professionals to join our mental health staff in an urban detention facility. Opportunities to be involved in creative program development and provide assessment, treatment, and a variety of forensic mental health evaluations to a diverse population. Candidates should have a background in testing, skills in rapid assessment and crisis intervention, experience in forensic mental health, and knowledge of brief therapy. Positions available at several levels (e.g., MSW, LCSW, doctorate in psychology). Specialized forensic supervision available, competitive salary and benefits.

The Department of Corrections is seeking to fill two positions to provide direct treatment services to female inmates in a medium-security facility where rehabilitation is emphasized. Both crisis intervention and short- and long-term treatment skills are required. Experience working with women offenders and experience in substance abuse treatment preferred. The ideal candidate will hold a PhD/PsyD in psychology, but other degrees combined with relevant experience will be considered.

We now turn our attention to the main tasks performed by correctional psychologists. For purposes of organization, these will be divided into two distinct but interrelated topic areas, assessment and treatment.

Psychological Assessment in Corrections

Psychological assessment refers to all of the techniques used to measure and evaluate an individual's past, present, or future psychological status. Assessment usually includes but is not limited to the use of psychological tests or measuring devices. The last two decades of the 20th century saw a large increase in the number of commercially available measures and tests specifically intended for use in forensic settings. This includes a variety of tests that are presently in use in prisons and jails across the United States. In addition to tests and other measurement instruments, assessment involves interviews with the individuals being assessed, interviews with others, direct observations, and reviews of case records.

In corrections, assessment is warranted *at a minimum* at several points in an inmate's career: (1) at the entry level, when he or she enters the correctional system; (2) when decisions are to be made concerning the offender's exit into the community; and (3) at times of psychological crisis. A more specialized type of assessment is also performed in death penalty cases, when questions are raised about an offender's competency to be executed. Beyond these very minimal requirements, however, reassessments should be done on an ongoing basis. "Behavioral changes in inmates, which occur as time is served, demand constant reassessment and reassignment" (Palmer & Palmer, 1999, p. 307).

For the correctional system intent on pursuing both security needs and rehabilitative goals, assessment also is a key component to providing treatment. James Bonta (1996) has identified three generations of assessment for the purpose of offering treatment. During the first generation, assessment was performed chiefly by individual clinicians who relied on their own professional experience and judgment. In the second generation, standardized assessment instruments were adopted, although these included primarily static risk factors (such as prior record or number of violent incidents within a facility) focused primarily on making decisions about an offender's custody level. The third and present generation of assessment includes both risk and needs factors. Thus, a standardized risk/needs assessment instrument takes into consideration both prior violent incidents (a risk factor) and an offender's attitude toward authority (a needs factor). We will discuss risk/needs assessments in more detail shortly.

Initial Inmate Screening and Classification

As a matter of institutional or systemwide policy, correctional facilities require entry-level assessments so that inmates can be "psychologically processed" and assigned to a particular facility or unit. Ideally, no individual should be placed in the general correctional population without having been screened for evidence of problem behaviors or mental states. Thus, screening should be done as soon as possible after entry into the facility.

In jails, especially for pretrial detainees, this screening process may be very cursory. It will focus on whether the inmate is a suicide risk, indications of substance abuse, history of hospitalizations and medications, and indicators of violence. Because few facilities have psychological staff available round the clock, initial screening may be done by corrections staff, such as caseworkers or corrections officers. The AACP (2000) standards condone this practice as long as these individuals have been trained by psychological staff and this staff reviews all written reports. If there is evidence of mental disorder, suicide ideation, or depression or anxiety greater than would be normally expected, the individual should be referred for a more extensive evaluation. It appears that initial psychiatric evaluations are available to inmates in virtually all jails (Steadman et al., 1989).

In prisons, screening and classification becomes more complex. In many states, an offender is first sent to a classification or reception center, which may or may not be within the facility to which the offender is eventually sent. States with large prison systems (e.g., Texas, New York, California, and Florida) have centralized processing centers. The new prisoner may spend several days or even many weeks in this assessment center, separated from those already in the system, until assigned to an institution based on security needs as well as to specific programs. The classification committee may recommend, for example, that a prisoner be assigned to an aggression management program or an educational program to improve his reading level. The committee might recommend that another prisoner be offered substance abuse treatment and that contacts with her children be facilitated.

The reception unit in many prisons includes psychologists, psychiatrists, social workers, or other professionals who administer tests, interview the offender, review records, and offer programming and treatment recommendations. The AACP (2000) standards recommend that all newly committed prison inmates be given a brief, routine psychological evaluation within 1 month of admission to the facility. Included in this evaluation should be behavioral observations, record reviews, group testing to screen for emotional and intellectual abnormalities, and a written report of initial findings (Standard 30). If the results of this brief screening indicate the need for further assessment, a comprehensive psychological evaluation should be completed within 14 days. The more detailed evaluation would include record reviews, contacting prior psychotherapists or family physicians, and an extensive diagnostic interview. Although recognizing that such an approach may well tax the staff and resources of a correctional facility, the standard indicates that this is crucial if psychologists are to conform with ethical and practice standards associated with their profession.

Needs Assessment

In corrections, it is important to assess both needs and risks, particularly if a treatment regimen is to follow. Andrews and Bonta (1994) have identified two main categories of needs: criminogenic and noncriminogenic. **Criminogenic needs** are dynamic factors (Gendreau, Cullen, & Bonta, 1994), subject to change. An offender's attitude toward employment or her or his degree of alcohol use is an example. "The importance of criminogenic needs is that they serve as treatment goals: when programs successfully diminish these needs we can reasonably expect reduction in recidivism" (Gendreau et al., 1994, p. 75). **Noncriminogenic needs** are those that may be subject to change but have been found to have little influence on an offender's criminal behavior. Psychological states such as depression, anxiety, or low self-esteem are examples. Although these states may lead to adjustment problems for the individual, they are not strongly correlated with criminal behavior in the great majority of offenders.

One of the foremost risk/needs scales available in corrections is the **Level of Service Inventory— Revised (LSI-R)** (Andrews & Bonta, 1995), which is widely used in Canadian correctional facilities and is slowly being introduced in American corrections. Surveys suggest that psychologists in the United States seem less inclined to use actuarial instruments (Boothby & Clements, 2000; Gallagher, Somwaru, & Ben-Porath, 1999). Nonetheless, there is indication that instruments with good predictive ability will increasingly be sought, particularly as courts demand more scientific accountability (Otto & Heilbrun, 2002). The LSI-R, an instrument that has garnered considerable research (e.g., Gendreau, Little, & Goggin, 1996; Simourd & Malcolm, 1998), samples 10 different domains relevant to criminal conduct, including personality characteristics, procriminal attitudes, family/ marital history, and substance abuse.

Unfortunately, too many correctional systems use the classification process primarily for management purposes. Classification for custody, rather than classification for treatment, becomes the dominant goal. Therefore, estimates of dangerousness and potential escape risks become very important. Furthermore, classification decisions are often based on the institution's needs more than those of the offender. Thus, although an offender might benefit from learning computer skills, she or he might be assigned to housekeeping duties because the facility has a great need for inmates performing institutional maintenance. Psychologists involved in the classification process, then, may find it extremely frustrating when their recommendations for treatment are not followed because resources are not available.

Release Decision Making

As prison inmates approach the end of their sentence, or as they approach a parole date, the psychologist may be called on to assess the inmates' risk of reoffending. Similar assessments also may be conducted when prison officials are considering a change in the offender's status, such as shifting him or her from a medium- to a minimum-security level. Because this is pertinent to the classification issues discussed above, it is important to keep in mind that the various assessment instruments to be covered below may be used for classification as well as release decision making.

Assessments for **release decisions** are usually prepared at the request of state parole boards (Brodsky, 1980), particularly in the case of inmates who have a history of mental disturbance or predatory behavior. The psychologist typically meets with the inmate, reviews his or her prison files, and administers psychological tests. As we have seen in previous chapters, psychology has made substantial progress in developing **risk assessment instruments** over the past 20 years (e.g., Monahan, Steadman, et al., 2001; Steadman et al., 1989). The Boothby and Clements (2000) survey, however, suggests that risk assessment *instruments* are not widely used. Nevertheless, instruments recommended for this purpose include the revised Psychopathy Checklist (PCL-R), discussed in Chapter 4, and the Violence Risk Appraisal Guide (VRAG) and the Historical/Clinical/Management Risk Scale (HCR-20), which were discussed in Chapter 10 (see Box 10.5). Also mentioned in Chapter 10 were the instruments developed specifically to assess sex offender risk, a particularly intractable problem.

Use of Risk Assessment Instruments

Despite the proliferation of risk assessment instruments, it is doubtful that they are being used extensively by many forensic psychologists working in correctional settings. In fact, risk assessments themselves may not be performed that frequently. In the Boothby and Clements (2000) study, respondents reported that their most frequent assessments were of personality characteristics (42%), followed by intellectual assessment (19%). Only 13% of their assessments were risk assessments. The few psychologists who reported conducting risk assessments typically did not specify the instruments they used; when they did, the most commonly indicated was the PCL-R. By far, the most common instrument used by the correctional psychologists in the study, though, was the

Minnesota Multiphasic Personality Inventory (MMPI), which was used in a variety of contexts by 87% of the respondents. "It seems that many correctional psychologists rely on instruments such as the MMPI regardless of the referral question" (Boothby & Clements, 2000, p. 724).

Crisis Intervention

Inmates in both jails and prisons are susceptible to facing a wide variety of psychological crises that may require the assessment and treatment skills of the forensic psychologist. Psychologist Hans Toch has written extensively about the "mosaic of despair" that can overwhelm some inmates and even lead them to injure themselves or take their own lives (e.g., Toch, 1992; Toch & Adams, 2002). Crises of self-doubt, hopelessness, fear, or abandonment are not unusual in an incarcerated population. In addition, any inmate may be confronted with a situation that warrants a psychological consultation. Victimization by other inmates, news of the death of a loved one, and denial of parole are all examples of situations that can precipitate a psychological crisis in an otherwise stable inmate. When such a crisis occurs, prison officials are interested in obtaining from the psychologist both an immediate resolution of the crisis and long-range solutions that will help avoid a similar problem in the future.

In their research on psychological crises that result in self-directed violence (such as self-mutilation or suicide attempts), Toch and Adams (2002) found age, cultural, and gender differences. They state that young, White and Latino inmates are the most likely groups to face acute psychological crises. Married inmates feel more vulnerable in jail, whereas single inmates suffer more in prisons. Women are most likely to have problems with loneliness, whereas Latino inmates are distressed if they face the abandonment of relatives. They emphasize, though, that response to the jail or prison environment is very individualistic, which suggests that correctional officials must be carefully attuned to the risks of suicide among particular inmates.

Assessment of Correctional Personnel

"For the most part, a psychologist's role in the employment selection process is not extensive" (Correia, 2001, p. 60). Although correctional officer candidates in prisons are likely to have taken entry-level examinations at correctional academies or at on-site facilities, these exams typically attempt to measure aptitude for the work and attempt to screen out major behavioral problems. Little research is available on the extent to which psychological tests are administered prior to employment. Those prison systems that administer psychological tests have predominantly used the MMPI and a test specifically designed for correctional officer use, the Inwald Personality Inventory (IPI) (Inwald, Knatz, & Shusman, 1982). Research on both suggests that they should be used with caution, however. The MMPI is intended primarily to identify gross mental disturbances; it is not helpful in "screening in" or identifying ideal characteristics in candidates for employment. The IPI, though validated for corrections officers, was found by its author to successfully predict the retention or termination of only 73% of the candidates in the research sample (Shusman, Inwald, & Landa, 1984). In the same study, MMPI profiles were found to predict 63%. No further published research on the IPI is apparently available, though Inwald has published a later study dealing with the IPI administered to law enforcement officers (Inwald, 1992).

Psychological screening of correctional officer candidates has also been resisted by correctional officer unions and challenged in a number of court cases. Psychological screening of officers in jail settings is rare. Although professional jail organizations such as the American Jail Association (AJA) recommend the careful selection of correctional officers, candidates for these positions are typically screened primarily for prior criminal records and aptitude for the work.

The AACP (2000) standards suggest that it is desirable for psychologists to be involved in staff screening (Standard 55), but no details are offered. Staff screening, staff training, and assignment of staff to various duties are all examples of the broad services that can be offered by psychologists to improve the jail or prison environment for the incarcerated offender. For example, psychologists can make recommendations—and sometimes even select—corrections officers for participation in a treatment program for certain offenders. Boothby and Clements (2000), in their review of the tasks performed by correctional psychologists, noted that less than 10% of their time was spent at staff training. It is unclear whether screening and selection were included in this figure.

Competency to Be Executed

One very specialized area demanding the assessment skills of some correctional psychologists revolves around the death penalty. The Constitution prohibits the execution of an offender who is so mentally disordered that he or she is unaware of the punishment that is about to be imposed and why he or she has to suffer it (*Ford v. Wainwright*, 1986). Most recently (*Atkins v. Virginia*, 2002), the Court also ruled that some mentally retarded persons could not be executed. Specifically, if they had IQ scores below 70 and were unable to care for themselves independently, it would be cruel and unusual punishment to put them to death. Thus, if an offender on death row challenges the execution on the basis of his or her mental disorder or retardation, the forensic psychologist may be called in to perform an assessment of the offender's competency for execution. Together, the two Supreme Court decisions reignited a longstanding philosophical debate on the critical role of mental health professionals with respect to offenders sentenced to die (e.g., Bonnie, 1990; Brodsky, 1980; Mossman,

1987; Radelet & Barnard, 1986). As we saw earlier in the chapter, a recent decision allowing the forced medication of such inmates will certainly keep the controversy raging.

The great majority of psychologists working in correctional settings will never be asked to conduct an evaluation of a death row inmate's competency to be executed. First, in states with the death penalty, the death row population is usually kept at one maximum-security facility, at least as these inmates approach their execution date. Only a small minority of psychologists work in or contract to these facilities. Second, prisoners under sentence of death are far more likely to appeal their death sentence on other grounds (e.g., inadequate assistance of counsel) than to raise the issue of incompetency. It is too early to tell whether the Court's recent case prohibiting execution of the mentally retarded will significantly increase the numbers of offenders who challenge their execution on this basis.

Both the American Psychological Association and the American Psychiatric Association say that the ultimate decision as to whether the offender is competent to be executed should be made by the court and that adversarial expert witnesses are essential in this context. In other words, the psychologist or psychiatrist conducting the evaluation should neither be the sole examiner nor the decision maker.

A number of forensic psychologists have offered suggestions to their colleagues who may be conducting evaluations of competency to be executed (e.g., Heilbrun, 1987; Heilbrun et al., 2002; Small & Otto, 1991). In a model report published by Heilbrun et al. (2002, p. 96), psychologist Mark Cunningham used the following techniques in his competency assessment:

- clinical and forensic interview of the prisoner;
- psychological testing, including the MMPI-2 and the Personality Assessment Inventory (PAI);
- interview of a corrections officer on the death row unit;

- cell observation;
- a second interview with the prisoner;
- telephone interviews with friends, relatives, the prisoner's ex-wife, and his spiritual adviser, which ranged in length from 70 minutes to 12 minutes; and
- reviews of numerous legal, health, military, and prison records, as well as journal entries and letters in support of clemency.

Small and Otto (1991) note that it is import to inform the prisoner of the purpose of the evaluation, describe its procedure, and explain who will get the results and the implications of the findings. In addition, they recommend videotaping the assessment to document that the above steps have been taken, under the assumption that a court may scrutinize the evaluation process itself. Central to the evaluation, they say, is the clinical interview, in which the clinician should try to determine whether the prisoner understands that he or she was convicted and is about to be executed.

Treatment and Rehabilitation in Correctional Facilities

A dominant task of the psychologist in the correctional system is to provide *psychological treatment*, a term that encompasses a wide spectrum of strategies, techniques, and goals. Boothby and Clements (2000) reported that direct treatment took up approximately 26% of psychologists' time, second only to administrative tasks. Among the most common treatments used within correctional institutions are person-centered therapy, cognitive therapy, behavior therapy, group and milieu therapy, transactional analysis, reality therapy, and responsibility therapy (Kratcoski, 1994; Lester, Braswell, & Van Voorhis, 1992). It should be noted that psychologists are just one of several professional groups providing this therapy. Psychiatrists, social workers, and mental health counselors are also involved in most correctional facilities.

This is an important point because the method of treatment used depends largely on the professional training and orientation of the clinician. Psychiatrists, for example, are more likely to favor psychoactive drugs as part of a treatment regimen, although recent studies suggest that this approach is increasingly being supplemented with individual therapy (Heilbrun & Griffin, 1999). Social workers are more likely to use group treatment approaches, in which inmates talk about their concerns, experiences, and anxieties while the clinician generally directs and controls the topic flow. As indicated by the Boothby and Clements (2000) study, group therapy does not seem to be the norm among psychologists in correctional facilities, but it is still widely used by other clinical professionals. Sixty percent of the treatment provided by the psychologists in that study was in an individual format. The researchers found this problematic, given the high need for mental health services in the nation's jails and prisons.

A different survey of 162 professionals representing a range of professional groups (Morgan, Winterowd, & Ferrell, 1999) indicated a far greater use of group therapy. In that study, 72% of the respondents offered group therapy to inmates, and their time was about equally divided between group and individual treatment. These practitioners also estimated that 20% of all inmates in their facilities received some group therapy. When delivered effectively, group therapy has several advantages over individual therapy in correctional settings. It is, of course, more practical, given the limited treatment staff and high prison population. In addition, group therapy provides inmates with opportunities for socializing, group decision making, developing altruism, and developing functional peer relationships that individual treatment typically does not provide (Morgan et al., 1999).

On a more negative note, few professionals in the above study (only 16%) reported that their departments were conducting research on the effectiveness of group or other therapy. Perhaps more sobering, 20% indicated that no supervision was offered to therapists who facilitated group therapy sessions.

Common Psychological Treatment in Corrections

A wide variety of treatment options are available to forensic psychologists offering therapy in correctional settings (Kratcoski, 1994). The treatment model—or treatment approach—adopted by a given professional may be influenced by a host of factors, including the psychologist's training, perceptions of "what works," and, of course, the available resources within the facility. In the Boothby and Clements (2000) study, a large majority of respondents (88%) reported using a cognitive model, whereas 69% used a **behavioral model** and 40% a rational-emotive approach. As is obvious from these percentages, psychologists used more than one model, depending on the situation.

Behavioral Models

In the 1960s, psychologists consulting with correctional facilities made extensive use of behavior modification as a means of encouraging inmates to change (Bartol, 1980). Behavior modification included rewarding inmates for "good behavior" within the facility and removing privileges when behavior was unacceptable. For example, an inmate who had no disciplinary violations for a month might be given an increase in visits to the commissary, or prison store. Disruptive behavior might result in a loss of visiting privileges. By themselves, approaches that are based on such reinforcement strategies have shown little effectiveness. The main objection to such approaches is that change generated within the facility did not generalize to the real world, once inmates were released. Furthermore, in some facilities, legal advocates argued that the punishments imposed were sometimes arbitrary and in violation of inmate rights. Behavior modification as the sole approach to treatment eventually lost favor.

Cognitive-Behavioral Models

Cognitive models seek to change the very beliefs and assumptions that are at the core of an individual's behavior. Strongly based on social learning theory, they encourage inmates to examine their beliefs and assumptions, recognize problems in judgment that have led them to criminal activity, develop self-awareness, and accept responsibility for their actions. Once this has been accomplished, inmates are taught decision-making strategies and social skills, as needed, for replacing behaviors that got them into trouble with prosocial behaviors. Because cognitive programs often have components that resemble aspects of behavioral programs, the term *cognitive-behavioral* is used. For example, many cognitive-behavioral programs make use of contracts and token economy systems, whereby individuals gain points when they demonstrate prosocial behaviors.

This **cognitive-behavioral approach** appears to have the most promise in a variety of treatment contexts. Pearson, Lipton, Cleland, and Yee (2002) performed a meta-analysis on the 69 primary research studies on the effectiveness of behavioral and cognitive behavioral treatment and found the latter significantly associated with lower recidivism rates. The effect was mainly due to the cognitive components rather than the behavior modification interventions, however. That is, such aspects as problem solving, interpersonal skills training, role-playing, and negotiation skills training—all associated with a cognitive approach—were linked with effectiveness. Token economies, contingency management, and behavioral contracts—all associated with behavior modification—had little effect.

Rational-Emotive Models

Nearly 50 years ago, psychologist Albert Ellis (1962) developed a model of therapy that has considerable similarity to the cognitive approaches discussed above. **Rational-emotive therapy (RET)** presumes that if a person holds "rational beliefs" rather than "irrational beliefs," the person will deal appropriately with difficulties in his or her life. Emotions such as sorrow, annoyance, or regret were considered appropriate; emotions such as depression, anxiety, and extreme anger were inappropriate (Haaga & Davidson, 1993). One goal of RET, then, is to teach patients to confront and forcefully dispute their irrational beliefs. An example of an irrational belief might be, "If I fail at this task, I must be a bad person." Another might be, "If I don't show her who's boss, she won't think I'm a real man." Therapists who use the RET approach often give their clients "homework assignments" aimed at disputing their beliefs.

According to Haaga and Davidson (1993), rational-emotive therapy was in the historical forefront of the cognitive trend and remains widely used in psychotherapy. Recall that this approach was used by 40% of the respondents in the Boothby and Clements (2000) survey. Nevertheless, its scientific status is less clear. Irrational beliefs are both difficult to define and difficult to measure, and evaluation results have been mixed. Haaga and Davidson note that the treatment has not been sufficiently tested. "Perhaps it is time to consider the possibility that RET is not susceptible to traditional scientific outcome evaluation" (Haaga & Davidson, 1993, p. 219).

Treatment of Special Populations

Like the general population, inmates vary widely in their background experiences and their needs. Although treatment should be individualized as much as possible to recognize these differences, programs are often established to address common needs of groups of offenders. For example, prisons—and to a lesser extent jails—may offer programs for inmates who are HIV positive, elderly inmates, women who killed their abusers, sex offenders, psychopaths, inmates who are parents, substance abusers, inmates with developmental disabilities, and inmates under sentence of death. Although we will not cover all of these categories below, readers are advised that a wide variety of literature in correctional psychology is available (e.g., Ashford, Sales, & Reid, 2001; Kratcoski, 1994).

Violent Offenders

Violent behavior has been defined as the intentional and malevolent physical injuring of another without adequate social justification (Blackburn, 1993). Psychological services to inmates who have committed violent crimes or who otherwise demonstrate propensities toward violent behavior are common in many correctional facilities. Corrections officials place a high priority on both controlling such behavior within prison and jail settings and reducing its likelihood once an inmate has been released. Therefore, programs that address this problem in the inmate population are appreciated, if not always well funded. As a group, however, violent offenders are extremely challenging. "When compared to other offenders, they tend to be less motivated for treatment, more resistant or noncompliant while in treatment, have higher attrition rates, demonstrate fewer positive behavioral changes while in treatment, and demonstrate higher recidivism rates posttreatment" (Serin & Preston, 2001, p. 254).

Serin and Preston (2001) note that a major impediment to treating violent offenders has been confusion over the definition of the population along with failure to recognize that violent individuals are not all alike. This lack of homogeneity, Serin and Preston emphasize, requires differential treatment, but differential treatment is rarely offered. Programs for violent offenders too often do not distinguish, for example, between offenders displaying instrumental aggression and offenders who have anger control problems. Instrumental aggression is coolly committed for the purposes of achieving a particular goal. Thus, it makes little sense to place an offender who commits his crimes using instrumental aggression into a program teaching him to control his anger. On the other hand, anger control is an important skill to develop in individuals who are impulsive, have substance abuse problems or mental disorders, or lack social, relationship, or parenting skills. Although differential treatment is an important goal, it is practically very difficult to achieve, particularly within an institutional setting. As Serin and Preston acknowledge, few settings have the resources—both financial and human—to provide multiple programs for different types of violent offenders. Even when more than one program is offered, the identification and matching of offenders with specific programs are challenging tasks. In addition, the population of violent offenders who qualify as psychopaths requires different strategies, as we will see shortly.

Programs vary widely in their approach. However, many have two common features: (a) teaching techniques for self-regulating aggression and (b) addressing cognitive deficits.

In the first category, motivated offenders are taught relaxation skills or "stress inoculation" approaches to reduce the arousal that results in inappropriate aggression. In the second category, motivated offenders are challenged to confront the irrational beliefs or biases that lead to violence. Defining problems in hostile ways or failing to anticipate the consequences of aggressive behavior are examples. Programs that address cognitive deficits, therefore, strive to change the thinking patterns of offenders by persuading them that the approaches they have used to this point have not resulted in successful outcomes in their relationships with society or with others in their environment. A prerequisite to a successful program outcome, however, is the motivation of the offender.

Although a variety of violent offender programs have produced some positive treatment effects, "few provide the rigor (i.e., control groups) to conclude that intervention for violent adults reduces violent recidivism" (Serin & Preston, 2001, p. 260). Advocates of violent offender programs maintain, however, that such programs at the least *reduce the risk* of future violence and should ideally be followed up with community supervision and treatment once inmates are released. Furthermore, even when studies do not demonstrate positive posttreatment effects, the design of the study itself—not the treatment offered—may be the problem. As always, more methodologically sound research is needed to continue the progress toward effective programming.

Interestingly, some research indicates that it is far more difficult to provide intensive treatment for high-risk offenders in the community than in a controlled prison environment. Despite the numerous challenges within an institutional setting that were discussed above, the clinician has more control within a residential program. In addition, milieu treatment—such as can be found in therapeutic communities within the facility—is a possibility. A major disadvantage of institutional treatment is the difficulty in generalizing it to noninstitutional settings (Quinsey et al., 1998).

It should be mentioned that pharmacological approaches are also used in the management of violent offenders, particularly those for whom violence can be attributed partially to biological factors. These would include some individuals with brain injuries, schizophrenia, dementia, and clinical depression, among other disorders. Antipsychotic medications are often used in prison settings to control acute violent behavior in a crisis situation, such as a psychotic episode. Nevertheless, the vast majority of violent offenders neither require nor would benefit from pharmacological treatment (Serin & Preston, 2001). When such treatment is indicated, it should also be accompanied by psychological interventions mentioned above.

Criminal Psychopaths

As we discussed in Chapter 4, individuals who qualify as criminal psychopaths present special challenges to society as well as to prison administrators. It has been a longstanding conclusion that psychopaths are essentially untreatable and continually demonstrate low motivation in treatment or rehabilitation programs. Hare (1996) asserts,

> There is no known treatment for psychopathy. . . . This does not necessarily mean that the egocentric and callous attitudes and behaviors of psychopaths are immutable, only that there are no methodologically sound treatments or "resocialization" programs that have been shown to work with psychopaths. Unfortunately, both the criminal justice system and the public routinely are fooled into believing otherwise. (p. 41)

Psychopaths often volunteer for various prison treatment programs, show "remarkable improvement," and present themselves as model prisoners. They are skillful at convincing therapists, counselors, and parole boards that they have changed for the better. Upon release, however, there is a high probability that they will reoffend, and their recidivism rate is not usually reduced following treatment (Porter et al., 2000). "Treatment participated in by many psychopaths may be superficial, intended mainly for impression management" (Porter et al., 2000, p. 219).

Some evidence even suggests that psychopaths who participate in therapy are more likely to engage in violent crime following treatment than psychopaths who did not receive treatment. Rice, Harris, and Cormier (1992) investigated the effectiveness of an intensive therapeutic community program offered in a maximum-security facility. (The concept of therapeutic communities will be discussed later in the chapter.) The study was retrospective, in that the researchers examined records and files 10 years after the program was completed. Results showed that psychopaths who participated in the therapeutic community exhibited higher rates of violent recidivism than psychopaths who did not. For nonpsychopaths, the results were the reverse: Nonpsychopaths were less likely to reoffend if they had participated in the program. Rice et al. admonish that the psychopaths in their study were an especially serious group of offenders, with 85% having a history of violent crimes. It is possible that a group of less serious offenders would show better results. Nevertheless, the researchers concluded, "The combined results suggest that a therapeutic community is not the treatment of choice for psychopaths, particularly those with extensive criminal histories" (Rice et al., 1992, p. 408). Hare (1996) suggests that group therapy and insight-oriented treatment programs may actually help the psychopath develop better ways of manipulating and deceiving others. It should be mentioned that the treatment program reported on in the Rice et al. (1992) article had controversial features, including emotion-laden encounter groups among inmates in the facility.

Some recent preliminary data by Skeem et al. (2002) do suggest, though, that *under certain conditions*, some psychopaths do benefit from treatment. Specifically, both the level of violence and the frequency of offending can be reduced. The key appears to be the intensity of the treatment. Skeem et al. found that psychopathic psychiatric patients who received seven or more treatment sessions during a 10-week period were approximately three times less likely to be violent than psychopathic patients who received six or fewer sessions. These results support earlier findings reported by Salekin (2002), who also discovered that a range of treatment interventions appeared to be moderately successful for psychopaths, especially if the treatment was lengthy and intensive.

Likewise, Bonta (2002) has suggested that psychopathy should be considered a dynamic factor, not a static variable. "Antisocial personality . . . does not need to be viewed as such a stable, intractable aspect of the person" (Bonta, 2002, p. 369). He argues that certain features of the antisocial personality—impulsiveness, risk taking, callous disregard for others, shallow affect,

pathological lying—can be linked with realistic treatment goals. Obviously, much more research is needed before we can make any far-reaching conclusions about the effectiveness of treatment programs directed at criminal psychopaths.

Sex Offender Treatment

As we discussed in Chapter 6, sex offenders are an extremely heterogeneous group. Most of the research has focused on two predominant groups, rapists and child molesters. These are the two sex offender groups that are the most likely to be imprisoned and the more difficult to treat, although within each group, some types of offenders are more amenable to treatment. Recall that we gave considerable attention in Chapter 5 to the typologies developed in an attempt to understand these offenders. It should be noted that extreme care should be used in applying these typologies, very few of which have been submitted to empirical validation (Heilbrun et al., 2002). As we stated in Chapter 10 while discussing sex offender evaluations, a negative label (e.g., sadistic rapist) may have unfair consequences for the individual so labeled. In prison, it may hinder his adjustment to incarceration, may affect his security level, or limit his chances for an early release. In addition, although many psychologists believe the risk assessment instruments specifically devised for sex offenders are useful, these instruments also have many limitations (Campbell, 2003).

The number of sex offenders under correctional supervision has reached alarming proportions. By the end of the 1990s, approximately 296,100 individuals convicted of rape or sexual assault—including assault of children—were in this category, with about 40% of them in jails or prisons (Bureau of Justice Statistics, 2001a). Observers have noted, however, that these figures represent the offense for which an offender was convicted and sentenced; an undetermined number of additional inmates also have offended sexually in the past but are not incarcerated for sex offenses (Burdon & Gallagher, 2002). In addition, some prison inmates are clinical sex offenders but not legal sex offenders. That is, they have a clinically diagnosable paraphilic disorder that may or may not have resulted in a conviction (Burdon & Gallagher, 2002). **Paraphilia** is a relatively new term for a variety of sexual deviations, where sexual arousal cannot occur without the presence of unusual imagination or behaviors.

Psychologists and other clinicians have responded to the above figures by continuing to search for effective strategies to prevent future crime among sex offenders who, as a group, are highly resistant to changing their deviant behavior patterns (Bartol, 2002). After an extensive review of the research and clinical literature on the subject, Furby, Weinroth, and Blackshaw (1989) were forced to conclude, "There is as yet no evidence that clinical treatment reduces rates of sex reoffenses in general and no appropriate data for assessing whether it may be differentially effective for different types of offenders" (p. 27). The Furby et al. review included all variants of therapeutic approaches.

Despite this pessimistic appraisal, other reviews have been more favorable. Recent meta-analyses of the sex offender treatment literature have indicated that, on the whole, sex offenders are better treated than untreated (e.g., Gallagher et al., 1999). In addition, some approaches have shown more promise than others. The cognitive-behavioral approaches discussed above, in particular, have received more favorable reviews (Laws, 1995). The cognitive-behavioral approach contends that maladaptive sexual behaviors are learned according to the same principles as normal sexual behaviors are learned and are largely the result of attitudes and beliefs. Cognitive-behavioral therapy, compared to traditional verbal, insight-oriented therapy, has demonstrated short-term effectiveness in eliminating exhibitionism and fetishism (Kilmann, Sabalis, Gearing, Bukstel, & Scovern, 1982), some forms of pedophilia (Marshall & Barbaree, 1990), and sexual violence and aggression (Hall, 1995; Polizzi, MacKenzie, & Hickman, 1999). Cognitive-behavioral treatment currently offers the most effective method in the temporary cessation of deviant sexual behavior in motivated individuals. (See Box 12.4 for common features of cognitive-behavioral treatment programs.)

BOX 12.4 The Cognitive-Behavioral Approach: Key Elements

Of the many therapeutic interventions that have been tried in corrections, the cognitive-behavioral approach seems to hold the most promise. It consists of counseling (group and individual) and training whereby offenders develop cognitive skills that will presumably help them to adopt alternative, prosocial behaviors rather than the antisocial behaviors that resulted in their criminal convictions. There is no universally implemented cognitive-behavioral treatment program; rather, treatment providers decide on an approach consistent with their own training and the needs of the offenders under their care. Any or all of the following elements might be found in a cognitive-behavioral treatment program:

- Social skills development training (e.g., learning to communicate, be assertive rather than aggressive, and resolve conflicts appropriately)
- Decision making (e.g., learning to weigh alternatives, learning to delay gratification)
- Identifying and avoiding "thinking errors"—misguided assumptions that facilitated criminal offending (e.g., "women want to be shown who's boss")

(Continued)

BOX 12.4 (Continued)

- Training at solving problems (e.g., interpersonal problems with one's intimate partner)
- Self-control training and anger management (e.g., avoiding hostile attribution)
- Building self-esteem (e.g., recognizing good qualities and providing self-reinforcement)
- Cognitive skills training (e.g., learning to reason)
- Relapse prevention (learning to avoid situations that might lead to further offending)
- Practical skills training (e.g., applying for work)

As noted in the text, the cognitive-behavioral approach has shown success when programs are properly implemented and carried out and offenders are motivated to change. It is not perfect. However, although other therapeutic approaches (e.g., behavior modification; therapeutic communities) have had unpromising results (with some exceptions), cognitive-behavioral therapy gives reason to hope.

The key words relative to the success of cognitive-behavioral treatment are *temporary cessation* and *motivated individual*. There is now widespread agreement among researchers and clinicians that sex offenders cannot be "cured." The problem of cognitive-behavioral therapy— and all therapies for that matter—is not in getting the motivated offender to stop the deviant sexual patterns but in preventing relapse across time and situations. It is analogous to dieting. Although most dieting regimens are effective in getting the motivated individual to lose weight initially, the real problem is the eventual relapse into old eating patterns. Thus, a treatment approach demonstrating much promise in the treatment of sex offenders is called Relapse Prevention (RP). "RP is a self-control program designed to teach individuals who are trying to change their behavior how to anticipate and cope with the problem of relapse" (George & Marlatt, 1989, p. 2). The program emphasizes self-management; clients are considered responsible for the solution of the problem.

Sex offender treatment programs exist in virtually every state and in the federal prison system, but the number of inmates who actually receive treatment is unknown (Burdon & Gallagher, 2002). They vary widely in approach,

in the extent to which they are evaluated, and in the degree of success when evaluation research is conducted. Treatment programs are less likely to be available to jail inmates because of the short-term nature of jail confinement. However, inmates who are subsequently released to the community may be referred to community treatment programs.

Women Offenders

In recent years, women's rates of incarceration have increased faster than men's rates, although very few scholars predict that they will ever "catch up." Presently, women make up 6.6% of all state and federal prison inmates and approximately 10% of all jail inmates and detainees (Bureau of Justice Statistics, 2001a). Although increasing research attention is now being given to women inmates, they still remain forgotten offenders compared with males.

Scholars agree that problems faced by female prisoners are similar to but also distinct from the problems faced by male prisoners. For example, due to the small numbers of women in prison, there are far fewer correctional facilities available, thus severely restricting opportunities to be near their families or to have occupational, educational, or social activities while incarcerated. More important, their relationships with their children are often severely hampered, resulting in a more severe deprivation than typically found for the male parent (MacKenzie, Robinson, & Campbell, 1989). This parent-child deprivation is especially severe for long-term women inmates, who may lose their major source of identity when they lose their parental role (Weisheit & Mahan, 1988). Weisheit and Mahan (1988) note that women inmates have on average two children and often are the head of their household. Moreover, they are likely to be poor, poorly educated, and members of a racial or ethnic minority. Female inmates are also more likely than male inmates to have experienced sexual abuse as a child and physical abuse as an adult (Owen, 2000).

Some observers have estimated that more than 60% of the female prison population requires mental health services and that a vast majority of women offenders have a need for substance abuse services (e.g., Owen, 2000). Many women serving time have had a history of victimization—often violent victimization and often at the hands of fathers, spouses, and/or intimate partners. As Owen (2000) observes, "Closely related to mental health problems is the need to recognize the impact of the physical, sexual, and emotional abuse experienced by women offenders" (p. 196). Approaches that increase their self-confidence, recognize their victimization but enable them to take charge of their lives, and teach them life skills offer the best hope for women incarcerated.

Treatment in Jail Settings

Psychological treatment of inmates in jail settings is considerably different from treatment in prisons. The short-term nature of the jail stay—on average 11 days—suggests that **crisis intervention** and limited treatment goals are typical. Moreover, treatment in jail settings is far more likely to consist of stabilizing medication rather than therapy. Nevertheless, the treatment models discussed above can still be implemented, even in short-term jail settings.

Steadman et al. (1989) have provided a helpful but dated description of mental health services offered in 43 jails in 26 states. All jails in their study offered psychotropic medication, and almost all offered psychological evaluation and competency examinations (98% and 93%, respectively). Far fewer (60%) offered drug and alcohol treatment. Therapy or counseling was offered by 30%, whereas a mere 16% provided case management services for general mental health at release. Steadman et al. (1989, pp. 48–49) identified, described in detail, and provided illustrations of four basic types of service arrangements for mentally disordered inmates:

- "ad hoc," in which services were offered only on an emergency basis;
- "identification," in which correctional officers only identified disturbed inmates;
- "identification and treatment," in which disturbed inmates were both identified and were provided with treatment; and
- "comprehensive," in which identification, treatment, and referral services were all available.

The above taxonomy was not the researchers' main concern, however. Rather, they wished to examine the linkages between community resources and the delivery of mental health services to the jailed population.

Instead of viewing the jail as a self-contained or closed system, an inter-organizational approach to program development and evaluation looks beyond the jail to its linkages with a variety of other organizations in its environment, such as state mental hospital, psychiatric units in general hospitals, community mental health centers, and other health and human service agencies. (Steadman et al., 1989, p. 73)

Many of the existing programs offered services outside the jail, such as by transporting inmates to community clinics or offices. Internal programs, which were less in evidence, place heavier demands on staffing, budgets, and institutional security.

A key finding of the research was that conflict between correctional staff and mental health staff was far less evident than the researchers had expected. Although some conflict existed, particularly when services were provided within the jail under the joint auspices of correctional and mental health personnel, the two professions shared the convergence of two goals: custody and therapy. Correctional staff indicated that therapists made their jobs easier, and therapists respected the needs of the custodial staff to keep the jail secure. Steadman and his colleagues (1989, p. 102) attributed this to the short-term nature of a jail stay, essentially leaving no time for the huge ascendancy of one type of goal over the other, such as is more likely to occur in prison settings. They note that the jail is truly the client:

> If individual treatment were more ambitious, much more therapy in the form of individual counseling and group sessions would become more pervasive, and conflict, as well as service costs, would probably increase dramatically. However, given the nature of the jail, such treatment goals are unrealistic, while safety management needs are acute. (p. 103)

Providing treatment services to the nonsentenced jail population—the detainees—is especially challenging. First, it is impossible to predict how long the individual will remain in detention because pretrial release is a continuing possibility for the majority of detainees. Other detainees may have charges dismissed or may plead guilty to their offenses, thus meaning that they will be placed on probation or transferred to prison. Second, even while in custody, numerous disruptions will occur in the individual's schedule. For example, court appearances, visits, meetings with attorneys,

population head counts, and even recreational opportunities are unpredictable. Third, treatment services must be generic and not tied to criminal activity because the detainee is only charged with, not convicted of, crime. Thus, sex offender treatment or a program for domestic abusers is inappropriate when applied to detainees who are presumed innocent until proven guilty. Even sentenced inmates provide challenges to the forensic psychologist, largely due to the short-term natures of their sentence. The therapist therefore must forgo long-term goals, even if he or she believes such goals are in the greater interest of the client. "Mental health professionals who are willing to work toward less traditional treatment goals can function within the jail with minimal goal conflict" (Steadman et al., 1989, p. 103). They are advised to develop release-planning goals that will link the individual to community-based mental health agencies. In addition, they are urged to keep in mind that the jail environment itself is crowded, noisy, and lacking in privacy and that inmates have very little control over their lives. Such conditions can exacerbate mental disorder. Not surprisingly, therefore, "the primary treatment goals for jail inmates will usually be crisis stabilization and maintenance at an appropriate level of functioning while in custody" (Cox, Landsberg, & Paravati, 1989, p. 223).

As discussed in the beginning of this chapter, jails—sometimes even more than prisons—have a number of features that can impede efforts to offer treatment. Today, limited budgets and overcrowding are major concerns. Bowker and Schweid (1992) have written about a program for retarded offenders in Cuyahoga County, Ohio. A mentally retarded offender (MRO) pod was started "to prevent more intelligent inmates from victimizing retarded offenders during their incarceration" (Bowker & Schweid, 1992, p. 499). A counselor would meet with the offenders weekly in group meetings to help them adjust to their environment and would consult with a team to address their needs. Overcrowding necessitated the closing of the special unit, and retarded inmates then were shifted to a medical/

psychological unit. Although the researchers noted there was hope that adding more space to the jail might revive the special unit, the problem that was faced is a common one in numerous jails that do not have the resources to separate inmates with special needs.

Treatment and Counseling of Correctional Officers

According to research and anecdotal reports, stress among correctional officers in both jails and prisons is widespread (Abt Associates, 2000; Huckabee, 1992). These officers face challenges ranging from threats of inmate violence to public derogation of their work. In the popular media, correctional officers are often depicted as callous, uneducated, and brutal. (Consider such contemporary films as *Shawshank Redemption, The Green Mile,* and *Monster's Ball.*) The professional, stable, intelligent officer is portrayed as the exception rather than the rule. These media stereotypes are reflected in public attitudes toward correctional work; officers not infrequently comment that, when asked what they do for a living, they reply that they "work for the state."

Within the prison or jails, correctional officers experience stress associated with understaffing and extensive overtime, low pay (particularly in jails), inmate violence, rotating shift work, and problems with coworkers (Abt Associates, 2000). Furthermore, overcrowding in many correctional facilities since the 1980s has been accompanied by an increasing number of attacks against correctional staff. The number of documented attacks in state and federal prisons rose by nearly one third between 1990 and 1995, from 10,731 to 14,165 (Stephan, 1997). The number of attacks in jail settings decreased during the same time period, but researchers still estimate an average of four assaults per week, with large jail systems experiencing the highest rates of attacks (Stephan, 1997). Despite the fact that most violence in prisons and in jails is believed to be inmate on inmate violence (Clear & Cole, 2000),

neither the victimization of inmates by staff nor the victimization of staff by inmates can be overlooked or tolerated.

For many reasons, psychological services to correctional officers are almost invariably delivered outside of the facility, on a contractual basis with the correctional system, and with guaranteed confidentiality. An exception might be on-site crisis counseling following a critical incident within the facility, such as a hostage-taking situation or the killing of a correctional officer. In such a situation, the facility's mental health professionals as well as professionals working in the community might conduct group debriefing sessions with affected correctional officers. For the most part, however, prison and jail systems contract with mental health professionals within the community. Alternately, correctional officers are left to seek help on their own. Peer counseling programs, with or without guidance from psychologists and other mental health professionals, are also becoming increasingly available in correctional facilities. A recent report prepared for the Department of Justice (Abt Associates, 2000) describes approximately a dozen programs designed to address correctional officer stress in prisons, jails, and youth facilities. Although we emphasize in this chapter the assessment and treatment offered to inmates, it is obvious that forensic psychologists must continue to make their services available to correctional staff as well.

Obstacles to the Treatment of Inmates and Staff

The correctional environment itself creates numerous challenges for the clinician offering services both to inmates and to staff. In this section, we discuss some of the main obstacles.

Confidentiality

As noted in earlier chapters, forensic psychologists often find that they cannot guarantee total confidentiality to the persons whom they assess or treat. This is especially true of psychologists working in correctional settings, particularly prisons and jails. For example, when the security of the institution is at stake, the inmate presents a threat of suicide, or a third party is in danger, confidentiality cannot be guaranteed. Limits of confidentiality include "knowledge of escape plans, intentions to commit a crime in prison, introduction of illegal items (e.g., contraband) into prison, in addition to suicidal or homicidal ideation and intention, court subpoenas, and reports of child or elder abuse or neglect" (Morgan et al., 1999, p. 602). As we noted earlier in the chapter, psychologists and other treatment providers are advised to inform inmates of these limitations on confidentiality prior to the provision of assessment and treatment services. As a result of these limits, the inmate may perceive the treatment provider as a representative of the administration. When this happens, the work of psychologists in correctional facilities becomes especially challenging (Milan, Chin, & Nguyen, 1999).

Confidentiality is also a critical factor when psychologists are treating correctional officers. There are countless anecdotal reports of correctional officers (as well as law enforcement officers) who resist seeking help for psychological problems—from mild to very severe—because they fear that supervisors or coworkers will learn of this and lose confidence in their abilities to do their job. For this reason, prison and jail systems sometimes go to great lengths to guarantee the anonymity of the officer being treated. In one program described in the Abt Associates (2000) report, for example, a chaplain assigns a number to an officer needing professional treatment. The officer then calls a psychologist, and all subsequent billing for services is done using only the number as identification. The chaplain serves as the intermediary, receiving bills and forwarding them to the appropriate fiscal office. In this way, correctional administrators presumably are never made aware of which officer has sought treatment.

Although patient-therapist confidentiality is sacrosanct, the fact that an individual has sought

treatment may eventually be revealed, however. This is particularly the case when a civil suit is brought against the facility or agency and an individual officer is an essential part of the legal action. When a clinician is called to testify as a witness in a legal proceeding, confidentiality is not protected. An officer sued for excessive force, for example, cannot expect to keep confidential the fact that he or she has sought psychological treatment, either before or after the alleged incident. Even an officer using justifiable force may be subjected to some legal scrutiny. The *content* of the therapist-patient communication is privileged, but the *fact* that such communication took place is not (*Jaffe v. Redmond*, 1996).

Coercion

Another obstacle to successful treatment, particularly treatment of inmates, is its coercive aspect. Institutional treatment often—although not invariably—operates on the principle that psychological change can be coerced. Conversely, traditional forms of psychological treatment have been successful only when subjects were willing and motivated to participate. This basic principle applies regardless of whether the person is living in the community or within the walls of an institution that has overwhelming power over the lives of its inmates. Thus, although inmates have a **right to refuse treatment**, their refusal can create far more problems than their grudging acceptance. For example, refusal may mean transfer to another facility, delay in being released, or a restriction on privileges (*McKune v. Lile*, 2002).

In recent years, however, some researchers have begun to question the conventional wisdom that coercion and treatment cannot coexist (see generally, Farabee, 2002). The critical variable appears to be not the fact that the individual is incarcerated but rather the individual's willingness to participate or perceived need for treatment. In addition, some studies indicate that even a recalcitrant inmate can eventually benefit from treatment programs (e.g., Burdon & Gallagher, 2002; Prendergast, Farabee, Cartier, & Henkin, 2002).

Environment

Another obstacle to effective treatment in prisons and jails is the unusual nature of the prison environment itself. The list of negative features ranges from overcrowding, violence, and victimization by both other prisoners and staff to isolation from families and feelings of a lack of control over one's life.

In the late 1950s and 1960s, a number of psychologists working in correctional settings helped establish "therapeutic communities" (TCs) for inmates facing adjustment problems in prisons (Toch, 1980). These TCs were special living quarters where inmates would be housed separately from the rest of the prison population and would be involved in decision making, group therapy, and operating their own living quarters within the broad prison setting. Although these inmates did not have significantly better recidivism rates than other inmates (Gendreau & Ross, 1984), prison life was made more tolerable for them, and job satisfaction for the staff improved. Today, few prison programs offer therapeutic community settings, primarily because of budgetary constraints and space limitations. When available, they are more likely to be offered to inmates with substance abuse problems. Recall from our discussion of psychopaths that they do not appear to be good candidates for a therapeutic community approach. In general, research has documented the effectiveness of therapeutic communities when they are intensive, behavior based, and focused on targeting an offender's drug use (MacKenzie, 2000).

Many observers note that prison environments are worse today than they were in the 1960s, when therapeutic communities were first proposed. Overcrowding, violence, and deteriorating physical conditions characterize a substantial number of the nation's prisons and jails. By the end of the 20th century, for example, state prisons as a group were operating between full capacity and 15% above capacity, and federal prisons were operating at 31% above capacity (Bureau of Justice Statistics, 2001a). The overcrowding problem in jails was even more severe. Violence is also endemic in many prisons. It has been estimated that about 25,000 nonsexual assaults and close to 300,000 sexual assaults occur each year in the nation's jails and prisons (Clear & Cole, 2000). It is impossible to know the true number because assaults may not be reported.

Living conditions for inmates who are kept in isolation for disciplinary reasons or presumably for their own protection (e.g., inmates with mental disorders) are particularly problematic. Although it would be unfair to suggest that the typical jail or prison faces these seemingly intractable problems, correctional psychologists encounter them all too often, and they contribute significantly to the stress experienced by both inmates and staff.

Treatment is also made difficult by other aspects of even the most humane jail or prison environment. Jail sentences are typically short, so continuous treatment is highly unlikely to occur. In both jails and prisons, inmates "miss" appointments with clinicians for a wide variety of reasons. Even when inmates themselves want to attend, they may be prevented from doing so for security or disciplinary reasons. A cellblock may be locked down for a day, for example, while officials conduct cell searches, investigate a disturbance, or conduct medical tests. An inmate involved in an altercation may be placed in disciplinary segregation, making it unlikely that visits to a therapist will be allowed. For security reasons, prison inmates are transferred to other facilities with little warning. Finally, budgetary constraints in many facilities result in cutbacks to all but the most essential services.

Community-Based Corrections

As we noted at the beginning of the chapter, the great majority of adults under correctional supervision remain within the community, either in their own homes or in transitional or group homes, camps, ranches, and similar facilities. Community-based placements other than one's own home generally hold individuals for less than 24 hours a day, allowing them opportunity to work, attend school, participate in job training, or attend counseling or treatment sessions. Community-based facilities are operated by state or federal governments or by private organizations under government contract. In the criminal justice literature, such placements are referred to as "intermediate sanctions," representing points on a continuum between probation and jail or prison, as well as between prison and parole. They may also be referred to as "probation plus," or "parole plus." The offender who lives in a halfway house upon release from prison, for example, is on parole with the added restrictions imposed by the rules and supervision of the halfway house administration. Interestingly, in February 2003, the federal government announced that it was removing from federal judges the authority to send sentenced offenders to halfway houses rather than to federal prisons when the federal sentencing guidelines prescribed a prison sentence. Offenders who were most likely to benefit from judicial discretion were those convicted of white-collar offenses. The government indicated its goal was to end favorable treatment for these individuals.

Intermediate sanctions are also used with offenders who remain in their own homes, such as offenders assigned to house arrest or electronic monitoring. The forensic psychologist offering services to offenders under community correctional supervision, therefore, soon learns that they have a variety of living arrangements as well as conditions of release.

A common condition of release is the requirement that an offender attend counseling or therapy. Thus, many community psychologists have on their caseload individuals who have been ordered to seek treatment. We will not revisit here the issue discussed earlier in the chapter, revolving around whether change can be coerced.

Although it is not irrelevant in this context, the coercion here is not as clear-cut as coercion within the institutional environment of the jail or prison, particularly the latter. Nevertheless, the forensic psychologist should be alert to the fact that her or his clients might not be seeking help but for the fear that they could be incarcerated if they do not meet the conditions of release.

Like the psychologist working with detainees and inmates, the psychologist working in community settings performs both assessment and treatment tasks. Evaluations of an individual's competency to stand trial or competency to participate in a variety of judicial proceedings are often performed in the community, as we noted in Chapter 10. In addition, the community psychologist may assess an offender's appropriateness for a particular treatment program, such as a program for sex offenders. Risk assessments are increasingly being performed within the community as well. For example, before downgrading a probationer from an **intensive supervision program** to "regular" probation, the court or the probation authority may ask the psychologist to assess the risk to the community if the probationer is no longer supervised as diligently as has been happening. The principles associated with risk assessment, as well as with risk/needs assessment discussed earlier in the chapter as well as in Chapter 9, will not be repeated here. As we will see shortly, recent commentators are strongly advocating an assessment of an offender's criminogenic needs before undertaking community treatment.

The role of the forensic psychologist in treating offenders in the community deserves our careful attention. In most ways, the principles applied and the standard of practice are no different from what the psychologist would adopt in the treatment of any other client. Nevertheless, a number of factors render the correctional client distinctive. The common thread among all of these factors is the importance of communication between the psychologist and the representatives of the criminal justice system. First, as noted above, the coercive nature of the treatment may create problems, although it is far less coercive than treatment in jails and prisons. Second, the psychologist may be placed in the untenable position of being an "enforcer," similar to the probation officer. Thus, if the client misses an appointment, the psychologist must decide whether to report this lapse to the probation officer, who may or may not see this as a serious problem. Third, in a somewhat related vein, the psychologist may be called on to make decisions involving privileges that he or she would rather not have to make. A parolee receiving treatment may wish to attend the out-of-state wedding of a sibling, for example, a decision that would typically be left to the supervising officer. Community psychologists are not infrequently called on to render opinions on such matters, which many believe are out of their purview. Fourth, the limits of confidentiality must be recognized and communicated to the individual. Typically, the client in these situations is not the offender but the supervising agency, which may be a court or a probation/parole department. In some jurisdictions, the court imposing the conditions of release may require periodic progress notes from the treating clinician. In addition, in the event that probation or parole is revoked, summary notes from the psychologist's records may be subjected to court scrutiny. Fifth, the criminogenic needs of the offender require continual assessment and addressing.

The last decade of the 20th century saw some promising work describing and evaluating the work of psychologists vis-à-vis conditionally released offenders in community settings. Heilbrun and Griffin (1999), describing a number of well-regarded programs in the United States, Canada, and the Netherlands, concluded that there was no single "ideal" program; rather, it was important to use

the full range of treatment modalities that have been developed during the past decade. . . . By employing treatments such as recently developed psychotropic medications, psychosocial rehabilitation,

skill-based psychoeducational interventions designed to improve relevant areas of deficits, and relapse prevention, it is likely that treatment response in a forensic program will be enhanced. (Heilbrun & Griffin, 1999, p. 270)

Heilbrun and Griffin (1999) provide illustrations of community-based programs in eight states as well as Canada. Most of the programs described provided services to a hybrid population of individuals with mental disorders, including individuals found not guilty by reason of insanity (NGRI) as well as probationers and parolees assigned to treatment programs as a condition of their release or referred by probation/ parole officers. Thus, most contacts were on an involuntary basis. Included were both outpatient and residential rehabilitation programs, with outpatient clinics offering both assessment and treatment. Some clinics offering substance abuse treatment also accepted voluntary clients.

In summarizing the programs they describe, Heilbrun and Griffin (1999) note that all emphasized the treatment of psychopathology and the management of aggressive behavior. "In order to meet both goals, programs may refuse to accept high-risk patients, who are generally regarded as more antisocial individuals" (p. 264). Interestingly, it is precisely high-risk offenders who benefit the most from intensive treatment programs.

This is a finding that has consistently emerged from research focusing on the variant of intermediate sanctions known as intensive supervision. Intensive supervision programs (ISPs) were intended for high-risk probationers and parolees who were nevertheless deemed not to require incarceration if a less costly alternative were available. (In reality, low-risk offenders were placed in these programs as well [Tonry, 1990].) Probation or parole officers supervising offenders on ISPs have smaller caseloads, provide around-the-clock team supervision, make frequent contacts, and presumably are less tolerant of any failure on the part of the offender to meet the conditions of release. Alcohol and illegal drug use are monitored closely and without notice. Despite these punitive conditions, evaluations of community ISPs have not been promising, and they have not proved cost-effective (Gendreau, Paparozzi, Little, & Goddard, 1993; Tonry, 1990).

Gendreau et al. (1994) have proposed **intensive rehabilitation supervision (IRS)** as a "second-generation" approach to community supervision. "Based on the existing empirical evidence, a persuasive case can be made for abandoning intensive supervision programs that seek only to control and punish offenders in favor of programs that give equal primacy to changing offenders" (p. 74).

Because of their potential for frequent contact with high-risk offenders, IRS programs are likely to be able to match the risk level of offenders with their criminogenic and noncriminogenic needs. Recall that many criminogenic needs are dynamic risk factors or factors that can change over time, such as an individual's attitude toward authority or employment. Recall also the following comment: "The importance of criminogenic needs is that they serve as treatment goals: when programs successfully diminish these needs, we can reasonably expect reduction in recidivism" (Gendreau et al., 1994, p. 75). Targeting noncriminogenic needs (e.g., anxiety, depression, and self-esteem) is less likely to produce significant reductions in recidivism (Andrews & Bonta, 1994).

Bonta, Wallace-Capretta, and Rooney (2000) conducted an experiment in which they assessed the effectiveness of an intensive rehabilitation approach operating in Newfoundland. The Learning Resources Program (LRP) provides such services to offenders as anger management, a cognitive-behavioral approach to substance abuse, individual counseling, and errors in thinking that might facilitate criminal activity. Bonta et al. compared three groups of offenders, two receiving treatment by the LRP and one receiving no treatment. The two groups receiving treatment were IRS participants and probationers who were chosen by probation officers as

needing treatment. The third group consisted of incarcerated inmates who did not receive treatment but who would have been considered eligible for IRS had it been available. In other words, they qualified as high-risk inmates. Results at first showed no significant differences in recidivism between the two treated groups and the nontreated inmate group. However, when researchers divided the groups into high-risk and low-risk participants (using the LSI-R), a significant interaction effect was found. "The high-risk offenders who received relatively intensive levels of treatment showed lower recidivism rates than untreated high-risk offenders (31.6% vs. 51.1%)" (p. 325). In addition, low-risk offenders who received intensive treatment demonstrated higher recidivism than nontreated low-risk offenders (32.3% vs. 14.5%). This last finding did not surprise researchers because prior studies have indicated that low-risk offenders do not seem to benefit by intensive treatment and may, in fact, be hurt by it (Andrews & Bonta, 1998; Andrews et al., 1990).

Gendreau and his colleagues (1994) have identified a number of features associated with the effective rehabilitation of high-risk offenders, including those in the community. For example, the intensive rehabilitation services provided to the high-risk offender should occupy 40% to 70% of the offender's time for 3 to 9 months. The goal of treatment should be to reduce criminogenic needs—thus obviously necessitating an initial risk/needs assessment. Both the style and the mode of treatment should be matched to the offender's personality—thus, an anxious offender might work better with a relaxed, calm clinician. Gendreau et al. suggest also that the treating psychologist should advocate for the offender and link the offender with other community agencies, as long as these agencies offer appropriate services.

Thus, Gendreau and his colleagues (1994) have faith in community corrections treatment, particularly if it is targeted specifically at high-risk offenders and uses the intensive treatment approach. "The empirical evidence regarding

ISP's is decisive: without a rehabilitation component, reductions in recidivism are as elusive as a desert mirage" (p. 77).

This is not to suggest that *nonintensive* treatment is not effective for low-risk offenders, however. As studies reviewed by Heilbrun and Griffin (1999) have demonstrated, substance abuse treatment and assistance in working toward independent living can be beneficial for motivated low-risk offenders. Programs with strong community ties, written contracts, group meetings, vocational resources, and assistance at tasks of daily living, such as managing money, have garnered positive research results.

Summary and Conclusions

The chapter has provided a description of the work of forensic psychologists working primarily with adult offenders (and sometimes with detainees) in both institutional and community settings. We began with an overview of jails and prisons, focusing on distinctions between the two that are most relevant to the psychologist. Because of their short-term nature, for example, jails offer fewer programs and are less likely to enable the psychologist to have long-range treatment goals. Jails also produce crisis situations, such as suicide attempts by detainees. The chapter also included an early review of those legal rights of inmates that are most likely to affect the work of psychologists. The right to treatment, the right to refuse treatment, and discussions of what constitutes cruel and unusual punishment are examples.

The work of psychologists in adult corrections can be divided into the two broad but overlapping areas of assessment and treatment. We reviewed the many situations under which psychologists are asked to assess various abilities of detainees and inmates, as well as their mental states. In recent years, psychology has seen the development of many assessment instruments for use in these forensic settings; studies indicate, however, that psychologists are not making

extensive use of these instruments, preferring more traditional measures such as the clinical interview and the MMPI. At a minimum, assessment is needed when inmates enter the facility, before they are released, and when they are in crisis situations. Ideally, though, assessment should be a continuing enterprise and should occur as indicated throughout the inmate's stay.

The assessment of a death row inmate's competency to be executed is unlikely to involve the typical correctional psychologist. Nevertheless, this is an area of immense importance and one that has engendered considerable debate. Some psychologists who are philosophically opposed to the death penalty believe they should not be involved in such assessments or in the subsequent treatment that may be needed. Others believe it is their professional duty to offer the services as they are required. Furthermore, because a federal court has now given authorities the go-ahead to force medication on a death row inmate to render him stable enough to be executed, this issue will undoubtedly trouble some clinicians even more. In states where psychologists have or will have prescription privileges, the matter will be especially salient. We did not cover this debate in detail within the chapter, but we discussed suggestions given to those forensic psychologists who conduct competency for execution assessments. With the Supreme Court's recent decision in *Atkins v. Virginia* (2002), assessments of cognitive ability may become more frequent as well.

Psychologists are only one of several professional groups offering treatment services to inmates, both individually and in groups. The treatment model—or treatment approach—that tends to be the most favored is the cognitive-behavioral approach, although others are also in evidence. Cognitive-behavioral approaches—which have received the most positive evaluation results—are based on social learning theory. They assume that criminal behavior is learned much like other behavior and that the motivated inmates can "unlearn" the behavior. Consequently, these approaches encourage inmates to identify their thinking patterns, their assumptions, and their expectations and to recognize the consequences of their behavior both on themselves and on their victims. Research indicates that motivated inmates can benefit by these approaches, which are often used with a wide range of offenders, including violent offenders, sex offenders, and substance abusers. Among the least motivated inmates for such treatment are persistent violent offenders and psychopaths, although we hesitate to draw generalizations, particularly about the first group.

Features of the prison and jail settings can present numerous obstacles to effective treatment, so much so that some psychologists prefer not to approach this challenge. Limitations on confidentiality, budgetary restraints, violence and overcrowding within the facility, inmate schedules and inmate transfers, and sometimes lack of support from administrators and correctional officers are not unusual. Yet many psychologists find immense satisfaction performing this work. Professional organizations, such as the American Association for Correctional Psychologists, have offered guidelines and provided support, and increasingly more research is published identifying effective strategies and approaches in a wide variety of situations.

The chapter ended with a review of community treatment programs with offenders who are on probation, on parole, or under intermediate sanctions, such as intensive supervision. In recent years, we have begun to see more descriptions and evaluations of community programs within the psychological literature. Although community programs provide their own special challenges (e.g., offenders not appearing for their treatment session), they also have the advantage of being in a more realistic environment that does not present the numerous obstacles of institutional settings.

CHAPTER 13

Juvenile Corrections

Like the adult corrections described in the previous chapter, juvenile corrections may be divided into two distinct approaches: community based and institutional. The great majority of juveniles under the correctional system are in community settings. In 1998, the most recent year for which national juvenile court statistics are available, probation was the most severe sanction ordered in 58% of adjudicated delinquency cases (Sickmund, 2003). Particularly in the case of juveniles, institutionalization is—or theoretically should be—considered a last resort. Still, again in 1998, in 26% of delinquency cases, courts ordered juveniles to out-of-home residential placements, such as training schools, treatment centers, boot camps, drug treatment, group homes, or private placements (Sickmund, 2003). More significantly, the total number of cases in which youth were placed out of their homes (176,700) rose 41% between 1989 and 1998.

Juveniles, like adults, also may be provided with intermediate sanctions, which are less restrictive than residential placement but more restrictive than the standard probation under which the juvenile remains in his or her own home with conditions attached. Examples of intermediate sanctions are day reporting centers and intensive supervision programs.

A major difference between juvenile and adult corrections is the number of private rather than public facilities available for juveniles. Although they do not hold as many juveniles, there are more privately operated than publicly operated facilities (Snyder & Sickmund, 1995). Private facilities have the advantage of restricting their populations to those juveniles they believe they are best able to help. Some innovative treatment programs have been tried and tested in such facilities and programs.

Also included under the rubric of juvenile corrections is **juvenile detention,** which is defined as a *temporary* secure or nonsecure placement pending adjudication or during adjudication proceedings, up to a final disposition. In other words, some youth are held in detention following arrest, through their delinquency hearing, and up until the time the judge decides whether to place them on probation, order them to residential treatment, or neither one. Although the term *detention* is widely used to pertain to placement at any point in time, it should technically be reserved in the above limited sense.

Like adults, juveniles are presumed innocent until proven guilty. Adults, though, have a greater presumption of being released prior to their next court appearance. Adults may be denied bail and held in preventive detention if they are charged with a capital crime or demonstrated to be dangerous (*U.S. v. Salerno*, 1987). Juveniles, however, may be held in preventive detention for their own protection or if there is a serious risk that they will commit *any* crime before their next court appearance (*Schall v. Martin*, 1984). This gives juvenile judges a wide leeway to detain juveniles. Most juveniles are not detained. In fact, the percentage of cases involving detention decreased over the 10-year period from 1989 to 1998. However, the number of cases involving detention increased 25%. Juvenile girls in particular experienced this increase. The number of cases involving the detention of juvenile girls

increased 56% (compared to a 20% increase for boys) (Puzzanchera et al., 2003). Such increases have contributed to the crisis in juvenile detention (see Box 13.1).

Juveniles in detention have not been adjudicated and thus cannot technically be placed in rehabilitation program. For example, a youth accused of sexual assault should not be placed in a treatment program for juvenile sex offenders. Many public juvenile facilities have detention and treatment wings, with treatment reserved for those juveniles who have been adjudicated delinquent. On the other hand, juveniles in detention can be provided with substance abuse treatment, sex education, remedial education, and other such services during the time they are held.

BOX 13.1 Crisis in Detention

The *proportion* of cases involving secure detention has remained stable or has dropped in recent years, but the *number* of cases has increased (Puzzanchera et al., 2003). This has placed a severe strain on detention facilities. In addition, as noted in the text, the disproportionate confinement of minority youth has been a major cause for concern. Fortunately, there is now a national movement—initiated in large part by the Annie E. Casey Foundation—to promote alternatives to detention for youth who do not truly need secure confinement. The Annie E. Casey Foundation is a private group dedicated to research and advocacy for the needs of children and adolescents.

In the mid-1990s, the foundation funded initiatives to reverse the trend of skyrocketing detention during the 1980s and early 1990s (Mendel, 2003). Various demonstration sites across the country obtained grants to perform better screening of youth at the intake stage, to determine whether secure detention was truly needed. For those youth not at risk of committing violent crime, alternatives such as the following have been adopted:

- Community custody, whereby youth are supervised by detention workers in their own homes or in unlocked group homes. Detention workers make frequent visits and link the youth with community services as needed.
- Youth reporting, whereby youth attend school during the day but check in with a reporting center after school or evenings. The reporting centers include activities and offer counseling and remedial skills as needed.
- Outpatient mental health clinics, where youth with emotional and behavioral problems are provided with counseling and/or medication as ordered by the juvenile courts.

Alternatives to the detention initiative have not reached all states, and many juvenile detention centers across the country remain overcrowded, understaffed, and lacking in sufficient services such as mental health screening, education, and recreational opportunities. Although the average length of stay in a detention facility is about 2 weeks, some youth remain in detention for months at a time. Because of the nature of detention, these juveniles are often emotionally upset, afraid, and resistant to staff, and violent behavior is not unusual. Although some juveniles clearly need secure confinement, it is also clear that many would benefit much more by the alternatives that are now being used.

Detention centers, compared with rehabilitation or treatment centers, also have come under scrutiny for their overcrowded conditions and disproportionate confinement of minority youth (though rehabilitation centers have not been totally absolved of problems in these regards either). Because of these important differences, we will preserve the "pure" meaning of *detention*. Whenever the word is used, the reader should realize that it refers to *temporary* placement and that the youth under these conditions have not yet been adjudicated delinquent, with the exception of those who have been and are awaiting the judge's disposition decision.

In this chapter, we will provide a brief historical overview of juvenile corrections that supplements the historical background relating to juvenile courts provided in Chapter 11. The assessment tasks of forensic psychologists that were discussed in that chapter (e.g., evaluating comprehension of constitutional rights, adjudicative competence, and amenability to rehabilitation) will not be repeated here, but they remain relevant. For example, evaluation of a youth's adjudicative competence or amenability for rehabilitation are often conducted on youth who are held in secure detention.

In addition, adjudicated delinquents both in the community and in treatment facilities still have a constitutional right of access to lawyers and consequently might be evaluated for their ability to communicate with these lawyers, as well as to participate in postconviction court proceedings (e.g., an appeal of the delinquency finding). Evaluations performed to determine whether the juvenile is a good candidate for a specific rehabilitation program are conducted for juvenile correctional officials as well as for the juvenile courts. Finally, the assessment enterprise is crucial to the treatment process. As McNeece, Springer, and Arnold (2001) have observed, assessment is the first active phase of treatment. It is also an ongoing activity that continues throughout treatment because the juvenile's needs as well as his or her situation may change.

The main focus of this chapter is the type of treatment options that are available to forensic psychologists working as treatment providers in the juvenile system, in both community and residential settings. A significant number of juveniles in correctional facilities are believed to have a spectrum of mental health needs, ranging from conduct disorders to severe depression and suicidal tendencies (LeCroy et al., 2001). Developmental disabilities and cognitive impairments also plague both institutionalized juveniles and those under community supervision (Day & Berney, 2001). Many juvenile offenders also are substance abusers, often with significant chemical dependency problems. Youth with multiple limitations abound. It is not unusual, for example, for a juvenile rehabilitation facility to receive a mildly mentally retarded sex offender who abuses alcohol and has attempted suicide.

On the other hand, some juvenile offenders do not have mental disorders, developmental disabilities, or substance abuse problems. They would, however, benefit from treatment programs addressing their violent behaviors or their chronic property offending. A substantial number of juvenile offenders have been victims of violence, including sexual assault, and many come from dysfunctional families. Consequently, programs that focus on treatment of juvenile offenders often address the effects of victimization. For example, they offer strategies for developing social skills and improving a self-concept that may have been shattered by years of abuse. A significant number of programs for juveniles incorporate family treatment along with individual and group treatment.

Historical Overview

As we reviewed in Chapter 11, the history of juvenile justice in both the 19th and 20th centuries is rife with sobering accounts of juveniles confined to various institutions where they were subjected to punitive treatment rather than rehabilitation (Bernard, 1992; Rothman, 1980). The last half of the 20th century saw some improvement in this regard, with significant efforts made to end unjustified confinement. The U.S. Supreme Court's decisions in *Kent v. U.S.* (1966) and *In re Gault* (1967) questioned the predilections of the juvenile courts to be too quick to send delinquents to institutions where they were more likely to be exploited than rehabilitated.

Shortly after these Court rulings were announced, Congress also began to scrutinize the juvenile justice system. In 1974, Congress passed the landmark **Juvenile Justice and Delinquency Prevention Act** (JJDPA), a law that encouraged states to do better by the juveniles in their care. The act strongly advocated the diversion of juveniles from formal court processing whenever this could be accomplished.

In addition, Congress was particularly concerned about two groups of juveniles. These were the juveniles who were being detained in adult jails, sometimes within sight and sound of adults, and the status offenders who had committed no "crimes" but were nevertheless being held in secure institutions, often with more serious delinquents. As described in Chapter 4, **status offenders** are juveniles whose offenses might include running away from home, "incorrigibility," or truancy (skipping school)—in other words, behaviors that only they can commit by virtue of their status as children or adolescents. The JJDPA mandated that states receiving funds for juvenile justice programs must remove all juveniles from adult jails and must also remove status offenders from secure institutions. The latter mandate is referred to as the DSO (**deinstitutionalization of status offenders**) requirement. Throughout the 1980s and 1990s, Congress passed numerous amendments to the JJDPA, some of which extended deadlines for states to meet the mandates of the law (I. M. Schwartz, 1989). Nevertheless, the JJDPA remains a strong piece of legislation supporting the rights of children in the juvenile justice system. A national office, the **Office of Juvenile Justice and Delinquency Prevention** (OJJDP), oversees the legislation, provides grants for research on juvenile issues, and helps set national juvenile justice policy.

By the end of the 20th century, both court decisions and legislation were in place to protect the rights of juveniles while also providing them with protection and treatment. Despite this, numerous observers commented that the juvenile justice system was in disarray (e.g., Amnesty International, 1998; Feld, 1999). Of particular concern was increasing evidence that racial and ethnic minorities were disproportionately detained and incarcerated (Leiber, 2002; Snyder & Sickmund, 1995). This problem became known as **disproportionate minority confinement** (DMC). In a provocative article, Sampson and Laub (1993) demonstrated that communities characterized by racial inequality and containing a high concentration of the "underclass" (defined as families in poverty, female-headed households, minorities, and families receiving welfare benefits) were significantly more likely to confine children of these population groups.

It should be noted that the latest available government statistics show some decline in the overall use of *detention* for Black versus White youth. However, racial variation persisted in drug cases, with detention used in 18% of drug cases involving White juveniles, 35% involving Blacks, and 20% involving other races. In addition, White youth were less likely than Black or other race youth to be ordered to *residential* placement (24% White, 30% Black, 25% other races) (Puzzanchera et al., 2003).

The treatment of girls and ethnic minorities also gained more attention as the century came to a close. Researchers and scholars noted that, although girls had benefited from the movement to deinstitutionalize status offenders (DSO), the needs of girls in detention and treatment were not being met by the juvenile justice system (Chesney-Lind & Shelden, 1998; Federle & Chesney-Lind, 1992). Still others pointed to the need for culturally sensitive programs within the juvenile justice system to recognize the needs of Native American, Black, Latino, and Asian American youth (Eron et al., 1994). Those who support such ethnocentric programming do not say that it alone will make a difference if other principles for facilitating positive change are not applied. As King, Holmes, Henderson, and Latessa (2001) observed, these programs are syringes rather than cures. "Syringes do not heal people by themselves; however, syringes are indispensable tools for delivering medicine" (p. 501).

The overall conditions in juvenile detention and treatment facilities also received considerable attention nationwide (Amnesty International, 1998; Parent et al., 1994; Puritz & Scali, 1998). By statute and case law, juveniles held in institutions have a variety of legal rights. They have a right to be in a sanitary environment and to be protected from other violent juveniles and abusive staff. They also may not be held in excessive isolation or under unreasonable restraints, but most institutions permit the use of isolation and restraints when needed (Snyder & Sickmund, 1995). Juveniles must receive adequate medical care, mental health care, and education, and they must have access to legal counsel, family communication, recreation, exercise, and programming (del Carmen, Parker, & Reddington, 1998; Puritz & Scali, 1998). Despite these rights, a review of conditions of confinement in detention centers, training schools,

camps, ranches, farms, and other facilities for juveniles nationwide indicated substantial and widespread problems in living space, health care, security, and control of suicidal behavior (Parent et al., 1994).

Finally, by the end of the 20th century, numerous questions continued to be raised about the efficacy of treatment provided to juveniles, particularly in institutional settings. A noteworthy meta-analytic review of juvenile treatment programs (Whitehead & Lab, 1989) produced discouraging results. The authors analyzed evaluations of juvenile correctional treatment that had appeared in professional journals from 1975 to 1984 and found little positive impact on recidivism. In fact, many of the programs appeared to exacerbate recidivism. The authors also found no support for the superiority of behavioral interventions over other forms. Diversionary approaches, those intended to steer juveniles away from formal court processing, did show some favorable results, however.

Not all reviewers were as pessimistic as the Whitehead and Lab (1989) meta-analysis would suggest. As we noted in the chapter on adult corrections, many scholars and researchers have not given up on rehabilitation and are intent on documenting the effectiveness of some programs for some individuals. In the juvenile context, Palmer (1991) argued that by the late 1980s, programs that involved rehabilitation and treatment were less often considered naive or futile. As we move forward into the 21st century, there continue to be sometimes fierce debates between those who believe rehabilitation is worth pursuing and those who are more pessimistic. Forensic psychologists, who are usually in the former camp, have uncovered a number of principles associated with effective treatment. For example, cognitive-behavioral approaches and "multimodal approaches" that integrate group, individual, and family treatment to the extent possible have received good reviews. We will discuss these in greater detail as we now turn to the treatment options available in juvenile correctional settings.

Approaches to Rehabilitation

Despite a trend toward punitiveness and a demand for greater accountability on the part of juveniles who commit crimes, the juvenile justice system in most states continues to be rehabilitative in orientation. Once processed through the juvenile courts—and often even before that point—juveniles are assigned to or placed in a wide variety of programs intended to prevent future offending as well as provide them with tools needed to move on to successful adult lives. Although some research evaluating these programs can be extremely discouraging (e.g., Greenwood & Turner, 1993), there is reason to hope, as the title of a recent work indicates (Eron et al., 1994).

Group Home Models

For a wide variety of reasons, many juveniles cannot remain in their own homes, yet they do not need to be placed in a secure treatment facility. Group homes are a common alternative, allowing juveniles to remain in their community, attend school, and be provided with services in the community on an outpatient basis (e.g., counseling, therapy, substance abuse prevention program). It is an important principle of juvenile justice that the least restrictive placement should be used, a principle that critics charge is too often not honored in practice.

One of the most common models for the treatment of adolescents in a group home setting is the **teaching-family model,** initiated in 1967 with the opening of Achievement Place in Kansas. Today, there are approximately 134 such group homes in the United States for delinquents, abused and neglected children, and autistic and developmentally challenged children and young adults (Bernfeld, 2001). In the typical "teaching-family home," the teaching parents are a couple with specialized training and usually with master's degrees in human services. They live in a family-like situation with up to seven youths and have assistants available on a daily basis. Consultants serve in a supervisory capacity and integrate treatment, training, and specialized services as needed. "Almost without exception, consultants started out as practitioners and then obtained the extra training to become consultants" (Fixsen, Blasé, Timbers, & Wolf, 2001, p. 163).

Fixsen et al. (2001) have candidly reviewed the growing pains of the teaching-family model, noting how earlier attempts to replicate the apparent success of Achievement Place produced discouraging results. In 1978, the first meetings of the Teaching-Family Association were held, and the association continues today to identify goals, produce ethical standards, and provide training and other services to individuals involved in this model (Teaching-Family Association, 1993, 1994).

Teaching-family homes originally operated primarily on a token-economy model—a behavior modification approach that was quite popular in psychology in the 1960s and 1970s for institutional settings. Residents would receive tokens or points for good behavior and could then exchange these points for privileges, such as longer recreation time or a more desirable work assignment. However, "bad" behavior resulted in loss of tokens and, consequently, the removal of privileges. Transferring the token economy to a natural setting, such as a group home, is more of a challenge (Reppucci & Saunders, 1974; Wolf, Kirigin, Fixsen, Blasé, & Braukmann, 1995). As a result, although reinforcement for good behavior and a system of points and privileges remain important aspects of the teaching-family home, additional treatment services are provided. The concept is usually not recommended, however, for adolescents with serious mental health problems or who have been charged with or found to have committed serious offenses.

The teaching-family home has many positive features that should be helpful to *nonserious* delinquents who are unable to remain in their own homes, at least temporarily. Warm and compassionate teaching parents, the maintenance of ties with natural family and with the community, and the opportunity to learn prosocial behaviors are among these features. Nevertheless, studies indicate that behavioral gains—including reductions in substance use and increases in prosocial behaviors—while adolescents are in the teaching-family home are typically not maintained when they have left (Mulvey, Arthur, & Reppucci, 1993).

In recent years, many have argued that group homes—like juvenile justice programs in general—should give more attention to cultural diversity and specific cultural needs of individual juveniles (e.g., Eron et al., 1994). Black, Latino, and Asian American youth, for example, can benefit from a group home placement that encourages them to acknowledge, learn about, and celebrate their cultural heritage. Evaluations of culturally sensitive programs indicate that they lower recidivism and increase self-efficacy (Eron et al., 1994; King et al., 2001). One such program, the House of Umoja in Philadelphia, provides education, cultural treatment, counseling, and substance abuse treatment to Black male

at-risk youth ages 15 to 18. They live in a strip of 23 row houses modeled after an ancient African city (see Box 13.2).

Likewise, gender-specific programming is critical. Girls, including delinquent girls, often have needs that are very different from those of boys. Delinquent girls are more likely than boys to have been victims of child sexual abuse and intimate violence and are more likely to be lacking in self-esteem (Budnick & Shields-Fletcher, 1998; Sorensen & Bowie, 1994). They are also less likely than boys to be charged with a violent offense (Snyder & Sickmund, 1999). Adolescent girls also are more likely than adolescent boys to suffer from mental disorders, particularly depression (Comer, 2004). However, girls also may be more likely than boys to self-report symptoms of depression. Although group home options may appear to be warranted for girls, they often come to these homes with family backgrounds that may be even more complex than those of delinquent boys.

BOX 13.2 House of Umojah

In the early 1970s, David and Falaka Fattah established the first House of Umojah (Swahili for *unity*) in a Philadelphia neighborhood. Concerned about the rising numbers of African American youth who were joining gangs, the couple wanted to provide boys at risk with a sense of belonging, identity, and self-worth as an alternative to gang membership. The House of Umojah provided a safe haven, mediated gang conflicts, and offered counseling and positive adult role models. In addition, it promoted pride in the traditional cultural norms of the African American community, such as the importance of the extended family.

Today, the House of Umojah occupies a strip of 23 row houses in Philadelphia. It accepts boys between the ages of 15 and 18 who are referred by various social service agencies in the city, including juvenile courts. Individual and group counseling, parent education, educational support, cultural activities, and family planning information are all included in the program. Residents learn leadership and conflict resolution skills and are encouraged to provide service to others. When possible, staff members work with the families of the youth to involve them in treatment. Although some boys return to their homes, others move into independent living arrangements, linked with community services.

Like other private organizations providing services to juveniles, the House of Umojah receives funding from federal, state, and local governments as well as from private foundations. Although

(Continued)

no published evaluation research is available, the House of Umojah has received positive reviews from such groups as the National Center for Neighborhood Enterprise (NCNE) and the Office of Juvenile Justice and Delinquency Prevention (OJJDP). According to the NCNE, the House of Umojah has "successfully transformed more than five hundred frightened, frustrated, and alienated young minority males into self-assured, competent, concerned, and productive citizens."

Source: www.ncjrs.org/html/ojjdp/summary_2000_8/prevention.html

Family Preservation Models

Many advocates for children maintain that children should be kept in their own homes, with their own parents or close relatives, if at all possible (e.g., Gordon, 2002; Henggeler, 1996). They believe that providing a wide range of support services, even to highly dysfunctional families, is in the best interest of the children and adolescents who are part of these families. It must be acknowledged, however, that family preservation is not in the best interest of all children and adolescents. Despite the optimistic appraisals and documented success of family preservation that will be covered below, some juveniles may not be well served by intense efforts to make their family situation work for them. This is particularly true of children and adolescents who have been victimized in their own homes, by parents or caretakers or by siblings. As Chesney-Lind and Shelden (1998) indicate,

> Family counseling that is grounded in the notion that maintenance of the family unit is uppermost needs to be critically reviewed in light of the extreme physical and sexual violence that some girls in the juvenile justice system report. In some instances, the victimized girl or boy must be allowed to live away from the parents. (p. 219)

With this caveat, we turn now to a discussion of the positive aspects of family preservation.

Homebuilders

One highly regarded family preservation approach is the **Homebuilders model,** an exemplary program for families in which one or more children are at risk of being removed from the home because of their antisocial behavior (Haapala & Kinney, 1988; Whittaker, Kinney, Tracy, & Booth, 1990). In the Homebuilders model, one or two caseworkers—typically social workers with master's degrees—work intensively with a family for a short period of time; they are available to the family around the clock and are highly proactive in obtaining needed services for the family. These services might be wide ranging. For example, they might include a job for one of the family members, transportation, tutoring, family therapy, after-school programming, or a mentor for a young adolescent. An evaluation of the Homebuilders program (Haapala & Kinney, 1988) produced highly favorable results, with 87% of the children avoiding out-of-home placement within a year. The forensic psychologist is most likely to come into contact with Homebuilders as a consultant offering evaluation or treatment services in the community. The youth involved in the program are not those with serious delinquency problems, however.

Multisystemic Therapy

Another program that has received extensive research attention is the family preservation approach advocated by social psychologist Scott

Henggeler, **multisystemic therapy (MST)**. MST was specifically developed for application with serious juvenile offenders, including those responsible for violent crimes. MST is heavily based on the systems theory pioneered by psychologist Urie Bronfenbrenner (1979). According to this view, behavior is multidetermined and influenced heavily by interactions with one's social environment. Children and adolescents are embedded in various social systems (their families, their peer groups, their schools, and their neighborhoods). Effective intervention requires that the child or adolescent and all of his or her social systems be considered. Thus, MST attempts to promote behavior change in the youth's natural environment and uses the strengths within each of the various social systems to bring this about.

Henggeler (1996; Henggeler & Borduin, 1990) argues that secure institutions should be avoided if at all possible because antisocial behaviors are only reinforced when serious offenders live among other serious offenders. Thus, in addition to keeping juveniles in their own homes, another goal of MST is to help juveniles break bonds with antisocial peers and develop bonds with prosocial peers. Henggeler has acknowledged that this is one of the most difficult goals to achieve.

Like Homebuilders, MST makes a small team of treatment providers—in this case, therapists—available to families around the clock and helps facilitate a wide range of services. Most treatment providers are master's-level mental health professionals specially trained in the multisystemic approach. Clinical psychologists supervise the therapist and provide intensive treatment if needed. Therapists meet with youth in natural settings (e.g., the home or school or even in a local park). They identify both risk and resilience factors in a juvenile's life, across all his or her social systems. For example, a risk factor at school may be an older boy who has goaded the juvenile into committing offenses in the past. A resilience factor at school may be an art class or a history class that the juvenile likes. Likewise, genuine affection among siblings is a resilience

factor in the family; the impending loss of a father's employment is a risk factor. The treatment providers then provide strategies for addressing the risk factors and capitalizing on the resilience factors.

MST may involve intensive individual counseling, a factor that distinguishes it from Homebuilders and other **family preservation models** that target youth whose behavioral problems are usually less serious. MST therapists are generalists. "Because of the varying demands of each family, [they] must be capable of applying a range of empirically-based therapeutic approaches . . . and tailoring interventions to the unique needs and strengths of each family" (Brown, Borduin, & Henggeler, 2001, p. 458). MST youth are often on probation after having been adjudicated delinquent, with offenses ranging from substance abuse to aggravated assault. However, MST also has been used for nonoffending child and adolescent populations and with youth from a variety of cultural and ethnic backgrounds (Brown et al., 2001; Edwards, Schoenwald, Henggeler, & Strother, 2001). Thus far, it has achieved favorable research reviews (e.g., Burns, Schoenwald, Burchard, Faw, & Santos, 2000; Henggeler, 2001). We should note, however, that virtually all of the research to date has been conducted by the individuals who developed the programs and deliver the services. Although this is not uncommon in evaluation research, the close oversight of the implementation and delivery of programs may affect the findings (MacKenzie, 2000). It is important that independent researchers in different settings also evaluate MST, along with other treatment programs for juveniles.

Functional Family Therapy

A program similar to MST is **functional family therapy (FFT)**, which was developed in the 1970s for behaviorally disturbed adolescents whose parents were unable to control their acting-out behaviors. It combines social learning, cognitive-behavioral theory, interpersonal theory, and family systems theories (Gordon, 2002). It should be recalled from Chapter 12 that cognitive-behavioral approaches focus on a person's expectations and appraisals. He or she is encouraged to examine how attitudes and beliefs may have contributed to his or her present situation. The individual works with the therapist to identify strategies for behavioral change. In functional family therapy, therapists work with the family as a unit and attempt to identify features of family dynamics that result in problematic interactions among members. Attention is focused away from the adolescent as the problem; rather, the family is viewed as a system, with members affecting one another's behaviors. Communication and problem-solving skills are taught, and participants are typically given homework assignments between sessions. Like MST, FFT is used in a wide variety of contexts, not just with youth who have come into conflict with the law. Although FFT has been used successfully with delinquents, including those referred by juvenile courts (Gordon, 2002), it seems less suited for serious delinquents remaining in the community than MST. The latter was specifically formulated to deal with serious delinquency, and it places considerable emphasis on intensive individual treatment as well as strengthening social systems both within and outside the family group. On the other hand, FFT may be better than MST at providing all members of the family group with skills and strategies to function effectively as a self-supporting group. Nonetheless, according to Brown et al. (2001), behavioral parent training approaches have not been demonstrably effective with serious juvenile offenders, primarily because of the multiple risk factors (e.g., marital distress, socioeconomic disadvantage, parental depression) that are relatively common in their families. Although FFT is not exclusively focused on parent training, it closely resembles that model.

MST and FFT—to ensure program integrity—require extensive training on the part of those who will deliver the services, but neither one requires that treatment providers hold terminal degrees in the field. Master's-level individuals—and sometimes less—are able to offer treatment when they are well trained and supervised by clinical psychologists. Edwards et al. (2001) and Gordon (2002) have summarized the challenges faced in implementing each of these approaches in communities that have expressed interest in them. Supporters of both approaches have emphasized the need for continual communication between developers of these programs and the service providers, as well as the extensive training and initial supervision required to ensure that treatment will be delivered effectively.

Substance Abuse Models

Like adult offenders, juvenile offenders very often have substance abuse problems that accompanied past offenses and are predictive of future delinquent activity (Snyder & Sickmund, 1999; Weekes, Moser, & Langevin, 1999). In the case of juvenile offenders, however, the treatment must take into account their rapid physiological, psychological, and sociocultural development (McNeece et al., 2001). In other words, treatment providers must factor in the emotional turmoil and search for identity and acceptance that are often characteristic of adolescence. Like the other treatment programs discussed, programs that provide individual, group, and family therapy—a multimodal approach—seem to be the most effective for substance abusers.

We should note that each of the approaches discussed thus far in this chapter might include a substance abuse component. For example, both group home and family preservation models frequently implement substance abuse treatment. Such treatment also is a component of virtually every publicly supported juvenile rehabilitation center. Private facilities, wherein parents enroll their adolescents for inpatient substance abuse treatment, are also common. Interestingly, Ira Schwartz (1989), a one-time head of the OJJDP, has argued forcefully that these private placements are overused and unwarranted for many youth, calling private treatment centers the new jail for middle-class kids. Moreover, there is very little evidence to support inpatient treatment over outpatient approaches for the vast majority of juvenile substance abusers (McNeece et al., 2001).

McNeece et al. (2001) reviewed the variety of programs available for both adult and juvenile substance abusers. These include individual, group, and family therapy; self-help programs; psychoeducational approaches; pharmacotherapy (e.g., Antabuse, methadone, and naltrexone); acupuncture; case management; and both inpatient and outpatient programs. They note that several states are developing specific assessment and receiving centers for juveniles with substance abuse problems. These centers may be attached to the juvenile court or a local drug court, or they may operate independently. Although such assessment and treatment centers may be a step in the right direction, follow-up services are desperately needed. In a study of six such assessment centers, McNeece and his colleagues (1997) learned that they provided short-term stabilization, but recommendations for extended treatment often were not followed due to lack of resources and shortage of staff. The crucial importance of follow-up services has been demonstrated in evaluation studies of many other juvenile programs as well.

The professional literature contains numerous descriptions and evaluations of substance abuse treatment programs for both adult and juvenile offenders. For our purposes, we will discuss two illustrations, one representing inpatient and one representing outpatient treatment.

Inpatient Substance Abuse Treatment: An Example

Mears and Kelly (2002) reviewed programs for chemically dependent adjudicated juvenile offenders under the supervision of the Texas Youth Commission (TYC). The youth were located in one of five inpatient treatment sites. In accordance with key principles of effective intervention, treatment was cognitive-behavioral in

approach and targeted dynamic/criminogenic needs (Cullen & Gendreau, 2000). Group counseling, peer accountability, and a low caseworker to youth ratio (1:8 to 1:10) were significant components of the program. In addition, staff worked with the youth to develop individualized **relapse prevention** and community reintegration plans. Treatment was provided for at least 6 continuous months. The 332 juveniles (all but 5 were male) were compared with a control group of 220 youth who were eligible for the treatment but did not receive it because of limited bed space.

Researchers analyzed both a juvenile's performance in the program and subsequent recidivism (measured by arrest, whether or not the arrest was drug related). Although there were no significant differences in recidivism between control and treatment groups (a discouraging finding, at the least), researchers did find that youth who performed better in treatment were somewhat less likely to recidivate (but again not significantly). More interestingly, researchers found differences among the treatment sites, with two of the sites demonstrating significantly greater success (with recidivism rates of 25% and 24%) and two significantly less (recidivism rates of 40% and 38%). The differences related to the quality of service delivery and the staff's commitment to carefully implementing the program. The two programs with the poorest results experienced staff turnover and seemed to suffer from "ongoing tension between emphasizing administrative and correctional versus rehabilitative concerns" (Mears & Kelly, 2002, p. 110). In other words, those who ran and worked in the program were not in agreement over its mission. Some believed it should be more punitive, whereas others were more dedicated to rehabilitation. The two best performing sites had unified and consistent support for rehabilitation. One was a new program with better funding for staff and resources; the other had a "long-standing reputation as having a culture of rehabilitation, despite the fact that it generally handles the most serious and violent youth at TYC" (Mears & Kelly, 2002, p. 110). Interestingly, psychologists were more involved at this site than at any of the others, suggesting that their presence may have made a difference. (The fifth site reported in the study had features of both the successful and less successful programs [e.g., commitment to rehabilitation but high staff turnover] and produced outcomes midway between the other two groups.)

Mears and Kelly (2002) concluded from their findings that evaluations of treatment programs must take into account how well youth participate in the programs, as well as how carefully the programs are implemented and operated on a day-to-day basis. In addition, they note, those programs that are found effective may become even more so if they improve their service delivery and carefully monitor youth progress in the program.

Outpatient Substance Abuse Treatment: An Example

A recent evaluation of an outpatient substance abuse treatment program produced mixed results. O'Neill, Lidz, and Heilbrun (2003) evaluated the effects of an outpatient substance abuse treatment program on adolescents with psychopathic characteristics. The treatment program was developed for adolescent substance abusers as a group, not just those with psychopathic characteristics. The program involved twice-weekly 1-hour sessions of individual therapy and daily group therapy sessions and was developed in accordance with a cognitive-behavioral model (Platt, Bux, Lamb, Lidz, & Husband, 1996). Among other things, the adolescents in the program would set goals for themselves; understand and modify their thoughts, feelings, and behaviors; and learn coping skills for maintaining appropriate behavior after discharge from the program. These are typical approaches taken by **cognitive-behavioral programs** and resemble the approach taken in the Texas sites discussed above. At this time, cognitive-behavioral principles are widely believed to be the most effective at facilitating positive change (Bartol, 2002; Cullen & Gendreau, 2000).

We must repeat, as we stated in Chapters 4 and 11, that **juvenile psychopathy** is a controversial construct. Many clinicians and researchers are reluctant to label adolescents in this way. As Edens, Skeem, et al. (2001) have noted, some characteristics that are considered psychopathic in adults (e.g., impulsivity, poor behavioral controls, need for stimulation, callousness) may be normative in the adolescent developmental sequence. Furthermore, adolescents often appear callous and unfeeling to hide their fear and anxiety (Barnum, 2000). O'Neill et al. (2003) concede these points but consider the concept of juvenile psychopathy as one that merits more study, particularly if psychopathic characteristics are found to be related to treatment outcomes.

In the O'Neill et al. (2003) research, higher scores on the Psychopathy Checklist: Youth Version (PCL:YV) were positively associated with four behaviors: (1) rearrest risk, (2) high attrition from the program, (3) lower quality ratings of participation in the program, and (4) more frequent use of alcohol and drugs throughout the treatment program. "The majority of participants with a high level of psychopathic characteristics did not respond favorably to the treatment interventions provided in this program" (O'Neill et al., 2003, p. 309). Nevertheless, they cautioned that the concept of juvenile psychopathy should be limited to the research arena until research can better differentiate those adolescents with psychopathic characteristics who will maintain those characteristics into adulthood. "The premature application [of research results] for clinical and forensic purposes could inhibit the development of potentially promising interventions and could also significantly mislead legal decision-makers" (p. 309).

It is important to note that many of the participants, particularly those with low Psychopathy Checklist: Screening Version (PCL:SV) scores, did benefit from the program described in the O'Neill et al. (2003) research. Moreover, like the Mears and Kelly (2002) study discussed above, *quality of participation* in the program was a significant variable. Juveniles with high PCL:SV scores were rated lower on their level of cooperation while in treatment. The other variables found significant in the Mears and Kelly review—staff-related variables such as commitment to rehabilitation and turnover—were not assessed in the O'Neill et al. research. However, the program included daily "community" meetings during which participants and staff discussed rules, expectations, and problems and recognized accomplishments. We might infer that these meetings would facilitate staff satisfaction, discourage turnover, and contribute to the program's positive effect on those youth who did not have psychopathic characteristics.

Boot Camps

Beginning in the early 1980s, boot camps gained popularity in adult corrections as a way of reducing overcrowding in adult prisons while providing nonviolent offenders with discipline and structure over an intense but short period of time (e.g., 30 to 120 days). In the late 1980s, they began to appear in juvenile corrections as well.

Boot camps are so called because they have many parallels to the military model. They are highly structured programs that, according to their supporters, instill discipline, respect for authority, and self-esteem in juveniles who generally have not been given the opportunity to learn these values. Boot camps are typically operated and staffed by correctional personnel who are not inclined to favor a therapeutic, rehabilitative approach with juvenile delinquents. There

are exceptions. In some juvenile boot camps, for example, substance abuse treatment or violence prevention programs are provided.

The boot camp approach has lost support in recent years because of highly publicized abuses (see Box 13.3) and because the evaluation research has not been positive (Cullen, Wright, & Applegate, 1996). A review of juvenile boot camp programs at three sites, sponsored by the Office of Juvenile Justice and Delinquency Prevention (1996), indicated that there was some hope for boot camps in which juveniles were offered substance abuse treatment and were provided with aftercare services for a 3-year period. Otherwise, the boot camp experience did not appear to significantly affect recidivism or self-efficacy. Negative effects of the boot camp experience were discovered at all three sites. The California Youth Authority (1997) published the results of its evaluation of its own boot camp program, with similar discouraging results. Boot camps have also been criticized as being the wrong approach to take, particularly with juvenile girls (Chesney-Lind & Shelden, 1998). The boot camp experience includes heavy doses of demeaning and shouting on the part of staff. This "in-your-face" approach, critics say, is the last thing that girls need because too many girls have been subjected to this far too much in their own backgrounds. On the whole, although boot camps remain appealing to some who believe that juveniles benefit from structure and discipline, boot camps are not obtaining rave reviews. The research simply does not support their continued use as a rehabilitative strategy for juveniles.

BOX 13.3   Juvenile Boot Camps: Lessons Learned?

In the year 2000, the state of Maryland disbanded its juvenile boot camps and fired top juvenile justice officials after publicity surrounding allegations of physical and emotional abuse of juveniles. One news story recounted split lips and bloody noses inflicted by guards who slammed teens to the ground (Nelson, 2003). Maryland was only 1 of 27 states that operated juvenile boot

---

(Continued)

BOX 13.3 (Continued)

---

camps in the 1990s, despite warnings from juvenile justice researchers that such punitive quick fixes do not reduce recidivism.

Even boot camps that include a rehabilitative aspect—such as educational programming and substance abuse treatment—have not produced highly favorable results. An evaluation of three sites sponsored by the Office of Juvenile Justice and Delinquency Prevention (OJJDP, 1996) indicated that some positive change occurred while the youth were in the 3-month camps. Once they graduated, however, positive change persisted only when they remained in aftercare for at least 5 months. However, nearly one half of the juveniles who entered aftercare dropped out, were arrested for new offenses, or were terminated for not complying with aftercare rules. On balance, the very small positive change reflected in the research pales beside the evidence that—for the great majority of boot camp participants—the experience is negative.

The OJJDP was initially supportive of juvenile boot camps, even to the point of producing model guidelines to states interesting in opening such camps. Even after the 1996 evaluation, the OJJDP indicated that the problems could be fixed by attention to the model guidelines and improved aftercare services. In 1997, though, the U.S. Department of Justice concluded that the efficacy of boot camps was questionable at best (Nelson, 2003).

Wilderness and Adventure Programs

Wilderness and adventure experiences are different from boot camps and seem to offer more hope as an effective strategy for *some* youth. A wide range of camps, ranches, and outdoor programs—most privately operated—are offered for juveniles. Among the most well known are those offered by the Eckerd Foundation, a private organization based in Florida. Associated Marine Industries (AMI) is another such enterprise.

Like many other private programs, **wilderness and adventure programs** accept both juveniles who are at risk of committing delinquency and those who are already adjudicated. (At-risk juveniles are often the status offenders who are runaways or are considered incorrigible by their parents or guardians.) The offenses of adjudicated delinquents range from drug offenses to violent crime. Some but not all accept juvenile sex offenders. Also like other private programs, and unlike public training schools or treatment centers, wilderness programs need accept only juveniles who meet their criteria—that is, those

they believe would be helped by their program. Wilderness camps are often the "last chance" for juveniles before being sent to a secure training school. However, like boot camps, wilderness programs have received some negative publicity relating to their treatment of the youth in their care.

Wilderness and adventure programs, compared with boot camps, have received some favorable research reviews, but the studies are rarely empirically sound and almost never include a control group (Brown et al., 2001). In addition, as noted above, the programs are not limited to delinquents, making it impossible to gauge treatment efficacy for that group. Brown et al. (2001) report that only one study (Sale, 1992) included a delinquent sample of 30 adolescent offenders. Although the self-concept of the adolescents improved as a result of being in the program, there was no comparison group.

Published descriptions of these programs suggest that, although they do not subscribe to a common model, they have some things in common: They de-emphasize traditional classroom education and emphasize the progressive development of physical skills that are intended to improve self-efficacy. Self-efficacy is the belief that one is competent and can get things accomplished, and self-esteem is "one's attitude toward oneself along a positive-negative dimension" (Baron & Byrne, 2000, p. 169). Wilderness and adventure programs do, however, include some educational component, which responds to an individual educational plan (IEP) formulated for each juvenile. They attempt to develop a positive peer culture, wherein youth support one another's prosocial behaviors and confront one another when antisocial behavior is displayed. They are far more likely than boot camps to include therapeutic components, such as drama therapy, development of communication and problem-solving skills, or individual counseling. Staff in these programs are typically young, idealistic, and supportive of the youth yet demand accountability and adherence to rules. However, it is unknown to what extent psychologists or other clinicians provide treatment services. One major criticism of wilderness programs is that the skills that might be obtained by youth in an outdoor environment do not necessarily translate to skills they will need to survive in an urban, suburban, or even rural environment. Also, like boot camp programs, wilderness programs rarely have intensive aftercare services.

From an evaluation viewpoint, it is extremely difficult to gauge the extent to which wilderness and adventure programs have a positive effect on recidivism or on the lives of juveniles who participate in them. There is a dearth of solid empirical research thus far available, even on individual programs. An early review (Kelly & Baer, 1978) compared boys in a traditional training school to boys in a wilderness-type program. A significant difference in recidivism over a 1-year period was found—with the wilderness boys doing significantly better—but the differences washed out over a 5-year period. Wilderness programs are very different from one another, defying an attempt at meaningful comparisons. However, evaluation research of individual programs is

warranted and needed, particularly because this approach continues to have considerable appeal as a rehabilitative strategy for some juvenile offenders and at-risk youth.

Violence Prevention Programs

Violence is commonly defined as physical force exerted for the purpose of inflicting injury, pain, discomfort, or abuse to a person or persons. Some definitions include damage to or destruction of property in the definition of violence. Thus, vandalism—an offense often seen in juvenile crime statistics—would be included. Programs for juveniles that are aimed at preventing and controlling violence focus primarily on physical harm done to others person. In addition, although sexual assault is clearly a violent crime, it is typically approached in a separate (or additional) treatment program, as we will discuss shortly.

As we discussed in Chapter 4, violence may begin very early in a child's life and often occurs as a result of modeling significant individuals in the child's social network—particularly parents, caretakers, peers, or media heroes. In recent years, increasing attention is given to violent video games that are thought by many to desensitize children to brutality and encourage them to adopt violent strategies in their own lives. Also gaining attention is the **biological/neurological perspective,** with some researchers suggesting that biological, genetic, and/or neuropsychological factors make a significant contribution to aggression (e.g., Fishbein, 2000; Moffit, 1993a; Raine, 1993). Although these researchers do not suggest that these factors "cause" violent crime or delinquency, they do indicate that some individuals may be predisposed to committing violent acts. Consequently, they urge the early identification and intervention into the lives of individuals who may be at risk.

Violent behavior may suddenly appear in adolescence—for example, the 14-year-old who takes a gun to school and kills the principal or the

15-year-old who stabs his father to death. However, this one-time violence is highly atypical. Far more typical is the progression from early, aggressive behavior to more serious aggression as a child develops. Psychologist Arnold Goldstein (2002a) was fond of saying, "Catch it low to prevent it high," indicating that low-level aggression could, if not nipped, turn into more serious behavior later on.

> My central belief—a belief increasingly finding at least initial empirical support—is that we, as a society, have far too often ignored the very manifestations of low-level aggression which, when rewarded, grow (often rapidly) into those several forms of often intractable high-level aggression which are currently receiving a great deal of society's attention. (Goldstein, 2002a, p. 169)

According to Goldstein (2002a), cursing, threats, insults, incivilities, vandalism, bullying, and harassment are all precursors to serious aggression. Thus, the 6- or 7-year-old who bullies, bites, or bops his playmates will likely, if reinforced, move on to more serious assaultive behavior as an adolescent. Reinforcement may be in the form of internal or external rewards. Gaining status on the playground or having other children afraid of him may be sufficient reinforcement, even if adult authority figures "punish" him for his misbehavior.

Most children who reach the juvenile courts on delinquency petitions are older than 10 years old, and most are between the ages of 12 and 17. Even so, approximately 9% of juvenile arrests involve children age 14 and younger. In addition, the most recent statistics indicate that the proportion of delinquency cases involving *crimes against persons* (e.g., assault, rape, robbery, violent sexual offenses) increased substantially among the under-12 age group. In 1989, 19% of such offenses involved children younger than 12; in 1998, the percentage had increased to 31% (Sickmund, 2003). By the teen years, the individual has already "learned" that his or her violent

behavior brings some rewards. Therefore, the treatment of violent behavior usually involves "unlearning" strategies that have seemingly worked up to that point.

Most violence prevention programs geared at juveniles adopt a cognitive-behavioral or social learning perspective. "Cognitive interventions assume that an angry, aggressive state is mediated through a person's expectations and appraisals and that the likelihood of violence is increased or decreased as a result of this process" (Tate, Reppucci, & Mulvey, 1995, p. 778). Violent youth often see hostility where none is intended. Therefore, they are encouraged to reassess their assumptions that others are a threat to them. In some programs, these cognitive distortions are referred to as "thinking errors," a concept proposed by Yochelson and Samenow (1976). Youth—particularly those in residential treatment programs—may be asked to write down their thoughts and emotions as they occur. In group therapy sessions, they reveal what they have written, and the group and the treatment provider identify the "thinking errors" and suggest strategies for thinking differently.

A victim empathy component may be part of the treatment. For example, the juveniles are encouraged to put themselves in the place of the victim to appreciate what the victim suffered, sometimes through role-playing exercises. Violence prevention programs also typically provide juveniles with alternatives to violent behavior, teaching them decision-making skills to put to use when a potentially violent situation erupts. They are encouraged also to avoid placing themselves in volatile situations. Alcoholic substances, for example, are known to facilitate violent behavior, so substance abuse prevention is an important component of many violence prevention programs.

Goldstein and Glick (1987, 2001) describe **aggression replacement training** (ART), an approach taken with children and adolescents in a variety of settings, including community and residential treatment programs for delinquents. They note that adolescents who display highly aggressive behaviors are often also deficient or inadequate in socially desirable behaviors, such as identifying their own feelings or responding appropriately to slights or anger. The ART curriculum consists of (1) skillstreaming (teaching a broad range of prosocial behaviors), (2) anger control training, and (3) moral reasoning. In small groups, chronically aggressive adolescents are taught such skills as asking permission, having a conversation, giving a compliment, and dealing with embarrassment. They are also taught to identify triggers to their aggression and provided with techniques for reducing the level of their anger (e.g., counting backward, imagining a peaceful scene). The juveniles are also presented with moral dilemmas and encouraged to find a solution that is fair and just. The ART curriculum has been implemented in numerous residential and community facilities, as well as in a variety of school systems and gang prevention programs (see Goldstein & Glick, 2001, for a review). Although ART has produced cognitive-behavioral changes in violent adolescents, it has not yet been demonstrated to reduce violent behavior in juveniles after release from correctional facilities (Tate et al., 1995). Goldstein and Glick acknowledge that maintaining anger control beyond facility walls can be problematic. Nevertheless, they maintain that positive effects of the program persist, although not as strongly as in a controlled environment.

Guerra, Tolan, and Hammond (1994) observe that a common element related to treatment effectiveness for adolescent violence is the development of social interaction skills. "Improved social skills not only help individuals resolve conflict-producing situations with their peers, but enable them to get along in multiple social contexts" (p. 397).

In the juvenile justice system, programs for serious violent offenders generally operate within institutional settings, primarily in secure settings for youth. From a therapeutic perspective, institutionalization has the obvious advantages of intervening in a controlled setting, away from criminogenic influences in the youth's

natural environment. It also allows intensive treatment, using both group and individual models. Unfortunately, evaluations of institutional treatment have produced mixed results, which is not surprising because the youth themselves are the most challenging to work with. Critics of institutionalization also point out, however, that a major disadvantage of secure treatment is the tendency of adolescents to align with one another and reinforce their own deviant behaviors (Henggeler, 1996). Interestingly, Jackson and Springer (1997) recommend taking advantage of this tendency to align; they suggest that those working with juveniles in incarcerated settings encourage the forming of "therapeutic gangs," which incorporate positive aspects of the juvenile gangs to which many incarcerated youth belonged. The "therapeutic gang" works together to identify negative attitudes and values and look for positive alternatives.

Institutional programs also are unable to place much emphasis on working with the family, the environment to which the adolescent frequently returns. Supporters of multisystemic therapy, discussed earlier, make a good case for its use with violent youth who are allowed to remain in the community and within their own family environment.

Paint Creek

One institutional treatment program for serious (including violent) offenders that has received avid research attention is Ohio's **Paint Creek** Youth Center, which was developed as an experimental program in 1984 (Greenwood & Turner, 1994). Delinquent youth are randomly assigned to Paint Creek or to other, more traditional training schools in the state, allowing a control population for purposes of comparison. Under the direction of a clinical psychologist, Paint Creek staff are trained to provide treatment that includes well-defined behavioral goals and reinforcements for meeting them. Role-playing exercises to encourage **victim empathy,** reality therapy, development of a positive peer culture, and the identification of "thinking errors" are all critical components of the treatment.

The program is small—serving 30 to 35 boys at a time (compared with several hundred in the traditional programs). It involves daily group sessions, family group therapy twice a month, and intensive aftercare. In other words, the program appears to have many features of a model approach to treating juveniles in an institutional setting. Unfortunately, the first published results of the Paint Creek program (Greenwood & Turner, 1994) were disconcerting. Although both youth and staff from Paint Creek were more favorable toward their program than were youth and staff from the traditional facilities, and although Paint Creek youth were held in confinement about 27% longer, there were no significant differences in either officially recorded or self-reported recidivism. Any reported gains (e.g., Paint Creek youth who completed the program reported less drug use) were modest at best. Greenwood and Turner (1994) suggested a number of possible interpretations for these findings. They reported, for example, that the youth in this study returned to disruptive environments; approximately one quarter experienced family deaths, deaths of friends, or being fired or laid off from their jobs within a 1-year period. It is possible that the chaotic environment of the more traditional training school did just as good a job preparing youth for the outside because it represented more accurately the life they would be leading. The researchers also suggested that more attention should be devoted to the aftercare component because the supervision and support provided by Paint Creek were not enough to make a significant difference.

The results of the Paint Creek experiment do not surprise those who are pessimistic about the prospects of rehabilitation, particularly within institutional settings (e.g., Feld, 1999; Whitehead & Lab, 1989). As we noted above, intensive treatment within the community is often preferred, even for serious offenders (Henggeler, 1996). Nevertheless, many if not most juvenile justice professionals believe that treatment in a secure juvenile facility is warranted for some youth who commit serious crime—including violent crime—but who should not be transferred to the adult criminal justice system.

Juvenile Sex Offender Treatment Programs

It is believed that a high percentage of all juvenile sex offenders were themselves sexually abused. Gray, Pithers, Busconi, and Houchens (1997) found that 86% of the children in their sample of serious juvenile offenders had been sexually abused themselves. As we discussed in Chapter 7, however, children who are sexually abused typically do not become abusers. Rather, the devastating effects of sexual abuse are more likely to be internalized and displayed in adjustment problems such as depression, self-destructive behavior, anxiety, and poor self-esteem in both children and adults (Browne & Finkelhor, 1986). Those victims who do become abusers also suffer many of these adjustment problems as well. If we consider the well-documented effects of childhood sexual abuse, it is clear that juvenile sex offenders need not only a treatment program to prevent future offending but also one that recognizes and addresses the emotional trauma they are likely to have experienced.

Adolescent sex offenders, left untreated, are highly likely to continue to offend into adulthood. It has been estimated that 47% to 58% of adult sex offenders committed their first offense during adolescence (Cellini et al., 1993). Becker and Johnson (2001) note that researchers and clinicians are becoming increasingly aware also that prepubescent children commit sexual offenses and that many of these offenses start in early adolescence. Recent juvenile court data show a slight decrease in the percentage of sex offenses (Puzzanchera et al., 2003), but over the 10-year period from 1989 to 1998, they increased quite dramatically (26% for forcible rape; 53% for other violent sex offenses). In addition, clinicians report increasing numbers of juvenile sex offenders in their own private practices (Cellini, 1995). Consequently, sex offender treatment, much like substance abuse treatment, is an essential component of many clinical practices. It is available in most public and many private juvenile rehabilitation facilities.

The assessment that precedes treatment for juvenile sex offenders often occurs before they have been adjudicated, however. Youth suspected of or charged with sexual offenses may be referred for evaluation, both by juvenile courts and by social service agencies. In these situations, "it is the job of the assessor to determine the probability that a deviant sexual act occurred, the reason for its occurrence, and whether or not there is need for intervention" (Becker & Johnson, 2001, p. 274).

Whether it occurs before or after a juvenile has been adjudicated delinquent, assessment of sex offenders is controversial. Because of the nature of sexual offending, courts and other juvenile justice officials are particularly interested in knowing not only whether the juvenile is likely to respond to treatment but also whether the juvenile is likely to reoffend. However, most assessment guidelines offered in the clinical literature have not been systematically evaluated. Cellini (1995) notes that, due to this absence of validated research instruments and assessment protocols, clinicians must be extremely cautious in making predictions or assessing risk. "There simply is no way to make clinical assumptions about the risk of re-offense or progression of adolescents' deviant sexual patterns" (Cellini, 1995, p. 6-4).

Practicing forensic psychologists and researchers recommend the gathering of extensive background and clinical information in any evaluations of juvenile sex offenders. According to Becker and Johnson (2001), the psychologist conducting the assessment should obtain the following:

- family social, medical, and mental histories;
- developmental history of the juvenile, including information about temperament as infant and toddler;

- school information;
- history of violent behavior;
- alcohol and other substance abuse history;
- a detailed sexual history; and
- information about mental status.

"One should assess the youth's general fund of knowledge and intelligence as well as insight and judgment" (Becker & Johnson, 2001, p. 276).

A very wide range of treatment modalities is available for juvenile sex offenders, including individual and group treatment, family counseling, and psychoeducational classes. According to Cellini (1995), "Peer groups are the preferred method of treatment for 98% of the juvenile and adult programs currently being offered for sex offenders" (p. 6-6). The typical peer group program takes a cognitive-behavioral approach, with sex offenders discussing their offenses and the effects on their victims, under the direction of a clinical moderator. Sex education is an important component; juvenile sex offenders are given factual information about human sexuality, and nondeviant sexual interests are promoted. They are encouraged to identify **thinking errors**—mistaken assumptions regarding their crimes or their victims—and to develop strategies to avoid future offending. Social skills and assertive skills training are important components of many sex offender treatment programs as well. Although peer group treatment may be dominant, the literature also highly advocates individual and family therapy when possible (Becker & Johnson, 2001). As is the case with programs for violent offenders, a multimodal approach, emphasizing group, individual, and family treatment is most likely to be effective.

One controversial aspect of sexual offender treatment is the use of pharmacological agents to suppress libido and reduce sexual offending. These are not recommended for use with adolescents before the age of 16, who have not yet completed puberty (Becker & Johnson, 2001; Bradford, 1993). Becker and Johnson (2001) review the effects of other biological agents (e.g., antipsychotic medication, mood stabilizers, and various antidepressants) that may be indicated for some juveniles, though never in the absence of psychotherapeutic interventions.

It is widely believed that sex offenders are never completely "cured" but are always suscepti- ble to reoffending (Cellini, 1995; Pithers et al., 1995). Thus, an important component of sex offender treatment programs is relapse preven- tion, whereby offenders are taught strategies for recognizing situations and avoiding stimuli that have led to their offenses in the past (e.g., visit with a particular acquaintance; playground; violent pornography).

As Becker and Johnson (2001) indicate, the literature on sex offender treatment is long on description and short on careful evaluation. Although many articles are published outlining the treatment methods used, there are very few controlled studies of effectiveness. In addition, the literature discusses primarily the sex offend- ing of adolescent males, with very little written regarding female sex offenders or prepubescent children. This, too, is changing, though, as more researchers become aware that the sexual offend- ing of women and girls is a topic worthy of atten- tion (Becker et al., 2001).

Summary and Conclusions

At the cusp of the 21st century, the juvenile jus- tice system celebrated its 100th anniversary, if one marks the system with the establishment of the first juvenile court in 1899. As would be expected, the juvenile justice process of today hardly resembles the process of the first half of the 20th century. Or does it? Early juvenile courts were informal, paternalistic, often very judgmen- tal, and nonadversarial, with children rarely being represented by lawyers. Clinicians— primarily psychiatrists and psychologists— consulted regularly with these courts, providing wide-ranging evaluations of a juvenile's emo- tional, cognitive, and mental status, as well as background information on the youth's social history. Although the courts were supposedly

intended to "save" children from a life of poverty, they too often placed them in institutions that failed to provide the education, nurturing, and overall physical and emotional care that children need. In the 1960s, a rights-oriented Supreme Court recognized these deficiencies in the juve- nile system and attempted to correct them by providing juveniles with legal representation and other due process rights. In the 1970s, Congress passed the Juvenile Justice and Delinquency Prevention Act, landmark legislation that, among many other things, began to address conditions in juvenile facilities.

It is important for forensic psychologists working with the juvenile system to be aware of its history, which was reviewed in the present chapter as well as in Chapter 11. Many concerned advocates for juveniles today fear that problems with similarities to the problems of old have reoccurred or, in some cases, never really disap- peared. In this chapter, we focused on issues that relate to juveniles while they are in detention or after they have been adjudicated delinquent. Conditions of confinement in many secure facil- ities are appalling. There is documented overrep- resentation of minority youth, particularly in secure confinement. The needs of juvenile girls have been overlooked, and the needs of juveniles from ethnic, racial, or sexual orientation minori- ties have been ignored. The effectiveness of many treatment programs has not been documented. These and many other problems have led to calls ranging from complete abolition of a separate system for juveniles to increasing its financial resources and making drastic changes in its pro- cedures. Nevertheless, good juvenile facilities exist, and numerous professionals find juvenile work highly rewarding, believing they can help make significant changes in the lives of juveniles. Psychologists provide an extremely wide range of consulting services to juvenile justice. Although we reviewed their assessment tasks in Chapter 11, here we concentrated on the provision of treat- ment. It is important to emphasize once again, though, that treatment cannot be offered without both initial and ongoing assessment.

Programs abound, both in community and institutional settings, but the great majority of them have not been submitted to empirical investigation. When they are, the results are often disappointing, particularly for programs based in residential settings. However, the evaluation research of the past had many shortcomings, including failure in some cases to include control groups. There is a great need for additional, well-designed evaluation research in juvenile as well as adult corrections.

Many researchers and clinicians today advocate community treatment if at all possible for a wide range of juvenile offenders, including substance abusers, sexual offenders, and some violent offenders. Family preservation models try intensely to keep juveniles within their own families. Critics of this approach maintain that it fails to recognize adequately that some children and adolescents are not well served by this emphasis.

Similar to what has been found with adult treatment programs, some common features of successful programs can be identified. Those based on cognitive-behavioral models, for example, have received very favorable reviews. Multimodal programs—those that attempt to incorporate group, individual, and family treatment—also produce good results. Programs that target offenders with high risks and high needs, work intensively with those offenders, and include a follow-up component are also well rated. The follow-up component is particularly important for juveniles because they so frequently return to an environment that facilitates their antisocial behavior. This may be why multisystemic therapy—the community-based approach that attempts to address strengths and weaknesses in the juvenile's various social systems (e.g., individual, family, school, community, employment setting)—is highly promising.

Key Concepts and Review Questions

Chapter 1

Key Concepts

American Association for Correctional Psychologists (AACP)

American Psychological Association (APA)

American Psychological Society (APS)

Availability heuristic

Computer evidence recovery

Diplomate

Ethical Principles of Psychologists and Code of Conduct—2002

Family forensic psychology

Forensic entomology

Forensic psychiatry

Forensic psychology

Forensic school psychology

Questioned document examination or analysis

Specialty Guidelines for Forensic Psychologists

Questions for Review

1. Contrast the narrow and broad definitions of forensic psychology.

2. Contrast forensic psychology and other forensic sciences.

3. Identify the five subspecialties of forensic psychology covered in this text and provide illustrations of the contributions of forensic psychologists in each one.

4. Briefly describe the three levels of forensic psychologists proposed by Otto and Heilbrun.

5. What occurred at each of the following historical benchmarks in forensic psychology: 1893, 1908, 1917, 1931, 1968, 1972, 1974, 1978, 1991, and 2001?

6. What (a) degrees, (b) licenses, and (c) career opportunities are available to psychologists at the master's level?

7. Explain the difference between the PhD and the PsyD.

8. What are the five *applied* branches of psychology?

9. How has the American Psychological Association responded to the need to provide services to a diverse client population?

10. According to recent surveys, where do new doctorates in psychology find employment?

Chapter 2

Key Concepts

Americans With Disabilities Act (ADA)

Concurrent validity

Coerced-compliant false confessions

Coerced-internalized false confessions

Early warning systems

Excessive force

External stress

Face validity

False confessions

Fitness-for-duty evaluation (FFDE)

Job analysis

Organizational stress

Personal stressors

Personality assessment

Postshooting traumatic reaction (PSTR)

Predictive validity

Screening-in procedures

Screening-out procedures

Situational testing

Task-related stress

Questions for Review

1. What has job analysis revealed about police work?

2. List and describe briefly the six personality measures currently most used in police screening.

3. Can personality measures predict police corruption? Explain your answer.

4. What are the four historical trends in police psychology?

5. Give examples of each of the four types of stressors common in law enforcement.

6. Provide examples of five gender issues relating to law enforcement.

7. Identify the two stages relating to disability inquiries under the ADA.

8. Give examples of questions that may and may not be asked at each of these stages. Other than screening, describe any three special evaluations that might be conducted by a police psychologist.

9. In the Scrivner study, what five different officer profiles were prone to excessive force complaints?

10. Discuss the common psychological reactions police may have to a shooting incident.

Chapter 3

Key Concepts

Acute dynamic factors

Autoerotic asphyxia

Behavioral Science Unit (BSU)

Cognitive-behavioral viewpoint

Confirmation bias

Commitment bias

Contagion or copycat effect

Control question technique (CQT)

Countermeasures

Crime scene analysis

Criminal profiling

Differential experience hypothesis

Disorganized crime scene

Dynamic risk factors

Employee Polygraph Protection Act

Equivalent death analysis

Facial composites

Functional size (lineup)

Geographical mapping

Geographical profiling

Hypnotic hypermnesia

Hypnotic trance theory

Idiographic approach

Mixed crime scene

Modus operandi (MO)

Nominal size (lineup)

Nomothetic approach

Nonhypnotic hypermnesia

Organized crime scene

Own-race bias

Psychological autopsy

Reconstructive psychological evaluation

Relevant/irrelevant question technique

Show-up

Signature

Stable dynamic factors

Staging

Static risk factors

Trophy

Typology

Unconscious transference

Undoing

Questions for Review

1. What three questions are central to the process of investigative psychology?

2. Distinguish between criminal profiling, crime scene analysis, and racial profiling.

3. How does the psychological autopsy differ from criminal profiling? What are the two basic types of psychological autopsy?

4. Distinguish between geographical profiling and geographical mapping.

5. According to Rossmo, what are the four "hunting patterns" of serial offenders?

6. Give at least three reasons why psychological profiling is so often inaccurate.

7. List any five findings from the research on the polygraph.

8. What are the advantages and disadvantages of using forensic hypnosis?

9. What were the four recommendations made by researchers regarding lineups and photospreads in the *Police Lineups* white paper?

10. Contrast the various methods of constructing facial composites from witness identification.

Chapter 4

Key Concepts

Adolescent-limited offenders (ALs)

Antisocial personality disorder

Attention deficit hyperactivity disorder (ADHD)

Clearance rate

Conduct disorder

Crime (definition of)

Factor analysis

Hierarchy rule

Hostile attribution bias

Index crimes

Juvenile delinquent

Life course–persistent offenders (LCPs)

National Incident-Based Reporting System (NIBRS)

Oppositional defiant disorder (ODD)

Psychopath

Psychopathy Checklist (PCL) series

Status offenses

Threat assessment

QUESTIONS FOR REVIEW

1. Discuss the differences between legal and psychological definitions of delinquency.

2. What are the main sources of youth crime data?

3. Explain how Moffitt's original dichotomy of juvenile offending has been modified in recent years.

4. What are at least three explanations of ADHD?

5. What are any three alternative explanations for the IQ-delinquency connection?

6. What is intelligence? How has Howard Gardner contributed to psychology's understanding of this concept?

7. What are any five commonly held myths about school shooters?

8. How does threat assessment differ from criminal profiling?

9. List Cleckley's behavioral features of the psychopath.

10. State the controversy over labeling juveniles as psychopaths.

Chapter 5

Key Concepts

Aggression

Availability heuristic

Bias crimes

Criminal homicide

Cyberstalking

Erotomania stalking

Hate Crime Statistics Act

Hedonistic type

Instrumental violence

Love obsession stalkers

Mass murder

Manslaughter

Mission-oriented type

Murder

Observational learning

Power-control

Reactive violence

Serial murder

Simple obsession stalkers

Spree murder

Vengeance stalkers

Violence

Violent Criminal Apprehension Program (ViCAP)

Visionary type

Workplace violence

Questions for Review

1. Identify and provide examples of the two tracks of psychological research on violence.

2. Provide illustrations of gender, race, and ethnic differences in violence.

3. What are the four categories of causes of violence?

4. Summarize the negative effects of constant viewing of violence in the media.

5. Distinguish among single murder, serial murder, mass murder, and spree murder.

6. List the typologies of serial killers.

7. What are the two major types of mass murder?

8. Why is the term *workplace violence* somewhat of a misnomer?

9. Describe the four major categories of workplace violence.

10. List any five findings from the research on stalking.

Chapter 6

Key Concepts

Anger rape

Date rape

Groth rape typology

Groth child molester typology

Hostile attribution bias

Incest

MTC:CM3

Nonsadistic rapists

Opportunistic rapist

Paraphilias

Pedophilia

Pervasively angry rapist

Phallometry

Power rape

Psychosexual evaluations

Rape

Rape by fraud

Rape myths

Recidivism

Risk assessment measures

Sadistic rape

Sexually motivated rapist

Statutory rape

Type 0

Type 1

Type 2

Typology

Vindictive rapist

Questions for Review

1. Define *rape* and explain how and why the term is being replaced in many criminal statutes.

2. What are the demographic features of men who rape?

3. Briefly summarize the MTC classification system, along with what it is based on.

4. What six variables have consistently been found to play an important role in the behavior, emotional, and thought patterns of rapists?

5. Contrast the MTC and the Groth rapist typologies on both (a) classification system and (b) research support.

6. What are the two basic dimensions on which child molesters are classified according to the MTC:CM?

7. Contrast the MTC and Groth child molester typologies on both (a) classification system and (b) research support.

8. Discuss juvenile sex offenders according to their antisocial conduct, the victims they choose, and their own history of victimization.

9. Are female juvenile sex offenders different from male juvenile sex offenders? Explain your answer.

10. What is the MASA?

Chapter 7

Key Concepts

Allocution

Burglary

Child sexual abuse accommodation syndrome (CSAAS)

Covictim

Compensation

Death notification

Empirically supported treatments

Multiculturalism

National Crime Victimization Survey (NVCS)

Notification

Posttraumatic stress disorder (PTSD)

Rape trauma syndrome

Restitution

Victimless crimes

Questions for Review

1. What is monocultural psychology, and what challenges does it present to forensic psychologists?

2. Are persons with disabilities more likely to be victims of crime? Explain your answer.

3. What are the two venues in which victims of crime may seek recourse?

4. List any five rights granted to victims as a result of the victims' rights movement.

5. What type of information about victimization is available from the NCVS?

6. List some of the common psychological effects of crime on its victims.

7. What role do forensic psychologists play in dealing with the co-victims of criminal homicide?

8. What role do forensic psychologists play in dealing with adult victims of sexual assault?

9. What role do forensic psychologists play in dealing with victims of child sexual abuse?

10. Describe Summit's child sexual abuse accommodation syndrome and state the controversy associated with it.

Chapter 8

Key Concepts

Battered woman syndrome (BWS)

Battering

Child abduction

Elder abuse

Dysphoric/borderline batterer

Family-only batterer

Family violence

Filicide

Flashbulb memory

Generally violent/antisocial batterer

Geropsychology

Iatrogenic effect

Infanticide

Intimate partner violence

Munchausen syndrome by proxy (MSBP)

Neonaticide

Reconstructive theory of memory

Repressed memory

Spousal Assault Risk Assessment (SARA)

Shaken baby syndrome (SBS)

State-dependent memory

Vicarious traumatization

Questions for Review

1. Summarize Meuer, Seymour, and Wallace's stage theory of domestic violence.

2. What obstacles are placed in the path of victims of intimate partner violence who want to leave the relationship?

3. Why is the term *battered woman syndrome* controversial?

4. What progress has been achieved in the treatment of batterers?

5. What are the major differences between same-sex domestic violence (SSDV) and opposite-sex domestic violence (OSDV)?

6. List five measures used to assess symptoms of PTSD.

7. List and describe briefly the four major types of child maltreatment.

8. What are the key psychological features of Munchausen's syndrome by proxy?

9. What conclusions were reached by the APA Working Group on Investigation of Memories of Childhood Abuse?

10. What is the role of the forensic psychologist in child abuse? In parental abduction? In elder abuse?

Chapter 9

Key Concepts

Actuarial data

Amicus curiae

Appellate jurisdiction

Arraignment

Bench trial or court trial

Challenge for cause

Civil case

Criminal case

Daubert standard

Defendant

Depositions

Discovery process

Disposition

Dual-court system

Duty to warn or protect

General jurisdiction

Geographical jurisdiction

Grand jury

Initial appearance

Judgment

Jurisdiction

Limited jurisdiction

Peremptory challenge

Plaintiff

Presentence investigation

Risk assessment

Scientific jury selection

Specialized courts

Subject-matter jurisdiction

Ultimate issue

Voir dire

Witness preparation

Questions for Review

1. What is the significance of *Jenkins v. U.S.* to forensic psychology?

2. Review the main steps or stages of the judicial process and provide illustrations of tasks forensic psychologists might perform at each one.

3. Distinguish between tasks psychologists might perform in scientific jury selection and witness preparation.

4. Why is the forensic psychologist's participation in witness preparation controversial?

5. List three findings from research on the influence of expert testimony on jurors.

6. Thus far, what has research shown about the effects of the *Daubert* standard on the admission of expert testimony?

7. Identify the cases in the *Daubert* trilogy and state the key holding or rule in each one.

8. What has changed about the release of test data in the most recent APA code of conduct?

9. Summarize each side of the argument as to whether an expert should provide an opinion on the "ultimate issue."

10. What are the pros and cons of using actuarial instruments in forensic assessment?

Chapter 10

Key Concepts

Adjudicative competence

Aggravating factors

Capital sentencing

Clear and convincing proof

Competency Screening Test

Criminal responsibility evaluations

Dual-purpose evaluations

Dual relationship

Forensic mental health assessment (FMHA)

Georgia Court Competency Test (GCCT)

Guilty but mentally ill

Insanity

Involuntary civil commitment

MacArthur Competency Assessment Tool—Criminal Adjudication (MacCAT-CA)

Malingering

Mitigating factors

Preponderance of the evidence

Psychoactive medication

Rogers Criminal Responsibility Assessment Scales (R-CRAS)

Restoration to competency

Sexually violent predator statutes

Questions for Review

1. List at least five competencies in criminal suspects and defendants that might have to be assessed by forensic psychologists.

2. State and explain the differences between the three burdens of proof discussed in this chapter.

3. List at least five aspects that are common to all FMHAs.

4. Why are dual and multiple relationships problematic?

5. Why are the following cases significant to forensic psychology: *Riggins v. Nevada*, *Jackson v. Indiana*, and *Foucha v. Louisiana*?

6. Compare and contrast the cases of Charles Sell and Rusty Weston.

7. Provide illustrations of how changes in federal and state statutes have made it more difficult for defendants pleading not guilty by reason of insanity.

8. Compare the assessment of competence to stand trial and sanity/criminal responsibility.

9. List the instruments commonly used in the assessment of risk.

10. What is the role of the forensic psychologist in (a) capital sentencing and (b) sexually violent predator proceedings?

Chapter 11

Key Concepts

Advanced directives

Amenability to rehabilitation

Best interest of child standard (BICS)

Content analysis

Decisional competency

Disposition

Employment compensation claims

Family forensic psychology

Houses of refuge

Involuntary civil commitment

Judicial waivers

Least detrimental alternative standard

Legislative waiver/statutory exclusion or waiver by statute

MacArthur Competence Assessment Tool—Treatment (MacCAT-T)

MacArthur Juvenile Competence Study

Miranda rights

Outpatient treatment orders

Parens patriae

Petition

Preventive outpatient treatment

Prosecutorial waiver

Sexual harassment

Sexual Experiences Questionnaire (SEQ)

Tender years doctrine

Testamentary capacity

Tort

Questions for Review

1. Summarize the positive and negative features of juvenile courts from the turn of the 20th century to the 1960s.

2. State the significance of *U.S. v. Kent* and *In re Gault* for juveniles charged with crime.

3. What type of information is commonly gathered in a juvenile assessment?

4. What has research uncovered about the ability of juveniles to understand *Miranda* rights?

5. List at least five findings from the MacArthur Juvenile Competence Study.

6. Compare and contrast the various forms of "waiving" juveniles to criminal courts.

7. Provide three findings from the research literature on custody evaluations and the effects of custody arrangements on children.

8. Provide illustrations of when a forensic psychologist might be asked to assess competence to consent to treatment.

9. What are three different forms of outpatient civil commitment?

10. What is the role of the forensic psychologist in evaluating mental injury and sexual harassment cases?

Chapter 12

Key Concepts

Administrative segregation

Behavioral models

Cognitive-behavioral approach

Community-based facilities

Community corrections

Competency to be executed

Correctional psychologists

Criminogenic needs

Crisis intervention

Detention centers

Disciplinary segregation

Federal Bureau of Prisons (BOP)

Incarceration rate

Institutional corrections

Intensive rehabilitation supervision

Intensive supervision programs

Intermediate sanctions

Jails

Level of Service Inventory—Revised (LSI-R)

Mandatory sentences

Noncriminogenic needs

Paraphilia

Pretrial detainees

Prisons

Prison transfer

Protective custody

Psychological assessment

Rational-emotive therapy (RET)

Recidivism

Rehabilitation

Release decisions

Right to refuse treatment

Right to treatment

Risk assessment instruments

Super-max prisons

Questions for Review

1. Explain the difference between institutional and community corrections.

2. List any five topics covered in the AACP standards.

3. List the main differences between prisons and jails.

4. Does the constitutional right to treatment include a right to psychiatric/psychological treatment? Explain your answer.

5. Which two categories of offenders have been found to be incompetent to be executed?

6. Why is it important for forensic psychologists working in correctional settings to be aware of both constitutional and state law relating to inmates?

7. Identify the tasks that might be assumed by psychologists in relation to both *screening* and *classification* of inmates.

8. Are forensic psychologists involved in the *screening* and *treatment* of correctional personnel? Explain your answer.

9. Provide an illustration of a treatment program for each of the following special populations: violent offenders, criminal psychopaths, women offenders, sex offenders, and inmates in jail.

10. What are three major obstacles to the treatment of prisoners and staff in prison settings?

Chapter 13

Key Concepts

Aggression replacement training (ART)

Biological/neurological perspective

Boot camps

Cognitive-behavioral programs

Deinstitutionalization of status offenders (DSO)

Disproportionate minority confinement (DSM)

Family preservation models

Functional family therapy (FFT)

Homebuilders model

Juvenile detention

Juvenile psychopathy

Juvenile Justice and Delinquency Prevention Act (JJDPA)

Multisystemic therapy (MST)

Office of Juvenile Justice and Delinquency Prevention (OJJDP)

Paint Creek

Relapse prevention

Status offenders

Teaching-family model

Thinking errors

Victim empathy

Wilderness and adventure programs

Questions for Review

1. Define *juvenile detention* and summarize the major concerns relative to detention today.

2. Why is it important to distinguish between detention and treatment/ rehabilitation?

3. What are the strengths and weaknesses of the teaching-family approach?

4. Compare and contrast Homebuilders, FFT, and MST on such factors as population served, treatment approaches, and evaluation research.

5. Provide illustrations of an inpatient and an outpatient substance abuse treatment program and summarize the advantages and disadvantages of each approach.

6. From a psychological perspective, what are the main problems with boot camps?

7. What is ART? Briefly summarize its curriculum.

8. Describe the Paint Creek treatment program.

9. Describe the Paint Creek evaluation study, focusing on the methodology and the results.

10. Based on the research literature, what conclusions can be drawn about juvenile sex offender (a) assessment and (b) treatment?

Cases Cited

Addington v. Texas, 99 S.Ct. 1804 (1979).
Atkins v. Virginia, U.S. (2002).

Barefoot v. Estelle, 463 U.S. 880 (1983).
Batson v. Kentucky, 476 U.S. 79 (1986).
Bell v. Wolfish, 441 U.S. 520 (1979).
Bowers v. Hardwick, 478 U.S. 186 (1986).
Boy Scouts of America v. Dale, U.S. (2000).

Chevron v. Echazabal, U.S. (2002).
Cooper v. Oklahoma, 116 S. Ct. 1373 (1996).
Cruzan v. Director, Missouri Department of Health, 497 U.S. 261 (1990).

Daubert v. Merrill Dow Pharmaceuticals, Inc., 509 U.S. 579 (1993).
Drope v. Missouri, 420 U.S. 162 (1975).
Dusky v. U.S., 362 U.S. 402 (1960).

Estelle v. Gamble, 429 U.S. 97 (1976).
ex parte Crouse, 4 Whart. 9 (Pa. Supreme Court, 1838).

Fare v. Michael C., 442 U.S. 707 (1979).
Farmer v. Brennan, 511 U.S. 725 (1994).
Feliciano v. Gonzales, 13 F.Supp.2d 151 (D.P.R. 1998).
Ford v. Wainwright, 477 U.S. 399 (1986).
Foucha v. Louisiana, 504 U.S. 71 (1992).
Frye v. U.S., 54 app. D.C., 46, 47; 293 F 1013, 1014 (1923).
Furman v. Georgia, 408 U.S. 238 (1972).

General Electric Co. v. Joiner, 522 U.S. 136 (1997).
Godinez v. Moran, 113 S.Ct. 2680 (1993).

Harris v. Forklift Systems, Inc., 510 U.S. 17 (1993).
Hellstrom v. Commonwealth, 825 S.W.2d 612 (Ky. 1992).
Hudson v. Palmer, 468 U.S. 517 (1984).

In re Gault, 387 U.S. 1 (1967).
In re Quinlan, 70 N.J. 10, 355 A.2d. 647, cert. denied sub nom. (1976).

J. E. B. v. Alabama ex rel T. B., 511 U.S. 127 (1994).
Jackson v. Indiana, 406 U.S. 715 (1972).
Jaffe v. Redmond, 116 S.Ct. 1923 (1996).
Jenkins v. U.S., 307 F.2d 637 (D.C. Cir. 1962 en banc).

Kansas v. Crane, U.S. (2002).
Kansas v. Hendricks, 521 U.S., 117 S.Ct. 2072 (1997).
Kent v. U.S., 383 U.S. 541 (1966).
Kumbo Tire Co. Ltd. v. Carmichael, 119 S. Ct. 1167 (1999).

Lawrence and Garner v. Texas, U.S. (2003).

Madrid v. Gomez, 889 F. Supp. 1149 (N.D. Cal. 1995).
Maryland v. Craig, 497 U.S. 836 (1987).
McKune v. Lile, U.S. (2002).
Meritor Savings Bank FSB v. Vinson, 477 U.S. 57 (1986).
Miranda v. Arizona, 384 U.S. 436 (1966).

North Dakota ex rel. Schuetzle v. Vogel, 537N.W.2d 358 (N.D. 1995).

Payne v. Tennessee, 501 U.S. 808 (1991).
People v. Hickey, 86 Ill. App. 20 (1889).

Perri v. Coughlin, WL 395374 (N.D.N.Y. 1999).

Riggins v. Nevada, 504 U.S. (1992).

Schall v. Martin, 467 U.S. 253 (1984).
Sell v. U.S., U.S. (2003).
State v. Driver, 88 W.Va. 479, 107 S.E. 189 (1921).
Stogner v. California, U.S. (2003).

Thor v. Superior Court, 855 P.2d 375 (Cal. 1993).
Toyota v. Williams, U.S. (2002).
Troxel v. Granville, 530 U.S. 57 (2000).

U.S. v. Salerno, 481 U.S. 739 (1987).

Vitek v. Jones, 445 U.S. 480 (1980).

Washington v. Harper, 494 U.S. 210 (1990).

Zinermon v. Burch, 110 S.Ct. 975 (1990).

References

Aamodt, M., & Stalnaker, H. (2001). Police officer suicide: Frequency and officer profiles. In D. C. Sheehan & J. I. Warren (Eds.), *Suicide and law enforcement.* Washington, DC: FBI Academy.

Abel, G. G., Lawry, S. S., Karlstrom, E., Osborn, C. A., & Gillespie, C. F. (1994). Screening tests for pedophilia. *Criminal Justice and Behavior, 21,* 115–131.

Abraham, H. J. (1998). *The judicial process* (7th ed.). New York: Oxford University Press.

Abrams, K. M., & Robinson, G. E. (2002). Occupational effects of stalking. *Canadian Journal of Psychiatry, 47,* 468–472.

Abt Associates, Inc. (2000). *Addressing correctional officer stress: Programs and strategies.* Washington, DC: U.S. Department of Justice, National Institute of Justice.

Acierno, R. H., Resnick, H., & Kilpatrick, D. G. (1997, Summer). Prevalence rates, case identification and risk factors for sexual assault, physical assault and domestic violence in men and women: Part 1. *Behavioral Medicine, 23,* 53–67.

Ackerman, M. J., & Ackerman, M. C. (1997). Custody evaluation practices: A survey of experienced professionals (revisited). *Professional Psychology: Research and Practice, 28,* 137–145.

Adams, J. H. (1997). Sexual harassment and Black women: A historical perspective. In W. O'Donahue (Ed.), *Sexual harassment: Theory, research and treatment.* Boston: Allyn & Bacon.

Adams, K., Alpert, G. P., Dunham, R. G., Garner, J. H., Greenfield, L. A., Henriquez, M. A., et al. (1999, October). *Use of force by police: Overview of national and local data series: Research report.* Washington, DC: National Institute of Justice and Bureau of Justice Statistics.

Administration on Aging. (1998, September). *The national elder abuse incidence study: Final report.* Washington, DC: U.S. Department of Health and Human Services, Administration on Aging.

Agopian, M. W. (1984). The impact on children of abduction by parents. *Child Welfare, 63,* 511–519.

Alexander, M. A. (1999). Sexual offender treatment efficacy revisited. *Sexual Abuse: A Journal of Research and Treatment, 11,* 101–116.

Alexander, R. A., Smith, W., & Stevenson, R. (1990). Serial Munchausen syndrome by proxy. *Pediatrics, 8,* 581–585.

Alison, L., Bennell, C., Ormerod, D., & Mokros, A. (2002). The personality paradox in offender profiling: A theoretical review of the processes involved in deriving background characteristics from crime scene actions. *Psychology, Public Policy, and Law, 8,* 115–135.

Alison, L., Smith, M. D., Eastman, O., & Rainbow, L. (2003). Toulmin's philosophy of argument and its relevance to offender profiling. *Psychology, Crime & Law, 9,* 173–183.

Alison, L., Smith, M. D., & Morgan, K. (2003). Interpreting the accuracy of offender profiles. *Psychology, Crime & Law, 9,* 185–195.

Alison, L. J., & Canter, D. V. (1999). Professional, legal and ethical issues in offender profiling. In D. V. Canter & L. J. Alison (Eds.), *Profiling in policy and practice.* Aldershot, England: Ashgate.

Allen, R. S., & Shuster, J. L. (2002). The role of proxies in treatment decisions: Evaluating functional capacity to consent to end-of-life treatments within a family context. *Behavioral Sciences and the Law, 20,* 235–252.

Allison, K. W., Crawford, I., Echemendia, R., Robinson, L., & Kemp, D. (1994). Human diversity and professional competence: Training in clinical and counseling psychology revisited. *American Psychologist, 49,* 792–796.

Alpert, J., Brown, L. S., & Courtois, C. A. (1998). Symptomatic clients and memories of childhood abuse: What the trauma and sexual abuse literature tells us. *Psychology, Public Policy, and Law, 4,* 941–945.

Althouse, R. (2000). AACP standards: A historical overview (1978–1980). *Criminal Justice and Behavior, 27,* 430–432.

American Association for Correctional Psychology. (2002). Standards for psychology services in jails, prisons, correctional facilities, and agencies. *Criminal Justice and Behavior, 27,* 433–493.

American Bar Association. (1979). *Juvenile justice standards project.* Chicago: Author.

American Psychiatric Association. (1994). *Diagnostic and statistical manual of mental disorders* (4th ed.). Washington, DC: Author.

American Psychiatric Association. (2000). *Diagnostic and statistical manual of mental disorders* (4th ed., text rev.). Washington, DC: Author.

American Psychological Association. (1978). *APA policy related to graduate education: Resolution on the master's-level issue.* Washington, DC: Author.

American Psychological Association. (1987). Model act for state licensure of psychologists. *American Psychologist, 42,* 696-703.

American Psychological Association. (1992). Ethical principles of psychologists and code of conduct. *American Psychologist, 47,* 1597–1611.

American Psychological Association. (1993). Guidelines for providers of psychological services to ethnic, linguistic, and culturally diverse populations. *American Psychologist, 48,* 45–48.

American Psychological Association. (1994). Guidelines for child custody evaluations in divorce proceedings. *American Psychologist, 49,* 677–680.

American Psychological Association. (1996). *Reducing violence: A research agenda.* Washington, DC: Author.

American Psychological Association. (2002a, December). Amicus curiae brief in *Sell v. U.S.,* no. 02–5664.

American Psychological Association. (2002b). Ethical principles of psychologists and code of conduct. *American Psychologist, 57,* 1060–1073.

American Psychological Association. (2003a). *Ethical principles of psychologists and code of conduct—2002.* Washington, DC: Author.

American Psychological Association. (2003b). Guidelines on multicultural education, training, research, practice, and organizational change for psychologists. *American Psychologist, 58,* 377–402.

American Psychological Association. (2003c). Is youth violence just another fact or life? In *APA Online: Public Interest Initiatives.* Washington, DC: Author. Available at www.APA. org.

American Psychological Association. (2003d). APA survey on undergraduate education. *APA Online*. Washington, DC: Author. Available at: www.APA.org.

American Psychological Association Committee on Professional Practice and Standards. (1998). *Guidelines for psychological evaluations in child protection matters*. Washington, DC: Author.

Amick-McMullen, A., Kilpatrick, D. G., & Resnick, H. S. (1991). Homicide as a risk factor for PTSD among surviving family members. *Behavioral Modification, 15,* 545–559.

Amick-McMullen, A., Kilpatrick, D. G., Veronen, L. J., & Smith, S. (1989). Family survivors of homicide victims: Theoretical perspectives and an exploratory study. *Journal of Traumatic Stress, 2,* 21–35.

Amnesty International. (1998). *Betraying the young* (Special report). New York: Author.

Anastasi, A. (1988). *Psychological testing* (4th ed.). New York: Macmillan.

Anderson, C. A., & Bushman, B. J. (2001). Effects of violent video games on aggressive behavior, aggressive cognition, aggressive affect, physiological arousal, and prosocial behavior: A meta-analytic review of the scientific literature. *Psychological Science, 12,* 353–359.

Anderson, S. D., & Hewitt, J. (2002). The effect of competency restoration training on defendants with mental retardation found not competent to proceed. *Law and Human Behavior, 26,* 343–351.

Andrews, D. A., & Bonta, J. (1994). *The psychology of criminal conduct*. Cincinnati, OH: Anderson.

Andrews, D. A., & Bonta, J. (1995). *The Level of Service Inventory—Revised*. Toronto, ON: Multi-Health Systems.

Andrews, D. A., & Bonta, J. (1998). *The psychology of criminal conduct* (2nd ed.). Cincinnati, OH: Anderson.

Andrews, D. A., Bonta, J., & Hoge, P. D. (1990). Classification for effective rehabilitation: Rediscovering psychology. *Criminal Justice and Behavior, 17,* 19–52.

Appelbaum, P. S., & Grisso, T. (1995). The MacArthur treatment competence study: I. Mental illness and competence to consent to treatment. *Law and Human Behavior, 19,* 105–126.

Arey, J. A. (1972). *The sky pirates*. New York: Scribner's.

Arkow, P. (1998). The correlations between cruelty to animals and child abuse and the implications for veterinary medicine. In R. Lockwood & F. R. Ascione (Eds.), *Cruelty to animals and interpersonal violence: Readings in research and application*. West Lafayette, IN: Purdue University Press.

Armstrong, D., & Pereira, J. (2001, October 23). Nation's airlines adopt aggressive measures for passenger profiling. *Wall Street Journal*, p. A12.

Ascione, R. R. (1997). *Animal welfare and domestic violence*. Logan: Utah State University.

Asher, R. (1951). Munchausen's syndrome. *The Lancet, 1,* 339–341.

Ashford, J. B., Sales, B. D., & Reid, W. H. (Eds.). (2001). *Treating adult and juvenile offenders with special needs*. Washington, DC: American Psychological Association.

Ault, R., Hazelwood, R. R., & Reboussin, R. (1994). Epistemological status of equivocal death analysis. *American Psychologist, 49,* 72–73.

Ault, R., & Reese, J. T. (1980). A psychological assessment of criminal profiling. *FBI Law Enforcement Bulletin, 49,* 22–25.

Bachman, R. (1992). *Death and violence on the reservation*. New York: Auburn House.

Bailis, D., Darley, J., Waxman, T., & Robinson, P. (1995). Community standards of criminal liability and the insanity defense. *Law and Human Behavior, 19,* 425–446.

Baker, R. R., Lichtenberg, P. A., & Moye, J. (1998). A practice guideline for assessment of competency and capacity of the older adult. *Professional Psychology: Research and Practice, 29,* 149–154.

Balkin, J. (1988). Why policemen don't like policewomen. *Journal of Police Science and Administration, 16,* 29–37.

Ballie, R. (2001, December). Where are the new psychologists going? *Monitor on Psychology, 32*, 24–25.

Barbaree, H. E., & Serin, R. C. (1993). Role of male sexual arousal during rape in various rapist subtypes. In G. C. Nagayama, G. C. N. Hall, R. Hirchman, J. R. Graham, & M. S. Zaragoza (Eds.), *Sexual aggression: Issues in etiology, assessment, and treatment.* Washington, DC: Taylor & Francis.

Barbaree, H. E., Seto, M. C., Serin, R. C., Amos, N. L., & Preston, D. L. (1994). Comparisons between sexual and nonsexual rapist subtypes: Sexual arousals to rape, offense precursors, and offense characteristics. *Criminal Justice and Behavior, 21*, 95–114.

Barber, T. X., Spanos, N. R., & Chaves, J. F. (1974). *Hypnosis, imagination, and human potentialities.* New York: Pergamon.

Bardone, A. M., Moffitt, T. E., & Caspi, A. (1996). Adult mental health and social outcomes of adolescent girls with depression and conduct disorder. *Development and Psychopathology, 8*, 811–829.

Barkley, R. (1997). Behavioral inhibition, sustained attention, and executive functions: Constructing a unifying theory of ADHD. *Psychological Bulletin, 121*, 65–94.

Barkley, R. (1998). *Attention deficit hyperactivity disorder* (2nd ed.). New York: Guilford.

Barland, G. H. (1988). The polygraph use in the USA and elsewhere. In A. Gale (Ed.), *The polygraph test: Lies, truth and science.* London: Sage.

Barland, G. H., & Raskin, D. C. (1973). Detection of deception. In W. F. Prokasy & D. C. Raskin (Eds.), *Electrodermal activity in psychosocial research.* New York: Academic Press.

Barling, J., Rogers, A. G., & Kelloway, E. (2000). Behind closed doors: In-home workers' experience of sexual harassment and workplace violence. *Journal of Occupational Health Psychology, 6*, 255–269.

Barnard, G. W., Thompson, J. W., Freeman, W. C., Robbins, L., Gies, D., & Hankins, G. (1991). Competency to stand trial: Description and initial evaluation of a new computer-assisted assessment tool (CADCOMP). *Bulletin of the American Academy of Psychiatry and the Law, 19*, 367–381.

Barnum, R. (2000). Clinical and forensic evaluation of competence to stand trial in juvenile defendants. In T. Grisso & R. G. Schwartz (Eds.), *Youth on trial.* Chicago: University of Chicago Press.

Baron, R. A., & Byrne, D. (2000). *Social psychology* (9th ed.). Boston: Allyn & Bacon.

Barrick, M. R., & Mount, M. K. (1991). The Big Five personality dimensions and job performance: A meta analysis. *Personnel Psychology, 44*, 1–26.

Barsky, A. E., & Gould, J. W. (2002). *Clinicians in court: A guide to subpoenas, depositions, testifying, and everything else you need to know.* New York: Guilford.

Bartol, C. R. (1980). *Criminal behavior: A psychosocial approach.* Englewood Cliffs, NJ: Prentice Hall.

Bartol, C. R. (1991). Predictive validation of the MMPI for small-town police officers who fail. *Professional Psychology: Research and Practice, 22*, 127–132.

Bartol, C. R. (1996). Police psychology: Then, now, and beyond. *Criminal Justice and Behavior, 23*, 70–89.

Bartol, C. R. (2002). *Criminal behavior: A psychosocial approach* (6th ed.). Upper Saddle River, NJ: Prentice Hall.

Bartol, C. R., & Bartol, A. M. (1987). History of forensic psychology. In I. B. Weiner & A. K. Hess (Eds.), *Handbook of forensic psychology.* New York: John Wiley.

Bartol, C. R., & Bartol, A. M. (1998). *Delinquency and justice: A psychosocial approach.* Upper Saddle River, NJ: Prentice Hall.

Bartol, C. R., & Bartol, A. M. (1999). History of forensic psychology. In A. K. Hess & I. B. Weiner (Eds.), *Handbook of forensic psychology* (2nd ed.). New York: John Wiley.

Bartol, C. R., & Bartol, A. M. (2004). *Psychology and law: Theory, research, and application* (3rd ed.). Belmont, CA: Wadsworth/Thomson.

Bashore, T. R., & Rapp, P. E. (1993). Are there alternatives to traditional polygraph procedures? *Psychological Bulletin, 113,* 3–22.

Bates, J. E., Marvinney, D., Kelly, T., Dodge, K. A., Bennett, D. S., & Pettit, G. S. (1994). Child-care history and kindergarten adjustment. *Developmental Psychology, 30,* 690–700.

Bauer, P. J. (1996). What do infants recall of their lives? Memory for specific events by one- to two-year-olds. *American Psychologist, 51,* 29–41.

Bauserman, R. (2002). Child adjustment in joint-custody versus sole-custody arrangements: A meta-analytic review. *Journal of Family Psychology, 16,* 38–53.

Beatty, D., Hickey, E.,& Sigmon, J. (2002). Stalking. In A. Seymour, M. Murray, J. Sigmon, M. Hook, C. Edwards, M. Gaboury, & G. Coleman (Eds.), *2002 National Victim Assistance Academy textbook.* Washington, DC: U.S. Department of Justice, Office of Victims of Crime.

Beauchaine, T. P., Katkin, E. S., Strassberg, Z., & Snarr, J. (2001). Disinhibitory psychopathology in male adolescents: Discriminating conduct disorder from attention-deficit/ hyperactivity disorder through concurrent assessment of multiple autonomic states. *Journal of Abnormal Psychology, 110,* 610–624.

Becker, J. V. (1990). Treating adolescent sexual offenders. *Professional Psychology: Research and Practice, 21,* 362–365.

Becker, J. V., Hall, S. R., & Stinson, J. D. (2001). Female sexual offenders: Clinical, legal and policy issues. *Journal of Forensic Psychology Practice, 1,* 29–50.

Becker, J. V., & Johnson, B. R. (2001). Treating juvenile sex offenders. In J. B. Ashford, B. D. Sales, & W. H. Reid (Eds.), *Treating adult and juvenile offenders with special needs.* Washington, DC: American Psychological Association.

Behnke, S. (2003). Release of test data and APA's new ethics code. *Monitor on Psychology, 34,* 70–72.

Bell, D. J. (1982). Policewomen: Myths and reality. *Journal of Police Science and Administration, 10,* 112–120.

Bem, D. J., & Allen, A. (1974). On predicting some of the people some of the time: The search for cross-situational consistencies in behavior. *Psychological Review, 81,* 506–520.

Ben-Shakhar, G. (2002). A critical review of the Control Question Test (CQT). In M. Kleiner (Ed.), *Handbook of polygraph testing.* San Diego: Academic Press.

Ben-Shakhar, G., & Dolev, K. (1996). Psychophysiological detection through the guilty knowledge technique: The effects of mental countermeasures. *Journal of Applied Psychology, 81,* 273–281.

Benson, E. (2002, November). The perils of going solo. *Monitor on Psychology, 33,* 25.

Berliner, L. (1998). The use of expert testimony in child sexual abuse cases. In S. J. Ceci & H. Hembrooke (Eds.), *Expert witnesses in child abuse cases.* Washington, DC: American Psychological Association.

Bernal, G., & Sharrón-Del-Río, M. R. (2001). Are empirically supported treatments valid for ethnic minorities? Toward an alternative approach for treatment research. *Cultural Diversity and Ethnic Minority Psychology, 7,* 328–342.

Bernard, T. (1992). *The cycle of juvenile justice.* New York: Oxford University Press.

Bernat, J. A., Cahoun, K. S., Adams, H. E., & Zeichner, A. (2001). Homophobia and physical aggression toward homosexual and heterosexual individuals. *Journal of Abnormal Psychology, 110,* 179–187.

Bernfeld, G. A. (2001). The struggle for treatment integrity in a "dis-integrated" service delivery system. In G. A. Bernfeld, D. P. Farrington, & A. W. Leschied (Eds.), *Offender rehabilitation in practice.* Chichester, UK: Wiley.

Bersoff, D. N., Goodman-Delahunty, J., Grisso, J. T., Hans, V. P., Poythress, N. G., & Roesch, R. G. (1997). Training in law and psychology: Models from the Villanova Conference. *American Psychologist, 52,* 1301–1310.

Beutler, L. E. (1998). Identifying empirically supported treatments: What if we didn't? *Journal of Consulting and Clinical Psychology, 66,* 113–120.

Bingham, R. P., Porché-Burke, L., James, S., Sue, D. W., & Vasquez, M. J. T. (2002). Introduction: A report on the National Multicultural Conference and Summit II. *Cultural Diversity and Ethnic Minority Psychology, 8,* 75–87.

Bishop, D. M. (2000). Juvenile offenders in the adult criminal justice system. In M. Tonry (Ed.), *Crime and justice: A review of research* (Vol. 27). Chicago: University of Chicago Press.

Black, H. C. (1990). *Black's law dictionary* (6th ed.). St. Paul, MN: West.

Black, J. (2000). Personality testing and police selection: Utility of the "Big Five." *New Zealand Journal of Psychology, 29,* 2–9.

Blackburn, R. (1993). *The psychology of criminal conduct.* Chichester, UK: Wiley.

Blanchard, R., Klassen, P., Dickey, R., Kuban, M. E., & Blak, T. (2001). Sensitivity and specificity of the phallometric test for pedophilia in nonadmitting sex offenders. *Psychological Assessment, 13,* 118–126.

Blumberg, M. (1997). Controlling police use of deadly force: Assessing two decades of progress. In R. G. Dunham & G. P. Alpert (Eds.), *Critical issues in policing: Contemporary readings* (3rd ed.). Prospect Heights, IL: Waveland.

Bobo, L. D., & Kluegel, J. (1997). The color line, the dilemma, and the dream: Racial attitudes and relations in American at the close of the twentieth century. In J. Higham (Ed.), *Civil rights and social wrongs: Black-White relations since World War II.* University Park: Pennsylvania State University Press.

Boccaccini, M. T. (2002). What do we really know about witness preparation? *Behavioral Sciences & the Law, 20,* 161–189.

Boccaccini, M. T., & Brodsky, S. L. (2002). Believability of expert and lay witnesses: Implications for trial consultation. *Professional Psychology: Research and Practice, 33,* 384–388.

Boes, J. O., Chandler, C. J., & Timm, H. W. (2001, December). *Police integrity: Use of personality measures to identify corruption-prone officers.* Monterey, CA: Defense Personnel Security Research Center.

Boeschen, L. E., Sales, B. D., & Koss, M. P. (1998). Rape trauma experts in the courtroom. *Psychology, Public Policy, and Law, 4,* 414–432.

Bohm, R. M. (1999). *Deathquest: An introduction to the theory and practice of capital punishment in the United States.* Cincinnati, OH: Anderson.

Boney-McCoy, S., & Finkelhor, D. (1995). Psychosocial sequelae of violent victimization in a national youth sample. *Journal of Consulting and Clinical Psychology, 63,* 726–736.

Bonnie, R., & Grisso, T. (2000). Adjudicative competence and youthful offenders. In T. Grisso & R. Schwartz (Eds.), *Youth on trial: A developmental perspective on juvenile justice.* Chicago: University of Chicago Press.

Bonnie, R. J. (1990). Dilemmas in administering the death penalty: Conscientious abstentions, professional ethics, and the needs of the legal system. *Law and Human Behavior, 14,* 67–90.

Bonnie, R. J. (1992). The competence of criminal defendants: A theoretical reformulation. *Behavioral Sciences & the Law, 10,* 291–316.

Bonta, J. (1996). Risk-needs: Assessment and treatment. In A. T. Harland (Ed.), *Choosing correctional options that work: Defining the demand and evaluating the supply.* Thousand Oaks, CA: Sage.

Bonta, J. (2002). Offender risk assessment: Guidelines for selection and use. *Criminal Justice and Behavior, 29,* 355–379.

Bonta, J., Wallace-Capretta, S., & Rooney, J. (2000). A quasi-experimental evaluation of an intensive rehabilitation supervision program. *Criminal Justice and Behavior, 27,* 312–329.

Boothby, J. L., & Clements, C. B. (2000). A national survey of correctional psychologists. *Criminal Justice and Behavior, 27,* 716–732.

Boothby, J. L., & Clements, C. B. (2002). Job satisfaction of correctional psychologists: Implications for recruitment and retention. *Professional Psychology: Research and Practice, 33,* 310–315.

Borum, R. (1996). Improving the clinical practice of violence risk assessment: Technology, guidelines, and training. *American Psychologist, 51,* 945–956.

Borum, R., Deane, M. W., Steadman, H. J., & Morrissey, J. (1998). Police perspectives on responding to the mentally ill people in crisis: Perceptions of program effectiveness. *Behavioral Sciences and the Law, 16,* 393–405.

Borum, R., Fein, R., Vossekuil, B., & Berglund, J. (1999). Threat assessment: Defining an approach for evaluating risk of targeted violence. *Behavioral Sciences and the Law, 17,* 323–337.

Borum, R., & Fulero, S. M. (1999). Empirical research on the insanity defense and attempted reforms: Evidence toward informed policy. *Law and Human Behavior, 23,* 375–394.

Borum, R., & Grisso, T. (1995). Psychological tests used in criminal forensic evaluations. *Professional Psychology: Research and Practice, 26,* 465–473.

Borum, R., & Philpot, C. (1993). Therapy with law enforcement couples: Clinical management of the "high-risk life style." *American Journal of Family Therapy, 21,* 122–135.

Borum, R., & Strentz, T. (1993, April). The borderline personality: Negotiation strategies. *FBI Law Enforcement Bulletin,* pp. 6–10.

Bow, J. N., & Quinnell, F. A. (2001). Psychologists' current practices and procedures in child custody evaluations five years after American Psychological Association guidelines. *Professional Psychology: Research and Practice, 32,* 261–268.

Bradford, J. M. W. (1993). *The pharmacological treatment of the adolescent sex offender.* New York: Guilford.

Braffman, W., & Kirsch, I. (1999). Imaginative suggestibility and hypnotizability: An empirical analysis. *Journal of Personality and Social Psychology, 77,* 578–587.

Brakel, S. J. (2003). Competency to stand trial: Rationalism, "contextualism" and other modest theories. *Behavioral Sciences and the Law, 21,* 285–295.

Brent, D. A. (1989). The psychological autopsy: Methodological issues for the study of adolescent suicide. *Suicide and Life Threatening Behavior, 19,* 43–57.

Bricklin, B., & Elliot, G. (1995). Postdivorce issues and relevant research. In B. Bricklin (Ed.), *The child custody evaluation handbook: Research-based solutions and applications.* New York: Bruner/Mazel.

Briere, J. (1988). The long-term clinical correlates of childhood sexual victimization. In R. A. Prentky & V. L. Quinsey (Eds.), *Human sexual aggression: Current perspectives.* New York: New York Academy of Sciences.

Briere, J., Malamuth, N., & Ceniti, J. (1981). *Self-assessed rape proclivity: Attitudinal and sexual correlates.* Paper presented at the American Psychological Association meeting, Los Angeles.

Briere, J., & Runtz, M. (1989). University males' sexual interest in children: Predicting potential indices of "pedophilia" in a non-forensic sample. *Child Abuse & Neglect, 13,* 65–75.

Brigham, J. C. (1999). What is forensic psychology, anyway? *Law and Human Behavior, 23,* 273–298.

British Psychological Society. (1995). *Recovered memories: The report of the working party of the British Psychological Society.* Leicester, UK: Author.

Brodsky, S. L. (1980). Ethical issues for psychologists in corrections. In J. Monahan (Ed.), *Who is the client? The ethics of psychological intervention in the criminal justice system.* Washington, DC: American Psychological Association.

Bronfenbrenner, U. (1979). *The ecology of human development: Experiment by nature and design.* Cambridge, MA: Harvard University Press.

Brooks, L. W. (1997). Police discretionary behavior: A study of style. In R. G. Dunham & G. P. Alpert (Eds.), *Critical issues in policing: Contemporary readings* (3rd ed.). Prospect Heights, IL: Waveland.

Brown, B. B., & Harris, P. B. (1989). Residential burglary victimization: Reactions to the invasion of a primary territory. *Journal of Environmental Psychology, 9,* 119–132.

Brown, M. L. (1997). Dilemmas facing nurses who care for Munchausen syndrome by proxy. *Pediatric Nursing, 23,* 416–418.

Brown, R., & Kulik, J. (1977). Flashbulb memories. *Cognition, 5,* 73–99.

Brown, S. L., & Forth, A. E. (1997). Psychopathy and sexual assault: Static risk factors, emotional precursors, and rapists subtypes. *Journal of Consulting and Clinical Psychology, 65,* 848–857.

Brown, T. L., Borduin, C. M., & Henggeler, S. W. (2001). Treating juvenile offenders in community settings. In J. B. Ashford, B. D. Sales, & W. H. Reid (Eds.), *Treating adult and juvenile offenders with special needs.* Washington, DC: American Psychological Association.

Browne, A., & Finkelhor, D. (1986). Impact of child sexual abuse: A review of the research. *Psychological Bulletin, 99,* 66–77.

Bruck, M., Ceci, S. J., & Francoeur, E. (2000). Children's use of anatomically detailed dolls to report genital touching in a medical examination. *Journal of Experimental Psychology: Applied, 6,* 74–83.

Budd, J. W., Arvey, R. D., & Lawless, P. (1996). Correlates and consequences of workplace violence. *Journal of Occupational Health Psychology, 1,* 197–210.

Budd, K. S., Felix, E. D., Poindexter, L. M., Naik-Polan, A. T., & Sloss, C. F. (2002). Clinical assessment of children in child protection cases: An empirical analysis. *Professional Psychology: Research and Practice, 33,* 3–12.

Budnick, K. J., & Shields-Fletcher, E. (1998). *What about girls?* Washington, DC: U.S. Department of Justice, Office of Juvenile Justice and Delinquency Prevention.

Bumby, K. M. (1993). Reviewing the guilty but mentally ill alternative: A case of the blind "pleading" the blind. *Journal of Psychiatry and Law, 21,* 191–220.

Bumby, K. M., & Bumby, N. H. (1997). Adolescent female sexual offenders. In H. R. Cellini & B. Schwartz (Eds.), *The sex offender: New insights, treatment innovations and legal developments* (Vol. 2). Kingston, NJ: Civil Research Institute.

Burdon, W. M., & Gallagher, C. A. (2002). Coercion and sex offenders: Controlling sex-offending behavior through incapacitation and treatment. *Criminal Justice and Behavior, 29,* 87–109.

Bureau of Justice Assistance. (2001, June). *Recruiting & retaining women: A self-assessment guide for law enforcement.* Washington, DC: U.S. Department of Justice, Bureau of Justice Assistance.

Bureau of Justice Statistics. (1993). *Law Enforcement Management and Administrative Statistics (LEMAS) survey.* Washington, DC: U.S. Department of Justice, Bureau of Justice Statistics.

Bureau of Justice Statistics. (2001a). *Prisoners in 2000.* Washington, DC: U.S. Department of Justice, Bureau of Justice Statistics.

Bureau of Justice Statistics. (2001b, December). *Violence in the workplace, 1993–1999.* Washington, DC: U.S. Department of Justice, Bureau of Justice Statistics.

Bureau of Justice Statistics. (2002a). Corrections statistics. Available: www.ojp.usdoj.gov/bjs/correct.htm

Bureau of Justice Statistics. (2002b). *National Crime Victimization Survey.* Washington, DC: U.S. Department of Justice, Bureau of Justice Statistics.

Bureau of Justice Statistics. (2002c). *Recidivism of prisoners released in 1994.* Washington, DC: U.S. Department of Justice, Bureau of Justice Statistics.

Bureau of Labor Statistics. (1999). *National census of fatal occupational injuries, 1998.* Washington, DC: U.S. Department of Labor.

Burgess, A. W., Hartman, C. R., & Ressler, R. K. (1986). Sexual homicide: A motivational model. *Journal of Interpersonal Violence, 1,* 251–272.

Burgess, A. W., & Hazelwood, R. (Eds.). (1995). *Practical aspects of rape investigation: A multidisciplinary approach* (2nd ed.). New York: CRC Press.

Burgess, A. W., & Holmstrom, L. L. (1974). Rape trauma syndrome. *American Journal of Psychiatry, 131,* 981–986.

Burns, B. J., Schoenwald, S. K., Burchard, J. D., Faw, L., & Santos, A. B. (2000). Comprehensive community-based interventions for youth with severe emotional disorders: Multisystemic therapy and the wraparound process. *Journal of Child and Family Studies, 9,* 283–314.

Buss, E. (2000). The role of lawyers in promoting juveniles' competence as defendants. In T. Grisso & R. G. Schwartz (Eds.), *Youth on trial: A developmental perspective on juvenile justice.* Chicago: University of Chicago Press.

Butcher, J. N., & Miller, K. B. (1999). Personality assessment in personal injury litigation. In A. K. Hess & I. B. Weiner (Eds.), *The handbook of forensic psychology* (2nd ed.). New York: John Wiley.

Butler, W. M., Leitenberg, H., & Fuselier, G. D. (1993). The use of mental health professional consultants to police hostage negotiation teams. *Behavioral Sciences and the Law, 11,* 213–221.

California Occupational Safety and Health Administration. (1995). *Guidelines for workplace security.* Sacramento: Author.

California Youth Authority. (1997). *LEAD: A boot camp and intensive parole program: Final impact evaluation.* Sacramento: State of California, Department of Youth Authority.

Callahan, L. A., Steadman, H. J., McGreevy, M. A., & Robbins, P. C. (1991). The volume and characteristics of insanity defense pleas: An eight-state study. *Bulletin of Psychiatry and the Law, 19,* 331–338.

Campbell, J. C. (1995). Prediction of homicide of and by battered women. In J. C. Campbell (Ed.), *Assessing dangerousness: Violence by sexual offenders, batterers, and child abusers.* Thousand Oaks, CA: Sage.

Campbell, T. W. (2003). Sex offenders and actuarial risk assessments: Ethical considerations. *Behavioral Sciences and the Law, 21,* 269–279.

Canter, D. (1995). *Criminal shadows: Inside the mind of the serial killer.* London: HarperCollins.

Canter, D. (1999). Equivocal death. In D. Canter & L. J. Alison (Eds.), *Profiling in policy and practice.* Burlington, VT: Ashgate.

Canter, D., & Alison, L. (2000). Profiling property crimes. In D. Canter & L. J. Alison (Eds.), *Profiling property crimes.* Burlington, VT: Ashgate.

Castle, T., & Hensley, C. (2002). Serial killers with military experience: Applying learning theory to serial murder. *International Journal of Offender Therapy and Comparative Criminology, 46,* 453–465.

Ceci, S. J., & Bruck, M. (1993). The suggestibility of the child witness: A historical review and synthesis. *Psychological Bulletin, 113,* 403–439.

Ceci, S. J., Ross, D. F., & Toglia, M. P. (1987). Suggestibility of children's memory: Psycholegal implications. *Journal of Experimental Psychology: General, 116,* 38–49.

Cellini, H. R. (1995). Assessment and treatment of the adolescent sexual offender. In B. Schwartz & H. R. Cellini (Eds.), *The sex offender: Corrections, treatment and legal practice* (Vol. 1). Kingston, NJ: Civil Research Institute.

Cellini, H., Schwartz, B., & Readio, S. (1993, December). *Child sexual abuse: An administrator's nightmare.* Washington, DC: National School Safety Center.

Chaiken, J. M. (1999, February). Foreword. In *American Indians and crime.* Washington, DC: U.S. Department of Justice.

Chaiken, M. R. (2000, March). Violent neighborhoods, violent kids. *Juvenile Justice Bulletin,* pp. 6–18. Washington, DC: U.S. Department of Justice.

Chandler, J. T. (1990). *Modern police psychology: For law enforcement and human behavior professionals.* Springfield, IL: Charles C Thomas.

Chappelle, W., & Rosengren, K. (2001). Maintaining composure and credibility as an expert witness during cross-examination. *Journal of Forensic Psychology Practice, 1,* 51–67.

Chenoweth, J. H. (1961). Situational tests: A new attempt at assessing police candidates. *Journal of Criminal Law, Criminology, and Police Science, 52,* 232–238.

Chesney-Lind, M., & Shelden, R. G. (1998). *Girls, delinquency, and juvenile justice* (2nd ed.). Belmont, CA: West/Wadsworth.

Chiancone, J. (2001, December). Parental abduction: Review of the literature. *Juvenile Justice Bulletin,* pp. 14–18. Washington, DC: Office of Juvenile Justice and Delinquency Prevention.

Child Abuse Prevention Center. (1998). *Shaken baby syndrome fatalities in the United States.* Ogden, UT: Author.

Chiroro, P., & Valentine, T. (1995). An investigation of the contact hypothesis of the own-race bias in face recognition. *Quarterly Journal of Experimental Psychology, 48A,* 979–894.

Cirincione, C., Steadman, H., & McGreevy, M. (1995). Rates of insanity acquittals and the factors associated with successful insanity pleas. *Bulletin of the American Academy of Psychiatry and Law, 23,* 399–409.

Civil Aeronautics Board. (1975). *Supplement to the handbook of airline statistics.* Springfield, VA: National Information Service.

Clark, K. (2002, May/June). Data recovery: The forensics wave of the future. *The Forensic Examiner, 11,* 36–37.

Clear, T. R., & Cole, G. F. (2000). *American corrections* (5th ed.). Belmont, CA: West/Wadsworth.

Cleckley, H. (1941). *The mask of sanity.* St. Louis, MO: C. V. Mosby.

Cochrane, R. E., Grisso, T., & Frederick, R. I. (2001). The relationship between criminal charges, diagnoses, and psycholegal opinions among federal defendants. *Behavioral Sciences & the Law, 19,* 565–582.

Cochrane, R. E., Tett, R. P., & VandeCreek, L. (2003). Psychological testing and the selection of police officers: A national survey. *Criminal Justice and Behavior, 30,* 511–527.

Cohen, F. (1998). *The mentally disordered inmate and the law.* Kingston, NJ: Civic Research Institute.

Cohen, F. (2000). *The mentally disordered inmate and the law, 2000–2001 supplement.* Kingston, NJ: Civic Research Institute.

Cohen, F. (2003). *The mentally disordered inmate and the law, 2003 cumulative supplement.* Kingston, NJ: Civic Research Institute.

Cohen, M., Garafalo, R., Boucher, R., & Seghorn, T. (1971). The psychology of rapists. *Seminars in Psychiatry, 3,* 307–327.

Cohen, M., Seghorn, T., & Calmas, W. (1969). Sociometric study of the sex offender. *Journal of Abnormal Psychology, 74,* 249–255.

Cohen, M. E., & Carr, W. J. (1975). Facial recognition and the von Restorff effect. *Bulletin of the Psychonomic Society, 6,* 383–384.

Cohen, P., Cohen, J., & Brook, J. (1993). An epidemiological study of disorders in late childhood and adolescence: II. Persistent disorders. *Journal of Child Psychology and Psychiatry, 34,* 869–877.

Cohn, Y. (1974). Crisis intervention and the victim of robbery. In I. Drapkin & E. Viano (Eds.), *Victimology: A new focus.* Lexington, MA: Lexington Books.

Coid, J. W. (2003). Formulating strategies for the primary prevention of adult antisocial behaviour: "High risk" or "population" strategies. In D. F. Farrington & J. W. Coid (Eds.), *Early prevention of adult antisocial behaviour.* Cambridge, UK: Cambridge University Press.

Coie, J. D., Belding, M., & Underwood, M. (1988). Aggression and peer rejection in childhood. In B. Lahey & A. Kazdin (Eds.), *Advances in clinical child psychology* (Vol. 2). New York: Plenum.

Coie, J. D., Dodge, K., & Kupersmith, J. (1990). Peer group behavior and social status. In S. R. Asher & J. D. Coie (Eds.), *Peer rejection in childhood.* Cambridge, UK: Cambridge University Press.

Coie, J. D., Underwood, M., & Lochman, J. E. (1991). Programmatic intervention with aggressive children in the school setting. In D. J. Pepler & H. Rubin (Eds.), *The development and treatment of childhood aggression.* Hillsdale, NJ: Lawrence Erlbaum.

Cole, G. F., & Smith, C. E. (2001). *The American system of criminal justice* (9th ed.). Belmont, CA: Wadsworth/Thompson.

Comas-Díaz, L. (2001). Hispanics, Latinos, or Americanos: The evolution of identity. *Cultural Diversity and Ethnic Minority Psychology, 7,* 115–120.

Comer, R. J. (2004). *Abnormal psychology* (5th ed.). New York: Worth.

Committee on Ethical Guidelines for Forensic Psychologists. (1991). Specialty guidelines for forensic psychologists. *Law and Human Behavior, 15,* 655–665.

Conley, J. M. (2000). Epilogue: A legal and cultural commentary on the psychology of jury instructions. *Psychology, Public Policy, and Law, 6,* 822–831.

Consigli, J. E. (2002). Post-conviction sex offender testing and the American Polygraph Association. In M. Kleiner (Ed.), *Handbook of polygraph testing.* San Diego: Academic Press.

Cooke, D. J., & Michie, C. (1997). An item response theory analysis of the Hare Psychopathy Checklist—Revised. *Psychological Assessment, 9,* 3–14.

Cooke, D. J., & Michie, C. (2001). Refining the construct of psychopathy: Toward a hierarchical model. *Psychological Assessment, 13,* 171–188.

Cooke, D. J., Michie, C., Hart, S. D., & Hare, R. D. (1999). Evaluation of the screening version of the Hare Psychopathy Checklist—Revised (PCL-SV): An item response theory analysis. *Psychological Assessment, 11,* 3–13.

Cornwell, P. (2002). *Portrait of a killer: Jack the Ripper—case closed.* New York: Putnam.

Correctional Services of Canada. (1990). *Forum on corrections research, 2*(1). Ottawa, Ontario: Author.

Correia, K. M. (2001). *A handbook for correctional psychologists.* Springfield, IL: Charles C Thomas.

Cortina, L. M. (2001). Assessing sexual harassment among Latinas: Development of an instrument. *Cultural Diversity and Ethnic Minority Psychology, 7,* 164–181.

Costa, P. T., & McCrae, R. R. (1992). *NEO PI-R: The Revised NEO Personality Inventory.* Odessa, FL: Psychological Assessment Resources.

Cox, J. F., Landsberg, G., & Paravati, M. P. (1989). A practical guide for mental health providers in local jails. In H. J. Steadman, D. W. McCarty, & J. P. Morrissey (Eds.), *The mentally ill in jail: Planning for essential services.* New York: Guilford.

Crabtree, P. (2003). [L.O.] appears in court. Available: www.rutlandherald.com/search/categories/article/63112

Crawford, N. (2002, November). Science-based program curbs violence in kids. *Monitor on Psychology, 33,* 38–39.

Crespi, T. D. (1990). School psychologists in forensic psychology: Converging and diverging issues. *Professional Psychology: Research and Practice, 21,* 83–87.

Cromwell, P. F., Jr., Killinger, G. C., Kerper, H. B., & Walker, C. (1985). *Probation and parole in the criminal justice system* (2nd ed.). St. Paul, MN: West.

Cromwell, P. F., Olson, J. F., & Avary, D. W. (1991). *Breaking and entering: An ethnographic analysis of burglary.* Newbury Park, CA: Sage.

Cruise, K., & Rogers, R. (1998). An analysis of competency to stand trial: An integration of case law and clinical knowledge. *Behavioral Sciences and the Law, 16,* 35–50.

Cullen, F. T., & Gendreau, P. (2000). Assessing correctional rehabilitation: Policy, practice, and prospects. In J. Horney (Ed.), *Criminal justice 2000: Vol. 3. Policies, processes, and decisions of the criminal justice system.* Washington, DC: National Institute of Justice.

Cullen, F. T., Wright, J. P., & Applegate, B. K. (1996). Control in the community: The limits of reform? In A. T. Harland (Ed.), *Choosing correctional options that work: Defining the demand and evaluating the supply.* Thousand Oaks, CA: Sage.

Cunningham, M. D., & Reidy, T. J. (1998). Integrating base rate data in violence risk assessments at capital sentencing. *Behavioral Sciences & the Law, 16,* 71–96.

Cunningham, M. D., & Reidy, T. J. (1999). Don't confuse me with the facts: Common errors in violence risk assessment at capital sentencing. *Criminal Justice and Behavior, 26,* 20–43.

Cutler, B. L., & Penrod, S. D. (1995). *Mistaken identification: The eyewitness, psychology, and law.* New York: Cambridge University Press.

Cutler, B. L., Penrod, S. D., & Dexter, H. R. (1989). The eyewitness, the expert psychologist, and the jury. *Law and Human Behavior, 13,* 311–322.

Cutler, B. L., Penrod, S. D., & Martens, T. K. (1987). Improving the reliability of eyewitness identification: Putting content with context. *Journal of Applied Psychology, 72,* 629–637.

Dailey, J. T., & Pickrel, E. W. (1975a, April). Federal Aviation Administration's behavioral research program for the defense against hijacking. *Aviation, Space and Environmental Medicine,* pp. 423–427.

Dailey, J. T., & Pickrel, E. W. (1975b). Some psychological contributions to defenses against hijackers. *American Psychologist, 30,* 161–165.

Davies, G., Morton, J., Mollon, P., & Robertson, N. (1998). Recovered memories in theory and practice. *Psychology, Public Policy, and Law, 4,* 1079–1090.

Davies, G., van der Willik, P., & Morrison, L. J. (2000). Facial composite production: A comparison of mechanical and computer driven systems. *Journal of Applied Psychology, 85,* 119–124.

Day, K., & Berney, T. (2001). Treatment and care for offenders with mental retardation. In J. B. Ashford, B. D. Sales, & W. H. Reid (Eds.), *Treating adult and juvenile offenders with special needs.* Washington, DC: American Psychological Association.

Dean, K. E., & Malamuth, N. M. (1997). Characteristics of men who aggress sexually and of men who imagine aggressing: Risk and moderating variables. *Journal of Personality and Social Psychology, 72,* 449–455.

DeHaan, J. (1997). *Kirk's fire investigation* (4th ed.). Upper Saddle River, NJ: Prentice Hall.

del Carmen, R. V., Parker, M., & Reddington, F. P. (1998). *Briefs of leading cases in juvenile justice.* Cincinnati, OH: Anderson.

Delprino, R. P., & Bahn, C. (1988). National survey of the extent and nature of psychological services in police departments. *Professional Psychology: Research and Practice, 19,* 421–425.

Department of Veterans Affairs. (1996). *Geropsychology assessment resource guide, 1996 revision.* Milwaukee, WI: National Center for Cost Containment.

Detrick, P., Chibnall, J. T., & Luebbert, M. C. (in press). The NEO PI-R as predictor of police academy performance. *Criminal Justice and Behavior.*

Developmental Disabilities Branch. (2000, December). *Attention-deficit/hyperactivity disorder.* Atlanta, GA: Centers for Disease Control and Prevention.

Diliman, E. C. (1963). Role-playing as a technique in police selection. *Public Personnel Review, 24,* 116–118.

Dishion, T. J., & Bullock, B. M. (2002). Parenting and adolescent problem behavior: An ecological analysis of the nurturance hypothesis. In J. G. Borkowski, S. L. Ramey, & M. Bristol-Power (Eds.), *Parenting and the child's world: Influences on academic, intellectual, and social-emotional development.* Mahwah, NJ: Lawrence Erlbaum.

Dittmann, M. (2002, December). Attracting more school psychology faculty. *Monitor on Psychology, 33,* 46–47.

Ditton, P. M. (1999). *Mental health and treatment of inmates and probationers.* Washington, DC: U.S. Department of Justice, Bureau of Justice Statistics.

Dixon, L., & Gill, B. (2002). Changes in the standards for admitting expert evidence in federal civil cases since the *Daubert* decision. *Psychology, Public Policy, and Law, 8,* 251–308.

Dobash, R. P., & Dobash, R. E. (2000). Feminist perspectives on victimization. In N. H. Rafter (Ed.), *Encyclopedia of women and crime.* Phoenix, AZ: Oryx.

Dobson, V., & Sales, B. (2000). The science of infanticide and mental illness. *Psychology, Public Policy, and Law, 4,* 1098–1112.

Dodge, K. A. (1993). Social-cognitive mechanisms in the development of conduct disorder and depression. *Annual Review of Psychology, 44,* 559–584.

Dodge, K. A., & Pettit, G. S. (2003). A biopsychological model of the developmnet of chronic conduct problems in adolescence. *Developmental Psychology, 39,* 349–371.

Donn, J. E., Routh, D. K., & Lunt, I. (2000). From Leipzig to Luxembourg (via Boulder and Vail): A history of clinical training in Europe and the United States. *Professional Psychology: Research and Practice, 31,* 423–428.

Donnellan, M. B., Ge, X., & Wenk, E. (2000). Cognitive abilities in adolescent-limited and life-course-persistent criminal offenders. *Journal of Abnormal Psychology, 109,* 396–402.

Doren, D. M. (2002). *Evaluating sex offenders.* Thousand Oaks, CA: Sage.

Dougher, M. J. (1995). Clinical assessment of sex offenders. In B. K. Schwartz & H. R. Cellini (Eds.), *The sex offender: Corrections, treatment and legal practice.* Kingston, NJ: Civic Research Institute.

Douglas, J. E., & Munn, C. (1992). The detection of staging and personation at the crime scene. In J. E. Douglas, A. W. Burgess, & R. K. Ressler (Eds.), *Crime classification manual.* New York: Lexington Books.

Douglas, J. E., Ressler, R. K., Burgess, A. W., & Hartman, C. R. (1986). Criminal profiling from crime scene analysis. *Behavioral Sciences and the Law, 4,* 401–421.

Dovidio, J., Gaertner, S., Kawakami, K., & Hodson, G. (2002). Why can't we just get along? Interpersonal biases and interracial distrust. *Cultural Diversity and Ethnic Minority Psychology, 8,* 88–102.

Dowdell, E. B., & Foster, K. L. (2000). Munchausen syndrome by proxy: Recognizing a form of child abuse. *Nursing Spectrum.* Available: www.nsweb.nursingspectrum.com

Dudycha, G. J., & Dudycha, M. M. (1941). Childhood memories: A review of the literature. *Psychological Bulletin, 38,* 668–682.

Duhaime, A., Christian, C. W., Rorke, L. B., & Zimmerman, R. A. (1998). Nonaccidental head injury in infants: The "shaken-baby syndrome." *New England Journal of Medicine, 338,* 1822–1829.

D'Unger, A. V., Land, K. C., McCall, P. L., & Nagin, D. S. (1998). How many latent classes of delinquent/criminal careers? Results from mixed Poisson regression analysis. *American Journal of Sociology, 103,* 1593–1630.

Durand, V. M., & Barlow, D. H. (2000). *Abnormal psychology: An introduction*. Belmont, CA: Wadsworth.

Dutton, D., & Golant, S. K. (1995). *The batterer: A psychological profile*. New York: Basic Books.

Dutton, M. A. (1992). *Empowering and healing the battered woman*. New York: Springer.

Dutton, M. A. (1996, May). *Validity and use of evidence concerning battering and its effects in criminal trials: NIJ Report to Congress*. Washington, DC: U.S. Department of Justice, National Institute of Justice and U.S. Department of Health and Human Services, National Institute of Mental Health.

Duwe, G. (2000). Body-count journalism: The presentation of mass murder in the news media. *Homicide Studies, 4*, 364–399.

Ebert, B. W. (1987). Guide to conducting a psychological autopsy. *Professional Psychology: Research and Practice, 18*, 52–56.

Eddy, D., & Edmunds, C. (2002). Compensation. In A. Seymour, M. Murray, J. Sigmon, M. Hook, C. Edmunds, M. Gaboury, & G. Coleman (Eds.), *National Victim Assistance Academy textbook*. Washington, DC: US. Department of Justice, Office of Victims of Crime.

Edens, J. F., Petrila, J., & Buffington-Vollum, J. K. (2001). Psychopathy and the death penalty: Can the Psychopathy Checklist—Revised identify offenders who represent "a continuing threat to society?" *Journal of Psychiatry and Law, 29*, 433–481.

Edens, J. F., Skeem, J. L., Cruise, K. R., & Cauffman, E. (2001). Assessment of "juvenile psychopathy" and its association with violence: A critical review. *Behavioral Sciences and the Law, 19*, 53–80.

Edwards, D. L., Schoenwald, S. K., Henggeler, S. W., & Strother, K. B. (2001). A multi-level perspective on the implementation of multisystemic therapy (MST): Attempting dissemination with fidelity. In G. A. Bernfeld, D. P. Farrington, & A. W. Leschied (Eds.), *Offender rehabilitation in practice*. Chichester, UK: Wiley.

Ehrlichman, H., & Halpern, J. N. (1988). Affect and memory: Effects of pleasant and unpleasant odors on retrieval of happy and unhappy memories. *Journal of Personality and Social Psychology, 55*, 769–779.

Eich, E. (1989). Theoretical issues in state dependent memory. In H. L. Roediger & F. I. M. Craik (Eds.), *Varieties of memory and consciousness.* . Hillsdale, NJ: Lawrence Erlbaum.

Einhorn, J. (1986). Child custody in historical perspective: A study of changing social perceptions of divorce and child custody in Anglo-American law. *Behavioral Sciences & the Law, 4*, 119–135.

Elliott, D. M. (1997). Traumatic events: Prevalence and delayed recall in the general population. *Journal of Consulting and Clinical Psychology, 65*, 811–820.

Elliott, D. S., Ageton, S. S., & Huizinga, D. (1980). *The National Youth Survey*. Boulder, CO: Behavioral Research Institute.

Elliott, D. S., Dunford, T. W., & Huizinga, D. (1987). The identification and prediction of career offenders utilizing self-reported and official data. In J. D. Burchard & S. N. Burchard (Eds.), *Prevention of delinquent behavior*. Newbury Park, CA: Sage.

Ellis, A. (1962). *Reason and emotion in psychotherapy*. Secaucus, NJ: Citadel.

Ellis, C. A., & Lord, J. (2002). Homicide. In A. Seymour, M. Murray, J. Sigmon, M. Hook, C. Edmunds, M. Gaboury, & G. Coleman (Eds.), *National Victim Assistance Academy textbook*. Washington, DC: US. Department of Justice, Office of Victims of Crime.

Ellsworth, P. C., & Reifman, A. (2000). Juror comprehension and public policy: Perceived problems and proposed solutions. *Psychology, Public Policy, and Law, 6*, 788–821.

Emerson, R. M., Ferris, K. O., & Gardner, C. B. (1998). On being stalked. *Social Problems, 45*, 289–314.

Emery, R. E., & Laumann-Billings, L. (1998). An overview of the nature, causes, and consequences of abusive family relationships. *American Psychologist, 53,* 121–135.

Epperson, D. L., Kaul, J. D., & Hesselton, D. (1998, October). *Final report of the development of the Minnesota Sex Offender Screening Tool—Revised (MnSOST-R).* Paper presented at the 17th Annual Research and Treatment Conference of the Association for the Treatment of Sexual Abusers, Vancouver, British Columbia, Canada.

Erickson, C. D., & Al-Timini, N. R. (2001). Providing mental health services to Arab Americans: Recommendations and considerations. *Cultural Diversity and Ethnic Minority Psychology, 7,* 308–327.

Eron, L., Gentry, J. H., & Schlegel, P. (Eds.). (1994). *Reason to hope: A psychosocial perspective on violence and youth.* Washington, DC: American Psychological Association.

Eron, L., Huesmann, R., Spindler, A., Guerra, N., Henry, D., & Tolan, P. (2002). A cognitive-ecological approach to preventing aggression in urban settings: Initial outcomes for high-risk children. *Journal of Consulting and Clinical Psychology, 70,* 179–194.

Eron, L., & Slaby, R. G. (1994). Introduction. In L. D. Eron, J. H. Gentry, & P. Schlegel (Eds.), *Reason to hope: A psychosocial perspective on violence and youth.* Washington, DC: American Psychological Association.

Evans, G. D., & Rey, J. (2001). In the echoes of gunfire: Practicing psychologists' responses to school violence. *Professional Psychology: Research and Practice, 32,* 157–164.

Ewing, C. P. (2003). False credentials cause extensive fallout. *Monitor on Psychology, 34,* 84.

Farabee, D. (Ed.). (2002). Making people change [Special issue]. *Criminal Justice and Behavior, 29.*

Faraone, S. V., Biederman, J., & Friedman, D. (2000). Validity of *DSM-IV* subtypes of attention-deficit/hyperactivity disorder: A family study perspective. *Journal of the American Academy of Child and Adolescent Psychiatry, 39,* 300–309.

Farrington, D. P. (1979). Environmental cues, delinquent behavior, and conviction. In I. G. Sarason & C. D. Spielberger (Eds.), *Stress and anxiety* (Vol. 6). Washington, DC: Hemisphere.

Farrington, D. P. (1987). Predicting individual crime rates. In D. M. Gottfredson & M. Tonry (Eds.), *Prediction and classification* (Vol. 10). Chicago: University of Chicago Press.

Farrington, D. P. (1991). Childhood aggression and adult violence: Early precursors and later life outcomes. In D. J. Pepler & K. H. Rubin (Eds.), *The development and treatment of childhood aggression.* Hillsdale, NJ: Lawrence Erlbaum.

Farrington, D. P., Loeber, R., & Stouthamer-Loeber, M. (2003). How can the relationship between race and violence be explained? In D. F. Hawkins (Ed.), *Violent crime: Assessing race and ethnic differences.* Cambridge, UK: Cambridge University Press.

Farrington, D. P., Ohlin, L. E., & Wilson, J. Q. (1986). *Understanding and controlling crime.* New York: Springer.

Federal Bureau of Investigation. (2000). *Uniform Crime Reports—1999.* Washington, DC: U.S. Department of Justice.

Federal Bureau of Investigation. (2001). *Uniform Crime Reports—2000.* Washington, DC: U.S. Department of Justice, Federal Bureau of Investigation.

Federal Bureau of Investigation. (2002a). *Hate crime statistics, 2001.* Washington, DC: U.S. Department of Justice, Federal Bureau of Investigation.

Federal Bureau of Investigation. (2002b). *Uniform Crime Reports—2001.* Washington, DC: U.S. Department of Justice, Federal Bureau of Investigation.

Federle, K. H., & Chesney-Lind, M. (1992). Special issues in juvenile justice: Gender, race and ethnicity. In I. M. Schwartz (Ed.), *Juvenile justice and public policy: Toward a national agenda.* New York: Maxwell-Macmillan.

Fehrenbach, P. A., & Monasterky, C. (1988). Characteristics of female sexual offenders. *American Journal of Orthopsychiatry, 58,* 148–151.

Fein, R. A., & Vossekuil, B. (1999). Assassination in the United States: An operational study of recent assassins, attackers, and near-lethal approaches. *Journal of Forensic Sciences, 50,* 321–333.

Feindler, E. L., Rathus, J. H., & Silver, L. B. (2003). *Assessment of family violence: A handbook for researchers and practitioners.* Washington, DC: American Psychological Association.

Feld, B. (Ed.). (1999). *Readings in juvenile justice administration.* New York: Oxford University Press.

Feld, B. C. (1988). *In re Gault* revisited: A cross-state comparison of the right to counsel in juvenile court. *Crime & Delinquency, 34,* 393–424.

Feld, B. C. (2000). Juveniles' waiver of legal rights: Confessions, *Miranda,* and the right to counsel. In T. Grisso & R. G. Schwartz (Eds.), *Youth on trial.* Chicago: University of Chicago Press.

Felson, R. B. (2002). *Violence and gender reexamined.* Washington, DC: American Psychological Association.

Ferguson, G. E., Eidelson, R. J., & Witt, P. H. (1998). New Jersey's sex offender risk assessment scale: Preliminary validity data. *Journal of Psychiatry and Law, 26,* 327–351.

Fernald, G. M., & Sullivan, E. B. (1924, October). Psychology and public safety. *California Monthly,* pp. 81–83.

Final conclusions of the American Psychological Association working group on investigation of memories of childhood abuse. (1998). *Psychology, Public Policy, and Law, 4,* 931–940.

Finkelhor, D., Hotaling, G., & Sedlak, A. (1990). *Missing, abducted, runaway, and thrownaway children in America: First report.* Washington, DC: Juvenile Justice Clearinghouse.

Finkelhor, D., & Lewis, I. A. (1988). An epidemiologic approach to the study of child molestation. In R. A. Prentky & V. L. Quinsey (Eds.), *Human sexual aggression: Current perspectives.* New York: New York Academy of Sciences.

Finkelhor, D., & Ormrod, R. (2000, June). *Kidnapping of juveniles: Patterns from NIBRS.* Washington, DC: U.S. Department of Justice, Office of Juvenile Justice and Delinquency Prevention.

Finkelhor, D., & Ormrod, R. (2001a, September). *Crimes against children by babysitters.* Washington, DC: U.S. Department of Justice, Office of Juvenile Justice and Delinquency Prevention.

Finkelhor, D., & Ormrod, R. (2001b, October). *Homicides of children and youth.* Washington, DC: U.S. Department of Justice, Office of Juvenile Justice and Delinquency Prevention.

Finley, L. M. (1996). The pharmaceutical industry and women's reproductive health. In E. Szockyj & J. G. Fox (Eds.), *Corporate victimization of women.* Boston: Northeastern University Press.

Finn, P., Talucci, V., & Wood, J. (2000, January). On-the-job stress in policing: Reducing it, preventing it. *National Institute of Justice Journal,* pp. 18–25.

Finn, P., & Tomz, J. E. (1997, March). *Developing a law enforcement stress program for officers and their families.* Washington, DC: U.S. Department of Justice.

Fischler, G. L. (2001). Psychological fitness-for-duty examinations: Practical considerations for public safety departments. *Illinois Law Enforcement Executive Forum, 1,* 77–92.

Fishbein, D. (2000). Neuropsychological function, drug abuse, and violence: A conceptual framework. *Criminal Justice and Behavior, 27,* 139–159.

Fisher, B. S., Cullen, F. T., & Turner, M. G. (2000). *Sexual victimization of college women.* Washington, DC: U.S. Department of Justice, National Institute of Justice.

Fisher, J. C. (1997). *Killer among us: Public reactions to serial murder.* Westport, CT: Praeger.

Fitzgerald, L. F., Buchanan, N. T., Collinsworth, L. L., Magley, V. J., & Ramos, A. M. (1999). Junk logic: The abuse defense in sexual harassment litigation. *Psychology, Public Policy, and Law, 5,* 730–759.

Fitzgerald, L. R., & Shullman, S. L. (1985). *Sexual Experiences Questionnaire.* Kent, OH: Kent State University.

Fixsen, D. L., Blasé, K. A., Timbers, G. D., & Wolf, M. M. (2001). In search of program implementation: 792 replications of the teaching-family model. In G. A. Bernfeld, D. P. Farrington, & A. W. Leschied (Eds.), *Offender rehabilitation in practice.* Chichester, UK: Wiley.

Fizel, D. (1997, February 26). *The suspect confessed. Case closed? Not necessarily, researcher says* [APA News Press Release]. American Psychological Association, Washington, DC.

Flory, K., Milich, R., Lynam, D. R., Leukefeld, C., & Clayton, R. (2003). Relation between childhood disruptive behavior disorders and substance use and dependence symptoms in young adulthood: Individuals with symptoms of attention-deficit/hyperactivity disorder and conduct disorder are uniquely at risk. *Psychology of Addictive Behaviors, 17,* 151–158.

Foa, E. B., Cashman, L., Jaycox, L., & Perry, K. (1997). The validation of a self-report measure of posttraumatic stress disorder: The Posttraumatic Diagnostic Scale. *Psychological Assessment, 9,* 445–451.

Foa, E. B., Riggs, D. S., Dancu, C. V., & Rothbaum, B. O. (1993). Reliability and validity of a brief instrument for assessing posttraumatic stress disorder. *Journal of Traumatic Stress, 6,* 459–474.

Foa, E. B., Rothbaum, B. O., Riggs, D. S., & Murdock, T. B. (1991). Treatment of posttraumatic stress disorder in rape victims: A comparison between cognitive-behavioral procedures and counseling. *Journal of Consulting and Clinical Psychology, 59,* 715–723.

Forth, A. E., Kosson, D. S., & Hare, R. D. (1997). *Hare Psychopathy Checklist: Youth Version.* Toronto, Ontario: Multi-Health Systems.

Fox, J. A., & Levin, J. (1998). Multiple homicide: Patterns of serial and mass murder. In M. Tonry (Ed.), *Crime and justice: A review of research* (Vol. 23). Chicago: University of Chicago Press.

Fox, J. A., & Zawitz, M. A. (2001). *Homicide trends in the United States.* Washington, DC: U.S. Department of Justice, Bureau of Justice Statistics.

Franklin, C. L., Sheeran, T., & Zimmerman, M. (2002). Screening for trauma histories, posttraumatic stress disorder (PTSD), and subthreshold PTSD in psychiatric outpatients. *Psychological Assessment, 14,* 467–471.

Frazier, P. A., & Borgida, E. (1992). Rape trauma syndrome: A review of case law and psychological research. *Law and Human Behavior, 16,* 293–311.

Freud, S. (1957). Repression. In J. Strachey (Ed. and Trans.), *The standard edition of the complete psychological works of Sigmund Freud* (Vol. 14). London: Hogarth. (Original work published 1915)

Freund, K. (1963). A laboratory method for diagnosing predominance of homo- and hetero-erotic interests in the male. *Behavior Research and Therapy, 1,* 85–93.

Frick, P. J., Bodin, S. D., & Barry, C. T. (2000). Psychopathic traits and conduct problems in community and clinic-referred samples of children: Further development of the psychopathy screening device. *Psychological Assessment, 12,* 382–393.

Frick, P. J., Cornell, A. H., Bodin, S. D., Dane, H. E., Barry, C. T., & Loney, B. R. (2003). Callous-unemotional traits and developmental pathways to severe conduct problems. *Developmental Psychology, 39,* 246–260.

Frick, P. J., O'Brien, B. S., Wootton, J., & McBurnett, K. (1994). Psychopathy and conduct problems in children. *Journal of Abnormal Psychology, 103,* 700–707.

Furby, L., Weinroth, M. R., & Blackshaw, L. (1989). Sex offender recidivism: A review. *Psychological Bulletin, 105,* 3–30.

Fuselier, G. D. (1981, June/July). A practical overview of hostage negotiations. *FBI Law Enforcement Bulletin,* pp. 1–11.

Fuselier, G. D. (1988). Hostage negotiation consultant: Emerging role for the clinical psychologist. *Professional Psychology: Research and Practice, 19,* 175–179.

Fuselier, G. D., & Noesner, G. W. (1990, July). Confronting the terrorist hostage taker. *FBI Law Enforcement Bulletin*, pp. 9–12.

Gaboury, M., & Edmunds, C. (2002). Civil remedies. In A. Seymour, M. Murray, J. Sigmon, M. Hook, C. Edwards, M. Gaboury, & G. Coleman (Eds.), *National Victim Assistance Academy textbook*. Washington, DC: U.S. Department of Justice, Office of Victims of Crime.

Gacono, C. B., Nieberding, R. J., Owen, A., Rubel, J., & Bodholdt, R. (1997). Treating conduct disorder, antisocial, and psychopathic personalities. In J. B. Ashford, B. D. Sales, & W. H. Reid (Eds.), *Treating adult and juvenile offenders with special needs*. Washington, DC: American Psychological Association.

Gallagher, R. W., Somwaru, D. P., & Ben-Porath, Y. S. (1999). Current usage of psychological tests in state correctional settings. *Corrections Compendium, 24*, 1–3, 20.

Gardner, H. (1983). *Frames of mind: The theory of multiple intelligences*. New York: Basic Books.

Gardner, H. (1986). The waning of intelligence tests. In R. J. Sternberg & D. K. Detterman (Eds.), *What is intelligence?* Norwood, NJ: Ablex.

Gardner, H. (1993). *Multiple intelligences*. New York: Basic Books.

Geberth, V. (1996). *Practical homicide investigation* (3rd ed.). New York: CRC Press.

Gendreau, P., Cullen, F. T., & Bonta, J. (1994). Intensive rehabilitation supervision: The next generation in community corrections? *Federal Probation, 58*, 72–78.

Gendreau, P., Little, T., & Goggin, C. (1996). A meta-analysis of the predictors of adult recidivism: What works! *Criminology, 34*, 401–433.

Gendreau, P., Paparozzi, M., Little, T., & Goddard, M. (1993). Punishing smarter: The effectiveness of the new generation of alternative sanctions. *Forum on Correctional Research, 5*, 31–34.

Gendreau, P., & Ross, R. R. (1984). Correctional treatment: Some recommendations for effective intervention. *Juvenile and Family Court Journal, 34*, 31–39.

Gentile, S. R., Asamen, J. K., Harmell, P. H., & Weathers, R. (2002). The stalking of psychologists by their clients. *Professional Psychology: Research and Practice, 33*, 490–494.

George, W. H., & Marlatt, G. A. (1989). Introduction. In D. R. Laws (Ed.), *Relapse prevention with sex offenders*. New York: Guilford.

Gibbons, D. (1988). Some critical observations on criminal type and criminal careers. *Criminal Justice and Behavior, 15*, 8–23.

Gibbs, J. J. (1992). Jailing and stress. In H. Toch (Ed.), *Mosaic of despair: Human breakdown in prison*. Washington, DC: American Psychological Association.

Gill, C. J., Kewman, D. G., & Brannon, R. W. (2003). Transforming psychological practice and society: Policies that reflect the new paradigm. *American Psychologist, 58*, 305–312.

Gillis, J. W. (2001). *First response to victims of crime 2001*. Washington, DC: U.S. Department of Justice, Office for Victims of Crime.

Going, M., & Read, J. D. (1974). Effects of uniqueness, sex of subject, and sex of photograph on facial recognition. *Perceptual and Motor Skills, 39*, 109–110.

Golding, S. L., & Roesch, R. (1987). The assessment of criminal responsibility: A historical approach to a current controversy. In I. B. Weiner & A. K. Hess (Eds.), *Handbook of forensic psychology*. New York: John Wiley.

Golding, S. L., Skeem, J. L., Roesch, R., & Zapf, P. A. (1999). The assessment of criminal responsibility: Current controversies. In A. K. Hess & I. B. Weiner (Eds.), *The handbook of forensic psychology* (2nd Ed.). New York: Wiley.

Goldkamp, J. S., & Irons-Guynn, C. (2000). *Emerging judicial strategies for the mentally ill in the criminal caseload: Mental health courts in Fort Lauderdale, Seattle, San Bernardino, and Anchorage*. Washington, DC: U.S. Department of Justice, Office of Justice Programs, Bureau of Justice Assistance.

Goldstein, A. M. (2002a). Low-level aggression: Definition, escalation, intervention. In J. McGuire (Ed.), *Offender rehabilitation and treatment*. Chichester, UK: Wiley.

Goldstein, A. M. (2002b). Teaching point: What kinds of cases do you avoid accepting because they would make it too difficult for you to remain impartial? In K. Heilbrun, G. R. Marczyk, & D. DeMatteo (Eds.), *Forensic mental health assessment.* New York: Oxford University Press.

Goldstein, A. P., & Glick, B. (1987). *Aggression replacement training.* Champaign, IL: Research Press.

Goldstein, A. P., & Glick, B. (2001). Aggression replacement training: Application and evaluation management. In G. A. Bernfeld, D. P. Farrington, & A. W. Leschied (Eds.), *Offender rehabilitation in practice.* Chichester, UK: Wiley.

Good, G. E., Heppner, P. P., Hillenbrand-Gunn, T. L., & Wang, L. (1995). Sexual and psychological violence: An exploratory study of predictors in college men. *Journal of Men's Studies, 4,* 59–71.

Goodman-Delahunty, J. (1999a). Civil law: Employment and discrimination. In R. Roesch, S. D. Hart, & J. R. P. Ogle (Eds.), *Psychology and law: The state of the discipline.* New York: Kluwer Academic/Plenum.

Goodman-Delahunty, J. (1999b). Pragmatic support for the reasonable victim standard in hostile workplace sexual harassment cases. *Psychology, Public Policy, and Law, 5,* 519–555.

Goodman-Delahunty, J. (2000). Psychological impairment under the Americans With Disabilities Act: Legal guidelines. *Professional Psychology: Research and Practice, 31,* 197–205.

Gordon, C. C. (1969). *Perspectives on law enforcement: I. Characteristics of police applicants.* Princeton, NJ: Educational Testing Service.

Gordon, D. A. (2002). Intervening with families of troubled youth: Functional family therapy and parenting wisely. In J. McGuire (Ed.), *Offender rehabilitation and treatment.* Chichester, UK: Wiley.

Gorman, W. (2001). Refugee survivors of torture: Trauma and treatment. *Professional Psychology: Research and Practice, 32,* 443–451.

Gothard, S., Rogers, R., & Sewell, K. W. (1995). Feigning incompetency to stand trial: An investigation of the Georgia Court Competency Test. *Law and Human Behavior, 19,* 363–373.

Gough, H. G. (1987). *California Psychological Inventory administrator's guide.* Palo Alto, CA: Consulting Psychologists Press.

Gray, A. S., Pithers, W., Busconi, A. J., & Houchens, P. (1997). Children with sexual behavior problems: An empirically derived taxonomy. *Association for the Treatment of Sexual Abusers, 3,* 10–11.

Greenfeld, L. A. (1997). *Sex offenses and offenders: An analysis of data on rape and sexual assault.* Washington, DC: U.S. Department of Justice, Bureau of Justice Statistics.

Greenfeld, L. A., Langan, P. A., & Smith, S. K. (1997, November). *Police use of force: Collection of national data.* Washington, DC: U.S. Department of Justice, Bureau of Justice Statistics.

Greenwood, P. W., & Turner, S. (1993). Evaluation of the Paint Creek Youth Center: A residential program for serious delinquents. *Criminology, 31,* 263–279.

Gregorie, T. (2000). *Cyberstalking: Dangers on the information highway.* Arlington, VA: National Center for Victims of Crime.

Gregorie, T., & Wallace, H. (2000). Workplace violence. In A. Seymour, M. Muray, J. Sigmon, M. Hook, C. Edmonds, M. Gaboury, & G. Coleman (Eds.), *2000 National Victim Assistance Academy textbook.* Washington, DC: U.S. Department of Justice, Office for Victims of Crime.

Gregorie, T., & Wallace, H. (2002). Workplace violence. In A. Seymour, M. Murray, J. Sigmon, M. Hook, C. Edmonds, M. Gaboury, & G. Coleman (Eds.), *National Victim Assistance Academy textbook.* Washington, DC: U.S. Department of Justice, Office for Victims of Crime.

Greif, G. L., & Hegar, R. L. (1993). *When parents kidnap: The families behind the headlines.* New York: Free Press.

Gretton, H. M., McBride, M., Hare, R. D., O'Shaughnessy, R., & Kumka, G. (2001). Psychopathy and recidivism in adolescent sex offenders. *Criminal Justice and Behavior, 28,* 427–449.

Grisso, T. (1981). *Juveniles' waiver of rights: Legal and psychological competence.* New York: Plenum.

Grisso, T. (1986). *Evaluating competencies: Forensic assessments and instruments.* New York: Plenum.

Grisso, T. (1988). *Competency to stand trial evaluations: A manual for practice.* Sarasota, FL: Professional Resource Exchange.

Grisso, T. (1996). Society's retributive response to juvenile violence: A developmental perspective. *Law and Human Behavior, 20,* 229–247.

Grisso, T. (1998). *Forensic evaluation of juveniles.* Sarasota, FL: Professional Resource Press.

Grisso, T. (1999). Dealing with juveniles' competence to stand trial: What we need to know. *Quinnipiac Law Review, 18,* 371–383.

Grisso, T., Appelbaum, P., Mulvey, E., & Fletcher, K. (1995). The MacArthur Treatment Competence Study: II. Measures of abilities related to competence to consent to treatment. *Law and Human Behavior, 19,* 127–148.

Grisso, T., & Saks, M. J. (1991). Psychology's influence on constitutional interpretation. *Law and Human Behavior, 15,* 205–211.

Grisso, T., & Schwartz, R. G. (Eds.). (2000). *Youth on trial: A developmental perspective on juvenile justice.* Chicago: University of Chicago Press.

Grisso, T., Steinberg, L., Woolard, J., Cauffman, E., Scott, E., Graham, S., et al. (2003). Juveniles' competence to stand trial: A comparison of adolescents' and adults' capacities as trial defendants. *Law and Human Behavior, 27,* 333–364.

Gross, A. M., Bennett, T., Sloan, L., Marx, B. P., & Jurgens, J. (2001). The impact of alcohol and alcohol expectancies on male perceptions of female sexual arousal in a date rape analog. *Experimental and Clinical Psychopharmacology, 9,* 380–388.

Grossman, N. S., & Okun, B. F. (2003). Family psychology and family law: Introduction to the special issue. *Journal of Family Psychology, 17,* 163–168.

Groth, A. N. (1979). *Men who rape: The psychology of the offender.* New York: Plenum.

Groth, A. N., & Burgess, A. W. (1977). Motivational intent in the sexual assault of children. *Criminal Justice and Behavior, 4,* 253–271.

Groth, A. N., Burgess, A. W., & Holmstrom, L. (1977). Rape: Power, anger, and sexuality. *American Journal of Psychiatry, 134,* 1239–1243.

Grove, W. M., & Barden, R. C. (1999). Protecting the integrity of the legal system: The admissibility of testimony from mental health experts under *Daubert/Kumho* analyses. *Psychology, Public Policy, and Law, 5,* 224–242.

Grove, W. M., Barden, R. C., Garb, H. N., & Lilienfeld, S. O. (2002). Failure of Rorschach-Comprehensive-System-based testimony to be admissible under the *Daubert-Joiner-Kumho* standard. *Psychology, Public Policy, and Law, 8,* 216–234.

Gudjonsson, G. H. (1988). A new scale of interrogative suggestibility. *Personality and Individual Differences, 5,* 303–314.

Gudjonsson, G. H. (1992). *The psychology of interrogations, confessions and testimony.* London: Wiley.

Guerra, N. G., Tolan, P. H., & Hammond, W. R. (1994). Prevention and treatment of adolescent violence. In L. D. Eron, J. H. Gentry, & P. Schlegel (Eds.), *Reason to hope: A psychosocial perspective on violence and youth.* Washington, DC: American Psychological Association.

Gunnoe, M. L., & Braver, S. L. (2001). The effects of joint legal custody on mothers, fathers, and children: Controlling for factors that predispose a sole maternal versus joint legal award. *Law and Human Behavior, 25,* 25–43.

Guy, L. S., & Edens, J. F. (2003). Juror decision-making in a mock sexually violent predator trial: Gender differences in the impact of divergent types of expert testimony. *Behavioral Sciences and the Law, 21,* 215–237.

Haaga, D. A. F., & Davidson, G. C. (1993). An appraisal of rational-emotive therapy. *Journal of Consulting and Clinical Psychology, 61,* 215–220.

Haapala, D. A., & Kinney, J. M. (1988). Avoiding out-of-home placement of high-risk status offenders through the use of intensive home-based family preservation services. *Criminal Justice and Behavior, 15,* 334–348.

Haber, R. N., & Haber, L. (2000). Experiencing, remembering, and reporting events. *Psychology, Public Policy, and Law, 6,* 1057–1097.

Hall, C. I. (1997). Cultural malpractice: The growing obsolescence of psychology with the changing U.S. population. *American Psychologist, 52,* 642–651.

Hall, N. G. C. (1995). Sexual offender recidivism revisited: A meta-analysis of recent treatment studies. *Journal of Consulting and Clinical Psychology, 63,* 802–809.

Halligan, S. L., Michael, T., Clark, D. M., & Ehlers, A. (2003). Posttraumatic stress disorder following assault: The role of cognitive processing, trauma memory, and appraisals. *Journal of Consulting and Clinical Psychology, 71,* 410–431.

Hamel, M., Gallagher, S., & Soares, C. (2001). The Rorschach: Here we go again. *Journal of Forensic Psychology Practice, 1,* 79–87.

Hanson, R. K. (2001). *Age and sexual recidivism: A comparison of rapists and child molesters.* Ottawa, ON: Department of Solicitor General Canada.

Hanson, R. K., & Bussière, M. T. (1998). Predicting relapse: A meta-analysis of sexual offender recidivism studies. *Journal of Consulting and Clinical Psychology, 66,* 348–362.

Hanson, R. K., & Harris, A. J. R. (1998). *Dynamic predictors of sexual recidivism—1998.* Ottawa, Canada: Public Works and Government Services, Department of the Solicitor General.

Hanson, R. K., & Harris, A. J. R. (2000). Where should we intervene? Dynamic predictors of sexual offense recidivism. *Criminal Justice and Behavior, 27,* 6–35.

Hanson, R. K., & Thornton, D. (2000). Improving risk assessments for sex offenders: A comparison of three actuarial scales. *Law and Human Behavior, 24,* 119–136.

Hare, R. D. (1980). A research scale for the assessment of psychopathy in criminal populations. *Personality and Individual Differences, 1,* 111–119.

Hare, R. D. (1991). *The Hare Psychopathy Checklist—Revised.* Toronto: Multi-Health Systems.

Hare, R. D. (1996). Psychopathy: A clinical construct whose time has come. *Criminal Justice and Behavior, 23,* 25–54.

Hare, R. D. (1998). Psychopathy, affect, and behavior. In D. Cooke, A. Forth, & R. Hare (Eds.), *Psychopathy: Theory, research, and implications for society.* Dordecht, The Netherlands: Kluwer.

Hare, R. D., Clark, D., Grann, M., & Thornton, D. (2000). Psychopathy and the predictive validity of the PCL-R: An international perspective. *Behavioral Sciences and the Law, 18,* 623–645.

Hare, R. D., Forth, A. E., & Strachan, K. E. (1992). Psychopathy and crime across the life span. In R. D. Peters, R. J. McMahon, & V. L. Quinsey (Eds.), *Aggression and violence throughout the life span.* Newbury Park, CA: Sage.

Hare, R. D., Hart, S. D., & Harpur, T. J. (1991). Psychopathy and the *DSM-IV* criteria for antisocial personality disorder. *Journal of Abnormal Psychology, 100,* 391–398.

Harley, K., & Reese, E. (1999). Origins of autobiographical memory. *Developmental Psychology, 35,* 1338–1348.

Harpur, T. J., Hakstian, A., & Hare, R. D. (1988). Factor structure of the Psychopathy Checklist. *Journal of Consulting and Clinical Psychology, 56,* 741–747.

Harris, G. T., Rice, M. E., & Quinsey, V. L. (1993). Violent recidivism of mentally disordered offenders: The development of a statistical prediction instrument. *Criminal Justice and Behavior, 20,* 315–325.

Harris, G. T., Rice, M. E., & Quinsey, V. L. (1994). Psychopathy as a taxon: Evidence that psychopaths are a discrete class. *Journal of Consulting and Clinical Psychology, 62,* 387–397.

Hart, S. D., Cox, D. N., & Hare, R. D. (1995). *The Hare Psychopathy Checklist: Screening Version.* Toronto, Ontario: Multi-Health Systems.

Hart, S. D., & Dempster, R. J. (1997). Impulsivity and psychopathy. In C. D. Webster & M. A. Jackson (Eds.), *Impulsivity: Theory, assessment, and treatment.* New York: Guilford.

Hart, S. D., Hare, R. D., & Forth, A. E. (1993). Psychopathy as a risk marker for violence: Development and validation of a screening version of the Revised Psychopathy Checklist. In J. Monahan & H. Steadman (Eds.), *Violence and mental disorder: Developments in risk assessment.* Chicago: University of Chicago Press.

Hart, S. D., Watt, K. A., & Vincent, G. M. (2002). Commentary on Seagrave and Grisso: Impressions of the state of the art. *Law and Human Behavior, 26,* 241–245.

Hasselbrack, A. M. (2001). Opting in to mental health courts (Sample issue). *Corrections Compendium,* pp. 4–5.

Hatcher, C., Mohandie, K., Turner, J., & Gelles, M. G. (1998). The role of the psychologist in crisis/hostage negotiations. *Behavioral Sciences and the Law, 16,* 455–472.

Haugaard, J. J., & Reppucci, N. D. (1988). *The sexual abuse of children.* San Francisco: Jossey-Bass.

Hawkins, D. F. (2003). Editor's introduction. In D. F. Hawkins (Ed.), *Violent crime: Assessing race and ethnic differences* Cambridge, UK: Cambridge University Press.

Hays-Thomas, R. L. (2000). The silent conversation: Talking about the master's degree. *Professional Psychology: Research and Practice, 31,* 339–345.

Hazelwood, R., & Burgess, A. (1987). *Practical aspects of rape investigation: A multidisciplinary approach.* New York: Elsevier.

Hazelwood, R., & Burgess, A. (1995). *Practical rape investigation: A multidisciplinary approach* (2nd ed.). Boca Raton, FL: CRC Press.

Hecker, T., & Steinberg, L. (2002). Psychological evaluation at juvenile court disposition. *Professional Psychology: Research and Practice, 33,* 300–306.

Heilbrun, K. (1987). The assessment of competency for execution: An overview. *Behavioral Sciences & the Law, 5,* 383–396.

Heilbrun, K. (2001). *Principles of forensic mental health assessment.* New York: Kluwer Academic/Plenum.

Heilbrun, K., & Griffin, P. (1999). Forensic treatment: A review of programs and research. In R. Roesch, S. D. Hart, & J. R. P. Ogloff (Eds.), *Psychology and law: The state of the discipline.* New York: Kluwer Academic/Plenum.

Heilbrun, K., Marczyk, G. R., & DeMatteo, D. (2002). *Forensic mental health assessment: A casebook.* New York: Oxford University Press.

Heilbrun, K., O'Neill, M. L., Strohman, L. K., Bowman, Q., & Philipson, J. (2000). Expert approaches to communicating violence risk. *Law and Human Behavior, 24,* 137–148.

Heilbrun, K., Philipson, J., Berman, L., & Warren, J. (1999). Risk communication: Clinicians' reported approaches and perceived values. *Journal of the American Academy of Psychiatry and the Law, 27,* 397–406.

Hellkamp, D. T., & Lewis, J. E. (1995). The consulting psychologist as an expert witness in sexual harassment and retaliation cases. *Consulting Psychology Journal: Practice and Research, 47,* 150–159.

Henderson, N. D. (1979). Criterion-related validity of personality and aptitude scales. In C. D. Spielberger (Ed.), *Police selection and evaluation: Issues and techniques.* Washington, DC: Hemisphere.

Henggeler, S. W. (1996). Treatment of violent juvenile offenders—we have the knowledge. *Journal of Family Psychology, 10,* 137–141.

Henggeler, S. W. (2001). Multisystemic therapy. *Residential Treatment for Children and Youth, 18,* 75–85.

Henggeler, S. W., & Borduin, C. M. (1990). *Family therapy and beyond: A multisystemic approach to treating the behavior problems of children and adolescents.* Pacific Grove, CA: Brooks/Cole.

Henker, B., & Whalen, C. K. (1989). Hyperactivity and attention deficits. *American Psychologist, 44,* 216–244.

Herek, G. M., Gillis, J. R., & Cogan, J. C. (1999). Psychological sequelae of hate-crime victimization among lesbian, gay, and bisexual adults. *Journal of Consulting and Clinical Psychology, 67,* 945–951.

Herndon, J. S. (2001). Law enforcement suicide: Psychological autopsies and psychometric traces. In D. C. Sheehan & J. I. Warren (Eds.), *Suicide and law enforcement.* Washington, DC: FBI Academy.

Hess, A. K. (1999). Serving as an expert witness. In A. K. Hess & I. B. Weiner (Eds.), *Handbook of forensic psychology* (2nd ed.). New York: John Wiley.

Hickey, E. W. (1997). *Serial murderers and their victims.* Belmont, CA: Wadsworth.

Hiday, V. A. (2003). Outpatient commitment: The state of empirical research on its outcomes. *Psychology, Public Policy, and Law, 9,* 8–32.

Hilgard, E. R. (1986). *Divided consciousness: Multiple controls in human thought and action* (Expanded ed.). New York: John Wiley.

Hill, J. (2000). The effects of sexual orientation in the courtroom: A double standard. *Journal of Homosexuality, 39,* 93–111.

Hill, M. S., & Fischer, A. R. (2001). Does entitlement mediate the link between masculinity and rape-related variables? *Journal of Counseling Psychology, 48,* 39–50.

Hillbrand, M. (2001). Homicide-suicide and other forms of co-occurring aggression against self and against others. *Professional Psychology: Research and Practice, 32,* 626–635.

Hirschi, T., & Hindelang, M. J. (1977). Intelligence and delinquency. *American Sociological Review, 42,* 571–587.

Hoge, S. K., Bonnie, R. G., Poythress, N., Monahan, J., Eisenberg, M., & Feucht-Haviar, T. (1997). The MacArthur Adjudicative Competence Study: Development and validation of a research instrument. *Law and Human Behavior, 21,* 141–179.

Holmes, R. M., & DeBurger, J. (1985). Profiles in terror: The serial murderer. *Federal Probation, 39,* 29–34.

Holmes, R. M., & DeBurger, J. (1988). *Serial murder.* Newbury Park, CA: Sage.

Holmes, R. M., & Holmes, S. T. (1998). *Serial murder* (2nd ed.). Thousand Oaks, CA: Sage.

Holmes, S. T., Hickey, E., & Holmes, R. M. (1991). Female serial murderesses: Constructing differentiating typologies. *Contemporary Journal of Criminal Justice, 7,* 245–256.

Holmes, S. T., & Holmes, R. M. (2002). *Sex crimes: Patterns and behavior* (2nd ed.). Thousand Oaks, CA: Sage.

Holtzworth-Munroe, A., & Stuart, G. L. (1994). Typologies of male batterers: Three subtypes and the differences among them. *Psychological Bulletin, 116,* 476–497.

Honts, C. R. (1987). Interpreting research on polygraph countermeasures. *Journal of Police Science and Administration, 15,* 204–209.

Honts, C. R., & Amato, S. L. (2002). Countermeasures. In M. Kleiner (Ed.), *Handbook of polygraph testing.* San Diego: Academic Press.

Honts, C. R., Devitt, M. K., Winbush, M., & Kircher, J. C. (1996). Mental and physical countermeasures reduce the accuracy of the concealed knowledge test. *Psychophysiology, 33,* 84–92.

Honts, C. R., Hodes, R. L., & Raskin, D. C. (1985). Effects of physical countermeasures on the physiological detection of deception. *Journal of Applied Psychology, 70,* 177–187.

Honts, C. R., & Perry, M. V. (1992). Polygraph admissability: Changes and challenges. *Law and Human Behavior, 16,* 357–379.

Honts, C. R., Raskin, D. C., & Kircher, J. C. (1987). Effects of physical countermeasures and their electromyographic detection during polygraph tests for deception. *Journal of Psychophysiology, 1,* 241–247.

Horowitz, M., Wilner, N., & Alvarez, W. (1979). Impact of Event Scale: A measure of subjective stress. *Psychometric Medicine, 41,* 209–218.

Horvath, F. S. (1977). The effect of selected variables on interpretation of polygraph records. *Journal of Applied Psychology, 62,* 127–136.

Horvath, L. S., Logan, T. K., & Walker, R. (2002). Child custody cases: A content analysis of evaluations in practice. *Professional Psychology: Research and Practice, 33,* 557–565.

Howarth, J., & Lawson, B. (Eds.). (1995). *Trust betrayed: Munchausen syndrome by proxy, inter-agency child protection and partnership with families.* London: National Children's Bureau Enterprises.

Howe, M. L., & Courage, M. L. (1997). The emergence and early development of autobiographical memory. *Psychological Review, 104,* 499–523.

Howell, J. C. (1998). A new approach to juvenile crime. *Corrections Compendium, 23,* 1–4, 24–25.

Hubbard, D. (1972, November 13). Title unknown. *Time,* 51.

Huckabee, R. G. (1992). Stress in corrections: An overview of the issues. *Journal of Criminal Justice, 20,* 479–486.

Huesmann, L. R., Moise-Titus, J., Podolski, C. L., & Eron, L. D. (2003). Longitudinal relations between children's exposure to TV violence and their aggressive and violent behavior in young adulthood: 1977–1992. *Developmental Psychology, 39,* 201–221.

Hunter, J. A., & Becker, J. V. (1999). Motivators of adolescent sex offenders and treatment perspectives. In J. Shaw (Eds.), *Sexual aggression.* Washington, DC: American Psychiatric Press.

Iacono, W. G., & Lykken, D. T. (1997). The validity of the lie detector: Two surveys of scientific opinion. *Journal of Applied Psychology, 82,* 426–433.

Iacono, W. G., & Patrick, C. J. (1999). Polygraph ("lie detector") testing: The state of the art. In A. K. Hess & I. B. Weiner (Eds.), *The handbook of forensic psychology* (2nd ed.). New York: John Wiley.

International Association of Chiefs of Police (IACP). (2002). *Fitness for duty evaluation guidelines.* Alexandria, VA: Author.

Inwald, R. E. (1992). *Inwald Personality Inventory technical manual* (Rev. ed.). Kew Gardens, NY: Hilson Research.

Inwald, R., Knatz, H., & Shusman, E. (1982). *The Inwald Personality Inventory manual.* New York: Hilton Research.

Iowa Injury Prevention Research Center. (2002, February). *Workplace violence: A report to the nation.* Iowa City: University of Iowa Press.

Jackson, M. S., & Springer, D. W. (1997). Social work practice with African-American juvenile gangs: Professional challenge. In C. A. McNeece & A. R. Roberts (Eds.), *Policy and practice in the justice system.* Chicago: Nelson-Hall.

Jackson, T. L., Petretic-Jackson, P. A., & Witte, T. H. (2002). Mental health assessment tools and techniques for working with battered women. In A. R. Roberts (Ed.), *Handbook of domestic violence intervention strategies.* New York: Oxford University Press.

Janus, E. S. (2000). Sexual predator commitment laws: Lessons for law and the behavioral sciences. *Behavioral Sciences and the Law, 18,* 5–21.

Janus, E. S., & Walbek, N. H. (2000). Sex offender commitments in Minnesota: A descriptive study of second generation commitments. *Behavioral Sciences and the Law, 18,* 343–374.

Jenkins, P. (1988). Serial murder in England, 1940–1985. *Journal of Criminal Justice, 16,* 1–15.

Jenkins, P. (1993). Chance or choice: The selection of serial murder victims. In A. V. Wilson (Ed.), *Homicide: The victim/offender connection.* Cincinnati, OH: Anderson.

Johnson, C. C., & Chanhatasilpa, C. (2003). The race/ethnicity and poverty nexus of violent crime: Reconciling differences in Chicago's community area homicide rates. In D. F. Hawkins (Ed.), *Violent crime: Assessing race and ethnic differences.* Cambridge, UK: Cambridge University Press.

Johnson, L. B. (1991). Job strain among police officers: Gender comparisons. *Police Studies, 14,* 12–16.

Johnson, R. (1996). *Hard time: Understanding and reforming the prison* (2nd ed.). Belmont, CA: Wadsworth.

Johnston, J. R. (1995). Research update: Children's adjustment in sole custody compared to joint custody families and principles for custody decision making. *Family and Conciliation Courts Review, 33,* 415–425.

Johnston, J. R., & Girdner, L. K. (2001, January). Family abductors: Descriptive profiles and prevention interventions. *Juvenile Justice Bulletin,* pp. 3–9. Washington, DC: Office of Juvenile Justice and Delinquency.

Jouriles, E. N., McDonald, R., Norwood, W. D., Ware, H. S., Spiller, L. C., & Swank, P. R. (1998). Knives, guns, and interparent violence: Relations with child behavior problems. *Journal of Family Psychology, 12,* 178–194.

Juvenile arrests 1999. Washington, D.C: U.S. Department of Justice.

Kalmbach, K. C., & Lyons, P. M. (2003). Ethical and legal standards for research in prisons. *Behavioral Sciences and the Law, 21,* 671–686.

Kaplan, M. S., & Green, A. (1995). Incarcerated female sexual offenders: A comparison of sexual histories with eleven female nonsexual offenders. *Sexual Abuse: A Journal of Research and Treatment, 7,* 287–300.

Kapp, M. B., & Mossman, D. (1996). Measuring decisional capacity: Cautions on the construction of a "Capacimeter." *Psychology, Public Policy, and Law, 2,* 45–95.

Karmen, A. (2001). *Crime victims: An introduction to victimology* (4th ed.). Belmont, CA: Wadsworth.

Karon, B. P., & Widener, A. J. (1999). Repressed memories: Just the facts. *Professional Psychology: Research and Practice, 30,* 625–626.

Kassin, S. M. (1997). The psychology of confession evidence. *American Psychologist, 52,* 221–233.

Kassin, S. M., Goldstein, C. G., & Savitsky, K. (2003). Behavior confirmation in the interrogation room: On the dangers of presuming guilt. *Law and Human Behavior, 27,* 187–203.

Kassin, S. M., & Kiechel, K. L. (1996). The social psychology of false confessions: Compliance, internalization, and confabulation. *Psychological Science, 7,* 125–128.

Kassin, S. M., & Wrightsman, L. S. (1985). Confession evidence. In S. M. Kassin & L. S. Wrightsman (Eds.), *The psychology of evidence and trial procedure.* Beverly Hills, CA: Sage.

Kaufer, S., & Mattman, J. W. (2002). *Workplace violence: An employer's guide.* Palm Springs, CA: Workplace Violence Research Institute.

Kebbell, M. R., & Wagstaff, G. G. (1998). Hypnotic interviewing: The best way to interview eyewitnesses. *Behavioral Sciences and the Law, 16,* 115–129.

Keeler, E. (1984). *Lie detector man.* Boston: Telshare.

Keilin, W. G., & Bloom, L. J. (1986). Child custody evaluation practices: A survey of experienced professionals. *Professional Psychology: Research and Practice, 17,* 338–346.

Kelly, D. H. (1980). The educational experience and evolving delinquent careers: A neglected institutional link. In D. Schichor & D. H. Kelly (Eds.), *Critical issues in juvenile delinquency.* Lexington, MA: Lexington Books.

Kelly, F., & Baer, D. (1978). *Outward Bound: An alternative to institutionalization for adolescent delinquent boys.* New York: Fandel.

Kelman, H. (1958). Compliance, identification, and internalization. *Journal of Conflict Resolution, 2,* 51–60.

Kendall, P. C., & Hammen, C. (1995). *Abnormal psychology.* Boston: Houghton Mifflin.

Kenrick, D. T., & Springfield, D. O. (1980). Personality traits and the eye of the beholder: Crossing some traditional philosophical boundaries in the search for consistency in all the people. *Psychological Review, 87,* 88–104.

Kessler, R. C., Sonnega, A., Bromet, E., Hughes, M., & Nelson, C. B. (1995). Posttraumatic stress disorder in the National Comorbidity Survey. *Archives of General Psychiatry, 52,* 1048–1060.

Kihlstrom, J. F. (2001). Martin T. Orne (1927–2000). *American Psychologist, 56,* 754–755.

Kilmann, P. R., Sabalis, R. F., Gearing, M. L., Bukstel, L. H., & Scovern, A. W. (1982). The treatment of sexual paraphilias: A review of the outcome research. *Journal of Sex Research, 18,* 193–252.

Kilpatrick, D. G., Best, C. L., Saunders, B. E., & Veronen, L. J. (1988). Rape in marriage and in dating relationships: How bad is it for mental health? In R. A. Prentky & V. L. Quinsey (Eds.), *Human sexual aggression: Current perspectives.* New York: New York Academy of Sciences.

Kilpatrick, D. G., Best, C. L., Veronen, L. J., Amick, A. E., Villepontreaux, L. A. & Ruff, G. A. (1985). Mental health correlates of criminal victimization: A random community survey. *Journal of Consulting and Clinical Psychology, 53,* 866–873.

Kilpatrick, D. G., Edmunds, C., & Seymour, A. (1992). *Rape in America: A report to the nation.* Arlington, VA: National Center for Victims of Crime.

Kilpatrick, D. G., & Saunders, B. E. (1997, November). *Prevalence and consequences of child victimization: Results from the National Survey of Adolescents: Final report.* Washington, DC: U.S. Department of Justice, Office of Justice Programs, National Institute of Justice.

Kilpatrick, D. G., Saunders, B. E., Veronen, L. J., Best, C. L., & Von, J. M. (1987). Criminal victimization: Lifetime prevalence, reporting to police, and psychological impact. *Crime and Delinquency, 33,* 479–489.

Kilpatrick, D. G., Seymour, A., & Boyle, J. (1991). *America speaks out: Citizens' attitudes about victims' rights and violence.* Arlington, VA: National Center for Victims of Crime.

Kilpatrick, D. G., Whalley, A., & Edmunds, C. (2002). Sexual assault. In A. Seymour, M. Murray, J. Sigmon, M. Hook, C. Edwards, M. Gaboury, & G. Coleman (Eds.), *National Victim Assistance Academy textbook.* Washington, DC: U.S. Department of Justice, Office for Victims of Crime.

King, W. R., Holmes, S. T., Henderson, M. L., & Latessa, E. J. (2001). The community corrections partnership: Examining the long-term effects of youth participation in an Afrocentric diversion program. *Crime & Delinquency, 47,* 558–572.

Kinports, K. (2002). Sex offenses. In K. L. Hall (Ed.), *The Oxford companion to American law.* New York: Oxford University Press.

Kircher, J. C., & Raskin, D. C. (2002). Computer methods for the psychophysiological detection of deception. In M. Kleiner (Ed.), *Handbook of polygraph testing.* San Diego: Academic Press.

Kirk, T., & Bersoff, D. N. (1996). How many procedural safeguards does it take to get a psychiatrist to leave the lightbulb unchanged? A due process analysis of the MacArthur Treatment Competence Study. *Psychology, Public Policy, and Law, 2,* 45–72.

Kirkland, K., & Kirkland, K. (2001). Frequency of child custody evaluation complaints and related disciplinary action: A survey of the association of state and provincial psychology boards. *Professional Psychology: Research and Practice, 32,* 171–174.

Kliewer, W., Lepore, S. J., Oskin, D., & Johnson, P. D. (1998). The role of social and cognitive processes in children's adjustment to community violence. *Journal of Consulting and Clinical Psychology, 66,* 199–209.

Kluckhohn, C., & Murray, H. A. (1953). Personality formation: The determinants. In C. Kluckhohn, H. Murray, & D. Schneider (Eds.), *Personality in nature, society, and culture.* New York: Knopf.

Knapp, S., & VandeCreek, L. (2000). Recovered memories of child abuse: Is there an underlying professional consensus? *Professional Psychology: Research and Practice, 31,* 365–371.

Knight, R. A. (1989). An assessment of the concurrent validity of a child molester typology. *Journal of Interpersonal Violence, 4,* 131–150.

Knight, R. A., Carter, D. L., & Prentky, R. A. (1989). A system for the classification of child molesters: Reliability and application. *Journal of Interpersonal Violence, 4,* 3–23.

Knight, R. A., & Cerce, D. D. (1999). Validation and revision of the Multdimensional Assessment of Sex and Aggression. *Psychologica Belgica, 39,* 135–161.

Knight, R. A., & Prentky, R. A. (1987). The developmental antecedents and adult adaptations of rapist subtypes. *Criminal Justice and Behavior, 14,* 403–426.

Knight, R. A., & Prentky, R. A. (1990). Classifying sexual offenders: The development and corroboration of taxonomic models. In W. L. Marshall, D. R. Laws, & H. E. Barbaree (Eds.), *The handbook of sexual assault: Issues, theories, and treatment of the offender.* New York: Plenum.

Knight, R. A., & Prentky, R. A. (1993). Exploring characteristics for classifying juvenile offenders. In H. E. Barbaree, W. L. Marshall, & S. M. Hudson (Eds.), *The juvenile sex offender.* New York: Guilford.

Knight, R. A., Prentky, R. A., & Cerce, D. D. (1994). The development, reliability, and validity of the multidimensional assessment of sex and aggression. *Criminal Justice and Behavior, 21,* 72–94.

Knight, R. A., Rosenberg, R., & Schneider, B. A. (1985). Classification of sexual offenders: Perspectives, methods, and validation. In A. W. Burgess (Ed.), *Rape and sexual assault.* New York: Garland.

Knight, R. A., Warren, J. I., Reboussin, R., & Soley, B. J. (1998). Predicting rapist type from crime-scene variables. *Criminal Justice and Behavior, 25,* 46–80.

Kocsis, R. N., Cooksey, R. W., & Irwin, H. J. (2002). Psychological profiling of offender characteristics from crime behaviors in serial rape offenses. *International Journal of Offender Therapy and Comparative Criminology, 46,* 144–169.

Koehn, C. E., & Fisher, R. P. (1997). Constructing facial composites with the Mac-A-Mug Pro system. *Psychology, Crime & Law, 3,* 209–218.

Koocher, G. P., Goodman, G. S., White, C. S., Friedrich, W. N., Sivan, A. B., & Reynolds, C. R. (1995). Psychological science and the use of anatomically detailed dolls in child-sexual assessments. *Psychological Bulletin, 118,* 199–222.

Koss, M. P., & Dinero, T. E. (1988). Predictors of sexual aggression among a national sample of male college students. In R. A. Prentky & V. L. Quinsey (Eds.), *Human sexual aggression: Current perspectives.* New York: New York Academy of Sciences.

Kosson, D. S., Cyterski, T. D., Steuerwald, B. L., Neuman, C. S., & Walker-Matthes, S. (2002). The reliability and validity of the Psychopathy Checklist Youth Version (PCL:YV) in nonincarcerated adolescent males. *Psychological Assessment, 14,* 97–109.

Kosson, D. S., Smith, S. S., & Newman, J. P. (1990). Evaluating the construct validity of psychopathy in Black and White male inmates: Three preliminary studies. *Journal of Abnormal Psychology, 99,* 250–259.

Kovera, M. B., & Cass, S. A. (2002). Compelled mental health examinations, liability decisions, and damage awards in sexual harassment cases: Issues for jury research. *Psychology, Public Policy, and Law, 8,* 96–114.

Kovera, M. B., & McAuliff, B. D. (2000). The effects of peer review and evidence quality on judge evaluations of psychological science: Are judges effective gatekeepers? *Journal of Applied Psychology, 85,* 574–586.

Kovera, M. B., Penrod, S. D., Pappas, C., & Thill, D. L. (1997). Identification of computer-generated facial composites. *Journal of Applied Psychology, 82,* 235–246.

Kovera, M. B., Russano, M. B., & McAuliff, B. D. (2002). Assessment of the commonsense psychology underlying *Daubert:* Legal decision makers' abilities to evaluate expert evidence in hostile work environment cases. *Psychology, Public Policy, and Law, 8,* 180–200.

Kozu, J. (1999). Domestic violence in Japan. *American Psychologist, 54,* 50–54.

Krafka, C., Dunn, M. A., Johnson, M. T., Cecil, J. S., & Miletich, D. (2002). Judge and attorney experiences, practices, and concerns regarding expert testimony in federal civil trials. *Psychology, Public Policy, and Law, 8,* 309–332.

Krapohl, D. J. (2002). The polygraph in personnel selection. In M. Kleiner (Ed.), *Handbook of polygraph testing.* San Diego: Academic Press.

Kratcoski, P. C. (1994). *Correctional counseling and treatment* (3rd ed.). Prospect Heights, IL: Waveland.

Krauss, D. A., & Sales, B. D. (2000). Legal standards, expertise, and experts in the resolution of contested child custody cases. *Psychology, Public Policy, and Law, 6,* 843–879.

Krauss, D. A., & Sales, B. D. (2001). The effects of clinical and scientific expert testimony on juror decision making in capital sentencing. *Psychology, Public Police, and Law, 7,* 267–310.

Krisberg, B. (1995). The legacy of juvenile corrections. *Corrections Today, 57,* 122–126.

Kropp, P. R., & Hart, S. D. (2000). The Spousal Assault Risk Assessment (SARA) guide: Reliability and validity in adult male offenders. *Law and Human Behavior, 24,* 101–118.

Kropp, P. R., Hart, S. D., Webster, C. E., & Eaves, D. (1998). *Spousal Assault Risk Assessment: User's guide.* Toronto, ON: Multi-Health Systems.

Kubany, E. S., Haynes, S. N., Leisen, M. B., Ownes, J. A., Kaplan, A. S., Watson, S. B., et al. (2000). Development and preliminary validation of a brief broad-spectrum measure of trauma exposure: The Traumatic Life Events Questionnaire. *Psychological Assessment, 12,* 200–224.

Kubany, E. S., Leisen, M. B., Kaplan, A. S., & Kelly, M. P. (2000). Validation of a brief measure of posttraumatic stress disorder: The Distressing Event Questionnaire (DEQ). *Psychological Assessment, 12,* 197–209.

Kurt, J. L. (1995). Stalking as a variant of domestic violence. *Bulletin of the American Academy of Psychiatry and Law, 23,* 219–230.

Laboratory of Community Psychology. (1974). *Competency to stand trial and mental illness* (DHEW Pub. No. ADM 74–103). Rockville, MD: U.S. Department of Health, Education, & Welfare.

La Fon, D. S. (2002). The psychological autopsy. In B. E. Turvey (Ed.), *Criminal profiling: An introduction to behavioral evidence analysis.* San Diego: Academic Press.

La Fond, J. Q. (2000). The future of involuntary civil commitment in the U.S.A. after *Kansas v. Hendricks. Behavioral Sciences and the Law, 18,* 153–167.

La Fond, J. Q. (2002). Criminal law principles. In K. L. Hall (Ed.), *The Oxford companion to American law .* New York: Oxford University Press.

La Fond, J. Q. (2003). Outpatient commitment's next frontier: Sexual predators. *Psychology, Public Policy, and Law, 9,* 159–182.

LaFortune, K. A., & Carpenter, B. N. (1998). Custody evaluations: A survey of mental health professionals. *Behavioral Sciences & the Law, 16,* 207–224.

Lahey, B. B., Loeber, R., Hart, E. L., Frick, P. J., Applegate, B., Zhang, Q., et al. (1995). Four-year longitudinal study of conduct disorder in boys: Patterns and predictors of persistence. *Journal of Abnormal Psychology, 104,* 83–93.

Laird, R. D., Jordan, K., Dodge, K. A., Pettit, G. S., & Bates, J. E. (2001). Peer rejection in childhood, involvement with antisocial peers in early adolescence, and the development of externalizing problems. *Development and Psychopathology, 13,* 337–354.

Langan, P. A., & Levin, D. J. (2002, June). *Recidivism of prisoners released in 1994.* Washington, DC: U.S. Department of Justice, Bureau of Justice Statistics.

Langevin, R. (1983). *Sexual strands.* Hillsdale, NJ: Lawrence Erlbaum.

Lanyon, R. I. (1986). Theory and treatment in child molestation. *Journal of Consulting and Clinical Psychology, 54,* 176–182.

Laws, D. R. (1995). Central elements in relapse prevention procedures with sex offenders. *Psychology, Crime, and Law, 2,* 41–53.

LeBlanc, M. M., & Kelloway, K. E. (2002). Predictors and outcomes of workplace violence and aggression. *Journal of Applied Psychology, 87,* 444–453.

LeCroy, C. W., Stevenson, P., & MacNeil, G. (2001). Systems considerations in treating juvenile offenders with mental disorders. In J. B. Ashford, B. D. Sales, & W. H. Reid (Eds.), *Treating adult and juvenile offenders with special needs.* Washington, DC: American Psychological Association.

Lee, M. (2002). Asian battered women: Assessment and treatment. In A. R. Roberts (Ed.), *Handbook of domestic violence: Intervention strategies.* New York: Oxford University Press.

Lefkowitz, J. (1975). Psychological attributes of policemen: A review of research and opinion. *Journal of Social Issues, 31,* 3–26.

Leiber, M. J. (2002). Disproportionate minority confinement (DMC) of youth: An analysis of state and federal efforts to address the issue. *Crime & Delinquency, 48,* 3–45.

Leitenberg, H., & Henning, K. (1995). Sexual fantasy. *Psychological Bulletin, 117,* 469–496.

Leo, R. A. (1996). Miranda's revenge: Police interrogation as a confidence game. *Law & Society Review, 30,* 259–288.

Leo, R. A., & Ofshe, R. J. (1998). The consequences of false confessions: Deprivations of liberty and miscarriages of justice in the age of psychological interrogation. *Journal of Criminal Law & Criminology, 88,* 429–440.

Lester, D., Braswell, M., & Van Voorhis, P. (1992). *Correctional counseling* (2nd ed.). Cincinnati, OH: Anderson.

Levesque, R. J. R. (2001). *Culture and family violence: Fostering change through human rights law.* Washington, DC: American Psychological Association.

Lewinsohn, P. M., & Rosenbaum, M. (1987). Recall of parental behavior by acute depressives, remitted depressives, and nondepressives. *Journal of Personality and Social Psychology, 52,* 611–619.

Lewis, J. A., Dana, R. Q., & Blevins, G. A. (1994). *Substance abuse counseling: An individualized approach* (2nd ed.). Pacific Grove, CA: Brooks/Cole.

Lidz, C. W., Mulvey, E. P., & Gardner, W. (1993). The accuracy of prediction of violence to others. *Journal of the American Medical Association, 269,* 1007–1011.

Lilienfeld, S. O., & Loftus, E. F. (1998). Repressed memories and World War II: Some cautionary notes. *Professional Psychology: Research and Practice, 29,* 471–475.

Lipton, D. N., McDonel, E. C., & McFall, R. M. (1987). Heterosocial perception in rapists. *Journal of Consulting and Clinical Psychology, 55,* 17–21.

Litwack, T. R. (2003). The competency of criminal defendants to refuse, for delusional reasons, a viable insanity defense recommended by counsel. *Behavioral Sciences and the Law, 21,* 135–156.

Loeber, R. (1990). Development and risk factors of juvenile antisocial behavior and delinquency. *Clinical Psychological Review, 10,* 1–41.

Loeber, R., & Dishion, T. (1983). Early prediction of male delinquency: A review. *Psychological Bulletin, 94,* 68–99.

Loftus, E. F. (1979). *Eyewitness testimony.* Cambridge, MA: Harvard University Press.

Lonsway, K. A., & Fitzgerald, L. F. (1994). Rape myths: In review. *Psychology of Women Quarterly, 18,* 133–164.

Lonsway, K. A., & Fitzgerald, L. F. (1995). Attitudinal antecedents of rape myth acceptance: A theoretical and empirical reexamination. *Journal of Personality and Social Psychology, 68,* 704–711.

Lord, J. (1997). *Death notification: Breaking the bad news with concern for the professional and compassion for the survivor.* Washington, DC: U.S. Department of Justice, Office for Victims of Crime.

Lord, J. (2001). Death notification training of trainers seminars. *OVC Bulletin.* Washington, DC: U.S. Department of Justice, Office for Victims of Crime.

Lunt, I., & Poortinga, Y. H. (1996). Internationalizing psychology. *American Psychologist, 51,* 504–508.

Lykken, D. T. (1981). *A tremor in the blood.* New York: McGraw-Hill.

Lynam, D. (1997). Pursuing the psychopath: Capturing the fledgling psychopath in a nomological net. *Journal of Abnormal Psychology, 106,* 425–438.

Lynam, D., Moffitt, T., & Stouthamer-Loeber, M. (1993). Explaining the relation between IQ and delinquency: Class, race, test motivation, school failure, or self-control? *Journal of Abnormal Psychology, 102,* 187–196.

Maccoby, E., Buchanan, C., Mnookin, R., & Dornsbusch, S. (1993). Postdivorce roles of mother and father in the lives of their children. *Journal of Family Psychology, 1,* 24–38.

MacKain, S. J., Tedeschi, R. G., Durham, T. W., & Goldman, V. J. (2002). So what are master's-level psychology practitioners doing? Surveys of employers and recent graduates in North Carolina. *Professional Psychology: Research and Practice, 33,* 408–412.

MacKenzie, D. L. (2000). Evidence-based corrections: Identifying what works. *Crime & Delinquency, 46,* 457–471.

MacKenzie, D. L., Robinson, J. W., & Campbell, C. S. (1989). Long-term incarceration of female offenders: Prison adjustment and coping. *Criminal Justice and Behavior, 16,* 223–238.

MacLin, O. H., MacLin, M. K., & Malpass, R. S. (2001). Race, arousal, attention, exposure, and delay: An examination of factors moderating face recognition. *Psychology, Public Policy, and Law, 7,* 134–152.

MacLin, O. H., & Malpass, R. S. (2001). Racial categorization of faces: The ambiguous race face effect. *Psychology, Public Policy, and Law, 7,* 98–118.

Madigan, L., & Gamble, N. C. (1989). *The second rape: Society's continued betrayal of the victim.* New York: Lexington Books.

Malamuth, N. M. (1981). Rape proclivity among males. *Journal of Social Issues, 37,* 138–157.

Malamuth, N. M., & Brown, L. M. (1994). Sexually aggressive men's perceptions of women's communications: Testing three explanations. *Journal of Personality and Social Psychology, 67,* 699–712.

Malamuth, N. M., Heavey, C. L., & Linz, D. (1993). Predicting men's antisocial behavior against women: The "interaction model" of sexual aggression. In N. G. Hall & R. Hirschman (Eds.), *Sexual aggression: Issues in etiology and assessment treatment and policy.* New York: Hemisphere.

Malamuth, N. M., Linz, D., Heavey, C. L., Barnes, G., & Acker, M. (1995). Using the confluence model of sexual aggression to predict men's conflict with women: A 10-year follow-up study. *Journal of Personality and Social Psychology, 69,* 353–369.

Malamuth, N. M., Sockloskie, R., Koss, M., & Tanaka, J. (1991). The characteristics of aggressors against women: Testing a model using a national sample of college students. *Journal of Consulting and Clinical Psychology, 59,* 670–681.

Mandler, J. M. (1988). How to build a baby: On the development of an accessible representational system. *Cognitive Development, 3,* 113–136.

Mandler, J. M. (1990). Recall of events by preverbal children. In A. Diamond (Ed.), *The development and neural bases of higher cognitive functions*. New York: New York Academy of Science.

Mannuzza, S., Klein, R. G., Bessler, A., Malloy, P., & LaPadula, M. (1998). Adult psychiatric status of hyperactive boys grown up. *American Journal of Psychiatry, 155*, 493–498.

Maremont, M. (2003, July 1). In corporate crime, paper trail leads to ink analyst's door. *Wall Street Journal*, pp. 1, A4.

Markesteyn, T. (1992). *The psychological impact of nonsexual criminal offenses on victims*. Ottawa: Ministry of the Solicitor General of Canada, Corrections Branch.

Marshall, C. E., Benton, D., & Brazier, J. M. (2000). Elder abuse: Using clinical tools to identify clues of mistreatment. *Geriatrics, 55*, 42–53.

Marshall, G. N., & Schell, T. L. (2002). Reappraising the link between peritraumatic dissociation and PTSD symptom severity: Evidence from a longitudinal study of community violence survivors. *Journal of Abnormal Psychology, 111*, 626–636.

Marshall, W., & Barbaree, H. (1990). Outcome of comprehensive cognitive-behavioral treatment programs. In W. L. Marshall & H. E. Barbaree (Eds.), *Handbook of sexual assault: Issues, theories, and treatment of offenders*. New York: Plenum.

Marshall, W. B. (1996). Assessment, treatment, and theorizing about sex offenders. *Criminal Justice and Behavior, 23*, 162–199.

Marshall, W. L., & Mazzucco, A. (1995). Self-esteem and parental attachments in child molesters. *Sexual Abuse: A Journal of Research and Treatment, 7*, 229–285.

Marshall, W. L., Barbaree, H. E., & Fernandez, M. (1995). Some aspects of social competence in sexual offenders. *Sexual Abuse: A Journal of Research and Treatment, 7*, 113–127.

Martin, S. E. (1989). Women on the move? A report on the status of women in policing. *Women and Criminal Justice, 1*, 21–40.

Martin, S. E. (1992). The effectiveness of affirmative action: The case of women in policing. *Justice Quarterly, 8*, 489–504.

Martinez, R., Jr. (2002). *Latino homicide: Immigration, violence, and community*. New York: Routledge.

Martinez, R., Jr. (2003). Moving beyond Black and White violence: African American, Haitian, and Latino homicides in Miami. In D. F. Hawkins (Ed.), *Violent crime: Assessing race and ethnic differences*. Cambridge, UK: Cambridge University Press.

Mason, M. A., & Quirk, A. (1997). Are mothers losing custody? Read my lips: Trends in judicial decision-making in custody disputes—1920, 1960, 1990, and 1995. *Family Law Quarterly, 31*, 215–236.

Matarazzo, J. D., Allen, B, V., Saslow, G., & Wiens, A. (1964). Characteristics of successful policemen and firemen applicants. *Journal of Applied Psychology, 48*, 123–133.

Mathews, J. K., Hunter, J. A., & Vuz, J. (1997). Juvenile female sexual offenders: Clinical characteristics and treatment issues. *Sexual Abuse: A Journal of Research and Treatment, 9*, 187–199.

Mayfield, M. G., & Widom, C. S. (1996). The cycle of violence. *Archives of Pediatric and Adolescent Medicine, 150*, 390–395.

McCann, J. T. (1998). A conceptual framework for identifying various types of confessions. *Behavioral Sciences and the Law, 16*, 441–453.

McCann, L., & Pearlman, L. A. (1990). Constructivist self-development theory as a framework for assessing and treating victims of family violence. In S. M. Stith & M. B. Williams (Eds.), *Violence hits home: Comprehensive treatment approaches to domestic violence*. New York: Springer.

McFarland, B., Faulkner, L., Bloom, J., Hallaux, R., & Bray, J. (1989). Chronic mental illness and the criminal justice system. *Hospital and Community Psychiatry, 40*, 718–723.

McMahon, M. (1999). Battered women and bad science: The limited validity and utility of battered women syndrome. *Psychiatry, Psychology, and Law, 6,* 23–49.

McNally, R. J. (1991). Assessment of posttraumatic stress disorder in children. *Psychological Assessment, 3,* 531–537.

McNeece, C. A., Springer, D. W., & Arnold, E. M. (2001). Treating substance abuse disorders. In J. B. Ashford, B. D. Sales, & W. H. Reid (Eds.), *Treating adult and juvenile offenders with special needs.* Washington, DC: American Psychological Association.

McNeece, C. A., Springer, D. W., Shader, M. A., Malone, R., Smith, M. A., Touchton-Cashwell, S., & Antalek, M. (1997). *An evaluation of juvenile assessment centers in Florida.* Tallahassee: Florida State University, Institute for Health and Human Services Research.

McWhirter, P. T. (1999). La violencia privada: Domestic violence in Chile. *American Psychologist, 54,* 37–40.

Meadow, R. (1977). Munchausen syndrome by proxy: The hinterland of child abuse. *Lancet, 2,* 343–345.

Mears, D. P., & Kelly, W. R. (2002). Linking process and outcomes in evaluating a statewide drug treatment program for youthful offenders. *Crime & Delinquency, 48,* 99–115.

Meesig, R., & Horvath, F. (1995). A national survey of practices, policies and evaluative comments on the use of pre-employment polygraph screening in police agencies in the United States. *Polygraph, 24,* 57–136.

Megargee, E. I. (1974). Applied psychological research in a correctional setting. *Criminal Justice and Behavior, 1,* 43–50.

Meissner, C. A., & Brigham, J. C. (2001). Thirty years of investigating the own-race bias in memory for faces: A meta-analytic review. *Psychology, Public Policy, and Law, 7,* 3–35.

Meloy, J. R., & Gothard, S. (1995). Demographic and clinical comparisons of obsessional followers and offenders with mental disorders. *American Journal of Psychiatry, 152,* 258–263.

Meloy, M. (2000). Police organizations. In N. H. Rafter (Ed.), *Encyclopedia of women and crime.* Phoenix, AZ: Oryx.

Melton, G. B., Petrila, J., Poythress, N. G., & Slobogin, C. (1997). *Psychological evaluations for the courts: A handbook for mental health professionals and lawyers* (2nd ed.). New York: Guilford.

Mendel, D. (2003). *And the walls keep tumbling down.* Baltimore, MD: Annie E. Casey Foundation Newsletter. Available: www.aecf.org/publications/advocasey/spring2003

Merrill, G. S., & Wolfe, V. A. (2000). Battered gay men: An exploration of abuse, help-seeking, and why they stay. *Journal of Homosexuality, 39,* 1–30.

Merrill, M. A. (1927). Intelligence of policemen. *Journal of Personnel Research, 5,* 511–515.

Merry, S., & Harsent, L. (2000). Intruders, pilferers, raiders, and invaders: The interpersonal dimension of burglary. In D. Canter & L. Alison (Eds.), *Profiling property crimes.* Dartmouth, UK: Ashgate.

Merz-Perez, L., Heide, K. M., & Silverman, I. J. (2001). Childhood cruelty to animals and subsequent violence against humans. *International Journal of Offender Therapy and Comparative Criminology, 45,* 556–573.

Meuer, T., Seymour, A., & Wallace, H. (2002, June). Domestic violence. In A. Seymour, M. Murray, J. Sigmon, M. Hook, C. Edwards, M. Gaboury, & G. Coleman. (Eds.), *National Victim Assistance Academy textbook.* Washington, DC: U.S. Department of Justice, Office for Victims of Crime.

Milan, M. A., Chin, C. E., & Nguyen, Q. X. (1999). Practicing psychology in correctional settings: Assessment, treatment, and substance abuse programs. In A. K. Hess & I. B. Weiner (Eds.), *Handbook of forensic psychology* (2nd ed.). New York: John Wiley.

Milgram, S. (1974). *Obedience to authority: An experimental view.* New York: Harper & Row.

Miller, L. (1995). Tough guys: Psychotherapeutic strategies with law enforcement and emergency services personnel. *Psychotherapy, 32*, 592–600.

Miller, R. D. (2003). Hospitalization of criminal defendants for evaluation of competence to stand trial or for restoration of competence: Clinical and legal issues. *Behavioral Sciences & the Law, 21*, 369–391.

Millon, T. (1994). *MCMI-III: Manual.* Minneapolis, MN: National Computer Systems.

Mills, R. B. (1969). Use of diagnostic small groups in police recruit selection and training. *Journal of Criminal Law, Crimininology, and Police Science, 60*, 238–241.

Mills, R. B. (1976). Simulated stress in police recruit selection. *Journal of Police Science and Administration, 4*, 179–186.

Mills, R. B., McDevitt, R. J., & Tonkin, S. (1966). Situational tests in metropolitan police recruit selection. *Journal of Criminal Law, Criminology, and Police Science, 57*, 99–104.

Miner, M. H., Day, D. M., & Nafpaktitis, M. K. (1989). Assessment of coping skills: Development of situational competency test. In D. R. Laws (Eds.), *Relapse prevention with sex offenders.* New York: Guilford.

Mischel, W. (1968). *Personality and assessment.* New York: John Wiley.

Mischel, W., & Peake, P. K. (1982). Beyond déjà vu in the search for cross-situational consistency. *Psychological Review, 89*, 730–755.

Moffitt, T. E. (1990). The neuropsychology of juvenile delinquency: A critical review. In M. Tonry & N. Morris (Eds.), *Crime and justice: A review of research.* Chicago: University of Chicago Press.

Moffitt, T. E. (1993a). Adolescent-limited and the life-course persistent antisocial behavior: A developmental taxonomy. *Psychological Review, 100*, 674–701.

Moffitt, T. E. (1993b). The neuropsychology of conduct disorder. *Development and Psychopathology, 5*, 135–151.

Moffitt, T. E., Caspi, A., Dickson, N., Silva, P., & Stanton, W. (1996). Childhood-onset versus adolescent-onset antisocial conduct problems in males: Natural history from ages 3 to 18. *Development and Psychopathology, 8*, 399–324.

Moffitt, T. E., & Silva, P. A. (1988). Self-reported delinquency, neuropsychological deficit, and history of attention deficit disorder. *Journal of Abnormal Child Psychology, 16*, 553–569.

Molina, B. S. G., Bukstein, O. G., & Lynch, K. G. (2002). Attention-deficit/hyperactivity disorder and conduct disorder symptomatology in adolescents with alcohol use disorder. *Psychology of Addictive Behaviors, 16*, 161–164.

Monahan, J. (1996). Violence prediction: The past twenty years and the next twenty years. *Criminal Justice and Behavior, 23*, 107–120.

Monahan, J., Bonnie, R. J., Appelbaum, P. S., Hyde, P. S., Steadman, H. J., & Swartz, M. S. (2001). Mandated community treatment: Beyond outpatient commitment. *Psychiatric Services, 52*, 1198–1205.

Monahan, J., & Steadman, H. (1996). Violent storms and violent people: How meteorology can inform risk communication in mental health law. *American Psychologist, 51*, 931–938.

Monahan, J., Steadman, H. J., Silver, E., Appelbaum, P. S., Robbins, P. C., Mulvey, E. P., et al. (2001). *Rethinking risk assessment: The MacArthur Study of Mental Disorder and Violence.* New York: Oxford University Press.

Money, J., & Werleas, J. (1976). Folie a deux in the parents of psychosocial dwarfs: Two cases. *Bulletin of the American Academy of Psychiatry and the Law, 4*, 351–362.

Morawetz, T. H. (2002). Homicide. In K. L. Hall (Ed.), *The Oxford companion to American law.* New York: Oxford University Press.

More, H. W. (1992). *Special topics in policing.* Cincinnati, OH: Anderson.

Morey, L. C. (1991). *The Personality Assessment Inventory: Professional manual.* Odessa, FL: Psychological Assessment Resources.

Morgan, R. D., Winterowd, C. L., & Ferrell, S. W. (1999). A national survey of group psychotherapy services in correctional facilities. *Professional Psychology: Research and Practice, 30,* 600–606.

Morris, A. (1996). Gender and ethnic differences in social constraints among a sample of New York City police officers. *Journal of Occupational Health Psychology, 1,* 224–235.

Morris, E. F. (2001). Clinical practices with African Americans: Juxtaposition of standard clinical practices and Africentricism. *Professional Psychology: Research and Practice, 32,* 563–572.

Morris, R. (2000). *Forensic handwriting identification: Fundamental concepts and principles.* San Diego: Academic Press.

Morris, S. M., Steadman, H. J., & Veysey, B. M. (1997). Mental health services in United States jails: A survey of innovative practices. *Criminal Justice and Behavior, 24,* 3–19.

Morry, M. M., & Winkler, E. (2001). Student acceptance and expectation of sexual assault. *Canadian Journal of Behavioural Science, 33,* 188–192.

Morse, S. J. (2003). Involuntary competence. *Behavioral Sciences and the Law, 21,* 311–328.

Mosher, D. L., & Anderson, R. D. (1986). Macho personality, sexual aggression, and reactions to guided imagery of realistic rape. *Journal of Research in Personality, 20,* 77–94.

Mossman, D. (1987). Assessing and restoring competency to be executed: Should psychologists participate? *Behavioral Sciences & the Law, 5,* 397–409.

Mossman, D. (2003). *Daubert,* cognitive malingering, and test accuracy. *Law and Human Behavior, 27,* 229–249.

Mulder, R.T., Wells, J. E., Joyce, P. R., & Bushnell, J. A. (1994). Antisocial women. *Journal of Personality Disorders, 8,* 279–287.

Mullen, P. E., Pathé, M., & Purcell, R. (2001). Stalking: New constructions of human behaviour. *Australian and New Zealand Journal of Psychiatry, 35,* 9–16.

Mulvey, E. P., Arthur, M. W., & Reppucci, N. D. (1993). The prevention and treatment of juvenile delinquency: A review of the research. *Clinical Psychology Review, 13,* 133–167.

Mumley, D. L., Tillbrook, C. E., & Grisso, T. (2003). Five year research update (1996–2000): Evaluations for competence to stand trial (adjudicative competence). *Behavioral Sciences and the Law, 21,* 329–350.

Murphy, J. J. (1972). Current practices in the use of psychological testing by police agencies. *Journal of Criminal Law, Criminology, and Police Science, 63,* 570–576.

Murphy, K. R., & Davidshofer, C. O. (1998). *Psychological testing: Principles and applications* (4th ed.). Upper Saddle River, NJ: Prentice Hall.

Murphy, W. D., Coleman, E. M., & Haynes, M. R. (1986). Factors related to coercive sexual behavior in a nonclinical sample of males. *Violence and Victims, 1,* 255–278.

Murray, B. (2000, January). The degree that almost wasn't: The PsyD comes of age. *Monitor on Psychology, 31,* 25–26.

Murray, B. (2002a, June). Good news for bachelor's grads. *Monitor on Psychology, 33,* 30–32.

Murray, B. (2002b, June). More students blend business and psychology. *Monitor on Psychology, 33,* 34–35.

Murray, J. B. (1997). Munchausen syndrome/Munchausen syndrome by proxy. *Journal of Psychology, 131,* 343–350.

Murray, M., & O'Ran, S. (2002). Restitution. In A. Seymour, M. Murray, J. Sigmon, M. Hook, C. Edwards, M. Gaboury, & G. Coleman (Eds.), *National Victim Assistance Academy textbook.* Washington, DC: U.S. Department of Justice, Office of Victims of Crime.

Murrie, D. C., & Cornell, D. G. (2002). Psychopathy screening of incarcerated juveniles: A comparison of measures. *Psychological Assessment, 14,* 390–396.

Myers, B., & Arena, M. P. (2001). Trial consultation: A new direction in applied psychology. *Professional Psychology: Research and Practice, 32,* 386–391.

Myers, J. E. B. (1991). Psychologists' involvement in cases of child maltreatment: Limits of role and expertise. *American Psychologist, 46,* 81–82.

Nagayama-Hall, G. (1992, November/December). Inside the mind of the rapist. *Psychology Today, 25,* 12.

Nagin, D. S., Farrington, D. P., & Moffitt, T. (1995). Life-course trajectories of different types of offenders. *Criminology, 33,* 111–139.

Nagin, D. S., & Land, K. C. (1993). Age, criminal careers, and population heterogeneity: Specification and estimation of a nonparametric mixed Poisson model. *Criminology, 31,* 163–189.

Narrol, H. G., & Levitt, E. E. (1963). Formal assessment procedures in police selection. *Psychological Reports, 12,* 691–694.

National Center for Victims of Crime. (1999). *The NCVC does not support the current language of the proposed crime victims' rights constitutional amendment.* Arlington, VA: Author.

National Center for Victims of Crime and Crime Victims Research and Treatment Center. (1992). *Rape in America: A report to the nation.* Arlington, VA: Author.

National Center for Women and Policing. (2000). *Equality denied: The status of women in policing.* Los Angeles: Author.

National Center on Elder Abuse. (1999). *Types of elder abuse in domestic settings.* Washington, DC: Author.

National Council of Juvenile and Family Court Judges. (1993). The revised report from the National Task Force on Juvenile Sexual Offending. *Juvenile and Family Court Journal, 44,* 1–120.

National Organization for Victim Assistance. (1998). *Community crisis response team training manual* (2nd ed.). Washington, DC: Author.

National Resource Center on Child Sexual Abuse. (1996, March/April). *NRCCSA news.* Huntsville, AL: Author.

Neisser, U., Boodoo, G., Bouchard, T., Boykin, A. W., Brody, N., Ceci, S. J., et al. (1996). Intelligence: Knowns and unknowns. *American Psychologist, 51,* 77–101.

Nelson, D. W. (2003). *On adolescent crime: Trend to end fad justice.* Baltimore, MD: Annie E. Casey Foundation Newsletter. Available: www.aecf.org/publications/advocasey/ spring2003

Neubauer, D. W. (1997). *Judicial process* (2nd ed.). Fort Worth, TX: Harcourt Brace.

Neubauer, D. W. (2002). *America's courts and the criminal justice system* (7th ed.). Belmont, CA: Wadsworth.

Newman, G. (1979). *Understanding violence.* New York: J. B. Lippincott.

Nicholson, R. (1999). Forensic assessment. In R. Roesch, S. D. Hart, & J. R. P. (Eds.), *Psychology and law: The state of the discipline.* New York: Kluwer Academic/Plenum.

Nicholson, R., & Norwood, S. (2000). The quality of forensic psychological assessments, reports, and testimony: Acknowledging the gap between promise and practice. *Law and Human Behavior, 24,* 9–44.

Nietzel, M. T., McCarthy, D. M., & Kerr, M. J. (1999). Juries: The current state of the empirical literature. In R. Roesch, S. D. Hart, & J. R. P. Ogloff (Eds.), *Psychology and law: The state of the discipline.* New York: Kluwer Academic.

Nigg, J. T. (2000). On inhibition/disinhibition in developmental psychopathology: Views from cognitive and personality psychology and a working inhibition taxonomy. *Psychological Bulletin, 126,* 220–246.

Nigg, J. T., Butler, K. M., Huang-Pollock, C. L., & Henderson, J. M. (2002). Inhibitory processes in adults with persistent childhood onset ADHD. *Journal of Consulting and Clinical Psychology, 70,* 153–157.

Nigg, J. T., John, O. P., Blaskey, L. G., Huang-Pollock, C., Willcutt, E. G., Hinshaw, S. P., et al. (2002). Big Five dimensions and ADHD symptoms: Links between personality traits and clinical symptoms. *Journal of Personality and Social Psychology, 83,* 451–469.

Norris, F. H., & Kaniasty, K. (1994). Psychological distress following criminal victimization in the general population: Cross-sectional, longitudinal, and prospective analysis. *Journal of Consulting and Clinical Psychology, 62,* 111–123.

Norris, F. H., Kaniasty, K., & Scheer, D. A. (1990). Use of mental health services among victims of crime: Frequency, correlates, and subsequent recovery. *Journal of Consulting and Clinical Psychology, 58,* 538–547.

O'Neill, M. L., Lidz, V., & Heilbrun, K. (2003). Adolescents with psychopathic characteristics in a substance abusing cohort: Treatment process and outcomes. *Law and Human Behavior, 27,* 299–313.

Oberlander, L. B., Goldstein, N. E., & Ho, C. N. (2001). Pre-adolescent adjudicative competence: Methodological considerations and recommendations for standard practice standards. *Behavioral Sciences & the Law, 19,* 545–563.

Occupational Safety and Health Administration. (2001). *Workplace violence.* Washington, DC: U.S. Department of Labor.

Office of Juvenile Justice and Delinquency Prevention. (1996). *Juvenile boot camps: Lessons learned.* Washington, DC: U.S. Department of Justice.

Offord, D. R., Boyle, M. C., & Racine, Y. A. (1991). The epidemiology of antisocial behavior in childhood and adolescence. In D. J. Pepler & H. Rubin (Eds.), *The development and treatment of childhood aggression.* Hillsdale, NJ: Lawrence Erlbaum.

Ogawa, B., & Belle, A. S. (2002). Respecting diversity: Responding to underserved victims of crime. In A. Seymour, M. Murray, J. Sigmon, M. Hook, C. Edwards, M. Gaboury, & G. Coleman (Eds.), *National Victim Assistance Academy textbook.* Washington, DC: U.S. Department of Justice, Office of Victims of Crime.

Ogle, R. S. (2000). Battered women and self-defense, USA. In N. H. Rafter (Ed.), *Encyclopedia of women and crime.* Phoenix, AZ: Oryx.

Ogloff, J. R. P. (1999). Ethical and legal contours of forensic psychology. In R. Roesch, S. D. Hart, & J. R. P. Ogloff (Eds.), *Psychology and law: The state of the discipline.* New York: Kluwer Academic.

Olkin, R. (2002). Could you hold the door for me? Including disability in diversity. *Cultural Diversity and Ethnic Minority Psychology, 8,* 130–137.

Olkin, R., & Pledger, C. (2003). Can disability studies and psychology join hands? *American Psychologist, 58,* 296–304.

Orne, M. T. (1970). Hypnosis, motivation and the ecological validity of the psychological experiment. In W. J. Arnold & M. M. Page (Eds.), *Nebraska Symposium on Motivation.* Lincoln: University of Nebraska Press.

Orne, M. T., Dinges, D. F., & Orne, E. C. (1984). On the differential diagnosis of multiple personality in the forensic context. *International Journal of Clinical and Experimental Hypnosis, 32,* 118–169.

Orne, M. T., Whitehouse, W. G., Dinges, D. F., & Orne, E. C. (1988). Reconstructing memory through hypnosis: Forensic and clinical implications. In H. M. Pettinati (Ed.), *Hypnosis and memory.* New York: Guilford.

Ornstein, P. A., Ceci, S. J., & Loftus, E. F. (1998a). Adult recollections of childhood abuse: Cognitive and developmental perspectives. *Psychology, Public Policy, and Law, 4,* 1025–1051.

Ornstein, P. A., Ceci, S. J., & Loftus, E. F. (1998b). Comment on Alpert, Brown, and Courtois (1998): The science of memory and the practice of psychotherapy. *Psychology, Public Policy, and Law, 4,* 996–1010.

O'Tool, M. E. (2000). *The school shooter: A threat assessment perspective.* Quantico, VA: National Center for the Analysis of Violent Crime, Criminal Incident Response Group.

Otto, R. K., & Heilbrun, K. (2002). The practice of forensic psychology: A look toward the future in light of the past. *American Psychologist, 57,* 5–18.

Otto, R. K., Poythress, N. G., Nicholson, R. A., Edens, J. F., Monahan, J., Bonnie, R. I., Hoge, S. K., & Eisenberg, M. (1998). Psychometric properties of the MacArthur Competence Assessment Tool—Criminal Adjudication. *Psychological Assessment, 10,* 435–443.

Owen, B. (2000). Prison security. In N. H. Rafter (Ed.), *Encyclopedia of women and crime.* Phoenix, AZ: Oryx.

Ozer, E. J., Best, S. R., Lipsey, T. L., & Weiss, D. S. (2003). Predictors of posttraumatic stress disorder and symptoms in adults: A meta-analysis. *Psychological Bulletin, 129,* 52–73.

Palerea, R., Zona, M. A., Lane, J. C., & Langhinrichsen-Rohling, J. (1999). The dangerous nature of intimate relationship stalking: Threats, violence, and associated risk factors. *Behavioral Sciences and the Law, 17,* 269–283.

Palmer, J. W., & Palmer, S. E. (1999). *Constitutional rights of prisoners* (6th ed.). Cincinnati, OH: Anderson.

Palmer, T. (1991). The effectiveness of intervention: Recent trends and current issues. *Crime and Delinquency, 37,* 330–346.

Parent, D. G., Leiter, V., Kennedy, S., Livens, L., Wentworth, D., & Wilcox, S. (1994). *Conditions of confinement: Juvenile detention and corrections facilities.* Washington, DC: U.S. Department of Justice, Office of Justice Programs, Office of Juvenile Justice and Delinquency Prevention.

Parry, J., & Drogan, E. Y. (2000). *Criminal law handbook on psychiatric and psychological evidence and testimony.* Washington, DC: American Bar Association.

Partlett, D. F., & Nurcombe, B. (1998). Recovered memories of child sexual abuse and liability: Society, science, and the law in a comparative setting. *Psychology, Public Policy, and Law, 4,* 1253–1306.

Patrick, C. J., & Iacono, W. G. (1989). Psychopathy, threat, and polygraph test accuracy. *Journal of Applied Psychology, 74,* 347–355.

Patterson, G. R. (1982). *Coercive family processes.* Eugene, OR: Castalia Press.

Pearl, P. T. (1995). Identifying and responding to Munchausen syndrome by proxy. *Early Child Development and Care, 106,* 177–185.

Pearson, F. S., Lipton, D. S., Cleland, C. M., & Yee, D. S. (2002). The effects of behavior/cognitive-behavioral programs on recidivism. *Crime & Delinquency, 48,* 476–496.

Pease, T., & Frantz, B. (1994). *Your safety . . . your rights and personal safety and abuse prevention education program to empower adults with disabilities and train service providers.* Doylestown, PA: Network of Victim Assistance.

Penrod, S., & Cutler, B. L. (1995). Witness confidence and witness accuracy: Assessing their forensic relation. *Psychology, Public Policy, and Law, 1,* 817–845.

Pepler, D. J., Byrd, W., & King, G. (1991). A social-cognitively based social skills training program for aggressive children. In D. J. Pepler & K. H. Rubin (Eds.), *The development and treatment of childhood aggression.* Hillsdale, NJ: Lawrence Erlbaum.

Perlin, M. L. (1991). Power imbalances in therapeutic and forensic relationships. *Behavioral Sciences & the Law, 9,* 111–128.

Perlin, M. L. (1994). *The jurisprudence of the insanity defense.* Durham, NC: Carolina Academic Press.

Perlin, M. L. (1996). "Dignity was the first to leave": *Godinez v. Moran,* Colin Ferguson, and the trial of mentally disabled criminal defendants. *Behavioral Sciences and the Law, 14,* 61–81.

Perlin, M. L. (2003). Beyond *Dusky* and *Godinez:* Competency before and after trial. *Behavioral Sciences and the Law, 21,* 297–310.

Perlin, M. L., & Dorfman, D. A. (1996). Is it more than "dodging lions and wastin' time"? Adequacy of counsel, questions of competence, and the judicial process in individual right to refuse treatment cases. *Psychology, Public Policy, and Law, 2,* 114–136.

Petee, T. A., & Jarvis, J. (2000). Analyzing violent serial offending. *Homicide Studies, 4,* 211–218.

Peters, S. D., Wyatt, G. E., & Finkelhor, D. (1986). Prevalence. In D. Finkelhor (Ed.), *Sourcebook on child sexual abuse.* Beverly Hills, CA: Sage.

Peterson, D. R. (1968). The doctor of psychology program at the University of Illinois. *American Psychologist, 23,* 511–516.

Petretic-Jackson, P. A., Witte, T. H., & Jackson, T. L. (2002). Battered women: Treatment goals and treatment planning. In A. R. Roberts (Ed.), *Handbook of domestic violence intervention strategies: Policies, programs, and legal remedies.* New York: Oxford University Press.

Pfiffner, L. J., McBurnett, K., Lahey, B. B., Loeber, R., Green, S., Frick, P. J., et al. (1999). Association of parental psychopathology to the comorbid disorders of boys with attention deficit–hyperactivity disorder. *Journal of Consulting and Clinical Psychology, 67,* 881–893.

Pierce, C. S., & Brodsky, S. L. (2002). Trust and understanding in the attorney-juvenile relationship. *Behavioral Sciences and the Law, 20,* 89–107.

Pillemer, K., & Finkelhor, D. (1988). The prevalence of elder abuse: A random sample survey. *Gerontologist, 28,* 51–57.

Pinizzotto, A. J. (1984). Forensic psychology: Criminal personality profiling. *Journal of Police Science and Administration, 12,* 32–40.

Pinizzotto, A. J., & Finkel, N. J. (1990). Criminal personality profiling: An outcome and process study. *Law and Human Behavior, 14,* 215–234.

Pithers, W. D., Becker, J. V., Kafka, M., Morenz, B., Schlank, A., & Leombruno, P. (1995). Children with sexual behavior problems, adolescent sexual abusers, and adult sexual offenders: Assessment and treatment. *American Psychiatric Press Review of Psychiatry, 14,* 779–819.

Platt, A. (1969). *The child savers: The invention of delinquency.* Chicago: University of Chicago Press.

Platt, J. J., Bux, D. A., Lamb, R. J., Lidz, V., & Husband, S. D. (1996). *Twenty-four session cognitive-behavioral treatment manual for adolescent substance abusers.* Philadelphia: MCP Hahnemann University.

Podkopacz, M. R., & Feld, B. C. (1996). The end of the line: An empirical study of judicial waiver. *Journal of Criminal Law and Criminology, 86,* 449–492.

Poland, J. M. (1978). Police selection methods and the prediction of police performance. *Journal of Police Science and Administration, 6,* 374–393.

Polizzi, D. M., MacKenzie, D. L., & Hickman, L. J. (1999). What works in adult sex offender treatment: A review of prison- and non-prison-based treatment programs. *International Journal of Offender Therapy and Comparative Criminology, 43,* 357–374.

Polusny, M., & Follette, V. (1996). Remembering childhood sexual abuse: A national survey of psychologists' clinical practices, beliefs, and personal experiences. *Professional Psychology: Research and Practice, 27,* 41–52.

Pope, H. S., Butcher, J. N., & Seelen, J. (2000). *The MMPI, MMPI-2, & MMPI-A in court: A practical guide for expert witnesses and attorneys* (2nd ed.). Washington, DC: American Psychological Association.

Porter, S., Fairweather, D., Drugge, J., Hervé, H., Birt, A., & Boer, D. P. (2000). Profiles of psychopathy in incarcerated sexual offenders. *Criminal Justice and Behavior, 27,* 216–233.

Potoczniak, M. J., Mourot, J. E., Crosbie-Burnett, M., & Potoczniak, D. J. (2003). Legal and psychological perspectives on same-sex domestic violence: A multisystematic approach. *Journal of Family Violence, 17,* 252–259.

Poythress, N. G. (1979). A proposal for training in forensic psychology. *American Psychologist, 34,* 612–621.

Poythress, N. G., Otto, R. K., Darnes, J., & Starr, L. (1993). APA's expert panel in congressional review of the USS *Iowa* incident. *American Psychologist, 48,* 8–15.

Prendergast, M. L., Farabee, D., Cartier, J., & Henkin, S. (2002). Involuntary treatment within a prison setting. *Criminal Justice and Behavior, 29,* 5–26.

Prentky, R. A., Burgess, A. W., & Carter, D. L. (1986). Victim responses by rapist type: An empirical and clinical analysis. *Journal of Interpersonal Violence, 1,* 73–98.

Prentky, R. A., Burgess, A. W., Rokous, F., Lee, A., Hartman, C., Ressler, R., et al. (1989). The presumptive role of fantasy in serial sexual homicide. *American Journal of Psychiatry, 146,* 887–891.

Prentky, R. A., & Edmunds, S. B. (1997). *Assessing sexual abuse: A resource guide for practitioners.* Brandon, VT: Safer Society Press.

Prentky, R. A., Harris, B., Frizzell, K., & Righthand, S. (2000). An actuarial procedure of assessing risk in juvenile sex offenders. *Sexual Abuse: A Journal of Research and Treatment, 12,* 71–93.

Prentky, R. A., & Knight, R. A. (1986). Impulsivity in the lifestyle and criminal behavior of sexual offenders. *Criminal Justice and Behavior, 13,* 141–164.

Prentky, R. A., & Knight, R. A. (1991). Identifying critical dimensions for discriminating among rapists. *Journal of Consulting and Clinical Psychology, 59,* 643–661.

Prentky, R. A., Knight, R. A., & Lee, A. F. S. (1997, June). *Child sexual molestation: Research issues.* Washington, DC: U.S. Department of Justice, Office of Justice Programs.

President's Commission on Law Enforcement and the Administration of Justice. (1967). *The challenge of crime in a free society.* Washington, DC: Government Printing Office.

Puritz, P., & Scali, M. A. (1998). *Beyond the walls: Improving conditions of confinement for youth in custody.* Washington, DC: Office of Juvenile Justice and Delinquency Prevention.

Puzzanchera, C., Stahl, A. L., Finnegan, T. A., Tierney, N. J., & Snyder, H. N. (2003, June). *Juvenile court statistics 1998.* Washington, DC: National Center for Juvenile Justice, Office of Juvenile Justice and Delinquency Prevention.

Qualls, S. H. (1998). Training in geropsychology: Preparing to meet the demand. *Professional Psychology: Research and Practice, 29,* 23–28.

Qualls, S. H., Segal, D. L., Norman, S., Niederche, G., & Gallagher-Thompson, D. (2002). Psychologists in practice with older adults: Current patterns, sources of training, and need for continuing education. *Professional Psychology: Research and Practice, 33,* 435–442.

Quay, H. C. (1965). Psychopathic personality: Pathological stimulation-seeking. *American Journal of Psychiatry, 122,* 180–183.

Quinsey, V. L. (1986). Men who have sex with children. In D. N. Weisstub (Ed.), *Law and mental health: International perspectives* (Vol. 2). New York: Pergamon.

Quinsey, V. L., & Chaplin, T. C. (1988). Preventing faking in phallometric assessment of sexual preference. *Annals of the New York Academy of Sciences, 528,* 49–58.

Quinsey, V. L., Harris, G. T., Rice, M. E., & Cormier, C. A. (1998). *Violent offenders: Appraising and managing risk.* Washington, DC: American Psychological Association.

Quinsey, V. L., Rice, & Harris (1995). Actuarial prediction of sexual recidivism. *Journal of Interpersonal Violence, 10,* 85–105.

Radelet, M. L., & Barnard, G. W. (1986). Ethics and the psychiatric determination of competency to be executed. *Bulletin of the American Academy of Psychiatry and Law, 14,* 37–53.

Raine, A. (1993). *The psychopathology of crime: Criminal behavior as a clinical disorder.* San Diego: Academic Press.

Ramirez, D., McDevitt, J., & Farrell, A. (2000, November). *A resource guide on racial profiling data collection systems: Promising practices and lessons learned.* Boston: Northeastern University Press.

Raspe, R. E. (1944). *The surprising adventures of Baron Munchausen.* New York: Peter Pauper.

Redding, R. E., Floyd, M. Y., & Hawk, G. L. (2001). What judges and lawyers think about the testimony of mental health experts: A survey of the courts and bar. *Behavioral Sciences & the Law, 19,* 583–594.

Redlich, A. D., & Goodman, G. S. (2003). Taking responsibility for an act not committed: The influence of age and suggestibility. *Law and Human Behavior, 27,* 141–156.

Redlich, A. D., Silverman, M., & Steiner, H. (2003). Pre-adjudicative and adjudicative competence in juveniles and young adults. *Behavioral Sciences and the Law, 21,* 393–410.

Reed, G. M., Levant, R. F., Stout, C. E., Murphy, M. J., & Phelps, R. (2001). Psychology in the current mental health marketplace. *Professional Psychology: Research and Practice, 32,* 65–70.

Reid, J. B. (1993). Prevention of conduct disorders before and after school entry: Relating interventions to developmental findings. *Development and Psychopathology, 5,* 243–262.

Reid, J. E., & Inbau, F. E. (1977). *Truth and deception: The polygraph ("lie detector") technique* (2nd ed.). Baltimore, MD: Williams & Wilkins.

Reidel, M. (2003). Homicide in Los Angeles County: A study of Latino victimization. In D. F. Hawkins (Ed.), *Violent crime: Assessing race and ethnic differences.* Cambridge, UK: Cambridge University Press.

Reiser, M. (1972). *The police psychologist.* Springfield, IL: Charles C Thomas.

Reiser, M. (1982). *Police psychology: Collected papers.* Los Angeles: LEHI.

Reiser, M., & Klyver, N. (1987). Consulting with police. In I. B. Weiner & A. K. Hess (Eds.), *Handbook of forensic psychology.* New York: John Wiley.

Reitzel, L. R. (2003, January). Sexual offender update: Juvenile sexual offender recidivism and treatment effectiveness. *Correctional Psychologist, 35,* 1, 3–4.

Rennison, C. (2001, March). *Violent victimization and race, 1993–1998.* Washington, DC: U.S. Department of Justice, Bureau of Justice Statistics.

Rennison, C. (2002, April). *Hispanic victims of violent crime, 1993–2000.* Washington, DC: U.S. Department of Justice, Bureau of Justice Statistics.

Reno, J. (1999). Message from the Attorney General. In Technical Working Group for Eyewitness Evidence (Ed.), *Eyewitness evidence: A guide for law enforcement.* Washington, DC: National Institute of Justice.

Renzetti, C. M. (1992). *Violent betrayal: Partner abuse in lesbian relationships.* Newbury Park, CA: Sage.

Reppucci, N. D., & Saunders, J. T. (1974). Social psychology of behavior modification: Problems of implementation in natural settings. *American Psychologist, 29,* 649–660.

Resnick, H. S., Kilpatrick, D. G., Dansky, B. S., Saunders, B. E., & Best, C. L. (1993). Prevalence of civilian trauma in posttraumatic stress disorder in a representative national sample of women. *Journal of Consulting and Clinical Psychology, 61,* 984–991.

Resnick, P. J. (1970). Murder of the newborn: A psychiatric review of neonaticide. *American Journal of Psychiatry, 120,* 1414–1420.

Ressler, R. K., Burgess, A., & Douglas, J. E. (1988). *Sexual homicide: Patterns and motives.* Lexington, MA: Lexington Books.

Ressler, R. K., Burgess, A., Hartman, C. R., Douglas, J. E., & McCormick, A. (1986). Murderers who rape and mutilate. *Journal of Interpersonal Violence, 1,* 273–287.

Rice, M. E., & Harris, G. T. (2002). Men who molest their sexually immature daughters: Is a special explanation required? *Journal of Abnormal Psychology, 111,* 329–339.

Rice, M. E., Harris, G. T., & Cormier, C. A. (1992). An evaluation of a maximum security therapeutic community for psychopaths and other mentally disordered offenders. *Law and Human Behavior, 16,* 399–412.

Richardson, G., Gudjonsson, G. H., & Kelly, T. P. (1995). Interrogative suggestibility in an adolescent forensic population. *Journal of Adolescence, 18,* 211–216.

Richardson, L. (2003). *Opportunities in correctional psychology.* Washington, DC: American Psychological Association. Available: www.apa.org/apags/profdev/corrpsyc.html

Righthand, S., & Welch, C. (2001, March). *Juveniles who have sexually offended: A review of the professional literature.* Washington, DC: U.S. Department of Justice, Office of Juvenile Justice and Delinquency Prevention.

Ritzler, B., Erard, R., & Pettigrew, G. (2002a). A final reply to Grove and Barden: The relevance of the Rorschach Comprehensive System for expert testimony. *Psychology, Public Policy, and Law, 8,* 235–246.

Ritzler, B., Erard, R., & Pettigrew, G. (2002b). Protecting the integrity of Rorschach expert witnesses: A reply to Grove and Barden (1999) Re: The admissibility of testimony under *Daubert/Kumho* analyses. *Psychology, Public Policy, and Law, 8,* 201–215.

Robins, P. M., & Sesan, R. (1991). Munchausen syndrome by proxy: Another women's disorder. *Professional Psychology: Research and Practice, 22,* 285–290.

Roediger, H. L., & Bergman, E. T. (1998). The controversy over recovered memories. *Psychology, Public Policy, and Law, 4,* 1091–1109.

Roesch, R., Zapf, P. A., Golding, S. L., & Skeem, J. L. (1999). Defining and assessing competency to stand trial. In A. K. Hess & I. B. Weiner (Eds.), *The handbook of forensic psychology* (2nd ed.). New York: John Wiley.

Rogers, R. (1984). *Rogers Criminal Responsibility Assessment Scales (R-CRAS) and test manual.* Odessa, FL: Psychological Assessment Resources.

Rogers, R. (1992). *Structured interview of reported symptoms.* Odessa, FL: Psychological Assessment Resources.

Rogers, R. (1997). *Clinical assessment of malingering and deception* (2nd ed.). New York: Guilford.

Rogers, R., & Ewing, C. P. (1989). Ultimate issue proscriptions: A cosmetic fix and plea for empiricism. *Law and Human Behavior, 13,* 357–374.

Rogers, R., & Sewell, K. W. (1999). The R-CRAS and insanity evaluations: A re-examination of construct validity. *Behavioral Sciences & the Law, 17,* 181–194.

Rogers, R., & Shuman, D. W. (1999). *Conducting insanity evaluations* (2nd ed.). New York: Guilford.

Rohde, L. A., Barbosa, G., Polanczyk, G., Eizirik, M., Rasmussen, R. R., Neuman, R. J., et al. (2001). Factor and latent class analysis of *DSM-IV* ADHD symptoms in a school sample of Brazilian adolescents. *Journal of the American Academy of Child and Adolescent Psychiatry, 40,* 711–718.

Romans, J. S. C., Hays, J. R., & White, T. K. (1996). Stalking and related behaviors experienced by counseling center staff members from current and former clients. *Professional Psychology: Research and Practice, 27,* 595–599.

Root, R. W., & Resnick, R. J. (2003). An update on the diagnosis and treatment of attention-deficit/hyperactivity disorder in children. *Professional Psychology: Research and Practice, 34,* 34–41.

Rosenfeld, B., & Harmon, R. (2002). Factors associated with violence in stalking and obsessional harassment cases. *Criminal Justice and Behavior, 29,* 671–691.

Rossmo, D. K. (1997). Geographical profiling. In J. T. Jackson & D. A. Bekerain (Eds.), *Offender profiling: Theory, research and practice.* Chichester, UK: Wiley.

Rostow, C. D., Davis, R. D., Levy, J. P., & Brecknock, S. (2001, June). Civil liability and psychological services in law enforcement administration. *Police Chief,* pp. 18–24.

Rothman, D. (1980). *Conscience and convenience.* Boston: Little, Brown.

Rubin, K. H., Bukowski, W., & Parker, J. G. (1998). Peer interactions, relationships, and groups. In N. Eisenberg (Ed.), *Handbook of child psychology: Vol. 3. Social, emotional, and personality development* (5th ed.). New York: John Wiley.

Rubinstein, M., Yeager, C. A., Goodstein, C., & Lewis, D. O. (1993). Sexually assaultive male juveniles: A follow-up. *American Journal of Psychiatry, 150,* 262–265.

Saks, M. J. (1993). Improving APA science translation amicus briefs. *Law and Human Behavior, 17,* 235–247.

Sale, P. L. (1992). Ego and self-concept development among juvenile delinquent participants in adventure-based programs. *Dissertation Abstracts International, 53,* 2253A.

Salekin, R. (2002). Psychopathy and therapeutic pessimism: Clinical lore or clinical reality? *Clinical Psychology Review, 22,* 79–112.

Salekin, R. T., Rogers, R., & Sewell, K. W. (1997). Construct validity of psychopathy in a female offender sample: A multitrait-multimethod evaluation. *Journal of Abnormal Psychology, 106,* 576–585.

Salekin, R. T., Rogers, R., Ustad, K. L., & Sewell, K. W. (1998). Psychopathy and recidivism among female inmates. *Law and Human Behavior, 22,* 109–128.

Salter, D., McMillan, D., Richards, M., Talbot, T., Hodges, J., Arnon, B., et al. (2003). Development of sexually abusive behaviour in sexually victimised males: A longitudinal study. *The Lancet, 361,* 108–115.

Sampson, R. J., & Laub, J. H. (1993). Structural variations in juvenile court processing: Inequality, the underclass, and social control. *Law & Society Review, 27,* 285–311.

Satterfield, J. H., Swanson, J., Schell, A., & Lee, F. (1994). Prediction of antisocial behavior in attention-deficit hyperactivity disorder boys from aggression/defiance scores. *Journal of the American Academy of Child and Adolescent Psychiatry, 33,* 185–191.

Saunders, B. E., Arata, C., & Kilpatrick, D. (1990). Development of a crime-related post-traumatic stress disorder scale for women within the Symptom Checklist-90—Revised. *Journal of Traumatic Stress, 3,* 439–448.

Schafer, W. E., & Polk, K. (1967). Delinquency and the schools. *Task force report: Juvenile delinquency and youth crime.* Washington, DC: Government Printing Office.

Scheflin, A. W., Spiegel, H., & Spiegel, D. (1999). Forensic uses of hypnosis. In A. K. Hess & I. B. Weiner (Eds.), *The handbook of forensic psychology* (2nd ed.). New York: John Wiley.

Scherer, M., Maddux, J. E., Mercandante, B., Prentice-Dunn, S., Jacobs, B., & Rogers, R. W. (1982). The Self-Efficacy Scale: Construction and validation. *Psychological Reports, 51,* 663–671.

Schmidt, M. G., Reppucci, N. D., & Woolard, J. L. (2003). Effectiveness of participation as a defendant: The attorney-juvenile client relationship. *Behavioral Sciences and the Law, 21,* 175–198.

Schopp, R. F. (2003). Outpatient civil commitment: A dangerous charade or a component of a comprehensive institution of civil commitment? *Psychology, Public Policy, and Law, 9,* 33–69.

Schramke, C. J., & Bauer, R. M. (1997). State-dependent learning in older and younger adults. *Psychology and Aging, 12,* 255–262.

Schwartz, B. K. (1995). Characteristics and typologies of sex offenders. In B. K. Schwartz & H. R. Cellini (Eds.), *The sex offender: Corrections, treatment and legal practice.* Kingston, NJ: Civic Research Institute.

Schwartz, I. M. (1989). *(In)Justice for juveniles: Rethinking the best interests of the child.* Lexington, MA: Lexington Books.

Scrivner, E. M. (1994, April). *The role of police psychology in controlling excessive force.* Washington, DC: National Institute of Justice.

Seagrave, D., & Grisso, T. (2002). Adolescent development and measurement of juvenile psychopathy. *Law and Human Behavior, 26,* 219–239.

Seligman, M. E. (1975). *Helplessness: On depression, development, and death.* San Francisco: W. H. Freeman.

Selkin, J. (1975). Rape. *Psychology Today, 8*(8), 70–73.

Selkin, J. (1987). *Psychological autopsy in the courtroom.* Denver, CO: Author.

Selkin, J. (1994). Psychological autopsy: Scientific psychohistory or clinical intuition? *American Psychologist, 49,* 74–75.

Serin, R. C., & Amos, N. L. (1995). The role of psychopathy in the assessment of dangerousness. *International Journal of Law & Psychiatry, 18,* 231–238.

Serin, R. C., Peters, R. D., & Barbaree, H. E. (1990). Predictors of psychopathy and release outcome in a criminal population. *Psychological Assessment, 2,* 419–422.

Serin, R. C., & Preston, D. L. (2001). *Managing and treating violent offenders.* In J. B. Ashford, B. D. Sales, & W. H. Reid (Eds.), *Treating adult and juvenile offenders with special needs.* Washington, DC: American Psychological Association.

Seto, M. C., & Barbaree, H. E. (1999). Psychopathy, treatment behavior, and sex offender recidivism. *Journal of Interpersonal Violence, 14,* 1235–1248.

Seto, M. C., Lalumière, M. L., & Blanchard, R. (2000). The discriminative validity of a phallometric test for pedophilic interests among adolescent sex offenders against children. *Psychological Assessment, 12,* 319–327.

Seymour, A., Hook, M., & Grimes, C. (2002). Hate and bias crimes. In A. Seymour, M. Murray, J. Sigmon, M. Hook, C. Edwards, M. Gaboury, & G. Coleman (Eds.), *National Victim Assistance Academy textbook.* Washington, DC: U.S. Department of Justice, Office of Victims of Crime.

Shahinfar, A., Kupersmidt, J. B., & Matza, L. S. (2001). The relation between exposure to violence and social information processing among incarcerated adolescents. *Journal of Abnormal Psychology, 110,* 136–141.

Shapiro, D. L. (1999). *Criminal responsibility evaluations: A manual for practice.* Sarasota, FL: Professional Resource Press.

Shepherd, J. W., & Ellis, H. D. (1973). The effect of attractiveness on recognition memory for faces. *American Journal of Psychology, 86,* 627–633.

Sheridan, L., & Davies, G. M. (2001). Stalking: The elusive crime. *Legal and Criminological Psychology, 6,* 133–147.

Shneidman, E. S. (1994). The psychological autopsy. *American Psychologist, 49,* 75–76.

Showers, J. (1997). *Executive summary: The National Conference on Shaken Baby Syndrome.* Alexandria, VA: National Association of Children's Hospitals and Related Institutions.

Showers, J. (1999). *Never never never shake a baby: The challenges of shaken baby syndrome.* Alexandria, VA: National Association of Children's Hospitals and Related Institutions.

Shuman, D. W., & Sales, B. D. (2001). Daubert's wager. *Journal of Forensic Psychology Practice, 1,* 69–77.

Shusman, E., Inwald, R., & Landa, B. (1984). A validation and cross-validation study of correction officer job performance as predicted by the IPI and MMPI. *Criminal Justice and Behavior, 11,* 309–329.

Sickmund, M. (2003, June). *Juveniles in court* (Juvenile Offenders and Victims National Report Series). Washington, DC: U.S. Department of Justice, Office of Juvenile Justice and Delinquency Prevention.

Siegel, A. M., & Elwork, A. (1990). Treating incompetence to stand trial. *Law and Human Behavior, 14,* 57–65.

Simon, L. M. J. (2000). An examination of the assumptions of specialization, mental disorder, and dangerousness in sex offenders. *Behavioral Sciences and the Law, 18,* 275–308.

Simon, T., Mercy, J., & Perkins, C. (2001, June). *Injuries from violent crime, 1992–1998.* Washington, DC: U.S. Department of Justice, Bureau of Justice Statistics.

Simourd, D. J., & Hoge, R. D. (2000). Criminal psychopathy: A risk-and-need perspective. *Criminal Justice and Behavior, 27,* 256–272.

Simourd, D. J., & Malcolm, P. B. (1998). Reliability and validity of the Level of Service Inventory—Revised among federally incarcerated offenders. *Journal of Interpersonal Violence, 13,* 261–274.

Sinclair, J. J., Pettit, G. S., Harrist, A. W., & Bates, J. E. (1994). Encounters with aggressive peers in early childhood: Frequency, age differences, and correlates of risk for behaviour problems. *International Journal of Behavioural Development, 17,* 675–696.

Singer, M. T., & Nievod, A. (1987). Consulting and testifying in court. In I. B. Weiner & A. K. Hess (Eds.), *Handbook of forensic psychology.* New York: John Wiley.

Sipe, R., Jensen, E. L., & Everett, R. S. (1998). Adolescent sexual offenders grown up: Recidivism in young adulthood. *Criminal Justice and Behavior, 25,* 109–124.

Skeem, J. L., Edens, J. F., & Colwell, L. H. (2003, April). *Are there racial differences in levels of psychopathy? A meta-analysis.* Paper presented at the 3rd annual conference of the International Association of Forensic Mental Health Services, Miami, FL.

Skeem, J. L., Edens, J. F., Sanford, G. M., & Colwell, L. H. (2003). Psychopathic personality and racial/ethnic differences reconsidered: A reply to Lynn (2002). *Personality and Individual Differences, 34,* 1–24.

Skeem, J. L., Monahan, J., & Mulvey, E. P. (2002). Psychopathy, treatment involvement, and subsequent violence among civil psychiatric patients. *Law and Human Behavior, 26,* 577–603.

Skeem, J. L., Poythress, N., Edens, J., Lilienfeld, S., & Cale, E. (in press). Psychopathic personality or personalities? Exploring potential variants of psychopathy and their implications for risk assessment. *Aggression and Violent Behavior.*

Skilling, T. A., Quinsey, V. L., & Craig, W. M. (2001). Evidence of a taxon underlying serious antisocial behavior in boys. *Criminal Justice and Behavior, 28,* 450–470.

Skrapec, C. A. (1996). The sexual component of serial murder. In T. O'Reilly-Fleming (Ed.), *Serial and mass murder: Theory, research and policy.* Toronto, ON: Canadian Scholars' Press.

Skrapec, C. A. (2001). Phenomenology and serial murder: Asking different questions. *Homicide Studies, 5,* 46–63.

Slobogin, C. (1999). The admissibility of behavioral science information in criminal trials: From primitivism to *Daubert* to voice. *Psychology, Public Policy, and Law, 5,* 100–119.

Slobogin, C., & Mashburn, A. (2000). The criminal defense lawyer's fiduciary duty to clients with mental disability. *Fordham Law Review, 68,* 1581–1642.

Slot, L. A. B., & Colpaert, F. C. (1999). Recall rendered dependent on an opiate state. *Behavioral Neuroscience, 113,* 337–344.

Slovenko, R. (1999). Civil competency. In A. K. Hess & I. B. Weiner (Eds.), *Handbook of forensic psychology* (2nd ed.). New York: John Wiley.

Small, M. H., & Otto, R. K. (1991). Evaluations of competency to be executed: Legal contours and implication for assessment. *Criminal Justice and Behavior, 18,* 146–158.

Smith, B. C., Penrod, S. D., Otto, A. L., & Park, R. C. (1996). Jurors' use of probabilistic evidence. *Law and Human Behavior, 20,* 49–82.

Smith, B. M. (1967). The polygraph. *Scientific American, 216,* 25–31.

Smith, D. (2002a, June). Helping mentally ill offenders. *Monitor on Psychology, 33,* 64.

Smith, D. (2002b, June). On call, 24–7. *Monitor on Psychology, 33,* 65.

Smith, D. (2002c, June). Where are recent grads getting jobs? *Monitor on Psychology, 33,* 28–29.

Smithey, M. (1998). Infant homicide: Victim-offender relationship and causes of death. *Journal of Family Violence, 13,* 285–287.

Snyder, H. N. (2000, June). *Sexual assault of young children as reported to law enforcement: Victim, incident, and offender characteristics.* Washington, DC: U.S. Department of Justice, Bureau of Justice Statistics.

Snyder, H. N., & Sickmund, M. (1995). *Juvenile offenders and victims: A national report.* Washington, DC: Office of Juvenile Justice and Delinquency Prevention.

Snyder, H. N., & Sickmund, M. (1999). *Juvenile offenders and victims: 1999 national report.* Washington, DC: Office of Juvenile Justice and Delinquency Prevention.

Solomon, R. M., & Horn, J. M. (1986). Post-shooting traumatic reactions: A pilot study. In J. T. Reese & H. A. Goldstein (Eds.), *Psychological services for law enforcement.* Washington, DC: Government Printing Office.

Sorensen, S. B., & Bowie, P. (1994). Girls and young women. In L. D. Eron, J. H. Gentry, & P. Schlegel (Eds.), *Reason to hope: A psychosocial perspective on violence and youth.* Washington, DC: American Psychological Association.

Spaccarelli, S., Bowden, B., Coatsworth, J. D., & Kim, S. (1997). Psychosocial correlates of male sexual aggression in a chronic delinquent sample. *Criminal Justice and Behavior, 24,* 71–95.

Spence, J., & Helmreich, R. (1978). *Masculinity and femininity.* Austin: University of Texas Press.

Spiegel, D., & Spiegel, H. (1987). Forensic uses of hypnosis. In I. B. Weiner & A. K. Hess (Eds.), *Handbook of forensic psychology.* New York: John Wiley.

Spielberger, C. D. (Ed.). (1979). *Police selection and evaluation.* Washington, DC: Hemisphere.

Spielberger, C. D., Ward, J. C., & Spaulding, H. C. (1979). A model for the selection of law enforcement officers. In C. D. Spielberger (Ed.), *Police selection and evaluation: Issues and techniques.* Washington, DC: Hemisphere.

Sporer, S. L. (2001). The cross-race effect: Beyond recognition of faces in the laboratory. *Psychology, Public Policy, and Law, 7,* 170–200.

Sprang, M. V., McNeil, J. S., & Wright, R. (1989). Psychological changes after the murder of a significant other. *Social Casework: The Journal of Contemporary Social Work, 70,* 159–164.

Stack, S., & Kelley, T. (1999). Police suicide. In D. J. Kenney & R. P. McNamara (Eds.), *Police and policing: Contemporary issues* (2nd ed.). Westport, CT: Praeger.

Standards Committee, American Association for Correctional Psychology. (2000). Standards for psychology services in jails, prisons, correctional facilities, and agencies. *Criminal Justice and Behavior, 27,* 433–494.

Stark, E. (2002). Preparing for expert testimony in domestic violence cases. In A. R. Roberts (Ed.), *Handbook of domestic violence intervention strategies: Policies, programs, and legal remedies.* New York: Oxford University Press.

Stavis, P. F. (1999). The nexum: A modest proposal of self-guardianship by contract: A system of advance directives and surrogate committees-at-large for the intermittently mentally ill. *Journal of Contemporary Health Law & Policy, 1,* 21–22.

Steadman, H. J., Davidson, S., & Brown, C. (2001). Mental health courts: Their promise and unanswered questions. *Psychiatric Services, 54,* 457–458.

Steadman, H. J., Gounis, K., & Dennis, D. (2001). Assessing the New York City involuntary outpatient commitment pilot program. *Psychiatric Services, 52,* 330–336.

Steadman, H. J., McCarty, D. W., & Morrissey, J. P. (1989). *The mentally ill in jail: Planning for essential services.* New York: Guilford.

Steadman, H. J., & Veysey, B. M. (1997). *Providing services for jail inmates with mental disorders.* Washington, DC: U.S. Department of Justice, National Institute of Justice.

Stefan, S. (1996). Race, competence testing, and disability law: A review of the MacArthur competence research. *Psychology, Public Policy, and Law, 2,* 31–44.

Stehlin, I. B. (1995, July/August). FDA's forensic center: Speedy, sophisticated sleuthing. *FDA Consumer Magazine,* pp. 17–28.

Stephan, J. J. (1997). *Census of state and federal correctional facilities, 1995* (NCJ 166582). Washington, DC: U.S. Department of Justice, Bureau of Justice Statistics.

Stockdale, M. S., O'Connor, M., Gutek, B. A., & Geer, T. (2002). The relationship between prior sexual abuse and reactions to sexual harassment: Literature review and empirical study. *Psychology, Public Policy, and Law, 8,* 64–95.

Stone, A. V. (1995). Law enforcement psychological fitness for duty: Clinical issues. In M. Kurke & E. Scrivner (Eds.), *Police psychology into the 21st century.* Hillsdale, NJ: Lawrence Erlbaum.

Stone, M. H. (1998). Sadistic personality in murders. In T. Millon, E. Simonsen, M. Burket-Smith, & R. Davis (Eds.), *Psychopathy: Antisocial, criminal, and violent behavior.* New York: Guilford.

Stratton, J. G., Parker, D., & Snabbe, J. (1984). Post-traumatic stress: Study of police officers involved in shooting. *Psychological Reports, 55,* 127–131.

Strier, F. (1999). Whither trial consulting? Issues and projections. *Law and Human Behavior, 23,* 93–115.

Strom, K. J. (2001, September). *Hate crimes reported in NIBRS, 1997–1999.* Washington, DC: U.S. Department of Justice, Bureau of Justice Statistics.

Studebaker, C. L., & Goodman-Delahunty, J. (Eds.). (2002). Expert testimony in the courts: The influence of the *Daubert, Joiner,* and *Kumho* decisions, part 3 [Special issue]. *Psychology, Public Policy, and Law, 8.*

Sue, D. W., Arredondo, P., & McDavis, R. J. (1992). Multicultural counseling competencies and standards: A call to the profession. *Journal of Counseling and Development, 70,* 477–486.

Sue, D. W., Bingham, R. P., Porché-Burke, L., & Vasquez, M. (1999). The diversification of psychology: A multicultural revolution. *American Psychologist, 54,* 1061–1069.

Summit, R. C. (1983). The child sexual abuse accommodation syndrome. *Child Abuse & Neglect, 7,* 177–193.

Summit, R. C. (1992). Abuse of the child sexual abuse accommodation syndrome. *Journal of Child Sexual Abuse, 1*(4), 153–163.

Super, J. T. (1999). Forensic psychology and law enforcement. In A. K. Hess & I. B. Weiner (Eds.), *The handbook of forensic psychology* (2nd ed.). New York: John Wiley.

Swartz, M. S., Swanson, J. W., & Hiday, V. A. (2001). Randomized controlled trial of outpatient commitment in North Carolina. *Psychiatric Services, 52,* 325–329.

Tagatz, G. E., & Hess, L. R. (1972). *Police entry tests and their predictability of score in police academy and subsequent job performance.* Milwaukee, WI: Center for Criminal Justice.

Tappan, P. W. (1947). Who is criminal? *American Sociological Review, 12,* 100–110.

Tappan, P. W. (1949). *Juvenile delinquency.* New York: McGraw-Hill.

Task Force on Promotion and Dissemination of Psychological Procedures. (1995). *The Clinical Psychologist, 48,* 3–23.

Tate, D. C., Reppucci, N. D., & Mulvey, E. P. (1995). Violent juvenile delinquents: Treatment effectiveness and implications for future directions. *American Psychologist, 50,* 777–781.

Teaching-Family Association. (1993). *Standards of ethical conduct of the Teaching-Family Association.* Asheville, NC: Author.

Teaching-Family Association. (1994). *Elements of the teaching-family model.* Asheville, NC: Author.

Teplin, L. A. (1986, April). *Keeping the peace: The parameters of police discretion in relation to the mentally disordered.* Washington, DC: U.S. Department of Justice, National Institute of Justice.

Teplin, L. A. (2000, July). Police discretion and mentally ill persons. *National Institute of Justice Journal,* pp. 8–15.

Terman, L. M. (1917). A trial of mental and pedagogical tests in a civil service examination for policemen and firemen. *Journal of Applied Psychology, 1,* 17–29.

Terr, L. (1979). Children of Chowchilla: A study of psychic trauma. *Psychoanalytic Study of the Child, 34,* 547–623.

Terr, L. (1982). Psychic trauma in children: Observations following the Chowchilla school bus kidnapping. *Annals of Progress in Child Psychiatry and Child Development, 2,* 384–396.

Terr, L. (1983). Chowchilla revisited: The effects of psychic trauma four years after a school-bus kidnapping. *American Journal of Psychiatry, 140,* 1543–1550.

Terr, L. (1991). Childhood traumas: An outline and overview. *American Journal of Psychiatry, 148,* 10–20.

Terr, L. (1994). *Unchained memories.* New York: Basic Books.

Thurstone, L. L. (1922). The intelligence of policemen. *Journal of Personnel Research, 1,* 64–74.

Till, F. (1980). *Sexual harassment: A report on the sexual harassment of students.* Washington, DC: National Advisory Council on Women's Educational Programs.

Tingle, D., Barnard, G. W., Robbins, L., Newman, G., & Hutchinson, D. (1986). Childhood and adolescent characteristics of pedophiles and rapists. *International Journal of Law and Psychiatry, 9,* 103–116.

Tjaden, P. (1997, November). The crime of stalking: How big is the problem? *NIJ Research Preview.* Washington, DC: U.S. Department of Justice.

Tjaden, P., & Thoennes, N. (1998a, November). *Prevalence, incidence, and consequences of violence against women: Findings from the National Violence Against Women Survey* (Research in brief). Washington, DC: U.S. Department of Justice, National Institute of Justice.

Tjaden, P., & Thoennes, M. (1998b). *Stalking in America: Findings from the National Violence Against Women Survey* (NCJ 169592). Washington, DC: U.S. Department of Justice.

Tobey, A., Grisso, T., & Schwartz, R. (2000). Youths' trial participation as seen by youths and their attorneys: An exploration of competence-based issues. In T. Grisso & R. G. Schwartz (Eds.), *Youth on trial: A developmental perspective on juvenile justice.* Chicago: University of Chicago Press.

Toch, H. (Ed.). (1980). *Therapeutic communities in corrections.* New York: Praeger.

Toch, H. (Ed.). (1992). *Mosaic of despair: Human breakdown in prisons.* Washington, DC: American Psychological Association.

Toch, H., & Adams, K. (2002). *Acting out: Maladaptive behavior in confinement.* Washington, DC: American Psychological Association.

Tombaugh, T. N. (1997). *TOMM: Test of Memory Malingering manual.* Toronto, ON: Multi-Health Systems.

Tonry, M. (1990). Stated and latent functions of ISP. *Crime & Delinquency, 36,* 174–190.

Topp, B. W., & Kardash, C. A. (1986). Personality, achievement, and attrition: Validation in a multiple-jurisdiction police academy. *Journal of Police Science and Administration, 14,* 234–241.

Trovillo, P. V. (1939). A history in lie detection. *Journal of Criminal Law and Criminology, 29,* 848–881.

Truman, D. M., Tokar, D. M., & Fischer, A. R. (1996). Dimensions of masculinity: Relations to date-rape supportive attitudes and sexual aggression in dating situations. *Journal of Counseling and Development, 74,* 555–562.

Tucillo, J. A., DeFilippis, N. A., Denny, R. L., & Dsurney, J. (2002). Licensure requirements for interjurisdictional forensic evaluations. *Professional Psychology: Research and Practice, 33,* 377–383.

Tucker, H. S. (2002). Some seek attention by making pets sick. *Archives of Disease in Childhood, 87,* 263.

Turrell, S. C. (2000). A descriptive analysis of same-sex relationship violence for a diverse sample. *Journal of Family Violence, 15,* 281–293.

Turvey, B. (2002). *Criminal profiling: An introduction to behavioral evidence analysis* (2nd ed.). San Diego: Academic Press.

Tyiska, C. G. (1998). *Working with victims of crime with disabilities.* Washington, DC: U.S. Department of Justice, Office of Victims of Crime.

U.S. Advisory Board on Child Abuse and Neglect. (1995). *A national shame: Fatal child abuse and neglect in the U.S.* (5th report). Washington, DC: Government Printing Office.

U.S. Department of Health and Human Services. (2003, April 1). *Child abuse prevention: An overview.* Washington, DC: Author.

U.S. Department of Justice. (1988). *Report to the nation on crime and justice: The data* (2nd ed.). Washington, DC: Government Printing Office.

U.S. Department of Justice, Bureau of Justice Statistics. (2003). *Visitation risk assessment.* Available: www.psychologyinfo.com/forensic/vistation_risk.html

U.S. Secret Service. (2000). *Safe School Initiative: An interim report on the prevention of targeted violence in schools.* Washington, DC: National Threat Assessment Center.

Van der Kolk, B. A., & Fisler, R. E. (1994). Childhood abuse and neglect and loss of self-regulation. *Bulletin of the Menninger Clinic, 58,* 145–158.

Van der Kolk, B. A., & Fisler, R. E. (1995). Dissociation and the fragmentary nature of traumatic memories: Overview and exploratory study. *Journal of Traumatic Stress, 8,* 505–525.

Van Maanen, J. (1975). Police socialization: A longitudinal examination of job attitudes in an urban police department. *Administrative Science Quarterly, 20,* 207–228.

Varela, J. G., Boccaccini, M. T., Scogin, F., Stump, J., & Caputo, A. (in press). Personality testing in law enforcement settings: A meta-analytic review. *Criminal Justice and Behavior.*

Vermeiren, R., De Clippele, A., Schwab-Stone, M., Ruchkin, V., & Deboutte, D. (2002). Neuropsychological characteristics of three subgroups of Flemish delinquent adolescents. *Neuropsychology, 16,* 49–55.

Vila, B., & Kenney, D. J. (2002). Tired cops: The prevalence and potential consequences of police fatigue. *National Institute of Justice Journal, 248,* 16–21.

Violanti, J. M. (1996). *Police suicide: Epidemic in blue.* Springfield, IL: Charles C Thomas.

Vitale, J. E., Smith, S. S., Brinkley, C. A., & Newman, J. P. (2002). The reliability and validity of the Psychopathy Checklist—Revised in a sample of female offenders. *Criminal Justice and Behavior, 29,* 202–231.

Viteles, M. S. (1929). Psychological methods in the selection of patrolmen in Europe. *Annals of the American Academy, 146,* 160–165.

Voltz, A. G. (1995). Nursing interventions in Munchausen syndrome by proxy. *Journal of Psychosocial Nursing, 10,* 93–97.

Vossekuil, B., Fein, R. A., Reddy, M., Borum, R., & Mozeleski, W. (2002, May). *The final report and findings of the safe school initiative.* Washington, DC: U.S. Secret Service and the U.S. Department of Education.

Walker, L. E. (1979). *The battered woman.* New York: Harper Colophone Books.

Walker, L. E. (1984). *The battered woman syndrome.* New York: Springer.

Walker, L. E. (1989). *Terrifying love: Why battered women kill and how society responds.* New York: HarperCollins.

Walker, L. E. (1999). Psychology and domestic violence around the world. *American Psychologist, 54,* 21–29.

Walker, S., Alpert, G. P., & Kenney, D. J. (2001, July). *Early warning systems: Responding to the problem police officer.* Washington, DC: U.S. Department of Justice, National Institute of Justice.

Walker, S. D., & Kilpatrick, D. G. (2002). Scope of crime/historical review of the victims' rights discipline. In A. Seymour, M. Murray, J. Sigmon, M. Hook, C. Edwards, M. Gaboury, & G. Coleman (Eds.), *National Victim Assistance Academy textbook.* Washington, DC: U.S. Department of Justice, Office of Victims of Crime.

Wallerstein, J. S. (1989, January 23). Children after divorce: Wounds that don't heal. *New York Times Magazine,* pp. 19–21, 41–44.

Waltz, J., Babcock, J. C., Jacobson, N. S., & Gottman, J. M. (2000). Testing a typology of batterers. *Journal of Consulting and Clinical Psychology, 68,* 658–669.

Warren, J. I., Fitch, W. L., Dietz, P. E., & Rosenfeld, B. D. (1991). Criminal offense, psychiatric diagnosis, and psycholegal opinion: An analysis of 894 pretrial referrals. *Bulletin of the American Academy of Psychiatry and Law, 19,* 63–69.

Warren, J. I., Hazelwood, R. R., & Reboussin, R. (1991). Serial rape: The offender and his rape career. In A. Burgess (Ed.), *Rape and sexual assault III.* New York: Garland.

Warren, J. I., Reboussin, R., Hazelwood, R. R., & Wright, J. A. (1989). Serial rape: Correlates of increased aggression and relationship of offender pleasure to victim resistance. *Journal of Interpersonal Violence, 4,* 65–78.

Waschbusch, D. A. (2002). A meta-analytic examination of comorbid hyperactive-impulsive-attention problems and conduct problems. *Psychological Bulletin, 128,* 118–150.

Webster, C. D., Harris, G. T., Rice, M. E., Cormier, C., & Quinsey, V. L. (1994). *The violence prediction scheme: Assessing dangerousness in high-risk men.* Toronto, Ontario: University of Toronto Press.

Weekes, J. R., Moser, A. E., & Langevin, C. M. (1999). Assessing substance-abusing offenders for treatment. In E. J. Latessa (Ed.), *Strategic solutions.* Lanham, MD: American Correctional Association.

Weiner, I. B. (2000). Making Rorschach interpretation as good as it can be. *Journal of Personality Assessment, 74,* 164–174.

Weiner, I. B. (2001). Advancing the science of psychological assessment: The Rorschach Inkblot Method as exemplar. *Psychological Assessment, 13,* 423–432.

Weingartner, H. J., Putnam, F., George, D. T., & Ragan, P. (1995). Drug state-dependent auto-biographical knowledge. *Experimental and Clinical Psychopharmacology, 3,* 304–307.

Weisheit, R., & Mahan, S. (1988). *Women, crime, and criminal justice.* Cincinnati, OH: Anderson.

Weiss, D. S., Marmar, C. R., Schlenger, W. E., Fairbank, J. A., Jordan, B. K., Hough, R. L., et al. (1992). The prevalence of lifetime and partial post-traumatic stress disorder in Vietnam theater veterans. *Journal of Traumatic Stress, 5,* 365–376.

Wells, G. L. (2001). Police lineups: Data, theory, and policy. *Psychology, Public Policy, and Law, 1,* 791–801.

Wells, G. L., Small, M., Penrod, S., Malpass, R. S., Fulero, S. M., & Brimacombe, C. A. E. (1998). Eyewitness identification procedures: Recommendations for lineups and photospreads. *Law and Human Behavior, 22,* 603–647.

Werth, J. L., Benjamin, G. A. H., & Farrenkopf, T. (2000). Requests for physician-assisted death: Guidelines for assessing mental capacity and impaired judgment. *Psychology, Public Policy, and Law, 6,* 348–372.

Wessler, S., & Moss, M. (2001, October). *Hate crimes on campus: The problem and efforts to confront it.* Washington, DC: U.S. Department of Justice, Office of Justice Programs.

West, C. M. (1998). Leaving a second closet: Outing partner violence in same-sex couples. In J. L. Jasinski & L. M. Williams (Eds.), *Partner violence: A comprehensive review of 20 years of research.* Thousand Oaks, CA: Sage.

Whitcomb, D., Hook, M., & Alexander, E. (2002). Child victimization. In A. Seymour, M. Murray, J. Sigmon, M. Hook, C. Edwards, M. Gaboury, & G. Coleman (Eds.),

National Victim Assistance Academy textbook. Washington, DC: U.S. Department of Justice, Office for Victims of Crime.

White, H. R., Bates, M. E., & Buyske, S. (2001). Adolescence-limited versus persistent delinquency: Extending Moffitt's hypothesis into adulthood. *Journal of Abnormal Psychology, 110,* 600–609.

Whitehead, J. T., & Lab, S. P. (1989). A meta-analysis of juvenile correctional treatment. *Journal of Research in Crime & Delinquency, 26,* 276–295.

Whittaker, J. K., Kinney, J., Tracy, E. N., & Booth, C. (1990). *Reaching high-risk families: Intensive family preservation in human services.* New York: Aldine de Gruyter.

Williamson, S., Hare, R. D., & Wong, S. (1987). Violence: Criminal psychopaths and their victims. *Canadian Journal of Behavioral Science, 19,* 454–462.

Wilson, J. J. (2001, January). From the administrator. In J. R. Johnson & L. K. Girdner (Eds.), *Family abductors: Descriptive profiles and preventive interventions.* Washington, DC: U.S. Department of Justice, Office of Juvenile Justice and Delinquency.

Wilson, M., & Daly, M. (1993). Spousal homicide risk and estrangement. *Violence and Victims, 8,* 3–16.

Winick, B. J. (1996). The MacArthur Treatment Competence Study: Legal and therapeutic implications. *Psychology, Public Policy, and Law, 2,* 137–166.

Winick, B. J. (2003). Outpatient commitment: A therapeutic jurisprudence analysis. *Psychology, Public Policy, and Law, 9,* 107–144.

Winick, B. J., & Kress, K. (2003a). Foreword: A symposium on outpatient commitment dedicated to Bruce Ennis, Alexander Brooks, and Stanley Herr. *Psychology, Public Policy, and Law, 9,* 3–7.

Winick, B. J., & Kress, K. (Eds.). (2003b). Preventive outpatient commitment for persons with serious mental illness [Special issue]. *Psychology, Public Policy, and Law, 9.*

Witt, A. (2001, June 5). False confessions–Day 3–Police bend, suspend rules. *Washington Post,* p. A01.

Wolf, M. M., Kirigin, K. A., Fixsen, D. L., Blasé, K. A., & Braukmann, C. J. (1995). The teaching-family model: A case study in data-based program development and refinement (and dragon wrestling). *Journal of Organizational Behavior Management, 15,* 11–68.

Wong, S. (2000). Psychopathic offenders. In S. Hodgins & R. Muller-Isberner (Eds.), *Violence, crime and mentally disordered offenders: Concepts and methods for effective treatment and prevention.* New York: John Wiley.

Wood, J. M., Nezworski, M. T., Stejskal, W. J., McKinzey, R. K. (2001). Problems of the Comprehensive System for the Rorschach in forensic settings: Recent developments. *Journal of Forensic Psychology Practice, 1,* 89–103.

Wood, R. M., Grossman, L. S., & Fichtner, C. G. (2000). Psychological assessment, treatment, and outcome with sex offenders. *Behavioral Sciences and the Law, 18,* 23–41.

Woodworth, M., & Porter, S. (2002). In cold blood: Characteristics of criminal homicides as a function of psychopathy. *Journal of Abnormal Psychology, 111,* 436–445.

Worden, A. P. (1993). The attitudes of women and men in policing: Testing conventional and contemporary wisdom. *Criminology, 31,* 203–242.

Yarmey, A. D. (1979). *The psychology of eyewitness testimony.* New York: Free Press.

Yochelson, S., & Samenow, S. E. (1976). *The criminal personality* (Vol. 1). New York: Jason Aronson.

Zapf, P. A., Hubbard, K. L., Galloway, V. A., Cox, M., & Ronan, K. A. (2002). *An investigation of discrepancies between forensic examiners and the courts in decisions about competency.* Manuscript submitted for publication.

Zapf, P. A., & Viljoen, J. L. (2003). Issues and considerations regarding the use of assessment instruments in the evaluation of competency to stand trial. *Behavioral Sciences and the Law, 21,* 351–367.

Zeling, M. (1986). Research needs in the study of post shooting trauma. In J. T. Reese & H. A. Goldstein (Eds.), *Psychological services for law enforcement.* Washington, DC: Government Printing Office.

Ziskin, J., & Faust, D. (1994). *Coping with psychiatric and psychological testimony* (5th ed.). Marina Del Rey, CA: Law and Psychology Press.

Zoccoulillo, M. (1993). Gender and the development of conduct disorder. *Development and Psychopathology, 5,* 65–78.

Zona, M. A., Sharma, K. K., & Lane, J. A. (1993). A comparative study of erotomanic and obsessional subjects in a forensic sample. *Journal of Forensic Sciences, 38,* 894–903.

Author Index

Subject Index

About the Authors

Curt R. Bartol has been a college professor for more than 30 years, teaching a wide variety of both undergraduate and graduate courses, including biopsychology, criminal behavior, juvenile delinquency, introduction to forensic psychology, social psychology, and psychology and law. He earned his PhD in Personality/Social Psychology from Northern Illinois University in 1972. He was instrumental in creating and launching Castleton State College's graduate program in Forensic Psychology and served as its Director for 6 years. As a licensed clinical psychologist, he has been a consulting police psychologist to local, municipal, state, and federal law enforcement agencies for nearly 25 years. He is also the Editor of *Criminal Justice and Behavior,* the international journal of the American Association for Correctional Psychologists.

In addition to *Introduction to Forensic Psychology,* he has written *Criminal Behavior: A Psychosocial Approach,* now in its sixth edition, and coauthored, with Anne Bartol, *Juvenile Delinquency: A Systems Approach, Delinquency and Justice: A Psychosocial Approach* (2nd edition), and *Psychology and Law: Theory, Research, and Application* (3rd edition). He has published extensively in the field of forensic psychology.

Anne M. Bartol earned an MA and a PhD in Criminal Justice from State University of New York at Albany. She also holds an MA in journalism from the University of Wisconsin–Madison. She has taught criminal justice, sociology, and journalism courses over a 20-year college teaching career, primarily at Castleton State College, and has worked as a journalist and a social worker in child and adolescent protective services. In addition to *Introduction to Forensic Psychology,* she coauthored, with Curt Bartol, *Juvenile Delinquency: A Systems Approach, Delinquency and Justice: A Psychosocial Approach* (2nd edition), and *Psychology and Law: Theory, Research, and Application* (3rd edition). She has served as book review editor of *Criminal Justice and Behavior* and has published articles on women and criminal justice, rural courts, and the history of forensic psychology.